THE OXFORD HAND[

PAPYROLOGY

THE OXFORD HANDBOOK OF

PAPYROLOGY

Edited by

ROGER S. BAGNALL

OXFORD

UNIVERSITY PRESS

OXFORD
UNIVERSITY PRESS

Oxford University Press, Inc., publishes works that further
Oxford University's objective of excellence
in research, scholarship, and education.

Oxford   New York
Auckland   Cape Town   Dar es Salaam   Hong Kong   Karachi
Kuala Lumpur   Madrid   Melbourne   Mexico City   Nairobi
New Delhi   Shanghai   Taipei   Toronto

With offices in
Argentina   Austria   Brazil   Chile   Czech Republic   France   Greece
Guatemala   Hungary   Italy   Japan   Poland   Portugal   Singapore
South Korea   Switzerland   Thailand   Turkey   Ukraine   Vietnam

Published by Oxford University Press, Inc.
198 Madison Avenue, New York, New York 10016
www.oup.com

First issued as an Oxford University Press paperback, 2011

Oxford is a registered trademark of Oxford University Press

Library of Congress Cataloging-in-Publication Data
The Oxford handbook of papyrology / edited by Roger S. Bagnall.
p. cm.
Includes bibliographical references and index.
ISBN 978-0-19-517838-8 (hardcover); 978-0-19-984369-5 (paperback)
1. Manuscripts (Papyri). 2. Paleography. 3. History, Ancient—Historiography.
4. Middle East—Historiography. I. Bagnall, Roger S. II. Title: Handbook of papyrology.
Z110.P36O98 2009
091—dc22   2008031679

Printed in the United States of America
on acid-free paper

CONTENTS

....

Contributors

Roger S. Bagnall Professor of Ancient History and Director of the Institute for the Study of the Ancient World, New York University

Adam Bülow-Jacobsen Former Carlsberg Research Professor, University of Copenhagen

Guglielmo Cavallo Professor of Palaeography, University of Rome–La Sapienza

Willy Clarysse Professor of Ancient History, Katholieke Universiteit Leuven

Raffaella Cribiore Professor of Classics, New York University

Hélène Cuvigny Directeur de recherches, Centre National de la Recherche Scientifique (Institut de Recherche et d'Histoire des Textes)

Eleanor Dickey Associate Professor of Classics, University of Exeter

Maria Rosaria Falivene Associate Professor of Papyrology, Faculty of Letters and Philosophy, University of Rome Tor Vergata

Jean-Luc Fournet Directeur d'Études en papyrologie grecque, École Pratique des Hautes Études, Section des sciences historiques et philologiques, Paris

Jaakko Frösén Professor of Greek Philology, University of Helsinki

Jean Gascou Professor of Papyrology, University of Paris-Sorbonne

Nikolaos Gonis Reader in Papyrology, University College London

Todd M. Hickey Assistant Professor of Classics, University of California, Berkeley

William A. Johnson Associate Professor of Classics and Head of the Department of Classics, University of Cincinnati

Alexander Jones Professor of the History of the Exact Sciences in Antiquity, Institute for the Study of the Ancient World, New York University

James G. Keenan Professor of Classical Studies, Loyola University Chicago

David G. Martinez Associate Professor, Department of Classics and the Divinity School, University of Chicago

Bernhard Palme Professor of Ancient History and Papyrology, University of Vienna

Timothy Renner Professor of Classics and General Humanities, Montclair State University

Cornelia Römer Director of the Papyrus Collection and Papyrus Museum, Austrian National Library, Vienna

Paul Schubert Professor of Greek Language and Literature, University of Geneva

David Sider Professor of Classics, New York University

Petra M. Sijpesteijn Professor of Arabic Language and Culture, Leiden University

Dorothy J. Thompson Former Newton Trust Lecturer and affiliated lecturer in ancient history, and Life Fellow of Girton College, University of Cambridge

Katelijn Vandorpe Professor of Ancient History, Katholieke Universiteit Leuven

Peter van Minnen Associate Professor of Classics and Ancient History, University of Cincinnati

Uri Yiftach-Firanko Assistant Professor of Classics, Hebrew University of Jerusalem

FIGURES

ABBREVIATIONS

....

AJA	*American Journal of Archaeology*
AncSoc	*Ancient Society*
ANRW	*Aufstieg und Niedergang der römischen Welt*
APF	*Archiv für Papyrusforschung und verwandte Gebiete*
ARAM	*ARAM periodical*
BASP	*Bulletin of the American Sociey of Papyrologists*
BCH	*Bulletin de correspondance hellénique*
BIFAO	*Bulletin de l'Institut français d'archéologie orientale*
BSAC	*Bulletin de la Société d'Archéologie Copte*
BSOAS	*Bulletin of the School of Oriental and African Studies*
Cd'É	*Chronique d'Égypte*
CErc	*Cronache ercolanesi*
CRAI	*Comptes rendus de l'Académie des Inscriptions et Belles-Lettres*
CRIPEL	*Cahiers de recherches de l'Institut de Papyrologie et d'Égyptologie de Lille III*
CSCA	*California Studies in Classical Antiquity*
EVO	*Egitto e vicino oriente*
GRBS	*Greek, Roman and Byzantine Studies*
JEA	*Journal of Egyptian Archaeology*
JHS	*Journal of Hellenic Studies*
JJP	*Journal of Juristic Papyrology*
JRA	*Journal of Roman Archaeology*
JRAS	*Journal of the Royal Asiatic Society*
JRS	*Journal of Roman Studies*
MBAH	*Münstersche Beiträge zur antiken Handelsgeschichte*
MDAIK	*Mitteilungen des Deutschen Archäologischen Instituts (Abt. Kairo)*
OLA	*Orientalia Lovaniensia analecta*
QDAP	*Quarterly of the Department of Antiquities of Palestine*

QS	*Quaderni di storia*
RAssyr	*Revue assyriologique*
RBi	*Revue biblique*
REB	*Revue des études byzantines*
RHR	*Revue de l'histoire des religions*
RIDA	*Revue internationale des droits d'antiquité*
SCI	*Scripta classica Israelica*
SDHI	*Studia et documenta historiae iuris*
TR	*Tijdschrift voor Rechtsgeschiedenis*
ZPE	*Zeitschrift für Papyrologie und Epigraphik*
ZSav	*Zeitschrift der Savigny-Stiftung für Rechtsgeschichte: Romanistische Abteilung*

Internet Resources

The following list gives only a selection of tools mentioned in this volume. For lists of additional resources, with links, see the following two Web sites:
http://www.columbia.edu/cu/lweb/digital/pn/resources.html
http://www.ulb.ac.be/assoc/aip/liens.htm

Advanced Papyrological Information System (APIS). A union catalogue of metadata and images from many papyrus collections, including a set of links to other online catalogues of papyrus collections, http://www.columbia.edu/cu/lweb/projects/digital/apis/index.html; also through http://www. papyri.info

Catalogue of Paraliterary Papyri (CPP). Katholieke Universiteit Leuven, Departement Klassieke Studies. http://cpp.arts.kuleuven.ac.be/

Checklist of Arabic Documents. http://www.ori.uzh.ch/isap/isapchecklist.html

Checklist of Editions of Greek, Latin, Demotic, and Coptic Papyri, Ostraca, and Tablets. http://scriptorium.lib.duke.edu/papyrus/texts/clist.html

Cologne Mani-Codex. Images, http://www.uni-koeln.de/phil-fak/ifa/NRWakademie/papyrologie/Manikodex/mani.html

Demotistische Literaturübersicht, Katholieke Universiteit Leuven. http://www.trismegistos.org/dl/index.html

Duke Data Bank of Documentary Papyri. A full-text database only for Greek and Latin documents. http://www.papyri.info

Fayyum Villages Project. Now included in Trismegistos: places. http://www.trismegistos.org/geo/index.php

Heidelberger Gesamtverzeichnis der griechischen Papyrusurkunden aus Ägypten. A database (without texts) of Greek and Latin documentary papyri and ostraca. http://www.rzuser.uni-heidelberg.de/~gvo/gvz.html; also through http://www.papyri.info

Homer and the Papyri, Harvard Center for Hellenic Studies. http://chs.harvard.edu/chs/homer___the_papyri

Leuven Database of Ancient Books (LDAB). A guide to Greek, Latin, and Coptic literary texts, including school exercises. http://www.trismegistos.org/ldab/index.php

Mertens-Pack, 3d ed. A digital update of Roger A. Pack, *Index of Greek and Latin Literary Texts from Greco-Roman Egypt,* 2d ed. Ann Arbor: University of Michigan Press, 1965. A listing of literary papyri with full references. http://www2.ulg.ac.be/facphl/services/cedopal/

Nag Hammadi Library. http://www.gnosis.org/naghamm/nhl.html

Namen in koptischen dokumentarischen Texten (by M. Hasitzka). A repertory of personal names attested in Coptic documents. http://www.onb.ac.at/sammlungen/papyrus/publ/kopt_namen.pdf

Oxyrhynchus Papyri. Metadata and images of the more recent volumes. http://www.papyrology.ox.ac.uk/POxy/

Papyrus Archives in Graeco-Roman Egypt. Database with description of archives and dossiers. http://www.trismegistos.org/arch/index.php

Thesaurus Linguae Graecae. A comprehensive database of Greek literary texts from Homer to Byzantine times (license required). http://www.tlg.uci.edu

Vindolanda Tablets. Metadata, translations, and images. http://vindolanda.csad.ox.ac.uk/

INTRODUCTION

ROGER S. BAGNALL

In a broad sense, papyrology is a discipline concerned with the recovery and exploitation of ancient artifacts bearing writing and of the textual material preserved on such artifacts. For the most part it focuses on what can be called the spectrum of everyday writing rather than forms of writing intended for publicity and permanence, most of which were inscribed on stone or metal and belong to epigraphy, in the scholarly division of labor. The edges of these domains, however, are fuzzy. Papyrology cannot actually be defined by the material support: Potsherds can belong to epigraphy or papyrology, depending on their origin and nature, while the great parchment codices of the fourth and fifth centuries are not usually thought of as papyrological texts. Technique of writing is not an adequate discriminant, for not all epigraphical texts are incised, and some papyrological texts are. A public/private dichotomy is undermined by papyri put up as public notices, and many types of content are found in both epigraphical and papyrological texts—edicts of Roman governors, to give only one obvious example. Nor does geography divide the fields: Both papyrological and epigraphical texts can be found from Britain to Afghanistan, although, for environmental reasons, most papyrological material comes from Egypt. Material that in Egypt would be considered papyrological finds a home in the *Corpus inscriptionum iranicarum* when written in a Persian language. In one sense, none of this is a problem unless one wants to close oneself into a discipline with clear boundaries. But for the editor of a handbook it poses certain challenges.

Publishing a handbook for a field such as papyrology presupposes some sense of approximate boundaries. A generation ago, "papyrology" meant Greek and Latin papyrology, and the borders were thus clear at least in linguistic terms. Neither Coptic nor Arabic papyrology had more than a handful of practitioners, and demotic Egyptian unquestionably belonged to the Egyptologists. In the summer seminar in papyrology in 1968, at which I received my first training, I think none of these languages was ever mentioned. The papyrology of the rest of the ancient world was hardly an issue, either; apart from Herculaneum, Dura-Europos, and a scattering of other texts, papyrology meant Egypt. The papyrological textbooks of that era, most notably Turner (1968, 1980²) and Montevecchi (1973, 1988²), are essentially and even avowedly about the Greek (and Latin, to some extent) papyri of Egypt, just as had been the case already for Mitteis and Wilcken (1912), and the same is explicitly true of Rupprecht (1994).

Today, a broader concept, already partly visible long ago in Peremans and Vergote (1942), is unavoidable. One may trace the change in the *Checklist of Editions,* which between its first edition in 1974 and its most recent in 2001 (Oates et al. 2001) has added demotic and Coptic, and an analogous Arabic checklist has come into being (online). It seems only a matter of time before the papyri in other Semitic languages are added. Will the Bactrian documents (Sims-Williams 2000) be next? Papyrologists trained on Egyptian material have found themselves working on papyri from Petra and tablets from Vindolanda. Several volumes of one papyrological series have now been titled "From Herculaneum to Egypt" *(Papyrologica lupiensia).* All of this has in some ways not so much left behind the old contest between methodological and substantive concepts of the field of papyrology as relocated them to a broader plane.

It is, however, all too easy to see these developments uncritically as the papyrological manifestations of the egalitarian, multicultural spirit of the present. No matter how fuzzy a set papyrological texts constitute, they do have a core. Greek is still the dominant language of papyrology, and the Roman empire its fulcrum. Nearly 80 percent of published papyri are Greek and Latin (mostly Greek; cf. chapter 27), texts from the period of Roman rule greatly outnumber those of the Hellenistic period, and the numbers among the unpublished may not be vastly different. The "normality" of the Roman period for papyrology is probably not just a matter of the chance of survivals, however; or, to look at it from another point of view, the survival of documents is probably not simply the product of archaeological contingency. Roman rule brought with it the development of a society of "notables," the prosperous elites of both villages and cities who governed them—the cities especially after Septimius Severus granted them city councils. These groups, the property they owned, and the public duties they carried out generated an immense amount of paperwork, much of which had not been there in the Ptolemaic period, and these papyri are a large part of what gives us our impression of the "middle-class" (but really upper middle or lower upper class) society to which the modern middle-class reader connects so easily. It is the village societies of the Fayyum and the bourgeoisie of Oxyrhynchos that have generated most of the stories papyrologists tell about life in Graeco-Roman Egypt. Greek was the language of power and business in these societies.

The Roman Empire—in an expansive sense, including late antiquity—is also the period in which the geographical range of papyrological finds outside Egypt is at its greatest. From the first to the early second centuries there are important finds from the pre-Hadrianic forts at Vindolanda in northern Britain (*Tab. Vindol.* I–III), with their snapshot of frontier military life, and the fort of Masada by the Dead Sea, where, near the other end of the empire, the Roman army was engaged in putting down a rebellion (*Doc.Masada*). Second- and third-century documents from the Dead Sea (*P.Yadin*) and the Euphrates valley (*P.Euphr., P.Dura*) have also helped prevent too Egyptocentric a view of the papyrological world, as the interplay of

Roman, Greek, and local languages and legal norms has given more specificity, bite, and controversy to questions all too easily buried in generalizations. The army is documented again in third-century Libya with a large find of ostraca (*O.Bu Njem*). Later still, Petra and Nessana give us city and village documents linked to church and military but also highly revealing about private property transactions in the sixth and seventh centuries (*P.Petra, P.Ness.*). Yet none of this takes away from the overwhelming numerical dominance of Egyptian texts.

This handbook reflects these changes in papyrology over the last third of a century; it also reflects the lack of any universally accepted view of the discipline to replace the consensus of the past. The Greek papyri still dominate the book, just as they do the subject. Limitations of space, differences in the developmental stages of various fields, and sometimes a lack of available contributors have made it impossible to treat all possible subjects. I particularly regret the absence of any substantial discussion of Coptic palaeography, a subject much in need of systematic treatment, and the lack of a planned chapter on hieratic and demotic papyri (although chapters 12 and 17 deal with part of that territory). Fortunately, these topics will be treated extensively in the forthcoming *Oxford Handbook of Egyptology* and *Oxford Handbook of Coptic Studies*. Readers should in any case recognize that any seeming incoherences of boundaries and coverage accurately reflect the nature of papyrology today in the midst of change.

The divide between the methodological and substantive sides of the discipline will also be evident. Some chapters are more practical in character, aiming to help the reader understand how papyrologists go about reading, editing, and making sense of their texts. Others give some of the results of that process. This divide too was evident in Peremans and Vergote's *Handboek,* which contained an entire chapter on the definition of the subject, then other chapters on writing material, conservation, and decipherment, as well as chapters on political history, language, administration, law, religion, social life, economy, culture, and private life. The balance is clearly toward the results of papyrology, perhaps not a surprising outcome in a book written by two scholars who were not editors of papyri. If the present handbook attempted to cover the full range of these subjects, it would have required at least two volumes (if it could have been produced at all). It has no sections on class, ethnicity, economy, trade, gender, family, Hellenization, Romanization, and many other subjects on which a great deal of good work has been done in recent decades. Space has been used instead to widen the linguistic range and break "religion" out into more of its varied constituents. This was hardly an inevitable choice, but it seemed to me more important to cover papyrology's development into those directions, even if incompletely, than to try to provide a history of Egypt (let alone the entire ancient world) through the lens of the papyri.

As a collective work, this handbook has of necessity a different character from previous handbooks or textbooks of papyrology. The twenty-seven authors represented here and their subjects overlap from time to time, and they do not agree about everything. Although some repetition has been excised, some remains, and contention remains, too. There would be no point in pretending that all of the authors speak with the same voice. One of the purposes of a multiauthor volume of this kind, in fact, is to give the reader a sense of the debates that animate the field. Moreover, different authors have different conceptions of their audience; that again seems to me inevitable in such a work and perhaps even desirable. Most of the chapters require no knowledge of any ancient language, but it was hard to imagine a chapter on the Greek and Latin of the papyri addressed to an audience that knew nothing of either language.

Handbooks tend to be consulted or read in part rather than continuously. Many different arrangements of the chapters could have been envisaged, naturally; the one adopted here made sense to me, but nothing prevents readers from reading chapters in any order they find helpful.

This is certainly the first papyrological handbook in which electronic research tools play a significant part. There are few chapters not marked in one way or another by the availability of major resources in digital form, mainly on the World Wide Web but some still only on CD-ROM. The authors have somewhat diverse things to say about this revolution, and I have thought that here particularly some repetition was a good thing. The addresses of these tools are given above (pages xv– xvi), where the reader will find all of these resources listed with information on access to them.

This book has benefited from the help of many individuals. I want to acknowledge particularly the valuable comments of the participants in the Summer Seminar in Papyrology held at Columbia University in 2006, who had drafts of the volume available to them. Eduard Iricinschi, of Princeton University, read the entire copyedited volume and improved it in many particulars, a service for which I am deeply grateful. The financial support of the Andrew W. Mellon Foundation and of the Institute for the Study of the Ancient World of New York University has made possible the seminar and this editorial work.

BIBLIOGRAPHY

Editions of papyri and papyrological reference works are cited throughout this volume according to the abbreviations in Oates et al. (2001) or its electronic version.

Mitteis, L., and U. Wilcken. 1912. *Grundzüge und Chrestomathie der Papyruskunde.* 4 vols. Berlin.

Montevecchi, O. 1988. *La papirologia,* 2d ed. Milan: Vita e pensiero.

Oates, J. F., R. S. Bagnall, S. J. Clackson, A. A. O'Brien, J. D. Sosin, T. G. Wilfong, and K. A. Worp. 2001. *Checklist of Editions of Greek, Latin, Demotic, and Coptic Papyri, Ostraca, and Tablets,* 5th ed. Oakville, Conn.: American Society of Papyrologists. For up-to-date electronic version, see p. xv.

Peremans, W., and J. Vergote. 1942. *Papyrologisch Handboek.* Leuven: Beheer van Philologische Studiën.

Pestman, P. W. 1990. *The New Papyrological Primer.* Leiden: Brill.

Rupprecht, H.-A. 1994. *Kleine Einführung in die Papyruskunde.* Darmstadt: Wissenschaftliche Buchgesellschaft.

Sijpesteijn, P. M., and L. Sundelin, eds. 2004. *Papyrology and the History of Early Islamic Egypt.* Leiden: Brill.

Sims-Williams, N. 2000. *Bactrian Documents from Northern Afghanistan.* Vol. 1: *Legal and Economic Documents.* Studies in the Khalili Collection; vol. 3: *Corpus inscriptionum iranicarum,* II.6. Oxford: Nour Foundation.

Turner, E. G. *Greek Papyri: An Introduction,* 2d ed. 1980. Oxford: Clarendon Press.

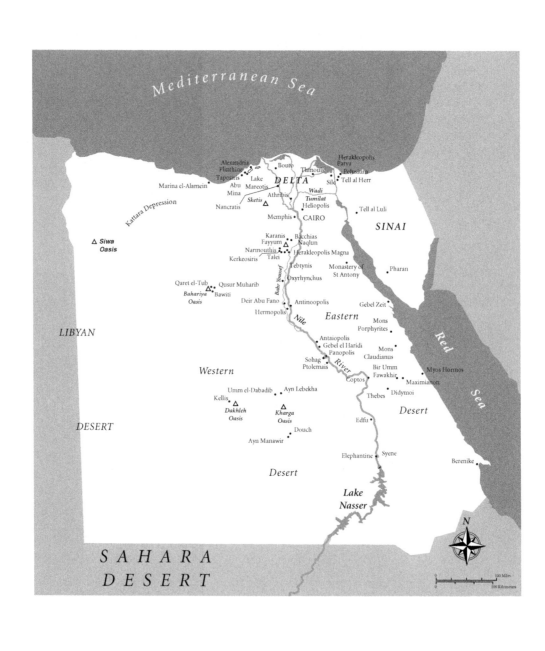

THE OXFORD HANDBOOK OF

PAPYROLOGY

CHAPTER 1

WRITING MATERIALS IN THE ANCIENT WORLD

ADAM BÜLOW-JACOBSEN

Paper, as we know it today, did not exist in the ancient Mediterranean world.[1] Instead, people wrote on an enormous variety of other materials. While almost every substance imaginable has been used as writing material at one time or another,[2] in this chapter I focus on the common ones. First, I naturally consider papyrus since the overwhelming majority of ancient texts are written on this material. Parchment, ostraca, and wooden tablets also receive considerable attention, while linen (e.g., mummy bandages) and stone (mainly Coptic limestone ostraca inscribed with ink) receive minimal attention.

An overall view of the use of various writing materials for Greek documentary texts can easily be acquired from the *Heidelberger Gesamtverzeichnis der griechischen Papyrusurkunden Ägyptens einschließlich der Ostraka usw., der lateinischen Texte, sowie der entsprechenden Urkunden aus benachbarten Regionen* (hereinafter *HGV*).[3] Out of a total (as of April 2004) of 54,312 published documents, the distribution on writing materials is given in table 1.1. In columns 4 and 5 I have added the figures and percentages for literary texts, which are taken from the total of 9,875 items incorporated in the *Leuven Database of Ancient Books* (hereinafter *LDAB*).[4]

The aforementioned figures are for texts in Greek and Latin. If we look at Coptic documentary texts,[5] which extend past the end of antiquity, ostraca are the most important medium (47.5 percent), while papyrus is second (40.5 percent). Limestone accounts for 10.5 percent, while skin (leather/parchment), paper, and wood represent less than 1 percent each.

Table 1.1. The Frequency of Various Writing Materials

Material	Documents	% of Documents	Literary Texts	% of Literary Texts
papyrus	35,591	65%	7,100	71%
ostraca[1]	15,195	28%	339	3%
wood[2]	2,500	5%	148	1%
parchment	349	0.6%	2,575	25%
graffiti	234	0.4%		
linen	84			
wax tablet	73			
stone	67		30	
cloth (mummy linen, etc.)	30			
leather, etc.	25			
various semiprecious stones	9			
limestone	7			
bone	7			
gold and silver	6			
bronze	6			
lead	1			
iron	1			
schist	1			
reed	1			

1. This category includes fragments of ceramic on which the text is written in ink or engraved after firing.

2. A good many of these are mummy labels. One could also include wax tablets and the description *Klapptafel* (4 items in *HGV*). For reasons of geography the *HGV* includes neither the Vindolanda (*T.Vindol.*, 853 items) nor the Vindonissa tablets (*T.Vindon*, 90 items). Otherwise, the wooden tablets would account for 6 percent of the total.

PAPYRUS

Where and How Did Papyrus Grow?

According to Theophrastus, whom Pliny copies without acknowledgement,[6] papyrus grew in water no deeper than 90 centimeters (two cubits). Pliny adds on his own account (or from another source) that it grows in the swamps of Egypt, which are stagnant after the floods. This was certainly true in his day and at the time of

Theophrastus as well, but before man interfered with the floods of the Nile, where would papyrus have grown in Egypt? Without human intervention, the floods did not leave stagnant pools for very long, and the annual change in the water level would not have agreed with the papyrus plant. It is thus no surprise that *Cyperus papyrus L.* died out in Egypt when it was no longer cultivated for paper making, and I suspect that it never grew there spontaneously but was imported from tropical Africa at a very early period. In the 1960s a surviving specimen was discovered in Wadi Natrun but typically not on the Nile.[7] The papyrus that now grows in Egypt and is used by modern papyrus makers was imported from the Jardin du Luxembourg, Paris, in 1872 and planted in front of the Egyptian Museum in Cairo. From there, a number of plants came to the Cairo Zoo and were in turn transplanted by Dr. Hassan Ragab to his plantation on Jacob's Island. The origin of these plants appears to be Syracuse, where papyrus was introduced (or rediscovered) by the Arabs during the Middle Ages. In any case, the origin of the plants must have been Egypt.[8] Pliny (*HN* 13, 72–73) also mentions papyrus in Syria and Mesopotamia.

How Was Papyrus Made?

We have three sources of information on papyrus making: analysis of ancient papyri, ancient descriptions, and modern experiments with manufacture. If we start with the simplest form of analysis, looking at a piece of papyrus paper, it is obvious that it is made of two layers of fibers placed perpendicularly to one another. As for descriptions, I consider that we have no good description from antiquity of how papyrus was made. The Egyptians apparently never recorded the process, and the only classical author who describes it is Pliny (*HN* 13, 74–82), whose account is problematical in several ways. The principles of textual criticism dictate that we try to reconstitute what the author wrote, but our natural tendency is to try to make sense of what Pliny wrote since we tend to assume that he knew what he was talking about. This is, however, not necessarily the case, since Pliny had never been to Egypt and papyrus paper must be made from fresh papyrus; thus, it can be made only where papyrus grows. It is therefore almost certain that he had never witnessed the manufacture of a papyrus sheet, and it is consequently difficult to determine how we should deal with the obvious shortcomings of Pliny's text. He must have been excerpting a written source, but we have no idea what it was or whether it was correct. So, in general, emendations of Pliny's text should be avoided. What we can do (and what several commentators, including myself, have done) is to try to interpret the words in such a way that they can be harmonized with what we believe to be the truth. This procedure contains an obvious danger of circular argumentation. To complicate matters, I believe that Pliny is mixing personal experience of papyrus he had bought and used in Rome with whatever source he was using to describe its manufacture, and I believe that, while his source must have given an account of papyrus making in pharaonic times, his own experience was, of course, of papyrus as produced in his own day.[9]

I quote a translation of the relevant passage, adapted from Lewis (1974: 37–41):

74. Paper is made from the papyrus plant by separating it carefully[10] into very thin strips as broad as possible. The choice quality comes from the middle, and after that come the other cuts in order. The (choice) quality, in former times called "hieratic" because it was devoted only to religious books has, out of flattery, taken on the name of Augustus, and the next quality that of Livia, after his wife, so that the "hieratic" has dropped to third rank.

75. The next had been named "amphitheatric" from its place of manufacture. At Rome, Fannius' clever workshop took it up and refined it by careful processing, thus making a first-class paper out of a common one and renaming it after him; the paper not so reworked remained in its original grade as "amphitheatric."

76. Next is the "Saitic," so called after the town where it is most abundant, made from inferior scraps, and, even more like bark, there is the "Taeneotic," named after a nearby place (this is sold, in fact, by weight, not by quality). The "emporitic," being useless for writing, provides envelopes for papers and wrappings for merchandise, and its name accordingly comes from [the Greek for] merchants. After this there is the end of the papyrus stalk, which is similar to a rush and useless even for rope except in moisture.

77. Paper of whatever grade is fabricated on a board moistened with water from the Nile: the muddy liquid serves as the bonding force. First there is spread flat on the board and quite straight a layer consisting of strips of papyrus of whatever length they may be. When the ends are squared off a cross layer completes the construction. Then it is pressed in presses, and the sheets thus formed are dried in the sun and joined one to another, in declining order of excellence down to the poorest. There are never more than twenty sheets in a roll.

78. There is great variation in their breadth, the best thirteen digits, the "hieratic" two less, the "Fannian" measures ten, the "amphitheatric" one less, the "Saitic" a few less—and it is not strong enough for malletting—and the narrow "emporitic" does not exceed six digits. Beyond that, the qualities esteemed in paper are fineness, firmness, whiteness, and smoothness.

79. The Emperor Claudius changed the order of preference. The "Augustan" paper was too thin for writing with a pen; in addition, as it let the ink through there was always the fear of a blot from the back, and in other respects it was unattractive in appearance because excessively translucent. Consequently the vertical (under) layer was made of second-grade material and the horizontal layer of first-grade. He also increased its width to measure a foot.

80. There was also the "macrocolumn," a cubit wide, but experience revealed the defect that when one strip tears off it damages several columns of writing. For these reasons the "Claudian" paper is preferred to all others; the "Augustan" retains its importance for correspondence, and the "Livian," which never had any first-grade elements but was all second-grade, retains its same place.

81. Rough spots are rubbed smooth with ivory or shell, but then the writing is apt to become scaly: the polished paper is shinier and less absorptive. Writing is also impeded if (in manufacture) the liquid was negligently applied in the first place; this fault is detected with the mallet, or even by odour if the application was too careless. Spots, too, are easily detected by the eye, but a strip inserted between two others, though bibulous from the sponginess of (such) papyrus, can scarcely be detected except when the writing runs—there is so much trickery in the business! The result is the additional labour of reprocessing.

82. Common paste made from finest flour is dissolved in boiling water with the merest sprinkle of vinegar, for carpenter's glue and gum are too brittle. A more painstaking process percolates boiling water through the crumb of leavened bread; by this method the substance of the intervening paste is so minimal that even the suppleness of linen is surpassed. Whatever paste is used ought to be no more or less than a day old. Afterwards it is flattened with the mallet and gone over with paste, and wrinkles are again removed and smoothed out with the mallet.

In general this description corresponds well to what we may deduce from observation of existing papyri, but a few obscure points remain. The papyrus stalk was harvested and cut into sections, separating sections from the lower, the middle, or the upper parts. Pliny becomes a little confusing when describing the qualities resulting from these various cuts because the criteria for the qualities combined both the firmness and opacity of the writing material and the width of the sheets. The lower part of the stalk contains relatively more pulp between the fibers than the higher part, so the sections from the lower part of the stem produce a thinner papyrus sheet than the middle.[11] Because of the change of writing implements from reed brush (as used for Egyptian) to reed pen ($\kappa\acute{\alpha}\lambda\alpha\mu o\varsigma$) (as used for Greek and Latin), the very fine papyrus favored in pharaonic times was less attractive for the Greeks and Romans.[12] However, the qualities also differed in the width of the individual sheets.[13] When the papyrus was sold in roll form, one asked for a roll of a given quality, and since the width of the twenty sheets was fixed, the length of the roll (i.e. twenty sheets of the width appropriate to that quality) was also known for every quality. The height, on the other hand, could vary. The somewhat confusing statement in 77 would give the impression that every roll contained all the qualities, which of course is nonsense. What Pliny means is that the best sheets of the quality in question were put first in the roll for the customer to see, rather as strawberries tend to be arranged for sale in the punnet.[14]

Another point that may need some explanation concerns the procedures of "Fannius's clever workshop." The posttreatment of Fannius has long excited commentators. Pliny does not tell us what the method involved and the reason may be that he did not know. The only thing Pliny *does* say is that the sheets or rolls were made larger. Fannius presumably guarded his professional secret. Lewis "speculates within the bounds of reason" that Fannius may have added a third layer of better quality in order to produce a better writing surface.[15] I find it difficult to see how this would enlarge the sheets. C. H. Roberts is quoted by Lewis for a similar idea, namely that the original papyrus was split and a layer of better quality was substituted as writing surface.[16] Again, I do not see that this would enlarge the sheet/roll. Besides, such a procedure would have been difficult, not to say impossible. If I, too, may be allowed to speculate within reason, I believe that the only way to make an existing sheet or roll larger is to beat it with a mallet.[17] This would inevitably make a dry papyrus sheet more brittle, but if the sheet was first moistened, it might be possible to increase its size by about 10 percent while making the paper thinner. The main risk when moistening papyrus, as all restorers know, is that the ink may run, which is not pertinent in this case. Anyone who has tried his hand at restoration will have noticed that the fibers regain much of their original flexibility when wet. In fact, I believe that in 78 Pliny is telling us that the paper was hammered out; he writes that the Saitic quality is even smaller *nec malleo sufficit* (and is not strong enough to be malleted). Why else would he mention the mallet in connection with the size?

Modern Experiments

The best-known modern experiments are those of Hassan Ragab, Cairo, and Corrado Basile, Syracuse. Both have produced papyrus of a useable quality, and both are sure they have recreated the ancient procedure, although it is obvious to anyone who handles their paper that something is wrong. The few examples I have seen of the Sicilian papyrus are very soft, white, and pliable but do not feel like papyrus at all. The Ragab papyrus feels like ancient papyrus but has the characteristic "grid pattern," that is, the individual strips are seen very clearly, which is not the case with ancient papyrus. The problem is whether to place the strips side by side (with the risk of gaps forming between them as they dry), or placing them with an overlap, as Ragab did, thus producing the grid pattern. Pliny's description (given earlier) does not mention any overlap, and the ancient papyri do not show any grid pattern. So we still do not know exactly how papyrus was made. In an attempt to find a solution, I. Hendriks proposed that Pliny's *diviso acu* meant exactly that—with a needle—and that the papyrus stalk was unrolled by the so-called peeling method.[18] The theory created a certain amount of interest at the time,[19] but as I have shown, Pliny's text contains too many counterindications. Besides, having tried it myself, I know that a papyrus stalk does not react kindly to being peeled. It breaks whenever one tries to "go around a corner" in order to open the next side of the triangle, and using a needle instead of a knife tends to tear the pulp. Besides, it has never been clear to me why using a needle would lead to the peeling method (see figures 1.1–1.4).

Figure 1.1. An ancient papyrus on the lightbox (*P.Sorb.* inv. 2245). There are no overlaps or bare patches between the papyrus strips. We clearly see a *kollêsis* somewhat to the left of the middle of the image. Photo by Adam Bülow-Jacobsen.

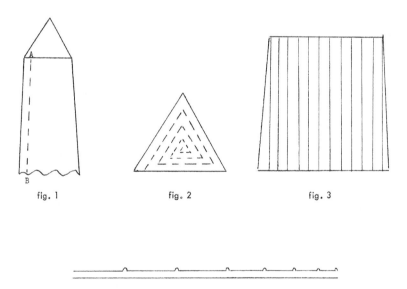

Figure 1.2. Diagrams from Hendriks's original article: 1. the initial cut into the triangular stem; 2. the peeling schematized on a cross-section of the stalk; 3. the peeled section; 4. a peeled section seen from the edge. Reproduced courtesy of Habelt Verlag.

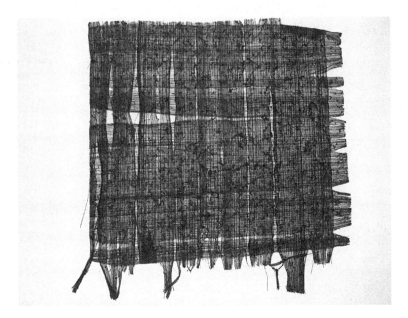

Figure 1.3. Papyrus made by Hendriks's peeling method. Overlapping between the strips has been avoided, but there are far too many holes in the sheet where the fibers have shrunk while drying. Photo by Adam Bülow-Jacobsen.

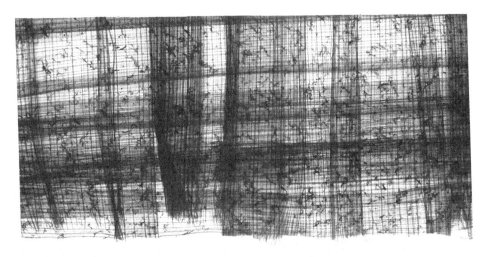

Figure 1.4. Papyrus made by H. Ragab. The overlaps between the strips are much too obvious. Photo by Adam Bülow-Jacobsen.

PARCHMENT

In Latin, parchment was called *pergamena* (n. pl.) or, much more often, *membrana* (f.). The most common Greek word is διφθέρα, but in the fourth century περγαμηνὴ (διφθέρα) and δέρμα were also used.[20] The word *parchment* comes from the name of the city of Pergamon in Asia Minor, and the ancients believed that the use of untanned skins originated there. Pliny quotes Varro as the origin of the following well-known story: King Ptolemy (V Epiphanes, 205–180 BCE) of Egypt and King Eumenes (II, 197–159 BCE) of Pergamon competed on creating the best library. To thwart his adversary, Ptolemy stopped the exportation of papyrus, and so the Pergamenes invented parchment.[21] The story is unlikely to be true, however, for skins were used for writing long before that period: Aramaic parchment documents from Bactria from the fourth century BCE have been found (Shaked 2004), and documents on parchment from the early second century BCE have been found at Dura-Europos.[22]

Contrary to papyrus, the method of making parchment is well known. Skins, mostly of calf, goat, or sheep, are cleaned, scraped free of hair, stretched while drying, and treated with alum and chalk.[23] Parchment, or vellum, as it is also called, is different from leather in that it is not tanned.

When looking at a parchment codex, it is a sobering thought that every double folio page represents a whole sheep or goat.

WOOD

Wood in several forms was regularly used for writing.[24] Wax tablets, wooden boards (whitened or not), and concertina leaves are the most important of these. In Greek a wooden tablet is called πίναξ, πινακίς, δελτίον, δελτίδιον, πυκτίον, or γραμματεῖον. In Latin *tabula* or *tabella* is used, or, for a wax tablet, *cera*.

Wax Tablets

The surface of a wooden board was gouged out, leaving a border at the edge, and the hollow thus created was filled with beeswax. The writing was scratched into the wax with a γραφίς (Latin *stilus*), which was a pointed pin of wood, bone, or bronze, whose opposite end was normally formed as a spatula for smoothing out when the scribe wanted to correct something.[25] Quintilian recommends writing on wax tablets, although older people may have difficulties because of the low contrast between the writing and the background. Writing on parchment with a pen and ink, however, disturbs the flow of thought—so Quintilian says—because of the frequent need to dip the pen. Also, he says, it is easier to correct on wax tablets.[26] Wax tablets were clearly the everyday notebook for bookkeeping, business correspondence, and literary drafts. The problem is that the wax does not often survive, and the writing is then preserved only in the scratchings left in the wood underneath the wax.[27] If holes were drilled in the edge and a string passed through them, wax tablets could be arranged in a kind of codex. The "pages" between the first and the last tablet could be hollowed out and waxed on both sides.

Wax tablets were often written in lines parallel to the long side of the tablet. Thus, when they were bound together into a codex, the notebook would not open with a left and a right page, but with an upper and a lower page.

Wooden Boards

A wooden board covered with white paint presents a very good writing surface for pen and ink and must always have been used. We know that such boards, σανίδες, were used in Athens for the publication of official texts, either impermanent ones or before they could be carved in stone.[28]

In Egypt such boards, whitened or not, are found occasionally, first of all as mummy labels; these are small wooden tablets (never whitened as far as I know) on which the name of the deceased was written in pen and ink or very occasionally incised. The label was attached to the mummy with a piece of string that passed through a hole in the label. Labels of similar design were also attached to sacks or baskets that were sent, for example, to people working away from their families (figure 1.5).

The most spectacular wooden tablets are the codices from the oasis of Dakhla.[29] These recent finds are unique in their genre so far and also interesting because of their perfect condition. They are sawn from a block of acacia wood, the

Figure 1.5. Ἀμμώνις Ἀμμωνίου. Wooden label with its string intact (*O.Claud.* inv. 4271). Photo by Adam Bülow-Jacobsen.

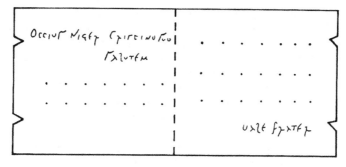

Leaf-tablet: letter format.

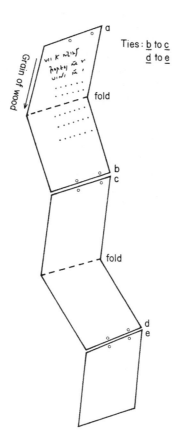

Leaf-tablets, concertina format.

Figure 1.6a–b. A letter written on a folded leaf tablet and a concertina tablet. From *T.Vindol.* I 3839. Reproduced by permission of A. K. Bowman.

norm apparently being eight leaves from a block. The two outer leaves were sawn to a thickness of about 5 mm, while the inner leaves are 2–3 mm. The separated leaves were marked with notches by the carpenter, so that the original order could be maintained. Holes were drilled at the edge, and a string was passed through them. The boards are normally not whitened, but an inserted leaf in the Isocrates codex is. The text is written in ink in lines parallel to the short side of the tablets.

Wooden Leaf Tablets

This type of tablet is known from Vindolanda in northern England, where many have been preserved in anaerobic and humid conditions. Apart from ordinary wax tablets, the site also yielded these unique specimens. They are very thin slices (some as thin as 0.25 mm), but most are 1–2 mm thick and are of alder or birch. The surface, where it is preserved or can be reconstructed, is 16–20 cm by 6–9 cm. If such a slice were to be used for a letter, the lines of writing would normally be parallel to the longest side (thus parallel to the grain of the wood) and in two columns. The leaf was then scored lightly in the middle and folded, and it could be closed and sealed by a string drawn through holes near the left and right edges. The address could be written on the outside.[30] If the text was an account, the writing would often be parallel to the short side of the leaf (i.e., across the grain of the wood). The tablets were again scored and folded, but if the account was a long one, several such diptychs could be tied together to form a "concertina list" (figure 1.6).[31]

OSTRACA

Potsherds were everywhere in the ancient world, since pots, although they can be reused, cannot be recycled like glass or metal once they are broken.

We must distinguish several types of ostraca (in the modern usage of the term): (1) the Athenian type; mostly black glaze (i.e., red-figure) pottery on which ostracisms were written by scratching through the black glaze so that letters are shown by the pink pottery below; (2) the ancient Egyptian type of flat limestone with writing in ink; (3) sherds of broken pots written on with pen and ink (or brush and ink for the demotic ones); (4) whole pots inscribed with the contents, the origin, the name of the recipient, or similar information.

The regular Greek word for *ostracon* is ὄστρακον, whereas Latin does not seem to have a word that covers all the meanings of the Greek term. *Testa* or *testula* are used to translate ὄστρακον in the Athenian sense (type 1 above) of a voting ballot. *Ostracum* is found very occasionally in texts from Egypt.

Figure 1.7. Athenian ostracon (Kerameikos Museum). Photo by
Adam Bülow-Jacobsen.

Ostraca of the Athenian type are of course preserved under most climatic
conditions, while the other two types, even if the ostracon itself is preserved, need a
relatively dry climate if the ink is to remain legible (figure 1.7).

Ostraca of the Athenian type do not seem to have been used for purposes other
than balloting. Type 3 ostraca, on the other hand, were used for most kinds of writing
in Egypt, although they were considered a surrogate for papyrus.[32] Obviously,
ostraca were suited only for short texts and could not easily be archived, nor could
they be bound together if more than one was needed for a longer text, and letters on
ostraca could not be sealed to protect the text from prying eyes. In addition, they were
much heavier than papyrus. Nevertheless, all these disadvantages were outweighed
by one important advantage: Ostraca were completely free. In many places one only
had to bend down and pick them up. However, in places like Mons Claudianus,
where stonemasons were employed, we sometimes find ostraca that were prepared
for writing with much more care. In a suitable sherd, holes were drilled to mark the
circumference of the desired ostracon, and the worker then carved out the writing
ostracon using these holes as a guide. In this way one could obtain a pleasant oval or a
rounded square. Edges were then beveled, and the writing surface often smoothed,
presumably by polishing it in sand. Such ostraca were sometimes washed and used
again, but this shaping-procedure was exceptional and is not found in sites where
military personnel were predominant (figures 1.8 and 1.9).

The best-known use of Greek and demotic ostraca was for tax receipts,
especially in southern Egypt, but there is mounting evidence of their use for all
kinds of writing in the desert. In particular, the many Roman sites in the Eastern
Desert that have been excavated during the last twenty years continue to produce
large amounts of ostraca and very few papyri. This is not difficult to explain:
Provisions of wine, salt fish, olives, oil, and even pickled meat and fish for the
people who lived and worked in the desert arrived in jars, mostly the standard
Egyptian amphora of about 6½ liters with pitch on the inside, which may have
been reused on site but were mostly broken (figure 1.10). So there was never any
shortage of ostraca. On the other hand, papyrus had to be brought from the valley.

Figure 1.8. Ostracon from Mons Claudianus in preparation. Here the craftsman has chosen a piece of an amphora that already has an inscription. The project appears to have been abandoned because the sherd broke. Photo by Adam Bülow-Jacobsen.

Letters on papyrus that had arrived from the valley must also have been a temptation when one was in need of kindling. In Coptic, ostraca were also used for tax receipts, but the great mass of surviving ostraca, which come from monasteries, contain letters. It is striking how few Arabic ostraca have been found so far.

Figure 1.9. A good example of a shaped ostracon (*O.Claud.* III 522, natural size). Photo by Adam Bülow-Jacobsen.

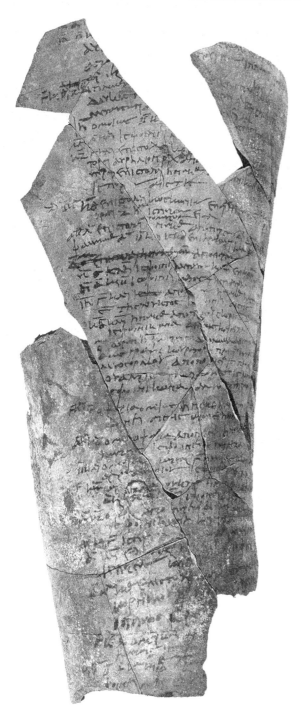

Figure 1.10. A giant ostracon (40.5 cm tall) using an almost complete amphora to write a register of post riders. (*O.Krok.* I 1). Photo by Adam Bülow-Jacobsen.

INK (μέλαν, ATRAMENTUM)

In antiquity, ink was what we now call India ink: soot with a little gum arabic suspended in water.[33] Both in China and in pharaonic Egypt ink was kept in blocks, and the writing brush could be inked directly on the block if a little water (spittle) was applied to its surface. Since Greek and Latin were written with a calamus (a reed pen), which had to be dipped into the ink, the scribe had to prepare a quantity of ink every day.[34] The earliest occurrence of metallic ink is from the third century BCE,[35] but from the second century CE and particularly from the third century onward, the mordant metallic inks make their appearance. These are made from powdered gallnuts, a metallic salt (iron or copper), gum arabic, and water. While the India inks do not fade, iron-gall inks turn from black to brown with time. They may fade to almost the same shade of brown as the papyrus and become very difficult to read. The mordant quality of iron-gall ink makes it more penetrating, but may also eventually damage the papyrus or parchment.

BOOKS IN ANTIQUITY: THE VOLUMEN AND THE CODEX

Book (*liber*, βιβλίον), as far as the ancients were concerned, meant a roll (Lat. *volumen*). Although the codex format was known at a fairly early time, it was not until the second century CE that it really appeared in Egypt, but already in the fourth century the majority of literary works were written on codices.

The situation is well illustrated by Ulpian (†228 CE) commenting on Sabinus (first half of the first century) and Gaius Cassius (mid–first century). The discussion is about what constitutes "a book" when donated in a will:

> Under the term books (*librorum appellatione*) are included all rolls, whether of papyrus or parchment or any other material. And even if they are of rind of the lime or linden tree (as made by some) or of some other bark, the same must be said. But are they due if they are in codex-form, either of parchment or papyrus or ivory or some other material, or of waxed-tablets? Let us see. Gaius Cassius wrote that [loose] parchments are due also, when books have been bequeathed. Therefore, it follows that the others too will be due, unless this is contrary to the testator's intentions.[36]

So, in Rome, in the first century of our era, a jurist's response was required to decide whether a codex was a book. Yet, when Ulpian wrote in the early third century, the codex was gaining steadily on the roll and in another century would

Figure 1.11. Bookroll with calamus and inkwell and polyptych with stylus. (From Praedia di Iulia Felix, Museo Nazionale, Napoli, inv. 8598). Photo by J.-P. Brun.

replace it almost completely. Why would that be ? Before trying to answer this question, we must look at the anatomy of the roll and the codex respectively.

The Bookroll

The roll was the normal unit in which papyrus was produced and sold.[37] As we have already seen from Pliny *HN* 13.77, the papyrus sheets were pasted together, twenty at a time, and sold as rolls. When a scribe wanted to write a document, he cut a sheet of an appropriate size from the roll, but when writing literature, the scribe presumably used the roll as it was. If the length of the work he was transcribing did not correspond to the length of the roll—and there was no reason it should—he would add on or cut off in order to obtain the right length.

As Pliny has told us, papyrus was commercialized as rolls made up of sheets pasted together. The reason for this was probably that the individual sheets would each present four edges, and the edges are the weakness of papyrus, always presenting a risk of fraying. Pasted together into a roll, the twenty sheets would present only four edges in all, and additional measures were taken to protect the ends. At the beginning of the roll was the *protokollon*, an unwritten sheet, while at the end there was probably the ὀμφαλός or *umbilicus*, the wooden stick around which the papyrus was rolled, but even if no *umbilicus* was present, the end was protected inside the roll. The sheets of the roll were pasted together in such a way that the left sheet was always over the right one in any given join. The joins are called *kollēseis* (singular *kollēsis*). If the roll was to be used for demotic writing (from right to left), it was turned 180 degrees. In this way the writer would always write "downward" over the join and feel a minimum of resistance when passing over a "step." The face used first was always the inside of the roll, where the fibers

Figure 1.12. A muse reading from a bookroll (Attic red-figure lekythos from ca. 435–425. Louvre, Collection Pozzi, inv. CA 2220). Photo by RMN/H. Lewandowski, courtesy of the Musée du Louvre.

were parallel to the length of the roll and to the lines of writing. This is not because it is easier to write with the fibers rather than across them, nor is it normally because the surface on the "back" is less well suited for writing. Given a fragment of papyrus without original edges, writing, or *kollêseis,* papyrologists (even experienced ones) will have trouble telling which side is the front and which the back. When a *kollêsis* is present on a fragment, it is easy to see which side is the front and which side is the back since the *kollêsis* on the front makes a break in the fiber pattern. However, it is much more difficult to see the join from the back, where the edge of the sheet follows the same direction as the fibers ("vertical"). The reason for having the "horizontal" fibers on the inside and the "vertical" on the outside was probably that vertical fibers would be squeezed together and risk detachment if they were on the inside.

The writing would be on the inside, front, in columns ($\sigma\epsilon\lambda\acute{\iota}\delta\epsilon\varsigma$, *paginae*) unless the document was written *transversa charta* (i.e., "having turned the papyrus"), in which case it would present one long column running down the roll with lines of writing across the fibers (figure 1.13).[38]

For practical reasons, a bookroll could be written on one side only. When we find, as we often do, that there is writing on both sides of a papyrus, we are dealing with an example of reuse. Quite often a roll would be turned inside out when the primary writing was no longer of interest, and the back could be used for further writing. Of 3,365 literary rolls listed in the *LDAB,* more than 400 are examples of literature written on the back of documentary rolls that have been turned over. There are also several examples of demotic literature that was written on the back of Greek rolls, although demotists have a tendency to consider the demotic text as the "recto" or the front, regardless of the fiber direction and other evidence.

The height of the roll depended on the constituent sheets, not, as we have seen, on the quality of the papyrus, and ranges from 15 cm to more than 40 cm (a height of 20–30 cm is normal). The length of the bookroll was theoretically unlimited, and Ulpian mentions, for the sake of the argument, the possibility of getting all forty-eight books of Homer onto one roll.[39] Ancient Egyptian rolls could be very long (the longest known exceeds 40 meters), but most of these very long rolls are ornamental copies of the Book of the Dead, meant to be buried with the deceased, not to be read in this world. Greek rolls were no longer than 10–11 meters and generally much shorter, but few complete Greek rolls exist, and the original length of a fragmentary roll is mostly a theoretical projection on the basis of letters per line and lines per column calculated against a known text.

To modern people who are used to the codex format, the disadvantages of the roll seem many: It does not readily contain more than part of a prose work, like, for example, a book of an historian; it has to be rolled back when read; and it is difficult to refer to a passage. Besides, the roll is fragile. The edges fray, especially the lower edge, which may rub against the reader's clothing, and the roll is easily torn.

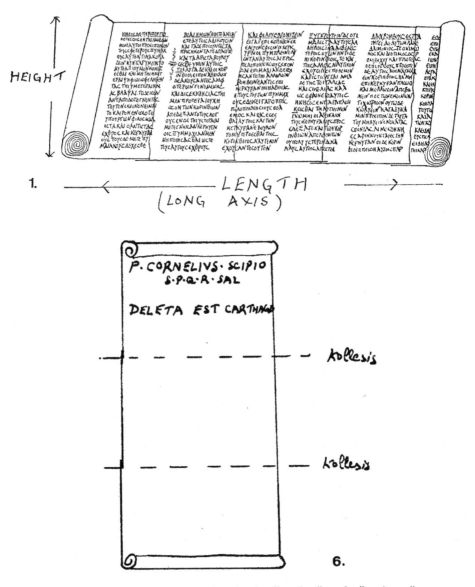

Figure 1.13a–b. Drawings of, respectively, a bookroll and a "rotulus" written "transversa charta" (W. E. H. Cockle and E. G. Turner in Turner 1978, 14, 33).

Parchment sheets can be made into rolls, the best-known examples being the Hebrew Torah rolls. However, the one example of a parchment roll that I know and which must originate from Egypt is clearly an amateurish creation.[40] Altogether I know of eighteen parchment rolls in Greek or Latin, of which seven are Old Testament texts that were clearly influenced by the Torah format; two are New Testament; and the remainder are a few fragments of classical authors. However, none of these were unquestionably written in Egypt, and most of them were probably not. I believe that these texts may give us a glimpse of what books in the Pergamon library looked like.

The Codex

To understand the development of the codex,[41] consider that, if the material is not papyrus but rather tablets or parchment, the bookroll is not a natural result. Neither tablets nor parchment have frail edges that need protection, and they are more difficult to concatenate. Parchment rolls are sewn together, not glued. The "concertina" tablets from Vindolanda (mentioned earlier) have been regarded as precursors of the codex but could also have been an attempt to make a roll. Wooden or waxed tablets might also have been concatenated like sheets in a roll.[42]

The format adopted when a longer text was to be written on tablets or parchment was the codex (*caudex, pugillares, membranae*), which began its career far from the bookroll's world of classical literature. Letters, drafts, and accounts were routinely written in this form, not least, of course, outside Egypt, where papyrus was less easily obtained.

A natural way to link tablets together is to bore holes in one edge and bind them with a piece of string or a leather thong. This way, both sides of the tablet are useable, the inner surfaces are protected, the "book" can be sealed if it contains a letter, and it is easily transportable. Such books, with as many as fifteen leaves (thirty pages), are well known from a number of places in the Roman Empire. The special case of the Dakhla tablet books has already been described, but waxed tablets were undoubtedly more common.

Latin authors also mention notebooks made of parchment, called *membranae*.[43] The point of departure here would be a large sheet of parchment that was folded and cut at the edges, precisely like modern printed books before the

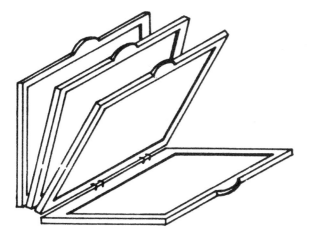

Figure 1.14. Reconstruction of a polyptych from "Villa dei papiri" in Herculaneum. From Capasso, "Le tavolette della Villa dei papiri ad Ercolano" in Lalou, ed. (1992). Reproduced courtesy of M. Capasso.

bookbinders began to do it for us. A sheet folded once in each direction will produce four leaves or eight pages, a "quarto" format. Folding once more makes an "octavo" format of eight leaves, and so on. These folded sheets, called "quires" in English (derived from Latin *quaternio* [a set of four]), are then sewn together with other quires to form a codex. By following this procedure one automatically obtains the aesthetically pleasant effect that any opening of the finished, cut book presents two pages of "flesh side" or two pages of "hair side."

All this is quite different, however, if you want to make your codex of papyrus, as would be natural in Egypt.[44] Here the starting point is the roll made of sheets pasted together. This roll must be cut into sheets twice the width of the desired page and folded once in the middle. The early papyrus codices were often made as "single quire" codices, in which the cut sheets were placed in a pile (normally all with the front up), which was folded in the middle. This method put great stress on the outer leaves and produced an irregular and fragile front edge. Every possible method seems to have been tried, and, besides the single-quire codices, there are papyrus codices that range from one to at least five sheets per quire. Eventually, however, a preference for the *quaternio* (four sheets per quire) was established.[45] The principle of facing pages having the same surface was, as we saw, automatic with parchment, but with papyrus it was not. Apart from the single-quire codices, a practice seems to have developed in which the outside leaf in a quire normally had horizontal fibers and the following ones alternated, so that an opening always showed two facing pages with the same fiber direction. Sometimes the codex is well enough preserved to permit reconstruction of the roll from which the leaves were cut (figure 1.15).

The competition between the roll and the codex lasted a couple of centuries but was eventually completely won by the codex. It seems that the Christians took to the codex with alacrity, perhaps because the roll was associated with classical elite, literary culture, while the first Christians were mostly humble people who were more used to accounts and business letters than to Homer and Aeschylus. Presumably they also wanted their books to be different from the Jewish Torah rolls. The codex was also easier to refer to, simpler to transport, and more economical since the back of the sheet could also be used. As early as the second century, when the struggle had just begun, only about 4 percent of 1,772 papyri of classical literature were codices, whereas 75 percent of 37 Christian works were codices. In the third century, 13 percent of classical texts were written in codex form, while 75 percent of the Christian works were codices. In the fourth century the codex had already claimed 64 percent of classical literature and 81 percent of Christian. By the fifth century 90 percent of classical and 95 percent of Christian literature was in codex form (table 1.2). The era of the literary bookroll had definitely ended.[46]

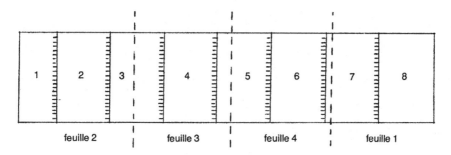

Figure 1.15. A reconstruction of the roll from which the first four sheets for a codex were cut. As is evident, no account is taken of the original *kollêseis*. From J. Scherer, *Extraits des livres I et II du Contre Celse d'Origène d'après le Papyrus no. 88747 du Musée du Caire*, Cairo (1956).

Table 1.2. The replacement of the volumen by the codex

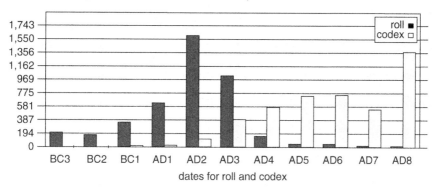

Source: *Leuven Database of Ancient Books*, http://www.trismegistos.org/ldab/.

NOTES

1. Brashear (1997).

2. See, for example, Pliny *HN* 13, 69.

3. Http://www.rzuser.uni-heidelberg.de/~gv0/gvz.html.

4. Http://www.trismegistos.org/ldab/.

5. Alain Delattre, *Banque de données des textes coptes documentaires*, http://dev.ulb.ac.be/philo/bad/copte/base.php?page=rechercher.php.

6. Theophr. *HP* 4, 8, 3; Pliny *HN* 13, 70.

7. Täckholm (1974, 790).

8. Ragab (1980, 52–53). Contrast, however, Ragab (1988, 514–515), who states that the plants in his plantation came from the Sudan. Moreover, Basile (1998, 29) claims that, around 250 BCE, Hieron II had transported the plant from Egypt to Sicily, where it was used only for cordage since the Sicilians did not know the secret of paper making.

9. Thompson (1965, 23): "His description applies specially to the system of his own day; but no doubt it was essentially the same as had been followed for centuries."

10. This translation is based on a correction of the text, which I propose with some hesitation. The manuscripts have *diviso acu* (divided by a needle). Attempts to make sense of this has led to various interpretations, such as Hendriks (1980) (discussed later) or Łukaszewicz (1997), but all difficulties would disappear if we were to accept *diviso ac<c>u<rate>* and assume a lacuna in the archetype.

11. Bülow-Jacobsen (1976).

12. Tait (1988). See also Clarysse (1993). Delange (1990) gives examples of demotic papyri written with carbon ink and a reed brush, while, in the same document, the Greek subscription is written in metallic ink with a calamus.

13. Johnson (1993).

14. Cf. Lewis (1974, 53n27).

15. Lewis (1989, 21–22).

16. Lewis (1974, 45n13).

17. Lewis (1989, 22): "How did the 'clever workshop' make the papyrus thinner? By malleting?"

18. Hendriks (1980).

19. See, for example, Turner (1980) but also Lewis (1981).

20. In the sense of "parchment book," δέρμα appears in P.Ashm. inv. 3 (fourth century), republished by Otranto (1997). I thank Simona Russo for this reference.

21. Pliny *NH* 13, 70.

22. Roberts and Skeat (1983, 5–7) do not believe that the story can be true; they cite arguments from a thesis by Richard R. Johnson, "The Role of Parchment in Greco-Roman Antiquity" (PhD. diss., University of California, Los Angeles, 1968), which I have not seen.

23. For references to more detailed descriptions, see Turner (1968, 9 and 9n41).

24. Lalou (1992) contains articles by experts on most kinds of tablets.

25. Quintilian (*Inst. Or.* X 4, 1) even claims that the erasing capacity of the stilus is at least as important as its capacity to write.

26. Quintilian, *Inst. Or.*, X, 3, 31.27. See, for example, *T.Vindon.* = Speidel (1996).

28. See, for example, Andokides, περὶ τῶν μυστηρίων 83; Lysias XXVI 10.

29. See J. L. Sharp, "The Dakhleh Tablets," in Lalou, ed. (1992, 127–148), and Sharp's very full codicological descriptions in *P.Kellis* IV pp.17–20, and *P.Kellis* III pp.9–21.

30. A perfect example is *T.Vindol.* II 310 (figure 1.6a). A similar type of folded leaf tablet is *P.Yadin* 54.

31. See *T.Vindol.* I 4. (figure 1.6b).

32. Cuvigny et al. (2003 II 470–473) present a more thorough analysis of the use of ostraca than the space here permits. There are also quotations from unpublished ostraca that present excuses for not writing on papyrus.

33. See also Cockle (1983, 150).

34. τὸ μέλαν τρίβειν ("to grind the ink"); see, for example, Demosthenes, *De Corona* 258.

35. See Delange (1990).

36. Justinian, *Digesta* 32.1.52, trans. A. Watson.

37. The most recent and comprehensive description of the bookroll is Turner (1978).

38. This was apparently customary when writing to the senate in Rome; cf. Suetonius, *Div. Iul.* 52.6.

39. Justinian, *Digesta*. 32.1.52.1.1. On a conservative estimate such a roll would have been a monster of about 140 meters.

40. Chester Beatty Library, inv. W 145. See the description in Quecke (1975). See also *P.Köln* IV 174, which is part of the same roll and where the full bibliography may be found.

41. Greek κῶδιξ, but no proper Greek word seems to have existed.

42. This format is in fact found in Nimrud, where waxed ivory tablets of the late eighth century BCE were hinged together to make a concertina (Wiseman 1955; Howard 1955). These waxed tablets were made of wood and ivory and contain writing on both sides. Wiseman (1955, 6–8) appears to assume that both the front and the back were used for the same text.

43. Passages illustrating books and reading are conveniently collected in Kenyon (1951: 121–134).

44. To me, there is little doubt that the papyrus codex is derived from the parchment codex, but the great specialists on the matter, Roberts and Skeat (1983), see it differently. Two chapters of their book are devoted to various theories about both this and the Christian preference for the codex.

45. For makeup and statistics on the early codex see Turner (1977).

46. *LDAB*.

BIBLIOGRAPHY

Basile, C. 1977. "Metodo usato dagli antichi Egizi per la fabbricazione e la preservazione della carta papiro." *Aegyptus* 57: 190–199.

———. 1998. "New Discoveries concerning the Fabric of Papyrus." *Annales du Service des Antiquités de l'Egypte* 73: 28–34.

Bierbrier, M. L., ed. 1986. *Papyrus: Structure and Usage.* London: British Museum.

Blanchard, A., ed. 1989. *Les débuts du codex: Actes de la journée d'étude* (Bibliologia 9). Turnhout: Brepols.

Brashear, W. M. 1997. "Egyptian Papyrus Then, Chinese Paper Today (or: of Mummies in Maine and Tea from Cathay)." In *Akten des 21. Internationalen Papyrologenkongresses*, ed. B. Kramer et al., vol. 1, 113–131. Stuttgart: Teubner.

———, and F. A. J. Hoogendijk. 1990. "Corpus tabularum lignearum ceratarumque Aegyptiarum." *Enchoria* 17: 21–54.

Bülow-Jacobsen, A. 1976. "Principatus medio. Pliny *NH* XIII, 72 sqq." *ZPE* 20: 113–116.

———. 1985. "Magna in latitudine earum differentia" (Pliny *NH* XIII, 78). *ZPE* 60: 273–274.

Černy, J. 1952. *Paper and Books in Ancient Egypt.* London. (Repr. *s.a.* Chicago: Ares Publishers.)

Clarysse, W. 1993. "Egyptian Scribes Writing Greek." *CdÉ* 68: 186–201.

Cockle, W. E. H. 1983. "Restoring and Conserving Papyri." *Bulletin of the Institute of Classical Studies* 30: 147–165.

Cuvigny, H. (ed.), Jean-Pierre Brun, Adam Bülow-Jacobsen, Dominique Cardon, Jean-Luc Fournet, Martine Leguilloux, Marie-Agnès Matelly, and Michel Reddé. 2003. *La route de Myos Hormos: L'armée romaine dans le désert oriental d'Egypte. Praesidia du désert de Bérénice*. 2 vols. Fouilles de l'Institut français d'archéologie orientale 48/1–2. Cairo.

Delange, E., M. Grange, B. Kusko, and E. Menei. 1990. Apparition de l'encre métallogallique en Égypte à partir de la collection de papyrus du Louvre. *Revue d'Égyptologie* 41: 213–217.

Hendriks, I. H. M. 1980. "Pliny, Historia Naturalis XIII, 74–82, and the Manufacture of Papyrus." *ZPE* 37: 121–136.

——. 1984. "More about the Manufacture of Papyrus." *Atti del XVII Congresso Internazionale di Papirologia*, vol. 1, 31–37. Naples: Centro Internazionale per lo Studio dei Papiri Ercolanesi.

Holwerda, D. 1982. "Plinius über die Anfertigung von 'charta.' " *ZPE* 45: 257–262.

Howard, M. 1955. "Technical Description of the Ivory Writing-boards from Nimrud." *Iraq* 17: 14–20.

Irmscher, J. 1997. "Moderne Papyrusproduktion: Siracusa." In *Akten des 21. Internationalen Papyrologenkongresses*, ed. B. Kramer et al., vol. 2, 1113–1115. Stuttgart: Teubner.

Johnson, R. R. 1970. "Ancient and Medieval Account of the 'Invention' of Parchment." *CSCA* 3: 115–122.

Johnson, W. A. 1992. The Literary Papyrus Roll: Formats and Conventions. An Analysis of the Evidence from Oxyrhynchus. PhD. diss., Yale University.

——. 1993. "Pliny the Elder and Standardized Roll Heights in the Manufacture of Papyrus." *Classical Philology* 88: 46–50.

Kenyon, F. G. 1951. *Books and Readers in Ancient Greece and Rome*, 2d ed. New York: Oxford University Press.

Lalou, É., ed. 1992. *Les tablettes à écrire de l'antiquité à l'époque moderne* (Bibliologia 12). Turnhout: Brepols.

Leach, B., and J. Tait. 2000. "Papyrus." In *Ancient Egyptian Materials and Technology*, ed. P. T. Nicholson and I. Shaw, 227–253. Cambridge: Cambridge University Press.

Lewis, N. 1974. *Papyrus in Classical Antiquity*. Oxford: Clarendon.

——. 1981. "Open Letter to I. H. M. Hendriks and E. G. Turner (More on ZPE 39, 1980, 113–14)." *ZPE* 42: 293–294.

——. 1989. *Papyrus in Classical Antiquity: A Supplement* (Papyrologica Bruxellensia 23). Brussels: Fondation égyptologique Reine Elisabeth.

——. 1992. "Papyrus in Classical Antiquity: An Update." *CdÉ* 67: 308–318.

Łukaszewicz, A. 1997. "Diviso acu. Was a Needle Used in Papyrus Manufacturing?" *Journal of Juristic Papyrology* 27: 61–67.

Menci, G. 1988. "Fabbricazione, uso e restauro antico del papiro: Tre note in margine a Plinio, NH XIII 74–82." *Proceedings of the XVIII International Congress of Papyrology*, ed. B. Mandilaras. 2 vols. Vol. 2, 497–504. Athens: Greek Papyrological Society.

Otranto, R. 1997. "*Alia tempora, alii libri*: Notizie ed elenchi di libri cristiani su papiro." *Aegyptus* 77: 101–124.

Pliny HN = Ernout, A. 1956. Pline l'Ancien *Histoire naturelle* Livre XIII. (*Des Plantes exotiques*). Paris: Les Belles Lettres, Collection des Universités de France.

Quecke, H. 1975. *Die Briefe Pachoms: Griechischer Text der Handschrift W. 145 der Chester-Beatty Library*. Regensburg: Pustet.

Ragab, H. 1980. *Le papyrus* [Contribution à l'étude du papyrus (*Cyperus papyrus. L*) et à sa transformation en support de l'écriture (papyrus des anciens)]. Cairo: Dr. Ragab Papyrus Institute.

———. 1988. "The Quality of the Recently Manufactured Papyrus as Compared with Ancient Egyptian Papyrus." In *Proceedings of the XVIII International Congress of Papyrology,* ed. B. Mandilaras. 2 vols. Vol. 2, 513–523. Athens: Greek Papyrological Society.

Roberts, C. H., and T. C. Skeat. 1983. *The Birth of the Codex.* London: Oxford University Press.

Shaked, S. 2004. *Le satrape de Bactriane et son gouverneur: Documents araméens du IVe s. avant notre ère provenant de Bactriane* (Persika 4). Paris.

Skeat, T. C. 1982. "The Length of the Standard Papyrus Roll and the Cost Advantage of the Codex." *ZPE* 45: 169–175.

———. 1990. "Roll versus Codex: A New Approach?" *ZPE* 84: 297–298.

———. 1994. "The Origin of the Christian Codex." *ZPE* 102: 263–268.

———. 1995. "Was Papyrus Regarded as 'Cheap' or 'Expensive' in the Ancient World?" *Aegyptus* 75: 75–93.

Speidel, M. A. 1996. *Die römischen Schreibtafeln von Vindonissa: Lateinische Texte des militärischen Alltags und ihre geschichtliche Bedeutung.* Brugg: Veröffentlichungen der Gesellschaft Pro Vindonissa.

Täckholm, V. 1974. *Students' Flora of Egypt,* 2d ed. Cairo: Cairo University.

Tait, W. J. 1988. "Rush and Reed: The Pens of Egyptian and Greek Scribes." In *Proceedings of the XVIII International Congress of Papyrology,* ed. B. Mandilaras. 2 vols. Vol. 2, 477–481. Athens: Greek Papyrological Society.

Thompson, E. M. 1965. *An Introduction to Greek and Latin Palaeography.* New York: B. Franklin. (Orig. pub. 1912.)

Turner, E. G. 1952. *Athenian Books in the Fifth and Fourth Centuries* B.C. London: H. K. Lewis.

———. 1968. *Greek Papyri: An Introduction.* Oxford: Clarendon.

———. 1977. *The Typology of the Early Codex.* Philadelphia: University of Pennsylvania Press.

———. 1978. "The Terms Recto and Verso: The Anatomy of the Papyrus Roll." In *Actes du XVe Congrès international de papyrologie.* Part 1, Papyrologica Bruxellensia 16, ed. J. Bingen and G. Nachtergael. Brussels: Fondation égyptologique Reine Élisabeth.

———. 1980. "An Open Letter to Dr. I. Hendriks." *ZPE* 39: 113–114.

Whitehorne, J. E. G. 1994. "A Postscript about a Wooden Tablet Book (P. Kellis 63)." In *Proceedings of the 20th International Congress of Papyrologists,* ed. A. Bülow-Jacobsen, 277–283. Copenhagen: Museum Tusculanum Press.

———. 1996. "The Kellis Writing Tablets: Their Manufacture and Use." *JRA* Suppl. 19, *Archaeological Research in Roman Egypt:* 240–245.

Wiseman, D. J. 1955. "Assyrian Writing-Boards." *Iraq* 17: 3–13.

CHAPTER 2

THE FINDS OF PAPYRI: THE ARCHAEOLOGY OF PAPYROLOGY

HÉLÈNE CUVIGNY

(TRANSLATED BY ADAM BÜLOW-JACOBSEN)

FROM "SMASH-AND-GRAB" JOBS TO SUBTLE STRATIGRAPHY

The Time of the Consuls

Until Napoleon Bonaparte's expedition to Egypt (1798–1801), the papyri had slumbered undisturbed in their tombs and the ruins of ancient settlements. There were only rare exceptions, like the roll that came to be known as Charta Borgiana (reputedly found with fifty others), which was bought by an anonymous Italian merchant at Giza in 1777.

Greek papyri completely escaped the attention of the scholars of the French expedition, who brought back only papyri written in Egyptian. This military campaign, however, precipitated Egypt's entry into the modern world. The expedition left behind political chaos, out of which emerged Mohamad Ali, who reigned from 1805 to 1848 and opened the country to Western influence. France and England then entered into a devious power struggle. Merchants, diplomats, spies, adventurers, tourists, engineers, and technical counselors were everywhere in Egypt. They discovered an archaeological El Dorado and became antiquities hunters and dealers. Some of them (not least the consuls) financed excavations, whether from passion or greed, and assembled fabulous collections, which they sold in Europe, especially to museums.[1]

Frédéric Cailliaud, a French mineralogist who had been sent by Mohamad Ali to find the ancient emerald mines in the Eastern Desert, describes the feverish atmosphere in Thebes in 1818: "The whole area of the ruins of Karnak was covered with demarcation-lines that separated French, English, Irish, Italian, &c. excavations from each other. European ladies and other travelers ran around in the ruins and in the catacombs. All were trying to find or buy antiquities, and nobody thought of the heat and the fatigue" (Cailliaud 1821, 82). The Greek papyri found during this period are collection pieces and generally Ptolemaic.

This archaeological fervor did not prevent the destruction of other antiquities. At Antinoopolis and Hermopolis, the limestone and marble monuments, known today only from engravings in the *Description de l'Égypte*,[2] became quarries: Blocks were reused in modern buildings or disappeared into the lime kilns. During his journey in Egypt in 1828–1829, Champollion was horrified to see that the monuments no longer existed.

In 1835, under the influence of Egyptian thinker Rifa'a Al-Tahtawi,[3] Mohamad Ali ordered the suspension of all excavations in Egypt and forbade the exportation of antiquities. This order was ineffectual, however, because the demand was too great and the authorities were indifferent to the plundering.

In 1858 the French obtained from Viceroy Saïd Pasha permission to create a *Service de conservation des antiquités de l'Égypte,* or Conservation Service. The idea came from Auguste Mariette, who had become famous in 1851 by finding the Serapeum of Memphis. Mariette was sincerely concerned about the pillaging of antiquities, but for him the Conservation Service was also a means of staying in Egypt. Although he was assistant conservator at the Louvre, he did not see himself as an armchair scholar. For France, this "archaeological protectorate," which the French managed to maintain until 1952, was a low-cost way of acquiring more influence in Egypt.[4] As founder and first director of this agency, Mariette put an end to the unbridled pillaging and to a large extent managed to acquire for the Service the sole right to excavate. This practice enriched the holdings of the Egyptian Museum, which he founded.

Sebâkh and Cartonnage: The Papyrological Excavations

The First Fayyum Find

Mohamad Ali had begun an ambitious program of modernization in Egypt, which was carried on by his successors and much encouraged by the English, who took over administration of the country in 1882. Mohamad Ali's program had important consequences for the history of papyrology. First of all, Egypt's irrigation system was completely restructured. The traditional basins, in which water from the floods was retained in order to soak the soil, were partly replaced by canals that made perennial irrigation possible. This brought about a significant extension of the cultivable land and resulted in double or even triple harvests. Cash crops were introduced, the most important of which were sugarcane and cotton. Already at the end of the nineteenth century, archaeologists began worrying about the deterioration of archaeological sites that came to be surrounded by cultivated land. In addition, archaeologists and scholars are now concerned about an unforeseen consequence of the building of the Aswan high dam (inaugurated in 1969): the rising water table. But the archaeologists of the late nineteenth century also had to contend with the much more pressing competition from the *sebbâkhîn* (*sebâkh* diggers) and the powerful economic interests that made the peasants excavate for *sebâkh*.

In Egyptian Arabic, *sebâkh* is the powdery, saltpeter-rich earth that is characteristic of Egyptian ruins and is used for manure. *Sebâkh* consists of decomposed organic matter mixed with the fine clay that results from the destruction of mud-brick architecture. In addition, the mud bricks were also salvaged in order to fire them (Bailey 1999, 211). From the 1830s on, the peasants *(fallâhîn)* were also put to work digging for *sebâkh* in the mounds (*kimân*, singular *kôm*) of archaeological sediment into which the Egyptian climate had transformed ancient settlements. These were sometimes as much as twenty meters high. In 1910 an official inventory of the *kimân* from which *sebâkh* could be extracted numbered 545; most of these were located in the delta, many in Middle Egypt, and a few in Upper Egypt, which was less populated (Bailey 1999, 213). The industrial crops were not the only "consumers" of *sebâkh*, which was also collected in order to extract the saltpeter and produce gunpowder. In the second half of the nineteenth century, large gunpowder factories were constructed next to Antinoopolis and Hermopolis, and the mud-brick city walls of Antinoopolis were swallowed up.

Whole buildings and everything in them were carried off by the camels and donkeys of the *sebbâkhîn*, who inevitably also found marketable antiquities. During the winter of 1877–1878 they attacked the *kimân Faris*, the ruins of the ancient metropolis of the Arsinoite nome. Papyri were found by the thousands, constituting the "first Fayyum find," most of which was bought by the Austrian dealer and collector Theodor Graf, who sold them in 1884 to Archduke Rainer. The first

Fayyum find marked the beginning of illicit excavations in the whole province, and the antiquities market in Cairo was swamped by enormous quantities of Fayyum papyri. In the last decade of the nineteenth century the site of Soknopaiou Nesos was plundered by both the *fallâhîn* and two local antiquarians, who for some time had been granted exclusive "rights" to these excavations. No papyri from the Fayyum or the neighboring Herakleopolis and Hermopolis found in the urban ruins during this period are older than the Roman principate. The earlier levels of occupation had been covered by the Roman and Byzantine levels, and the rising humidity had destroyed the earlier, lower levels, which were thus less likely to yield papyri.

The Excavations for Papyri

In 1882 nationalist troubles led to a British military occupation of Egypt. England took charge of the country's administration, with the result that every Egyptian minister was under the control of a British counselor. The Egypt Exploration Fund (EEF), a private, learned society whose purpose was to finance excavations in Egypt, had just been created.[5] Unlike Mariette, his successor, the French Egyptologist Gaston Maspero happily granted authorizations for excavations, and he quickly persuaded the Egyptian government to divide the antiquities that excavators brought to light between the excavators and the Egyptian Museum, of which he was also the director. The EEF's first project, directed by Swiss Egyptologist Edouard Naville, was initiated in 1883 at Tell el-Masquta, ancient Pithom. The choice of a place mentioned in the Scriptures, in order to prove the historical validity of the Bible, was meant to attract donors. When Naville was temporarily unavailable the following year, the EEF sent W. M. Flinders Petrie, who was to excavate in Egypt until 1926.

A bitter rivalry grew up between the EEF's two prime excavators. Petrie had received an unconventional education and had developed a passion for measuring and surveying; his archaeological recordings and attention to the humblest objects were indications of the coming of modern archaeology. On the other hand, Professor Naville, a distinguished academic, was interested only in inscribed blocks and, when on site, spent part of every day in his tent. When Petrie accused him of not marking the findspot of every object, he defended himself by saying, "You might as well make a plan of the position of raisins in a plum-pudding" (Drower 1985, 283).

In 1889, in the Ptolemaic cemetery of Gurob, Petrie found mummies covered in cartonnage of demotic and Greek papyri.[6] From then on, Ptolemaic cemeteries were systematically plundered, but the raiders were frequently disappointed because humidity had often affected the cartonnage in such a way that it turned to dust at the slightest touch. In 1902–1905 the tombs excavated by O. Rubensohn at Abusir al-Malaq produced cartonnage from both the first century BCE and the reign of

Augustus. It contained papyri from the Herakleopolite nome, as well as Alexandria, a great rarity. Among the latter is a royal ordinance that perhaps carries Cleopatra's signature, which made headlines in 2000 (van Minnen 2000).

In 1893 a young Oxford classicist, Bernard P. Grenfell, came to Egypt for the first time. He worked with Petrie in Koptos, bought some papyri (the future *P.Grenfell*), and understood the importance of excavating postpharaonic sites in order to save as much as possible from the *sebbâkhîn*. With support from Petrie he obtained financing for excavations in the Fayyum. The excavations of 1895–1896, which he undertook with D. G. Hogarth and A. S. Hunt, were the first papyrological excavations made by Western scholars. The EEF also financed Grenfell and Hunt's first campaign at Oxyrhynchus (1897). After three weeks of work in the Roman necropolis and the much-destroyed ancient town, they decided to concentrate on the enormous, ancient rubbish mounds. During their four months of excavation there, Grenfell and Hunt found two thousand documentary and three hundred literary texts. This first season (see chapter 3) was such a success that the EEF immediately created the Graeco-Roman branch, which was intended to finance the papyrological excavations and the publication of the texts they brought to light.

The so-called Oxford Dioscuri immediately acquired a following. In 1899 the great Ulrich Wilcken excavated at Herakleopolis. Unfortunately, the papyri he found there went up in smoke when the ship on which they had been sent to Europe burned in the harbor of Hamburg. From 1902 to 1906 Otto Rubensohn excavated on behalf of the Berlin museums at Hermopolis (al-Ashmunayn), where he had to contend with competition from the Italians, who excavated there until 1909. However, their harvests were modest compared to that of Grenfell and Hunt at Oxyrhynchus. The *sebbâkhîn* had already made great finds at Hermopolis before organized excavations began.

Sebbâkhîn vs. Archaeologists

The competing economic interests were too important to allow the Antiquities Service to curb the relentless destruction of the *kimân*. At the end of his campaign at Antinoopolis in 1913, J. de M. Johnson noted that all attempts to protect the *kimân* would meet with opposition from the ministries of the interior, finances, agriculture, and public works (the Antiquities Service had been part of public works since 1883) (Johnson 1914, 173*m*). Against such powers, the resources of the Antiquities Service counted for nothing, but at least it tried to limit the extraction of *sebâkh*. The first decree, inspired by Maspero, was issued in 1901, and the following ones were in the same spirit: *Sebâkh* digging was subject to authorization and must be carried out under surveillance, and the antiquities found must be handed over to the service.

But worse was in store: the great landowners began to use railways to transport the *sebâkh*. In 1910 Maspero complained, "Until today, the method of transporting the

Figure 2.1. Karanis. The northwestern corner of the area excavated by the *sebbâkhîn*. Photo by G. R. Swain. Kelsey Museum Archives, 5.1707. Courtesy of The Kelsey Museum, University of Michigan.

sebâkh on camels and donkeys allowed the farmers the time to sift the manure and consequently to collect what they found in it, so that we received our part. With the present procedure the manure is loaded directly into the dumping wagons. Precious objects are crushed or broken, papyri are reduced to smithereens and only large pieces resist destruction" (Maspero 1910, 321). In fact, as early as 1884 a dump wagon track laid by a sugar company led right into the heart of the ruins of Hermopolis. In 1925 at Karanis, the American excavators from the University of Michigan had to come to an agreement with the *daira* Agnelli, an Italian company that was authorized to extract two hundred cubic meters of *sebâkh* per day (figure 2.1). Going into what used to be the center of the village, A. E. R. Boak had the impression of being in "the crater of some extinct volcano." After negotiations, the Italians agreed to take only the dirt from the excavations, while the Americans grudgingly consented to choose their excavation sites with regard to their richness in *sebâkh* and proximity to the tracks (Boak and Peterson 1931, 3). However, they soon came to appreciate the fact that their dirt was removed for free; after the second season, when *sebâkh* output had been unacceptably low and the Italians had threatened to switch to chemical manure, the Americans promptly concentrated again on more productive locations (*Kelsey Museum Newsletter* [Fall 2005]: 5). It was not until the 1930s that *sebâkh* digging became illegal.

Saving Papyri

The excavations conducted before the First World War with the sole purpose of finding papyri and ostraca had common traits. The concession areas allotted to the excavators were very large, which permitted them to leave disappointing sites after only a few days in search of more promising ones. They were poorly financed by public or, in the case of the Graeco-Roman branch of the EEF, private funds exclusively to find papyri; thus, the excavators could never be sure they would be able to return the following year. They were therefore always under pressure to produce immediate results and did not waste time making plans before beginning to dig. They observed the color of the earth or the feel of it under the boots, which can indicate the presence of a good layer of *afsh,* a mixture of earth with straw and other dry, vegetable matter, which experience had taught them often contained papyri (Grenfell and Hunt somewhat pompously called these indicators "the principles of *afsh*"). Their global view of the site was vague, and they had no precise idea of the position of their ditches. In a description to Wilcken of the findspot of an important cluster of fiscal ostraca, Maspero told him to draw two lines on Mariette's plan. The house of the ostraca "was roughly at the intersection of the two lines. . . . Of course, this is only an approximation, and I could be wrong even by a hundred metres."[7] Plans of buildings are rare and are not indicated in a general plan because those were never made. Moreover, uninscribed objects were not placed in a context, and the concept of stratigraphy was absent.

Today archaeologists shudder at the thought of Grenfell and Hunt's "methods," but we must take into account the conditions at the time. First, there was no clear distinction between archaeologists and philologists, and scientific archaeology[8] was typically directed by philologists, who were more interested in written documents than objects. Petrie, who demonstrated the scientific importance of even the humblest objects, looks like a visionary in this connection. Further, Grenfell, Hunt, and their followers felt the pressure of competition with the *sebbâkhîn,* the illicit diggers, and the steadily growing areas of cultivation. These were rescue excavations, a concept that is still with us. The papyrus excavation was not unlike a race in which the "teams" tried to overtake each other: The papyrologists constantly frequented the dealers to obtain new leads to where papyri might be found. As soon as the papyrologists had left, the illicit diggers inevitably took over.

In addition to having to work faster than the local population, the papyrologists of the EEF also had to satisfy their donors. Several excavation reports from Grenfell and Hunt end with an expression of their hope of having enough money to return to Egypt the following year. This is why they unashamedly preferred the papyri that most interested the donors to the EEF Graeco-Roman branch (among whom there were seven bishops), namely, the literary and the theological texts. This consideration of their donors' preferences, which apparently coincided with their personal inclinations, entered into their archaeological choices. Grenfell and Hunt even

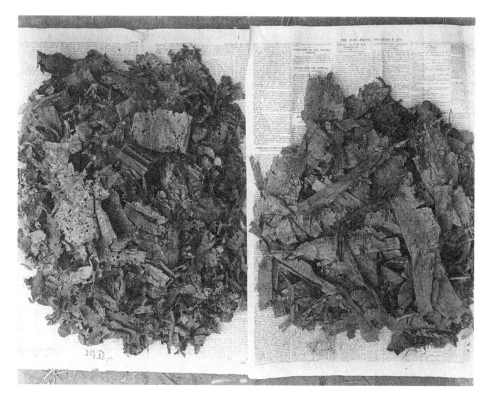

Figure 2.2. Papyrus fragments found at Oxyrhynchus. Courtesy of the Egypt Exploration Society.

gave up excavating potentially rich (but Byzantine) zones, as they explain in their report of the fourth season in Oxyrhynchus: "The mounds which accumulated in the sixth or seventh century or later have been merely scratched, and to any one who cares for early and medieval Arabic documents there is plenty of virgin ground to be explored. But the interest and importance of Greek papyri after the fourth century wanes rapidly" (*EEF Archaeological Report* 14 [1904–1905]: 14).

The archaeological methods of Grenfell and Hunt may seem crude, but, thanks to the papyri, they were nevertheless able to date the layers they were excavating. They also scrupulously collected the uninscribed material (Grenfell had been trained by Petrie), and the large number of coins found—even if coins would not normally be thrown away—shows that their workers were careful. Where papyri were concerned, they were aware of the archaeological context and made an effort to keep together those that had been found together (figure 2.2):

> Since this rubbish mound had proved so fruitful I proceeded to increase the number of workmen gradually up to 110, and, as we moved northwards over other parts of the site, the flow of papyri soon became a torrent which it was difficult to cope with. Each lot found by a pair, man and boy, had to be kept separate; for the knowledge that papyri are found together is frequently of the greatest importance

for determining their date, and since it is inevitable that so fragile a material should sometimes be broken in the process of extricating it from the closely-packed soil, it is imperative to keep together, as far as possible, fragments of the same document. We engaged two men to make tin boxes for storing the papyri, but for the next ten weeks they could hardly keep pace with us. (*EEF Archaeological Report* 6 [1896–1897]: 6 f)

The existence of a legal antiquities trade with the possibility of exporting[9] must have made the excavators' life even more difficult since the Egyptian workers were seriously tempted to hide the best finds and sell them to the dealers, who often came right up to the edge of the excavation. For this reason the *bakshish* principle, invented by Petrie, was practiced, through which each worker was paid extra for his finds. One can imagine that the poor scholars must have spent more time keeping track of the finds of their numerous workers than following the excavation step by step. Friday payment was a nightmare for Hogarth when he was with Grenfell and Hunt in the Fayyum (Montserrat 1996, 142). Moreover, J. de M. Johnson reports that there was a constant need of arbitration between the teams of diggers, since the practice was to give each one a strip several meters wide to excavate (Johnson 1914, 175).

Egypt has fallen victim to its extraordinary archaeological riches and is undoubtedly the least well excavated of the ancient Mediterranean cultures. But let us not forget that papyrology as a discipline would not exist without the massive finds made by the *fellahîn* and the somewhat uninhibited excavations carried out by a number of lucid and pragmatic scholars of the late nineteenth and early twentieth centuries.

The Scientific Excavations

The Coming of the Archaeologists

Was it the diminishing abundance of papyri that made salvage excavations less urgent and led to making a virtue of necessity? Or was it the progress in archaeological technique and in social and economic history, which made for an understanding that precious archaeological contexts had been destroyed in the unbridled race for *sebâkh* and papyri? No doubt both reasons were pertinent.

From the 1920s on, the excavations of Graeco-Roman sites no longer had the finding of papyri as their sole objective. This new trend was initiated in the United States by the philologist Francis W. Kelsey, who was professor of Latin at the University of Michigan. Kelsey saw the faults of Graeco-Roman archaeology in Egypt and decided that the United States had a duty to do something about it. The Americans' choice fell on Karanis, which, thanks to Egypt's unique climatic conditions, turned out to be an ideal site for the study of people in antiquity not only through the writings they had left but also by the analysis of the material world in which they had lived.

Figure 2.3. Rolls of papyrus found in the threshold between rooms D and E of 5026 at Karanis: a documentary cache? Worms feasted on them before papyrologists could do so, and they are all still unpublished (unless *P.Mich.* IX 551, a donkey sale, is one of them, but layer indications are contradictory). Photo by G. R. Swain. Kelsey Museum Archives, 5.1801. Courtesy of the Kelsey Museum, University of Michigan.

The excavation of Karanis, carried out by the University of Michigan from 1924 to 1935, was exemplary for its time.[10] While we wait for the recent excavations of Tebtynis and Bacchias to progress, Karanis is still the best-known urban conglomerate in the Fayyum. For the first time, the excavators worked to distinguish different levels of occupation, carefully mapped the excavated zones, made plans and cross-sections of houses, and scrupulously recorded the location and level of each object or papyrus (figure 2.3). This was a vast improvement over previous excavations and one that would remain unparalleled for a long time.

Now that modern archaeology demands a very high degree of technical skills, it is no longer possible to become an excavator just by excavating. And yet, although the papyrologists hardly dare touch a trowel nowadays, many Graeco-Roman sites are still opened on their initiative. In fact, Graeco-Roman sites in Egypt have not been very attractive to archaeologists unless they have a bearing on a larger historical problem like central power, commerce,[11] or the environment.[12] In other cases, Graeco-Roman layers have to be removed in order to gain access to pharaonic sites, as is the case with D. Bailey's excavation at Hermopolis, which is essentially a by-product of an Egyptological excavation. The exploration of villages or middle-sized towns that the *metropoleis* were (which were allowed to call themselves cities only at a late date and even then relatively briefly) does not lead directly into the mainstream of historical research. There is no prestige attached to these sites. Their monuments have been dismantled, Egypt is notoriously poor in Greek or Latin inscriptions, and what is left for the archaeologist are modest mud-brick structures, rubbish dumps with difficult and unrewarding stratigraphies, and overwhelming quantities of commonplace material, not the least of which is pottery.

The excavations of Tebtynis (begun in 1988 in collaboration with the Institut français d'archéologie orientale and under the direction of Claudio Gallazzi, professor of papyrology at the Università Statale of Milan) have shown that papyrology has nothing to lose by a methodical excavation, provided that adequate financing is available; thus, several large-scale seasons can be conducted without fear of disruption. There are no more large concentrations of papyri, and excavations must be conducted over a large area in order to gather a good crop. Although Tebtynis has been excavated since the end of the nineteenth century by a succession of official and illicit diggers (not to mention the *sebbâkhîn*), the site is rich in ostraca, a commonplace writing material in Upper Egypt but which was thought to be rare in the Fayyum. This discovery is the result of a more careful and methodical excavation. The earlier papyrus hunters made soundings in order to find a layer of *afsh,* which they then followed as one would a vein of ore. Since they were primarily interested in papyri, they paid no attention to the potsherds, which are always abundant in Egyptian excavations (Gallazzi 2000, 31). Incidentally, it is interesting that, in the deontologically correct excavations of Bacchias, ostraca are handled more casually than papyri. Papyri are individually located in three dimensions, while ostraca are treated as potsherds and recognized as written sources only when the potsherds are washed and sorted. Ostraca are thus identified with only a layer number (Davoli 2000, 17–18). A final difference between today's excavations and those of the early papyrus hunters is that the latter were not interested in the lower layers, where the pressure and the mounting humidity made the presence of good papyri less likely. In this way they cut themselves off from earlier material and depended, at least in the Fayyum, only on mummy cartonnage for Ptolemaic papyri.

The exploration of Mons Claudianus, begun a year before that of Tebtynis, on the initiative of a group of papyrologists, of whom I was one, is a special case.[13] There the papyrologists found themselves in a situation similar to that of the papyrus hunters before World War I. In a remote location between the Nile and the Red Sea, Mons Claudianus had remained almost undamaged for nearly two thousand years, but with the tourism boom on the Red Sea coast beginning in the 1980s, it was exposed to illicit digging, which in turn gave the Bedouin ideas. Moreover, because of its isolation, the site was impossible to guard.[14] Mons Claudianus was very rich in texts (not papyri but mostly ostraca), which were concentrated in the rubbish mounds and easy to find, so there was a great temptation to dig just to find the ostraca. However, the team was strengthened by the participation of several archaeologists, who added some archaeological respectability.

From the point of view of human experience and method, the seven years of excavation at Mons Claudianus were not free from friction, but they were all the more interesting in that the archaeologists had high principles, while we, the papyrologists, were simply excited by all these ostraca that were there for the taking. Our colleagues could but regard us as looters, while we tended to see them as killjoys. We undoubtedly learned a lot from each other. In any case, the experience of Mons Claudianus has shown that the interests of papyrology and modern archaeology are not necessarily easy to reconcile. Understandably, the archaeologists are loath to dig in places that suggest no other prospect than the presence of texts. Modern archaeologists are very conscious of the destruction caused by excavation. Like surgeons, the archaeologists endeavor to use nonintrusive methods in order to leave unspoiled samples for exploration by future generations of archaeologists with newer and even better techniques. Their efforts are concentrated on mapping, planning, and measuring. Now magnetometry permits analysis of remains under the soil before (or without) digging. Trial trenches are reduced to a minimum, and soil samples are taken for analysis and study. It is thus possible to obtain a comprehensive visualization of a site without destroying it. In Egypt, however, the problem is that the "future generations" are already at work.

Archaeological Multidisciplinarity as Seen by a Papyrologist

No archaeological course of study fails to point out that it involves multiple disciplines. However, the joint study of anepigraphic artifacts, soil samples, and texts that have been collected with the strictest observance of archaeological stratigraphy does not automatically lead to fruitful conclusions. Texts and objects do not always illuminate each other. Often there is little common ground, and various types of material present different problems. Often one gets the impression of parallel, unconnected worlds. Sometimes the data are redundant; sometimes they are supplementary. The collaboration between specialists is necessary but can be disappointing.

The specialists in uninscribed material who work in the Eastern Desert never fail to ask us how their type of material is reflected in the ostraca. The confrontation of the data gives varying results depending on the types of material. It is without a doubt the archaeobotanists who profit most from the texts.[15] Food and provisions are among the most common subjects in the ostraca, whether they are private letters or administrative. Most of the cultivated species that the archaeobotanists have identified are also mentioned in the ostraca, which, on the other hand, give details about the organization of the provisioning. For instance, we learn that certain herbs and vegetables were cultivated in desert gardens. At Mons Claudianus a number of quarriers' and blacksmiths' pay chits provide much detail on the workers' diet.

Meat and butchering are also mentioned in the ostraca, although to a lesser degree, but as meat was rare, the information is more anecdotal (e.g., "buy three suckling pigs," "I send you a donkey leg"). The study of the faunal remains gives precious quantitative information: We learn that donkey was the meat most commonly eaten at Mons Claudianus, while pork was more common in the forts along the roads to Myos Hormos and Berenike. This difference is explained by the many work donkeys in the quarries. Archaeozoologists have also been able to state that significant quantities of fish were eaten at Mons Claudianus and that they came almost exclusively from the Red Sea, not from the Nile. The only Nile fish that has been identified is the catfish, whose presence is certainly not explained by their fine taste but rather by the fact that these amphibious creatures could arrive alive at Mons Claudianus. The ostraca give the impression that fresh fish were a rare delicacy and do not inform us of the quantities involved. On the other hand, they put a perspective on the means of obtaining fish: At Mons Claudianus, according to one ostracon, fish from the sea were brought by Bedouin, who are probably to be identified with the coastal dwellers called "Arab-Egyptian fish eaters" by the geographer Ptolemy. On the Myos Hormos road the relay post riders of the military stations helped to provide fine fish for the table of the prefect of Egypt when he was in Koptos.

With regard to leather and textiles, a comparison between the data of the texts and archaeology is of no particular interest. The leather specialists have been able to identify a variety of types of shoes, but these are described in the texts by only two words: *sandalion* and the generic *hypodêma*. The variety in the leather objects is nothing compared to that of the textiles, where the richness of color and the complexity of weaving dazzle the experts. Analysis of colors is beginning to show just how advanced dyers from Roman Egypt were, especially in imitating real purple with vegetable dyes. But, of course, there is nothing on the subject in the texts written by those who wore these clothes.

By contrast, it is not useless to search the ostraca for names of the ceramic containers that the ceramologists classify and draw. At Mons Claudianus it goes without saying that the ubiquitous *keramion* of the texts is the common Nile silt amphora, which constitutes 90 percent of the pottery found (the so-called AE3 bitronconique). Since complete specimens have been found, it has been possible to measure the contents at 6.5 liters, which is extremely important for a calculation of wine consumption because the *keramion* is used to measure rations. From the middle of the second century, the ostraca from the sites in the Eastern Desert—at least those that continued to function after about 150 CE—mention a new kind of ordinary container, the *kolophônion*. It so happens that, at the same time and from the same sites, large quantities of costrels appear. It is almost inevitable that ceramologists identify these costrels with the *kolophônia*.

Since the ostraca are often precisely dated, they also permit dating of certain contemporary artifacts. The ostraca from Mons Claudianus have, for instance, allowed D. Bailey to date the so-called frog lamps to the second century, when they had hitherto been thought to be from a later period. On the other hand, at the site of Maximianon, where, as luck would have it, none of the fifteen hundred ostraca found could be dated, it was the typology of the glass that allowed a dating of the layers and hence the ostraca.

It is the collaboration with the actual excavator that is most productive for the papyrologist. In spite of the significant information derived from the written documents, we must not ignore the results of the excavator's austere examination of structures and layers. Certainly the texts normally tell us the ancient name of the site—except in cases where the papyri were recycled as mummy cartonnage and found in graveyards (the embalmers reused old papyri that could have come from anywhere). On the other hand, the texts can be deceptive with regard to the periods of occupation either because whole layers have disappeared or because the site has not yet been fully explored. This is the case in Tebtynis, where the latest papyri date from the third century CE but where the Byzantine part of the town has not yet been excavated (Bagnall 2001, 234).

In certain cases, the archaeological context in which a document was found can prove essential for its understanding. This is the case with an important group of ostraca found at Tebtynis in 2003. Their texts are short: a date, a name, and a quantity of beer measured in *dichôra*. A few similar texts were already known from stray finds or older excavations, and the editors had interpreted them either as receipts given to a brewery by those who had received beer or as delivery notes issued by the brewery. Now, the new texts from Tebtynis in some cases carry the additional mention of *posis zytou* (consumption of beer), which places them in the context of the ritual consumption of an association. In addition, the ostraca have been found in a banquet hall, which suggests that the names are those of association members who have presented the beer (Reiter 2005, 133–136). In isolation (i.e., in a museum or a collection), these documents made no sense and, given their brevity, would be of little interest except perhaps for some new proper names.

To give another example, let us go back to the letter by Maspero, in which he tries to explain to Wilcken, using a plan of Karnak, where he had found a group of tax receipts that had accumulated against the wall of a house. At the time of the discovery, Maspero did not know that these texts could have clarified the important problem of where tax receipts were kept. Often these are found, as we should expect, in the house of the taxpayer who received them when the taxes were paid. However, these receipts from the Theban region (most of them bought in the 1880s and 1890s) can often be organized into archives not of the taxpayer but of the tax collector as if they had been kept by the latter. To explain this apparent paradox, Wilcken suggests that the receipts were issued by the bank to the tax collectors. In fact, the taxpayer often did not pay the taxes directly to the public bank but instead to collectors, who then deposited the money. Unfortunately, these ostraca were not read on the spot and now appear to have disappeared without a trace in the stores of the Egyptian Museum, where Maspero had duly deposited them, so we do not know which formula they followed, and Wilcken's theory cannot be verified.

In What Archaeological Contexts Are Papyri Found?

The types of papyri that would most interest the historians, those of the offices of the central administration at Alexandria, or the classical philologist, the contents of the library of Alexandria, have disappeared. This is why papyrology still suffers from a comparative lack of recognition as an important discipline. The historian will have to make do with papyri found in the nome capitals and the villages south of the delta. As it happens, the delta, which was the richest and most populous region, has a geography and a climate that have not allowed papyri to survive as they have elsewhere in the country. There are only two exceptions to this, namely the carbonized papyri of Thmouis and Boubastos (see chapter 16). Moreover, archaeological contexts are neither all equally interesting nor equally favorable to the preservation of papyri.

Books in Tombs

Some beautiful literary rolls have been found in tombs. The oldest is the Timotheos papyrus (fourth century BCE), which was discovered by L. Borchardt in 1902 in a wooden sarcophagus in Abusir. A roll containing *Iliad* II (second century CE) was found by Petrie at Hawara under the head of the mummy of a young woman. The first editor of the papyrus, A. H. Sayce, credits her with an agreeable, intellectual physiognomy, undoubtedly Greek. Earlier, in 1858, Mariette had given to the Louvre a papyrus of Alcman found by the natives at Saqqara, rolled up in linen and placed between the legs of a mummy.[16] The manuscript of Herodas's *Mimes* (first–second century CE) appears to have been found north of Assiut (at Meir?), perhaps along with the *Constitution of Athens,* in the tomb of a couple. The wife, Sarapous (daughter of Sarapion), had died at the age of fourteen (Martin 2002, 23–26). This practice was not widespread; in February 1912 J. de M. Johnson, working for the EEF, spent several days opening approximately a hundred tombs at Qamadir, near Oxyrhynchus, "in the vain hope of a papyrus roll." The people who were sufficiently smitten with literature to be buried with an expensive book must have been statistically rare, for it seems necessary to interpret these pious gifts as a reflection of the deceased's personality rather than as an imitation of the

Figure 2.4. Cartonnage elements at Tebtynis (1899–1900). Courtesy of the Egypt Exploration Society.

Egyptian habit of giving the dead a book of religious-magical formulas as a passport to the hereafter. The Derveni papyrus (fourth–third century BCE), incidentally, attests to a similar concern in the Greek world. This papyrus, the only one to have been found in Greece, contains a philosophical-eschatological text and was found in 1962, carbonized among the remains of a funeral pyre (Betegh 2002).

Cartonnage and Crocodiles

During the whole of the Ptolemaic period and up to the end of the reign of Augustus, human mummies were wrapped in linen bands and often given a mask, sometimes also other separate elements such as a foot case, a pectoral, an apron, and leg guards (figure 2.4). These elements were made of a core of papyrus, linen, or palm fiber, which was covered with stucco and painted with standardized, protective images. The use of scrap paper for cartonnage does not seem to have been common before the reign of Ptolemy II Philadelphos (283–246). Most of the papyri of the third century BCE come from such cartonnage, with the notable exception of the Zenon archive. Most papyri from cartonnage are administrative documents, but literary texts are sometimes found as well. These papyri have the disadvantage of having been cut to fit the part of the body that they were intended to cover. Moreover, the writing is often weakened, first by the application of the stucco and then by its removal.

At Tebtynis, Grenfell and Hunt accidentally discovered that a number of crocodile mummies had been prepared with recycled administrative papers, either as wrapping or as filling but not as cartonnage proper (figure 2.5):

> On Jan. 16, 1900—a day which was otherwise memorable for producing twenty-three early Ptolemaic mummies with papyrus cartonnage—one of our workmen, disgusted at finding a row of crocodiles where he expected sarcophagi, broke one of them in pieces and disclosed the surprising fact that the creature was wrapped in sheets of papyrus. As may be imagined, after this find we dug out all the crocodile-tombs in the cemetery; and in the next few weeks several thousands of these animals were unearthed, of which a small proportion (about 2 per cent.) contained papyri. (Grenfell, Hunt, and Smyly 1902, vi)

These papyri were of the second century BCE and came from the office of the village scribe at Kerkeosiris. One might have thought that this was an isolated case, but in 1901 at Talit, a village neighboring Tebtynis, Grenfell and Hunt found

Figure 2.5. Crocodile mummies at Tebtynis (1899–1900). Courtesy of the Egypt Exploration Society.

other crocodiles wrapped in Greek and demotic documents of the first century BCE, just slightly later.[17] This practice has been related to the subventions from the Ptolemies toward the burial of sacred animals,[18] even though scrap paper from the administration is perhaps not what one imagines when reading about the "magnificent and famous gifts" that the Rosetta Stone mentions in this respect.

Buildings

Obviously, the dream of every papyrus hunter was to find the public archive still in place in the *bibliothêkê*. This miracle almost happened in 1892, when Naville came upon what must have been the archives of the Mendesian nome in the delta. The rooms of the building were filled with papyri burned in a fire in the late second century CE. Naville's description is depressing, although he may purposely have made it even more so:

> They are now quite carbonized, like those of Herculaneum, but even in a worse state. They are most difficult to take out, they crumble to pieces when they are loosened from the earth which covers them, but, by looking sideways the characters are still discernible; they generally are Greek, in good handwriting. As for those which have escaped the fire, they are quite hopeless. The moisture and the salt in the soil have reduced them to a kind of brownish paste, which seems to be very fertile, for roots of plants grow in it in abundance. (*EEF Archaeological Report* [1892–1893: 4])

Naville filled five boxes, which arrived at the British Museum with their contents reduced to crumbs. Since Petrie suspected that Naville, heavy handed as he was, had not done everything possible to save what could be saved, the EEF at once undertook a rescue operation directed by Howard Carter. Carter spent two months looking in vain among the ruins without finding the *bibliothêkê*. Naville's indications were not precise enough to find it (Drower 1985, 284). A number of rolls from illicit digging came into the hands of the Egyptologist Albert Daninos, who conceived the brilliant idea of softening them in rectified alcohol. He then cut the rolls open lengthwise and detached the sheets, which he glued onto cardboard. This is all that is left of the archive of the Mendesian nome.

The papyri from Dura-Europos in Syria are the only other example of an archive uncovered by an official excavation. And yet, even they do not represent the whole of the archive of the *Cohors XX Palmyrenorum,* whose camp had been installed in part of the town. The room in which the texts were found is just a place where one stored documents that were no longer of interest. It opened onto another room where the walls were covered with dipinti, graffiti, and "a great many smudges of ink as if one had used the plaster for wiping pens and fingers" (Rostovtzeff 1934, 152), probably the *officium* of the scribes of the general staff.

Grenfell and Hunt established a hierarchy of archaeological contexts in which one might find papyri. The best are abandoned houses that have collapsed, thus sealing both papyri and objects of daily use where the inhabitants had left them.[19] But the interest, according to them, was that the papyri were better preserved than in the rubbish dumps, not, as we would now think, that they were part of a coherent archaeological context in which the various elements could elucidate each other. Strangely, the first editors of the papyri from Karanis, which had been found in advanced excavations with multidisciplinary aspirations, showed the same inhibition and did not take the archaeological context into consideration in order to explain their texts. As an example, the ostraca found in the same house were published separately, while the editor did not realize that they could establish the genealogy of the family that had lived there (van Minnen 1992). The archaeologists in turn let precious stratigraphic information slip away because they did not know that a group of papyri found in a trench were homogeneous and consequently belonged to the same stratigraphic unit (van Minnen 1994). At least the registration of the finds was so well conceived (even if somewhat rough according to today's standards) that it is still operational, and now, sixty years later, allows one to make use of the data and show what can be deduced from what Peter van Minnen has called "a house-to-house approach," a method that he has applied to house 17 in state B. Taking into account all the papyri, published or unpublished, and all the objects from this house, he has demonstrated that house B17 was inhabited by a tax collector *(praktôr argyrikôn)* by the name of Socrates, who not only lived but also worked there. Thanks to a draft of a petition in Socrates' handwriting, van Minnen has been able to identify him as the writer of a Karanis tax roll in which he leaves a personal mark by amusing himself by inventing Greek equivalents of the taxpayers' Egyptian names. Some of these names testify to a high degree of erudition (e.g., ἀνδίκτης, which is otherwise attested only in Callimachus, where it means "mousetrap"). Socrates uses this name here instead of the Egyptian name, Panpin, which means "he of the mice." Callimachus was not among the books found in Socrates' library in house B17, but a fragment with text by this author has in fact been found in the house opposite it. Van Minnen further remarks that Socrates did not live with the woman who was probably the mother of his twin sons, a Roman citizen who lived several blocks away and who had declared her sons as of an unknown father in order for them to inherit her juridical status.

The texts found in Socrates' house were only what was left by chance after abandonment. Earlier I discussed public archives; on their own level, private archives, which people guarded carefully in jars or boxes, also have a much greater importance than documents found in isolation (see chapter 10). Unfortunately, these nests of papyri, the private archives, are rarely found by archaeologists. We may think of the archives of Zenon, which were found in Philadelphia under unknown circumstances somewhat before World War I, or the archive of

Heroninos, which was reportedly found at Theadelphia by *fellahîn* in a wooden box a short time after Grenfell and Hunt's excavations. One of the curses of papyrology is, in fact, that so many of the important discoveries have been clandestine; thus, the archaeological context is unknown. Predictably, the natives were often luckier than the professionals. Numbers were in their favor, and they were impeded neither by time and financing nor by methodological scruples. Of course, scholars have also made some discoveries of archives, but these were in older excavations of a period when the excavators were often philologists who saw no farther than the contents of their texts and did not think of looking for help in the material context.

At Kôm Ishqaw in 1905, the classicist Gustave Lefebvre, who was also inspector of antiquities, found the archive of Dioskoros of Aphrodite. His report gives a good impression of a less pedantic way of doing archaeology: "For a few pounds the owner sold us the right to turn his plot of land inside out. We excavated right into the road, on the other side of the wall. Everything was done in three days." One meter below the surface they came upon a house with three rooms, in one of which "there stood a jar with the neck broken off, 0,90 m high, full of papyri.... The inventory was quickly made: at the top of the jar there came to light, all crumpled up, a codex of eleven leaves: it was the Menander manuscript.... In the jar there were also some hundred and fifty rolls, mostly Greek, business papers, wills, contracts, letters &c." (Lefebvre 1907, x). Unfortunately, there is not even a photograph of the discovery.[20] The excavation reports from the heroic age of papyrus hunting make much more agreeable reading than today's terse archaeological reports, but they leave us unsatisfied if we are looking for useful information to elucidate our texts. When one considers all this wasted archaeological potential, one may perceive some irony in the technical refinement that is deployed today on the tatters that remain after the two hundred years of devastation to which Egyptian antiquities have been subjected.

The Document Caches

The documents found in 1960 and 1961 by Yigael Yadin in the Judean desert are to this day the only archive found by someone worthy of being called an archaeologist and in the condition in which the owners left them. This brings us to the concept of "document cache," which Alain Martin has proposed adding to the roster of archaeological contexts that produce papyri (Martin 1994). The most famous examples of these treasure troves not of gold but of documents are undoubtedly the two archives found in the "cave of letters," one of the inaccessible strongholds in which survivors of the Bar Kochba revolt took refuge in 132 CE or shortly thereafter.[21] The first cache found was a bundle of fourteen letters on papyrus and one on a folded, wooden leaf tablet (see chapter 1), all of which was tied up with string and sealed with a clay seal. The documents are written in Greek,

Aramaic, and Hebrew and contain orders, especially instructions for confiscation, issued by Bar Kochba himself, addressed to several of the persons who had taken refuge in the cave and who had found it prudent to keep these documents in order to cover themselves later on, if need be (Yadin 1961).

The other archive is that of Babatha, twice widowed and a strong-willed woman. She had not undertaken the climb up the cliff in Nahal Hever without the thirty-five documents that proved, first of all, her ownership of various disputed properties. The archaeological report shows with what care she had classified and protected these precious documents (Yadin 1962), which were found in a leather pouch, itself wrapped in linen and tied with a string (figures 2.6 and 2.7). Finally, the bundle had been put into a water skin, like the Bar Kochba letters.

The discovery of other caches of personal objects (keys, a bird net, everyday utensils) in the cave seems to indicate that its inhabitants left with the intention of coming back for their belongings.

The Rubbish Deposits

Rubbish deposits represent the type of ground most likely to produce massive finds of papyri, even though the proportion of inscribed material will be less in a village mound than in that of a metropolis. The depositories can be public dumps (some of which are as much as nine meters high) or private accumulations of garbage in an unused space, whether a room in a house, an empty cistern, or a silo. The depositories contain domestic, industrial, and agricultural garbage, rubble, ashes, rags, discarded objects, and masses of potsherds. It is surprising to see that the various kinds of debris have been thrown out according to type. The papyri (and in the Eastern Desert the ostraca) are no exception. They are rarely isolated in the dump but were thrown away several at a time. The papyri that a person decided to discard were not important documents that ought to be kept, like contracts, title deeds, or literary works. Nevertheless, the excavations at Oxyrhynchus show that from time to time, in circumstances that we should like to know, it was decided to clean out documents and rolls in quantity. Some of them were even still in the baskets in which they had been brought to the dump. Grenfell and Hunt also remark that rolls were systematically torn before being thrown away.

The abundance of texts from Oxyrhynchus (or to a lesser degree, from the mounds of the Eastern Desert) must not blind us to the fact that they are only an infinitesimal part of what was thrown away in antiquity. It took only a shower and then something thrown onto the humid surface to seal it, and all of the sealed-up material would rot—turn from *afsh* into *sebâkh*. Even in the climatic conditions of Egypt, the perfect excavation of an undamaged ancient site would yield only a fraction of the texts it once contained. It often happens that one can join parts of

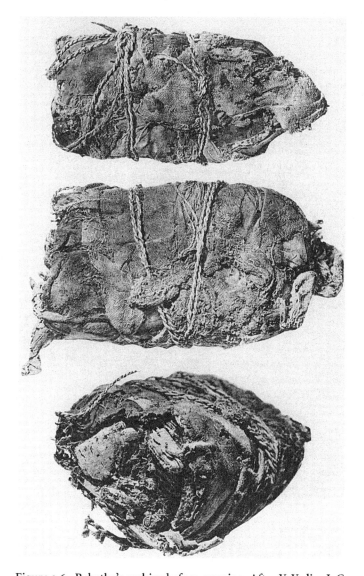

Figure 2.6. Babatha's archive before opening. After Y. Yadin, J. C. Greenfield, A. Yardeni, and B. Levine, *The Documents from the Bar Kokhba Period in the Cave of Letters. Hebrew, Aramaic, and Nabatean Aramaic Papyri,* Jerusalem 2002, II, pl. 1. Courtesy of the Israel Exploration Society.

excavated ostraca that are in very different states of preservation. Even if they have spent the intervening years a few centimeters apart, they have been subjected to very different conditions of preservation.

The garbage dumps are the least interesting type of context from the point of view of what the archaeological context can contribute to an understanding of the

Figure 2.7. Babatha's pouch, opened. After Yadin et al. 2002
(figure 2.6), pl. 2. Courtesy of the Israel Exploration Society.

text. This is why the rough-and-ready archaeology of Grenfell and Hunt as applied
to the mounds at Oxyrhynchus has not really done much harm in this respect and
the less so since they took care not to separate papyri that were found together.
These rubbish mounds are mass graves, where the links between objects that used
to share a context have been dissolved. When three inkwells are found in house B17
at Karanis, it is significant because we know that the house was occupied by a father
and two sons. But the same three inkwells found in a dump are just material for a

Figure 2.8. A layer with ostraca in the garbage dump at Krokodilô (Eastern Desert). Photo by J.-P. Brun.

typology of inkwells. Only the contents of the texts and/or the knowledge that they were found together allow us to reconstitute archives.

A dump that has formed in the open is infinitely more complex in stratigraphy than a room filled with rubbish, where the layers are contained by the walls and are formed more or less horizontally on top of each other. It is formed by successive dumpings, juxtaposed or superimposed, which will have stayed together or spilled down the sides of the heap. The lower layers are more or less horizontal, but layers become more and more unpredictable and oblique as the heap grows. Even hardened archaeologists can get lost in them.[22] Today garbage dumps are excavated like any other archaeological ground, in other words, by removing the layers separately, which demands a high degree of concentration when they cross over or under each other (figure 2.8). In the excavations of the great age before 1914 this was done differently: One attacked the mound laterally, caused slices of it to fall one by one, and sorted out the papyri after each "landslide." Grenfell was sometimes alone "supervising" two hundred workers (figure 2.9), while today archaeologists feel stressed if they have to follow a dozen workers on a mound (figure 2.10). The ungratifying work of analyzing a refuse heap is undoubtedly an important factor in influencing scrupulous archaeologists not to search for texts. It is a great deal of work, and afterward one has little to write about it; moreover, the descriptions are indigestible for the reader and, for the author, boring and academically unrewarding.

Figure 2.9. Oxyrhynchus, 1902–1903. Men at work, with B. P. Grenfell observing.

Figure 2.10. Didymoi 1999 (Eastern Desert). Men at work on the garbage dump. Photo J.-P. Brun.

CONCLUSION

From the first Fayyum find until the First World War, the period of miraculous discoveries lasted barely forty years. Even in 1913 Hunt felt that this period was coming to an end: "Failing the emergence of a fresh fertile source, costly excavations may before long be found to be not sufficiently remunerative, and there will be a gradual return to the conditions of the first period of discovery.[23] Isolated finds will of course continue to be made for an indefinite time" (Hunt 1914, 91). Perhaps Hunt had not foreseen that the progress in archaeology and the evolution of ancient history under the influence of social anthropology would soon make the humblest excavated object important. And yet he was right, for in the present era of slavery to the mass media, the benefactors and institutions who provide financial support do not have an understanding of archaeology much different from that of the nineteenth century. Treasure hunting and necrophilia are still the order of the day. It is better to find a royal mummy than a papyrus and better to find a papyrus than domestic garbage, however great its informational value. Except for the special case of the Eastern Desert, it is no longer possible to be sure where to look in order to find texts, but it is still quite possible that extended excavation of what is left of urban conglomerates will produce impressive finds. One might think of the enormous deposits of papyri that were found at Tebtynis in 1931 and 1934 during the Italian excavations (Begg 1998; Gallazzi 1990). But it is a matter of urgency, for under the pressure of an exploding demography, the archaeological sites most likely to yield papyri, already threatened by the rising water table, may soon be sacrificed to the extension of urbanization and agriculture (Gallazzi 1994).

NOTES

1. Bernardino Drovetti, French consul in Alexandria, pretended to work for the enrichment of the French cultural heritage but primarily wanted to pay off some substantial debts by trying to sell his collection to the French government.

2. This monumental work (first edition 1809–1828) is a sum of all the observations made by the artists, scientists, and technicians who accompanied Bonaparte's expedition.

3. He had been among the first group of Egyptian students who were sent to study in France, where he was residing in 1822, the year Champollion announced that he had solved the riddle of the hieroglyphs.

4. This fortunate expression was coined by R. S. Poole and is quoted by M. S. Drower (1982, 312).

5. James (1982, 9–36). In 1919 the EEF was renamed the Egypt Exploration Society.

6. Petrie (1891, 28). Recycled papyrus from cartonnage was already known; it was mentioned by Letronne in 1826 in connection with fragments of cartonnage from the Passalacqua collection (*P.Paris*, pp. 410 ff.).

7. Letter of Oct. 22, 1888, quoted in Wilcken (1899, 26).

8. Their descriptions make us smile today, but this is how Grenfell and Hunt report excavations directed by scholars as opposed to *sebbâkhîn* and other looters (Grenfell, Hunt, and Hogarth 1900, 20).

9. This trade and the possibility of exportation were not made illegal until Law 117 was enacted in 1983.

10. See Davoli (1998, 76) for a good evaluation of this excavation.

11. I am thinking of the excavations of the Red Sea harbors by S. E. Sidebotham, W. Wendrich, and D. P. S. Peacock, as well as of J.-Y. Empereur, archaeologist and epigraphist, at Alexandria. The exploration of Mons Porphyrites by D. P. S. Peacock and V. Maxfield is linked to the study of imperial power. It is a model of nondestructive excavation, in which the search for papyrological documents was a secondary consideration.

12. This is also the case with the Dakhleh Oasis Project which has studied that oasis in the Western desert since 1978 from both a long-term geological and climatic point of view and a historical perspective.

13. Located in the Eastern Desert, Mons Claudianus is a group of grano-diorite quarries that were exploited by the Roman emperors beginning around the time of Claudius or Nero. The peak of activity occurred under Trajan, who used the quarries for the numerous monolithic columns in the Basilica Ulpia. Mons Claudianus has also produced most of the columns in front of the Pantheon in Rome, which was reconstructed under Hadrian.

14. The "rabbit holes" left by illicit diggers expose the mounds to the rain, which is not so rare in the Eastern Desert as elsewhere in Egypt, and the previously sealed layers are quickly penetrated and destroyed. The proximity of modern works–mining, quarries, road building projects, and so on—also presents risks. Several garbage heaps from ancient forts have been disturbed by bulldozers or simply removed. Recently somebody took a bulldozer right through the walls of the fort Iovis, mentioned in the *Itinerarium Antoninianum*.

15. See what Marijke van der Veen (1988) deduces from the texts.

16. Pack² 78 (first century CE). The circumstances of the find were reported by Mariette; see *P.Paris*, p. 417.

17. The practice remains a local one, however, since Talit and Tebtynis are no more than five kilometers apart as the crow flies.

18. See *P.Mich.* XVIII pp. 91 ff.

19. Grenfell, Hunt, and Hogarth (1900, 24 ff.). Second best were rooms that had been transformed into garbage deposits, and third the actual rubbish mounds. The latter two categories are discussed later.

20. There may be a good reason for this: In scrutinizing unpublished letters exchanged between Lefebvre and Maspero, Jean-Luc Fournet has recently realized that the archive had been found by illicit diggers *before* Lefebvre's excavations, which were fruitless.

21. The cave is in a cliff of the Nahal Hever, one of the valleys on the west side of the Dead Sea. The exploration of the caves was undertaken in 1960 after it was discovered that Bedouin had found documents there that they were selling on the Jordanian antiquities market. The Israeli authorities were enthusiastic about the project, which was carried out in style. The army arranged the logistics for four parallel expeditions with helicopters, aerial

photography, electricity in the caves, mountaineering equipment, mine detectors, and even a number of soldiers who participated in the excavations.

22. On this subject, read the pages full of humor and humility by Jean-Pierre Brun, an expert "garbologist" ("Méthodes et conditions de fouilles des fortins et des dépotoirs, ou les affres d'un Gallo-Romain en Égypte," in Cuvigny, ed. 2003, 61–71).

23. That is the period before the first Fayyum find.

BIBLIOGRAPHY

Bagnall, R. S. 2001. "Archaeological Work on Hellenistic and Roman Egypt, 1995–2000." *AJA* 105: 227–243.

Bailey, D. M. 1999. "*Sebakh*, Sherds, and Survey." *JEA* 85: 211–218.

Begg, D. J. I. 1998. "It Was Wonderful, Our Return in the Darkness with . . . the Baskets of Papyri! Papyrus Finds at Tebtunis from the Bagnani Archives, 1931–1936." *BASP* 35: 185–210.

Betegh, G. 2002. "Papyrus on the Pyre: The Derveni Papyrus and Its Archaeological Context." *Acta Antiqua* 42: 51–56.

Boak, A. E. R., and E. E. Peterson. 1931. *Karanis, Topographical and Architectural Report of Excavations during the Seasons 1924–28.* Ann Arbor: University of Michigan Press.

Cailliaud, F. 1821. *Voyage à l'oasis de Thèbes.* Paris: Imprimerie royale.

Cuvigny, H., ed. 2003. *La route de Myos Hormos: L'armée romaine dans le désert Oriental d'Égypte.* Cairo: Institut français d'archéologie orientale.

Davoli, P. 1998. *L'archeologia urbana nel Fayyum di età ellenistica e romana.* Naples: Procaccini.

——. 2000. *Archeologia e papiri.* Naples: Eurocomp.

Johnson, J. de M. 1914. "Antinoë and its Papyri." *JEA* 1: 168–181.

Jomard, E.-F. and J. B. J. Fourier, ed. 1809–1828. *Description de l'Égypte, ou, Recueil des observations et des recherches qui ont été faites en Égypte pendant l'expédition de l'armée française,* Paris: Imprimerie Impériale.

Drower, M. S. 1982. "Gaston Maspero and the Birth of the Egypt Exploration Fund (1881–3)." *JEA* 68: 299–313.

——. 1985. *Flinders Petrie: A Life in Archaeology.* London: Gollancz.

Gallazzi, C. 1990. "La 'Cantina dei Papiri' di Tebtynis e ciò che essa conteneva." *ZPE* 80: 283–288.

——. 1994. "Trouvera-t-on encore des papyrus en 2042?" In *Proceedings of the 20th International Congress of Papyrologists,* ed. A. Bülow-Jacobsen, 131–135. Copenhagen: Museum Tusculanum Press.

——. 2000. "La reprise des fouilles." In *Tebtynis I. La reprise des fouilles et le quartier de la chapelle d'Isis-Thermouthis,* ed. C. Gallazzi and G. Hadji-Minaglou, 3–39. Cairo: Institut français d'archéologie orientale.

Grenfell, B. P., A. S. Hunt, and D. G. Hogarth. 1900. *Fayûm Towns and Their Papyri.* London: Egypt Exploration Fund.

Grenfell, B. P., A. S. Hunt, and J. G. Smyly. 1902. *The Tebtunis Papyri* I. London: Oxford University Press.

Hunt, A. S. 1914. "Papyri and Papyrology." *JEA* 1: 81–92.

James, T. G. H., ed. 1982. *Excavating in Egypt: The Egypt Exploration Society 1882–1982.* Chicago: University of Chicago Press.

Lefebvre, G. 1907. *Fragments d'un manuscrit de Ménandre découverts et publiés*. Cairo: Institut français d'archéologie orientale.

Martin, A. 1994. "Archives privées et cachettes documentaires." In *Proceedings of the 20th International Congress of Papyrologists*, ed. A. Bülow-Jacobsen, 569–577. Copenhagen: Museum Tusculanum Press.

———. 2002. "Heurs et malheurs d'un manuscrit: Deux notes à propos du papyrus d'Hérondas." *ZPE* 139: 22–26.

Maspero, G. 1910. *Rapports sur la marche du Service des Antiquités*. Cairo: Imprimerie nationale.

Montserrat, D. 1996. " 'No Papyrus and No Portraits': Hogarth, Grenfell, and the First Season in the Fayyum, 1895–6." *BASP* 33: 133–176.

Pack, R. A. 1965. *The Greek and Latin Literary Texts from Greco-Roman Egypt. Second Revised and Enlarged Edition*. Ann Arbor: University of Michigan Press.

Petrie, W. M. F. 1891. *Illahun, Kahun, and Gurob (1889–90)*. London: David Nutt.

Reiter, F. 2005. "Symposia in Tebtynis: Zu den griechischen Ostraka aus den neuen Grabungen." In *Tebtynis und Soknopaiu Nesos: Leben im römerzeitlichen Fajum. Akten des Internationalen Symposions vom 11. bis 13. Dezember 2003 in Sommerhausen bei Würzburg*, ed. S. Lippert and M. Schentuleit, 131–140. Wiesbaden: Harrassowitz.

Rostovtzeff, M. I. 1934. *The Excavations at Dura-Europos: Preliminary Report of the Fifth Season of Work*. New Haven, Conn.: Yale University Press.

van Minnen, P. 1992. "A Closer Look at *O. Mich.* I 126." *BASP* 29: 169–171.

———. 1994. "House-to-House Enquiries: An Interdisciplinary Approach to Roman Karanis." *ZPE* 100: 227–251.

———. 2000. "An Official Act of Cleopatra (with a Subscription in Her Own Hand)." *Ancient Society* 30: 29–34.

Veen, Marijke van der. 1988. "A Life of Luxury in the Desert? The Food and Fodder Supply to Mons Claudianus." *JRA* 11: 101–116.

Wilcken, Ulrich. 1899. *Griechische Ostraka aus Ägypten und Nubien: Ein Beitrag zur antiken Wirtschaftsgeschichte*. Vol. 1. Berlin: Gieseke & Devrient.

Yadin, Y. 1961. "Expedition D." *Israel Exploration Journal* 11: 36–52.

———. 1962. "Expedition D: The Cave of the Letters." *Israel Exploration Journal* 12: 227–257.

CHAPTER 3

THE HISTORY OF
THE DISCIPLINE

JAMES G. KEENAN

THE development of papyrology as a discipline presumes the existence in substantial numbers of finds like those described in the preceding chapter. That being so, a strong case can be made (Gigante 1984) for dating the beginning of papyrology to 1752, the year in which papyri were first discovered at Herculaneum, the south Italian city buried by the eruption of Vesuvius in 79 CE (see chapter 13). These papyri came in the form of cigar-shaped rolls, crisp and fragile from their ancient incineration. Thus, the earliest history of papyrology is dominated by the tale of the frustrating and sometimes ruinous attempts to unroll these recalcitrant pieces (Deuel 1965, chapters 9–10).

Nevertheless, perhaps because papyrology came to be associated with Egypt and documents, not Italy and philosophical texts, papyrologists came to identify 1788 as marking the beginning of their discipline. In that year Danish classicist Niels Iversen Schow (1754–1830) published a Greek papyrus that recorded a series of receipts for work performed in 193 CE on the irrigation dikes in the Fayyum district of Egypt. The papyrus itself, a roll with twelve and a half surviving columns, had been bought in 1778 near Memphis by an anonymous merchant. As legend has it, the merchant bought only this one papyrus of the fifty offered for sale; "the Turks" proceeded to burn the rest, delighting in the resulting aroma. Details of the story, especially its olfactory coda, have been contested, but it is certain that the papyrus that escaped destruction was donated to Cardinal Stefano Borgia. Hence, it is sometimes known after the cardinal as the Charta Borgiana, but it is also called the Schow papyrus after its editor (full details, Martin 2000b; see Litinas 2007 for a new fragment found in

Lisbon). Initially housed in the cardinal's museum at Velitri, it now resides in the Museo Nazionale Archeologico in Naples (Preisendanz 1933, 69–73).

If credit for the first edition of a papyrus belongs to Schow, credit for the first modern edition of an integrated series of papyri goes to Amedeo Angelo Maria Peyron (1785–1870), an Italian Jesuit scholar of Coptic and Greek, for his *Papyri graeci regii Musei Taurinensis* (Greek Papyri of the Royal Museum at Turin) (1826–1827). In this volume Peyron published a set of papyri from the so-called *choachytai* dossier. These were long, well-preserved Ptolemaic-period documents concerned with litigation between Egyptian mortuary priests ("choachytai" are literally "water pourers" in Greek) and two Hellenized Egyptians. Not long ago, Peyron's edition was judged a "miracle" (Bingen 1994, 43) not just by the nonexistent standards of his own day but by universal standards as well. Although other papyrus editions sporadically followed, none matched Peyron's in editorial skill or in sensitivity to what documentary papyri reveal about human history (Bingen 1994; Montevecchi 1994). Nevertheless, great as it was, Peyron's achievement was overshadowed by the expectations raised by Champollion's decipherment of Egyptian hieroglyphs. In contrast to what the new decipherment promised, the contents of documents like Peyron's were regarded as "vulgar" and "negligible" (Montevecchi 1994, 27, quoting Angelo Cardinal Mai [1782–1854])—a prejudice against which papyrology has had to struggle ever since.

Because it appeared at a time when the word papyrology did not exist and the discipline had not yet been distinguished from what is now called Egyptology, Peyron's edition belongs, like the Herculaneum discoveries, to the protohistory of papyrology. During these early years, most papyri that were shipped to Europe were acquired (rather ruthlessly by today's standards) as parts of collections of other, more valued antiquities. The driving forces, both through purchase and rough-and-ready excavation, were often diplomats like Giovanni Anastasi (1780–1860), Bernardino Drovetti (1776–1852), and Henry Salt (1780–1827) (Fagan 1975; Reid 2002).

The number of acquisitions grew exponentially in 1877 when peasants digging for fertilizer in the ancient mounds of Kimân Faris, north of the modern capital of the Fayyum province, discovered thousands of papyri; to distinguish it from a second, somewhat less spectacular, clandestine discovery, this event came to be called "the first Fayyum find." Most of these papyri, along with others of Herakleopolite provenance, were purchased in Cairo by Austrian businessman and antiquities dealer Theodor Graf (1840–1903) (Preisendanz 1933, 110–124). Graf sold the papyri in lots, first to the Louvre and the Berlin Museum and then, in 1883 (or 1884), to Archduke Rainer (1827–1913). Rainer commissioned Graf to make further purchases in his behalf, a working arrangement that lasted until 1889. Ten years later, the archduke donated his acquisitions to the Austrian National Library, creating in one stroke what is now the world's second or third (after Berlin) largest collection. Importantly for their recovery and preservation, papyri had come to be valued as artifacts in and of themselves.

If the Austrians and others assembled collections largely through purchase, the English, encouraged by the successful efforts of William Matthew Flinders Petrie (1853–1942) in the Fayyum in the late 1880s, led the field in excavating for papyri. There soon followed another major turning point in papyrology's late nineteenth-century history. This was not a single event but a series of events over two years, 1891–1892, that served to put papyrology on the map. The year 1891 is often referred to in papyrological circles as the "miracle year" (*annus mirabilis*). It witnessed Swiss-born Irishman John P. Mahaffy's (1839–1919) publication of the first volume of Petrie papyri, as well as editions by Englishman Frederic G. Kenyon (1863–1952) of the British Museum's "Constitution of Athens" and, in separate publications, papyrus rolls with mimes of Herondas and speeches by the Athenian orator Hypereides. In 1892 there appeared the first fascicle in the extensive series of Greek documentary papyri from the Berlin Museum (*Aegyptische Urkunden aus den Königlichen* [later *Staatlichen*] *Museen zu Berlin, Griechische Urkunden*). This led to the coining of the word papyrologist by Jules Nicole (1842–1921) of Geneva, who in 1896 referred (in French) to the editors of the Berlin papyri as "papyrologistes" (van Minnen 1993, 7, 7n11). In English, "papyrology," after a hesitant appearance in 1898 ("In the department of *papyrology, if we may use such a word"), achieved full acceptance by 1900 ("Papyrology is the Greek study which is devouring all the rest") (*Oxford English Dictionary* [1933], vol. 7, 442; both citations from anonymous reviews in the literary journal *Athenæum*). A year later it had become a "science" (Robinson 1901, 212).

At first papyrology denoted specifically the decipherment and presentation of texts written on papyrus (and ostraca), especially in Greek. Texts in the Egyptian language in whatever script—hieroglyphic, hieratic, demotic—remained the preserve of the field that came to be called Egyptology. So did texts in Coptic (Egyptian written in a predominantly Greek script), at least until recent times, when papyrologists (and New Testament scholars) have increasingly tried to master Coptic without experiencing the traditional, and some think essential, initiation to the earlier forms of Egyptian language and scripts. Papyrology, however, soon also developed a meaning that extends beyond the editing of papyrus texts to include their use in the study of Egyptian history, society, and economy from approximately the third century BCE until the early eighth century CE. This is sometimes referred to as "the papyrological millennium."

An enormous boost to papyrology in both senses is owed to the discoveries of Bernard P. Grenfell (1869–1926) and Arthur S. Hunt (1871–1934). These young Oxford classicists had, under the auspices of the Egypt Exploration Fund (later, Society), undertaken excavations in Egypt in specific quest of papyri with a special mandate for seeking out Christian and literary texts. They first excavated in surveylike fashion at various sites in the Fayyum. But in 1896, with a geographically extended permit, they turned their attention beyond the Fayyum to the ancient city of Oxyrhynchus, a site conceded to them by Petrie. Failing on the basis of past experience to uncover papyri in either of the most obvious locations, the Graeco-Roman cemetery and the town proper, they decided to dig in the ancient town's rubbish dumps. On January 11, 1897, they hit the mother lode, recovering numerous papyrus fragments of all kinds. The next day they uncovered a special prize, a small, crumpled codex leaf containing a series of "sayings of Jesus," later identified as coming from the apocryphal Gospel of Thomas. And the finds kept on coming in enormous quantities, not just in 1897 but in later years as well, until 1907, when Grenfell and Hunt's excavations at Oxyrhynchus, after six seasons of digging, ceased (Deuel 1966, chapters 9–10; Turner 1982). (These excavations were the source of the world's largest collection of papyri.)

Almost as impressive as the Oxyrhynchus finds themselves was the swiftness of their publication. In 1898, within eleven months of the arrival in England of the first batch of papyri, Grenfell and Hunt produced the first volume of *Oxyrhynchus Papyri*. Besides the "sayings of Jesus," previously published in pamphlet form, other prizes in *P.Oxy.* I included poetic fragments of Alcaeus and Sappho. In all, 158 texts were edited in full, and another 49 in brief description.

Significantly, the first volume of *Oxyrhynchus Papyri* adopted a new format for exhibiting papyri in print. Grenfell and Hunt gave every papyrus a number and a title; a heading giving measurements and date; a concise introduction to the text's contents; Greek text in modern form (accents included); critical apparatus indicating scribal aberrations and linguistic anomalies; and line-by-line commentary. Positioned before the commentary—and revolutionary at the time—were translations for most of the texts, provided, as Grenfell and Hunt say in their preface, "at the request of several subscribers to the Graeco-Roman branch" of the Egypt Exploration Fund.

For both the interested public and scholars, this template made the Oxyrhynchus papyri more accessible than those published in antiquated, less congenial formats. Today, any edition of a papyrus without translation is deemed incomplete: The translation, in effect, completes the edition. In this view (Youtie 1973, vol. 1, 12), the translation is not added "for its own sake" but rather to let the reader know "at any moment what meaning the editor attributed to any and every passage of the text.... [I]t is there as additional and almost certainly more effective commentary."

Grenfell and Hunt are therefore rightly credited with having created a "style," at once a hallmark of the Oxyrhynchus editions and a model for modern editions in general. It is, nonetheless, a particular style that is dominated by the text-based interests of philology and typology. It does not normally allow for extension into the wider social or historical ramifications of individual texts or groups of texts. Moreover, within the Oxyrhynchus volumes, papyri were (and still are) grouped in an established order by type (literary, subliterary, documentary); they were thereby detached from their archaeological context and dissociated from related papyri of different type (Gagos, Gates, and Wilburn 2005). In the later publication of literary papyri from Oxyrhynchus, this style reached its ideal in the impeccable but austere editions of Edgar Lobel (1888–1982): "[N]o parade of scholarship, no clutter of bibliography, ... an insistence on fact and precision, a distaste for easy solutions and grandiose speculations" (preface to *P.Oxy.* L).

It happened that while Grenfell and Hunt were migrating between Egypt and Oxford, excavating and deciphering, there lived in Germany a scholar who found fascination in even the most pedestrian of tax receipts scrawled on potsherds (Wilcken 1899). This was Ulrich Wilcken (1862–1944), a devoted student of Theodor Mommsen (1817–1903). Mommsen has long been credited with originating the prediction that just as the nineteenth century had been the century of epigraphy, so the twentieth would be the century of papyrology (the credit perhaps belongs to Ludwig Mitteis [1859–1921], Martin 2000a). It was Wilcken who decided to found the first journal devoted exclusively to papyrology, the *Archiv für Papyrusforschung,* whose first fascicle appeared in 1900; the first volume was completed in 1901. Earlier, papyrologists had found homes for their shorter writings in a variety of specialist journals. Now, by Wilcken's intention, papyrological research would have its own *Vereinigungspunkt* (concentration point) not only for papyrological research in the strict sense but also for all studies related to papyrology (ancient history, epigraphy, numismatics, theology, philology). In his foreword to the first issue, Wilcken enunciated a program for the new periodical. Though not excluding literary papyri, the focus was to be on documents, both in and of themselves and in their relation to ancient history and culture. Submissions were not restricted to those in German. Articles in English, French, Italian, and Latin were also invited.

Wilcken, then at Würzburg, was the journal's sole editor, but as associates he had assembled an international cast of papyrological "all-stars": Otto Gradenwitz (Königsberg), B. P. Grenfell and A. S. Hunt (Oxford), Pierre Jouguet (then at Lille), Frederic Kenyon (London, British Museum), Giacomo Lumbroso (Rome), J. P. Mahaffy (Dublin), Ludwig Mitteis (Leipzig), Jules Nicole (Geneva), and Paul Viereck (Berlin). Many contributions to *Archiv*'s first volume seem to have been by invitation. It contained a series of articles (*Aufsätze*), reports and reviews (*Referate und Besprechungen*), and brief communications (*Mitteilungen*). Wilcken and nearly all of the associates contributed to the first volume, which also included articles by Mommsen and Ulrich von Wilamowitz-Moellendorff (1848–1931), respectively the premier ancient historian and the foremost philologist of their time (and quite likely of all time). Among the articles was Wilcken's "general register" of papyri published to date. Among the reports was one of Wilcken's firm but gracious critiques of recent papyrus editions; there were also reports on Christian texts by Carl Schmidt (1868–1938) and on new legal documents from Oxyrhynchus by Mitteis. The brief communications included Grenfell and Hunt's description of their excavations at Tebtynis for the University of California in the winter of 1899–1900.

Wilcken intended to organize the new discipline of papyrology on an international scale. If *Archiv* was to be devoted largely to documents, it was also to connect the results of papyrological research with those of other subfields of *Altertumswissenschaft* and to establish a form of quality control over papyrological editions. Once a papyrologist was assured that documents had been well edited, the next step was to see to their use in other disciplines, to the mutual illumination of papyri, literature, inscriptions, ostraca, and coins. But the still higher goal consequent to the foregoing was, as Wilcken put it, "to grasp ancient culture in all its manifestations in the liveliest possible way" (1901, v).

Conscious of how difficult it was for nonpapyrologists to access the results of papyrological research, Wilcken later collaborated with Mitteis, the leading jurist among papyrologists, to create in 1912 a monumental assessment of the documentary papyri published to date. This was the *Grundzüge und Chrestomathie der Papyruskunde*. It appeared in two halves, one historical, one juristic, each containing a volume introducing its subject and a volume containing hundreds of illustrative documents. These four volumes, still authoritative today, defined papyrology's major concerns while simultaneously enshrining the division of Egypt's papyrological millennium into Ptolemaic, Roman, and Byzantine periods and identifying juristic papyrology as the discipline's principal subfield. Also influential over the long term was Wilcken's view (1912, xv) that Egypt held a "special place" (*Sonderstellung*) both in the Hellenistic world during the Ptolemaic period and later on under the Roman Empire. General conclusions could therefore be drawn from the Egyptian evidence only with the greatest caution.

Wilcken's magisterium cast a long shadow, so it is no surprise that the young Marcel Hombert (1900–1992) assimilated this brief passage from Wilcken, incorporated it verbatim into his own inaugural lecture in Brussels on October 27, 1925 ("La papyrologie grecque," http://www.ulb.ac.be/philo/cpeg/hombert. htm), and there referred to Egypt in the Hellenistic world and under the Roman Empire as having "une position toute particulière." Wilcken's measured adoption of the idea that Egypt was a "special place" therefore had an impact that was specific and practically immediate. It was also lasting and sometimes exaggerated. Though not Wilcken's intention, it has served to diminish or exclude the use of Egyptian evidence for the general study of ancient (namely, classical) history. This is most apparent in work on the Roman imperial period, where on many occasions Egypt with its papyrus evidence was judged to be so "untypical" that it could be readily dismissed. Moreover, what may be called the "*Sonderstellung* problem" is also inextricably bound to the problem of historical continuity, especially that from the Ptolemaic period into the Roman. On the one hand, simply put, if the Romans adopted Ptolemaic forms, then Egypt remained as peculiar under the Romans as it had been under the Ptolemies; on the other hand, if the Romans introduced their own forms, then Egypt's place was not so "special" after all, and its evidence could not be casually set aside. In the past generation, criticism of the model of

Ptolemaic-to-Roman continuity (Lewis 1970, 1984) naturally led to some erosion of the "Sonderstellung" model (e.g., Bowman and Rathbone 1992). In the meantime, papyrologists have composed detailed defenses of the value of the Egyptian evidence both for the Hellenistic world (Heinen 1989) and for the Roman Empire (Geraci 1989). Nevertheless, from a programmatic standpoint, perhaps the most balanced assessment is that advanced years ago by Cambridge ancient historian A. H. M. Jones (Jones 1942, esp. 286–287) in a succinct but pointed statement on the need to bring history and papyrology together based on the latter's contributions to the former and the belief that the papyrus evidence had significance that transcended particularities of place. Jones, of course, amply honored his own recommendation in numerous articles (e.g., Jones 1974) and, most extensively, in his massive *The Later Roman Empire, 284–602* (1964).

Another, perhaps even more important consequence of Wilcken's research agenda is that the study of papyrus *documents* came to signify papyrology as a whole. The result was a lasting tendency to separate, or marginalize, the study of literary papyri, even though classical scholars, many of whom have only passing familiarity with the documents, display enormous enthusiasm each time a new literary papyrus is published. All of this aside, Wilcken was obviously a magnificent synthesizer, justly credited as the first scholar to develop a vision of the field as a whole. Nevertheless, if Wilcken was papyrology's first (and perhaps only) truly great synthesizer, its first great organizer was his slightly older contemporary Friedrich Preisigke (1856–1924) (Montevecchi 1988, 35–36), longtime director of the Post Office and Telegraph in (then) Straßburg. In retirement Preisigke initiated, collaborated upon, and supervised four major projects: "la grande tétralogie de Preisigke" (Bingen 1977, 42; cf. Preisendanz 1933, 199–202):

1. the *Sammelbuch* (1913–), a series of volumes to reprint documents (papyri, ostraca, inscriptions) that had been published piecemeal in periodicals
2. the *Berichtigungsliste* (1922–), volumes that record corrections made to already published texts
3. the exhaustively titled *Namenbuch* (1922), an alphabetical list of personal names
4. the multivolume *Wörterbuch* (1925–), a dictionary of the documentary papyri

The generosity of Preisigke's endeavors matched the internationalism of Wilcken's vision of the field. In truth, papyrology has a long tradition of international cooperation. Originally this was due to the efforts of scholars like Wilcken and Preisigke as just described and to lively correspondence across national borders. Two examples of more formal international cooperation are the so-called papyrus cartels and the international meetings that have been held under the auspices of the Association Internationale de Papyrologues (International Association of Papyrologists).

Papyrus Cartels

In the 1920s and 1930s numerous papyri were being offered for sale on the antiquities market—an expectedly unregulated market in which papyri were sold at high prices and scattered worldwide with little tracking. In response, there was formed what has been called a "cartel," although it was more precisely "a syndicate of buyers" (Turner 1980, 36). The idea was not new: The Germans had tried something like it earlier in the Deutsches Papyruskartell, which functioned between 1902 and 1914, purchasing papyri from local dealers in Egypt and distributing them to German member institutions, including, between 1903 and 1906, papyri that turned out to have been filched from Grenfell and Hunt's site at Oxyrhynchus (Preisendanz 1933, 210–211; Martin 2007).

The new cartel, begun in or shortly after 1920, continued to operate through the mid-1930s, headed by the British Museum with H. I. Bell (1879–1967) as the principal keeper of records. Bell inventoried and oversaw the dispersal of papyri to a number of member institutions, mainly American, according to their particular interests and respective purchasing powers. These at first included Cornell, Michigan, Princeton, and Wisconsin; Columbia and Yale joined later. Geneva and Oslo were European members, as was, of course, the British Museum. This was a rather fluid association whose history, in the interests of what is called "museum archaeology" (Vandorpe 1994)—the virtual reassembling of papyrus archives and dossiers physically scattered through illegal excavations and the antiquities market—would be worth reconstructing based on the surviving correspondence between representatives of the member institutions. The most active of these was the University of Michigan, whose collection was initiated before the syndicate's creation through purchases made by Francis W. Kelsey (1858–1927), namesake of today's Kelsey Museum of Archaeology. The University of Michigan's purchases through and apart from the syndicate continued even during its excavations at Karanis and Soknopaiou Nesos (1924–1935) (Gagos 2001, esp. 517–525). When buying independently, Michigan seems to have bought mainly from Maurice Nahman (1868–1948), in whose "petit palais de style arabe" (Capart 1947; photo: Pintaudi 1993, 165) at 27 Madebegh Street, Cairo, antiquities were displayed as in a gallery (WWWE 305 [see acknowledgments, this chapter]; photos: Pintaudi 1993, 157 [Nahman], 167 and 169 [the gallery]).

Part of the syndicate's purpose was to keep a lid on prices. Nonetheless, competition from nonsyndicate institutions and amateur buyers, together with the wealth and alleged ignorance of the U.S. member institutions, which seemed liable to "spoil the market" (letter from Hunt to Bell, BL Add MS 59512, item 202), continued to drive prices skyward. A glimpse at buyers' competitiveness is provided by a handful of letters written by Nahman, three from Paris (Le Grand Hotel, 12, Boulevard des Capucines) and two from Cairo (27, Rue el-Madabegh; later 27, rue Cherif Pacha), to Medea Norsa (1877–1952) between 1932 and 1935. At this time the site of Oxyrhynchus was being stripped by illegal excavations whose finds Nahman refused on principle to buy (Pintaudi 1993, 156–169). It is true that Nahman's customers included American institutions represented by A. E. R. Boak and Michael Rostovtzeff, but the villain in Nahman's letters turns out to be not the Americans but an Italian archaeologist-papyrologist from Milan.

A crisis having been reached, Marcel Hombert published in the Belgian periodical *Chronique d'Égypte* a brief but passionate treatment of the subject (Hombert 1933). In a largely forgotten but minor classic of Orientalist writing, Hombert pointed to the competition among institutions to acquire papyri, a limited resource obtainable only in Egypt. He credited the syndicate with partial success in price control and considerable success in substance, singling out for special mention its acquisition of the Roman emperor Claudius's famous letter to the Alexandrians. Hombert continued with an imaginative sketch in which an amateur, would-be purchaser of papyri, having failed to make any acquisitions from European dealers in Alexandria or Cairo, turns to native antiquities shops near the fashionable Shepheard's Hotel (Reid 2002, 73, photo on 74). There the hapless buyer becomes a target for disinformation. He quickly finds himself a neighborhood celebrity, hassled by salesmen hawking postcards, walking canes, and flyswatters. He is then cozened by a shady dragoman out into the primitive countryside into the presence of a surly villager dealer. There he is eventually offered coffee and shown some dust-covered terracotta lamps, belle époque bronze figurines, and scarabs of dubious authenticity. When papyri are finally brought out, they prove to be as expensive in the abode of "this obscure peasant" as "in the most luxurious antiquities gallery in Cairo."

But despite the frustrations visited upon Hombert's notional purchaser, buyers still went, and they still bought—at exorbitant prices. What could be done? The only hope seemed to lie in the equally expensive alternative of excavation—in which a small country like Belgium could hardly expect to compete on its own. At this very time, the University of Michigan, for example, was still excavating at Karanis (1924–1935), Yale was midway through its excavations at Dura-Europos (1928–1937), a small city in Syria on the bank of the Euphrates River (Hopkins 1979), and Italian excavations at Tebtynis for the Società italiana per la ricerca dei papiri in Egitto were also in full swing (1929–1936) (e.g., Begg 1998).

INTERNATIONAL ORGANIZATIONS
AND "SCHOOLS"

If Hombert's pleas seemed fruitless and if the cartel was relatively short-lived, the institution of international congresses of papyrology has been useful and lasting. Papyrologists as a group first came together at an international meeting in Brussels in 1930. At the invitation of Jean Capart (1877–1947), famed Belgian Egyptologist (*WWWE* 82–83, with photo), a special papyrology session was held as part of an "Egyptological week" celebrating the centenary of Belgium's independence. After the fact this came to be reckoned as the First International Congress of Papyrologists. At this meeting an International Committee of Papyrology, with Cairo-based Frenchman Pierre Jouguet (1869–1949) as president and Marcel Hombert as permanent secretary in Brussels, was established to oversee future meetings. The following year, at Leiden, papyrologists met in "an autonomous session," once again as part of a larger meeting, this time the Eighteenth International Congress of Orientalists, now credited as the Second International Congress of Papyrologists.

By the standards of today's congresses, both meetings were modest affairs in terms of the number of participants and the number of papers given, but the names of almost all the participants are those who were, or became, giants in the field (Habermann 2001, 102–103, with notes). Many of the papers at the first meeting, whether delivered in person or by proxy, were progress reports on papyrology in the various countries represented. Of the others, for example, Victor Martin (1886–1964) of Switzerland provided an update on a project to reedit the papers of Flavius Abinnaeus, a fourth-century military commander; a young Belgian, Claire Préaux (1904–1979), spoke on the Zenon papyri, the largest and most famous archive of the Ptolemaic period; and the eminent ancient historian and Russian emigré Michael Rostovtzeff (1870–1952) presented results of the Yale excavations at Dura-Europos.

For the Leiden meeting, the International Committee of Papyrology had set itself the task of establishing a system of symbols for use in editing texts, partly modeled on those used in editing inscriptions. In the morning session of September 10, 1931, B. A. van Groningen (1894–1987) of Holland made the principal proposal but also read supplementary recommendations from H. I. Bell and A. S. Hunt, who were not in attendance. After discussion, the proposals of Bell and Hunt were accepted as friendly amendments to van Groningen's proposal. The following day, the papyrologists in attendance unanimously approved not only what has come to be called "the Leiden system" (i.e., system of editorial signs) but also the more general standardization of editions recommended by Bell.[1]

After the Leiden meeting, papyrologists met three more times on their own (Munich, 1933; Florence, 1935; Oxford, 1937), but the politics of the late 1930s and the Second World War interrupted the series. The meeting planned for Vienna in 1939 (Habermann 2001) was never held. The war itself, based on reports gathered afterward by Marcel Hombert (Hombert 1947, 1948), wrought terrible personal loss: A young Austrian papyrologist and the conservator of the Vienna papyrus collection were both killed in battle; a well-known French papyrologist from

---

1. The "Leiden conventions" can be found in most volumes of papyri, for example, at the start of each volume of *P.Oxy.*

Strasbourg (Paul Collomp, 1885–1943) was murdered by the German police in Clermont-Ferrand (the University of Strasbourg's place of exile); a German went missing in action on the Russian front in the war's final months; a young Dutch papyrologist was executed for his role in the Resistance. In addition to these tragedies, significant material and cultural destruction was sustained: Papyri were lost or destroyed, libraries were bombed and burned, and tremendous disruption occurred, including the shipping of the British Museum's great collection to Aberystwyth, Wales, for safekeeping, which was just one event in the mass relocation of all kinds of valuable collections at the time (Nicholas 1994).

All of this notwithstanding, several papyrologists met in Brussels in August 1947 with the intention of restoring international relations among colleagues and devising a plan to recommence regular meetings. The first such meeting took place in Paris in 1949 (Bingen 1977, 35). There a decision was approved to formalize the organization of the international congresses through the creation, under the auspices of UNESCO, of the Association Internationale de Papyrologues (AIP). As before, the secretariat was to be in Brussels but with elected officers and board members representing many countries. A major force in the organizational effort was (once again) Marcel Hombert, who became the association's first secretary-treasurer, serving until 1961 when he was succeeded by Jean Bingen (1920–). Since 1949, with the exception of one four-year interlude, papyrologists have held their congresses every three years. (The 2007 meeting was held in Ann Arbor, Michigan; Geneva, Switzerland, is the site for the 2010 meeting.)

The coining of what became the association's motto, "amicitia papyrologorum," is attributed to juristic papyrologist Leopold Wenger (1874–1953), who as host of the festivities on the evening of the last day (September 7, 1933) of the Third International Congress (Munich) toasted "the friendship of papyrologists." By the fourth congress (Florence, 1935), as the political horizon darkened, "the friendship of papyrologists" could be said to have become proverbial (*sprichwörtlich*). This was perhaps in part because of the (in retrospect desperate?) faith in what was then referred to as the "new humanism," a firm belief in human progress based on a renaissance in classical scholarship, somehow much dependent upon the "fraternity" of papyrologists, sentiments glowingly expressed during the Florence congress (*Aegyptus*, serie scientifica 5, Milan [1936]; cf. Keenan 2002, 226–227).

The meaning of the motto is usually assumed but rarely defined. It is an ideal that clearly implies that the field of papyrology is larger than individual papyrologists, no matter what their several contributions. It alludes to a code of courtesy even in cases of strong disagreement, where criticism is directed at an anonymous "editor" and polemics are frowned-upon exceptions. It acknowledges that the field is in a constant state of growth and revision in which all papyrologists are partners. It suggests that the friendship is personal as much as professional. It also points to the internationalism of the field. As Wenger put it somewhat later, in 1940, in still darker days, "A realm of knowledge like papyrology, built to so great a degree upon the collaboration of the international community of learning, makes it extraordinarily difficult, nay impossible, to separate neatly the share of the work of an individual nation from the great totality" (http://www.ulb.ac.be/assoc/aip/amicitia.htm). A few years later, in a symbolically significant gesture, H. I. Bell, at the beginning of an article in the *Journal of Egyptian Archaeology* (31 [1945]: 75), was pleased to announce that he had received an offprint and with it news from Italian papyrologist Medea Norsa that she was alive and well despite the current fighting in northern Italy in and around Florence. Within recent memory, the career that probably best exemplifies the ideals of the "amicitia" was that of Sir Eric G. Turner (1911–1983) (Parsons 1987), worthy successor in Great Britain to H. I. Bell in this regard (Thomas 1966).

There is an irony in all this, I think. That is, despite friendships across real and sometimes ideological battle lines (Gigante 1986; Habermann 2001), despite Wenger's credo, and despite the AIP's statute (article 1) codifying the ideal of "fostering international collaboration in the field of papyrology," papyrology's accomplishments have tended to be presented and assessed, as in the modern Olympics, according to the boundaries of nation-states (e.g., Preisendanz 1933, 160–300). So, for example, the Belgians (Montevecchi 1988, 37–38) and the Dutch may justly be credited with being in the forefront of combining documents in Greek and in demotic Egyptian for the study of Ptolemaic Egypt. Such is their conjoined contribution that it has been possible to refer to the accomplishments of the "*schools* of Leuven, Brussels, and Leiden" (Bagnall 1982–1983, 17; my emphasis). A monumental product of this fusion of Greek and demotic studies in the Low Countries is the *Guide to the Zenon Archive* produced by six scholars under the editorship of P. W. Pestman (Pestman 1981).

The Germans, along with the Poles (especially Raphael Taubenschlag [1881–1958] and the University of Warsaw's *Journal of Juristic Papyrology*), have made the most substantial contributions in juristic papyrology (e.g., Rupprecht 1989), a tradition especially strong at Marburg. In the wake of one of papyrology's pioneering editors, Carl Wessely (1860–1931) (Gerstinger 1932; Hopfner 1933), Austrian papyrologists and their associates have contributed immensely to knowledge of the Byzantine and early Islamic periods, based on editions of papyri from the Vienna collection, whose origins were sketched above. French papyrologists have made and continue to make exceptional contributions to study of these late-period papyri, especially in their historical interpretation. In this they carry on the tradition of Jean Maspero (1885–1915), initiator with H. I. Bell of the specialty known as "Byzantine papyrology." (Maspero, in one of papyrology's greatest losses, was mortally wounded during an assault at Vauquois on the Lorraine front on February 18, 1915; G. Maspero 1916, *WWWE* 278–280.)

Soviet papyrology as revealed by I. F. Fikhman (Fikhman 1999, to cite only the longest in a series of archival studies) came to center upon Grigorij F. Zereteli (1870–1939), a half-Georgian (but cultural Russian) later in life based in Tbilisi.

Though politically unengaged, he was arrested on May 24, 1938 (earlier arrests had occurred in 1918 and 1930), and is presumed to have died in 1939 (I. F. Fikhman, letter, September 25, 2005), a blow from which Russian papyrology has never recovered. Finally, many Italian scholars, inspired in Naples by the leadership and dynamism of Marcello Gigante (1923–2001), founder in 1969 of the Centro Internazionale per lo Studio dei Papiri Ercolanesi, are dedicated to research on the Herculaneum papyri, a phenomenon amply attested in the published *atti* (proceedings) of the Florence Congress of 1998 (Keenan 2002, 222–223). The Italians have also been indefatigable excavators of archaeological sites of papyrological interest (Bonacasa 1989; Casini 2001) and remarkably successful in bringing women into the discipline.

Whether this rough, incomplete classification of interests should lead to extensive consideration of national schools of papyrology in either the institutional or the intellectual sense is quite another matter. This is something that awaits systematic sorting out. Montevecchi's compact list (1988, 33–40), outdated despite its addenda (540–541), includes many items that hardly qualify as schools. It identifies numerous schools in the institutional sense but makes only a few nods in the direction of schools as intellectually conceived. A leading example in both senses is the "Istituto Vitelli," the first of several Italian schools or institutes of papyrology (Montevecchi 1988, 37). When founded in 1908 in Florence as the "Società Italiana per la Ricerca dei Papiri Greci e Latini in Egitto," it was intended as a school dedicated on a national, even nationalistic, basis to the excavation and publication of papyri (Carozzi 1982). Its principal founder, Girolamo Vitelli, sensed the Italians were entering the field belatedly. In the end, he left a strong imprint on the institute: in approach, through his distinguished earlier career as a philologist; in fashion, through his devotion to the severe style in editing (Gigante 1986); and on posterity, through a directly traceable line of papyrological descendants, including Medea Norsa and Vittorio Bartoletti (1912–1967) (Pintaudi 1993).

The French scene is both complicated and enriched by the Institut Français d'Archéologie Orientale (IFAO) in Cairo, formally established in 1898 in succession to the school that had existed since 1880 (Reid 2002, 173–175). The institute was geared primarily toward the study of the Near East in a wide, multidisciplinary sense, with an emphasis on archaeology. Papyrology has had an important but not a dominant role. Traditionally important for the institute have been its links in France, especially with Paris. For example, an American, Naphtali Lewis (1911–2005), after a seminar at Columbia on the Zenon archive under William Linn Westermann (1873–1954), went to the Sorbonne to earn his doctorate. There in 1933–1934 he worked under Paul Collart (1878–1946); the following year, he studied in Cairo under Pierre Jouguet (1869–1949) and assisted in the decipherment of the Fouad papyri, published in 1939 (Bagnall 1999). In a telephone conversation (February 28, 2005), Lewis respectfully inclined to view the French combination as more "atelier" (his label) than school, with Collart—a kind, paternal, and caring teacher—as the guiding light in Paris and Jouguet the major figure in Cairo, assisted by Octave Guéraud (1901–1987), who first worked as conservator at the Egyptian Museum, then as secretary general of IFAO. In Cairo with Lewis, also working on the Fouad edition, was Jean Scherer (1911–2001), Lewis's exact contemporary and IFAO "pensionnaire" until his return to France in 1954, where he was soon to become director of the Sorbonne's Institute of Papyrology (Chamoux 2002).

In Germany, to give in brief a third and more recent example, the Institut für Altertumskunde at the University of Cologne, initiated by Joseph Kroll and Reinhold Merkelbach, dates to the mid-1960s. Though many of its early associates have scattered geographically and institutionally, the institute has remained an important center for documentary and literary study and has been responsible for what has become the world's leading and certainly most prolific journal of papyrology, the *Zeitschrift für Papyrologie und Epigraphik*, whose first issue appeared in 1967.

Of course, there cannot be schools without sufficient numbers of teachers and students in some form of physical and intellectual association. Thus, it must have seemed shocking to some in the audience when Herbert Youtie, in his Henry Russel lecture at Ann Arbor in 1962, estimated papyrologists to be "a very small group of scholars, about half a dozen in the United States and Canada, another half dozen in Great Britain, two or three in the Scandinavian countries, a dozen or more dispersed over the continent of Europe, one or two perhaps in the Near East—shall we say a maximum of thirty?" The other 270 or so then members of the AIP were scholars with other interests. They did not edit papyri themselves but made ample use of papyrus evidence in their various studies. Youtie effectively distinguished between a "private papyrology," inhabited by an inner circle (it seems) of papyrus editors, and a "public papyrology," with a far greater number of "students of ancient literature, ancient historians, jurists, grammarians, palaeographers, theologians, Egyptologists, Copticists, Arabists, archaeologists" (Youtie 1973, vol. 1, chapter 1, esp. 11–12).

Youtie's purpose in his 1962 lecture was, I believe, to narrow the scope of his subject so as to explain the papyrus-editing process to a general audience. Not quite fifteen years later, in a lecture given in 1976 at an international meeting of classicists (Bingen 1977), Jean Bingen defined papyrology in more generous terms: "There are nearly as many papyrologies as there are papyrologists, and they [papyrologists] are numerous," said Bingen. Decipherment remains the center of the enterprise, but papyrological activities are diverse, including, for example, literary studies, Ptolemaic chronology, economic history, and New Testament textual criticism. The unity of these activities resides principally in the papyrological origin of their data. The ultimate goal, after all, is the kind of synthesis Wilcken envisaged. In this way, papyrology, as redefined by Bingen, becomes "a kind of sociology, in the widest sense," one that is especially focused on the Greek presence in Egypt's particular geographic and ethnic milieu.

Of course, as we have glimpsed, this tension between papyrology strictly construed (by Youtie) and papyrology catholically extended (by Bingen) has been present for more than a century. It is the tension between the editing of papyri and the wider use of those editions or between philological examination and historical exploitation. In the United States, one might, roughly, see this as represented in turn by what can be called the Michigan tradition and the Yale tradition of papyrology. These can properly be called schools in both senses of the term, institutional and intellectual; they are epitomized respectively by Herbert C. Youtie and C. Bradford Welles. The two may be conveniently paired as friendly foils.

Herbert C. Youtie (1904–1980) was hired by the University of Michigan in 1929 specifically for the purposes of the papyrus collection it was acquiring, as already described, through purchase inside and outside the cartel and through excavations at Karanis (Koenen 2007). He received his AB degree from the University of Cincinnati in 1927 and an MA from Columbia in 1928. He trained for a year in Paris under Paul Collart (D'Arms 1980), whom he fondly recalled (this is a personal reminiscence) as gently rebuking those students who began to transcribe their papyri in ink: Collart (significantly) insisted on pencil. Youtie earned a diploma in Paris but had no time to spend on a doctorate: The Michigan papyri required immediate editorial attention. An honorary degree from Cologne, where his influence became considerable (L. Koenen, e-mail, January 17, 2006), would come forty years later (1969).

In the meantime, Youtie established a reputation as the consummate editor and critic of papyrus editions, the main successor to Wilcken in these enterprises. His own editorial masterpiece, in collaboration with A. E. R. Boak (1888–1962), was *The Archive of Aurelius Isidorus* (1960), a set of papers of a local official and landowner in the village of Karanis in the early fourth century CE. Youtie's interests were almost exclusively editorial; it was Boak who was concerned with the archive's historical ramifications (Gagos 2001, 522–523). Similarly, the Michigan scholar who in the long run was most open to the archaeological possibilities of the Karanis materials was Elinor M. Husselman (1900–1996), curator of manuscripts and papyri of the Michigan Library and curator also at the Kelsey Museum from 1925 until 1965 (Gagos 2001, 523–524; Wilfong 1996).

Youtie was not interested in such things per se. Rather, he was a philologist who focused on texts in and of themselves and in relation to other texts. He was also just about the only papyrologist openly fascinated by the psychological aspects of reading papyri (for editing and correcting, see also Turner 1980, chapter 5, "How a Papyrus Text Is Edited," and Schubart 1970; cf. Turner 1973). So, in the 1950s and 1960s he delivered lectures in London, Ann Arbor, and Cologne (Youtie 1974, 1973, vol. 1, chapters 1 and 2) on what might these days be called "metapapyrology." These lectures, taken together in their published forms, have established themselves as "the papyrologist's Bible."

The Ann Arbor lecture, subsequently printed as "The Papyrologist: Artificer of Fact" (Youtie 1973, vol. 1, chapter 1), is probably the best introduction to the general public of what those papyrologists whose deepest commitment is to the editing of texts actually do—or should do. Probably all papyrologists, at one time or another, in conversation with curious nonpapyrologists, have had to explain that they do not (at least initially) "translate" papyri; rather, they edit them, and in that process the most difficult task is *transcription,* the decipherment of ancient writing in often difficult hands on usually very damaged surfaces. Youtie, while enunciating what might properly be called an ethics of papyrology, saw the transcribing of texts as an intense form of reading, much slower and almost infinitely more arduous but in essence the same as everyday reading. Both, for example, require or (better) are facilitated by stores of acquired cultural knowledge and strategies based on prediction. Much of this knowledge Youtie seems to have stored in his mind or recorded on index cards. It was there not for its own sake but to aid in decipherment and commentary.

The story of C. Bradford Welles (1901–1969) (Bagnall 2007) follows a radically different trajectory from Youtie's. Welles was entirely Yale educated; he earned his BA in 1924 and his PhD in 1928. He had therefore been at Yale for several years before the arrival of Michael Rostovtzeff, the premier ancient historian of the first half of the twentieth century, in 1925. This led to a long and productive professional collaboration and father-son relationship. As a scholar, Welles had begun as a philologist but later moved into epigraphy. It was under Rostovtzeff's influence that his dissertation was turned into the distinguished epigraphical study, *Royal Correspondence in the Hellenistic Period* (1934).

Rostovtzeff's scholarly appetite was gargantuan. Archaeology and art were for him important historical sources. So were documents of all kinds. These needed to be edited, but mainly in order to serve the larger purposes of history. It was therefore natural for Rostovtzeff and Welles to collaborate on preliminary editions of the more important Dura papyri (Welles seems to have been self-taught in papyrology), always attended by extensive discussion and commentary, exhaustively exploring their full historical relevance. Those students brought to papyrology through Yale have tended to study the Egyptian papyri with the same historically driven intentions. This was not by chance, for as Welles once wrote me (September 5, 1969), "I am less interested myself in making papyrologists than in showing classical students what there is in the papyri, and how it relates to antiquity in general."

This tension between papyrology as focused on editing, represented by Youtie, and papyrology as concerned with historical expansion, represented by Welles, is inherent in the discipline—but it is only one aspect of papyrology's history. This is a history that remains to be written, largely because papyrologists have generally been too busy "doing papyrology" to reflect upon their own disciplinary past. There are always pauses for retrospection during the international congresses, sometimes in the papers given, always in necrologies delivered during the closing ceremonies. An exception to the rule is I. F. Fikhman's work on G. F. Zereteli. The extensive publication of correspondence relevant to Italian papyrology (e.g., Morelli and Pintaudi 1983 and recent issues of *Analecta Papyrologica*) is also especially noteworthy. But this merely taps an enormous international reservoir of letters and records. To read and assimilate all of this would be a long-term project, whose goal would be a book-length study akin to but more immediate and graphic than Preisendanz's worthy, encyclopedic *Papyrusforschung und Papyruskunde* (1933; for a different approach see Canfora 2005). As an alternative one might will Marcel Hombert back into life and in a long afternoon's conversation learn all that needed to be known.

ACKNOWLEDGMENTS

I am grateful to the editor for reasons too numerous to list and to Todd Hickey for advice on general substance, certain points of fact, and many bibliographical recommendations. I am also indebted for specific details to I. F. Fikhman, Traianos Gagos, Nikolaos Gonis, Ludwig Koenen, †Naphtali Lewis, Anthony A. Long, Herwig Maehler, Alain Martin, Fritz Mitthof, †John F. Oates, and Dirk Obbink. Any lingering mistakes, of course, are mine alone. Dates and bibliographical notices for many of the people mentioned in this chapter may be found in *Who Was Who in Egyptology*, ed. Morris L. Bierbrier (1995), abbreviated in my text as *WWWE*. Dates for papyrologists not included in *WWWE* are conveniently accessible on the website of the Association Internationale de Papyrologues (http://www.ulb.ac.be/assoc/aip), especially in its picture gallery. See also Capasso 2007, not available to me in full when this chapter was being written.

BIBLIOGRAPHY

Bagnall, R. S. 1982–1983. "Papyrology and Ptolemaic History." *Classical World* 76: 13–21.
——. 1999. Unpublished notes on a "Visit with Naphtali Lewis, Croydon, New Hampshire, 20–22 August 1999."
——. 2007. "Charles Bradford Welles." In *Hermae: Scholars and Scholarship in Papyrology*, ed. M. Capasso, 283–286. Pisa: Giardini Editori e Stampatori.
Begg, D. J. I. 1998. "It Was Wonderful, Our Return in the Darkness with . . . the Baskets of Papyri! Papyrus Finds at Tebtunis from the Bagnani Archives, 1931–1936." *BASP* 35: 185–210.
Bierbrier, M. L., ed. 1995. *Who Was Who in Egyptology*, 3d rev. ed. London: Egypt Exploration Society.

Bingen, J. 1977. "La Papyrologie grecque et latine: Problèmes de fond et problèmes d'organisation." In *Aspects des études classiques: Actes du colloque associé à la XVIe Assemblée Générale de la Fédération Internationale des Associations d'Études Classiques*, ed. J. Bingen and G. Cambier, 33–44. Brussels: Éditions de l'Université de Bruxelles.

——. 1994. "La papyrologie, d'avant-hier à demain." In *Proceedings of the 20th International Congress of Papyrologists*, ed. A. Bülow-Jacobsen, 42–47. Copenhagen: Museum Tusculanum.

Boak, A. E. R., and H. C. Youtie. 1960. *The Archive of Aurelius Isidorus in the Egyptian Museum, Cairo, and the University of Michigan*. Ann Arbor: University of Michigan Press.

Bonacasa, N. 1989. "Cento anni di archeologia italiana per la conoscenza dell'Egitto greco-romano." In *Egitto e storia antica dall'ellenismo all'età araba: Bilancio di un confronto*, ed. L. Criscuolo and G. Geraci, 291–299. Bologna: Cooperativa Libraria Universitaria Editrice Bologna.

Bowman, A. K., and D. W. Rathbone. 1992. "Cities and Administration in Roman Egypt." *JRS* 82: 107–127.

Canfora, L. 2005. *Il papiro di Dongo*. Milan: Adelphi Edizioni.

Capasso, M., ed. 2007. *Hermae: Scholars and Scholarship in Papyrology*. Pisa: Giardini Editori e Stampatori.

Capart, J. 1947. "Maurice Nahman." *CdÉ* 22: 300–301.

Carozzi, P. A. 1982. "Alle origini della Società Italiana per la Ricerca dei Papiri Greci e Latini (dal carteggio inedito di Girolamo Vitelli con Uberto Pestalozza, 1898–1908)." *Atene e Roma*, n.s. 27: 26–45.

Casini, M., ed. 2001. *One Hundred Years in Egypt: Paths of Italian Archaeology*. Milan: Electa.

Chamoux, F. 2002. "Jean Scherer (1911–2001)." *Association Amicale de Secours des Anciens Élèves de l'École Normale Supérieure*, vol. 1, 59–61.

Criscuolo, L., and G. Geraci, eds. 1989. *Egitto e storia antica dall'ellenismo all'età araba: Bilancio di un confronto*. Bologna: Cooperativa Libraria Universitaria Editrice Bologna.

D'Arms, J. H. 1980. "Research Professor Emeritus Herbert C. Youtie 1904–1980." Obituary entered into the minutes of the Faculty of Michigan's College of Literature, Science and the Arts, circulated with a cover letter, November 12, 1980.

Deuel, L. 1965. *Testaments of Time: The Search for Lost Manuscripts and Records*. New York: Alfred A. Knopf.

Fagan, B. M. 1975. *The Rape of the Nile: Tomb Robbers, Tourists, and Archaeologists in Egypt*. New York: Charles Scribner's Sons.

Fikhman, I. F. 1999. "G. F. Cereteli nei fondi archivistici dell'ex Unione Sovietica (Materiali per un ritratto socio-psicologico dello studioso)." *Communicazioni dell'Istituto G. Vitelli* 1: 1–73.

Gagos, T. 2001. "The University of Michigan Papyrus Collection: Current Trends and Future Perspectives." In *Atti del XXII Congresso Internazionale di Papirologia*, ed. I. Andorlini, G. Bastianini, M. Manfredi, and G. Menci, vol. 1, 511–537. Florence: Istituto Papirologico "G. Vitelli".

——, J. Gates, and A. Wilburn. 2005. "Material Culture and Texts of Graeco-Roman Egypt: Creating Context, Debating Meaning." *BASP* 42: 171–188.

Geraci, G. 1989. "L'Egitto romano nella storiografia moderna." In *Egitto e storia antica dall'ellenismo all'età araba: Bilancio di un confronto*, ed. L. Criscuolo and G. Geraci, 55–88. Bologna: Cooperativa Libraria Universitaria Editrice Bologna.

Gerstinger, H. 1932. "Carl Wessely (27-VI-1860–21-XI-1931)." *Aegyptus* 12: 250–255.

Gigante, M. 1984. "Per l'unità della scienza papirologica." *Atti del XVII Congresso Internazionale di Papirologia,* ed. M. Gigante, vol. 1, 5–28. Naples: Centro Internazionale per lo Studio dei Papiri Ercolanesi.

———. 1986. *Girolamo Vitelli e la nuova filologia.* Santa Croce del Sannio: Istituto Storico "Giuseppe M. Galanti".

Habermann, W. 2001. "Die deutsche Delegation beim Internationalen Papyrologenkongreß in Oxford im Jahre 1937 und der für das Jahr 1939 geplante Papyrologenkongreß in Wien." *APF* 47: 102–171.

Heinen, H. 1989. "L'Égypte dans l'historiographie moderne du monde hellénistique." In *Egitto e storia antica dall'ellenismo all'età araba: Bilancio di un confronto,* ed. L. Criscuolo and G. Geraci, 105–135. Bologna: Cooperativa Libraria Universitaria Editrice Bologna.

Hombert, M. 1933. "Le commerce des papyrus en Égypte." *CdÉ* 8: 148–154.

———. 1947. "L'état des études de papyrologie au lendemain de la guerre." *CdÉ* 22: 343–362.

———. 1948. "L'état des études de papyrologie au lendemain de la guerre." *CdÉ* 23: 181–190.

Hopfner, T. 1933. "Carl Wessely. Geboren 27. Juni 1860, gestorben 21. November 1931." *Jahresbericht über die Fortschritte der klassischen Altertumswissenschaft* 241B: 1–24.

Hopkins, C. 1979. *The Discovery of Dura-Europos.* New Haven: Yale University Press.

Jones, A. H. M. 1942. "Egypt and Rome." In *The Legacy of Egypt,* ed. S. R. K. Glanville, 283–299. Oxford: Clarendon Press.

———. 1964. *The Later Roman Empire, 284–602.* 2 vols. Norman: University of Oklahoma Press.

———. 1974. *The Roman Economy: Studies in Ancient Economic and Administrative History.* Oxford: Blackwell Publishing.

Keenan, J. G. 2002. Review of I. Andorlini et al., eds. *Atti del XXII Congresso Internazionale di Papirologia,* Florence. *BASP* 39: 213–227.

Koenen, L. 2007. "Herbert Chayyim Youtie (1904–1980)." In *Hermae: Scholars and Scholarship in Papyrology,* ed. M. Capasso, 295–305. Pisa: Giardini Editori e Stampatori.

Lewis, N. 1970. "Greco-Roman Egypt: Fact or Fiction?" In *Proceedings of the Twelfth International Congress of Papyrology,* ed. D. Samuel, 3–14. Toronto: Hakkert.

———. 1984. "The Romanity of Roman Egypt: A Growing Consensus." In *Atti del XVII Congresso Internazionale di Papirologia,* ed. M. Gigante, vol. 3, 1077–1084. Naples: Centro Internazionale per lo Studio dei Papiri Ercolanesi.

Litinas, N. 2007. "Habent sua fata fragmenta: 'Donum Borgianum.'" In *Akten des 23. Internationalen Papyrologenkongresses,* ed. B. Palme, 399–405. Vienna: Verlag der Österreichischen Akademie der Wissenschaften.

Martin, A. 2000a. "Das Jahrhundert der Papyrologie?" *APF* 46: 1–2.

———. 2000b. "En marge de la *Charta Borgiana.*" *CdÉ* 75: 118–125.

———. 2007. "The Papyruskartell: The Papyri and the Movement of Antiquities." In *Oxyrhynchus: A City and Its Texts,* ed. A. K. Bowman, R. A. Coles, N. Gonis, D. Obbink, and P. J. Parsons, 40–49. London: Egypt Exploration Society.

Maspero, G. 1916. Introduction to J. Maspero, *Papyrus grecs d'époque byzantine,* vol. 3. Reprint, Milan: Cisalpino-La Goliardica and Osnabrück: Otto Zeller, 1973.

Montevecchi, O. 1988. *La papirologia,* 2d ed. Milan: Vita e Pensiero.

———. 1994. "Problemi e prospettive della papirologia nelle intuizioni di un pioniere: Amedeo Peyron." In *Proceedings of the 20th International Congress of Papyrologists,* ed. A. Bülow-Jacobsen, 25–34. Copenhagen: Museum Tusculanum Press.

Morelli, D., and R. Pintaudi. 1983. *Cinquant'anni di papirologia in Italia: Carteggi Breccia-Comparetti-Norsa-Vitelli.* 2 vols. Naples: Bibliopolis.

Nicholas, L. H. 1994. *The Rape of Europa: The Fate of Europe's Treasures in the Third Reich and the Second World War.* New York: Alfred A. Knopf.

Parsons, P. J. 1987. "Eric Gardner Turner 1911–1983." *Proceedings of the British Academy* 73: 685–704.

Pestman, P. W., ed. 1981. *Guide to the Zenon Archive.* 2 vols. Leiden: E. J. Brill.

Pintaudi, R. 1993. "Documenti per una storia della papirologia in Italia." *Analecta Papyrologica* 5: 155–181.

Preisendanz, K. 1933. *Papyrusfunde und Papyrusforschung.* Leipzig: Verlag Karl W. Hiersemann.

Reid, D. M. 2002. *Whose Pharaohs? Archaeology, Museums, and Egyptian National Identity from Napoleon to World War I.* Berkeley: University of California Press.

Robinson, J. J. 1901. Review of Otto Gradenwitz, *Einführung in die Papyruskunde. American Journal of Philology* 22: 210–214.

Rupprecht, H. A. 1989. "Erwin Seidl als Papyrologe." In *Akademischer Gedächtnis für Professor Dr. Erwin Seidl, 1905–1987, am 9. Dezember 1988,* 7–15. Cologne: Verein zur Förderung der Rechtswissenschaft.

Schubart, W. 1970. "Herstellung schadhafter Texte." *APF* 20: 5–14.

Thomas, J. D. 1966. "H. I. Bell (1879–1967)." *Aegyptus* 66: 97–99.

Turner, E. G. 1973. *The Papyrologist at Work.* Greek, Roman and Byzantine Monographs, no. 6, ed. William H. Willis. Durham, N.C.: Duke University Press.

———. 1980. *Greek Papyri: An Introduction,* 2d ed. New York: Oxford University Press.

———. 1982. "The Graeco-Roman Branch." In *Excavating in Egypt: The Egypt Exploration Society 1882–1982,* ed. T. G. H. James, 161–176. Chicago: University of Chicago Press.

Van Minnen, P. 1993. "The Century of Papyrology (1892–1992)." *BASP* 30: 5–18.

Vandorpe, K. 1994. "Museum Archaeology or How to Reconstruct Pathyris Archives." In *Acta Demotica: Acts of the Fifth International Conference for Demotists, Pisa, 4th–8th September 1993* (Egitto e Vicino Oriente 17), ed. E. Bresciani, 289–300. Pisa: Giardini Editori e Stampatori.

Welles, C. B. 1934. *Royal Correspondence in the Hellenistic Period: A Study in Greek Epigraphy.* New Haven: Yale University Press.

Wilcken, U. 1899. *Griechische Ostraka aus Aegypten und Nubien: Ein Beitrag zur antiken Wirtschaftsgeschichte.* 2 vols. Reprint, Amsterdam: A. M. Hakkert, 1970.

———. 1901. "Vorwort." *APF* 1: iii–vi.

———. 1912. *Grundzüge und Chrestomathie der Papyruskunde.* Leipzig: B. G. Teubner.

Wilfong, T. G. 1996. "†Elinor Mullett Husselman." *BASP* 33: 5–10.

Youtie, H. C. 1973. *Scriptiunculae.* 2 vols. Amsterdam: A. M. Hakkert.

———. 1974. *The Textual Criticism of Documentary Papyri: Prolegomena.* 2d ed. Bulletin of the Institute of Classical Studies, Supplement no. 33. London: Institute of Classical Studies.

CHAPTER 4

CONSERVATION OF ANCIENT PAPYRUS MATERIALS

JAAKKO FRÖSÉN

DAMAGE AND SURVIVAL OF THE PAPYRI

From the moment that papyrus was used as writing material in antiquity it was subject to wear and tear at the hands of scribes and readers. Careless handling caused abrasion, and the edges became worn. In humid surroundings the papyrus suffered from hydrolysis and oxidation. When stored in unsuitable conditions, the papyrus could rot or grow mold, and it was sometimes eaten by rodents and/or insects, especially worms and ants. This phenomenon continued and even increased when the papyrus was buried either intentionally or by accident until the climate of the environment became absolutely dry as a result of the abandonment of habitation sites that were out of the reach of the annual Nile flood. Most collapsed buildings were afterward used as a dumping ground. The papyri found in ancient habitation sites are thus mostly quite worn and full of holes, and their surface is abraded or discolored. (For details about the finds see chapter 2, as well as M. Fackelmann 1985, 14–19. For the damage see, e.g., Donnithorne 1986, 1–4.)

Almost all of the papyri found in Egypt have been exposed to the desert sand, which contains small crystals of calcium, magnesium, and natron salts, which are visible under a low-powered microscope. These salts absorb moisture and thus eliminate the deteriorating effect of the humidity; on the other hand, when crystal-lized on the surface of the papyrus, they can cause decay or disintegration.

The best-preserved papyrus rolls or sheets have been found stored in jars, boxes, and chests in collapsed buildings in dry areas or in tombs in desert cemeteries. Similarly well preserved are papyrus rolls and sheets, as well as recycled papyri, deposited in desert tombs even though the funerary papyri lying alongside their owners in wooden mummy cases have often been prone to extensive staining from the resin or bitumen poured over the mummy at burial or from fluids from the body. In particular, animal mummies have from time to time been wrapped in pieces of rolls or sheets of papyrus, and the animal bodies, particularly the crocodiles, were sometimes stuffed with papyri. These papyri are equally well preserved, even if mostly cut or torn into pieces and crumpled for stuffing. The recycled papyri of the mummy cartonnages found in the cemeteries are described later in this chapter.

Quite well preserved are papyri found in collapsed buildings filled by their own debris and windblown sand (a soil low in organic material) in deserted town sites, temples, and monasteries that have not yet been soaked by the rising groundwater table and never been filled up with garbage. Those papyri were often deposited and buried in jars and boxes or between building stones. If they were found on the floor, they were mostly ignored as worthless since they were often already in a poor state of preservation when the building was abandoned.

In much worse condition are papyri found in ancient trash piles either in separate heaps or in collapsed buildings, where the objects were deliberately thrown away in antiquity. They are rarely whole scrolls and often only single leaves or fragments of leaves originating from a cleaning out of some local, often personal, dossier or library. Unfortunately, they were first torn to pieces and then broken, crushed, or crumpled when being thrown away. In the trash piles they were also exposed to other debris, liquids, insects, and microorganisms, partly rotten, moldy, very dusty, and torn. Sometimes baskets full of discarded papyrus have been found in excavations.

CONSERVATION OF NORMAL PAPYRUS MATERIAL

Physical Control

The purpose of papyrus conservation is twofold. The most important concern is to prevent further decomposition of the papyrus material, that is, to get physical control over the archaeological objects (for general conservation methods see, e.g., Viñas and Viñas 1988, 1.1–1.3; for the chemical consistency of the papyrus material see Wiedeman and Bayer 1983). Once taken from the formerly safe surroundings guaranteed by the extremely dry sand of the desert, the organic material immediately starts to oxidize and decompose. However, more often the objective is to retrieve the ancient texts written on the papyri for study and publication or for exhibition. Some 80–90 percent of all surviving papyri consist of the so-called normal papyrus material, which can be subjected to a simple, neither time-consuming nor expensive, conservation treatment.

Papyri from Excavations and Dealers

In most cases, the conservation of papyri recently found in excavations or stored afterward in the papyrus collections of museums and libraries is quite a simple action that does not call for special instruments or complicated chemicals. What is required is a steady hand, good nerves, and of course practice, which means knowledge of the material to be conserved and of the few chemicals used in papyrus conservation. Familiarity with ancient languages and ancient handwritings is certainly useful, too, but it is absolutely necessary only in special cases. The same is true for the papyri acquired by purchase. In general, texts that are obtained from uncontrolled illegal excavations have already been somehow conserved (or at least flattened), mostly by nonexperts, in order to give them a more attractive appearance (for more details see the section titled "Old Repairs" in this chapter).

In the first steps of restoration, reassembling, and arrangement of the fragments, one can use several aids that the papyrus itself offers, namely the continuity of the writing (on both front and back), the shape of the handwriting, the color of the material, the design of the fragments, the wormholes that reappear at successive intervals and in similar shape in the opened roll or unfolded papyrus leaf, the folds of the leaf, the pattern of the crisscrossed fibers, and the original joins and overlaps (*kollêseis*) of the papyrus. Further steps of restoration are possible only for a papyrologist who is able to read the handwriting and interpret the contents, which is part of the editing process.

Preparation

As in all conservation work, the first thing to do is to remove all of the loose soil and dirt. The next step is the documentation, both written and photographic. Every fragment should be inspected for damage. More often than not, the papyrus has been folded for carrying and storing, rolled in antiquity, or intentionally crumpled; it may also have become creased and distorted by another object, decayed, and eaten by worms or microorganisms as part of the archaeological stratum. The more or less three-dimensional dirty object has to be opened, flattened, and cleaned. It has to be softened by dampening in order to make it pliable (figures 2.2, 2.3 and 2.6, 2.7).

The Ink

First the ink has to be tested. There are two types of ink (as well as a mixture of those two) used in the papyrus texts. The typical one, carbon ink, is a mixture of soot and gum arabic. Very resistant and not soluble in water, it does not bleach when exposed to sunlight. The second, called iron-gall or ferro-gallic ink, has a metallic base. Originally black, it usually ages to a brownish color. It suffers from exposure to light but is not water soluble. A mixture of carbon ink and iron-gall ink is not stable and can be water soluble. Papyrus texts written with both iron-gall and the mixed ink, which fortunately occurred only infrequently in antiquity, must be handled with great care during the conservation process and must be stored in the dark. (See also, e.g., Cockle 1983, 150; M. Fackelmann 1985, 28–29; Viñas and Viñas 1988, 2.1–2.2.)

Dampening and Treatment

There are many dampening methods available. One can use a humidor, a moisture chamber (for details see, e.g., Lau-Lamb 2005, 6), a fine sprayer to sprinkle the water, or a wet piece of cloth positioned under and around the object. One can also place it between sheets of dampened blotting paper. The object is left in the humid surroundings under a transparent cover for up to twenty-four hours (or more) until the dry papyrus has absorbed enough water and become flexible but not totally wet. Then the moistened object is moved to clean, dry blotting paper, unrolled or unfolded and straightened with sharp-pointed tweezers, and finally sandwiched between two sheets of blotting paper. The parts that are folded under should be straightened. Some of the distorted and twisted fibers can be unbent and fixed in their right places by using tweezers and a thin paintbrush moistened in water. However, in order to avoid rubbing off either the ink or the thin surface of the damp papyrus, do not try to brush away the dirt at this stage. All brushing should be done when the papyrus is dry. The papyrus should be allowed to dry out and flatten under a light weight or in a clamp press; it can also be mounted between two sheets of glass secured with tight metal or plastic clips (M. Fackelmann 1985, 40–46).

Cellulose Treatment

A solution of cellulose (Klucel or hydroxypropyl celluloid) can be used to dampen the papyrus material. When absorbed by the papyrus material, it strengthens the cell tissue and the vascular bundles and thus increases its elasticity. (For more details see M. Fackelmann 1981, 659–660; Nielsen and Doblinger 1985, 22–28.) Other materials (e.g., papyrus juice, gum arabic) have also been applied to strengthen the papyrus (A. Fackelmann 1970, 145; Cockle 1983, 155–156; M. Fackelmann 1985, 20–24, 45).

Cleaning

After a few days the dry papyri are ready for their next treatment. After they are placed on dry blotting paper, they can be cleaned mechanically by brushing them lightly with a bristle brush in the direction of the fibers, from the middle toward the edges. The dirt (e.g., loose mud, dust, grains of sand, salt crystals) can easily be removed from the dry surface with sharp tweezers, a scalpel, or a spatula. A damp cotton swab or a ball of fresh-baked white bread also works well (Cockle 1983, 156). The delaminated and twisted fibers can be straightened and aligned in their correct position by using tweezers and two thin paintbrushes moistened in water. If needed, methyl cellulose or a flour-and-water paste can be used. The damp papyrus should be allowed to dry under a light weight. This treatment should be repeated until the papyrus is fully conserved. The blotters must be changed frequently. Both sides of the papyrus sheet should be cleaned with care even if no text is visible on the back.

Some of the literary papyri have been treated in antiquity with cedar oil, probably to strengthen the surface and prevent bookworms. This ancient fixative should not be removed (cf. Cockle 1983, 157).

Special Cases

In some special cases, the papyri need very painstaking care and scrupulous attention. The extracting of recycled papyri from the "cardboard" covers of the mummies, the so-called cartonnages, as well as the conservation of the paintings on those cartonnages, is a case in point. The method is similar to that of extracting recycled papyri from a bookbinding.

Another special case is the opening and the conservation of charred papyrus scrolls. Sometimes the so-called normal papyri have become brittle and have disintegrated to the point that dampening would totally destroy the material. Even if they have not been burned by fire and are not black, material exposed to the effects of a damp environment for too long will become pyrolized by the oxygen to the extent that it can no longer absorb moisture like normal papyrus. The natural adhesive of the papyrus has in this case totally disappeared, and decay has set in. This kind of material has to be treated like carbonized papyrus material. This is mostly the case with scrolls of a very fine and thin papyrus material used, for instance, for the Egyptian Book of the Dead, which have been exposed, after their retrieval from the extra dry tomb or sand, in a museum exhibition. Usually the

Figure 4.1. Unrolling a pyrolized papyrus scroll without dampening. The back of the roll has been partly consolidated by using Japanese paper. Photo by Jaakko Frösén, Egyptian Museum, Cairo (1987).

humidity and the temperature have not been kept constant for a long period of time (figure 4.1).

Fixing Ink and Pigments

When the ink or the pigment of the illustrations is flaky, a very thin methyl cellulose or wheat starch paste (for recipes see, e.g., Lau-Lamb 2005, 15–16) can be applied underneath it by means of a fine sable brush; then the pigment is gently tacked down with a small spatula (M. Fackelmann 1985, 44; Viñas and Viñas 1988, 2.2–2.3).

Joining Loose Fragments

Loose fragments can be identified as joining others by their form, the arrangement of their fibers, and the writing. The identification of loose fragments by the writing is, of course, more effective when the conservator can read the text or works closely with a papyrologist. During the conservation process, all of the identified joining fragments should be physically connected and attached to the main papyrus. The joining tape materials should expand and contract at the same rate as the papyrus itself, and the adhesive should never permeate the papyrus. The most ideal method is to use loose papyrus fibers and starch paste or cellulose as an adhesive. Small, finely cut strips of paper or Filmoplast on the back of the papyrus also work well. The adhesive, however, should be water soluble so that mistakes can easily be corrected (M. Fackelmann 1985, 46–55). Strips of Japanese paper with a water-soluble adhesive form a suitable tape.

Old Repairs

Removing old repairs and tape is the most time-consuming work of the papyrus conservator. In many cases, the nonexperts have used different kinds of tapes and adhesives "temporarily" and in a hurry. Some of them were attached at the archaeological site or by the dealers in antiquities in order to fix and secure the fragments or to make them more attractive, but an opportunity to remove them was never provided. The fragments are not always aligned correctly, and parts of the papyrus may be folded under. Sometimes the dealers have produced fakes by gluing together fragments of various original texts, thus achieving "whole leaves" or even fake rolls of papyrus. The oldest types of repairs made with, for instance, brown tape, stamp paper, or similar materials can easily be removed when dampened. However, in many cases, the adhesives have permeated the papyrus and caused severe problems and losses. Scotch tape can very seldom be totally removed. Usually the tape turns brownish and dry in four to five years, and in some cases the tape carrier comes off when the adhesive dries up, but the glue stays, more often than not, in the papyrus. Chemical solvents (e.g., ethanol diluted with water 50:50) can be used but only very carefully. Every adhesive has its own solvent, but chemicals that could harm the ink or the papyrus material cannot be used. Great care must be taken to free the papyrus of any traces of chemicals afterward (M. Fackelmann, 60–61).

Early Cardboard Backing

Some early conservation treatments are causing problems today. When a papyrus sheet is backed with cardboard, as was the custom in the nineteenth century, it should be separated. Most of the backing materials are of an inferior quality, and the rate at which they expand and contract is different from that of the papyrus materials, especially with humidity. Often the backing material is made of wood pulp, which is not acid free and contains many other harmful additives. Together they have already caused fatal and continuing changes in the otherwise neutral (pH 7) papyrus material. Different kinds of adhesives have also been used. When they are water soluble, they can easily be broken down even though it may take two to three days to soften the cardboard enough to remove the adhesive from the back of the papyrus (see, e.g., Donnithorne 1986, 8–9). In other cases, depending on the glue, boiling water or an enzyme treatment could be used rather than chemical solvents (cf., e.g., Cockle 1983, 156–157; M. Fackelmann 1985, 68–71).

Mounting and Storing Papyrus

Papyri can be stored in folders between sheets of acid-free blotting paper. If they are very fragile or very large or are often used by researchers or for exhibitions, the papyri should be mounted in a frame between glass plates with a backing of acid-free blotting paper. The blotting paper lessens the changes in the microclimate between the plates and prevents the papyrus fragments from slipping in the frame. Tags with information on the pieces (plate numbers, inventory numbers, fragment numbers, etc.) can be put under glass along with the papyrus. Before the final mounting between glass plates, the papyrus has to dry thoroughly for several weeks. The binding tape should allow a little air to flow in and out. When airproof binding material is used, airholes must be left for ventilation. This prevents the growth of mildew and the residue of other microorganisms in the papyrus. The papyri must be stored in a climate-controlled area where the humidity and temperature are kept as constant as possible (50–60 percent relative humidity and 17°–23°C).

The ultraviolet part of the daylight spectrum can cause reactions in certain materials; thus, when exposed to daylight, papyrus will fade. A special film or type of glass can be applied to frames of papyri in exhibitions to help protect them from the harmful rays.

Plexiglas

Plexiglas or similar acrylic plastic material presents several problems as a mounting medium for papyrus. The most critical danger is the static electricity that develops between the two sheets. Whenever the papyrus was mounted long ago between two sheets of Plexiglas, the static electricity must be discharged before they are opened (e.g., by using an ionizer). Otherwise, one runs the risk of splitting the thin front and back layers of the papyrus and of the ink sticking to the Plexiglas because the static electricity creates a harmful electrolysis in the somewhat humid atmosphere between the two plates (Cockle 1983, 155).

THE MUMMY CARTONNAGES

Production of Papyrus Cartonnages

Egyptian papyrus cartonnage is a kind of papier-mâché product for protecting the mummies of both humans and animals. They are whole mummy cases or two- or three-dimensional cover plates that were usually put inside a wooden coffin. The cartonnages were constructed in pharaonic times of layers of linen and in the Ptolemaic period of layers of linen and/or discarded, used rolls and sheets of papyrus. The waste papyrus was cut or torn to pieces and dampened with water to fit the piece of cartonnage, layered, and then stuck together, sometimes with a sort of plaster or glue. The cartonnage was coated on both sides with a layer of lime gesso plaster. An idealized image representing the deceased was often painted on the front of the cartonnage, as were representations of Egyptian divinities and ornaments. As a consequence of the dampening both during and after the production process, the outmost layers on both sides of the cartonnage, particularly the ink of the writings, covered with gesso, have generally been damaged by so-called calcium burns. In some cases the pigments of the painting have oozed through the plaster and stained and damaged the papyrus layer or at least the writing. Most disastrous have been the metallic colors, especially the green pigments containing copper, which have eaten through the papyrus material. Papyri removed from the cartonnage may have a thick layer of plaster on the surface, and because a lot of water has been used to dissolve the gesso in the process of dismantling the cartonnage, particles of calcium carbonate can always be seen under a low-powered microscope in all extracted papyri (Adams 1966; see chapter 2, figure 2.4).

Conservation of Recycled Papyri from Mummy Cartonnages

Since the first discoveries of the papyrus cartonnage and the realization of the potential of the cartonnage as a source of papyrus texts in the 1820s, the gesso of the cartonnage, together with the paintings, has been dissolved in a water with vinegar or hydrochloric acid bath and removed. The papyri were extracted and saved, but the process led to the complete loss of the painted gesso surface. Even if practiced occasionally, particularly in private collections even into the 1960s, this method has been abandoned for obvious reasons as unethical.

The new techniques of papyrus restoration, combined with methods of conserving wall paintings, have made it possible to extract papyrus successfully while safeguarding the mummy portraits and other paintings made on papyrus cartonnage. The frequently very bad state of preservation of the cartonnage has been caused partly by the archaeological surroundings and partly by poor storage conditions later on. A good deal of the cartonnage material still unconserved in the archaeological depots comes from excavations carried out at the beginning of the twentieth century. When the paintings have been removed from their papyrus support and fixed on a new, more stable support, the waste papyri of the gesso cartonnage can also be extracted and conserved (cf., e.g., M. Fackelmann 1985, 67–74).

The recovery of papyrus from cartonnage is still the subject of controversy. Admittedly it interferes with the integrity of the cartonnage as an artifact. However, as the adhesive in particular that is used in some cardboards is prone to attack by insects and microorganisms, the cartonnages are in many cases in a very poor state of preservation. More often than not, in order to save the paintings, the papyrus cardboard has to be replaced. (Cf. the later section titled "Conservation of Book Bindings." See Donnithorne 1986, 8; Frösén 1997; Horak 1997; and especially Janis 1997.)

The Greek and demotic Egyptian documentary papyrus texts from the Ptolemaic period are of significant value for investigating the historical outlines of Hellenistic Egypt, as well as specific topics of economic and social history. The dated papyrus documents also enable us to date the scattered literary fragments found in the same cartonnage *(terminus ad quem)* and the cartonnages themselves with their paintings *(terminus post quem)*.

Twenty Steps in Conserving the Paintings and the Papyri

This is a refined version of the method employed by Stohler-Zimmermann and Harrauer (Stohler-Zimmermann 1981; cf. Wright 1983). It works without complicated chemicals and without enzymes. The technique is inexpensive and, due to the drying, requires approximately one week to complete. Nevertheless, during this time several cartonnages can be handled.

1. Loose dirt is removed by brushing, and the painted surface is cleaned with acetone.
2. Holes in painted gesso or lime plaster are protected ("blocked off") with calcium carbonate (figure 4.2).
3. The paint layer is consolidated ("fixed") by using Paraloid B-48 (30 percent in acetone).
4. The paint layer is faced with a new temporary cartonnage by using pieces of (a) Japanese tissue paper (ca. 50 g) and a Paraloid B-48/acetone emulsion (20 percent)—one layer; (b) Japanese paper (ca. 70 g) and a Planatol BB/ water dilution (40 percent)—two layers; (c) linen cloth and a Planatol BB/ water dilution (40 percent)—one layer; and (d) Japanese paper (ca. 70 g) and a Planatol BB/water emulsion (40 percent)—one layer.

Figure 4.2. Conserving a mummy cartonnage, steps 1 and 2. The holes in the cleaned surface have been protected with calcium carbonate. Photo by Jaakko Frösén, Petrie Museum of Egyptian Antiquities, London (1985).

5. The object (three-dimensional only) is supported by a negative form by using, for example, fluid polyurethane.
6. The object in its negative form is placed in water (60°C) for about ten minutes (or longer if needed).
7. The inner layer of gesso is dampened with water and removed with a brush.
8. The papyrus cartonnage is removed from behind with a scalpel (figure 4.3).
9. The cartonnage is placed for a few minutes in a hot water bath (90°C). The use of acid in water will cause the gesso to effervesce and loosen the layers of papyrus, which are sometimes pasted together; afterward, however, they must be deacidified.
10. When wet, papyrus layers are mechanically separated with tweezers and scalpel.
11. Fragments of papyri are dried between sheets of blotting paper.
12. The painting with its gesso layer is consolidated from the back with Paraloid B-48 (20 percent in acetone).
13. The object is backed with a new cartonnage support consisting of Japanese paper (70–90 g), linen cloth, and a Planatol BB/water dilution (40 percent).
14. The negative form of the three-dimensional object is mechanically removed.
15. The temporary facing support is removed with tweezers and brush by using acetone.
16. The painted surface is cleaned with a brush and acetone (figure 4.4).

Figure 4.3. Conserving a mummy cartonnage, step 8: removing the papyrus cartonnage from behind the painted gesso layer. Photo by Tapio Tyni, Helsinki (1981).

17. When dry, papyri are cleaned with a brush.
18. Papyrus fragments are mechanically cleaned (by sandwiching them between pieces of wet cloth or blotting paper) using a brush, tweezers, and palette knives, leading to the final removal of the remaining pieces of gesso.
19. Papyrus fragments are dried between sheets of blotting paper under pressure.
20. Papyrus fragments are stored between glass plates.

The Paraloid B-48 is an ethyl acrylate/methyl methacrylate copolymer (made by Rohm and Haas Ltd., UK). The Planatol BB is a polyvinyl acetate (PVA) (made by Planatolwerk W. Hesselmann, Germany) that is used, for example, by book-binders. Instead of acetone, other solvents such as toluene or ethyl methyl ketone (which are easier and safer to use) can be substituted.

In some cases, especially in the earlier cartonnages, various glues have been used in forming the papyrus support. Depending on the glue, boiling water or an enzyme treatment could be utilized rather than chemical solvents in order to extract the glued papyrus layers (for more details see, e.g., Cockle 1983, 156–157; M. Fackelmann 1985, 68–71).

Figure 4.4. The conserved mummy cartonnage. The painted gesso layer has been backed with a new cartonnage support. Photo by Jaakko Frösén, Petrie Museum of Egyptian Antiquities, London (1985).

Conservation of Book Bindings

The boards of ancient and medieval book bindings are generally of poor quality as they were normally covered with leather or cloth. Instead of wooden boards, pasteboard was frequently used for covering the codices. The production of the pasteboard was similar to that of papyrus cartonnnages except that more glue was applied in order to make the product as solid as possible. When recycled literary or documentary papyri were used, they were cut from discarded remains of rolls; alternatively, whole sheets were glued together on top of each other so as to resemble cardboard. The covering leather and the animal glue adhesive or the starch paste of the cardboard are prone to attack by insects. Thus, more often than not, the boards have to be replaced, but in some cases the leather can be reused for covering the more solid new boards. In extracting the papyri from the cardboard of the bindings, an enzyme treatment is usually needed (Cockle 1983, 156–157; cf. Donnithorne 1986, 8). (For the book bindings, see, e.g., Viñas and Viñas 1988, 5.1–5.4.)

CONSERVATION OF CARBONIZED PAPYRI

The Carbonized Papyri of Herculaneum: An Exception

Carbonized rolls or codices can only rarely be unrolled or opened carefully, page by page. This kind of exceptional situation prevailed in respect to the carbonized rolls found in Herculaneum in 1752 (see chapter 13). The building and the room in which the papyri were stored did not collapse, and the papyrus rolls had been taken out of "bookshelves" and gathered (possibly for evacuation) in the middle of the floor before the fire broke out. During the eruption of Vesuvius, the Villa dei Papiri was also covered by a thick layer of eruption material, a concretelike tuff, which provided an effective obstacle to the subsequent penetration of, for example, water, air, and roots into the charred strata, which consisted of organic material. For more than two hundred fifty years, many attempts have been made to unroll these literary papyrus rolls. All kinds of physical (among them Antonio Piaggio's famous machine), chemical (solvents and gases), and biochemical (enzymes) procedures have been tested with varying success (A. Fackelmann 1970, 145–147; Cockle 1983, 158; M. Fackelmann 1985, 63–66). For the latest steps in conserving the Herculaneum rolls see Capasso (1990, 1991).

The Normal Finds of Charred Papyri

Usually the situation is quite different from that in Herculaneum: The charred papyrus material has been found in archaeological or illegal excavations in the middle of collapsed ruins. It has already been affected, immediately during and after the fire and perhaps later on (repeatedly) by oxygen and water; the papyri have been subjected to the pressure of stones, sand, and other collapsed materials for quite a long time. Roots of plants have found their way to the organic charred layers and worked their way into the papyrus lumps. Thus, the rolls or codices cannot typically be unrolled or opened simply by lifting the layers one after another. In most cases, the very thin charred layers of papyrus are stuck and more or less pasted together (ten or even twenty layers within one millimeter) and sometimes attached to each other by a net of tree and bush roots. The condition of the fragments of rolls or codices is thus by no means uniform.

The Carbonized Papyri from Egypt and Elsewhere

The carbonized papyri of Tanis and Thmouis in the Nile delta, found partly during the excavations of 1884 and 1902–1904 and between 1892–1893 and 1906, respectively, as well as partly in the "unofficial" excavations prior to and in between the official ones, fall into the category of normal finds of charred papyri. This was also the case of the charred literary roll of Derveni (Greece), found during systematic archaeological excavations in 1963, as was the case of the carbonized papyri of Boubastos (Nile delta), discovered during illegal excavations in the late 1950s or early 1960s and removed without any scientific control or documentation. The carbonized papyri of Petra (Jordan), which were exposed and removed with painstaking care, control, and documentation during the systematic archaeological excavations of the Byzantine church in the city center in December 1993 were also normal charred papyrus finds (figures 4.5–4.6).

Figure 4.5. Three carbonized rolls before conservation. The Petra papyri. Photo by Jaakko Frösén, American Center of Oriental Research, Amman (1995).

The Idea of Conservation

The principal idea of the conservation of carbonized papyri is to stop the harmful chemical process from continuing to destroy the delicate organic material: the burning process—the pyrolysis—as well as the deterioration caused by physical contact, pressure, and tremor. The conservation method applied to save the

Figure 4.6. Section of a loosely rolled Petra papyrus. Photo by R. Henry
Cowherd, American Center of Oriental Research, Amman (1995).

carbonized papyri is, in principle, the same as that used by Daninos Pasha at the end
of the nineteenth century for conserving a small part of the Thmouis papyri. It was
also employed by U. and D. Hagedorn, together with L. Koenen, in 1961 when
opening two lumps from the Boubastos archive in Cologne. In addition, it was
applied and described by Anton Fackelmann (Papyrus Collection of the Austrian
National Library) in the 1960s for dismounting some of the Herculaneum papyri in
Naples and the Derveni scroll in Thessaloniki and tested by him on the Boubastos

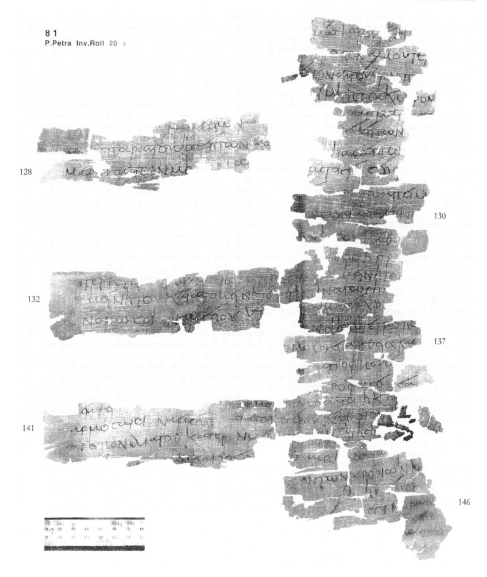

Figure 4.7. An assembled plate of Petra papyri. Digital image by Steven Booras and Gene Ware, American Center of Oriental Research, Amman (1998). Prepared for publication by Antti Nurminen and Vesa Vahtikari (2006).

scrolls in Vienna (A. Fackelmann 1970, 145–147). It was used (with some amendments by Michael Fackelmann [1981, 1985] after 1970 and by J. Kampichler [1984] from 1978 to 1983) on the Boubastos papyri in Vienna. I myself used it on the Boubastos papyri in Vienna and Cologne from 1982 to 1985, and my team applied it to the Petra papyri in Amman in 1994–1995 (Lehtinen 2002). The successful treatment of the material by this method demands special knowledge of the carbonized material and extensive practical experience. Moreover, a knowledge of ancient languages and ancient handwritings is indispensable for the restoration work.

The Method

Separating the Layers

One begins by mechanically separating first the scroll fragments and then the layers of these fragments one by one with a thin palette knife, scraper, or other tool and lifting them with tweezers. It is essential to record with care the order of the pieces. To facilitate the loosening process, it sometimes helps to dampen and warm the object, thus causing the papyrus to curl layer by layer. Often one's breath is enough ("just talk to them"); otherwise, one may carefully introduce some humidity with a thin paintbrush or by putting the object under a light bulb (approximately 40°C) or both. This is Anton Fackelmann's method, but it is not a question of static electricity or of "the electromagnetic action of the bulb" as stated by him (A. Fackelmann 1970, 145–146). Nevertheless, when working on large fragments, one usually cannot separate and lift the whole layer at once; this must be done piece by piece. In a later phase it is quite easy to put the pieces together to form a whole layer. If the layer is very fragile and does not react to slight moisture and heat, it can be fixed from the back by using a dilution of water and glue and, if needed, small pieces of Japanese paper (see the second step). Thereafter, one can loosen and lift the layer with the aid of the paper. This is, of course, possible only when the back is blank and when working on the outside of the object.

Fixing the Separated Layers

To provide some elasticity, one has to strengthen the fragile layers. The pieces have to be put together according to the writing on the front in order to reconstruct the whole layer. Then the layer is turned over in order to stabilize the entire construction from the back, which is usually blank. (If the back of the papyrus also contains writing, the pieces cannot be consolidated at all—sometimes only very carefully between the inscribed lines.) The reconstruction of the layer is best made on a piece of acid-free Japanese (or Indian) tissue paper (9–11 g) somewhat larger than the papyrus layer and placed on a sheet of glass. After that, one puts a piece of wax paper (or comparable material, e.g., plastic paper) over the whole reconstruction and then covers it with a glass plate. Sandwiched in this manner, the whole thing is easy to turn over.

The carbonized layer can be strengthened by carefully applying the diluted adhesive through the Japanese paper from the back with a thin paintbrush and letting the glass plate slide aside, step by step. The whole back must be glued (avoiding all air bubbles). The glue must not be allowed to seep deep into the charred material. The glue will dry to a thin clear film, thereby attaching the piece of papyrus to the Japanese paper and thus consolidating and protecting it. If the adhesive permeates the thin papyrus layer, it will form a reflective film surface on the front of the papyrus; this will eliminate the contrast between the dull black ink and the shiny black background and make the text invisible. For the glue, one can use cellulose or a dilution of neutral (pH 7) polyvinyl acetate glue and water (e.g., Planatol BB—1 part glue to 8–10 parts water, depending on the consistency of the adhesive). Then the reinforced piece of papyrus can be turned over by grasping the Japanese paper; one may make the indispensable notes in the blank corner of the paper. The layers must be sandwiched between two pieces of wax paper, and blotting paper or pasteboard under light pressure, letting them dry for a couple of days.

The Two-Dimensional Reconstruction or Jigsaw Puzzle

The two-dimensional reconstruction of the opened papyrus scroll—according to the written text of the papyrus, one's own notes, and the numbering of the fragments—must be made on acid-free paper. To facilitate the subsequent photography, gray acid-free paper should be used rather than white. When putting the fragments together, the superfluous margins of the Japanese paper must be removed with sharp scissors. The fragments of the opened layers can be glued together one after the other from the back (i.e., from the back of the Japanese paper glued on the back of the charred layers) with thin strips of an archive-safe Scotch tape or Filmoplast. Papyrus fragments that have writing on both sides cannot be consolidated or glued together.

Mounting between Glass Plates

The next step is to put the reconstructed sheet of charred papyrus on the acid-free paper and mount it in a frame of two glass plates. Plexiglas should be avoided not only because the elasticity and the static electricity it produces could make it very difficult to keep the fragments in their correct positions but also because the static electricity will create a harmful electrolysis in the somewhat humid atmosphere between the two plates; this in turn will destroy the charred papyrus layers. Along the edges, the plates may be sealed with tight metal or plastic clips or long-lasting, acid-free frame sealing tape, which adheres well to glass. The corners of the plates must be left unsealed for ventilation and to prevent an injurious and fungi-fertile microclimate from developing between the plates. Tags with information on the pieces can be put under glass along with the papyri. The plates can be used as double sided.

Storage

The plates of carbonized papyri should be kept, when not on exhibition or in working rooms, in a place where the climate can be kept as constant as possible (17–23°C and 50–60 percent relative humidity) since every change in temperature or humidity will create a movement in the charred material. The plates should be kept horizontally on cabinet shelves, not more than three plates in each stack and acid-free paper or pasteboard between the plates in order to avoid excessive pressure and scratches on the glass. Unpainted and unvarnished wooden cabinets and shelves are preferable because of the more constant conditions they provide for the conservation of organic material.

The Photographic Documentation

For documentation, the plates must be photographed by using special methods of black-and-white overexposure. An approximately two-thousand-watt light (preferably incandescent bulbs with a reddish light) is needed. It should come from three or four points at an angle of 45° to avoid reflection and be dispersed as evenly as possible over the whole object. When the plates are exposed to the lights, the heat will create a strong movement in the pieces and cause the carbonized papyrus fragments, which are glued to Japanese paper, to curl drastically. To avoid the curling and ensure stability, the fragments must be photographed under the sheet of glass. This increases the reflection of the lights and also of the ceiling, the camera, and other surrounding objects. In addition, the glass decreases the effectiveness of the infrared photographs. By using a high-contrast film for black-and-white prints (e.g., Kodak TechPan 25 ISO), one can use an exposure time of one second with an aperture of 11. These are, of course, only rough approximations. However, the best results can be achieved by using the multispectral digital technique (figure 4.7).

PAPYRUS CONSERVATION: PAST AND PRESENT

Papyrus conservation has a long history since the first attempts to open the carbonized Herculaneum rolls found in 1752 and to unroll the Charta Borgiana, acquired in 1778. New techniques have always been invented and tested, and old treatments have been revised. (For a short history of papyrus conservation and for old techniques see Cockle 1983, 153–158; Donnithorne 1986, 5–6; Parkinson and Quirke 1995, 74–83.) In this chapter I have recorded the methods I have used on papyrus materials. The sources in the bibliography discuss additional techniques and treatment of other materials. They will also lead to other procedures.

Although there is no systematic training program for papyrus conservators, various training programs in paper conservation provide some instruction. Otherwise, those who are interested in and want to take charge of treating the papyrus material in various collections share their experiences and knowledge both privately and at international conferences and thus build a common knowledge of best practices. The papyrus collection at the Austrian National Library in Vienna has played an important role in this process.

BIBLIOGRAPHY

Adams, C. V. A. 1966. "The Manufacture of Ancient Egyptian Cartonnage Cases." *Smithsonian Journal of History* 1: 55–66.

Bierbrier, Morris L., ed. 1986. *Papyrus: Structure and Usage.* British Museum Occasional Paper 60. London: British Museum.

Capasso, M. 1990. "Problemi di conservazione, restauro e svolgimento di papiri carbonizzati." *Rudiae* 2: 41–49.

———. 1991. "Problemi di conservazione, restauro e svolgimento di papiri carbonizzati II." *Rudiae* 3: 25–29.

Cockle, W. E. H. 1983. "Restoring and Conserving Papyri." *Bulletin of the Institute of Classical Studies* 30: 147–165.

Donnithorne, A. 1986. "The Conservation of Papyrus in the British Museum." In *Papyrus: Structure and Usage,* ed. M. L. Bierbrier, 1–23. British Museum Occasional Paper 60. London: British Museum.

Fackelmann, A. 1970. "The Restoration of the Herculaneum Papyri and Other Recent Finds." *Bulletin of the Institute of Classical Studies* 17: 144–147.

Fackelmann, M. 1981. "Neuerungen in der Papyrusrestaurierung." In *Proceedings of the XVI International Congress of Papyrology,* ed. R. S. Bagnall, G. M. Browne, A. E. Hanson, and L. Koenen, 657–663. American Studies in Papyrology 23. Chico, Calif.: Scholars Press.

———. 1985. *Restaurierung von Papyrus und anderen Schriftträgern aus Ägypten.* Studia Amstelodamensia 23. Zutphen, the Netherlands: Terra.

Frösén, J. 1997. "Der Wert des Kontextes für die Deutung der Kartonage-Papyri." *Akten des 21. Internationalen Papyrologenkongresses, Berlin 1995,* ed. B. Kramer et al., vol 2: 1079–1082. Stuttgart: Teubner.

Harrauer, H., ed. 1985. *Bericht über das 1. Wiener Symposion für Papyrusrestaurierung 4.–8.6.1984.* Mitteilungen aus der Papyrussammlung der Österreichischen Nationalbibliothek NF 19 (with an extensive bibliography by M. Doblinger, "Literaturübersicht zur Papyrusrestaurierung," 63–76). Vienna: Holzhausen.

Horak, U. 1997. "Die Bedeutung der Malerei auf Papyruskartonage aus ptolemäischer und augusteischer Zeit für die antike Ikonographie und für das Verständnis einer antiken Kunstindustrie." *Akten des 21. Internationalen Papyrologenkongresses, Berlin 1995,* ed. B. Kramer, W. Luppe, and H. Maehler, 1091–1096. Stuttgart: Teubner.

Janis, K. 1997. "Die Bearbeitung eines ptolemäischen Mumienpektorals im Interessenkonflikt zwischen Papyrologe und Restaurator." *Göttinger Miszellen* 161: 87–95.

Kampichler, J. 1985. "Konservierung verkohlter Papyri." In *Bericht über das 1. Wiener Symposion für Papyrusrestaurierung 4.–8.6.1984,* ed. H. Harrauer, 35–36. Vienna: Holzhausen.

Lau-Lamb, L. 2005. *Guidelines for Conservation of Papyrus.* Advanced Papyrological Information System (APIS). http://www.lib.umich.edu/pap/conservation/guidelines.html.

Lehtinen, M. 2002. "Conservation and Reconstruction." *The Petra Papyri* I, ed. J. Frösén, A. Arjava, and M. Lehtinen, 11–16. Amman, Jordan: American Center of Oriental Research.

Nielsen, I., and M. Doblinger. 1985. "Hydroxypropylcellulose zur Festigung von Papyrus." In *Bericht über das 1. Wiener Symposion für Papyrusrestaurierung 4.–8.6.1984,* ed. H. Harrauer, 22–28. Vienna: Holzhausen.

Parkinson, R., and S. Quirke (with contributions by U. Wartenberg and B. Leach). 1995. *Papyrus.* Austin: University of Texas Press.

Stohler-Zimmermann, A. 1981. "Das Ablösen der Malerei von Mumienkartonagen." In *Proceedings of the XVI International Congress of Papyrology,* ed. R. S. Bagnall, G. M. Browne, A. E. Hanson, and L. Koenen, 665–676. American Studies in Papyrology 23. Chico, Calif.: Scholars Press.

Viñas, V., and R. Viñas. 1988. *Traditional Restoration Techniques: A RAMP Study* (original in Spanish). General Information Programme and UNISIST. UNESCO, Paris (PGI-88/WS/17). http://www.unesco.org/webworld/ramp/html/r8817e/r8817e.jpg.

Wiedemann, H. G., and G. Bayer. 1983. "Papyrus: The Paper of Ancient Egypt." *Analytical Chemistry* 55: 1220–1230A.

Wright, M. M. 1983. "A Method of Extracting Papyri from Cartonnage." *Studies in Conservation* 28: 122–126.

CHAPTER 5

GREEK AND LATIN WRITING IN THE PAPYRI

GUGLIELMO CAVALLO

IT is difficult—both methodologically and in choice of material—to trace concisely the history of Greek and Latin writing in the papyri over many centuries, especially because it is impossible to discuss and defend adequately the dates proposed, the criteria for assessing handwritings, and one's acceptance or rejection of the views of other scholars. Instead, I first briefly set forth some methodological considerations.[1]

In the area of method, I have sought to avoid too drastic a distinction between documentary and literary hands, for handwriting is a unitary phenomenon, the various manifestations of which need to be assessed not so much on the basis of the use to which they are put—documents or books—as by a consideration of their development. The basic patterns of the letters always constitute the point of departure, patterns taught first at the elementary level and then, through successive exercises, developed either toward greater rapidity and cursiveness or toward calligraphic deliberateness. The writing exercises attested in papyri, ostraca, and tablets offer many examples of training at various levels.[2] The distinction that emerges from them is thus not between documentary and literary hands but between (1) cursive and semicursive writing styles, in which the greater or lesser velocity of the *ductus* modifies the traces and forms of the letters, and (2) regular or rather calligraphic handwritings, which remain closer to the original graphic structure of the letters.

A discussion limited to the Greek and Latin handwriting of the papyri (including parchment fragments) also suffers methodologically from being unable to take into account all of the graphic manifestations on other supports (not only papyrus and parchment but also tablets, ostraca, stone, marble, plaster, metal, and other materials). Nor can one ignore the fact that, starting with the fourth century, manuscripts preserved in libraries begin to be available alongside those found in archaeological excavations.

The choice of examples from the nonetheless vast range of material offered by the papyri has involved balancing two constraints: The first is the need to examine significant pieces; the second, that of selecting readily accessible material. Taking account of these two limitations, the choice of documents has fallen especially on dated or datable items, while literary materials, which generally lack explicit indications of date, have been chosen on the basis of various other criteria—archaeological, papyrological, and palaeographical. One type of archaeological criterion is provided by the discovery of mummy cartonnage in which both documents and books were used as raw material. Another instance, particularly fortunate because it offers not only archaeological but also textual evidence, is provided by the discoveries at Herculaneum. Because the majority of these contain works of Philodemus of Gadara, they must of necessity be dated in the middle of the first century BCE and in any case before 79 CE, the year of the catastrophic eruption of Mount Vesuvius. Papyrological evidence may come from considering the criterion of recto/verso in cases where a roll was written on both sides, one bearing a document, the other a literary work; if the document is dated or approximately datable, the literary hand will be older than the document if on the recto, later if on the verso.[3] More directly, palaeographical evidence can emerge from the comparison of dated or datable documentary writing and undated literary hands. In the absence of any other criterion for dating, only a palaeographical assessment remains.

THE ORIGINS OF GREEK HANDWRITING

Familiarity with writing and the ability to read and write go back in the Greek world to a period well before that to which we can assign the oldest documentary and literary papyri known so far, which are not older than the second half of the fourth century BCE and the opening decades of the third.[4] In these, we can identify some characteristics of Greek writing: alpha with horizontal bar; epsilon and sigma of an archaic type, with straight strokes; kappa with short oblique lines; and omega with a convex central curve. We encounter these characteristics in *SB* XIV 11942, a military order from the years between 331 and 323, which displays, all the same, a highly rigid writing, which can hardly be considered a typical hand of its day. A more normal hand appears in late fourth-century accounts found in the same necropolis at Saqqara (*SB* XIV 11963), written in two hands. A handwriting with a faster and more fluid ductus appears in the marriage contract *P.Eleph.* 1 (310 BCE), the oldest dated papyrus, and at the start of the third century in the contracts *P.Eleph.* 2 (285/284) and 3 (284/283). In these, besides a slight inclination of the letters to the right, one can even observe some forms that appear later, like alpha with an oblique cross stroke, beta with flattened curves, large mu, and nu with a raised middle stroke.

The same graphic characteristics and evolutionary phases reappear in the literary papyri assignable to the last decades of the fourth century or the first decade of the third. In *P.Derveni*, which is interesting because it comes from near Salonika, in Greece, and is archaeologically datable to around 340–320, we see alpha with horizontal crossbar, archaic epsilon and sigma, and omega with convex central curve. We can also see zeta with parallel outer horizontal strokes and vertical middle stroke and theta with its central element reduced to a point. Other examples of this early type of writing in literary papyri are *P.Berol.* inv. 9875, the *Persians* of Timotheos, found at Abousir, the so-called curse of Artemisia in *UPZ* I 1, *P.Hib.* I 6, and *BKT* V 2, 56–63, which contain scholia and elegies, the writing of which shows, like the documents of Elephantine, the transition from fourth-century to third-century forms. In the writing of the last of these, a constant characteristic of third-century scripts (especially in literary rolls) is visible: the contrasting sizes of large letters (alpha, eta, mu, tau, and sometimes nu and pi) and other narrower or smaller letters (epsilon, theta, omicron, sigma).

In the oldest examples, then, no substantial differences are visible between documentary and literary Greek hands or between papyrological and epigraphic hands. Perhaps a basic script had been taught at the elementary level as early as the end of the fifth century and was intended to be used for general purposes. Beginning around the fourth to third century, however, as the Elephantine papyri show, a process of differentiation began that, from around 275 BCE on, led to increasingly different styles of execution. The rigid writing of the old style remained in use, however, as we can see both from certain documents like the letter *P.Lille* I 17 (probably Ptolemy II Philadelphos) or literary papyri like *P.Petr.* II 50 and *P.Petr.* I 5–8, which contain, respectively, the *Laches* and the *Phaedo* of Plato. In documents dated a bit later we observe graphic forms becoming ever faster, as is evident in *P.Rev.* (259/258) and *P.Hamb.* II 187 (246/245).

A rather stylized script, called "Alexandrian chancery," is found in a series of documents from the Zenon archive produced in Alexandria, especially letters from the dioikêtês Apollonios to Zenon (*P.Lond.* VII 1973 [254] and *PSI* V 514 [251]) or circular letters from Apollonios to officials (e.g., *PSI* IV 324 and 325 [261] [figure 5.1] in the same hand). The most obvious characteristic of this script is the placement of letters along a guideline that determines their shape, so that the horizontal strokes of gamma, epsilon, pi, and tau are extended to touch the following letter, forming a kind of pseudo-ligature, with oblique strokes descending from the left of

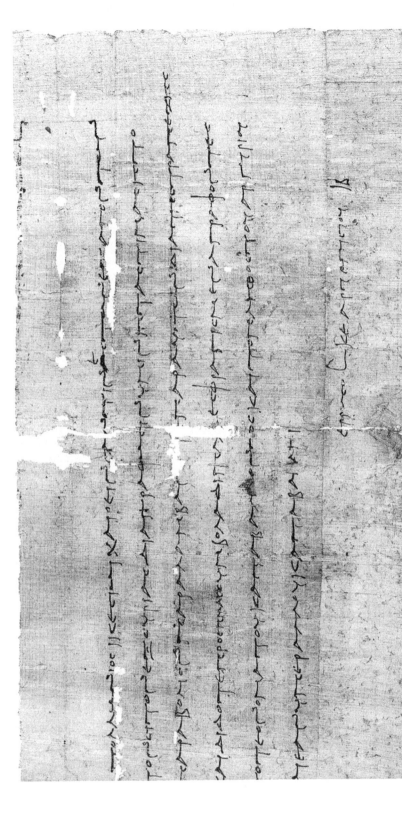

Figure 5.1. *PSI IV 325*. Photo courtesy of the Biblioteca Medicea Laurenziana.

alpha, delta, lambda, and nu, and the middle strokes of mu transformed as far as possible into horizontal strokes also aligned with the guideline. Curved strokes, like the bowl of upsilon and the second half of omega, undergo a similar transformation, and beta, iota, omicron, sigma, and rho, reduced in size, look as if hung from the horizontal guideline.[5]

Less formal chancery scripts are attested in documents written in Egypt, Caria, and Palestine, all of which are from the Zenon archive: *PSI* VI 616, *PSI* V 518, and *P.Cair.Zen.* I 59037.[6] In addition, the same Alexandrian chancery writing, in a less rigid and stylized form, was likely adopted in literary papyri, as in the two funerary epigrams commissioned by Zenon for his hunting dog, Tauron (*P.Cair.Zen.* IV 59532).

DEVELOPED PTOLEMAIC STYLE

The further lines of evolution of Greek writing from the middle of the third century to the early second century may be followed in hands that, although not completely devoid of elements drawn from the Alexandrian chancery style, differ from it in lacking the relentless horizontal linear drive of the writing as a whole, with individual letters taking on more regular proportions and softer strokes. The ductus is sometimes slower and more calligraphic, sometimes faster and informal. Examples include *PSI* IV 341 and *P.Lond.* VII 2011, with more rounded forms visible in *PSI* IV 383 (figure 5.2). This papyrus allows us to see characteristics of the period, such as a contrast in size between broader and narrower letters, alpha, lambda, and delta with a slightly concave oblique stroke descending from left to right, and mu and pi with their right hasta (i.e. the vertical stroke) transformed into a curved line; however, it shows no trace of stylization along the lines of the chancery style. Instead, small ornamental apices appear at the ends of right-hand strokes in some letters (mu, nu, omega), a habit that would later be extended to other letters. In the late third century we also find writing in an older style, as in *P.Eleph.* 17, *P.Hamb.* I 24, and *SB* XXII 15762, all from 223–210 BCE.

The same characteristics may be found with minor variations in the hands of literary papyri, beginning in the middle of the third century and lasting through the end of the century. Sometimes, however, the ductus is slower, and the forms more calligraphic and rounded. Good examples for these central decades are the pseudo-Epicharmus (*P.Hib.* I 1), the *Hippolytus* of Euripides (*P.Lond.Lit.* 73), the *Odyssey* fragment *PSI* VIII 979, Thucydides in *P.Hamb.* II 163, and the mathematical exercises *PSI* VII 763, this last showing similarities particularly with *P.Lond.* VII 2011 (244). The tetrameters of Archilochus in *P.Lond.Lit.* 54 and Menander's *Sicyonius* in *P.Sorb.* inv. 2772b, which show a letter axis slightly inclined to the right, may be dated a little later. The book hands of the later third century can also be represented by the

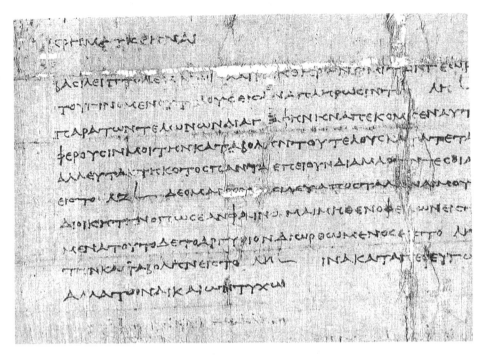

Figure 5.2. *PSI* IV 383. Photo courtesy of the Biblioteca Medicea Laurenziana.

Posidippus papyrus *P.Vogl.Mil.* VIII 307 (figure 5.3), which is associated with documents from the period 222–213,[7] the Odyssey papyrus *P.Sorb.* inv. 2245, and the tragic fragment *PSI* II 136.

The transition from the third to the second century brought no radical change in Greek writing, but evolution continued in the cursive and semicursive hands. In documents such as two petitions from the 160s (*P.Lond.* I 24 recto and *P.Lond.* I 44), as well as a judicial decision probably from 135/134 BCE (*PSI* XIII 1310), the writing recalls the more or less rigid forms of the third century, but semicursive hands also appear, as in *P.Mert.* 5 (149–135), *PSI* III 166 (118), and *P.Bad.* II 3 (109) (figure 5.4). At the same time, however, we witness the birth of the first true cursive writing, visible in documents like *P.Amh.* 35 (petition, 132) and *BGU* III 998 (contract, 101) (figure 5.5) and in receipts on ostraca (*BGU* VI 1440 [143/142], VI 1340 [120/119], VI 1341 [104]).

Along with these semicursive and cursive hands flourishes a line of skilled and regular hands, visible sometimes in the same documentary production and even more widely in book production. Such hands appear in documents like *P.Lond.* II 223, *P.Köln* V 222, and *P.Bad.* II 2, ranging from 179/178 (or 168/167) to 130. In the formal handwritings used in second-century book production, we can distinguish two basic tendencies: There are both accurate but fluid hands and more elaborate and elegant hands, characterized by more or less marked decorative apices more at the ends of strokes. We thus witness the birth of highly calligraphic hands. An example of the first class is the skeptical treatise *P.Louvre* E7733 recto (Pack[2] 2579),

Figure 5.3. *P.Mil.Vogl.* VII 307. Photo courtesy of the Istituto di Papirologia, Università degli Studi, Milan.

while a fluid ductus can be seen in *P.Par.* 2 (Chrysippus); examples of the style with apices are *P.Würzb.* 1 (history) and *P.Tebt.* I 4 (*Iliad*), while a particularly artificial style appears in *P.Oxy.* XV 1790.

FROM HELLENISTIC TO ROMAN

Graphic elements of an archaic type, like the horizontal orientation of strokes, sharp corners, contrast in size between broad and narrow letters, and the absence of ligatures, which all tend to disappear around the end of the second century BCE, vanish in the following century, during which we see a transition from Hellenistic handwriting to Roman. In the documents semicursive and cursive writings dominate, although there is a continuous grade between these two categories rather than

Figure 5.4. *P.Bad.* II 3. Photo courtesy of the Institut für Papyrologie, University of Heidelberg.

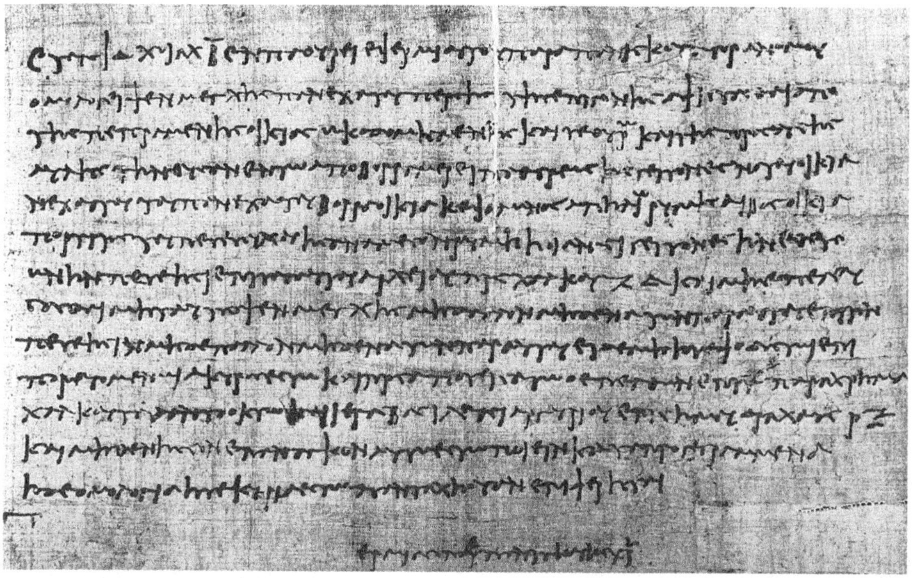

Figure 5.5. *BGU* III 998.

a clean distinction. In the semicursive part of the spectrum we may place *P.Lond.* III 833 (89/88) and *P.Oxy.* VII 1061 (22 BCE [figure 5.6]); toward the cursive end are *PSI* V 549 (41 BCE), *P.Ryl.* II 73 (33–30) (figure 5.7), and *PSI* X 1099 (6/5).

In the second half of the first century BCE, particularly from the reign of Augustus, the process of "cursivization" reaches full maturity. This period opens a phase of changes in the morphology of the letters, whereby the speed of the ductus brings about reductions and simplifications in the internal strokes of letters, and ligatures change the letters they join. The letters beta and kappa are a particular locus of change; in some cases these are written in a single movement and take on the form of two curved hastas joined by a curved base, rather like the Latin *u* (for beta, see *P.Ryl.* II 73 and, for kappa, *P.Oxy.* VII 1061 [figure 5.6]).[8]

In Egypt, the cursive that matured in the first century BCE, written more or less rapidly, continues in the following centuries. In the first century CE we can distinguish two types of cursive. One displays rounded strokes, characterized in some versions by a certain sinuosity; examples are *P.Ryl.* II 183a (16 CE) and *SB* I 3924 (= *P.Select.* II 221, 19 CE or shortly after). The other type of cursive shows more headlong forms and a more marked tendency toward leaning to the right. This is found in documents like *P.Ryl.* II 131 (31 CE), *P.Ryl.* II 119 (54–67 CE), and *BGU* I 197 (17 CE) (figure 5.8).

In the period from the first century BCE to the first CE, the panorama of skilled hands—those that retain a regular composition of the letters from strokes and sometimes reach a high level of formality—is more articulated and varied than in earlier centuries. In *P.Ryl.* IV 586 + *P.Oxy.* IV 802 (99 BCE), only a few cursive elements appear. Although less elegant, *P.Oxy.* XIV 1635 (44–37 BCE) offers a clear, regular hand,

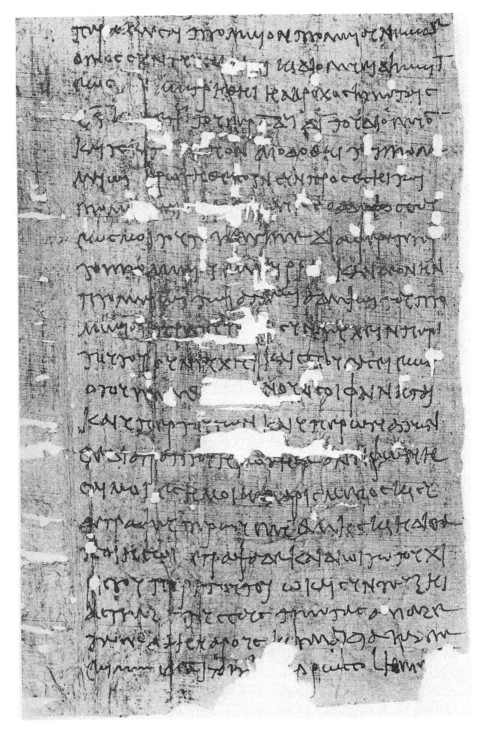

Figure 5.6. *P.Oxy.* VII 1061.

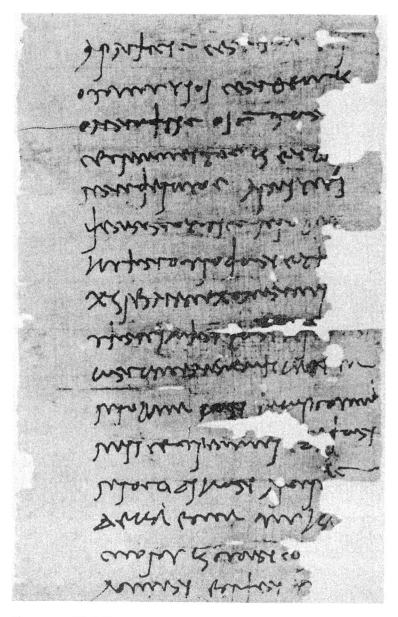

Figure 5.7. *P.Ryl.* II 73.

as does *BGU* IV 1114 (5 BCE). The narrow, headlong forms of *PSI* X 1160 (after 23 BCE; account of an Alexandrian embassy to Augustus), by contrast, imitate or are inspired by chancery forms: The letters are almost entirely detached, made with a rather slow ductus, sometimes with caudate hastas (particularly in kappa and upsilon). But in the Augustan period (7–4 BCE) we also find in *P.Lond.* II 354 a petition, a writing that, even if fluid and fluent, is also rather regular and even calligraphic.

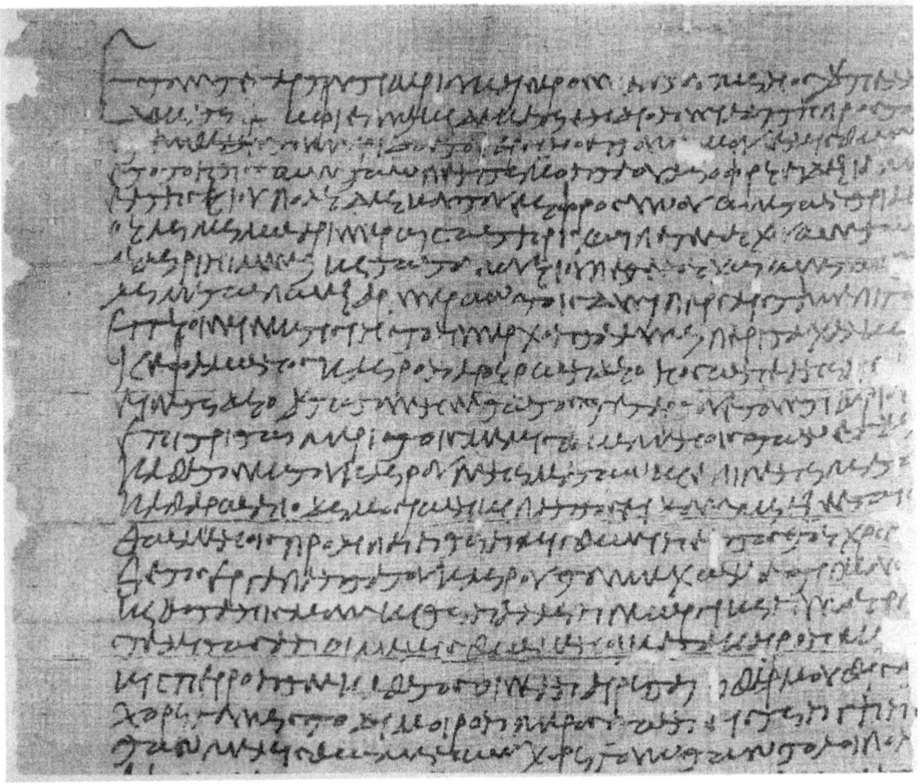

Figure 5.8. *BGU* I 197.

Turning from documents to contemporary literary rolls, we find a rich series of skilled and calligraphic hands. These, indeed, in the course of this period not only reach full maturity but also exhibit a typological variety that allows us to distinguish a whole series of graphic streams sometimes also visible in documents, thereby enabling us to arrive at better-founded dates.

A first and rather widespread graphic stream is represented by *P.Herc.* 1050, with its very regular hand, using elegantly rounded forms. This type of writing is found in the same century (the first BCE) not only in the Herculaneum papyri but also in *P. Louvre* E7733 verso (Pack² 2911) and in the following one in the document *P.Oxy.* II 246 (66 CE). The writing of *P.Mur.* 108 (a fragment perhaps of a philosophical text) (figure 5.9) is also close to these in type. Another graphic stream, identifiable also from the first century BCE, is evident in *BKT* V 2, 131–139 (anapests) (figure 5.10), which can be dated to the first half of the century, in which we find a round script adorned with marked apices at the ends of hastas, paralleled in a document from 99 BCE. The same graphic forms are found in a fragment of Deuteronomy, *P.Fouad* inv. 266 (Van Haelst 56, mid to late–first century BCE), and in the pinnacle of contemporary calligraphy, the famous papyrus of the *Coma Berenices* of Callimachus, *PSI* IX 1092.

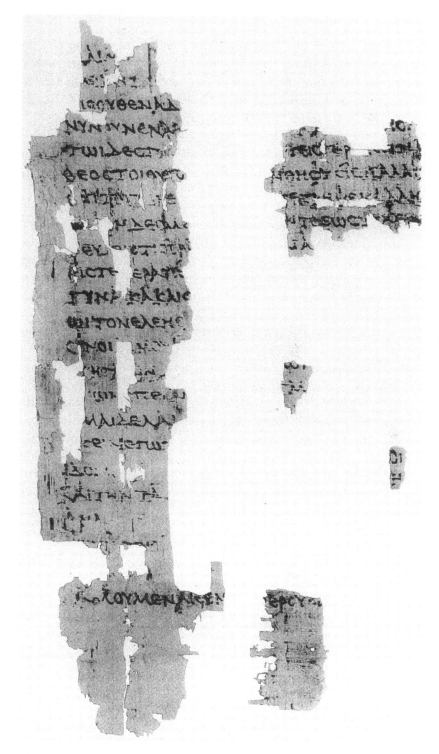

Figure 5.9. *P.Mur.* 108. Photo courtesy of the Israel Antiquities Authority.

The continuation of this style in the first century CE is evident in *PSI* XI 1214 (Sophron, *Mimes*) (figure 5.11). A related graphic stream is represented by the *Iliad* papyrus *P.Fay.* 6, the Epicurean fragment *P.Heid.* inv. 1740 recto, and the *Carchedonios* of Menander (*P.Oxy.* XXXIII 2654); *P.Oxy.* XXXIII 2654 is assigned to the first half of the first century CE, and the first two date to its beginning or even the end of the previous century. This writing has simple, even rough, forms, mostly devoid of apices; it appears first in some papyri from Herculaneum (e.g., *P.Herc.* 1005) and later in the *Iliad* papyrus *P.Lond.Lit.* 6, which displays a rather less formal script, which should be assigned to a date some decades before the reign of Domitian (81–96), when a document was written on the verso. A calligraphic script, but written with a fluid ductus, appears in a series of literary papyri connected to a graphic stream; it is also attested in a document from the end of the first century BCE, *P.Lond.* II 354, but is widespread above all in the following century in book production, as *P.Lond.Lit.* 30 (*Odyssey*), *PSI* XII 1285 (Alexandrian romance), and *P.Gen.* II 85 (Ninus romance, before 100/101 [verso]) show. Further examples are *PSI* IX 1091 (figure 5.12), *PSI* VIII 978, and *P.Berol.* inv. 6845, the script of which has a close parallel in *P.Fay.* 110, a document from 94 CE.

A graphic stream entirely different from those mentioned so far appears in the Herculaneum papyri, for example, *P.Herc.* 994 + 1676 + 1677 + 1074 + 1081, certainly from the first century BCE, as well as in Egyptian papyri like *P.Oxy.* XXIII 2359 (Stesichorus?) and *P.Oxy.* XXII 2318 (Archilochus). This graphic stream, beginning with the end of the first century CE and continuing throughout the second, has more rigid forms, even while sometimes using softer strokes, as the looped alpha, the mu with its middle strokes fused into a curve, and the omega with more curved lines illustrate. This phase is evident in papyri like the so-called Harris Homer (*P.Lond.Lit.* 25), *P.Oxy.* XVII 2066 (Sappho), *P.Oxy.* XV 1809 (Plato), and *PSI* IX 1088 (Isocrates), all of which were written not later than the first century CE, and in *P.Oxy.* VIII 1083 (Sophocles), a luxurious roll from the second century.

There are two final, particularly characteristic graphic typologies. The first picks up some forms from *P.Oxy.* XV 1790; one of its first exemplary instances is the Hyperides papyrus *P.Lond.Lit.* 134 (second century BCE) (figure 5.13), with its elaborate, fairly regular writing. In the same classification we can place the Philodemian *De libertate dicendi* (*P.Herc.* 1471) and the less elegant *P.Oxy.* IV 659 (Pindar) and *P.Oxy.* XXXI 2535 (*hypomnema;* to be assigned to the first century CE). The other rather characteristic script of this period is what we may call "epsilon-theta style," from the marked tendency in these letters to reduce the middle element to isolated central points, buttons, apices, or short curved strokes. The flourishing of this style, which may be dated to the second half of the first century BCE and the beginning of the first century CE, is reflected in papyri like *P.Herc.* 1044 (life of Philodemus), *P.Lond.Lit.* 48, and *P.Oxy.* XXXI 2545 (figure 5.14).

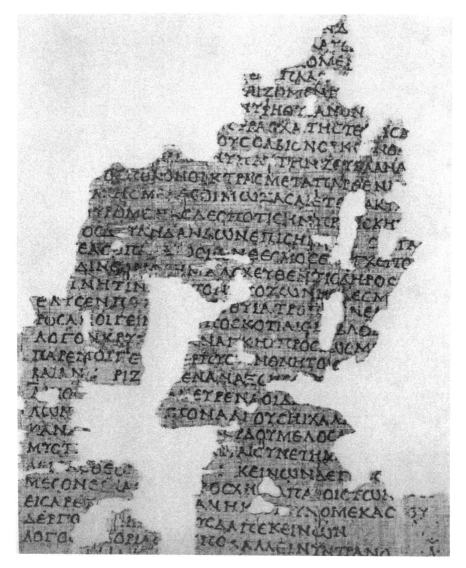

Figure 5.10. *BKT* V.2, 131–139.

THE IMPERIAL PEAK

The period from the first to the third centuries CE represents the peak in numbers of preserved papyri, with the pinnacle occurring in the second century. In the most common cursive scripts the two dominant tendencies observed even in the early Roman period continue. The cursive of a more rounded type is sometimes uneven and messy, with deforming ligatures and inversions of strokes, because of the practiced speed with which the vast quantity of documents was produced.

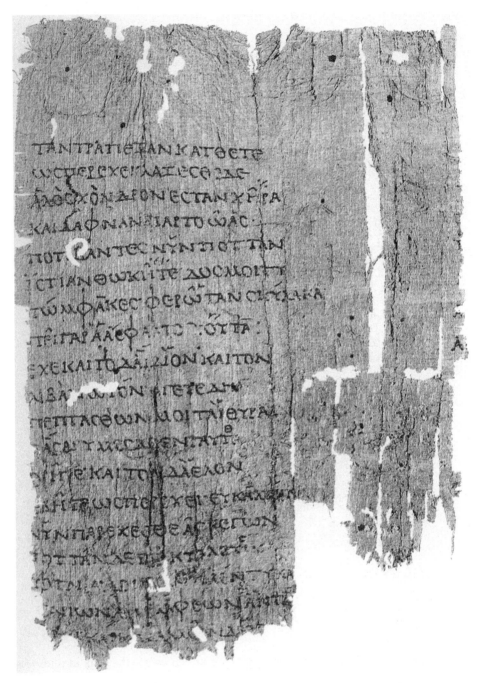

Figure 5.11. *PSI* XI 1214. Photo courtesy of the Biblioteca Medicea Laurenziana.

Figure 5.12. *PSI* IX 1091. Photo courtesy of the Biblioteca Medicea Laurenziana.

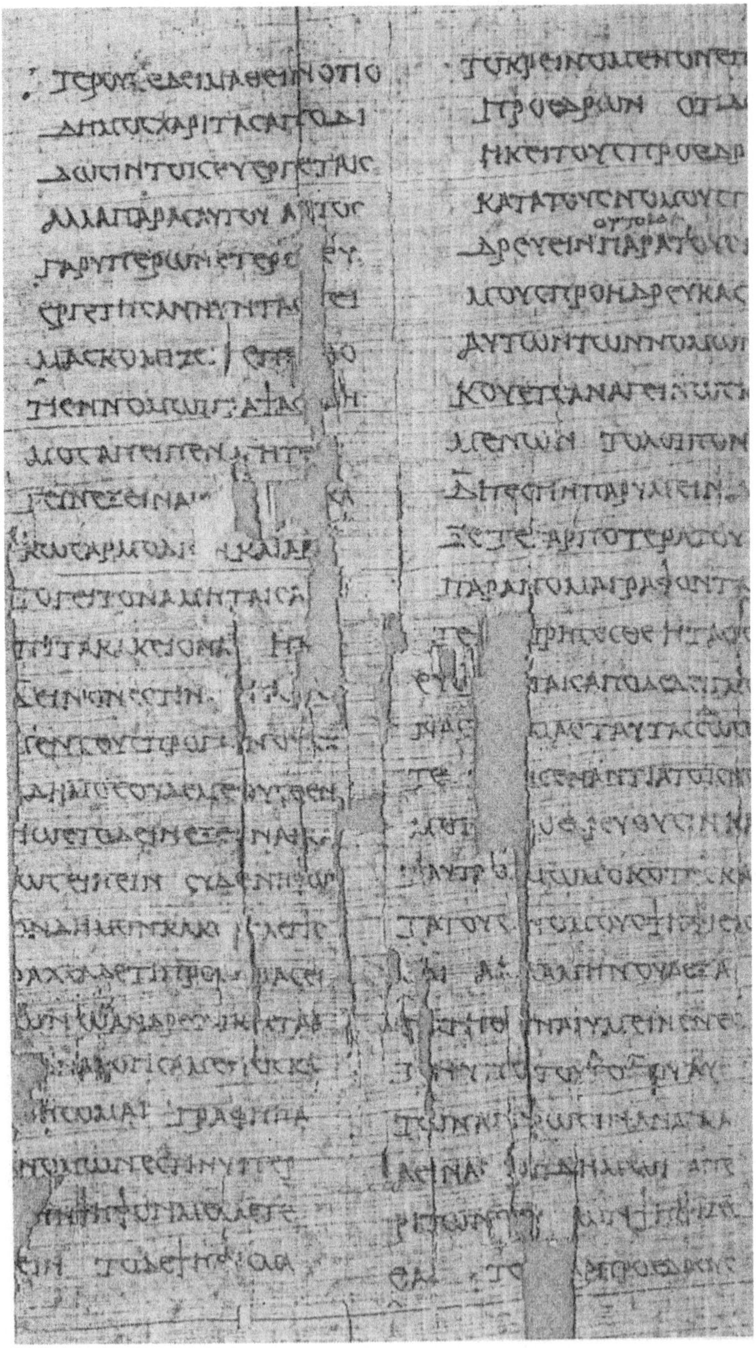

Figure 5.13. *P.Lond.Lit.* 134.

Figure 5.14. *P.Oxy.* XXXI 2545. Photo courtesy of the Egypt Exploration Society.

Although sometimes this writing keeps an upright axis, it increasingly acquires a more or less strong slant to the right. Good examples of the more upright variety are *PSI* X 1138 (107), *PSI* XII 1225 (156/157), and *BGU* III 807 (185). But more common, from the second century on, is the inclined variant of this cursive, as illustrated in *P.Bad.* II 22 (126), *P.Flor.* I 47 (213–217) (figure 5.15), and *P.Ryl.* II 117 (269). The same cursive is found also in the third-century *PSI* X 1173. The other cursive, which was documented in the first century but became more widespread in the second and particularly in the third century, is the more headlong, sharp variety with a more or less marked slant to the right; examples include *BGU* II 544 (ca. 138–161), *P.Flor.* I 23 (145), *BGU* I 92 (187), *CPR* I 32 (218) (figure 5.16), and *BGU* IV 1073 (275).

Many of the handwritings found in papyri outside Egypt in this period are similar to those of the Egyptian documents. There are, however, some distinctive characteristics, particularly the widespread use of semicursive scripts characterized by very rigid tracing, angularity, and compact strokes, which give the writing a coarse appearance. These characteristics appear in documents from Palestine and Mesopotamia.[9] Palestinian examples include (from Murabba'at) *P.Mur.* 116 (first half of the second century) and *P.Mur.* 114 (probably 171) (figure 5.17); the same awkward, heavy scripts are also attested in documents from Nahal Hever (e.g., *P.Yadin* 14, 15, 17, and 18 [figure 5.18], all from 125–128 CE). There are also examples from Dura-Europos, like *P.Dura* 18 (87), 23 (134) (figure 5.19), and 17 (second century).

Alongside the cursive hands there appear in the second century scripts in which the letters often have a cursive base but overall are traced with a more or less slow ductus. Generally these show an upright axis, with ligatures frequent at times but in any case not affecting letter shapes, and with some artificial shapes and extended hastas. These scripts were used particularly (although not exclusively) in bureaucratic settings. A more clearly distinctive stream is that inspired by the chancery style; it shows artificial strokes, frequent presence of cursive forms written with a more or less slow ductus, and a modest use of ligature. For the second and third centuries, examples are *PSI* XII 1227 (188), *P.Ryl.* II 196 (196), *P.Flor.* I 6 (210), and *P.Ryl.* II 110 (259).

This script sometimes shows hints of a rather characteristic chancery style, which asserts itself at the turn of the third century, a style of which the most exemplary witness is the well-known *P.Berol.* inv. 11532 (figure 5.20) and which exercised a more or less marked influence on contemporary documentary writing. The papyrus was written in Alexandria and is thus a rare example of writing from a central chancery. It is possible that this stylization (characterized by some narrow letters, as can be seen in official documents like *BGU* I 73) was already in use in chancery documents at the start of the second century. The letters, rigorously perpendicular to the baseline, at times have an exaggerated prolongation in their vertical dimension (beta, epsilon, theta, kappa, omicron) and sometimes a marked reduction in size (alpha, delta, omega). The script as a whole appears formal, artificial, severe, and thus highly stylized. The same forms appear in the third

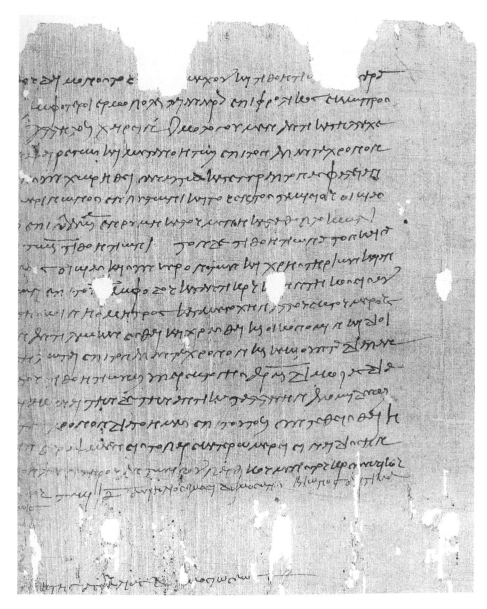

Figure 5.15. *P.Flor.* I 47. Photo courtesy of the Biblioteca Medicea Laurenziana.

century in the official communication *PSI* XII 1247, perhaps also the product of the
prefect's office in Alexandria, and in the official letter *P.Oxy.* XIX 2227 (probably
215/216). It also appears in less stylized forms, especially in copies made in minor
offices, military documents, fiscal and judicial reports, as well as in private letters,
contracts, and various other documents. For the period that encompasses the end
of the second century and all of the third, one may mention, for instance, *P.Flor.* II

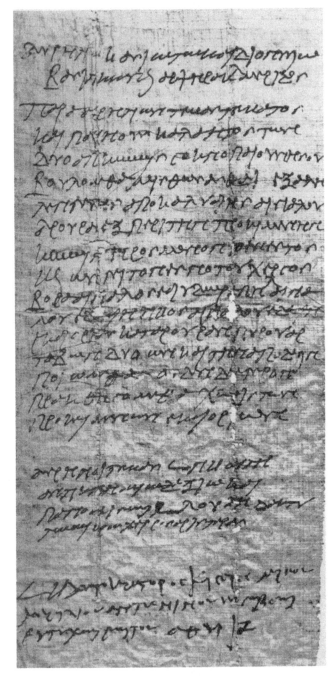

Figure 5.16. *CPR* I 32. Photo courtesy of the Papyrussammlung, Österreichische Nationalbibliothek.

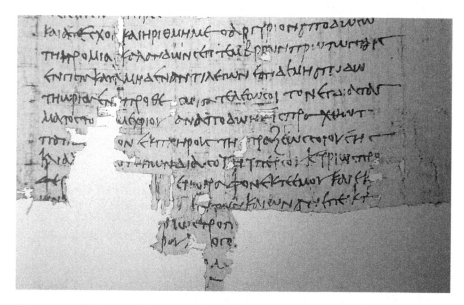

Figure 5.17. *P.Mur.* 114. Photo courtesy of the Israel Antiquities Authority.

278 (203/204), *P.Lond.* II 345 (194), *BGU* I 296 (219/220), and *P.Oxy.* XXXI 2612 (288–290). Chancery hands also appear in literary papyri, apparently written by functionaries: Examples are *P.Beatty* V (Genesis), *PSI* II 127 (Judges), and *PSI* VI 727 (astrology), all from the late second or early third century.

Formal scripts, devoid of any chancery stylization, are also found in documents from the same period, particularly in bureaucratic milieus; these are to be categorized with the rounded and sometimes calligraphic scripts such as those in the *Gnomon of the Idios Logos* (*BGU* V 1210, ca. 170) and *P.Oxy.* VIII 1100 (figure 5.21), a copy of an edict of the prefect (206). These resemble the scripts also found in literary papyri. The writing of the *Gnomon,* for example, is close to that in the famous papyrus of the Mimes of Herondas (*P.Lond.Lit.* 96), assignable to the start of the second century, while the script of *P.Oxy.* VIII 1100 is found in the same period in the papyrus of Favorinus (*P.Vat.* 11), later than 190/191, in *BKT* IX 58 *(Iliad),* before Septimius Severus, and in the Christian papyri *P.Ryl.* III 463 (Gospel of Mary) and *PSI* VIII 980 (Psalms). Elegant calligraphic hands that are also flowing appear particularly in *PSI* V 446 (prefect's edict, 133–136) (figure 5.22), *P.Oxy.* III 473 (138–160), and *P.Mur.* 113 (Murabba'at). A similar but more rigid and less elegant handwriting is found in *BGU* III 895 (138–161), a will probably written in Syria.

The skilled hands found in literary papyri of the second and third centuries display a great variety of graphic solutions. In this period the rise of new cultural currents, circles of readers, literary practices, texts, and public and private libraries drove a more extensive and varied production of books than the past. At this time, the most notable phenomenon in writing found in the domain of skilled and

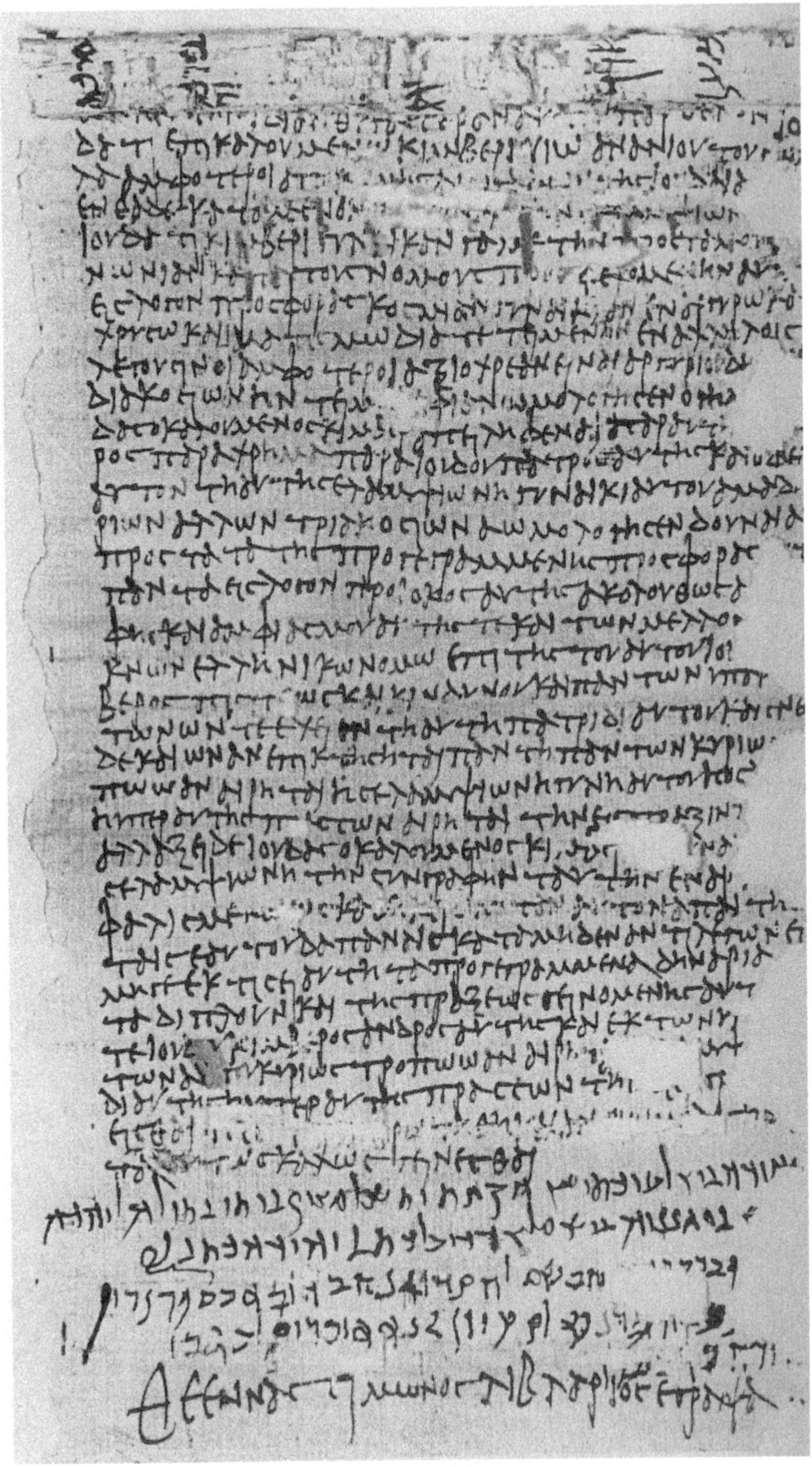

Figure 5.18. *P. Yadin* 18. Photo courtesy of the Israel Exploration Society.

Figure 5.19. *P.Dura* 23. Photo courtesy of the Beinecke Rare Book and Manuscript Library, Yale University.

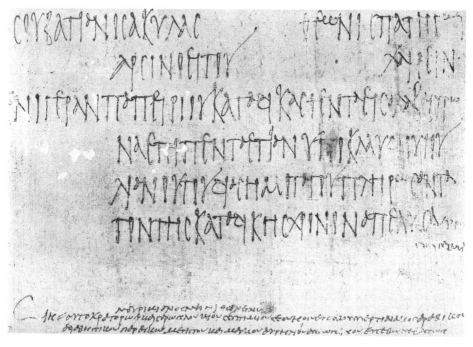

Figure 5.20. *P.Berol.* inv. 11532.

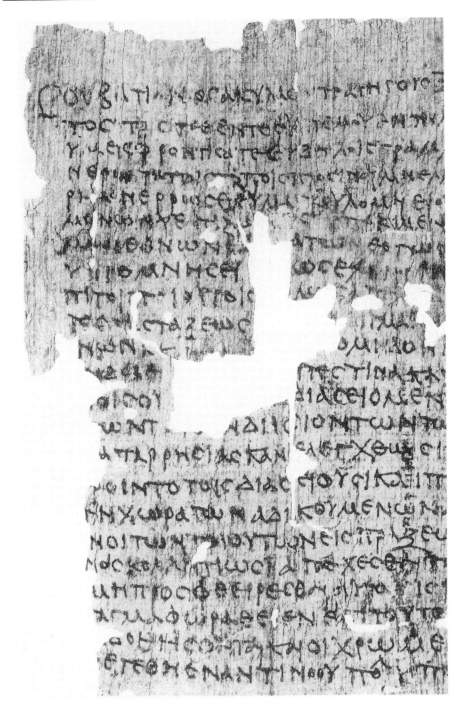

Figure 5.21. *P.Oxy.* VIII 1100.

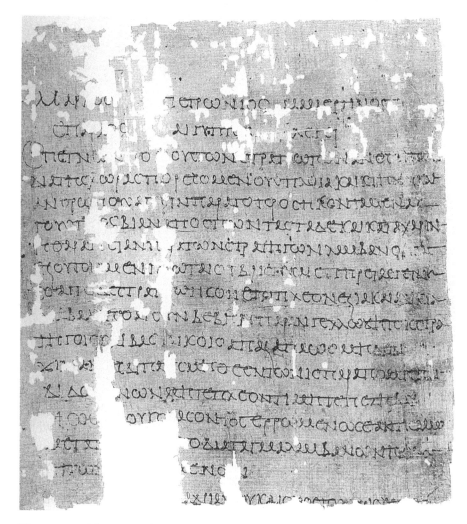

Figure 5.22. *PSI* V 446. Photo courtesy of the Biblioteca Medicea Laurenziana.

calligraphic hands is the development of normative scripts (i.e., handwritings that follow precise rules and are repetitively stable in their technique and manner of execution, with the result that they have great staying power).

The first group is made up of the regular and rounded scripts that constitute the continuation of analogous hands in previous centuries. Here, from the first half of the second century (or possibly the end of the first), we find *PSI* VIII 978 and *PSI* XI 1197 + *PSI Congr. XVII* 8 + *P.Oxy.* II 226; from the second century we find *P.Oxy.* III 454 and, in a less formal style, *PSI* IX 1095, *P.Oxy.* X 1231, and *P.Berol.* inv. 9782. The assignment of these hands to the second century is supported by the affinity they display with documents like *P.Berol.* inv. 6854 (Trajan) and the *Gnomon of the Idios Logos* (*BGU* V 1210, ca. 170). To the turn of the second to the third century and to the

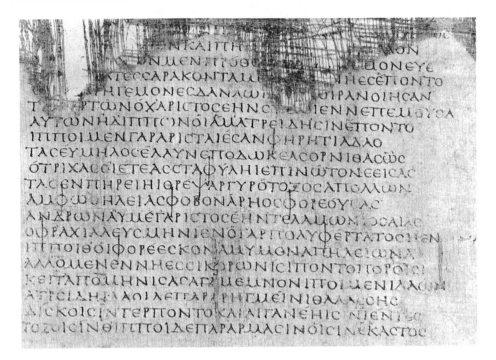

Figure 5.23. The Hawara Homer.

third century we attribute *P.Beatty* VI (Numbers), and to the turn of the third century to the fourth, *P.Beatty* IX (Ezekiel and Esther). Among these curvilinear hands the so-called round majuscule (also called the "Roman uncial") stands out, representing one of the pinnacles of Greek calligraphy. Because its characteristics (with only minor variation) are identical in many examples, it was clearly a normative script; the letters are drawn with maximum regularity, the strokes tend to curvilinear forms (note the mu), and even oblique lines sometimes present a slight curvature. The script as a whole is markedly bilinear and adorned with decorative apices.[10]

Among the most important examples are the famous Hawara Homer (*P.Haw.* 24–28) (figure 5.23), *PSI* XI 1213, *PSI* I 8, and *BKT* V 1, 28–30, all of the second century, the floruit of this remarkable calligraphy. This flourishing was, however, ephemeral, essentially limited to the Antonine period, with no examples after the second century. An imitation was produced in the late fifth century, perhaps in pagan Alexandrian circles. It appears, in fact, in the famous *Ilias Ambrosiana,* in the Iliadic fragments *PSI* VII 748 + 749 and in two Platonic fragments, *P.Duke* inv. 5 and *P.Ant.* II 78.

A new graphic grouping with normative claims, the so-called biblical majuscule, makes its appearance starting in the late second century.[11] Its basis was a sober and undecorated script, which can be observed at the turn of the second to the third century in *P.Oxy.* XVIII 2169 (Callimachus), *P.Berol.* inv. 9968 (Homer), as well as *P.Mich.* II 135 + *P.Mil.* I 13 (Ecclesiasticus). Among these scripts emerges the true biblical majuscule, which reflects in its penmanship the base models of the letters and is carried out with a visible contrast between thin horizontal strokes and fatter vertical ones (particularly gamma, pi, tau), while oblique strokes appear in between (alpha, delta, lambda). Rho and upsilon project below the baseline, and the hastas of phi and psi project both up and down.

The number of witnesses to the biblical majuscule—by no means all biblical—is very large. For the first centuries of its existence one may cite the classical texts in *P.Ryl.* I 16 (before 255/256), *PSI* IX 1086 (figure 5.24), *P.Berol.* inv. 7499 + 7502, *P.Oxy.* IX 1179, and *P.Oxy.* XXII 2334, the last of the third to the fourth century. This handwriting was widely adopted for Christian texts, in particular for the Scriptures, to the extent that it was used for the great biblical codices (Vaticanus, Sinaiticus [both fourth century] and Alexandrinus [fifth]). Its continuing use in book production is attested up to the eight century and beyond in numerous examples on both papyrus and parchment, secular and especially Christian. Besides the biblical codices already mentioned, important examples for the fourth century are the parchment leaf *P.Oxy.* XIII 1621 and *P.Beatty* IV (Genesis); for the fifth, *P.Oxy.* III 411 (Thucydides), and *P.Amh.* I 1 (ascension of Isaiah); for the sixth, the famous illustrated codex of Dioscorides in Vienna, produced at Constantinople in 513 or a bit later, and the parchment fragment of Jonah, *PSI* X 1164 + *BKT* VIII 18 (figure 5.25). Around the seventh century the biblical majuscule begins to disappear in the last Greek books produced in Egypt, while it survives, even if only sporadically, in Greek book production in other areas. Among the late examples, as can already be observed in the Vienna Dioscorides, the script shows a stronger contrast between fat and thin strokes and decorative buttons at the extremities of the latter, in particular on the horizontal strokes of gamma, delta, epsilon, pi, and tau.

Yet another type that emerged in the second century is that of a script showing curving strokes and a more fluid ductus, which appears from the reign of Antoninus in documents like *PSI* V 446 (figure 5.22) and *P.Oxy.* III 473. This type of handwriting later turned into a normative style, the "Alexandrian majuscule," which was also widely used in both classical and Christian book production.[12] The first signs of this script appear in the second-century gospel codex *P.Egerton* 2; in *P.Bodm.* II (John) and *P.Ant.* I 28 (Hippocrates) of the third century; in *PSI* II 125 (Acts, fourth century); *P.Ant.* I 12 (2 John, fifth century); and *PSI* I 1 (Matthew, fifth–sixth century) (figure 5.26). In the last of these, as in many other sixth-century manuscripts (e.g., *P.Amh.* II 191, 192; *BKT* VIII 4), the Alexandrian majuscule appears with all of its normative characteristics. The script is soft and flowing, with oblique lines descending from left to right and tending to be prolonged on the baseline to form pseudoligatures; alpha, mu (with internal strokes fused into a single curve), upsilon, and omega present variably open or closed loops; epsilon sometimes has its upper curve brought down to the middle stroke; and delta and lambda generally have a curl at the upper end of the right-hand oblique stroke.

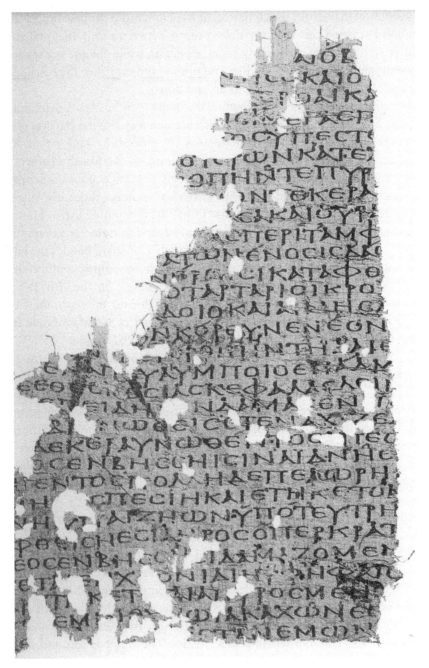

Figure 5.24. *PSI* IX 1086. Photo courtesy of the Biblioteca Medicea Laurenziana.

Figure 5.25. *PSI* X 1164. Photo courtesy of the Biblioteca Medicea Laurenziana.

This same script, with curved strokes and fluid ductus, appears in the second century in a narrower version, with epsilon, theta, omicron, and sigma particularly squeezed, eventually turning into an Alexandrian majuscule that differs from that just described in a sharper contrast between wide and narrow letters. Good early examples are *P.Oxy.* XXXII 2631 (second century, lyric) and *P.Lund.* IV 13 (260–270); nonetheless, this script remains rare until the fourth century and then comes into wider use from the fifth century on. Examples from this period are *P.Berol.* inv. 13418 (fifth century), *P.Oxy.* XV 1820 (fifth–sixth century), *P.Oxy.* XX 2258 (sixth century), *PSI* XIV 1400 (seventh century), *P.Louvre* E 7404 (seventh–eighth), and *P.Bad.* IV 58 (eighth). The dating of the Alexandrian majuscule has a series of pegs in some festal letters issued by the Alexandrian patriarchs assignable to precise or highly probable dates. The best known of these are *P.Grenf.* II 112 (577) and *BKT* VI 55–109 (713 or 719). This script was used not only by the patriarchal chancery of Alexandria but also (adapted to the Coptic alphabet) as an ecclesiastical script used for centuries for Coptic texts, such that it seems to have been particularly widely used in Egypt and its vicinity; there are examples from Nessana in the Negev.[13]

A further type of script that began spreading in the second century is that identified by Wilhelm Schubart, who called it "severe style," a term still sometimes used. It is a script based on rigid and angular hands, characterized by a contrast in size between broad letters (mu, nu, tau, omega) and narrow letters (epsilon, theta, omicron, sigma), and seen already in the Hellenistic period. The severe style has a greater degree of simplicity and a tendency not only to squeeze some letters but also to shrink them. Schubart mentioned as particularly significant examples of the severe style *P.Oxy.* X 1234 + XI 1360 + XVIII 2166 (Alcaeus) and especially the

Figure 5.26. *PSI* I 1. Photo courtesy of the Biblioteca Medicea
Laurenziana.

famous Bacchylides papyrus *P.Lond.Lit.* 46 + *PSI* XII 1278, to which one may add *P. Oxy.* IX 1174, *P.Oxy.* I 26 (both second century) (figure 5.27), and *P.Oxy.* VII 1016, *PSI* X 1170, and *P.Oxy.* XVII 2098 (early third century), where a slight inclination of the axis is noticeable. In the severe style, this slant toward the right is marked to the point of becoming a true sloping script. It appears both in documents (e.g., *P.Oxy.* XXII 2341 [202] and *P.Flor.* II 259 [before 260]) and in a considerable number of literary papyri, both classical and Christian. Examples are *PSI* XI 1203 (late second century), *P.Oxy.* V 842 (second–third), *P.Ryl.* I 57, *PSI* X 1169 (figure 5.28), and *P.Lond.Lit.* 5 (*verso*) + 182 (all third century).

In the following centuries, the upright severe style seems to evolve into the Byzantine script called "upright ogival majuscule," taking on a certain contrast in the thickness of the strokes and thus exhibiting a stylistic taste of a general nature ever more widely diffused in late antiquity.[14] Fourth-century examples are *P.Oxy.* XI 1352 (Psalms) and *PSI* X 1171 (Aristophanes), and fifth-century, *P.Flor.* III 389 (Sibylline oracles) (figure 5.29). However, instances from this period are rare; its floruit is middle Byzantine, thus rather later. By contrast, scripts that lean more to the right were widely diffused from the fourth century on. Prominent among these are the "inclined ogival majuscule," which, as the Byzantine period progresses, also

Figure 5.27. *P.Oxy.* I 26.

acquires some degree of contrast in the width of the strokes. A faster, more cursive version appears in the fourth century in *P.Herm.* 4 and 5 (ca. 320–325), *P.Oxy.* XXXIII 2656 (= LXIV 4408), and *P.Bodm.* IV; a slower and more rigid form that occurs in the same period appears in *P.Beatty* XI, *PSI* X 1165, and *P.Oxy.* XXXIV 2699. In this last papyrus the inclined ogival majuscule takes on an uncommonly marked contrast in the thickness of strokes. This characteristic becomes normal in the following centuries both in Egypt and in Palestine.[15] Examples include the famous Menander codex *P.Cair.* 43227 (fifth century), *P.Oxy.* XV 1817 and 1818 (sixth), *PSI* XIII 1296 (seventh), and *P.Ness.* 6 (eighth).

The more or less regular scripts (used particularly in book production) that we have examined so far, along with their successors in the seventh and eight centuries, do not exhaust the graphic range of the Roman period. They constitute only some of the more characteristic, widely diffused, and durable scripts of the period. The complex and varied range of other handwritings makes it impossible to give a detailed and ordered classification. Many are generic scripts that do not fall into well-defined typologies but reflect the diverse tendencies of the period and combinations of individual forms. Some are minute and densely written, like *P.Oxy.* V 843 or *P.Flor.* II 112; others are larger and more broadly spaced, as in *P.Lond.* I 130 or *P.Beatty* VII + *P.Mert.* I 2 + *PSI* XII 1273; while others are forms derived from cursive, as in *P.Oxy.* VII 1019 + *P.Oxy.* XLI 2948 and *PSI* X 1181. Still others resemble more formal scripts, like *P.Oxy.* X 1250, or are even inspired by chancery style, like *PSI* VIII 982.

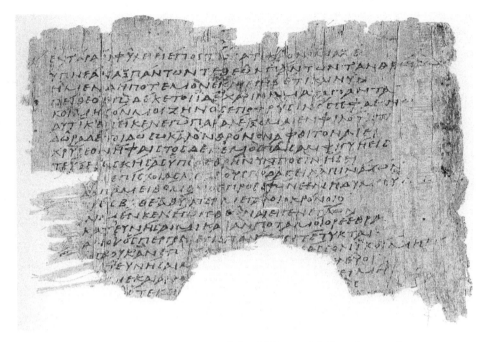

Figure 5.28 *PSI* X 1169. Photo courtesy of the Biblioteca Medicea Laurenziana.

Figure 5.29. *P.Flor.* III 389. Photo courtesy of the Biblioteca Medicea Laurenziana.

THE BYZANTINE PERIOD

In papyrological parlance, the Byzantine period for cursive and semicursive writing in Egypt begins with Diocletian. Although the documentation remains abundant, it is less diverse in type than that of the Roman period, concentrated as it is in groups connected with the great families of state functionaries and landowners and with the new institutions represented by the churches and monasteries. Over time, the production of books moves away from the texts of the classical tradition—apart from those used in education—to Christian scriptures and literature.

Bureaucratic and chancery usage of scripts in the fourth century, whether cursive, semicursive, or regular, witnesses both continuity with the hands of the second-to-third century and significant transformations. Continuity in the cursive is evident, for example, in the inclined writing of *BGU* II 408 (312), while in the tradition of older semicursive scripts with some chancery elements, we find documents like *PSI* X 1107 (336) and *P.Flor.* I 75 (380). More marked elements of second-to-third-century chancery script (but without elements like the contrast in letter size) appear in *BGU* II 405 (348), where a gentle slope in the axis of the letters is observable.

From Diocletian on, Greek majuscule bureaucratic handwriting comes increasingly into contact with Latin minuscule writing, resulting in the formation of certain graphically equivalent but often phonetically different signs; examples are d = delta (but also $t + i$ = rounded delta), h = eta, m = pi + iota. This phenomenon (the so-called Graeco-Latin graphic koinê) initiates a rapid process of the transformation of majuscule graphic forms into minuscule, even if the latter in some cases had already been found in Greek writing for a long time. The phases of this process are noticeable beginning in the fourth century in cursive and semicursive hands, whether upright or inclined. Particularly fine specimens of the rapprochement between Greek and Latin handwriting appear in judicial and administrative practice, like the bilingual *P.Lips.* I 38, a trial before the *praeses Thebaidis* in the year 390, and *PSI* XIII 1309 (early fifth century), similarly a trial. However, the same graphic phenomenon can be traced in purely Greek papyri written in bureaucratic hands. The archive of Abinnaeus furnishes interesting examples for the mid-fourth century; for the fifth, good illustrations are *PSI* XII 1265 (426) and *P.Flor.* III 315 (435).

Beginning at the latest with the fifth century, minuscule forms also enter the scripts in ordinary use. In documents like *PSI* XII 1239 (430) and *BGU* II 609 (442) we observe the substitution—still unsystematic—of some minuscule letters of the koinê for those of the traditional type. A more pervasive presence of minuscule elements, both letters and ligatures, is found, for instance, in *PSI* X 114 (454) and *P.Flor.* I 94 (491), which show that at the turn of the fifth to the sixth century the transition in Greek writing from majuscule to minuscule, at least in documentary practice, was essentially complete.

During the same time span, however, and even later, the traditional majuscule survives, even if sometimes mixed with certain minuscule forms. Its range includes semicursive and detached handwritings, both upright and inclined, used both for documents and for books, both classical and Christian. Documents include *SB* VIII 9907 (388), *P.Köln* III 151 (423), *SB* XVI 12865 (576), and *PSI* I 60 (595). These scripts also occur in literary papyri like *P.Köln* III 134 (fourth century) and *P.Oxy.* XIII 1614 and *P.Egert.* 5 (fifth century). These hands all appear very rough and disorderly. Calligraphic writing by this point is limited to styles long established by tradition—biblical majuscule, Alexandrian majuscule, upright and inclined ogival majuscule—which, as we have seen, continue in use.

As it emerged from the Graeco-Latin koinê by the sixth century, Byzantine minuscule cursive continued its life down to the Arab period in two parallel styles of writing. The most widely attested one is swift, decisively inclined to the right, rich in ligatures, and characterized by elongated strokes that extend above and below the line, along with artificial swirls and flourishes. Good examples are *BGU* I 255 (599), *P.Flor.* I 70 (627), and *P.Berol.* inv. 13371 (ca. 650), which bring us into the Arab period, during which the same type of writing appears in many papyri of the correspondence of Qurrah ben Sharik (e.g., *P.Lond.* IV 1348 [710]). The papyri from Petra and Nessana of the sixth and seventh centuries show that this manner of writing was in use also outside Egypt.

The other type is a stylized chancery script with a slower ductus and an upright or only slightly inclined axis, lacking deforming ligatures, tending to isolate and round the body of the letters, and exhibiting modestly elongated and hooked hastas. Some letters in particular (lambda, mu, pi, tau) show a form different from that encountered in the other stream of Byzantine cursive.[16] This stylization is in use and widely diffused above all in the Arab period, as is apparent in *P.Apoll.* 9 (675/676 or 660/661), *P.Lond.* IV 1408 (709), and above all *P.Lond.* I 32, an official letter of the *dux* Attyia ben Gu'aid (698/699, less probably 713/714), and *SB* I 5638 (710).[17] What is striking is that, in the course of the Arab period, this chancery stylization begins to be adopted also for nondocumentary use. It appears, in fact, even in some Christian papyri with devotional texts, like *MPER* n.s. IV 31 + XVII 7, *MPER* XVII 34, *MPER* XVII 53, or even *P.Aberd.* 72a.

When around 800 CE new cultural movements arose in the Byzantine world and the ancient and monumental majuscule scripts for book production, now regarded as slow and tiring in execution, began to disappear, it is the chancery stylization of the Byzantine cursive that, stripped of its most bureaucratic elements (e.g., its swirls and excessive elongation of hastas) is promoted to become also a book handwriting, thus turning into the normal Byzantine Greek minuscule. Nonetheless, in this period the torch of Greek culture and script had passed from the Nile and Alexandria to the Bosporus and Constantinople.

LATIN HANDWRITING

Latin papyri are relatively scarce compared to the immense number of Greek papyri; moreover, most of them come from Egypt, whereas Latin was written mostly in Italy and the western provinces of the Roman world. There is, all the same, enough material to document the course of Latin handwriting at least from the first century BCE.

To begin, cursive writing is not attested in the available material before the first century CE, when we meet it in *BGU* II 611, the famous papyrus of the *oratio Claudii* on reforming justice, which is later than 41–54. This is the oldest example of authentic Latin cursive. It shows that Latin writing had already, at least for some purposes, freed itself from the hard strokes natural to incision on tablets. In particular, certain characteristic forms of Latin cursive are evident, like *B* with its belly to the left, *E* with oblique middle stroke, and *Q* with a long tail. See *PSI* VI 729 (77 CE) (figure 5.30) for an illustration of the same type of writing.

Another type of writing is that which, even if executed in ink, seems to represent the transposition of an incised script meant for wax tablets. It shows a geometric course; isolated letters; an absence of ligatures; hard, cutting strokes; broken curves; and sometimes prolongation of hastas as in incised texts. This script appears in a fragmentary letter of ca. 29–22 BCE, *P.Vindob.* inv. L 1b (*ChLA* XLII 1241), *P.Berol.* inv. 8334 (*ChLA* X 417; 83–86, copy of imperial codicil), *P.Berol.* inv. 11649 (*ChLA* X 424; letter), all of the first century, and the Severan *BGU* II 628r. This rigid and disarticulated writing is found in the West in a number of tablets from Vindolanda and in the East in *P.Lond.* 229 (166, Seleucia). This script was that most commonly used on papyri from the first century BCE to the second century CE. In the same graphic track and contemporary to these documents we also find literary texts like *P.Heid.* L 1a, b (*CLA* VIII 1220) and *P.Mich.* VII 430. This same script is sometimes more compact and leans slightly on its axis, as in *P.Vindob.* inv. L 1c (*ChLA* XLIII 1241), *PSI* XIII 1307 and 1308, and *P.Mich.* VII 442 (second century).

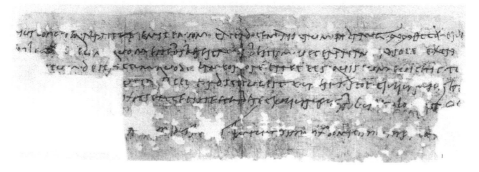

Figure 5.30. *PSI* VI 729. Photo courtesy of the Biblioteca Medicea Laurenziana.

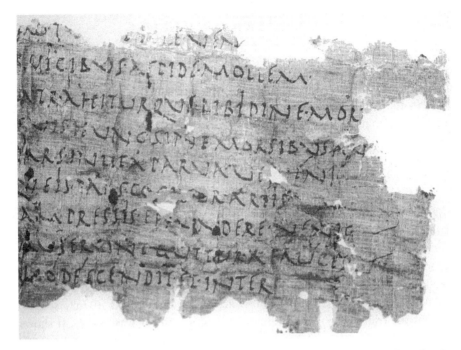

Figure 5.31. *P.Herc.* 817. Photo courtesy of the Biblioteca nazionale Napoli and Brig-ham Young University (Provo, Utah). All rights reserved. Courtesy of the Ministero per i Beni e le Attività Culturali, Italy.

Once again, Vindolanda's ink tablets offer parallels in the early second century (*Tab.Vind.* II 291, 310, 345). The presence of this script in a legal roll (*P.Mich.* VII 456, first century) and in a literary text of the second century, *P.Oxy.* XVII 2088, shows that it was also used in book production.

Before further considering the second and third centuries, let us look at the more formal and calligraphic scripts, which are among the oldest witnesses to Latin writing on papyrus, those that show, taken together, a normative handwriting. This is the capital normally used in books and whose characteristics can be summarized as follows: substantially epigraphic letter forms; soft drawing; usually a contrast in thickness between strokes; frequent addition of elegant apices at the ends of vertical strokes.[18] One of the first examples of these capitals is *P.Berol.* inv. 13956 (*ChLA* X 428; second half of the first century CE); in a more calligraphic form, the same script appears in *PSI* XI 1183 (45–54), with an outer text in book majuscule and an inner text (the same) in a harsh and broken cursive. If the same scribe wrote both, as seems likely, it seems clear that some Latin scribes were trained in two types of writing. A book majuscule is also attested in *BGU* VII 1689 (122–145) and *P.Cair.* Jd'E 39513 (*ChLA* XLI 1191; first–second century).

Figure 5.32. *P.Vindob.* inv. L 112. Photo courtesy of the Papyrussammlung, Österreichische Nationalbibliothek.

However, it is obviously in books that this capital writing is most amply
attested. The Herculaneum papyri offer examples that were certainly produced in
Italy, but so do Egypt and other Mediterranean areas. All of these were presumably
written in the Roman west or by hands trained there. Among the Herculaneum
finds the majuscule is sometimes more fluid, as in *P.Herc.* 817 (figure 5.31), the
famous *Carmen de bello Actiaco,* and sometimes more formal, as in *P.Herc.* 1475 and
1067, securely datable before 79 CE (the first after 46 BCE and the second after 27
BCE). Egyptian examples include *P.Oxy.* VI 871, *P.Hamb.* 167, and the Sallustian
fragments *P.Ryl.* I 42 and *P.Ryl.* III 473 (both second century). Particularly in the
oratorical fragments from Herculaneum and in *P.Ryl.* I 42 the writing demonstrates
a large, squared module characterized by soft, thick oblique lines from left to right
and by soft little strokes crowning the hastas, as if traced by a little pen. This is the
highest-quality majuscule used in Roman books from the time of Augustus on. A
particularly interesting instance is the "Cornelius Gallus papyrus," found at Qasr
Ibrim in Nubia.[19]

Another type of regular capital appears in documentary practice. Its most
distinctive characteristic is the absence of contrast between thick and thin strokes.
Instances are *P.Vindob.* inv. L 112 (*ChLA* XLV 1323; after 129) (figure 5.32), *P.Iand.*
inv. 209 (*ChLA* XI 491; second century), and *BGU* II 696 (156).

Among the scripts in use in chancery practice, which were developing already
in the late first century and continued to emerge and develop in the second, is a
headlong cursive with thin strokes decisively inclined to the right, in which certain
forms and ligatures gradually develop into a system. This particular hand emerges
fully in the third century in a near-normative documentary script.[20] The most

Figure 5.33. *P.Grenf.* II 110.

characteristic letters are *A* made with only outer oblique lines that meet along the stroke descending from left to right, *B* with its belly to the left, *D* with an open or "laced" eyelet, *E* in the shape of *V*, *M* and *N* with their middle strokes almost always elevated, *P* with the upper curve reduced to an oblique stroke and *R* with it turned into a wavy line, and *Q* with its descending hasta turned from the left.

Second-century examples are *P.Oxy.* VII 1012, *PSI* IX 1026, *P.Grenf.* II 108, and *P.Gen.Lat.* 8; third-century instances are *P.Ryl.* IV 553, *P.Dura* 59, 63, and *P.Oxy.* XLI 2951. These same chancery forms, although not so formal, are also found in many ostraca from Bu Njem in Libya, written in ink perhaps with a soft, small reed pen; *O.Bu Njem* 76–80, military letters of 259 written by a single hand, are good examples.[21] In addition, the same style of writing was sometimes used for paraliterary texts like *P.Oxy.* XI 1404. This chancery writing virtually disappears at the end of the third century and survives only in the imperial chancery, which alone was permitted to use the so-called *litterae caelestes*. The imperial rescripts from 436–450 in Paris and Leiden are notable examples.

It is possible to document a freer evolution of everyday cursive script between the first and the third centuries, a handwriting usually called "common script." This evolution may be followed in both incised and inked writing, which show a process of reduction or simplification of the letter strokes leading to the creation of the minuscule. This process can be observed already underway in some letters during the late first century in the wall inscriptions of Pompeii and on plates and bowls from La Graufesenque (ancient Condatomagos in Gaul),[22] as well as in some first–second-century tablets from Vindolanda, such as the epistolary diptych *Tab.Vind.* II 343. In the papyri, some minuscule forms appear as variants in less formal examples of the chancery style of the second–third century, like *P.Dura* 60 and 82. However, from the third to the beginning of the fourth century, other documents show more fully the evolution of the common script in the sense of the minuscule; an example is the cursive script, alternating with capitals, of *P.Mich.* III 164 (242–244), *P.Grenf.* II 110 (293) (figure 5.33), *PSI* I 111 (287–304), and *P.Argent. Lat.* 1 (317–324). The brief sections owed to an official in *P.Dura* 59 are also substantially in minuscule.

In all of these, apart from occasional appearances of residual forms of the majuscule, the script can be considered to be minuscule, which takes over definitively from the majuscule in the fourth century. In a petition of Flavius Abinnaeus, *P.Abinn.* 1 (341/342), the new cursive shows all of its characteristics. It is the final result of the evolution of the everyday cursive during the two previous centuries and the product of a more widespread literacy. If only a few examples from this period appear in the documentation, that is due to the dominance of official documents in the Egyptian evidence and to the near absence of the products of everyday writing in the West.

In the period from the late second to the fourth century, the evolution of Latin writing toward the minuscule and its replacement of the majuscule brought about changes as well in the use of more formal scripts, although calligraphic capitals continued to be used in various documents and books. Instances of the latter are the *Feriale Duranum* (*P.Dura* 54, 225–235) and the Aeneid codex *P.Ant.* I 30 (late fourth century). The majuscule still had a long life ahead of it, above all in high-quality books; the great late antique Vergilian codices of Italian origin and preserved in libraries, some of them elegantly illustrated, are sufficient to make the point.

In the skilled hands, minuscule forms *(d, h, q)* appear as early as the second century in the codex *P.Oxy.* I 30, but it is mainly from the third century that they appear ever more frequently alongside the majuscule as the latter falls into disuse. These hands are difficult to categorize, like the *Epitome* of Livy, *P.Oxy.* IV 668, assigned to the third century (but perhaps instead from the third–fourth), which displays a minuscule with traces of the majuscule *(A, G, N)*. Another such hand appears in a fragment of the *Sententiae* of Paul, *CLA* X 1577, and in the liturgical fragment *P.Ryl.* III 472, approximately contemporaneous.[23] Moreover, a number of versions of a genuine minuscule were carried out with slow ductus and more or less marked separation between letters. One example is *PSI* VII 848, as is the codex now in Montserrat, containing Cicero's *Catilinarians,* the so-called Latin *Alcestis,* and a responsory psalm: With these papyri we come to the fourth century. From this point on, especially in the fifth century, "papyrological" material properly speaking is joined by codices and documents preserved continuously in libraries and archives. I can give only a few references to the latter here.

In daily use and private documentation, the new cursive remains the dominant script after the fourth century. Starting in the fifth century, it shows a faster ductus and acquires some new characteristics, like a certain upward direction and a decided slant of the axis to the right. The best examples are not from Egypt but from Italy, particularly Ravenna: *P.Ital.* 1 (445/446), *P.Ital.* 35 (572), and *P.Ital.* 20 (590–602).

Chancery-type stylizations of the same new cursive are found from the fourth–fifth century on in both the East (where Latin continues to be used in bureaucratic practice) and the West.[24] The two regions share certain habits like a rigorously vertical axis, a contrast in size among letters, and a strong prolongation of some hastas even though everything suggests that in other stylistic respects the two differed considerably. In eastern provincial offices, the method of giving a recognizably bureaucratic appearance was making some letters rounder and larger, a trait visible in *P.Vindob.* inv. L 31 (after 386) (figure 5.34), a copy of an imperial rescript made in the office of the prefect of Egypt to be sent to the *praeses Arcadiae*, or in *P.Ryl.* IV 615 (fifth century). In provincial and local offices in the West, by contrast, a certain vertical direction in the writing marked official script, a trait already found in third-century chancery style; to it were added the compression of eyelets and the twisting of hastas, as *ChLA* I 5 (mid-sixth century) shows clearly. In the final analysis, the provincial and municipal offices of the East, like those in the West, were driven to adopt the *litterae communes*, the current minuscule, and to develop new stylistic variants of it in order to give their documents a distinctive graphic physiognomy in the wake of the imperial constitution issued at Trier in 367 (*CTh* 9.19.3), forbidding the use of the *litterae caelestes*, based on the old cursive and now reserved solely for the imperial chancery.

In the stream of formal scripts during the fourth and following centuries, the semiuncial and uncial were dominant. In the East, the semiuncial is attested several times in its variant with the axis leaning to the right. This is apparent in various legal texts, like *P.Bodl.Lat.* class. G 1 (*CLA* II 248; fourth century), *P.Vindob.* inv. L 90 (*CLA* VIII 1042; fourth–fifth century) (figure 5.35), and *P.Ryl.* III 474 and *P.Rein.* inv. 2219 (*CLA* V 700; both sixth century). The same semiuncial also occurs with an upright axis, as normally in the West, but it presents in general a rather crowded appearance, as in *P.Oxy.* 2401, or influences from Greek script as in *P.Oxy.* VI 884, both dated in the fifth–sixth century.

Uncial writing is attested in the papyri from the moment of its creation, but that remains problematic.[25] This script is a mixture of majuscule forms drawn from capitals, some replaced with minuscules (*h*, *p*, *q*, and *u*), and others from characteristic forms of *A*, *D*, *E*, and *M*. Even these last forms, however, appear in the Latin graphic tradition, even if only occasionally. The *D* and the *A* of the uncial can be observed respectively in *P.Oxy.* I 30 (perhaps second century) and *P.Oxy.* IV 668

Figure 5.34. *P.Vindob.* inv. L 31. Photo courtesy of the Papyrussammlung, Österreichische Nationalbibliothek.

Figure 5.35. *P.Vindob.* inv. L 90. Photo courtesy of the Papyrussammlung, Österreichische Nationalbibliothek.

(third–fourth century), while *E* and *M* (the latter still in the process of formation) are attested in *P.Berol.* inv. 6757 (*CLA* VIII 1033) and *P.Vindob.* inv. L 103 (*CLA* X 1537), dated to the beginning of the fourth century or even the end of the third; finally, *A, E,* and *M* appear in uncial form in *P.Oxy.* XI 1379, perhaps also from the start of the fourth century. The uncial seems altogether an artificial script, in which forms from majuscule and minuscule were combined and exhibiting various other influences as well, including possibly even biblical majuscule. The final product is visible in *PSI* XII 1272 (perhaps fifth century) and in manuscripts preserved in libraries (see British Library Add. MS 40165 A.1 [*CLA* II 178; late fourth century] or Marburg, Staatsarchiv Hr 1.1 [*CLA* suppl. 1728; fifth century]). In the East and in papyrological finds, the uncial is attested above all in juristic fragments and in a particular typology that E. A. Lowe has called the "B-R uncial" because of its most characteristic letters: the high *B* and the *R*, with its hasta descending beneath the baseline and its oblique stroke in a horizontal position. Besides various juristic texts one finds it in *PSI* XI 1182 (Gaius), *P.Strasb.* I 6b (Ulpian), *P.Oxy.* XV 1813 (*CTh*), *P.Oxy.* XV 1814 and *PSI* XIII 1347 (*CJ*, first and second editions, respectively), and *P.Ryl.* III 479 and *P.Heid.Lat.* inv. 4 (*CLA* VIII 1221; Justinian's *Digest*). All of these are dated to the Justinianic era or close to it and are written in a very formal B-R uncial. At the same time, other examples, although inspired by this uncial, display forms (e.g., *m* or *d* of minuscule type) that diverge from it.

The rupture between the East and the West that developed after Justinian and was concluded in the reign of Heraclius led to the disappearance of Latin writing in the eastern provinces of the empire.

NOTES

1. For further discussion of Greek writing see Schubart 1911, 1925; Norsa 1929, 1931; Roberts 1956; Cavallo 1967, 1983, 2005; Seider 1967, 1970, 1972, 1975, 1978, 1981, 1990; Turner 1987; Cavallo and Maehler 1987; Crisci 1996; Cavallo, Crisci, Messeri, and Pintaudi, eds. 1998; for Latin writing see *CLA* I–XI and suppl.; *ChLA* I–XLIX; Mallon, Marichal, and Perrat 1939; Marichal 1948; Mallon 1952, 1982; Tjäder 1955, 1982; Cencetti 1993. Printed reproductions of the papyri cited can easily be found by consulting the Leuven Database of Ancient Books (LDAB) and the Heidelberger Gesamtverzeichnis der griechischen Papyrusurkunden Ägyptens (HGV), both available online.

2. Cribiore (1996, especially 97–118).

3. Besides the classic work of Turner (1978), see most recently Messeri (2005).

4. On the oldest Greek writing on papyrus, see particularly Turner (1980) and Crisci (1999).

5. Messeri and Pintaudi (1998, 41–43).

6. Crisci (1996, 17–18).

7. Bastianini and Gallazzi (2001, 17).

8. On the evolution of these letters see Petrucci (1991, 472–477).

9. Crisci (1996, 44–49, 137–141).

10. Kern (1913, 48).

11. See Cavallo (1967); an update on biblical majuscule appears in Orsini (2005).

12. On the Alexandrian majuscule, besides Cavallo (2005) see Porro (1985).

13. Crisci (1996, 84–85).

14. On upright ogival majuscule see Crisci (1985).

15. Crisci (1996, 79–84).

16. Morelli (*CPR XXII*, 7) has called attention to these differences.

17. On the writing of these documents see De Gregorio (2000, 93–94).

18. Petronio Nicolai (1973) and Radiciotti (1998) have made studies of this type of capital.

19. See most recently Capasso (2003).

20. Besides Cencetti (1993), see Casamassima and Staraz (1977) and Tjäder (1979).

21. Marichal (1992, 182–188).

22. Petrucci (1962); Marichal (1988).

23. Marichal (1956).

24. On chancery stylization, besides Mallon (1982), Cencetti (1993), and Cavallo (2005), see Kresten (1966).

25. See at least Tjäder (1974).

BIBLIOGRAPHY

Bastianini, G., and C. Gallazzi. 2001. *Posidippo di Pella: Epigrammi (P. Mil. Vogl. VIII 309)*. Milan: Edizioni Universitarie Lettere Economia Diritto.

Capasso, M. 2003. *Il ritorno di Cornelio Gallo: Il papiro di Qaṣr Ibrîm venticinque anni dopo*. With a contribution by P. Radiciotti. Naples: Graus.

Casamassima, E., and E. Staraz. 1977. "Varianti e cambio grafico nella scrittura dei papiri latini. Note paleografiche." *Scrittura e civiltà* 1: 9–110.

Cavallo, G. 1967. *Ricerche sulla maiuscola biblica*. Florence: Le Monnier.

——. 1983. *Libri scritture scribi a Ercolano*. Naples: Macchiaroli.

——. 2005. *Il calamo e il papiro: La scrittura greca dall'età ellenistica ai primi secoli di Bisanzio*. Florence: Gonnelli.

——, E. Crisci, G. Messeri, and R. Pintaudi, eds. 1998. *Scrivere libri e documenti nel mondo antico*. Florence: Gonnelli.

Cavallo, G., and H. Maehler. 1987. *Greek Bookhands of the Early Byzantine Period*, A.D. 300–800. London: University of London. Institute of Classical Studies.

Cencetti, G. 1993. *Scritti di paleografia*, ed. G. Nicolaj. Dietikon-Zürich: Urs Graf Verlag.

Cribiore, R. 1996. *Writing, Teachers, and Students in Graeco-Roman Egypt*. Atlanta: Scholars Press.

Crisci, E. 1985. "La maiuscola ogivale diritta: Origine, tipologie, dislocazioni." *Scrittura e civiltà* 9: 103–145.

——. 1996. *Scrivere greco fuori d'Egitto: Ricerche sui manoscritti greco-orientali di origine non egiziana dal IV secolo a. C. all'VIII d. C.* Florence: Gonnelli.

——. 1999. "I più antichi libri greci: Note bibliologiche e paleografiche su rotoli papiracei del IV–III secolo A.C." *Scrittura e civiltà* 23: 29–62.

De Gregorio, G. 2000. "Materiali vecchi e nuovi per uno studio della minuscola greca fra VII e IX secolo." In *I manoscritti greci tra riflessione e dibattito: Atti del V Colloquio Internazionale di paleografia greca (Cremona, 4–10 ottobre 1998)*, ed. G. Prato, vol. 1, 83–151. Florence: Gonnelli.

Kern, O. 1913. *Inscriptiones graecae*. Bonn: Marcus and Weber.

Kresten, O. 1966. "Diplomatische Auszeichnungsschriften in Spätantike und Frühmittelalter." *Mitteilungen des Instituts für österreichische Geschichtsforschung* 74: 9–40.

Mallon, J. 1952. *Paléographie romaine*. Madrid: Consejo Superior de Investigaciones Cientificas.

———. 1982. *De l'écriture: Recueil d'études publiées de 1937 à 1981*. Paris: Éditions du Centre National de la Recherche Scientifique.

Mallon, J., R. Marichal, and C. Perrat. 1939. *L'écriture latine de la capitale romaine à la minuscule*. Paris: Arts et Métiers Graphiques.

Marichal, R. 1948. "De la capitale romaine à la minuscule." In *Somme typographique*, ed. M. Audin, vol. 1, *Les origines*, 61–111. Paris: Audin Editeur.

———. 1950. "L'écriture latine et l'écriture grecque du Ier au VIe siècle." *L'antiquité classique* 19: 113–144.

———. 1956. "L'écriture du Paul de Leyde." In *Pauli Sententiarum Fragmentum Leidense (Cod. Leid. B. P. L. 2589)*, ed. G. G. Archi, M. David, E. Levy, R. Marichal, and H. L. V. Nelson, 24–57. Leiden: Brill.

———. 1988. *Les graffites de La Graufesenque*. Paris: Éditions du Centre National de la Recherche Scientifique.

———. 1992. *Les ostraka de Bu Njem*. Tripoli: Grande Jamahira Arabe, Libyenne, Populaire et Socialiste, Département des Antiquités.

Messeri, G. 2005. "Relazioni fra papiri documentari e papiri letterari." *Nea Rhome* 2: 5–23.

Messeri, G., and R. Pintaudi. 1998. "Documenti e scritture." In *Scrivere libri: 39–53*.

———. 2000. "I papiri greci d'Egitto e la minuscola libraria." In *I manoscritti greci tra riflessione e dibattito: Atti del V Colloquio Internazionale di paleografia greca (Cremona, 4–10 ottobre 1998)*, ed. G. Prato, vol. 1, 67–82. Florence: Gonnelli.

Norsa, M. 1929. *Papiri greci delle collezioni italiane: Scritture documentarie dal III secolo a. C. al secolo VIII d. C.* Rome: Istituto di Filologia Classica.

———. 1939. *La scrittura letteraria greca dal secolo IV a. C. all'VIII d. C.* Florence: Tipografia E. Ariani.

Orsini, P. 2005. *Manoscritti in maiuscola biblica: materiali per un aggiornamento*. Cassino: Edizioni dell'Università degli Studi di Cassino.

Pack, R. A. 1965. *The Greek and Latin Literary Texts from Greco-Roman Egypt*, 2nd ed. Ann Arbor: University of Michigan Press.

Petronio Nicolai, G. 1973. "Osservazioni sul canone della capitale libraria romana fra I e III secolo." In *Miscellanea in memoria di Giorgio Cencetti*, 3–28. Turin: Bottega d'Erasmo.

Petrucci, A. 1962. "Per la storia della scrittura romana: i graffiti di Condatomagos." *Bullettino dell'Archivio Paleografico Italiano* 3(1): 85–132.

———. 1991. "Paleografia greca e paleografia latina: significato e limiti di un confronto." In *Paleografia e codicologia greca: Atti del II Colloquio internazionale (Berlino-Wolfenbüttel, 17–21 ottobre 1983)*, ed. D. Harlfinger and G. Prato, 463–484. Alessandria: Edizioni dell'Orso.

Porro, A. 1985. "Manoscritti in maiuscola alessandrina di contenuto profano: Aspetti grafici codicologici filologici." *Scrittura e civiltà* 9: 169–215.

Radiciotti, P. 1998. "Osservazioni paleografiche sui papiri latini di Ercolano." *Scrittura e civiltà* 22: 353–370.

Roberts, C. H. 1956. *Greek Literary Hands, 350 B.C.–A.D. 400*, 2d ed. Oxford: Clarendon.

Schubart, W. 1911. *Papyri Graecae Berolinenses*. Bonn: Marcus & Weber.

——. 1925. *Griechische Palaeographie*. Munich: Beck.

Seider, R. 1967. *Paläographie der griechischen Papyri*, vol. 1, *Tafeln*, Part 1, *Urkunden*. Stuttgart: Hiersemann.

——. 1970. *Paläographie der griechischen Papyri*, vol. 2, *Tafeln*, Part 2, *Literarische Papyri*. Stuttgart: Hiersemann.

——. 1972. *Paläographie der lateinischen Papyri*, vol. 1, *Tafeln*, Part 1, *Urkunden*. Stuttgart: Hiersemann.

——. 1975. "Zur Paläographie der frühen lateinischen Papyri." In *Proceedings of the XIV International Congress of Papyrologists*, 277–284. London: Egypt Exploration Society.

——. 1978. *Paläographie der lateinischen Papyri*, vol. 2.1, *Tafeln*, Part 2.1: *Literarische Papyri*. Stuttgart: Hiersemann.

——. 1981. *Paläographie der lateinischen Papyri*, vol. 2.2, *Tafeln*, Part 2.2: *Literarische Papyri*. Stuttgart: Hiersemann.

——. 1990. *Paläographie der griechischen Papyri*, vol. 3.1, *Text*, Part 1: *Urkundenschrift I. Mit einer Vorgeschichte zur Paläographie der griechischen Papyri*. Stuttgart: Hiersemann.

Tjäder, J.-O. 1955. *Die nichtliterarische lateinischen Papyri Italiens aus der Zeit 445–700*, vol. 1. Lund: Gleerup.

——. 1979. "Considerazioni e proposte sulla scrittura latina nell'età romana." In *Paleographica Diplomatica et Archivistica: Studi in onore di Giulio Battelli*, vol. 1, 31–62. Rome: Edizioni di Storia e Letteratura.

——. 1982. *Die nichtliterarische lateinischen Papyri Italiens aus der Zeit 445–700*, vol. 2. Stockholm: Aströms Förlag.

Turner, E. G. 1978. *The Terms Recto and Verso: The Anatomy of the Papyrus Roll*. Brussels: Fondation Égyptologique Reine Élisabeth.

——. 1980. "Ptolemaic Bookhands and Lille Stesichorus." *Scrittura e civiltà* 4: 19–40.

——. 1987. *Greek Manuscripts of the Ancient World*, 2d ed., ed. P. J. Parsons. London: University of London, Institute of Classical Studies.

Van Haelst, J. 1976. *Catalogue des papyrus littéraires juifs et chrétiens*. (Papyrologie, 1). Paris: Publications de la Sorbonne.

CHAPTER 6

THE GREEK AND LATIN LANGUAGES IN THE PAPYRI

ELEANOR DICKEY

INTRODUCTION

For the first thousand years after the end of the classical period, documentary papyri constitute our most important source of information on the development of the Greek language.[1] Papyri are also significant for our understanding of the development of Latin but less so, owing to the much smaller number of surviving Latin papyri and to the preservation of considerable amounts of subliterary Latin in other forms such as the Vindolanda writing tablets. By contrast, Greek writing tablets rarely survive, so that the vast majority of our extant corpus of subliterary Hellenistic and Roman Greek comes from documents written on papyri or ostraca in Egypt.

The Greek in which these documents were written is considered to be a form of koinê Greek. Koinê was created when the Macedonians exported an Ionicized form of the Attic dialect to their newly conquered empire and used it as the language of government and upper-class society. Most Hellenistic and some Roman-period Greek literature is also in koinê; thus, literary texts as disparate as Polybius's histories and the New Testament fall into this category. The Greek of the documentary papyri has some features in common with these literary texts, but in many respects it is considerably different from them.

Postclassical literature in both Greek and Latin tended to take the classical model as a goal to be imitated linguistically. The languages, as they were learned by children and used in ordinary conversation, were constantly evolving; this is a natural and inevitable process common to all languages. But authors of literary texts did not attempt to write in the language of everyday conversation; rather, they aimed at stylistic norms that in many cases had been established centuries earlier. Some Roman-period authors wrote in nearly flawless imitations of classical Attic, and others used a language that made more concessions to subsequent changes, but none of them reflected the contemporary spoken idiom. Writers of private documents such as letters, on the other hand, often used a language much closer to that of ordinary conversation and so reveal to us the changes that their language had undergone. Of course, such was not their intent; writing that simply reflected speech was stigmatized as a mark of lack of education, and the writers of papyrus documents usually tried hard to use classical spelling and grammar. It is their failures in this respect that have the most to teach us.

Literary papyri offer a different kind of insight into language. Some contain glossaries or linguistic commentary on particular texts, while others have been annotated with accents or other marks that enable us to know how their writers understood particular words and phrases. Such marks may also tell us how their writers pronounced words or thought they should be pronounced in classical usage.

GREEK PHONOLOGY

Since the fifth century BCE profound changes have occurred in the way the Greek language is pronounced.[2] Ancient Greek was on the whole written phonetically at the time the alphabet was originally introduced, and for a few centuries thereafter spelling tended to change to keep up with pronunciation, as is evident from surviving archaic inscriptions. After the classical period, however, spelling was largely standardized, and much of that standardization has persisted even to the present day despite major changes in pronunciation. (Something similar has occurred in English, where spellings standardized centuries ago are still the norm, but the English spelling system differs from the Greek both in having been standardized for a much shorter period of time and in having been less phonetic to begin with.) Thus, the letters ι, η, and υ, which originally represented very different sounds, are all pronounced the same way in the modern language, and the original diphthongs η, ει, οι, and υι are also pronounced like ι, η, and υ.

Before the discovery of the papyri there was considerable debate about the history of the Greek sound system. When Western scholars first rediscovered

ancient Greek, they initially shared the assumption of their Greek contemporaries that the ancient language must have been pronounced like modern (i.e.,
Renaissance) Greek. Soon, however, examination of ancient onomatopoeic
words and of transliterations between Greek and languages written in other
scripts (such as Latin and Aramaic) made it clear that Greek is no exception to
the general rule that the pronunciation of languages changes over time.[3] Progress
in determining the starting point of the changes, the sound system of the fifth
century BCE, was rapid, and the stage they had reached by the early modern period
(i.e., the Greek of Erasmus's contemporaries) had long been known. But until
significant numbers of papyrus documents became available for linguistic analysis,
scholars had very little understanding of how and when the different changes
took place.

The writers of papyrus documents were not trying to revise the spelling system
or to write phonetically; they attempted to use classical spellings, just as writers of
modern English attempt to use our standardized spelling system. But when the
same sound is spelled differently in different words (as is usually the case in a
language where sound change has led to the merging of two originally distinct
sounds), poor spellers have a tendency to confuse them and write one where they
intend the other. The misspellings thus produced can provide valuable clues about
homophony to someone without direct access to the spoken language. Thus a
linguist who had never heard English spoken but possessed a large corpus of letters
written by a representative cross-section of our society would quickly conclude
from the errors they contained that the same sound may be represented in English
by both *c* and *s* or by both *ie* and *ei*.

Fortunately for us, many Greek papyri were written by poor spellers, and their
errors provide the vast majority of our evidence for the pronunciation changes and
their chronology. Unfortunately, the interpretation of the evidence is not always
straightforward. When a spelling confusion is widespread, it clearly shows that the
sound change causing it had taken place in the community concerned. But what do
sporadic misspellings prove? They could be the few clues provided by a generally
well-educated group to changes that had indeed taken place but were almost never
visible in writing because of the writers' high level of education. Or they could
result from very different causes: a slip of the pen, a personal idiosyncrasy, a
foreigner's imperfect command of Greek. Sporadic misspellings are not uncommon in the papyri, and when they suggest sound changes that clearly have not
taken place in modern Greek, they are usually dismissed as not representative of the
spoken language. When rare misspellings are early examples of changes that later
become widespread, however, it is harder to know how seriously to take them.
There are thus several possible datings for most Greek sound changes, one the
point at which the first misspellings indicating that change are documented, the
other the point at which such misspellings become common; these points may
differ by several centuries.[4]

Vowels

The greatest changes involved the vowel system. During the Ptolemaic period the long diphthongs ᾳ, ῃ, and ῳ came to be pronounced like the simple long vowels ā, η, and ω. The ι of these diphthongs, which is now written subscript following a Byzantine convention, was written as a full letter in antiquity. After it ceased to be pronounced it was often omitted in writing, but sometimes it was written hyper-correctly after a long vowel that had never been a diphthong (e.g., ἐρωτῶι for ἐρωτῶ, "I ask"). The fact that the misspelling goes in both directions is the best proof of the complete merger of the sounds concerned. Also datable to the Ptolemaic period is the merger of ει and ι, which allowed either one to be written for the other (e.g., εἴνα for ἵνα, ἰς for εἰς).

The dating of the other vowel changes is disputed, as the papyrus evidence is not conclusive (and occasionally conflicts with evidence from transliterations, particularly those made elsewhere in the Greek-speaking world). A loss of distinctions of vowel length led to the merger of ο and ω; the diphthong οι merged with υ, and the short diphthong αι merged with ε, so that, for example, the verb endings -εσθαι (infinitive) and -εσθε (second-person plural) became confusable. These changes are normally dated to the second century CE, when the relevant mis-spellings become common, but it has also been argued that they started in the Ptolemaic period. Also traditionally dated to the Roman period is the merger of η and ι, but this change could be dated to the Byzantine period instead. Some Roman-period papyri also show confusion between υ and ι; it is, however, thought that this change may have been a peculiarity of Egypt that was not generalized in other parts of the Greek-speaking world until the Byzantine period.

Another vowel change of disputed date is the shift in the nature of the accent from a pitch accent to a stress accent. It is generally believed that this change was related to the loss of distinctive vowel length and the confusion between ο and ω, though there is disagreement about which change brought about the other. It is therefore likely that the accent shift occurred during the Roman period, but arguments in favor of an earlier dating have also been advanced. The change of the accent is not directly reflected in writing: not only are accents not normally written in documentary papyri, but when they were written, the same accent marks were used before and for many centuries after the accent shift. Nevertheless, the presence of a stress accent can sometimes be detected in late written texts by the omission of unaccented vowels, a process that can be caused by stress accents but not by pitch accents.

Consonants

Many of the consonants also changed their pronunciations radically, but because they remained distinct from one another, these changes did not on the whole lead to spelling confusions. Papyrus evidence is thus less important for our understanding of the consonant system than of the vowel system. Evidence for pronunciation changes affecting consonants can be found in transliterations, as when Latin or other foreign words are rendered into Greek; occasionally entire passages of Latin are written in Greek script by writers who knew how to speak Latin but not how to write it. Latin pronunciation, of course, also changed over time, and sometimes the same spellings can serve as evidence for either language or both: for example, when the Greek letter β is used to represent the Latin consonantal *u*, it tells us either that the Greek letter was no longer pronounced like our *b* or that the Latin letter was no longer pronounced like our *w* or both.[5]

The major consonant changes were the transformation of the voiced stops β, γ, and δ to voiced fricatives (e.g., δ pronounced like the *th* in *there* rather than like our *d*) and of the aspirated stops θ, ϕ, and χ to voiceless fricatives (e.g., ϕ pronounced like our *f* rather than our *p + h*). Double consonants ceased to be pronounced differently from single ones, so a general confusion of single and double letters (e.g., λ for $\lambda\lambda$ and vice versa) occurred. All these changes probably took place during the Roman or early Byzantine periods, but another one, that of ζ from a double consonant *zd* to a single fricative like our *z*, was probably Ptolemaic.

One change that did affect spelling was the weakening of the pronunciation of final *-ν*. In modern Greek *ν* has tended to disappear at the ends of words, so that the nominative and the accusative of second-declension neuter nouns ends in *-o*, as does (usually) the accusative of masculine second-declension nouns. This process was not completed until after the period represented by the papyri, but the weakened pronunciation is reflected in the fact that final *-ν* is sometimes omitted in the papyri.

Initial *h*, represented by a rough breathing in modern texts of ancient Greek and in many literary papyri, was not normally written in documentary papyri. Certain final consonants, however, were aspirated if the following word began with *h*; thus, one would expect οὐκ αὐτός but οὐχ οὗτος (similarly κατ' and καθ', ἀπ' and ἀφ', etc.). During the Roman period the writing of such aspiration becomes erratic, with οὐκ and so on not infrequently appearing before words that originally started with *h-* and οὐχ and so on before those that originally did not. Such spellings suggest that the writers no longer pronounced *h* at all and that their aspirations were the result of training in spelling (or, in the case of incorrect aspirations, hypercorrection). Something similar happens with Greek words borrowed into Coptic: hori, the Coptic equivalent of *h*, may be either used or omitted both where classical Greek had an *h* and where it did not, but the correct use of hori is frequent enough to indicate that, even as late as the third century CE, educated writers were still aware of which words began with *h* in classical Greek.

GREEK MORPHOLOGY AND SYNTAX

During the period for which we have papyrus evidence, the complex grammar of classical Greek underwent a radical process of simplification.[6] Some of that simplification was directly related to the phonological changes just described, for the vowel mergers sometimes caused different grammatical forms to be pronounced the same. For example, the vowel changes caused frequent homophony between the aorist subjunctive and the future indicative, and this in turn led to confusion of the two even in verbs where they had remained phonologically distinct.

At the same time, none of the changes affecting Greek grammar were universal. Just as the writers of some papyrus documents were sufficiently educated to avoid betraying their pronunciation by misspelling words, so there were some, even at late periods, who displayed a command of grammatical forms that had long since disappeared from the language of the less educated.

The morphology of nouns and adjectives was eventually simplified along two dimensions: a reduction in the number of distinct cases commonly used and a decrease in the number of different endings for each case. The case that was ultimately lost was the dative, which had more or less died out by the Byzantine period. It is generally believed that the papyri show early evidence of this loss, and sometimes (particularly in the later Roman period) one finds other cases used where one would have expected a dative in classical Greek. But for most of the period for which we have papyrus evidence, datives are in fact common in documentary papyri. The reduction of endings is more obvious in our documents; it was effected partly by the replacement of morphologically difficult words with ones of more regular formation (e.g., παῖς, παιδός was largely supplanted by παιδίον, παιδίου, which lost its diminutive force) and partly by the reconfiguration of the paradigms of existing words.

Third-declension nouns and adjectives often borrowed endings from the first and second declensions; this tendency eventually led to the almost complete loss of the third declension as a separate entity, though this final stage postdates the papyri. The most common such change is the addition of -ν to the -α of the third-declension accusative singular (e.g., μητέραν as the accusative of μήτηρ). A genitive singular in -ου is also attested, particularly for words that originally had a genitive in -ους (e.g., ἔτου as the genitive of ἔτος). Third-declension names in -ης were particularly likely to be declined like first-declension names in -ης; thus, one finds Σωκράτου, Σωκράτηι, and Σωκράτην as oblique forms of Σωκράτης, alongside the more traditional Σωκράτους, Σωκράτει, and Σωκράτη. In addition, the third-declension nominative plural ending -ες started to spread to the accusative plural (e.g., τὰς γυναῖκες), where it would eventually replace the classical -ας completely.

There was also a general tendency for unusual noun and adjective paradigms to be regularized and for the different declensional types within each declension to merge with one another. Thus, the Attic second declension (e.g., νεώς "temple") largely disappeared in favor of the normal second-declension inflection (e.g., $\bar{\nu}\alpha\acute{o}s$), and in the first declension, nouns and adjectives in -α may appear with stems in -η (e.g., $\mu o\acute{\iota}\rho\eta s$ as genitive of $\mu o\hat{\iota}\rho\alpha$, $\mu\iota\kappa\rho\hat{\eta}s$ as genitive of $\mu\iota\kappa\rho\acute{\alpha}$), or occasionally vice versa, while the distinctive -ου genitive of the first-declension masculines sometimes disappears. Contracted nouns and adjectives are occasionally found in their uncontracted forms (e.g., $\chi\acute{\alpha}\lambda\kappa\epsilon os$ for $\chi\alpha\lambda\kappa o\hat{\upsilon}s$). In the third declension one finds a preference for more regular forms such as $\chi\acute{\alpha}\rho\iota\tau\alpha$ rather than $\chi\acute{\alpha}\rho\iota\nu$ as the accusative singular of $\chi\acute{\alpha}\rho\iota s$ and for regularizations such as $\mu\acute{\epsilon}\rho os$ instead of $\mu\acute{\epsilon}\rho o\upsilon s$ as the genitive singular of $\mu\acute{\epsilon}\rho os$.

Two-termination adjectives may have a separate feminine in the papyri. Thus where Attic has masculine/feminine $\phi\rho\acute{o}\nu\iota\mu os$, neuter $\phi\rho\acute{o}\nu\iota\mu o\nu$, papyri sometimes have $\phi\rho\acute{o}\nu\iota\mu os$, $\phi\rho o\nu\acute{\iota}\mu\eta$, $\phi\rho\acute{o}\nu\iota\mu o\nu$. On the other hand, the masculine forms of active participles are often used for the feminine in papyri (e.g., $\acute{\eta}$ $\acute{o}\mu o\lambda o\gamma\hat{\omega}\nu$ for $\acute{\eta}$ $\acute{o}\mu o\lambda o\gamma o\hat{\upsilon}\sigma\alpha$[7]). Though these changes appear to go in opposite directions, both are fundamentally regularizations, as the first assimilates a minority group to the larger category of first- and second-declension adjectives, and the latter does the same with a minority group of third-declension adjectives.

Comparatives and especially superlatives are very common in the papyri, especially in the Byzantine period, indicating that their marginalization in modern Greek was a later phenomenon. But they are not always formed as they would have been in the classical period. Irregular comparative and superlative forms are often replaced by formations in -$\tau\epsilon\rho os$ and -$\tau\alpha\tau os$ (e.g., $\acute{\alpha}\gamma\alpha\theta\acute{\omega}\tau\alpha\tau os$ instead of $\acute{\alpha}\rho\iota\sigma\tau os$ as the superlative of $\acute{\alpha}\gamma\alpha\theta\acute{o}s$), and it was also possible to add these regular suffixes to the existing irregular forms (e.g., $\mu\epsilon\iota\zeta\acute{o}\tau\epsilon\rho os$, $\mu\epsilon\gamma\iota\sigma\tau\acute{o}\tau\alpha\tau os$ instead of $\mu\epsilon\acute{\iota}\zeta\omega\nu$, $\mu\acute{\epsilon}\gamma\iota\sigma\tau os$ as the comparative and superlative of $\mu\acute{\epsilon}\gamma\alpha s$).

Most of the simplifications occurred in the verb system, however, as this was more complex to begin with. Once again simplification involved both a reduction in the number of different grammatical forms each verb could have and a decrease in the number of different endings employed by various verbs to indicate those forms. The complexity of the verbal system as a whole was diminished by the decline of the optative mood, middle voice, and perfect tense. These losses were gradual, and none of them was completed within the period of the papyri; even the optative, which started to disappear well before the end of the Ptolemaic period, is sometimes used by well-educated writers of documentary papyri, and middle forms are not infrequent (though they sometimes need a reflexive pronoun to clarify their meaning). The loss of the perfect was particularly complex. It began in the Ptolemaic period with a loss of the distinction in meaning between aorist and perfect, so that either tense could be used in place of the other. For a while this merger resulted in an increased use of the perfect, but eventually the aorist, which had always been more common, prevailed, and the perfect largely disappeared from use. A periphrastic formation using a perfect or an aorist participle and the verb "be" came to fill the function originally performed by the old perfects, and the beginnings of that development are evident in some papyri.

The morphological alterations of the moods and tenses that remained were extensive. Verbs with irregular principal parts often developed new, more predictable stems (e.g., ἦξα and ἔλειψα instead of ἤγαγον and ἔλιπον as aorists of ἄγω and λείπω), a process that largely eliminated types like contract futures and root aorists (i.e., the ἔβην type). There was widespread amalgamation of endings, so that both first and second aorist endings were used for both types of aorist and for the perfect and imperfect. Thus, one finds forms like ἦλθα and ἔλαβα (for second aorists ἦλθον and ἔλαβον), ἔλεγαν (for imperfect third plural ἔλεγον), ἔγραψες (for first aorist ἔγραψας), and δέδωκες and εἴληφαν (for perfects δέδωκας and εἰλήφασι). The equivalence in meaning between perfect and aorist led to widespread morphological confusion, so that, in addition to the confusion of endings with both the aorists, perfects could be formed with an augment instead of reduplication (and sometimes aorists with reduplication instead of an augment), and so forth. The different types of contract verbs also showed a tendency to be conflated, particularly by the spread of the -εω endings to the -αω verbs (e.g., ἀγαποῦμεν for ἀγαπῶμεν), and the number of -οω contract verbs increased. In addition, the athematic (-μι) verbs started taking the same endings as the thematic (-ω) verbs, a tendency that eventually led to the complete loss of their distinctive conjugation.

Augments are sometimes omitted; this tendency was no doubt fueled by phonological changes such as the loss of distinction between o and ω, but it extended into verbs for which no phonological explanation is possible. Confusion over the use of the augment also led to the occasional use of augments on forms where they did not belong (e.g., subjunctive ἠξήλθης for ἐξέλθης).

The future had particular difficulties. Phonological changes led to a homophony of future forms such as πέμψεις, πέμψει, and πέμψομεν with aorist subjunctives such as πέμψῃς, πέμψῃ, and πέμψωμεν (the first person singular πέμψω had been homophonous from the beginning). In some verbs the future and the aorist had different stems, but the tendency to regularize principal parts reduced the number of those verbs. Because of ambiguity, the old future forms became difficult to use and were eventually replaced by periphrases with auxiliaries such as μέλλω or, much later, θέλω ἵνα plus subjunctive.

Though the overall decline in the use of non-indicative forms meant that morphological confusions were more immediately obvious in the indicative than elsewhere, the changes in non-indicative forms were even greater than those in the indicative. Present or future indicative forms were often used where we would expect subjunctives, seemingly indicating a genuine decline in the use of the subjunctive as well as phonological confusion. Imperatives underwent widespread alteration. Infinitive forms were particularly liable to confusion, so that endings appropriate to one tense are frequently found on stems appropriate to another tense, and a number of different tenses started to form an infinitive in -ει or -εν (e.g., πέμψεν as [aorist?] infinitive of πέμπω).

The morphological changes in the Greek of the papyri are often considered to be purely simplifications of the classical language, and as we have seen this generalization is largely true. Nonetheless, not every change was a simplification. One that went in the other direction was the creation of a new class of nouns in -ις (masculine) or -ιν (neuter), genitive -ιου, dative -ιῳ, and accusative -ιν. These were formed by dropping the ο from second-declension nouns in -ιος and -ιον; some have survived into modern Greek as nouns in -ι. Thus, the title κύριος can be found with the nominative κῦρις, accusative κῦριν, and vocative κῦρι, and ἀργύριον can become ἀργύριν.

GREEK VOCABULARY

The words that occur in documentary papyri are often unfamiliar to readers used to classical Attic. Some of the difference is an inevitable result of the subject matter: Egyptian documents often refer to physical, social, or political matters that did not exist in classical Athens and for which there were, consequently, no Attic words. Not all the new vocabulary can be explained in this fashion, however. Some classical words (particularly those that posed morphological difficulties) fell into disuse and were replaced by existing synonyms or by newer, often morphologically more regular, terms. Other ancient words survived but changed their meanings significantly. In many cases the vocabulary shifts visible in the papyri also turn up in low-register literature such as the New Testament, and not infrequently their results have persisted into modern Greek.

Thus, in the papyri, classical βούλομαι ("want") is marginalized by its synonym (ἐ)θέλω, while αἰσχύνομαι ("be ashamed") is starting to be replaced by the newer ἐντρέπομαι.[8] The classical word for "one," εἷς can be used like an indefinite article ("a," "an"), and the definite article (ὁ, ἡ, τό) is often used for the relative pronoun (ὅς, ἥ, ὅ). The pronoun αὐτός, which in classical Attic had an intensifying force in the nominative and so could be used as a simple anaphoric pronoun (i.e., as an equivalent of "him," "her," "them," etc.) only in the oblique cases, came to be used anaphorically in the nominative as well. Some distinctions were lost; for example, the pronoun ἕτερος, which originally meant "the other of two," became indistinguishable from ἄλλος, "other" of any number.

Prepositions are used more often in the papyri than in classical Greek and in new ways; some constructions that were originally expressed without a preposition, such as the partitive genitive or the genitive of price, are likely to use a preposition in papyrus documents. Thus, ἀπό plus genitive can replace the partitive genitive; ἐκ plus genitive, the genitive of price; διά plus genitive, the dative of means, and so on. There is also a loss of distinction between certain prepositions, so that εἰς can be used for ἐν, ἀπό for ἐκ, διά for περί, and so forth.

Many of these changes were the result of the language's natural development, which would have resulted in vocabulary changes even if Greek had been entirely isolated, but there were also pressures on postclassical Greek from the other languages with which it was in contact. The papyri show considerable evidence of influence from these languages. One major source of new vocabulary, particularly in the Ptolemaic period, was the local Egyptian language. Though the vast majority of preserved papyri are written in Greek, and though it is clear that Greek was the dominant language of both administration and culture beginning with the Macedonian conquest of Egypt, many Egyptian terms had to be taken into the language in order to describe pre-existing physical and cultural realities. In addition to Egyptian personal and place names, we find Egyptian months, Egyptian deities, and so on.

An even larger, but somewhat later, source of new vocabulary was Latin. Latin loanwords start appearing in the papyri in the second century BCE and become common after the Roman conquest in the later first century BCE; at their peak in the fourth and sixth centuries CE there is an average of one attestation of a loanword per preserved documentary fragment. Although Greek remained the language of most provincial administration after the Roman conquest, the presence of Roman officials and in particular of the Roman army introduced a large body of new terminology. This included titles such as Αὔγουστος (*Augustus*), military designations such as κεντυρίων (*centurio*), and eventually currency terms such as δηνάριον (*denarius*). The writers of some papyri, particularly in the later Roman period, used Latin loanwords even when a common Greek alternative was available: βέστη (*vestis*), πραῖδα (*praeda*), and ὅσπες (*hospes*).[9]

In many cases, however, the external influence on Greek was more subtle. Many Roman concepts were expressed either by the creation of new words from Greek roots and affixes or by the adaptation of older Greek words to new uses. Some of the most important Roman concepts had two representations in Greek, one a direct borrowing and one a Greek adaptation; thus we also find σεβαστός for *Augustus* and ἑκατόνταρχος for *centurio*. (For many words the Greek forms appear earlier than the direct borrowings and are commoner in the early imperial period, while the direct borrowings become more prevalent in later centuries, but this pattern is not always followed.) Other concepts were always represented primarily by an adapted Greek word, such as ὕπατος for *consul* or the address κύριε for *domine*.[10]

A SAMPLE GREEK DOCUMENT

This letter (*P.Oxy.* LXVII 4627) was written in the late third century CE and found at Oxyrhynchus; we know nothing about either the writer or the recipient beyond what we can deduce from the letter itself. Word divisions, capitalization, punctuation, accents, and breathings are editorial additions.

κυρίω μου ἀδελφῶ Ἱερακαπόλλωνι
Σερῆνος χαίρειν.
θαυμάζω 'πῶς' μέχρι σήμερον παρὰ σεαυ-
τῷ μεμένηκας. οὐκ εἰς ὀλίγην
5   γάρ με ἀγωνίαν ἐνέβαλας τοῦτο
ποιήσας. κἂν νῦν τοίνυν ἢ ταχέως κατάλαβέ με ἢ γράψον
μοι τί ἐστιν τὸ βράδος, πρό γε
δὲ πάντων περὶ τῆς σωτηρί-
10   ας ὑμῶν καὶ περὶ ὧν ἐνταῦ-
θα χρήζεται. ἀσπάζομαι τὴν
κυρίαν μου ἀδελφὴν καὶ τὴν κυρίαν μου μητέρα καὶ πάντας τοὺς
ἡμῶν. ἐρρῶσθαι ὑμᾶς εὔχομαι
15   πολλοῖς χρόνοις.
[date]   Παχὼν κ'
[address]   κυρίω μου ἀδελφῶι Ἱερακαπόλλωνι Σαράμμων.

To my lord brother Hierakapollon, Serenus [sends] greetings. I am surprised how you have stayed at your own place until today. For you threw me into not a little anguish by doing this. So even now [i.e., late as it is] either come quickly to me or write to me what the delay is, and at least before all [write] about your [pl.] health and about what you need [from?] here. I greet my lady sister and my lady mother and all our people. I pray that you [pl.] be well for many years.
[Written on the] 20th [day of the month] Pachon.
Sarammon [writes] to my lord brother Hierakapollon.

The letter was written by a relatively well-educated man (note his use of particles such as γε and γάρ, which are not common in papyrus letters); nevertheless, it shows several spelling errors characteristic of papyrus documents. Iota adscript is usually missing (κυρίω(ι)and ἀδελφῶ(ι) in line 1, σεαυτῷ(ι) in lines 3–4, etc.), but it is written correctly in one of the two datives in the address (ἀδελφῶι, but note the lack of iota in κυρίω(ι) two words earlier). There is also an interchange of αι and ε (χρήζεται for χρήζετε in line 11) and a morphological slip (ἐνέβαλας for second aorist ἐνέβαλες in line 5). The σ of σήμερον is not an error but one of the Ionic elements characteristic of the koinê dialect; the Attic form would be τήμερον.

But spelling and morphology are only a small part of what makes this letter immediately recognizable as a papyrus document rather than a classical one. The biggest clue is found in the vocabulary. The writer uses χρόνος to mean "year" rather than "time" (line 15), καταλαμβάνω to mean "arrive at" rather than "seize" (line 7), the Roman-period creation[11] βράδος for "delay" (line 8), and the Egyptian month-name Παχών to give a date according to the Egyptian calendar (line 16). The letter's recipient is given the title κύριος in both the heading and the address, and the two women to whom greetings are sent are both called κυρία (line 12), though in the classical period, titles would not normally have been used even to people of considerably elevated status, let alone to ordinary citizens.[12] Moreover, in the classical period κύριος had a few specific meanings, such as the guardian of a woman, and its general use as a polite term is a phenomenon characteristic of the Roman period (see Dickey 2004a).

The kinship terms used in this letter are likewise an indication of its date. In the classical period kinship terms tend to be used alone; their combination with names (as in the heading and address) and with titles (as in every instance in this letter) is a late feature. Moreover, there is a significant difference between the ways kinship terms are used in classical Greek and in papyrus letters: in the classical language ἀδελφός and ἀδελφή really mean "brother" and "sister," and μήτηρ means "mother," but in papyrus letters it is not uncommon for all these terms to be used in a more generalized sense for people with no genetic relationship to the writer. In particular, ἀδελφός can be used to friends and even distant acquaintances without conveying particular affection or intimacy. We know nothing about the people named in this letter beyond what we can deduce from the letter itself, so in this case it is possible that all the kinship terms indicate blood relationship, but, given the letter's date, such relationships cannot be assumed simply on the basis of the kinship terms (see Dickey 2004b).

This letter also has a number of syntactic features that mark it as a papyrus document. The dative is used instead of the accusative for extent of time (line 15). The κἄν in line 6 would in the classical period have been crasis for καὶ ἐάν, but in Hellenistic and later Greek it can be used simply as an equivalent for καί. The writer has hesitated over the construction to use after θαυμάζω in line 3. Originally he simply followed it by a sentence in the indicative, without any conjunction, but then went back and added πῶς ("how"). In the classical period the normal construction with θαυμάζω would be an indirect statement introduced by εἰ (normally meaning "if" but in this construction best translated as "that"); θαυμάζω ὅπως is possible but rare. The use of βράδος ("delay") where a classical writer would probably have preferred a verb is connected to a general tendency of the postclassical language, both literary and subliterary, to use more nouns and in particular more abstract nouns than classical authors employed. The phrase μέχρι τήμερον is unattested in classical Attic, though similar phrases such as μέχρι νυνί and εἰς τήμερον occur.[13]

The word order is also somewhat different from what one would expect to find in the classical period. The nonclassical particle combination γε δέ occurs in lines 8–9; a classical author might have used δέ γε, but since that combination is not found in contexts like the one here (see Denniston 1950, 152–156), most likely a classical writer would not have used both these particles in this passage. Also, the heading begins with the addressee's name, followed by the sender's, while the standard order for letter headings in the classical, Ptolemaic, and Roman periods puts the sender before the addressee. The reverse order is a late antique phenomenon of which this letter is a relatively early example; the change seems to have been motivated by considerations of politeness.

In addition to the features that unambiguously mark this letter as a product of its time and place, it contains a number of more doubtful elements, ones that were or might have been used in classical Attic but that are nevertheless slightly surprising for one reason or another. The particle γάρ would normally come in second position in its clause, but its use here (line 5) as the fourth word is not unparalleled, especially in poetry (see Denniston 1950, 95–98). Similarly, ὑγιαίνειν is used for "to be well" far more often than ἐρρῶσθαι in classical Attic, though the latter is also attested. The aorist participle ποιήσας (line 6) seems odd for an action that is both continuous in aspect and simultaneous in time with that of the main verb, so one might have expected the present ποιῶν instead, but the aorist participle could be defended as complementing the aorist main verb.

The last two sentences of this five-sentence letter consist of courtesies: sending greetings to two women and wishing the addressee continued health. Both these features are very common in papyrus letters; indeed some letters consist almost entirely of good wishes and greetings to long strings of friends and relatives. Such courtesies are considerably less prominent in the classical period, and this rarity can only partially be ascribed to a scarcity of preserved letters from that period. The Platonic epistles, those preserved with the works of Demosthenes, Isocrates, and Hippocrates (not that all of these are authentic, but in most cases they are probably not a great deal later than the period at which they purport to have been written), the letters embedded in the works of various historians,[14] and the few actual private documents that survive from an early period[15] make it clear that the culture of elaborate epistolary courtesy reflected in Roman-period letters did not exist in the fifth and fourth centuries BCE. Most letters from that period, if they contain any good wishes at all, have them in a one-word farewell such as ἔρρωσο ("be well") or εὐτύχει ("be fortunate"); more elaborate courtesies and greetings to third parties are rare.[16]

The sender's name is Serenus in the heading but Sarammon in the address. It is possible that two different people are involved but more likely that the sender had several names. Classical Greeks had only one name; if that did not suffice for precise identification, a patronymic or demotic could be added. After the Roman conquest, however, Greek men who acquired Roman citizenship adopted the Roman system of using three names, and in the imperial period even noncitizens often had multiple names.

This letter might have looked as follows had it been written by a well-educated fifth- or fourth-century Athenian:

Σερῆνος Ἱερακαπόλλωνι χαίρειν.
θαυμάζω εἰ μέχρι νυνὶ οἴκοι μένεις· εἰς γὰρ ἀγωνίαν οὐκ ὀλίγην μ' ἐνέβαλες τοῦτο ποιῶν. καὶ νῦν τοίνυν ἢ ταχέως ὥς με ἀφίκου ἢ γράψον μοι τίνος ἕνεκα βραδύνεις, πρὸ δὲ πάντων περὶ τῆς ὑγιείας ὑμῶν καὶ περὶ ὧν παρ' ἡμῶν χρῄζετε. ἔρρωσο.
Serenus to Hierakapollon, greetings.
I am surprised that you have stayed at home until now, for you threw me into not a little anguish by doing this. And now therefore either come quickly to me or

write to me why you are delaying, and before all [write] about your [pl.] health and about what you need from us. Farewell.

THE LATIN OF PAPYRI AND OSTRACA

The usual written language in Egypt was Greek, and therefore we have comparatively few documents in Latin; we also have fewer document types in Latin than in Greek.[17] Among the more common types of Latin document are army communications and private letters; we have a number of army documents and short letters on ostraca and a few longer letters on papyrus. Six of the latter group were written by one person, a bilingual soldier named Claudius Terentianus, who wrote to his family in the early second century CE. All these letters provide evidence for Latin as spoken under the Roman Empire, often referred to as Vulgar Latin; other evidence for Vulgar Latin comes from curse tablets, graffiti (especially at Pompeii), and numerous late Latin writings.

The Latin of papyrus letters contains misspellings that reveal a variety of phonetic changes similar to but less extensive than those visible in Greek papyri. In postclassical Latin, as in postclassical Greek, the phonemic distinction between long and short vowels disappeared. Since Latin had never had separate letters to indicate long vowels, this shift is not usually apparent in writing, but it was partially responsible for one visible spelling error: confusion between long *e* and short *i*. This confusion produced spellings like *nese* and *nesi* for *nisi* and *dicet* for *dicit*. Only one diphthong underwent substantial monophthongization in the period of the papyri: *ae*, which is often written *e*, as in *magne* for *magnae* or *Alexandrie* for the locative place name *Alexandriae*.

One can also find in the papyri spellings with short *o* where classical Latin had short *u*, such as *con* for *cum* and *nouom* for *nouum*, and it has sometimes been suggested that these spellings anticipate the late Latin confusion of *o* and *u*. But the words so spelled in papyri are ones that were written *o* rather than *u* in both early and very late Latin, so these papyrus spellings are more likely to be due to archaism than to anticipation of the late change.[18]

The Latin consonant changes also paralleled those of Greek to some extent. Final -*m*, which had disappeared from educated speech by the second century BCE, is frequently omitted in writing, producing forms like *scriba* for *scribam*, *unu* for *unum*, and *minore* for *minorem*; sometimes it is added by hypercorrection where it does not belong, as *factam* for *facta* or *ducerem* for *ducere*. Final -*t* may also be lost, as in *uendedi* for *uendidit*. Intervocalic stop consonants may be voiced, as *tridicum* for *triticum* (Adams 1994, 108). The letter *h*, which had early ceased to be pronounced in some varieties of Latin, is often omitted in papyri, as for example in *mi* for *mihi* and *abiturum* for *habiturum*. The sound traditionally written with *b*, which was originally pronounced like our *b*, become a fricative similar (but not identical) to our *v*, while the consonant traditionally written with *u*, which was originally pronounced like our *w*, changed to the same fricative. The resulting merged sound could be written with either letter, but *b* was more common: thus we find *bolt* for *uult*, *negabit* for *negauit*, *bia* for *uia*, and *benio* for *uenio*.

Final -*n* was normally assimilated in pronunciation to the initial consonant of the following word, even in educated speech (cf. Cicero, *Fam.* 9.22.2), but in standard Latin orthography the assimilation was not reflected in writing. At all periods writers with orthographic preferences other than those that later became standard produced assimilated spellings, for example, *im perpetuo* for *in perpetuo*; this tendency is particularly obvious in papyrus letters because of the low educational level of their writers. Also reflecting a widespread feature of standard pronunciation is the confusion between final -*t* and -*d* in certain short words, leading to the use of each letter for the other. Thus we find not only phrases like *ed domino* for *et domino* or *aput te* for *apud te* but also ones like *ud continuo* for *ut continuo* or *ed pater* for *et pater*.

The Latin of the papyri, like the Greek, differs from the classical language in morphology and syntax as well as in spelling. For example, the accusative is often found with prepositions that would take the ablative in the classical language, such as *con tirones* for *cum tironibus*. The comparative can be used where we would expect the positive, as in *celerius* for *celeriter*. And writers show some difficulties with verb endings, particularly in the future; many of these problems resulted from the sound changes that made endings like -*bit* and -*ēs* homophonous with ones like -*uit* and -*is*. Writers also tended to use the indicative instead of the subjunctive in certain constructions, such as indirect questions. But overall the Latin of the papyri differs less from classical Latin than the Greek of the papyri does from classical Greek in morphology and syntax as well as in phonology because of the shorter chronological gap between the two phases of the language being compared. Of course, one does not find Ciceronian oratory in soldiers' letters, but that is a question of register rather than date: even Cicero's own letters use a markedly more colloquial style than his speeches, and even in Cicero's day Romans with less education would have written their letters in less perfect Latin than his.

Word order in papyrus letters also differs from that in classical Latin, particularly in the later period. In the classical language the verb tends to come at the end of its clause, but in later Latin it normally comes earlier—before its object and any associated prepositional phrases.

The vocabulary of papyrus letters also diverges from that of classical Latin. As is only to be expected, given Latin's minority status in Egypt, Greek loanwords are abundant; personal and place names, deities, and so on may come from either Greek or Egyptian. Native Latin words may be used differently in Vulgar Latin from in the classical language (e.g., *fortis* for "healthy"). Moreover, writers of papyrus letters sometimes prefer one word for an object where writers of literary texts preferred another (e.g., preferring *epistula* to *litterae*). Sometimes words and usages found in the papyri or ostraca also occur in much earlier low-register texts and can be identified as persistent colloquialisms rather than postclassical innovations (e.g., *adiuto* instead of *adiuvo*).

A SAMPLE LATIN DOCUMENT

This letter (*P.Oxy.* XLIV 3208), which was found at Oxyrhynchus, was probably written in the Augustan age.[19] It is thus only slightly later than Cicero's letters and earlier than Seneca's and Pliny's. Though it contains nonstandard spellings and other unusual features, it is on the whole carefully written by someone with a certain amount of education. Word divisions are indicated on the papyrus, but capitalization and punctuation are editorial additions.

> Suneros Chio suo plur(imam) sal(utem). s(i) u(ales) b(ene). Theo adduxsit ad
>   me Ohapim,
> regium mensularium Oxsyrychitem, qui quidem mecum est locutus
> de inprobitate Epaphraes. itaque nihil ultra loquor quam ⟦no⟧
> "ne patiarus te propter illos perire." crede mihi, nimia bonitas
> 5   pernicies homin[i]bus est ʻuel maxsumaʼ. deinde ipse tibei de mostrabit
> qu[i]t rei sit qum illum ad te uocareis. set perseruera:
> qui de tam pusilla summa tam magnum lucrum facit,
> dominum occidere uolt. deinde ego clamare debeo, siquod uideo,
> "deuom atque hominum ⟦fidem." si tu [.] ista non cuibis⟧
> 10   tuum erit uindicare ne alio libeat facere.
> [address]   Chio Caesaris

> Suneros [sends] very many greetings to his own Chios. If you are well, [that's] fine.
> Theo brought to me Ohapim, the public banker of Oxyrhynchus, who spoke with me
> about the wickedness of Epaphras. And so I say nothing beyond "Don't allow
> yourself to be ruined on account of them." Believe me, excessive generosity is a source
> of disaster for men, altogether the biggest [source]. Then he himself will show you
> what it's about when you call him to you. But be persistent: someone who makes such
> a big profit from such a trifling sum is willing to kill his master. Then I ought to
> shout, if I [correctly] perceive anything, "by the faith of gods and men!" Punishment
> will be up to you, lest someone else should want to do it.
> To Chios, slave of Caesar.

In many ways the language of this letter is close to classical Latin: it follows classical word order; the verbs have their full range of inflection and (on the whole) the usual endings; and much of the vocabulary is standard. Though many of the words look odd to readers used to Latin literary texts, most of the unusual appearance is due simply to the presence of alternative spellings (also common in inscriptions) that do not indicate a pronunciation different from the standard one. In this category fall the learned spelling *xs* for *x* (*adduxsit*, line 1; *Oxsyrychitem*, line 2; and *maxsuma*, line 5); archaic *ei* for long *i* (*tibei* for *tibi*, line 5; and probably also (with the *i* omitted) *deuom* for *diuum*, line 9); *n* omitted before *s* in *Oxsyry(n)-chitem* (line 2) and *demo(n)strabit* (line 5); *o* written instead of *u* after consonantal *u* in *uolt* (line 8) and *deuom* (line 9); the archaic superlative in -*umus* rather than -*imus* (*maxsuma*, line 5); the unassimilated *n* in *inprobitate* (line 3); *qum* for *cum* (line 6); and the transliteration of the Greek upsilon in *Suneros* (line 1) with *u* rather than the *y* used in *Oxsyrychitem*. The word break after the initial element of *demostrabit* (line 5) and the lack of one between *si* and *quod* (line 8) do not fit with our Latin orthography but would not have been unusual in antiquity; in any case they are matters of writing rather than of pronunciation. The interchange of final *d* and *t*, which occurs in *set* for *sed* (line 8) and *quit* for *quid* (line 9), probably does not indicate any particular pronunciation either, as it is likely that *d* and *t* were not distinguished in pronunciation at the ends of such words.

This letter also contains some elements of nonstandard morphology. The dative of *alius* is given as *alio*, which would be the normal ending for a second-declension adjective, rather than the *alii* of standard Latin, which follows a special pronominal declension; this type of inflection is thought to be a colloquialism (Cugusi 1992, vol. 2, 24). The -*rus* for -*ris* ending of *patiarus* (line 4) is also found in graffiti at Pompeii and has been argued to be rustic or otherwise low register.[20] The use of *quod* where we would expect *quid* (line 8) is part of a general tendency in early and colloquial Latin not to make a rigid distinction between the use of *quis, quid* and that of *qui, quae, quod*.[21] The future perfect *uocareis* (= *uocaueris*) in line 6 uses the widely attested syncopation of -*ue*- in the perfect system, as well as the *ei* spelling for long *i*.[22] The -*aes* ending on the Greek name *Epaphraes* (line 3) is a partial Latinization of the Greek first-declension genitive ending -ηs; such -*aes* genitive endings are distinctly low register and not uncommon in Vulgar Latin contexts. Usually they are found on the Latin gentilicia of people with Greek cognomina rather than on the Greek name itself, as in this case (Adams 2003, 479–483). The ending has nothing to do with the actual Greek genitive of this word, Ἐπαφρᾶ.

Some of the vocabulary is revealing as well. *Pusilla* is classical but colloquial and occurs in Cicero's letters. The phrase *regius mensularius*, which uses a rare word for "banker," is a translation of the Greek term βασιλικὸς τραπεζίτης ("public banker") (Brown 1970, 141–142).

The letter contains numerous Greek names, all of which have been Latinized where possible. *Theo* has been given a Latin nominative ending (a straight translit-eration of the Greek would have been *Theon*); *Oxsyrychitem* has both a Latin suffix and a Latin accusative ending; and the oddly Latinized ending of *Epaphraes* has already been noted. *Suneros* and *Chio* are not susceptible of Latinization.[23] The language from which Ohapim's name comes is uncertain—there have even been attempts to make him into a Jewish banker named Joachim (cf. Brown 1970, 138)—but it is probably Egyptian and in any case clearly not Latin in origin.

This letter might have looked as follows had it been written by someone with Cicero's educational background:

> Syneros Chio suo s(alutem) p(lurimam) d(icit). s(i) u(ales) b(ene) e(st).
> Theo adduxit ad me Ohapim, argentarium publicum Oxyrhynchitem, qui quidem
> mecum est locutus de improbitate Epaphrae. itaque nihil ultra moneo quam
> "ne patiaris te propter illos perire." crede mihi, nimia bonitas pernicies hominibus
> est uel maxima. deinde ipse tibi demonstrabit quid rei sit cum illum ad te
> uocaueris. sed perseuera: qui de tam pusilla summa tantum lucrum facit, uel
> dominum occideret. deinde ego clamare debeo, si quid intellego, "pro diuum
> atque hominum fidem." tuum erit uindicare ne alii libeat facere.

Understanding the Latin and Greek of the Papyri

Because the language of documentary papyri is so often different from the classical languages that one traditionally learns, special resources are often needed to read them. For Greek vocabulary not covered by Liddell, Scott et al. (1940), one can look in Arndt et al. (2000), Moulton and Milligan (1930), Preisigke (1924–1993), and Sophokles (1870). Odd spellings can usually be explained by reference to Mayser (1926–1938) and Gignac (1976–1981); nonstandard morphology can sometimes be found in the same sources, but one may also need to consult Mandilaras (1973). Syntax is inadequately covered by existing reference works, though some information is given in the works listed above, particularly Mandilaras (1973).

Because Latin papyri are so much rarer than Greek ones, we do not have the same kind of specialized works on papyrological Latin as on papyrological Greek. Nevertheless some works on Vulgar Latin, although they concentrate on other types of source, are helpful in dealing with papyri. Latin words that do not appear in the *Oxford Latin Dictionary* (which deliberately excludes all sources after 200 CE) can often be found in Lewis and Short (1879). Common Vulgar Latin spellings, morphology, and so forth are discussed by Väänänen (1963) and Herman (2000), and anything that happens to occur in Terentianus's letters is covered by Adams (1977).

NOTES

1. I am grateful for the assistance of J. N. Adams, P. Probert, and others with the preparation of this chapter.

2. For a more complete description of the phonetic changes in the Greek of the papyri, with numerous examples of each, see Gignac (1976–1981, vol. 1).

3. Other types of evidence exist as well, including statements by grammarians; for a fuller discussion see Allen (1987, esp. xiii).

4. Exponents of the later dating, which is more widely accepted, include Allen (1987) and Gignac (1976–1981); the earlier dating is supported by Teodorsson (1977) and Horrocks (1997).

5. The evidence of transliterations must, however, be used with some caution. One cannot necessarily conclude from such spellings that the Greek and the Latin letters had exactly the same pronunciation at the time a given transliteration occurred, let alone that that common pronunciation was the same as the one their respective modern descendants now share (i.e., like English *v*). When transliterating from one alphabet into another, one often has to use the closest equivalent for sounds that have no exact match in the other alphabet; for example, someone who wants to transliterate "cherry" into the Greek alphabet might use τσ to represent the *ch* not because he thought the Greek consonant cluster was identical to the English sound but because he could not find anything in Greek closer to the English sound. Alternatively, he or she might use χ because that letter is often transliterated *ch* in English. Therefore, the most a transliteration like ου (the original Greek equivalent of Latin consonantal *u*) or β (the later equivalent) can tell us is that the letters used for the transliteration were closer than anything else that alphabet offered to the sound being transliterated.

6. For a more complete description of the morphological changes in the Greek of the papyri, with citations for the examples given here and many additional examples, see Gignac (1976–1981, vol. 2).

7. The motivation behind this example may be formulaic usage, as the writer probably saw ὁ ὁμολογῶν as a fixed formula.

8. For more such pairs see Shipp (1967).

9. See Cervenka-Ehrenstrasser (1996–), Daris (1991), and Dickey (2003).

10. See Mason (1974) and Dickey (2004a).

11. There are two possible attestations of this word before the Roman period, one classical and one Hellenistic, but see Meissner (2006, 100–104, 185, 224–225) for arguments against accepting their authenticity.

12. For example, Plato's letters to various important figures, which may be spurious but are linguistically classical enough that knowledgeable ancient writers like Cicero thought them genuine, mostly have simple headings like Πλάτων Διονυσίῳ εὖ πράττειν.

13. The former, for example, at Aristophanes, *Ran.* 1256; the latter, for example, at Plato, *Symp.* 174a. Demosthenes several times uses μέχρι τῆς τήμερον ἡμέρας (e.g., 19.297, 19.328), but this belongs to a more formal register than would be appropriate in a personal letter. The writer of this letter has used a perfect tense after μέχρι σήμερον, and this is also the tense Demosthenes uses with μέχρι τῆς τήμερον ἡμέρας, but both μέχρι νυνί and the more common but slightly later μέχρι (τοῦ) νῦν tend to take a verb in the present tense

(e.g., Demosthenes 19.336, Hecataeus (Jacoby 1923–, vol. 1a, author 1, fr. 119, line 13), Ctesias (Jacoby 1923–, vol. 3c, author 688, fr. 1b, line 363), Aristotle, *Poetics* 1447b 9).

14. For example, Hdt. 1.124, 3.40; Thuc. 1.128.7, 1.129.3; Xen., *Cyr.* 4.5.27–33.

15. See Jordan (2000, esp. 91–92).

16. For example, ἔρρωσο at Xen., *Cyr.* 4.5.33; and εὐτύχει at Plato, *Epistle* 4 (321c). Exceptions to this generalization include a greeting in Plato, *Epistle* 13 (τοὺς συσφαιριστὰς ἀσπάζου ὑπὲρ ἐμοῦ, 363d).

17. For a more detailed discussion of most of these phenomena, citations for the examples given here, and additional examples see Adams (1977).

18. See Väänänen (1966, 27), Adams (1977, 9–11), and Herman (1990, 138–139). The *o* spellings are particularly frequent after consonantal *u* and in such circumstances seem to be a graphic phenomenon that resulted from a reluctance to write *uu*.

19. For further information see the more detailed discussions in Brown (1970) and Cugusi (1992, vol. 1, 93; vol. 2, 21–24).

20. See Cugusi (1992, vol. 2, 19, 22) and Adams (2007, chap. 7.6).

21. See Löfstedt (1933, 79–96).

22. The *i* of this ending, though we normally think of it as short, is attested in classical poetry as both long and short; see Brown (1970, 140).

23. The *-os* ending of *Suneros* probably reflects Greek *-ως* rather than *-ος*, so one would not expect it to be Latinized as *-us* in the manner of second-declension nominative endings.

BIBLIOGRAPHY

Adams, J. N. 1977. *The Vulgar Latin of the Letters of Claudius Terentianus* (*P.Mich.* VIII, 467–72). Manchester: Manchester University Press.

——. 1994. "Latin and Punic in Contact? The Case of the Bu Njem Ostraca." *Journal of Roman Studies* 84: 87–112.

——. 2003. *Bilingualism and the Latin Language.* Cambridge: Cambridge University Press.

——. 2007. *The Regional Diversification of Latin, 200 BC–AD 600.* Cambridge: Cambridge University Press.

Allen, W. S. 1987. *Vox graeca: A Guide to the Pronunciation of Ancient Greek,* 3d ed. Cambridge: Cambridge University Press.

Arndt, W. F., W. Bauer, F. W. Gingrich, and F. W. Danker. 2000. *A Greek-English Lexicon of the New Testament and Other Early Christian Literature,* 3d ed. Chicago: University of Chicago Press.

Brown, V. 1970. "A Latin Letter from Oxyrhynchus." *Bulletin of the Institute of Classical Studies* 17: 136–143.

Cervenka-Ehrenstrasser, I.-M., with J. Diethart. 1996–. *Lexikon der lateinischen Lehnwörter.* Vienna: Hollinek.

Cugusi, P. 1992–2002. *Corpus epistularum latinarum: papyris tabulis ostracis servatarum.* 3 vols. Florence: Gonnelli.

Daris, S. 1991. *Il lessico latino nel greco d'Egitto,* 2d ed. Barcelona: Institut de Teologia fonamental.

Denniston, J. D. 1950. *The Greek Particles,* 2d ed., rev. K. J. Dover. Oxford: Clarendon.

Dickey, E. 2003. "Latin Influence on the Greek of Documentary Papyri: An Analysis of Its Chronological Distribution." *Zeitschrift für Papyrologie und Epigraphik* 145: 249–257.

———. 2004a. "The Greek Address System of the Roman Period and Its Relationship to Latin." *Classical Quarterly*, n.s., 54: 494–527.

———. 2004b. "Literal and Extended Use of Kinship Terms in Documentary Papyri." *Mnemosyne* 57: 131–176.

Exler, F. X. 1923. *The Form of the Ancient Greek Letter of the Epistolary Papyri*. Washington, D.C.: Catholic University of America.

Gignac, F. T. 1976–1981. *A Grammar of the Greek Papyri of the Roman and Byzantine Periods*. Vol. 1, *Phonology*; vol. 2, *Morphology*. Milan: Istituto editoriale Cisalpino–La Goliardica.

Herman, J. 1990. *Du latin aux langues romanes*. Tübingen: Niemeyer.

———. 2000. *Vulgar Latin*, trans. R. Wright. University Park: Pennsylvania State University Press.

Horrocks, G. 1997. *Greek: A History of the Language and Its Speakers*. New York: Longman.

Jacoby, F., ed. 1923–. *Fragmente der griechischen Historiker*. Berlin: Weidmann.

Jordan, D. R. 2000. "A Personal Letter Found in the Athenian Agora." *Hesperia* 69: 91–103.

Kapsomenakis, S. G. 1938. *Voruntersuchungen zu einer Grammatik der Papyri der Nachchristlichen Zeit*. Munich: Beck.

Lewis, C. T., and C. Short. 1879. *A Latin Dictionary*. Oxford: Clarendon.

Liddell, H. G., R. Scott, H. S. Jones, and R. McKenzie. 1940. *A Greek-English Lexicon*, 9th ed. Oxford: Clarendon.

Löfstedt, E. 1933. *Syntactica: Studien und Beiträge zur historischen Syntax des Lateins*. vol. 2. Lund: C. W. K. Gleerup.

Mandilaras, B. G. 1973. *The Verb in the Greek Non-literary Papyri*. Athens: Hellenic Ministry of Culture and Sciences.

Mason, H. J. 1974. *Greek Terms for Roman Institutions: A Lexicon and Analysis*. Toronto: Hakkert.

Mayser, E. 1926–1938. *Grammatik der griechischen Papyri aus der Ptolemäerzeit*. Berlin: De Gruyter.

Meissner, T. 2006. *S-stem Nouns and Adjectives in Greek and Proto-Indo-European: A Diachronic Study in Word Formation*. Oxford: Oxford University Press.

Moulton, J. H., and G. Milligan. 1930. *Vocabulary of the Greek Testament, Illustrated from the Papyri and Other Non-literary Sources*. London: Hodder and Stoughton.

Palmer, L. R. 1945. *A Grammar of the Post-Ptolemaic Papyri*. Vol. 1, pt. i. London: Oxford University Press, G. Cumberlege.

Preisigke, F. 1924–1993. *Wörterbuch der griechische Papyrusurkunden*. Wiesbaden: Harrassowitz.

Shipp, G. P. 1967. "Some Observations on the Distribution of Words in the New Testament." In *Essays in Honour of Griffithes Wheeler Thatcher*, ed. E. C. B. MacLaurin, 127–138. Sydney: Sydney University Press.

Sophokles, E. A. 1870. *Greek Lexicon of the Roman and Byzantine Periods from B.C. 146 to A.D. 1100*. Boston: Little, Brown.

Teodorsson, S. T. 1977. *The Phonology of Ptolemaic Koine*. Gothenburg: Acta Universitatis Gothoburgensis.

Väänänen, V. 1963. *Introduction au latin vulgaire*. Paris: Klincksieck.

———. 1966. *Le latin vulgaire des inscriptions Pompéiennes*, 3d ed. Berlin: Akademie-Verlag.

CHAPTER 7

ABBREVIATIONS AND SYMBOLS

NIKOLAOS GONIS

ABBREVIATIONS

A full collection of abbreviations in the papyri is not generally available (Blanchard's 1969 Sorbonne dissertation has not been published). The most comprehensive list one may consult is that offered by Bilabel (1923, 2296–2303), while the indexes to *P.Lond.* II–V and to the text volumes of *SPP* remain useful (but a good deal of caution is advisable; only *P.Lond.* IV–V are sufficiently reliable). Likewise, no detailed discussion exists, and the present chapter does not offer one (this would have required a monograph-length study). In setting out the material, I have consciously followed to a large extent Wilcken's treatment of the subject (1912, xxxix–xlvii), the first systematic and perhaps also the most lucid attempt to describe the phenomenon. Blanchard (1974) is fundamental, although it is not a systematic survey but two "essays in interpretative palaeography" (Parsons 1976, 265).

Here we are concerned with abbreviations found in Greek documentary papyri and ostraca (and occasionally wooden tablets); those in literary papyri are treated in McNamee (1981) (cf. also McNamee 1985; Bastianini 1992). Shorthand, of which we still understand very little, is not discussed (see the bibliography in Torallas Tovar and Worp 2006).

In writing, one "abbreviates," or shortens a word, to save effort, time, or even space. No rules need apply, but when the writing is meant to be read by another person, one has to ensure that what is abbreviated is also understood. Arbitrary choices cannot be absent, but everything usually falls under the umbrella of convention, part of the common writing ground that is taught or otherwise disseminated from generation to generation. We find abbreviations in writing of all kinds and ages: literary or documentary and on stone, wood, papyrus, or leather. The documents in which abbreviation is rife are predominantly those produced on a massive scale and bound to repeat the same words, such as tax accounts and receipts. We also find plentiful use of abbreviations in documents of informal character or where compactness was desired: private accounts and memoranda, drafts, notes, subscriptions, dockets, summaries, and so on.

Like letter forms, abbreviations change across the centuries; matters of taste and criteria of convenience do not remain the same, while the writing conventions of other languages also play an influential role. One may wish to see an organic development of the abbreviation system (cf. Blanchard [1974] with Parsons [1976, 266]). To be sure, one starts with a few simple abbreviations in the third century BCE, which increase in proportion to the growing cursive character of everyday script, while ten centuries later the system has acquired a daunting complexity. Nonetheless, evolution does not progress along the same single line; a practice may disappear, only to resurface, perhaps distorted but still recognizable, some centuries later.

The following is a list of practices and principles that apply to the great majority of abbreviations. Some of them are more specific to certain periods than others.

(1) The commonest method of abbreviation is by suspension, that is, to omit one or more of the final letters of a word, even all the letters after the first. Cases in which a suspension is effected but not signaled in one way or another ("unmarked abbreviations") are not unknown and occur at all times. But the reader should normally be alerted to the presence of an abbreviation: Suspension may be indicated by having the last remaining letter written directly above or to the upper right of the penultimate letter or by adding some sort of marker above or after the last remaining letter. These are the two commonest practices.

(2) Interpretation of an abbreviation depends on the context; more than one word will share the same beginning and be abbreviated identically or be represented by a single "symbol," which may lead to confusion. For example, in O.Strasb. 654.1, $\alpha\rho^{\gamma}$ was first resolved as $\dot{\alpha}\rho\gamma(\upsilon\rho\iota\kappa\hat{\omega}\nu)$ but should be read as $\dot{\alpha}\rho\gamma(\dot{\iota}\alpha\varsigma)$; or, in Ptolemaic texts, $\mu\epsilon\mu\dot{\epsilon}\tau\rho\eta\kappa\epsilon\nu$ and other words starting with $\mu\epsilon$- have more or less the same shortened graphic representation as $\pi\dot{\epsilon}\pi\tau\omega\kappa\epsilon\nu$, $\tau\dot{\epsilon}\tau\alpha\kappa\tau\alpha\iota$, and other words beginning with $\pi\epsilon$- or $\tau\epsilon$- (Blanchard 1974, 4–5).

Since the abbreviated words are often reduced to their bare essentials, little attention is paid to their declension; again, the context will make it clear whether, for instance, a genitive or an accusative is meant. We first witness departures from this practice in the later period (see item 10).

(3) In the simple forms of suspension, superscription predominates, but in the case of several two-letter abbreviations, chiefly in the Ptolemaic period, the last remaining letter may be written "inside" or under the penultimate one (but not under the baseline).

(4) Supralinear letters are often deformed. A leftward-facing curve, either big or small, usually represents pi in documents of the Roman period. In the later Ptolemaic and early Roman periods, alpha is often written as an acute angle *(Hakenalpha)*. In the Roman period, alpha, epsilon, mu, pi, and tau often end up as small supralinear horizontals. In the seventh and eighth centuries, overwritten alpha, epsilon, and tau "tend to become a mere line; the intermediate stage is a line slightly thickened at the beginning" (Bell 1910, xliv). (See also items 12 and 16).

(5) Two letters may be combined into a "monogram." These are most often the first two, and the only two remaining, letters of the word. Thus, for example, the crossbar of E may be placed between the arms of K to form an abbreviation transcribed as $\kappa\epsilon(\rho\acute{\alpha}\mu\iota o\nu)$; or, certain words beginning with ΓP or ΠP are represented by Γ or Π intersected by P. This practice is predominantly Ptolemaic and is attested as early as the third century BCE.

(6) A word may be reduced by abbreviation to a single letter (the first), often accompanied by a stroke that acts as a marker. Single-letter abbreviations occur at all times (they were earlier associated mainly with the Ptolemaic period, but this view no longer holds). Here belong the various representations of $\alpha\mathring{v}\tau\acute{o}s$, made of a sinusoid (originally a *Hakenalpha*), either capped by a short horizontal or curve or followed by a small, accentlike oblique.

It is worth adding that, unlike Latin, Greek did not use abbreviations consisting of strings of initials; there is nothing comparable, for instance, to Latin *SPQR.*

(7) A letter extended rightward or downward (or even upward, if it is iota) may indicate an abbreviation. In the later periods, this practice is usually in evidence when the scribe intends to abbreviate at the end of a line; the letter is followed "by a single stroke, curved or straight, with or without an over-written letter" (Bell 1951, 427).

(8) Groups of two words may be abbreviated in such a way that what remains of the second word is its first letter, which is superscript. As expected, we find it with pre- and postpositives (usually articles and prepositions); $\acute{o}$ $\kappa(\alpha\acute{\iota})$, a collocation mostly used for aliases, written as o^{κ}, is a classic

example. A more drastic abbreviation of this sort is τo^κ, representing
$\tau\grave{o}$ $\kappa(\alpha\tau'$ $\check{\alpha}\nu\delta\rho\alpha)$; on the face of it, one could also resolve $\tau(\grave{o}$ $\kappa\alpha\acute{\iota})$, but the
context guards against misunderstandings. Indicative of the extent of
the practice, though of limited occurrence, is the abbreviation
$\delta\eta^\gamma = \delta\eta(\mu\acute{o}\sigma\iota o s)$ $\gamma(\epsilon\omega\rho\gamma\acute{o}s)$. The remaining letters of two words may
also be merged into a monogram: In a common abbreviation of
$\gamma\hat{\eta}$ $\kappa(\alpha\tau o\iota\kappa\iota\kappa\acute{\eta})$, we have $\varGamma$ with a line through the top stroke.

(9) In compound words, abbreviation may affect both components
("double suspension"); for example, $\tau o\pi o\gamma\rho\alpha\mu\mu\alpha\tau\epsilon\acute{u}s$ may be rendered
as $\tau\gamma\rho$ or $\tau o\pi\gamma\rho$ (the more conventional $\tau o\pi o\gamma\rho$ also occurs). One of the
commonest abbreviations of this kind is $\kappa o\iota$ (or $\kappa^{o\iota}$) for $\kappa(\acute{\alpha}\tau)o\iota(\kappa o s)$,
$\kappa(\alpha\tau)o\iota(\kappa\iota\kappa\acute{o}s)$, and the like. This practice is attested as early as the
Ptolemaic period but becomes particularly common in late antiquity,
when the system acquires a new profile (see item 10).

In compounds that contain a numeral, the latter may be represented by
an ordinal: Thus, $\varPi\epsilon\nu\tau\alpha\kappa\omega\mu\acute{\iota}\alpha$ will appear as $\epsilon\kappa\omega\mu\iota\alpha$ and $\grave{o}\kappa\tau\acute{\alpha}\mu\eta\nu o s$ as
$\eta\mu\eta\nu o s$ (Youtie 1973–1975, i 153). One of the components may be repre-
sented by a symbol, as in compounds that include weights, measures, or
money: $\varsigma\int=\acute{\epsilon}\xi\alpha\delta\rho\alpha\chi\mu\acute{\iota}\alpha$.

(10) From the fourth century on (and especially after the sixth), we witness
the increasing use of abbreviations *à thème discontinu* ("of discontinuous
theme"; Blanchard 1974, 12),[1] a more fortunate term than the earlier
"abbreviation by contraction." This type of abbreviation has affinities
to practices described in item 9 but is not limited to compounds and
seems to be due to Latin influence. Here, the supralinear letter may
not be the last letter of the unabbreviated part of the word, but one
or more letters may have been omitted between the letter on the line
and that over it. The supralinear letter is virtually always
a consonant, most often the next consonant after the last letter on
the line, though in extreme abbreviations a scribe may choose to
write the consonant considered most significant, as, for instance,
$\zeta^\tau = \zeta(\upsilon\gamma o\sigma)\tau(\acute{\alpha}\tau\eta s)$. Sometimes we find two letters superscript, as
in $\nu\alpha\upsilon^{\pi\gamma} = \nu\alpha\upsilon\pi(\eta)\gamma(\acute{o}s)$. Naturally, not everything is straightforward;
for example, we may infer how $\kappa\omega\mu o\kappa\acute{\alpha}\tau o\iota\kappa o s$ came to be reduced
to $\kappa\omega\mu o\iota\kappa$, but the modern reader will stumble at first sight.

---

1. Whether contractions of the kind known from Latin writing (i.e., a word is reduced
to its initial and final letters) were in use in the papyri has been a controversial issue.
Wilcken (1912, xliii–xlv) regarded contractions as a special subgroup, but his evidence
relates mainly to *nomina sacra,* which are a case apart (see chapter 25). Blanchard
dismisses this "subgroup" altogether (1974, 2, 18–19).

Overwritten nonsequential vowels also occur, but they come from the end of the words and serve to indicate inflexions (Bell 1951, 431); $ινδ^o = ἰνδ(ικτίων)ο(ς)$ is the commonest such example.

(11) Abbreviation may be indicated by means of a separate stroke added at the end of the shortened word. This is the preferred practice in the later periods, though superscriptions never disappear. We mostly find short horizontals, sinusoids (or "double curves"), and obliques. The use of the single dot, a Latin influence, is very sporadic.

(12) The horizontals are largely simplified versions of supralinear letters, which progressively lost their defining characteristics and were reduced to single strokes (see item 3). Editors often waver between recognizing in such strokes the original letters and taking them just as abbreviation markers. Here much depends on personal taste, but it would be preferable to interpret such strokes as letters unless they have more than one function in the same text.

(13) The use of the sinusoid in abbreviations becomes common from the Roman period on. It is possible that the sinusoids written at the end of words initially represented the ligature alpha plus iota written increasingly cursively (with alpha in the form of *Hakenalpha*), so that in the end the original components are not distinguishable.

The sinusoid may also stand in its own right as a symbol with a plurality of meanings (see item 21).

(14) A short oblique stroke of varying angles may follow or intersect the final letter. Letters with long descenders (e.g., mu, rho, phi) or with elements that can be extended below the line (e.g., kappa) are prime targets for such intersections. This is by and large a feature of the later documentation.

Obliques may sometimes be very short and could be added high in the line (like acute accents). They sometimes occur with doubled letters, indicating plural forms (Islamic period only; see item 16).

Abbreviating obliques may occasionally be doubled (commonly after $ινδ = ἰνδ(ικτίωνος)$ and $μ = μ(όνον)$, but this entails no difference in meaning.

(15) From the late fifth century on, oblique strokes and sinusoids were often used in conjunction with superscription, even though this would seem to be redundant.

(16) From the sixth century on, the duplication of the final letter(s) of an abbreviated word signals the plural; this replicates a Latin convention. The abbreviation proper is marked by either a superscription or some other indicator. Thus $κάραβοι$ may be shortened as $καρρ$ or $καρ\overset{a}{ρ}\overset{a}{ρ}$ (*P.Lond.* IV 1414.56, 1416.41).

SYMBOLS

Most symbols stem from abbreviations by suspension; these may become reduced to monograms whose original constituents are sometimes no longer discernible (ingenuity in explaining some of them as suspensions of one sort or another has not been in short supply). This is the case with most symbols that represent weights and measures, as well as, in the later period, money, which naturally occurred very frequently. Blanchard has made a perceptive classification of the commonest symbols, which I follow (figure 7.1).

(17) A number of symbols go back to earlier Greek conventions, including those for the monetary values imported into Egypt (drachma, obol, and fractions), to which one may add the symbol for the year.
The origin of the L-shaped symbol representing the year ($\check{\epsilon}\tau o\upsilon s$) remains unclear despite attempts to explain it, for example, as a demotic derivation (Wilcken 1912, xlv; contrast Blanchard 1974, 42) or as a conflation of $E + T$ (Bell 1951, 425). It always precedes the numeral. We find it from the third century BCE to the fourth century CE, when dating by regnal years progressively disappears; after that, it is used only with datings in the Oxyrhynchite era, but there it is placed high in the line, approximating the shape of the documentary paragraphos at that time.

(18) Some other very familiar symbols that we find early enough seem to go back to demotic (analysis in Blanchard 1974, 30–31):

(i) the symbol used for the total ($\gamma\acute{\iota}\nu\epsilon\tau\alpha\iota$) in Ptolemaic and Roman papyri, usually an oblique stroke (/). In later times, $\gamma\acute{\iota}\nu\epsilon\tau\alpha\iota$ is commonly abbreviated as $\gamma\iota$: Whether this relates to the increased use of the oblique as an abbreviation indicator, which might have undermined the original function of the free-standing oblique, we do not know.

(ii) the symbol for "what remains" ($\lambda o\iota\pi\acute{o}\nu$), which looks like lambda with a tiny omicron under it (it is conceivable that its origin was not always known and that it was occasionally also considered as the shortening of a Greek word; it is interesting that in papyri of the Islamic period the abbreviation for the same word usually consists of lambda with pi underneath).

(iii) the L-shaped symbol indicating a "minus" out of a larger total ($\dot{\alpha}\varphi$ $\check{\omega}\nu$); in money accounts, it also introduces the uses of funds received.

(19) The Ptolemaic period sees the rise of certain symbols, originally straightforward monograms, which stand for some essential quantities: the talent, wheat ($\pi\upsilon\rho o\hat{\upsilon}$) (see further Blanchard 1974, 44n18, 45n21),

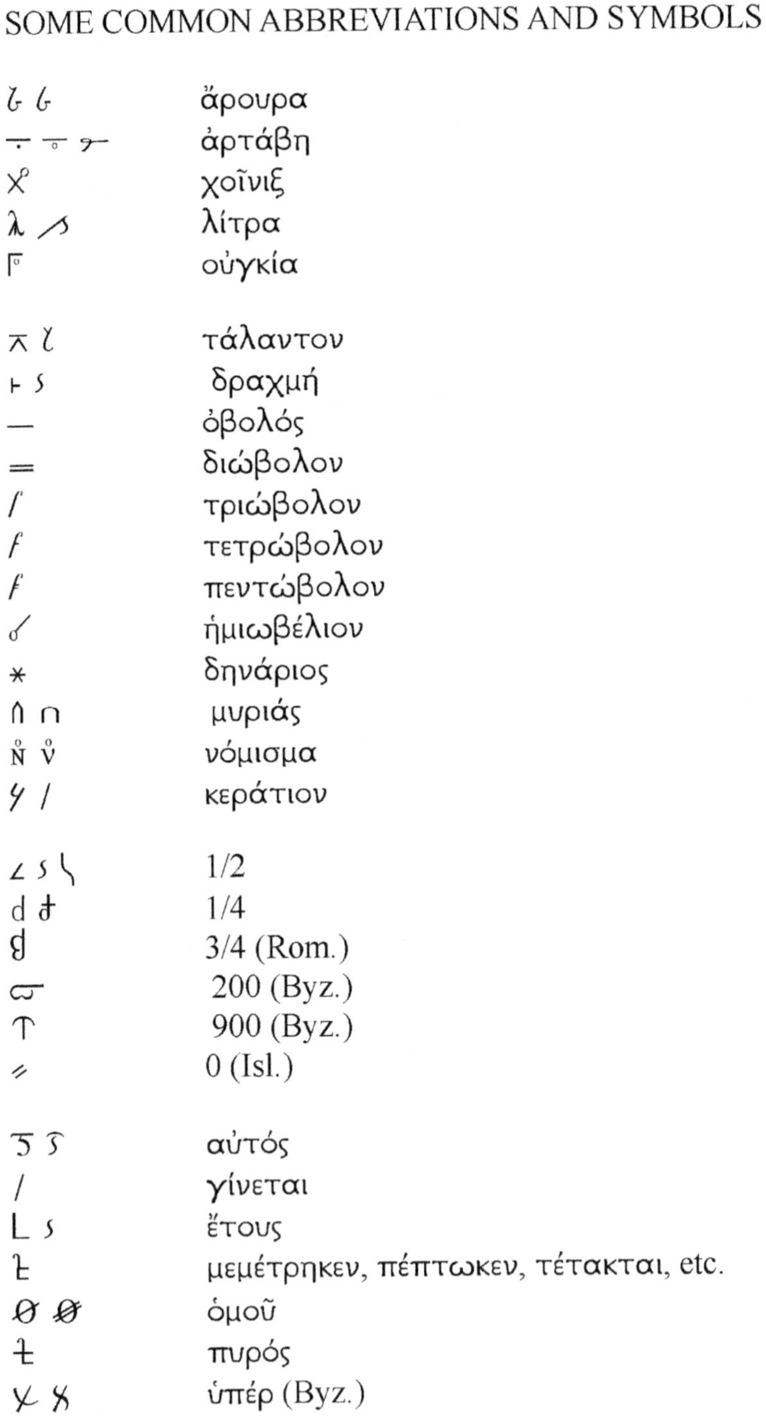
SOME COMMON ABBREVIATIONS AND SYMBOLS
ἄρουρα
ἀρτάβη
χοῖνιξ
λίτρα
οὐγκία
τάλαντον
δραχμή
ὀβολός
διώβολον
τριώβολον
τετρώβολον
πεντώβολον
ἡμιωβέλιον
δηνάριος
μυριάς
νόμισμα
κεράτιον
1/2
1/4
3/4 (Rom.)
200 (Byz.)
900 (Byz.)
0 (Isl.)
αὐτός
γίνεται
ἔτους
μεμέτρηκεν, πέπτωκεν, τέτακται, etc.
ὁμοῦ
πυρός
ὑπέρ (Byz.)

Figure 7.1. List of symbols.

and the *artaba* (on the origins and history of the sign see Blanchard 1974, 34–38).

(20) The Roman period introduces new abbreviations and symbols for certain fractions, for the *aroura* (analysis in Blanchard 1974, 38–40), and for the conjunction καί. In late antiquity, the repertoire increases: there are symbols for new monetary values (myriads, monads, solidi, carats), for fractions, and for common words in fiscal contexts (e.g., ὑπέρ).

(21) Meriting a note apart is a very common symbol in documents of the Roman and later periods: the sinusoid (or "double curve"). It has a plurality of meanings, of which the commonest are the following (Youtie 1974, 50):

(i) the drachma (on the development of the sign see Blanchard 1974, 32–34)

(ii) the one-half fraction (ἥμισυ), an evolution of the earlier angular form

(iii) the year (but only after the numeral; note that many of the sinusoids written after ordinal numbers, usually regnal, indictional, and con-sular iteration years, function only as markers)

(iv) καί.

The direction of the curves may be reversed (Youtie 1973, vol. 1, 132; Blanchard 1974, 33). This form occurs only sporadically in the Roman period but is particu-larly common in the eighth century, when the symbol usually stands for the concept one-half.

VERSCHLEIFUNGEN ("SLURS")

In the early days of papyrology, *Verschleifungen* were given the status of a particular subgroup of abbreviations (Wilcken 1912, xlii–xliii). The scribe "slurs" or pens the initial letters of a word and continues with a wavy or ribbonlike line in which no individual letters are distinguishable; the initial letters and the context suffice to identify the word meant. This practice is predominantly found with the names and titles of emperors and the names of months in date clauses, most often in tax receipts, but occasionally also in declarations to state authorities. Also in tax receipts, especially on ostraca, some set words such as διέγραψεν ("paid"), γενήματος ("produce"), and so on may be written in a similar fashion (Préaux 1954). However, *Verschleifungen* are no longer considered as abbreviations insofar as no letter was intentionally omitted (Bilabel 1923, 2281; Blanchard 1974, 1, 17). Thus, in transcribing *Verschleifungen*, no brackets should be used.

BIBLIOGRAPHY

Bastianini, G. 1992. "Le abbreviazioni." In *Corpus dei papiri filosofici greci e latini (CPF): Testi e lessico nei papiri di cultura greca e latina*. Parte I: *Autori noti*, vol. 1**: 276–281. Florence: Leo S. Olschki.

Bell, H. I. 1910. "§ 6. Palaeography, Diplomatic, etc." *P.Lond.* IV, pp. xlii–xlv. London. (On abbreviations in documents of the early Islamic period.)

———. 1951. "Abbreviations in Documentary Papyri." In *Studies Presented to David Moore Robinson on his Seventieth Birthday*, vol. 1, ed. G. E. Mylonas, 424–433. St. Louis: Washington University.

Bilabel, F. 1923. "Siglae." In *Paulys Realencyclopädie der classischen Altertumswissenschaft*, vol. 2A: 2279–2308. Stuttgart.

Blanchard, A. 1974. *Sigles et abréviations dans les papyrus documentaires grecs: Recherches de paléographie. Bulletin of the Institute of Classical Studies*, Suppl. 30. London: Institute of Classical Studies.

McNamee, K. 1981. *Abbreviations in Greek Literary Papyri and Ostraca. Bulletin of the American Society of Papyrologists*, Suppl. 3. Chico, Calif.: Scholars Press.

———. 1985. "Abbreviations in Greek Literary Papyri and Ostraca: Supplement, with List of Ghost Abbreviations." *Bulletin of the American Society of Papyrologists* 22: 205–225.

Parsons, P. J. 1976. Review of Blanchard 1974. *Journal of Hellenic Studies* 96: 265–266.

Préaux, C. 1954. "Sur l'écriture des ostraca thébains d'époque romaine." *Journal of Egyptian Archaeology* 40: 83–87.

Torallas Tovar, S., and K. A. Worp. 2006. *To the Origins of Greek Stenography (P. Monts. Roca I)*. Barcelona: Publicacions de l'Abbadia de Montserrat.

Wilcken, U. 1912. *Grundzüge und Chrestomathie der Papyruskunde*. Vol 1., *Historischer Teil*. Part 1, *Grundzüge*. Leipzig: B. G. Teubner.

Youtie, H. C. 1973–1975. *Scriptiunculae*, vols. 1–2. Amsterdam: A. M. Hakkert.

———. 1974. *The Textual Criticism of Documentary Papyri: Prolegomena*, 2d ed. *Bulletin of the Institute of Classical Studies*, Suppl. 33. London: Institute of Classical Studies.

CHAPTER 8

PRACTICAL HELP: CHRONOLOGY, GEOGRAPHY, MEASURES, CURRENCY, NAMES, PROSOPOGRAPHY, AND TECHNICAL VOCABULARY

ROGER S. BAGNALL

BOTH editors and readers of papyri, even if they know well the language in which their texts are written, constantly encounter reminders that these artifacts come from another society. These come in the form of a host of technical details. If a lease of land tells us that it was written in the fifth year of Nero, on Thoth 2, in Theadelphia in the Arsinoite nome; that the land measures five arouras and will have an annual rent of twenty-five artabas of wheat and fifty drachmas; and that the lessee is named Peteesis, son of Haryothes—how is the reader not only to make basic sense of all of this information but also to extract from it the maximum contribution to understanding the meaning of the text?

Most of these matters are not of much inherent interest to the average papyrologist; they are puzzles to be decoded, part of the specialized knowledge one acquires in the course of learning the discipline. To most readers who are not professional papyrologists, they are simply obstacles to understanding the transaction or some aspect of it that is of interest to them. When exactly was the lease concluded? How many hectares or acres of land were at stake? How much was the rent in terms that mean something to us? Who was the lessee, and why do his names sound so strange to our ears? This chapter explains the commonest and most important of these matters and provides some guidance to works where more detail can be found. These subjects are often unavoidably complicated, and many details must be left aside here. Even if we restrict ourselves to the documents from Egypt, we find Egyptian, Persian, Greek, Roman, and Semitic origins for the names, terms, and measures found in the papyri accumulating in layers over the centuries.

CHRONOLOGY: MEASURING TIME

The Year

The Egyptians used a solar year of 365 days, divided into twelve months of 30 days each and an additional 5-day festival period at the end of the year, which in Greek is called the (*hêmerai*) *epagomenai* ("added" days). Because it was about a quarter-day shorter than the true length of the solar year, the Egyptian calendar lost a day about every four years, thereby causing the starting date of the year, Thoth 1, to move backward against the actual solar year, returning to its starting point in a cycle of 1,460 years, the "Sothic" cycle. In Egyptian documents, the months are designated as the first through the fourth of the three successive seasons, harvest (*3ḥ.t*), winter (*pr.t*), and summer (*šmw*). (For the Egyptian calendar see Parker 1950.) The Greeks, accustomed to calling each month by a distinctive name usually connected with a festival that took place during it, adopted a set of twelve such names for these Egyptian months. These names survive today in the Coptic calendar.

Greek calendars, by contrast, were lunar, using twelve months alternately of 29 and 30 days, thus totaling 354 days. Each city or state had its own set of month names and periodically declared additional ("intercalary") months in order to keep the months in a roughly constant relationship to the solar year. Because Alexander the Great and Ptolemy, son of Lagos, were Macedonians, it was the Macedonian calendar that came to Egypt with the conquest of 332 BCE. Although it coexisted with the Egyptian calendar, few people found it easy to keep track of their relationship, which was constantly shifting because of the different bases and separate sources of instability. Early papyri show an attempt to use both calendars independently, but inconsistencies are common. Even under Ptolemy II, some well-informed individuals used an informal equation in which the count of days was maintained independently for only one of the calendars (for the Ptolemaic calendar see Samuel 1962 and Grzybek 1990). From the later third century BCE on, as a result of the difficulty of accurate maintenance of the dual calendars, people attempted various "assimilations" of the calendars (in which the lunar character of the Macedonian calendar—with its names equated to Egyptian months—disappeared), but the early history of these attempts is still a matter of controversy. The last system adopted, which remained in use in the Roman period, equated the Macedonian month Dios to the Egyptian month Thoth. The much simpler Egyptian calendar was thus the survivor of this competition.

This method, however, remained unstable against the solar year. An attempt in 238 BCE to reform the Egyptian calendar to eliminate this drift against the solar year was unsuccessful. It was not until the first decade of Roman rule, under Octavian (probably in 26/25 BCE), that a lasting reform was introduced. This approach created leap years by adding a sixth *epagomenê* every four years (in the year before that in which February acquired a twenty-ninth day according to the Roman calendar; thus, for example, in August 103, not February 104 [Skeat 1993]). From that point on, the relationship of Thoth 1 to the Roman calendar was fixed at August 29 in normal years and August 30 in leap years. The old reckoning

Table 8.1. Months

Egyptian	Macedonian	Roman Honorific	Julian Equivalent in Normal Year
Thôth	Dios	Sebastos, Germanikos	August 29–September 27
Phaôphi	Apellaios		September 28–October 27
Hathyr	Audnaios	Neos Sebastos	October 28–November 26
Choiak	Peritios	Ioulieus, Neroneios Sebastos, Hadrianos	November 27–December 26
Tybi	Dystros		December 27–January 25
Mecheir	Xandikos		January 26–February 24
Phamenôth	Artemisios		February 25–March 26
Pharmouthi	Daisios		March 27–April 25
Pachôn	Panemos	Germanikeios	April 26–May 25
Pauni	Lôios	Sotêrios	May 26–June 24
Epeiph	Gorpiaios	Drousieus	June 25–July 24
Mesorê	Hyperberetaios	Kaisareios	July 25–August 23
Epagomenai			August 24–August 28

without a leap year remained in use in some contexts, particularly religious, and dates "according to the ancients" or "according to the Egyptians" are found for some three centuries after Octavian's reform (Hagedorn and Worp 1994). Macedonian months are occasionally found in documents of the Roman imperial period, as are alternate names for the months named in honor of various members of the imperial household (Scott 1932). The Roman months and system of reckoning days themselves are rarely used in the papyri except for a short period in the late third and early fourth century (Bagnall and Worp 2004, 3) (table 8.1).

Counting Years

The Egyptians followed a system of counting the years of pharaohs' reigns within the framework of the civil year, which began on Thoth 1. At a king's accession, the time until the end of the next *epagomenai* was counted as the king's year 1, with year 2 starting on Thoth 1. A king who came to the throne near the end of one year and died soon after the start of another might thus have a "highest regnal year" that is higher by two than the number of complete years he had actually ruled. The regnal years of the Ptolemies were counted in the Egyptian calendar according to this system. In addition, in some third-century-BCE documents, a financial year began halfway through the Egyptian year. (For the Ptolemies' Egyptian regnal years, see Pestman 1967; to compute precise dates, use the tables in Skeat 1969.)

Macedonian practice, however, reckoned reigns from the actual date of accession to the throne until its anniversary. Depending on the date at which a king came to power, therefore, the Macedonian and Egyptian regnal years would be different for some part of each year. (On Macedonian years see Samuel 1962; for the Macedonian calendar from 260 to 221, see *Pap.Lugd.Bat.* XXI 220–263.) Documents from the Ptolemaic period often have prescripts giving the names of the ruling sovereigns and those of several holders of priesthoods connected to the royal cult (Clarysse and Van der Veken 1983).

The regnal years of Roman emperors through the fourth century are reckoned in the papyri according to the Egyptian system, although elsewhere in the empire people used the count of years for which they had held the official titles symbolizing their imperial power: imperator, consul, and holder of tribunician power. The papyri commonly, but not universally, give the names and titles of the ruling emperors. Until the later third century, coemperors used the regnal year count of the senior emperor; after that, separate counts were kept for each ruler. (For these regnal formulas and the beginning years of reigns, see Bureth 1964; Pestman 1967 has a list of regnal years and a table for converting months and days to their Julian equivalents. Grenier 1989 collects Roman titulature in Egyptian-language texts. Kienast 1990 is also useful for Roman imperial reckoning.)

After the beginning of the Tetrarchy in 293, in Diocletian's ninth year, dating by the Roman consuls, which had been rare except in documents in Latin or translated from Latin, started to be common, sometimes side by side with regnal years. Because the consulate ran with the Julian year (January 1), it changed at a different time from the regnal year. Consulates were used mostly for the official date at the beginning or end of a legal or official document. Because the names of consuls changed each year, they required dissemination from the court. As a result, scribes sometimes did not know the names of the new consuls and used "after the consulate" with the names from the previous year (Bagnall et al. 1987).

A further change came with the introduction of the indiction, initially a fiscal year, reckoned in fifteen-year cycles, with the first cycle beginning in 312. Indiction dates are thus not sufficient in themselves to identify a year uniquely for the historian; other dating criteria, internal or external, are also needed. Unfortunately for the papyrologist and historian, the indiction eventually supplanted the regnal year entirely except in Oxyrhynchus and perhaps a few other places, and even there the regnal year vanished before the end of the fourth century. The imperial indiction year coincided in Egypt with the old civil year, but in practice in the Thebaid and some other parts of the country it soon came to be reckoned from Pachon 1, or four months before the civil year. There are a number of local complexities in its use. (See generally Bagnall and Worp 2004, 22–35.)

The regnal year was reintroduced (and required in legal documents) by the Emperor Justinian in 537 CE but now reckoned from the date of accession. It thus became possible to have a regnal year, a consulate, and an indiction date all in the same document and each with a different starting date in the course of the year. In Oxyrhynchus there was in addition a local era year, based on the regnal years of Constantius and Julian and using a Thoth 1 year. Scribes in Oxyrhynchus tried various methods of simplifying this information overload; these are still not fully understood. Documents of the Byzantine period contain a considerable number of scribal inconsistencies between the different reckoning systems; the indiction year is usually the most reliable marker (see Bagnall and Worp 2004, index s.v. "blunders"). After the Arab conquest, an era dated by the accession of Diocletian (284), which is found for horoscopes and some private inscriptions under Roman rule, begins to appear in the documentary papyri (at least from the Arsinoite nome); still later the Hijra year (reckoned from 622) begins to be used, sometimes with the Egyptian months and occasionally with the Arabic calendar. The latter is lunar but does not use intercalary months as the Macedonians did, thus moving backward against the solar calendar by about eleven days each year. (For all aspects of year reckoning and the calendar in the period from Diocletian to after the Arab conquest see Bagnall and Worp 2004.)

GEOGRAPHY

Egypt was historically divided into forty nomes (Greek *nomoi*), half in Lower Egypt (the delta of the Nile) and half in Upper Egypt (the Nile valley from the head of the delta to the first cataract of the Nile at Aswan). The balanced duality of Upper and Lower Egypt was deeply rooted in the Egyptian consciousness. The Persians, Alexander, and the Ptolemies all in turn took over this basic structure, which reflected not only administrative convenience but also regional and local religious identity. The Greeks called the capitals of the nomes "cities" even though they were not autonomous, and they began to acquire standardized sets of institutions already in the Ptolemaic period. The Romans accelerated the civic development of these "metropoleis," culminating in Septimius Severus's grant of the right to have a city council (*boulê*) in 200 CE. As the delta gradually developed into the dominant part of the country, with perhaps two-thirds of Egypt's arable land and population, the number of nomes there grew.

Most of the nomes were subdivided into units called *toparchiai* (toparchies), representing a group of villages with their land. We know the full extent and number of toparchies for only a small number of nomes, but the average nome seems to have had six to ten of them referred to by their names. They were replaced in 307/308 with a system of *pagi*, in which nomes were typically divided into a larger number of subunits than before. These *pagi* were generally numbered. The Arsinoite nome, uniquely as far as we know, was divided in the third century BCE into three large subdivisions, the *merides* of Herakleides, Themistos, and Polemon, to which toparchies were subsidiary. During some parts of the Roman period these units had their own governors as if they were separate nomes. The large size of the Fayyum (perhaps about fifteen hundred square km at its peak) was presumably responsible for this unique structure.

The village (Greek *kômê*) was the next level of administration and geography; the villages varied greatly in population and amount of land within their control. Smaller units, often called *epoikion*, also existed. The character of these evidently varied and included both large private farmsteads and small hamlets with multiple households. Some evolved into villages, but others remained part of the territory of a larger village.

At the other end of the spectrum, the nomes were from time to time grouped into larger regional units with some form of government. Only the Thebaid in Upper Egypt plays an important regional role in the Ptolemaic documents, but, under the Romans, three or four units, each headed by an *epistrategos,* are found. After Diocletian, the province of Egypt was divided into smaller provinces headed by *praesides,* whose number and boundaries changed repeatedly. The subdivision of the delta marks its increasing importance. The imperial authority was in this way brought closer to the population.

Individuals are often identified in the papyri by their place of legal residence (*idia*). This description usually includes the city of residence or an adjective derived from it ("from Hermopolis" or "Hermopolite") in the case of urban residents. Villagers are generally identified as coming from a particular village of a specified nome, sometimes with toparchy or (from 307/308 onward) the *pagus* specified as well. On locally used documents, the nome name is sometimes omitted, and only the toparchy or *pagus* is given.

Most place names in the papyri are, as one would expect, of Egyptian origin. Sometimes equivalences between Greek and demotic or Coptic place names are known; in other cases, the Egyptian derivation of a Greek transcription may be apparent. Still others are so far unexplained. Many times the same name appears in more than one part of Egypt. The Arsinoite nome forms a special situation in which the large-scale expansion of settlement in the early Ptolemaic period produced a wave of new place names. Some of these were drawn from the ideological program also visible in the naming of the demes of Alexandria, encompassing Ptolemaic dynastic names and cultic names; others (Memphis, Boubastos, and the like) refer to the places from which Egyptian settlers had come to the Arsinoite.

Geographical names in Egypt are inventoried in Calderini and Daris (1935–). There are useful repertories specific to particular nomes, most notably, the Hermopolite (Drew-Bear 1979); Oxyrhynchite (Pruneti 1981); Herakleopolite (Falivene 1998); and Arsinoite (Leuven Fayum Villages Project). For topographical maps that show locatable places, see the *Barrington Atlas* (Talbert 2000).

MEASURES

Nowhere do we see the succession of influences on Egypt better than in weights and measures. Pharaonic, Persian, Greek, and Roman measures form cultural strata, with new measures being connected to old and local variants common and numerous. Only a selection can be treated here, but these account for the overwhelming majority of instances encountered in texts. (In the discussion, the figures given are approximate.)

The Land

Linear and square measurements are usually given by a system that dates back to pharaonic times, in which the basic unit of length was the cubit (Eg. *mḥ*, Gk. *pêchus*, Copt. *maje*), of .525 m. (Other cubits are also known, but "cubit" without description normally refers to this measure.) The cubit was divided into hands and fingers and served in turn as the basis for the principal unit of surface measurement or area, the *aroura* (Eg. *st3*, Copt. *sôt*), which was 100 cubits, or a *schoinion* (52.5 m) on a side, thus 2,756 square meters (1 square km = 363 arouras). Subdivisions of the

Table 8.2. Length and Land

1 sacred cubit (*mḥ*) = 7 hands = 28 fingers = .525 m
1 kalamos = 6 cubits (as square measure, 36 square cubits)
1 ground cubit (*mḥ-itn*) = 96 square cubits = 1/100 aroura
1 *hamma* = 144 square cubits = 1/64 aroura
10,000 square cubits = 1 aroura (*st3, sôt*) = 2756.25 square meters

aroura are usually given by fractions (1/2, 1/4, 1/8, 1/16, 1/32, 1/64), the smallest of which, 1/64, is called a *hamma*. However, units based on a decimal division were also known and used a notional unit that measured 1 × 100 cubits (the "ground cubit," or *mḥ-itn* in Demotic). These were probably reconciled by use of the *geometrikon*, or surveyor's measure, which was based on 96 rather than 100 cubits. An obscure measure called the *bikos* may have been 1½ *hammata*, but its equation to the *mḥ-itn* is not excluded. (See *T. Varie*, pp. 156–158.) The aroura and its subdivisions were the principal basis for the computation of taxes on land.

A volume of earth was measured by the *naubion*, which in the Ptolemaic period referred to a mass of 2 cubits in each dimension, or 1.158 cubic meters. In the Roman period, the *naubion* meant a volume of 3 cubits in each dimension, or 3.9 cubic meters (table 8.2).

Dry Measure

For wheat, barley, and other dry commodities the standard unit of reference was the *artaba*, a Persian measure that replaced the pharaonic *ḥ3r* (sack) of about 80 liters. The mentions in documents of many different measures and the varying information found in ancient metrological treatises have generated much controversy about the degree to which the artaba varied from place to place and time to time. It may initially have corresponded to about 60 Egyptian *hin* (30 liters) and thus to 30 Greek *choinikes* and perhaps equated to the Persian *hofen* (Vleeming 1980, 1981). In the Greek papyri of the Roman period, the artaba is consistently composed of 40 *choinikes*, which was the unit recognized by the government; it was also the commonest measure in the Ptolemaic period and perhaps corresponded roughly to half of the pharaonic sack. A unit called simply the "measure," short for "four-choinix measure," is often found; it is thus a tenth of an artaba. The Egyptian-derived term *mation* (*maje* in Coptic) was also used in the Roman and Byzantine periods for a tenth of an artaba. The artaba is also, however, measured in fractions down to 1/48. How the two different systems of subdivision were handled in practice is unclear, but the parallel of coexisting divisional systems for land is instructive. Although the successive governments aimed to enforce standardization in the measure used in tax payments (the "receiving measure," or *metron dochikon*)

Table 8.3. Dry Measure

1 artaba = 10 metra = 10 matia = 40 choinikes = 72 sextarii (xestai) = 38.808 liters
1 mation or metron = 3.88 liters
1 choinix = .97 liter
1 sextarius = .539 liter
1 artaba = 3 1/3 modii xystoi = 4.5 modii Italici
1 modius xystos (castrensis) = 21.6 sextarii = 11.64 liters
1 modius Italicus = 16 sextarii = 8.62 liters

and therefore checked shipments for conformity, there was no central control of the measures used in private transactions. Contracts often specify which measure to use in order to avoid possible doubt. One common measure, the Athenian, is at times equated to the "receiving measure" (Clarysse 1985).

Part of the controversy over the artaba and choinix arises from metrological tables of the Roman period and from equations between the artaba and Roman dry measures, which sometimes appear in the papyri. The Romans measured grain with the *modius,* but this too needed to be specified. The *modius Italicus* (Italian modius) equated to 16 *sextarii* (*xestai* in Greek), or 8.62 liters. The artaba generally equated to 4.5 modii Italici, or 72 sextarii. The other common modius, the *modius castrensis,* is usually called *xystos* in Greek, and ten of them equaled 3 artabas; its size was thus 21.6 sextarii. A slightly larger variant of the modius castrensis (at 22 sextarii) is also attested.

Because the sextarius held .539 liter, these Roman equivalences allow a calculation of the capacity of the artaba, which was thus 38.8 liters, and the standard choinix .97 liter. This capacity for the artaba has also been identified in the Rosetta Stone on the basis of the indication there that it was 4/15 of a cubic cubit. If Pliny's indication that the modius Italicus of Egyptian wheat weighed 20 5/6 Roman pounds is correct, the artaba of 4.5 modii must have weighed about 30.28 kg. It is impossible to be sure how far this standard artaba prevailed throughout Egypt at all times, but there is no good evidence for any normal use of a different artaba (Duncan-Jones 1976a, 1976b; Shelton 1977, 1981; Rathbone 1983) (table 8.3).

A very large number of other measures appear at different times and places for a variety of other goods; examples are the *môion* and *sarganê* for chaff, the *desmê* for hay, and the load, or *gomos,* for various goods. In most instances we neither know the size of these measures nor have a clear sense of how localized their capacity may have been.

Liquid Measure

The Greek system of liquid measurement was based on the *kotylê,* but this was itself not of fixed size. The Attic kotylê, the measure most often meant when another is

Table 8.4. Liquid Measures in the Great Oasis in the Fourth Century

1 *kotylê* = .27 liter
2 *kotylai* = 1 *sextarius* (.54 l)
12 *kotylai* = 6 *sextarii* = 1 *chous* (3.24 l)
9 sextarii = 1½ choes = 1 *boxion* (4.86 l)
18 sextarii = 3 choes = 1 *keramion* (9.72 l)
20 sextarii = 3 1/3 choes = 1 *marion* (10.8 l)
(1 metrêtês = 12 choes = 4 keramia [38.9 l])

not specified, was about .27 liter. The next larger unit was the *chous,* which had the following equations:

> 12 *kotylai* = 1 *chous* (3.24 liters)
> 12 *choes* = 1 *metrêtês* (39 liters).

An alternative system in use in the Arsinoite nome in the Ptolemaic period had a larger kotylê (.406 liter) and chous (4.875 liters), with a metrêtês of 6 choes, or 29.25 liters.

The papyri of the Ptolemaic and Roman periods offer a rich array of names for containers of wine and (to a lesser extent) oil (see Kruit and Worp 1999, 2000). Some of these are formed from place names like Rhodes, Knidos, Chios, and Samos. Originally they referred to jars of wine that originated in these places. The containers had varying capacities; for instance, Thasian jars have been estimated at 21 liters, Chian jars at 23, Rhodian ones at 26, and Milesian and Samian jars at 52 (thus 1.5 Attic metrêtai). Some of these jar names remained in use but apparently referred to locally made jars of distinctive capacities; the *knidion* had the longest life and was equated to the *diploun* ("double jar"). The commonest term, however, is *keramion,* which simply means "pottery jar" and does not of itself indicate any particular capacity. Within any household or enterprise, everyone would normally know what size keramion was in use. Where doubt could arise, adjectives referring to capacity were added. The commonest keramia corresponded to 3 (9.72 liters) and 4 choes (12.96 liters).

The Romans used a liquid and dry measure called the *sextarius,* which the Greeks translated as *xestês.* This was about .54 liter. It makes its appearance in Egypt well into the period of Roman rule; by the late fourth century it had become dominant and ousted the older Greek system entirely. Table 8.4 shows the set of equivalences of measures in use in a fourth-century context that continued to employ both choes and sextarii.

Weight

The Greek weight system was based on the *drachmê,* or drachma, a term also used for coins of this weight. In the Roman period, the drachma was treated as 1/96 of the Roman pound (about 323 g), or about 3.36 g (table 8.5). But different Greek

Table 8.5. Weights and Currency

8 chalkoi = 1 obol

6 obols = 1 drachma

2 drachmas = 1 qd (kite)

4 drachmas = 2 qd = 1 stater (tetradrachm) = 1 denarius

20 drachmas = 10 qd = 1 dbn

100 drachmas = 50 qd = 5 dbn = 1 mna

6000 drachmas = 3000 qd = 300 dbn = 1500 denarii = 60 mnai = 1 talent (Eg. krkr)

1 gold "quarter" (tetartê) = ½ drachma (a quarter of a didrachm or qd)

1 gold mnaieion = 8 drachmas (weight) = 16 "quarters"

1 Roman pound (litra) = 12 ounces (ounkiai) = 288 Roman grams (grammata) = 323 g

1 solidus (Diocletian to Constantine) = 1/60 pound = 4.8 grammata

1 solidus (post-Constantine) = 1/72 pound = 4 grammata = 24 carats

cities and other regions of the Greek world had their own weight standards, and one always needs to know what standard is in use in order to interpret figures in the texts. In general in the papyri one can presume that the drachma as a weight refers to the Ptolemaic standard (see the following section), which is close to but a bit higher than the figure given above. In Egyptian texts the drachma was reckoned as half of a qd (Copt. kite) and thus 1/20 of the dbn, which equated to 20 drachmas. In the Greek system of weights (described in the next section), the drachma was a subdivision in a system that included the mna and the talent, both also accounting terms for money. (For weights in jewelry see Ogden 1996.)

The Roman pound also had its own system of subdivisions and consisted of 12 unciae (Gk. ounkiai), or ounces, and grams (Gk. grammata), at 24 grams to the ounce. Thus 288 grams constituted a pound.

CURRENCY

Egypt used coinage only to a limited extent before the Macedonian conquest, but Egyptian documents both before and after the conquest readily express monetary value using a weight-based system, the deben and the kite.

Greek monetary systems were based on the weight unit called the drachma, with the following equivalences:

    100 drachmas = 1 mna
    60 mnai = 6,000 drachmas = 1 talent

The talent and the *mna*, however, were accounting units rather than minted coins. The drachma, as indicated earlier, varied according to local standards. During the last decade of the fourth century, Ptolemy I abandoned the heavier Athenian weight standard used by Macedonian kings up to this time in favor of a lighter Phoenician drachma of about 3.55 metric grams of silver, with the tetradrachm (four-drachma coin) weighing about 14.2 g. This weight standard remained in use through the remainder of Ptolemaic rule. Gold coins were also minted, with the eight-drachma coin valued the same as a *mina* of silver (the value ratio between the metals was 12 1/2:1).

Beginning in the reign of Ptolemy II, the role of bronze coinage became steadily more important. The stages of this development are controversial (Maresch 1996; Cadell and Le Rider 1997; von Reden 2007). At an early period, under Ptolemies II and III, the bronze coinage had a substantial fiduciary element, but the relationship of silver and bronze began to change from the reign of Ptolemy IV on in tandem with an increase in nominal prices expressed in bronze. The bronze-to-silver ratio eventually reached a level of 1:480, and additional charges were levied for exchange of bronze for silver. Most of the prices in later Ptolemaic papyri are expressed in bronze drachmas and talents. This development was not the result of the debasement of the silver tetradrachms, however, which did not begin until 149/148 and became substantial only under Ptolemy XII (Hazzard 1995). When working with prices in drachmas or talents in Ptolemaic texts, one must determine whether the figures are given in silver or bronze drachmas. If they are in silver, they can be compared across the Ptolemaic period with little risk of distortion; if in bronze, however, one must try to establish the period and the ratio of bronze to silver prevalent at that time (see Maresch 1996; Cadell and Le Rider 1997).

After the Romans acquired Egypt, Augustus minted bronze coins on the same denominational standard as the Ptolemies; from his year 28 on, these bear year dates, as do those of his successors. Tiberius introduced a tetradrachm of bronze with a small admixture of silver ("billon"), nominally equated to the Roman denarius, and Nero a bronze drachma equated to the sestertius. The drachma, as under the Ptolemies, was divided into six obols, and each obol into eight chalkoi, although the smallest fraction actually minted was usually the two-chalkoi coin. Tax payments were supposed to be made in billon tetradrachms, and a surcharge was levied for payment in the bronze drachmas and fractions. This policy gave rise to a number of complex accounting practices visible in the papyri, including the charging of supplements for exchange, discounting of the smaller coins, and the use of a tetradrachm with more than twenty-four obols in accounting. No gold was minted in Roman Egypt. This monetary system was separate from that of the rest of the Roman East and thereby kept Egypt in a kind of monetary isolation (West and Johnson 1944; Gara 1976).

That isolation was ended in 296 by Diocletian, who introduced into Egypt standard Roman coinage of his day; from this point on we begin to find references to denarii in the papyri. The old terminology, however, with drachmas and talents, remained in use for quite some time. A wave of price increases had occurred in the period after the Antonine plague in the later 160s, but prices then remained stable until about 275, when the papyri indicate an increase of nearly an order of magnitude. The successive waves of reduction in silver content in the imperial coinage after 296, coupled with the redenomination of coins, led to what looks like a massive price inflation between Diocletian and the third quarter of the fourth century. The nature, causes, and effects of this phenomenon are controversial, but there are good reasons to regard it essentially as a monetary phenomenon, the result of episodic pressures on imperial finances that led to debasement of the currency (Bagnall 1985). Just as the obol disappears in the papyri in the second half of the third century, the drachma vanishes in the fourth. Accounts come to be kept largely in talents or in myriads of denarii (a myriad, or ten thousand denarii, was equivalent to 6 2/3 talents).

The most decisive monetary phenomenon of the fourth century, however, was the rise of the gold coin called the solidus (mostly called *nomisma, nomismation,* or *holokottinos* in Greek), first issued by Diocletian at 1/60 of a Roman pound, subsequently set at four Roman *grammata,* or 1/72 of a pound, by Constantine and stable at that weight for the remainder of Roman rule in Egypt. Because we have no consistent series of data, price movements in gold are harder to track than those in bronze currency, although wheat seems to have become cheaper against gold between the fourth and the sixth century (see Banaji 2002). Most major transactions in the papyri of the fifth to the seventh centuries were denominated in solidi, and tax obligations in money were calculated in gold. The solidus had subdivisions in imperial coinage; the only one commonly referred to in the papyri is the *tremissis,* a third of a solidus. We find also the carat (*keration*), at 1/24 of a solidus, as an accounting unit rather than an actual coin. Most taxes were actually paid in bronze, however, thus giving rise to extensive opportunities for exchange transactions and, presumably, profits.

The papyri of the fifth to the seventh centuries quote many figures in the form of so many solidi minus (Gk. *para*) so many carats. The number subtracted varies from place to place and time to time, and the meaning of these sums remains controversial (see generally Maresch 1994). In part they seem to reflect local standards, which also led to accounting practices in which a total number of carats was divided by a figure lower than twenty-four to get the number of whole solidi. The standard of twenty-four, however, remained the "full-weight" standard.

NAMES

Stretching over nearly fifteen hundred years, the papyri record many names of individuals. Most of these are Egyptian, as one would expect, but many are Greek, Latin, and Semitic, along with fewer names of other origins. A number of volumes collect these names, but because these have been created according to the languages of the documents, none gives a comprehensive picture or is even current. For the Greek papyri, searching the Duke Data Bank of Documentary Papyri (DDbDP) is an indispensable supplement to the printed volumes of Preisigke (1922) and Foraboschi (1967–1971). For texts in other languages there is at present no such easy solution, but demotic texts are well covered by Lüddeckens and Thissen (1980–2000). A list of names in Coptic documentary texts by M. Hasitzka (2007) is available on the Internet.

Ancient names almost always have meanings that their etymologies reveal. Because many Egyptian names are known to us only in Greek transcription, the meanings of many are not yet known, but many are either known with certainty or conjectured with some likelihood. The collaboration of Greek papyrologists and Egyptologists has enabled much progress in this area (the index of names in Pestman 1981 is a good example), but a great deal remains to be done.

Most Egyptian names are nominal phrases, very often constructed with the name of a god, such as "he who has been given by Isis" (Peteesis) or "the daughter of Amoun" (Senamounis). Some are short sentences, and others are just the Egyptian definite article (masculine *p-*, feminine *t-*) with an adjective, noun, or ethnic (e.g., Pekysis, "the Nubian"). Some of these names (e.g., Horos) are common throughout Egypt, but most are local, limited to one or several places. This localism is mainly the product of variations in Egyptian religion; children were named after the gods particularly venerated in their home village, city, or nome, whom parents thanked for the gift of the child. Some also come from dialect differences among the regions of Egypt, as, for example, with the alternation between /a/ and /o/ in the vocalizations of the name of the god Shaï and of persons given names derived from it (Quaegebeur 1975).

Egyptian onomastic practice also changes over time; names come into or go out of fashion sometimes reflecting religious change as well. The result of this situation is that, when papyri from a provenance not previously well known come to light, they tend to yield a large number of previously unknown names. If no demotic texts are available to provide etymologies, Greek transcriptions may remain opaque. Editors of Greek texts have often been lulled by these difficulties into an attitude of "anything goes" with respect to Egyptian names, but the result of this approach is usually the reading of phantom names. At the same time, it is true that a large proportion of personal names occurs only once or twice in the documentation; rarity is thus not necessarily an indication of misreading.

The Greek settlers in Egypt brought with them their own names, some of them common throughout the Greek world but others particular to a given region or city. In particular, many Macedonian names occur in the papyri because of the importance of the Macedonian contingent among the earliest settlers. Ptolemaios is only the commonest of these. Among them were many formed from the names of Greek gods, for the Egyptians were hardly alone in constructing personal names in this manner; thus, we find names like Diodoros ("gift of Zeus"). Alongside this repertory developed a body of Greek names analogously formed from the appellations of Egyptian gods, like Besodoros ("gift of Bes") or Horion.

The papyri also contain numerous names from the Semitic languages, mostly brought by settlers from regions like Judaea and Idumaea, whether recruited for the Ptolemaic military or coming to Egypt for other economic reasons. The large Jewish population of Egypt used some relatively colorless Greek names alongside some of more distinctively Jewish character. After the large-scale slaughter of Egypt's Jewish population in the wake of the revolt under Trajan and Hadrian, distinctively Jewish names become rare in the papyri. Names found in the Hebrew scriptures, however, come back into prominence in late antiquity with the Christianization of Egypt and the rebuilding of a Jewish community in Alexandria and other Egyptian cities. With particular names, it is at times difficult to be certain whether an individual is a Christian or a Jew.

Christianity also brought a range of other names that provide specific indication of religious allegiance. Some of these are the names of apostles and martyrs in the New Testament (Peter and Paul, in particular); others refer to qualities (Adelphios), to theological doctrines or abstractions (Anastasia), or to saints and martyrs venerated throughout Egypt or more locally. It is mainly through this last category that some theophoric pagan names survive in late antiquity by means of their association with one or more saints (Apollos and Phoibammon are characteristic examples).

Papyri written after the Arab conquest (cf. chapter 19) also attest Arabic names. At first these are mainly those of high-ranking officials in the Arab administration, but as the population of Egypt began to convert to Islam, Arabic names are increasingly found among the Egyptian population in general. In the Coptic papyri, this phenomenon is evident especially from the ninth century on.

PROSOPOGRAPHY

The papyri mention many thousands of individuals bearing these varied names. The overwhelming majority of these (mostly ordinary taxpayers or other inhabitants but some of much higher status) are known from only one appearance. A smaller percentage are attested more often, and a relative handful appear in numerous documents, usually because these belong to archives constituted by these individuals. Papyrologists and historians have created some tools aimed at inventorying the identifiable people of various times and places, a scholarly subdiscipline called *prosopography* (the study of individuals), much used for Roman history and to a lesser extent for Greek history, but the sheer mass of material has limited such efforts. The most extensive is the *Prosopographia Ptolemaica,* now most fully available on the Internet.

Prosopographies of the Roman and the Byzantine periods have been less viable enterprises because the quantity of data is so much larger. They exist for particular periods for the Arsinoite and Oxyrhynchite nomes, as well as for the localities of Antinoopolis and Aphrodito; another prosopography is limited to the Coptic documentation from Thebes (mainly the West Bank) at the end of Byzantine rule and in the first century of Arab rule. No such works based on papyrological documents have been produced in the last twenty-five years except for the digitization of the *Prosopographia Ptolemaica* (print version: Peremans and Van 't Dack 1950–). (For other printed prosopographies see Diethart 1980; Jones and Whitehorne 1980; and Till 1954.) High-ranking officials in the papyri of the period from Diocletian to Heraclius can often be found in the *Prosopography of the Later Roman Empire* (Jones, Martindale, and Morris 1971–1992).

TECHNICAL VOCABULARY

Preferring variation in diction, literary Greek was on the whole averse to the use of technical vocabulary. The Greek of the documents, however, has a rich repertory of words used with specialized meanings for particular institutions, offices, taxes, legal acts, and other administrative and legal purposes. Many of these were adopted in Egyptian and appear in the Coptic texts as well. There has never been a full study of the technical vocabulary, and the only attempt to compile it is Preisigke (1915), now long out of date and perhaps the least successful of his research tools in that it requires considerable experience for profitable use. The specialized indexes of the *Wörterbuch* (Preisigke et al. 1925–) provide a kind of categorized listing of such vocabulary by domain but not always with definitions. Pestman (1994, 283–304) presents a handy glossary with English definitions. For Greek terms that represent Roman concepts or institutions, see Mason (1974), which, although flawed, is often useful. Frequently, however, the simplest way to understand the usage and meaning of technical terms is to search in the DDbDP for an attestation in a recent volume that is well edited and has translations.

BIBLIOGRAPHY

Bagnall, R. S. 1985. *Currency and Inflation in Fourth-century Egypt.* Atlanta: Scholars Press.
——, A. Cameron, S. Schwartz, and K. A. Worp. 1987. *Consuls of the Late Roman Empire.* Atlanta.

Bagnall, R. S., and K. A. Worp. 2004. *Chronological Systems of Byzantine Egypt*, 2d ed. Leiden: Brill.

Banaji, J. 2002. *Agrarian Change in Late Antiquity: Gold, Labour, and Aristocratic Dominance*. New York: Oxford University Press.

Bureth, P. 1964. *Les titulatures impériales dans les papyrus, les ostraca, et les inscriptions d'Égypte (30 a.c.–284 p.c.)*. Brussels: Fondation égyptologique Reine Elisabeth.

Cadell, H., and G. Le Rider. 1997. *Prix du blé et numéraire dans l'Égypte lagide de 305 à 173*. Brussels.

Calderini, A., and S. Daris. 1935–. *Dizionario dei nomi geografici e topografici dell'Egitto greco-romano*. 5 vols. and 3 supplements to date. Milan.

Clarysse, W. 1985. "The Athenian Measure at Hermopolis." *ZPE* 60: 232–236.

———, and G. van der Veken. 1983. *The Eponymous Priests of Ptolemaic Egypt (P.L. Bat. 24): Chronological Lists of the Priests of Alexandria and Ptolemais with a Study of the Demotic Transcriptions of Their Names*. Leiden: Brill.

Diethart, J. M. 1980. *Prosopographia Arsinoitica*. Vol. 1. Vienna: In Kommission bei Verlag Brüder Hollinek.

Drew-Bear, M. 1979. *Le nome Hermopolite: Toponymes et sites*. Missoula, Mont.: Scholars Press.

Duncan-Jones, R. P. 1976a. "The Choenix, the Artaba, and the Modius." *ZPE* 21: 43–52.

———. 1976b. "The Size of the Modius Castrensis." *ZPE* 21: 53–62.

Falivene, M. R. 1998. *The Herakleopolite Nome*. Atlanta: Scholars Press.

Foraboschi, D. 1967–1971. *Onomasticon alterum papyrologicum*. Milan.

Gara, A. 1976. *Prosdiagraphomena e circolazione monetaria*. Milan.

Grenier, J.-C. 1989. *Les titulatures des empereurs romains dans les documents en langue égyptienne*. Brussels.

Grzybek, E. 1990. *Du calendrier macédonien au calendrier ptolémaïque*. Basel.

Hagedorn, D., and K. A. Worp. 1994. "Das Wandeljahr im römischen Ägypten." *ZPE* 104: 243–255.

Hazzard, R. A. 1995. *Ptolemaic Coins: An Introduction for Collectors*. Toronto: Kirk & Bentley.

Jones, A. H. M., J. R. Martindale, and J. Morris. 1972–1992. *The Prosopography of the Later Roman Empire*. 3 vols. Cambridge: Cambridge University Press.

Jones, B., and J. Whitehorne. 1980. *Register of Oxyrhynchites*, 30 B.C.–A.D. 96. Chico, Calif.: Scholars Press.

Kienast, D. 1990. *Römische Kaisertabelle*. Darmstadt.

Kruit, N., and K. A. Worp. 1999. "Metrological Notes on Measures and Containers of Liquids in Graeco-Roman and Byzantine Egypt." *APF* 45: 96–127.

Kruit, N., and K. A. Worp. 2000. "Geographical Jar Names." *APF* 46: 65–146.

Lüddeckens, E., and H. J. Thissen. 1980–2000. *Demotisches Namenbuch*. Wiesbaden: Reichert.

Maresch, K. 1994. *Nomisma und Nomismatia : Beiträge zur Geldgeschichte Ägyptens im 6. Jahrhundert n. Chr.* Opladen.

———. 1996. *Bronze und Silber: Papyrologische Beiträge zur Geschichte der Währung im ptolemäischen und römischen Ägypten bis zum 2. Jahrhundert n. Chr.* Opladen.

Mason, H. J. 1974. *Greek Terms for Roman Institutions: A Lexicon and Analysis*. Toronto: Hakkert.

Ogden, J. 1996. "Weight Units of Romano-Egyptian Gold." In *Archaeological Research in Roman Egypt: The Proceedings of the Seventeenth Classical Colloquium of the Depart-*

ment of Greek and Roman Antiquities, British Museum, held on 1–4 December, 1993, ed. Donald M. Bailey, 191–196. Ann Arbor, Mich.: Journal of Roman Archaeology.

Parker, R. A. 1950. *The Calendars of Ancient Egypt.* Chicago: University of Chicago Press.

Peremans, W., and E. van 't Dack. 1950–. *Prosopographia Ptolemaica.* 10 vols. to date, arranged systematically with a name index. Leuven: Bibliotheca Universitatis. http://prosptol.arts.kuleuven.ac.be/.

Pestman, P. W. 1967. *Chronologie égyptienne d'après les textes démotiques (332 av. J.-C.–453 ap. J.-C.).* Leiden: Brill.

——. 1981. *A Guide to the Zenon Archive.* Vol. 1. Leiden: Brill.

——. 1994. *The New Papyrological Primer*, 2d ed. Leiden: Brill.

Preisigke, F. 1915. *Fachwörter des öffentlichen Berwaltungsdienstes Ägyptens in der griechischen Papyrusurkunden der ptolemäisch-römischen Zeit.* Göttingen.

——. 1922. *Namenbuch.* Heidelberg.

——, et al. 1925–. *Wörterbuch der griechischen Papyrusurkunden, mit Einschluss der griechischen Inschriften, Aufschriften, Ostraka, Mumienschilder, usw. aus Ägypten.* Berlin.

Pruneti, P. 1981. *I centri abitati dell'Ossirinchite: Repertorio toponomastico.* Florence.

Quaegebeur, J. 1975. *Le dieu égyptien Shaï dans la religion et l'onomastique.* Leuven.

Rathbone, D. W. 1983. "The Weight and Measurement of Egyptian Grains." *ZPE* 53: 265–275.

Samuel, A. E. 1962. *Ptolemaic Chronology.* Munich: Beck.

Scott, K. 1932. "Greek and Roman Honorific Months." *Yale Classical Studies* 2: 201–278.

Shelton, J. C. 1977. "Artabs and Choenices." *ZPE* 24: 55–67.

——. 1981. "Two Notes on the Artab." *ZPE* 42: 99–106.

Skeat, T. C. 1969. *The Reigns of the Ptolemies*, 2d ed. Munich: Beck.

——. 1993. *The Reign of Augustus in Egypt: Conversion Tables for the Egyptian and Julian Calendars, 30 B.C.–14 A.D.* Munich: Beck.

Talbert, R., ed. 2000. *Barrington Atlas of the Greek and Roman World.* Princeton, N.J.: Princeton University Press.

Till, W. 1954. *Datierung und Prosopographie der koptischen Urkunden aus Theben.* Vienna.

Vleeming, S. P. 1980. "Masse und Gewichte." *Lexikon der Ägyptologie* 3: 1209–1214.

——. 1981. "The Artaba and Egyptian Grain-Measures." In *Proceedings of the Sixteenth International Congress of Papyrology*, ed. R. S. Bagnall, 537–545. Chico, Calif.: Scholars Press.

Von Reden, S. 2007. *Money in Ptolemaic Egypt: From the Macedonian Conquest to the End of the Third Century BC.* Cambridge: Cambridge University Press.

West, L. C., and A. C. Johnson. 1944. *Currency in Roman and Byzantine Egypt.* Princeton, N.J.: Princeton University Press.

CHAPTER 9

EDITING A PAPYRUS

PAUL SCHUBERT

INTRODUCTION: THE TOOLS OF THE TRADE

The process of editing a papyrus is undeniably a central aspect in the field of papyrology. Starting often with little more help than the document itself, which is seldom completely preserved, a papyrologist must tackle many forms of writing. The edition of a papyrus should give readers from other fields of specialization access to this material in its original language, offer a translation in a modern language, and, most important, place the new text into its broader environment, be it historical or literary.

Although papyri are an abundant source of information for our knowledge of daily life in the ancient world, one could easily object that nobody needs yet another contract for the sale of a donkey or another scrap from the first book of the *Iliad*. On the other hand, one can argue that, when placed in the right setting, very few papyri lack any new information for the reader. It is therefore all the more desirable that the edition of a new papyrus not only provide readers with a sound text and internal commentary but also inform them of the text's addition to our knowledge about a particular topic.

As this chapter explains, the task of a scholar who undertakes the edition of a papyrus resembles that of a detective. Following some basic methodological principles, adding a certain amount of experience gained through contact with many texts, and using state-of-the-art tools to find their way around an increasingly vast corpus of primary sources, papyrologists must fit together various pieces of a puzzle. The emerging picture then needs to be interpreted in the light of findings made in related fields.

Several excellent introductions to the process of editing papyri have been written by some eminent specialists (Turner 1973, 1980; Youtie 1963, 1966, 1974). In the last three decades, however, the advent of electronic tools has made possible—and necessary—the quick handling of a huge mass of data, thus changing substantially many aspects of the way in which papyrologists edit their texts.

Until the last quarter of the twentieth century, scholars handling a literary papyrus resorted primarily to their general knowledge of ancient literature, thereby following in the path of the pioneers of papyrology, such as Bernard Grenfell and Arthur Hunt. Many had started learning Latin and Greek at secondary school and, by the time they were confronted with the task of deciphering a papyrus, displayed an intimate familiarity with the masterpieces of classical civilization. Excellent dictionaries were available, notably Liddell and Scott's (1940). Lexica and concordances pertaining to the major authors contributed to the identification of known texts; some had been produced by hand, while later the first computers helped to compile others. The now ubiquitous *Thesaurus Linguae Graecae (TLG)* created at the University of California–Irvine did not exist, and when it first came into being, it required the use of a computer dedicated almost exclusively to the task of reading Greek texts.

Papyrologists who were dealing with Greek documentary texts were better equipped, thanks mostly to the foresight of a retired German post office official, Friedrich Preisigke. He not only created the *Wörterbuch*, a specialized dictionary devoted to Greek documentary papyri, but also started a number of other useful tools (see chapter 3: the *Namenbuch* for personal names; the *Sammelbuch* for papyri not published in an indexed volume; the *Berichtigungsliste* for corrections to texts; and the *Fachwörter* for technical vocabulary).[1] To the list should be added Aristide Calderini's *Dizionario dei nomi geografici* (1935–2007), a dictionary of all place names in Egypt. Scholars in related fields (e.g., epigraphy) have often envied papyrologists for the diversity and thoroughness of their instruments. In Preisigke's day, papyrology was a relatively young discipline, and the bulk of material was of manageable proportion; thus, he could claim to have taken into account nearly every papyrus that was available to him.

Such was the setting in which previous introductions to the process of editing papyri were developed. Much of what was said then remains valid today. Nevertheless, it is now much easier for a papyrologist to sort through a vast number of papyri—tens of thousands of texts—at high speed, thus making it possible to look for parallels to a new item within a few minutes, where the same process would have required several hours not long ago. On the literary side, the *TLG* can be easily consulted either with a CD-ROM or on the Internet. Working on a small fragment, a papyrologist can now compare readings of even a short series of characters with nearly every text preserved from ancient Greek literature.

Another important aspect of the recent transition toward electronic tools is the increasing integration of these tools: The Duke Databank of Documentary Papyri (DDbDP), which contains the text of nearly every documentary text on papyrus in an easily readable form, is now linked to the *Heidelberger Gesamtverzeichnis der Papy-rusurkunden Ägyptens (HGV)*, where the user will find an exhaustive catalogue of Greek and Latin documentary papyri, including date, place, and contents. Similar databases are now available for Coptic documents and for demotic texts. Texts in the DDbDP also partially record corrections to the original edition. In the United States, major papyrus collections are presently catalogued in a standardized form through the Advanced Papyrological Information System (APIS). Every papyrus can be examined from anywhere in the world through the Internet; once a papyrus has been published, digital images are provided, as well as a translation and commentary. Since papyrus collections and archives tend to be scattered among many locations, such catalogues enable scholars from every country to compare these fragments and make sense of the apparent disorder.

Electronic tools will eventually supersede the main papyrological reference books. Supplements to Preisigke's *Wörterbuch* are becoming redundant now that scholars can search the same data on the Internet. The same can be said of R. A. Pack's *Greek and Latin Literary Texts from Greco-Roman Egypt*, which can be consulted in updated form as an online database from the *Centre de Documentation de Papyrologie Littéraire*, along with the *Leuven Database of Ancient Books*.

DECIPHERMENT: TO AND FRO
BETWEEN THE EYE AND THE MIND

The first phase in the process of editing a papyrus, however, does not require many sophisticated tools but rather a pair of sharp eyes and a certain amount of common sense. Before even starting to decipher a text, a papyrologist will look at the papyrus from a distance. Its general state of preservation will offer a first idea of the gaps that may have to be filled in later. The format of the sheet is also of importance: Obviously, there will be a difference between a tax receipt written on a small slip and a register for a whole village, which would require a roll of some length. In the case of literary papyri, the height of a roll or the layout of a codex page will give the editor a first impression of what they may contain. Margins are also worth taking into account; for instance, elaborate copies of books tend to have more generous margins (cf. chapter 11).

Papyri display a great variety of hands in both literary and documentary texts. Every level of proficiency appears, from the skilled professional scribe producing a book or working at the higher levels of administration in Egypt, to poorly trained individuals who can hardly write their own name (Youtie 1971). It can therefore be of great help to assess the quality of a hand before deciphering even a single word:

Does the scribe know how to write fluently? Is his hand fast? How easy would it be for his contemporary readers to reclaim the meaning of the written text?

A first glance at the writing will also allow a papyrologist to make a rough estimate of the date of a papyrus before starting to look for the possibility of an explicit date to confirm it. Styles vary considerably throughout the Ptolemaic and Roman periods, and, on that basis alone, a trained reader should in most cases be able to narrow the dating of a papyrus to within a century.[2]

Decipherment does not necessarily follow a straight path: Instead of starting at the upper left corner of a sheet, one may find it more helpful to look first for the most easily readable sections. As in a puzzle, every piece added to the picture contributes to the reading of more difficult parts. In a documentary text, the heading often provides crucial information on the type of document under scrutiny. For instance, the mere presence of the word παρά (para) at the beginning of the second line, followed by a name in the genitive (meaning "from X"), will suggest that this is a document that follows the form of a *hypomnema*, a memorandum, most often a request submitted to a person of higher standing by an individual in a subordinate position. In other cases, the presence of a telltale χαίρειν (chairein), or only the abbreviated form X⁻ in the first lines of a document may signal the format of a letter or perhaps a contract drafted in the form of a letter. Again, the presence of a date, accompanied by a titulature and a place name at the beginning of a document, may mean that a contract was written by a scribe working for an official notary, while private contracts usually show a date at the end of the document.

The same first quick assessment applies also to literary papyri. For instance, the presence of short horizontal strokes between the beginnings of two consecutive lines (paragraphos) may indicate that the text is a dialogue, possibly a drama, or a lemmatized commentary. *Nomina sacra*, the abbreviated forms of names like $\overline{\Theta\Sigma} = \theta\epsilon\acute{o}s$, or $\overline{I\Sigma} = \text{'}I\eta\sigma o\hat{u}s$, with a horizontal stroke above the letters, immediately indicate a Christian context (Paap 1959). When the whole width of a column is preserved, the length of lines may suggest a metrical unit: Hexameters are longer than iambic trimeters, and elegiacs alternate between longer and shorter lines. No single rule applies to each individual case, so common sense clearly plays a crucial role.

Much research has been done on the process of reading modern languages, notably English. Although not every result from such studies can indiscriminately be applied to the technique of deciphering ancient cursive scripts, certain findings can serve as useful guidelines to papyrologists. I therefore summarize the most relevant elements here and compare them with the technique of decipherment, which involves mostly trial and error.[3]

Starting with the shape of the letters, the "absolute legibility of a single letter is not what matters; it is relative confusability with other letters that is important" (Gibson and Levin 1975, 195). This is an experience that every papyrologist has had many times. In cursive scripts, confusion between *H* and *N*, *B* and *K*, or *N* and *TI*, for example, is very frequent. Beginners often start deciphering a papyrus one letter at a time, whereas in general one should concentrate on whole words. It is easier to read entire words than each letter sequentially. With modern languages, adults typically read in units of words, although this does not mean that we necessarily recognize a word only by its shape. According to Gibson and Levin (ibid., 197):

> Research on the effectiveness of global form or contour as a basis for recognition of the word has consistently tended to refute the idea. Overall word shape is not a good enough differentiator, and children (as well as adults) do not use it. Not only is differentiation poor without internal analysis, but without such analysis there would be no basis for transfer to new words.

In fact, many factors make a word recognizable. Graphic cues such as dominant letters (in modern languages, capital letters; in a papyrus, a φ, for instance) play an important role. The beginnings (and to a lesser degree the endings) of words seem to be more helpful than the middle in rendering a word recognizable. In reality, we seldom read single words but rather connected text, which implies that the meaning of the words affects our capacity to read the text as a whole.

When deciphering a papyrus, one is confronted not only with the straightfor-ward process of reading but also with the additional difficulty of having to restore the text where the papyrus has been damaged. In this, the psychology of modern reading allows us to draw a parallel with the decipherment of ancient texts. For historical reasons, the Latin alphabet used in many European languages bears a resemblance with Greek cursive script. Gibson and Levin (ibid., 170) state that "if the text is mutilated so that only the top half or the bottom half is visible, it is reasonably easy to read the top and very difficult to read the bottom. The prepon-derance of distinctive features exists on the top of the letters."

Coming back to the decipherment of papyri, if we leave aside very neat capital letters (where each letter is separated from the next and has an easily recognizable shape), it makes little sense to try to decipher words one letter at a time. Words are most often barely separated, and scribes use punctuation only rarely. Typically, in some documents from the end of the Ptolemaic period, a scribe often lifted his pen not between two letters but within a letter itself. He then linked it to the next without lifting his pen.[4]

The shape of letters, however, does matter. Although the same letter may have two different shapes in the same papyrus, one should look for the distinctive features of the most typical letters. For instance, if the scribe systematically ends the descending stroke of ρ with a hook but does not do so when writing a ϕ, this will become useful information when only the lower end of a descending stroke is preserved.

Moving away from the individual letters, a reader of papyri will try to grasp whole words, sometimes sequences of words. The process of deciphering then depends heavily on a movement from the eye to the mind and back again: Papyrologists incessantly check their readings against their prior knowledge of Greek (or whatever ancient language is involved) to match the signal caught by their eyes in a sequence of letters that makes sense in their memories, at least at the basic level of vocabulary and morphology. In ancient as in modern languages, "only certain combinations of letters or words *can* be a word. Knowledge of these rules even in the skilled reader is tacit rather than explicit" (Gibson and Levin 1975, 224). A sequence of strokes and curves will suggest to a papyrologist perhaps not a full word but a root or an ending. One then compares this first result with a number of possibilities and reverts to the papyrus, testing those hypotheses iteratively against the written material.

Because isolated words are seldom of much use, the next step obviously consists of trying to link several words into a sentence. Documentary papyri tend to use standard expressions that recur in many instances. A basic experience of the usual phraseology is therefore a great help to a papyrologist while reading new texts. Beginners will improve their deciphering skills by getting acquainted with a generous selection of texts in one of several available sourcebooks.[5] Even in the case of a perfectly preserved papyrus, a seasoned scholar may at first fail to comprehend certain passages because the cursive writing of particular scribes can be very confusing. For instance, imperial titulatures are often written in a fast scribble in which the individual letters are hardly recognizable. The most extreme cases show little more than a sharply undulating wave for words such as εὐτυχοῦς, εὐσεβοῦς, or σεβαστοῦ (corresponding to Latin *Felix, Pius,* and *Augustus*). With a basic knowledge of the expressions that frequently appear in such passages, the reader can hope to identify some words from the shape of one or two letters. For instance, the χ of εὐτυχοῦς usually stands out from the illegible scribble.

Deciphering a papyrus is of course only part of the process of editing; the next step is to transcribe the text into a form that other scholars will understand. For this purpose, papyrologists have agreed on a system of dots and brackets that indicate the state of the original papyrus and the level of confidence with regard to a particular word or phrase. Those rules were adopted in 1931 and are widely known as the "Leiden system" (table 9.1).[6]

Arguably the single most important item in this list is the dot, the purpose of which is to warn the reader of an uncertain reading. "Van Groningen [originator of the Leiden system] used to say with regard to the rule that uncertain letters should be dotted: 'The dot is a papyrologist's conscience'. "[7] Papyrologists, as well as nonspecialists, who use papyrological editions must therefore tread carefully when using a passage that has been heavily dotted—or bracketed. Simultaneous use of different types of brackets is also to be considered with caution.

When a text is badly corrupted, this is indicated in the apparatus, a section below the text where the reader will find relevant information on the state of the original papyrus. In the case of documentary papyri, editors do not correct spelling mistakes in the edited text but give the standard spelling in the apparatus. A single transcript is sufficient for most practical purposes. Words are separated, punctuation is supplied,

Table 9.1. Editorial Conventions of the Leiden System

1. letters about the reading of which there is a genuine doubt or that are so mutilated that without the context they might be read in more than one way	α̣β̣γ̣δ̣
2. illegible letters, the approximate number of which is known	... or −10− or ± 10
3. missing letters, the approximate number of which is known	[...] or [−10−] or [± 20]
4. missing letters, the number of which is unknown	] or [ ] or [
5. letters restored by the editor of the text	[αβγδ]
6. lacunae in the text (omissions of the scribe)	< > or ***
7. additions made by the editor in order to fill such lacunae	<αβγδ>
8. resolutions of abbreviations (e.g., γρ‾ = γρ(αμματεύς))	(αβγδ)
9. interpolations (i.e., letters or words wrongly added by the scribe and canceled by the editor of the text)	{αβγδ} or {...} or {αβχδ}
10. erasures by the scribe	⟦αβγδ⟧
11. interlinear additions that would be impractical to print between the lines	`αβγδ´

breathings and accents are added, and capital letters used for proper names. Accents, diaereses, or punctuation found in the papyrus are indicated in the apparatus.

With a literary papyrus, if this is a new text, it is advisable to produce two transcripts. The first ("diplomatic transcript") will provide the reader with the text precisely as it is read on the papyrus; it should retain the scribe's spelling, including errors. The second ("full transcript") will correct these errors and supply the reader with word breaks, punctuation, breathings, and accents. In the case of a well-known literary text (e.g., a fragment from the *Odyssey*), however, one transcript is enough; the spelling found on the papyrus is usually given in the text, with a note in the apparatus where necessary.

RESTORATION: THE SEARCH
FOR PARALLELS

Cursive writing in which the shape of every letter is not self-evident can by itself be cause for trouble, but it can also be aggravated by another frequent problem: holes of various sizes in the papyrus. Therefore, in deciphering a new text, a papyrologist often cannot rely solely on shape recognition and approximate feeling of the language to produce a decent transcript but must use parallels from previously published texts.

Looking for parallels has always been a tedious task that requires access to a well-furnished library. Until recently, references to possible parallels had to be located in standard dictionaries; after this, the papyrologist would go on to check the edition of the texts. Few university libraries possess a nearly complete set of classical Greek literature, let alone a generous selection of editions of documentary papyri. New electronic tools, however, have opened the field of papyrology to scholars working in universities of more modest means, where they now have access to texts from around the world. Electronic databases enable one to search not only for a specific word but also for a few letters in a word or for several words in the same context. A search can be further refined by specifying a time span (this is when a rough palaeographical estimate is most useful) or, in the case of Graeco-Roman Egypt, a particular village or nome. With literary fragments, one can also search by genre, date, or place. Recourse to those new tools, however, does not obviate the need to check the original editions later on, when the time comes to add some flesh to the skeleton: Reliance on electronic media alone too often proves treacherous and can lead to serious mistakes. Moreover, sound scholarship always relies on extensive reading of the original sources, regardless of technical progress.

At this point in the process of editing a papyrus, a scholar may follow different paths depending on the type of text under study. Literary and documentary papyri can present the editor with various situations, where the text under scrutiny either conforms to a previously known model or displays no immediate parallel.

A literary papyrus consisting of a fragment from a major work that was independently copied down to the Renaissance is probably the easiest case to handle. A search for parallels might show, for example, that a small scrap of papyrus dating from the second century CE contains a few broken lines from one of the speeches of Demosthenes, the orator most commonly found in Greek papyri. The papyrologist's task would then consist of restoring (with the help of a modern edition of Demosthenes) the appearance of the original papyrus roll; the reading of the papyrus is compared with the modern edition (i.e., with the testimony of Byzantine manuscripts); and variations in the transmitted text are identified. This is quite often a relatively straightforward process, which helps us mainly to evaluate the state of the textual transmission at a given period in relation to our Byzantine manuscripts.

Matters can become more difficult when a search for parallels with a literary fragment yields no suitable match. Complete rolls or codices were a rarity even when papyrology was in its infancy. Nowadays the typical unpublished literary fragment rarely contains a whole column of text. Faced with a previously unknown source, the editor focuses on smaller details in the search for parallels, even though this does not always lead to a complete text. Figure 9.1 is an example of

Figure 9.1. *P.Gen.* inv. 500.

a potentially interesting literary fragment (*P.Gen.* inv. 500) that still awaits a full interpretation.

Since *P.Gen.* inv. 500 is a previously unknown text, both a "diplomatic" and a "full" transcript are provided:

1 (1st hand)	]..[.]κτηρ [	]..[.].κτηρ[
2	].[.].αποτ.[	].[.].αποτ.[
3	]. γωκατασιτ[	].γω κατὰ σιτ[
4	]ερονερμουει.[	ἱ]ερὸν Ἑρμοῦ εἰ.[
5	].αθειναιξο[	ἀ]ναθεῖναι ξό[ανον
6	].υπο.[	].υπο.[
7	]ωιερ.[	]ωιερ.[
8	]ουθησεοτησκ[	ἐπηκολ]ούθησε ὁ τῆς κ[
9	]ουανοικοδομη[	]ου ἀνοικοδομη[
10 (2nd hand)	].ειωμελ[	].είῳ μελ[
11 (1st hand)	]ων.[	]ων.[

· · · · · · · ·

The restorations made in the full transcript suggest that we are dealing with a shrine of Hermes (line 4: ἱ]ερὸν Ἑρμοῦ). It seems that someone has been instructed to set up a statue (line 5: ἀ]ναθεῖναι ξό[ανον). There is also a mention of either building or rebuilding (line 9: ἀνοικοδομη[). Those elements point to a mythological narrative, perhaps explaining the erecting of a statue. The most promising parallel appears in the story of Hermes Perpheraios.[8] In a prose summary of one of Callimachus's *Iambi*, we learn that some fishermen from Ainos in Thracia found a statue in their net. Recognizing this as an image of a god, they set it up in their city. This is an interesting parallel, which could help a papyrologist in interpreting the new papyrus fragment, although the argument in favor of linking it to the Callimachean narrative remains rather weak. A firm conclusion can sometimes elude a papyrologist for many years until another clue shows up in a new papyrus.

Let us now return to documentary papyri. Not all texts are equally likely to conform to a given model. Scribes producing property returns, for instance, usually stick to a standardized phraseology that allows papyrologists to fill in considerable gaps in badly damaged papyri; the same can be said of petitions and many other types of documents. Contracts from the Ptolemaic period often begin with a long list of so-called eponymous priests who had charge of various dynastic cults in honor of the ruling family. These lists follow a standard form, and it is a relatively straightforward process to restore them to the full breadth of a column even when much is actually missing. Once a few lines are confidently filled in and one can estimate the width of the sheet, it is easier to work on the rest of the text, where the formulation may vary depending on the object of the contract.

The contents of mutilated private letters, on the other hand, are notoriously difficult to restore because of several factors that conspire to make a papyrologist's task more arduous: After the usual greetings that the sender shares with the addressee, the sender often continues by alluding to matters familiar to both parties but of which we have no direct knowledge. Because the contents of private letters frequently revolve around the daily life of Egypt's rural population, a myriad of scenarios may confront the modern reader, and a writer's inadequate knowledge of morphology and syntax can contribute to making the text still less intelligible.

Whatever the document's level of standardization and regardless of the quantity of parallels found in other documents, a few simple rules can help one avoid editorial errors:

- The scribes were no fools. When faced with phrasing that makes no sense, a papyrologist should consider what he has not understood before assuming that the scribe was under the influence of strong beer while writing the document. One must also remember that, at the receiving end, scribes expected their readers to be able to understand what they were writing. This general principle should, however, be mitigated by the fact that the level of instruction among scribes varied considerably. A particular scribe might have been incompetent, but a papyrologist should resort to such an explanation only after exhausting other hypotheses more respectful of the scribe's skills.

- The closer an editor is to a gap in the papyrus, the more careful he should be. The so-called Lex Youtie was formalized by Reinhold Merkelbach and neatly summarized by the Latin motto *iuxta lacunam ne mutaveris* ("next to a gap, thou shalt not alter [the text]").[9] In other words, assuming scribal error is most perilous when one does not know what was written next.

- A sheet of papyrus had its cost, and one can therefore expect scribes to use the full width of their page. Left and right margins in a document are not necessarily perfectly vertical, but one should nevertheless aim for a relatively even line length in the process of restoring a partially mutilated column. If, in a sequence of four lines, the text produces lines of 23, 25, 13, and 24 characters, the odds are good that the missing part of the text in line 3 has not been properly restored. This last rule should, of course, not be followed with excessive rigidity since exceptions are not infrequent.[10] For example, the layout of a heading sometimes requires that an element start on a new line, thus causing an indentation or a different spacing of the letters in the preceding line.

TRANSLATION: WHEN IT ALL MAKES SENSE

The early editors of many papyri did not bother to translate the texts they had deciphered, assuming that any decent scholar would know Greek (or any other ancient language) well enough to make this step unnecessary. It is all the more remarkable that Bernard Grenfell and Arthur Hunt, the founders of the *Oxyrhynchus Papyri* series, decided to include a translation of all of the texts they were editing. Did they believe that British readers had less command of the classical languages than their continental counterparts? It would seem that they had in fact two excellent reasons for translating their texts into English.

First, Grenfell and Hunt depended heavily on funding from the Egypt Exploration Fund (now known as the Egypt Exploration Society) for their excavations at Oxyrhynchus. Therefore, they had to appeal to a wide readership so as to convince their benefactors of the relevance of their work in Egypt. One can see how, in the first volumes of the series, they carefully included some new Christian texts, presumably in order to attract the interest of the British clergy. Numerous subscribers of the *Graeco-Roman Memoirs,* as the series (including the *Oxyrhynchus*

Papyri) was called, would have known some Greek and Latin without having pursued an academic career. Translations thus served the general purpose of making the highly specialized contents of the papyri available to a wide public of enlightened amateurs. It was a shrewd move on the part of the two Oxford scholars and one that classical scholars should not forget.

The second good reason was that a translation could be considered as the first step toward a commentary. Some papyrologists, considering the translation to be the ultimate result of editing a papyrus, place it at the end of the edition, after the commentary. No clear consensus has emerged on this practice. Things have not changed since the days of the pioneers: While editing a papyrus, one frequently finds that serious problems arise just as one starts translating the text into one's own language. What seemed obvious suddenly becomes more obscure, and one's brilliant conjectures for filling in a gap turn out to make little sense or even to contradict the rules of ordinary grammar. A translation thus serves a double purpose: to make the editor verify that the text makes proper sense and to convey the meaning to readers in a way that they can understand.

A good translation should fulfill several criteria that are not easily reconciled. Given the fact that we are most often dealing with an *editio princeps*, precision should take precedence over literary elegance. As much as possible, the translator should endeavor to keep the structure of the original sentence, although this is not always possible. Greek particles are very important for this purpose since they play the role of our modern punctuation and can quite often be interpreted as such in a modern language.

Technical terms provide the translator with a difficult challenge. What should we do with words like *epikrisis, dioikêtês,* or *embadikon?* A specialist will no doubt understand them in many cases without a proper translation, and some will claim that translating them can only obscure their meaning. Having sometimes made what I now believe to be the wrong choices, I would argue in favor of an appropriate translation and not a mere transliteration. Thus, for those who have not been initiated into the intricacies of papyrology, *epikrisis* will be more understandable if it is called "examination of civic status," and *dioikêtês* can be translated as "finance minister" or "financial manager," depending on the context. As for *embadikon,* which literally means "tax for moving in," one might consider using "real estate purchase tax."[11]

COMMENTARY: THE DETAILS THAT MATTER

Editors of papyri can differ greatly in the way in which they write a commentary, although they will likely agree on the basic purpose of the task: It should first provide justification for the choices made in the edition of the original text, especially when they rest upon conjecture; it should also explain to readers what is new in the papyrus and then give them information on certain technical matters. One can assume that the broad outline of interpretation has already been dealt with in an introduction.

Dating a papyrus is of course of the utmost importance. Documentary papyri often contain a date accurate to the day, and tables provide papyrologists with convenient means of translating various systems into our Julian calendar.[12] Geography also significantly affects the practice of scribes. The origin of a papyrus can be identified through not only the explicit mention of place names but also the presence of a specific personal name, a turn of phrase in an administrative document, or some phonological peculiarity. For instance, when a man bearing the name Stotoetis shows up in a papyrus, there is a high probability that the document comes from the village of Soknopaiou Nesos, on the northwestern shore of Lake Moeris, where this name is very common; again, the names Antiochos and Theon for a father and a son suggest Oxyrhynchus (*P.Louvre* II 100). Confusion between the sounds /r/ and /l/ (e.g., φόλετρον written for φόρετρον) is typical of the Egyptian dialect spoken in the Arsinoite nome and can therefore be taken as a clue that the scribe is a native Egyptian who lives in that particular area (Gignac 1976, 102–107).

When stumbling upon a technical term (i.e., a poorly attested office or a rare verb denoting a specific action in a procedure), readers expect to find some explanation in the commentary. The electronic version of the Brussels *Bibliographie papyrologique* (on CD-ROM only), now containing material for years starting in 1932, has made it much easier to locate the relevant information on many topics, although by using this method one will also miss much specific information lurking, for instance, within the commentary to previously published papyri.

The search for parallels has already been described. In the commentary, they are useful for explaining an unusual wording or for justifying the reconstruction of the text in a damaged section of the papyrus. Some editors choose to leave no stone unturned and offer exhaustive lists of parallels to their readers, who thus know that, in the work under consideration, no evidence has been overlooked; on the other hand, abundance of material can distract one's attention from substantive discussion or the most useful parallels.

ILLUSTRATIONS: UNLESS I SEE, I SHALL NOT BELIEVE

Because the image of a papyrus enables readers to check the decipherment for themselves, it can be considered an indispensable part of any papyrus edition. Unfortunately, plates are also the most expensive part of a book, which explains why some editors choose to display only the most important papyri in a volume. In the case of small scraps of little interest, this attitude is justifiable on the grounds that the cost of producing a plate exceeds its usefulness; such bits usually end up being only described rather than receiving a full edition.

The way in which papyri are illustrated has changed dramatically in the past two decades. For about a century, the standard illustration was a printed image in black and white. For most practical purposes, color mattered little because carbon ink, which is most widespread in papyri, contrasts well with the background of the papyrus sheet. Only recently has color been introduced on a regular basis in some papyrus editions.

The biggest change, however, lies not so much in the advent of color as in illustrations supplied by means other than paper. A short-lived attempt to provide readers with images on microfiche (e.g., *BGU* XV) met with limited success. Microforms are not always easy to handle, and reading them requires machines that libraries are becoming reluctant to maintain and that few individuals own.

The revolution in image-display technology was thus triggered by the advent of databases available on the Internet. Papyrus collections around the world are gradually being scanned and catalogued in such a way that external users can access the images and display them on their screens wherever they are working. Images can be produced in many different formats, depending on the intended use, and—with the proper software—can be treated so as to enhance contrast or move fragments around. This recent development will influence the working methods of papyrologists in several ways.

First, in the not-too-distant future, costly plates in papyrus editions will tend to be replaced by links to images accessible on the Internet. This will certainly make sense from a financial point of view, although one may worry about the long-term stability of such images and their references. This question, however, belongs to a debate that far exceeds the scope of the present discussion. Second, it will become increasingly easy to check almost instantly a reading on a papyrus stored anywhere in the world. Third, papyrologists will be able to browse through whole collections—in some cases also unpublished texts—and look for stray parts of a document or for papyri belonging to an archive.

MAJOR EDITIONS: OF DWARVES STANDING ON THE SHOULDERS OF GIANTS

The image of "dwarves standing on the shoulders of giants" was originally applied by Bernard de Chartres in the twelfth century to describe the debt that scholars of his day owed to the great minds of antiquity. The same image can be applied—mutatis mutandis—to present-day scholars in relation to the pioneers who produced the first editions of papyri more than a century ago.

In the vast field of papyrology, the hard core is made up of Greek—and to a lesser extent Latin—documentary texts, and not surprisingly it is around such texts that the process of editing papyri is most coherently organized. If one moves away from this center of gravity toward literary papyri (and especially toward other languages such as demotic, Coptic or Arabic), the editorial process has until recently been conducted in a less orderly and standardized manner. This situation, however, is evolving rapidly, as any user of the *Checklist of Editions* (Oates et al. 2001) will have noticed: In its latest printed version, it includes demotic and Coptic papyri; Arabic papyri are also registered in a separate checklist. The following survey therefore inevitably reflects the disproportionate amount of attention that was devoted to Greek documentary papyri for a little more than a century. The reader should nevertheless bear in mind that many things said about this particular category of papyri also apply to areas considered peripheral until quite recently.

With the exception of a few items, the publication of papyri on a systematic scale began only in the late nineteenth century. Not surprisingly, the institutions holding the largest collections started the most prestigious series, among which the *Oxyrhynchus Papyri* is probably the best known. Bernard Grenfell and Arthur Hunt edited both literary and documentary texts from the city of Oxyrhynchus in middle Egypt at the impressive rate of one volume a year without compromising on quality. Their very high standard of scholarship has been kept alive for more than a century, and many papyrologists from around the world contribute to keeping up with the yearly installments. The *Oxyrhynchus Papyri* have also served as a model for other papyrus editions with regard to general layout, translation, commentary, and indexes. This has led to the adoption of a number of editorial guidelines, together with the Leiden system of conventional signs (Bell 1932; Hunt 1932).

With less speed but comparable regularity and quality, the National Library in Vienna has edited the *Corpus Papyrorum Raineri* for more than a century. Other major series have met various destinies, following the fate of the institutions where the papyri were preserved. Thus the *Berliner Klassikertexte (BKT)* and *Berliner griechische Urkunden (BGU)* both had remarkable beginnings, but the Second World War and the Cold War took their toll in spite of the publication of several *BGU* volumes in recent years. The Strasbourg collection was established at the time when Alsace was German, and the first two volumes were produced by Friedrich Preisigke, the founder of most of the major papyrological instruments. After the Second World War, the output resumed under French authority. In Egypt, publication of papyri was in the hands of scholars from the former colonial powers—especially Britain and France—and virtually ceased after that time. In Italy, the *Papiri della Società Italiana* also stalled shortly after the Second World War.

On the whole, one can argue that today the liveliest series are those where the papyri are integrated in a center of higher learning. Whereas superb collections at the British Library in London and at the Louvre Museum in Paris receive only sporadic attention from scholars, some of the best papyrus editions are being produced at a steady rate by universities that possess large collections, as, for instance, those in Ann Arbor *(Michigan Papyri)*, Cologne, and Heidelberg.

There has never been a successful attempt to produce in print a unified corpus of all papyri. At an early period, Ulrich Wilcken gathered and reedited in his monumental *Urkunden der Ptolemäerzeit* many important Greek documentary papyri from the Ptolemaic period that were published in the nineteenth century. Although the material from that period has increased enormously since Wilcken's time, his edition remains one of the greatest achievements in papyrology. On an even more ambitious scale, a *Corpus Papyrorum Graecarum* started with two volumes in which the editors had assembled every text of a given type (in this case, notifications of death and contracts for wet nurses), but the project was then discontinued. The closest thing to a unified corpus of papyri is the electronic *Duke Databank of Documentary Papyri*. In the not-too-distant future, a complete network of digital tools should make it possible for any scholar to create a custom-made corpus on virtually any selection principles by drawing metadata from various sources and texts extracted from the *Duke Databank*.

One area where near exhaustiveness has been achieved is in the collecting of Greek documentary papyri scattered in various journals or more generally outside of standard text editions. We owe the so-called *Sammelbuch* to the initiative of Friedrich Preisigke; this instrument has been continued up to the present time in installments that cover several years.

The relative rarity of Latin papyri enabled Robert Cavenaile to cover the material in his *Corpus Papyrorum Latinarum,* a volume of fairly modest size. This book has, however, become in part obsolete as many more Latin papyri have been published in the half-century since its publication. A comprehensive survey of all Latin papyri and parchments that predate 800 CE has resulted in the publication of the magnificent *Chartae Latinae Antiquiores,* a series that will include (when completed) an edition and a plate of every single text.

TEXTUAL CRITICISM: NO TEXT IS PERFECT

A first edition of a papyrus is seldom flawless, as one can see from consulting the—as yet—eleven volumes of the *Berichtigungsliste,* where (in principle) all corrections to papyri are recorded. The editing of papyri is therefore an evolving process. A practical example taken from the revision of the first volume of the Geneva papyri illustrates how one can first spot a misreading, then correct the text, and finally draw some conclusions from the newly established interpretation. It also shows how the confrontation of two wrong readings can produce a better text and contribute to refining the prosopography of Roman Egypt.

Dating from ca. 87 CE, *P.Gen.* I 4 is a complaint sent to a high official, the *iuridicus Alexandreae,* by a man who claims that he was registered in the wrong civic category. He suggests that the *iuridicus* (judicial official) write to the *strategos* (governor) of the division of Herakleides in the Arsinoite nome to clear up the matter. The name of the strategos (lines 17–18) was first read as ... ηλίῳ | ι̣κι, and soon corrected to ... ηλίῳ | 'Ι[π]ποκράτει (Wilcken 1906, 380); Wilcken excluded Αὐρηλίῳ. A century later, closer examination of the original produced the *nomen* 'Ι̣ο̣υλίωι. It is, however, the reading of the cognomen that offers the most interesting insight into the process of correcting the text.

After Wilcken's time, this Hippocrates was found to have a near homonymous colleague, also a strategos of the same division, in a papyrus from Vienna (*P.Vind. Bosw.* 1.35), dated shortly after 87: Σωκρ̣ά̣της. The occurrence of two strategoi in the same division at virtually the same time, and bearing the names Socrates and Hippocrates, could only raise the suspicion that at least one of the two was misread. This is where the dots used to mark uncertain letters are most useful, despite the fact that their use often reflects an individual papyrologist's subjectivity. How can we reconcile 'Ι[π]ποκράτει with Σωκρ̣ά̣της? A close examination of the Geneva papyrus shows that the gap at the beginning of the word is too narrow for 'Ι[π]πο- but that another name will fit: 'Ι[σ]ο̣κράτε̣[ι]. An examination of the Vienna papyrus has confirmed that Isocrates is also to be read there. Having been given a false identity for more than a century, the strategos Iulius Isocrates is at last saved from oblivion.

In more general terms, documents on papyrus display a regularity that makes papyrologists beware of exceptions. If these occur, they should be justified as far as possible. Unparalleled personal names, grammatical oddities, and geographical or chronological inconsistencies should alert a reader to the possibility of an erroneous reading. The process of editing a papyrus therefore never ends.

NOTES

1. Reference to all of those standard reference books appears in Oates et al. 2001.
2. Useful sets of plates are listed in ibid. (74–75). The two first volumes of *P.Mert.* also offer numerous plates presented mostly in chronological order.

3. Gibson and Levin (1975). Although not the most recent work on the subject, Gibson and Levin's book focuses on many aspects that can—at least remotely—be connected with the practice of reading papyri.

4. See, for example, *P.Ryl.* II 73.8 (pl. 3; 32–31 BCE): χαίρειν. ἀπέχομεν παρ[ὰ σοῦ κτλ. Notice the ν of χαίρειν, which is written in three distinct strokes; the last is directly linked to the following α of ἀπέχομεν. Again, at the end of ἀπέχομεν, the ν is written in three strokes, the last of which is linked to the following παρ[ά.

5. Hunt and Edgar (1932–1934) with English translation; Pestman (1990) with no translation but a good commentary for beginners; Hengstl (1978) with German translation.

6. Van Groningen (1932). The English version presented here is from Turner (1980, 187–188).

7. Pestman (1990, 15). To avoid confusion with punctuation, the dot should always be set *below* line level, even when there is no letter above it.

8. Callimachus fr. 197; Rossum-Steenbeek (1998, 268).

9. Merkelbach (1980, 2003); for criticism of the principle underlying the Lex Youtie, see Fassino (1998).

10. See, for instance, *P.Hamb.* I 15, a contract from the early third century CE, where the width of the column varies considerably from one line to another. This can probably be explained by the fact that the papyrus is twice as wide as it is high (43 × 21 cm).

11. On ἐμβαδόν = ἐμβαδικόν, see Kramer (1997, 325).

12. For the Ptolemaic period, where leap years were not taken into account and the calendar therefore drifted by one day every four years, see Skeat (1954). The precise dating of documents during the reign of Augustus is also notoriously difficult.

BIBLIOGRAPHY

Bell, H. I. 1932. "Notes on Methods of Publication." *CdÉ* 7: 270–271.

Calderini, A., and S. Daris. 1935–2007. *Dizionario dei nomi geografici e topografici dell'Egitto greco-romano.* Cairo: Società Reale di Geografia d'Egitto; Madrid: Consejo superior de investigaciones cientificas; Bonn: R. Habelt; Milano: Fabrizio Serra.

Fassino, M. 1998. "Sulla cosiddetta 'lex Youtie.'" *Rivista di filologia* 126: 72–75.

Gibson, E. J., and H. Levin. 1975. *The Psychology of Reading.* Cambridge, Mass.: MIT Press.

Gignac, F. T. 1976. *A Grammar of the Greek Papyri of the Roman and Byzantine Periods.* Vol. 1. Milan: Istituto editoriale Cisalpino-La Goliardica.

Hengstl, J., ed. 1978. *Griechische Papyri aus Ägypten als Zeugnisse des öffentlichen und privaten Lebens.* Munich: Heimeran.

Hunt, A. S. 1932. "A Note on the Transliteration of Papyri." *CdÉ* 7: 272–274.

——, and C. C. Edgar, eds. 1932–1934. *Select Papyri.* Vols. 1–2. Cambridge, Mass.: Harvard University Press.

Kramer, B. 1997. "Der κτίστης Boethos, und die Einrichtung einer neuen Stadt I." *APF* 43: 315–339.

Liddell, H. G., and R. Scott (eds.), H. S. Jones. (rev.). 1940. *A Greek-English Lexicon,* 9th edition. Oxford: Oxford University Press.

Merkelbach, R. 1980. "Lex Youtie." *ZPE* 38: 29.

——. 2003. "Iuxta lacunam ne mutaveris." *ZPE* 142: 34.

Paap, A. H. R. E. 1959. *Nomina sacra in the Greek Papyri of the First Five Centuries* A.D. Leiden: Brill.

Pestman, P. W. 1990. *The New Papyrological Primer.* Leiden: Brill.

Rossum-Steenbeek, M. van. 1998. *Greek Readers' Digests?: Studies on a Selection of Sublit-erary Papyri.* Leiden: Brill.

Skeat, T. C. 1954. *The Reigns of the Ptolemies.* Munich: Beck.

Turner, E. G. 1973. *The Papyrologist at Work.* Greek, Roman, and Byzantine Monographs 6. Durham, N.C.: Duke University.

——. 1980. *Greek Papyri: An Introduction,* 2d ed. Oxford: Clarendon Press.

Van Groningen, B. A. 1932. "Projet d'unification des systèmes de signes critiques." *CdÉ* 7: 262–269.

Wilcken, U. 1906. "Zu den Genfer Papyri." *APF* 3: 369–404.

Youtie, H. C. 1963. "The Papyrologist: Artificer of Fact." *GRBS* 4: 19–32 [= *Scriptiunculae,* vol. 1, 9–23].

——. 1966. "Text and Context in Transcribing Papyri." *GRBS* 7: 251–258 [= *Scriptiunculae,* vol. 1, 25–33].

——. 1971. "Βραδέως γράφων: Between Literacy and Illiteracy." *GRBS* 12: 239–261 [= *Scriptiunculae,* vol. 2, 629–651].

——. 1974. *The Textual Criticism of Documentary Papyri: Prolegomena,* 2d ed. London: Institute of Classical Studies.

CHAPTER 10

ARCHIVES AND DOSSIERS

KATELIJN VANDORPE

DOCUMENTARY papyri lead us into the living rooms of ancient people. Where unrelated texts are like instant snapshots, archives present a coherent film of a person, a family, or a community and may span several months, years, or decades.[1] We may enjoy people's professional successes or feel sorry when they suffer misfortune. Contracts and wills may show how rich elite members were, and their business papers may give insight into the way their estates were run. Bilingual archives show how some Egyptians tried to become Hellenized, but their private accounts betray their native language. Private letters may testify to affectionate relationships or reveal marital problems.

An archive is bound to be of greater interest than isolated texts, and the possibilities of archival research for any aspect of life in Graeco-Roman Egypt (e.g., economy, institutions, history, gender, ethnicity) are practically unlimited; they can be illustrated here, however, only by way of numerous examples. This chapter offers a systematic approach to archival documents and explains what constitutes an archive, how archives come to light, how we can reconstruct them, what type of archives we may discern, and what types of documents we may find in them. Such an approach to archival documentation of the ancient world has in general been attracting increasing interest and brings together scholars who are studying different regions (Brosius 2003; Pantalacci 2008).

---

1. Archives discussed in this chapter are listed at the end with further information. Their names are preceded by an asterisk (*) in the text.

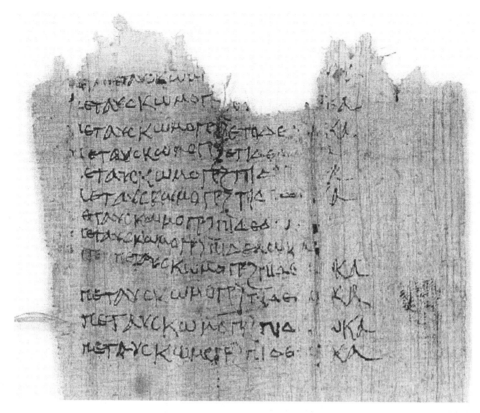

Figure 10.1. Petaus practicing the phrase "I, Petaus, village scribe, have *handed* in" (*Πεταῦς κωμογραμματεὺς ἐπιδέδωκα*); after four lines he forgets the first letter of the verb and writes "I, Petaus, village scribe, have *anded* in" (*πιδέδωκα*). Cologne, Papyrussammlung, inv. 328; *P.Petaus* 121.

TERMINOLOGICAL ISSUES

The Term *Archive* in Papyrological Jargon

Papyrologists use the term *archive* in a slightly different sense from modern historians, who think first of official records. The word *archive* is indeed derived from Greek *archeion* ("government house for official records"). Papers of a more private nature gained in significance in the second half of the twentieth century, and modern historians now draw on the archives of prominent individuals, politicians, aristocratic families, and businesses.

The ancient Greeks and Romans had extensive and well-organized public records, but with few exceptions these are now lost. Most papyrological archives are of a private nature; they belonged to various classes of society; an ordinary person, as well as an elite member of society, may have kept an archive. Consequently, papyrologists have always used "archive" to designate both public and private records and have anticipated the evolution in archival research (Martin 1994). By what other term than "family archive" could one stress the unity of papers that an individual maintained for his family and kept hidden in a closed jar in the cellar?

In addition, modern historians and papyrologists differ significantly in their approaches toward archival research. Unlike modern historians, who must ignore irrelevant documents from their archives in order to preserve focus, the rarity of ancient documents means that each and every text should be preserved and be welcomed by historians. Even the discovery of a new fragment may be front-page news in papyrology.

Archive versus Library, Archive versus Dossier

The term *archive* is clearly reserved for documentary groups of texts, whereas a public or personal *library* is a collection of literary texts (Martin 1994). Works of literature may, however, be included among documentary papers (discussed later).

There has been debate among papyrologists about the exact definition of the terms *archive* and *dossier*. Several scholars consider an archive "a *deliberate* collection of papers in antiquity by a single person, family, community (e.g., of priests) or around an office." An *arbitrary* collection, such as papers found together by accident on a rubbish dump from antiquity, is not included in this definition (Pestman, in *Prim.*[2]: 51, and 1995, 91–92; Martin 1994; for a summary and discussion of the different views see Van Beek 2007).

Where an archive is a collection made in *antiquity*, a dossier is "a group of texts brought together *today* concerning a particular person or family, or a particular subject." A dossier may include a person's archive, if available, as well as other texts that do *not* belong to the original archive but provide additional information on the archive holder (Pestman, in *Prim.*[2]: 51, and 1995, 91–92; Martin 1994).

To papyrologists, Zenon is a celebrity. He was born in Kaunos (in Asia Minor) and settled in Egypt, where he ran a large estate for the finance minister Apollonios under the second Ptolemy. Almost two thousand papyri from his personal archive have been unearthed at Philadelphia in the Fayyum, the town he helped develop. The majority of his documents are related to his management of the estate. When he started working for Apollonios, one of his main tasks was the irrigation of almost 2,750 hectares of land. Encountering difficulties, Zenon sent the chief engineer of the Fayyum the following letter: "Zenon to Kleon, greetings. The water in the canal has not risen more than a cubit, and so the land cannot be irrigated from it. Please, open the sluice-gates [at the entrance of the Fayyum] so that the land can be irrigated" (*P.Zen.Pestm.* B; see Van Beek 2005). As this letter was found among Kleon's papers, it is part of the dossier on Zenon, not part of his archive.

A dossier may include texts other than papyri and ostraca. The study of the "war of scepters," a conflict between Jews, Syrians, and Egyptians in the years 103–101 BCE, presents literary and epigraphical texts alongside the reedition of a small archive of Greek and demotic letters sent by soldiers on campaign to their home town. The study (*P.War of Sceptres*) has the appropriate subtitle "a multilingual dossier concerning a 'war of scepters'".

Because not all papyrologists have accepted the distinction between "archive" and "dossier," it is often ignored in practice. Furthermore, the difference is not always easy to make because information on the circumstances that surrounded the finding of documents is often lacking. In a well-argued article, Andrea Jördens proposes another, threefold classification that departs from the German word "Nachlass" and focuses on the find circumstances of the papyri (Jördens 2001; Van Beek 2007).

INTACT AND MIXED ARCHIVES

Archives in Their Original Depository

The ancient Egyptians kept their papers in a safe place; otherwise, their title deeds proving ownership might be stolen, as happened to a woman named Tapentos: "To Polemon, epistates of Kerkeosiris, from Tapentos daughter of Horos, of the same village. An attack was made upon my dwelling by Arsinoe and her son Phatres, who went off with the contract relating to my house and other business documents" (*P.Tebt.* I 52; ca 114 BCE).

Archives were kept in private houses, public buildings, temples, or monasteries. Within a building, several spots might be appropriate to deposit someone's papers: They could be hidden below a staircase or even under a doorstep (see the photograph of a house in Karanis, figure 2.3), but papers were, by preference, kept in the cellar. *Milon, who controlled the finances of the Egyptian temple of Edfu (225–222 BCE), took a number of business papers with him to the island of Elephantine, where they were found in a "round-bellied jar, which stood in a narrow cellar; the jar was badly damaged when the surrounding mud brick walls collapsed upon it and could not be preserved" (*P.Eleph.*, p. 34).

Choachytai, priests responsible for mummies after their embalming, and funerary priests in general instead put away their papers along with their tools in one of the tombs of the necropolis they worked in (for the Theban necropolis see *P.Choach.Survey,* pp. 10–13). Further archives have been hidden in caches such as the famous "cave of letters" in the Judean desert, where refugees of the Bar Kokhba revolt of 132 CE took shelter (see chapter 2 and figures 2.6–2.7).

Figure 10.2a. The demotic archive of the funerary priest Teos and his wife, Thabis, was bundled in three packets of papyri wrapped in cloth. The second (10.2b) and third (10.2c) photographs show the unwrapping of one of the packets in the Egyptian Department of the Musées Royaux d'Art et d'Histoire, Brussels (327/326–306 BCE, Thebes; Depauw 2000, pl. 1–3).

Papyri belonging to an archive could either be bound together into packets with strips or be wrapped in cloth (see figure 10.2a–c). Packed or not, archive papers might be put into a jar or box (see figure 10.3). The private archive of the *Melitian monks of Labla (511–513 CE), discovered in 1889 by Petrie in the church northwest of the Hawara pyramid, was carefully put away: "Each was rolled up separately; the rolls were then bound round, along with slips of reed, to prevent their being bent or broken; then tied up in a linen cloth; next in a large lump of old tattered woolen embroidery; and the bundle placed in a big jar sunk in the ground" (McGing 1990).

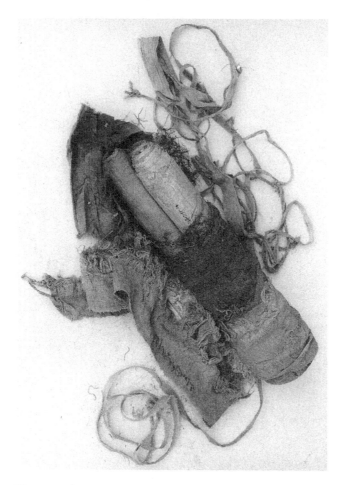

Figure 10.2b.

Archives Mixed Up in Antiquity

Papyri were, however, not always kept in their original depository, and even in antiquity archives sometimes fell into disarray. They might be thrown in the wastepaper basket and end up on rubbish dumps. The papyri in the dumps of Oxyrhynchus were often thrown away in groups; thus, the origin of a papyrus from a particular section may allow it to be linked with other texts (cf. chapter 2).

Further discarded papyri or archives, especially from government offices, were bought as secondhand paper and were reused for the fabrication of mummy cases or for wrapping and stuffing mummified crocodiles (chapter 2). During the excavations in the desert cemeteries of the site of Tebtynis, Ptolemaic papyri were unexpectedly discovered in several crocodile mummies. Among these reused texts, groups of interrelated documents have been reconstructed. Some smaller group-

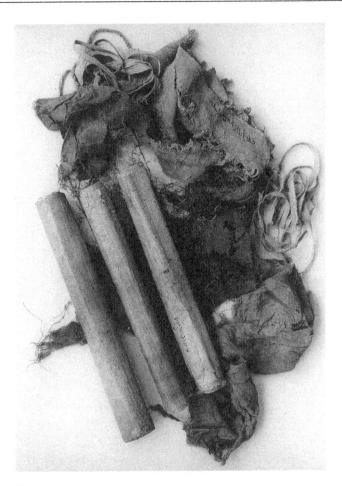

Figure 10.2c.

ings are evident, such as the correspondence of *Adamas, keeper of the public granary, spread over at least three different crocodiles. These original groupings are somewhat obscured in the edition of *P. Tebt.* because Grenfell and Hunt classified the documents according to text types. The best-known group is the so-called archive of *Menches, village scribe of nearby Kerkeosiris, which comprises almost two hundred published documents to date. As Verhoogt (1998b, 2005) has shown, we are actually dealing with documents discarded from the office of the village scribe and then used as secondhand paper by other people before ending up in the mummified crocodiles. Menches's papers were thus reused twice, once as paper and once as cartonnage, a circumstance that seriously hampers the reconstruction of the original archive.

These examples show that several archives that papyrologists cherish actually came out of a wastebasket. They help explain John D. Ray's reservations about

Figure 10.3. The bilingual archive of Totoes, priest of Hathor, was discovered in two large jars inside a house (probably his own house) near the temple of Hathor at Deir el-Medina (Thebes). The jars, of which one is shown, are well preserved and have a diameter of 23–24 cm and a height of 39 cm. The papyrus rolls, in general some 32 cm long, were placed upright in the container. The jars were closed by inserting a cup into the opening and were kept in place with a rope knotted around the small handles (189–100 BCE; Turin, Museo Egizio; for further examples of archives found in jars, see Depauw 2000, 3, 4n4).

Figure 10.4. One book, two archives. A special case of reuse involves the manufacture of a book from the secondhand paper of two long administrative rolls that contained official correspondence by Apollinarios, strategos of the Panopolite nome. Both rolls were cut up and pasted so that the blank versos made up a small codex whose pages were not sewn together. The new book belonged to a family (the *descendants of Alopex) who kept twenty-six tax receipts in it (Dublin, Chester Beatty Library; *P.Panop.* 19).

calling such groupings archives: "Archive, may the word be pardoned" (*O.Hor,* p. XIV).

Archives Mixed Up in Recent Times

Numerous archives were unfortunately not recovered during scientific excavations conducted by trained scholars but unearthed by sebbâkhîn and other native diggers who offered the texts for sale on the antiquities market (chapter 2). The antiquities dealers may have acquired a number of archives in one batch, but they rarely sold them intact. The bilingual archive of the Ptolemaic soldier *Horos, son of Nechouthes, for example, was purchased by Lord Adler, who noted: "I think the Hadj was trustworthy when he assured me that my potful had not been tampered with" (*P.Adl.,* p. 3); there are, however, reasons to believe that either the jar had actually been tampered with or that there was a second jar.

Most archives, however, were split up when they were brought onto the antiquities market. Even individual texts that belonged to an archive were, deliberately or through ignorance, torn into pieces (figure 10.5). The famous archive of

Figure 10.5. These four fragments of a single petition by Dryton, sold separately on the antiquities market and acquired by three different collections, had to be puzzled together (John Rylands Library inv. 67 + British Library inv. 686f + 687b + Heidelberg inv. G.1301; *P.Dryton* 31). Rylands fragment reproduced courtesy of the university librarian and director at John Rylands University Library, University of Manchester. Heidelberg fragment reproduced courtesy of the Institut für Papyrologie, Heidelberg.

*Zenon, agent to the finance minister Apollonios, is scattered over a series of collections. The first texts came on the market in 1911, and their price rose as Zenon became a celebrity. Almost two thousand texts are known to date, dispersed all over the world. The Museum of Cairo acquired the largest collection, published by C. C. Edgar in the five volumes of *P.Cair.Zen.*; other substantial parts of the archive have turned up in Europe (London, Florence, Manchester) and the United States (New York, Michigan). To this dispersion of the texts and fragments corresponds the fragmentation of publications; consequently, the "Guide to the Zenon Archive" (two volumes) has become an indispensable instrument (*Pap.Lugd.Bat.* XXI).

Certain archives have had an active life even after their initial publication. The demotic archive of the herdsman and soldier *Pabachtis was probably intact when Georg Hauswaldt (hence the name *P.Hauswaldt*) bought it for the Königliche Museen in Berlin. But during the Second World War one papyrus was destroyed in a bombardment, and other texts were seized by Soviet soldiers as war booty; fortunately, the majority have been returned to Berlin. A few texts, though, have turned up in Magdeburg and Warsaw (Manning in *P.Hausw.*, p. 1).

An additional problem is that, for a long time, purchasers were interested mainly in Greek papyri. The demotic papers of a bilingual archive thus often ended up in a different collection from the Greek documents. A special case in this respect is the archive of *Dionysios, son of Kephalas, of Egyptian descent and a priest of the local ibis cult. His family became Hellenized, and Dionysios was recruited as an infantryman of the Ptolemaic garrison at Tenis-Akoris. Reinach acquired this bilingual archive in Egypt in the winter of 1901–1902, but after the initial edition it was split up: The Greek portion went to Paris, and the Demotic batch to Munich (Pestman in *Pap.Lugd.Bat.* XXII, pp. V–VI).

RECONSTRUCTION OF ARCHIVES

When archives were intermingled with other texts in ancient rubbish dumps, mummy cases, or mummified crocodiles, or were split up by clandestine diggers or dealers, scholars may use several methods in reconstructing them (compare Martin 1994).

Relying on the Archaeological Context: A Solid Method

Information on the archaeological context, whenever available, is crucial. Van Minnen (1994) has demonstrated how productive a "house-to-house search" at Karanis might be, starting with the old (but for their time exemplary) excavation reports and taking into account all found objects, including papyri. He was thus able to identify the house and archive of the tax collector *Socrates (see chapter 2). Verhoogt (1998a) reconstructed a small Tebtynis archive starting from the editor's note in the introduction of *P. Tebt.* II 326: "This papyrus was found tied up in a bundle with 285, 319, 335, 378, 408 and 588." The papers appear to have belonged to *Sarapias, member of a family of Antinoite landowners in the Fayyum, who added some documents that belonged to her male relative Sarapammon (165–264/270 CE). Where information on the archaeological context is lacking, however, other methods are available.

Studying Prosopographical Data: A Successful Approach

Proposopographical data—information about individuals—and insight into the family tree are extremely helpful in sorting out which texts belong to which archive. As Bagnall rightly puts it, "Reconstructing the archive is itself an iterative process, in which clues allow the historian to delineate enough of an individual's characteristics to permit attribution of further documents to the archive" (Bagnall 1995, 40). It is ideal to dispose of a will that mentions grandparents and children or a census declaration filed by the householder, in which he lists himself and his family members, but this kind of information is scarce.

The archive of the descendants of *Alopex, kept at Dublin and Cologne, has been reconstructed mainly on prosopographical grounds. Because the name Alopex is rare and a few other names appear in both collections, Hagedorn (1970) concluded that these papers constitute an archive that belonged to a family descended from Alopex. Several texts refer to the family's olive yards, oil business, and taxes on oil production (308–355 CE).

In March 1934 Italian archaeologists made a spectacular discovery at the ancient site of Tebtynis in the Fayyum: A cellar of one of the houses harbored several hundred Roman papyri, thus earning the name *cantina dei papiri* (figure 10.6). Unfortunately, the findspots of the individual papyri were not described in detail; as a result, the archives of the cantina have had to be reconstructed solely by means of prosopography. The family archives known thus far belonged to (1) *Kronion, (2) the family of the *Patronids (formerly called the archive of Laches), and (3) the descendants of *Pakebkis. As Smolders (2005) proposes, Pakebkis's grandson Turbo can be identified as a manager or *phrontistes* of the Patronids, one of the wealthiest and most influential families of the nome at that time. If this identification is accepted, the second and third archives were probably in the hands of a single person before being dumped in the cantina.

This example shows the importance of detailed prosopographical research: A scholar not only has to definitively establish someone's identity but analyze the person's professional activities as well. Even the identification of the handwriting may be useful.

Figure 10.6. The "cantina dei papiri," shown here after it was emptied, is considered a storage area for discarded material (perhaps destined to be used as fuel) rather than an archival repository (Gallazzi 1990, 284; see also Davoli 1998, 186*n*313). Its archives are reconstructed on prosopographical grounds. Photo by Gallazzi (1990, pl. 18).

Identifying Real Estate: A Method Rarely Applied

Because they prove ownership, title deeds occupy a prominent place in family and personal archives of a private nature. When one person sold property to another, he turned over the older title deeds for the property to the new owner. In these cases, it is important to identify real estate through the remaining title deeds. Once the identification is completed and the last owner of the property is known, it is clear which archive the title deeds belong to. Pestman (1965) has developed this method for the bilingual archive of *Peteharsemtheus, son of Panobchounis, where title deeds account for one third of the documents.

The owner might bundle the papyri relating to his property. Around 83 CE *Apynchis, son of Tesenouphis, for instance, collected all of the papers concerning his house with a courtyard in Soknopaiou Nesos in the Fayyum: the most recent and the older title deeds, a copy of a bank receipt, and a declaration of property to the *bibliophylakes* of the metropolis. All these documents were probably pasted together into a *tomos synkollesimos* (see later description).

Museum Archaeology: A New Method

A more recent method is known as "museum archaeology": by tracing the routes of papyri and the dates of their acquisition by museums and other collections, one may draw several conclusions. For instance, if one and the same archive has been split up or if one and the same papyrus has been torn to pieces and if those papyri or fragments have turned up in different collections, there must be a link between the acquisitions of the collections in question. For a number of family archives from the Upper Egyptian town of Pathyris (modern Gebelein), this method has proven successful. The extension through museum archaeology, of the archive of the Greek cavalryman *Dryton and his wife, which had been reconstructed on purely prosopographical grounds, is significant and shows who inherited the papers on Dryton's death (Vandorpe 1994 and *P.Dryton*). Clackson (2004) successfully applied this method to Coptic documents as well.

A scholar will, however, never be certain of having found all of the pieces of the puzzle. Especially anonymous papers, like school exercises, accounts, or lists, are difficult to attribute to a specific archive. Papyri or fragments may lie concealed somewhere in an envelope or in the closet of a collection, waiting to be discovered a second time.

EDITIONS, GUIDES, AND LISTS OF ARCHIVES

Editions

An archive uncovered intact during a legal excavation and preserved as such in a museum is usually published in its entirety (e.g., *P.Adl.*, *P.Hausw.* by Spiegelberg; *P.Tor.Botti*). The documents of an archive that have been dispersed among several collections are, by contrast, often published in separate editions. The early Ptolemaic demotic archive of a woman named *Taienteus has been reconstructed from papyri scattered among several collections: The Manchester portion was published by Francis Griffith as *P.Ryl.Dem.* 10–14, and the London batch, by Stephen Glanville in 1939 (*P.Brit.Mus.* I), whereas other documents from Moscow still await publication (Pestman 1989, 14–24).

As Pestman (1989, 10) observes in a Dutch publication on family archives, an archive should be brought together and published as an entity before a thorough and reliable study can be written. The Roman archive of *Philosarapis was the first dispersed archive published as a whole (by van Groningen in 1950, *Pap.Lugd.Bat.* VI). Next was the Roman archive of *(Eutychides, son of) Sarapion (by Schwartz in 1961, *P.Sarap.*) and the archive of *Flavius Abinnaeus, of the early Byzantine period (by Bell and others in 1962, *P.Abinn.*). Those three archives are composed of Greek documents only.

Publications of bilingual (particularly Graeco-demotic) archives are not as numerous as single language collections. The Greek and demotic papers of *Horos, son of Nechouthes, were published together in 1939 but with editorial work divided by language competence. Pestman set an example by publishing the Greek and demotic documents of "L'archivio di Amenothes figlio di Horos" in 1981 (*P.Tor.Amen.*) and of "Les archives privées de Dionysios fils de Kephalas" in 1982 (*Pap.Lugd.Bat.* XXII, together with Boswinkel).

Guides

These publications have undoubtedly shown the value of a (re)edition of dispersed papyrus archives. When, however, an archive is composed of a large number of texts, an edition would constitute a lifetime project. It is then often more convenient to compose a guide to or survey of the archive, as was done for the *Zenon archive (*Pap.Lugd.Bat.* XXI) and that of the Theban *Choachytai Osoroeris and Panas (*P.Choach.Survey*). Such guides or surveys can be accompanied by a reedition of a part of the archive. The guide to the Zenon archive was preceded by a volume of the same series that incorporated, among other documents, editions of the bilingual papyri of Zenon's archive (*Pap.Lugd.Bat.* XX). The survey of the choachytes' archive appeared one year after Pestman's "Il processo di Hermias e altri documenti dell'archivio dei choachiti," a reedition of the archive's Greek and demotic texts preserved in Italian collections (*P.Tor.Choach.*). Many texts of these two archives still await publication.

Descriptions, Lists, and Studies of Archives

Several lists of archives, some accompanied by a brief description, are available. A long chronological list of 135 Greek archives, though certainly not pretending to be exhaustive, has been compiled by Montevecchi (1988, 248–261, 575–578). A similar initiative was undertaken for demotic and bilingual (Graeco-demotic and Graeco-Coptic) archives in 1986 by Lüddeckens (*Lexikon der Ägyptologie,* vol. 7, 876–886, s.v. *Urkundenarchive,* with sections for the Ptolemaic, Roman, and Byzantine periods) and in 1997 by Depauw, who included early demotic archives from the pre-Ptolemaic period (Depauw 1997, 153–162). Erwin Seidl presented a selection and a substantial description of Greek, demotic, and bilingual archives from Graeco-Roman Egypt (Seidl 1962, 15–49, for Hellenistic Egypt; Seidl 1973, 55–71, for Roman Egypt).

The Leuven project, "Leuven Homepage of Papyrus Collections," which began in 2002, is compiling an exhaustive list of all Greek, demotic, Coptic, and bilingual archives from Graeco-Roman and Byzantine Egypt. The results are presented in a database-driven website that offers several search options (directed by W. Clarysse and K. Vandorpe, see http://www.trismegistos.org/arch/index.php) and provides a systematic description of each archive (see also Van Beek 2007).

A list of archival studies in journals or in chapters of books would be long indeed, regardless of whether they concentrated on small archives or on particular aspects of large ones. Lewis (1986) has bundled several short portraits of individual archive keepers into his book *Greeks in Ptolemaic Egypt: Case Studies in the Social History of the Hellenistic World.* Among the book-length synthetic studies, Orrieux's two monographs on Zenon (1983, 1985) and Rathbone's *Economic Rationalism and Rural Society in Third-century AD Egypt* (1991) take a prominent place. In the latter study Rathbone deals with the extensive archive of *Heroninus, manager of a unit of the private estate of Appianus in the Fayyum. In it he "brings to the attention of historians of the ancient world a unique and so far neglected treasury of social and economic information whose significance, especially as regards the social structure of the estate and its system of management and accounting, is not confined to the history of Roman Egypt" (Rathbone 1991, 3).

TYPES OF ARCHIVES AND ARCHIVE KEEPERS

The jurist Erwin Seidl (1962) was the first to propose a typology of archives, distinguishing between official and private archives and, among the latter, between family and bookkeeping archives. The classification proposed later in the chapter builds on his typology. However, although official archives often appear to contain private correspondence and vice versa, it is not advisable to add an extra category called "hybrid archives" (Martin 1994). The introduction of the term "personal archive" may solve this problem, as Boussac (1993) suggests for Delian archives.

Official Archives and Personal Archives of Officials

Official archives (called "Amtsarchive" by Seidl) contain only or mainly papers belonging to a governmental agency or a state official. Few such archives have actually been found in a public building. In the winter of 1892–1893 Naville discovered several carbonized papyrus rolls in the ruins of the Roman *bibliothêkê*, or record office, in the ancient capital of the Mendesian nome, *Thmouis (*P.Thmouis*; compare chapter 2 for this and further examples).

The major part of the official archives, however, ended up on rubbish dumps or were used as secondhand paper in mummy cases and mummified crocodiles, such as the archive of *Menches (mentioned earlier), a village scribe. Other official papers were taken home by officials upon their retirement, for instance, and were found in their houses, as discussed later.

An official archive may center around a government office, such as a granary (e.g., at *Oxyrhyncha and *Pyrrheia), notarial office (e.g., at *Krokodilopolis and *Pathyris), or record office (*grapheion*, e.g., at *Theogonis). Other official archives are instead linked to a particular official and are generally named after this person and his title (e.g., the nomarches *Aristarchos, the toparches *Tesenouphis, or the village scribe *Isidoros). The archive of *Aurelius Heras, *praepositus pagi*, comprises nine documents addressed to Aurelius Heras (alias Dionysios) in his capacity as head of the administration (*praepositus*) of the eighth *pagus* (district) of the Oxyrhynchite nome.

The term *official archive* may in these cases be misleading, as these collections often include papers of a private nature. This should not surprise us, as our mailbox at work undoubtedly contains both business and private messages, and the ancients lacked our modern notions of separation between personal and professional. Such archives are thus best classified as "personal archives of officials." *Kleon, chief engineer in the Fayyum under the second Ptolemy, belonged to the Greek elite. His home city was Alexandria, where his wife and sons lived and where they had friends in high places. But for his job, Kleon was required to spend most of the year in the Fayyum, where he kept his official papers mixed up with his private correspondence, which composes about 15 percent of the archive (Van Beek 2005). His wife suggested coming to visit him, and his children begged him to come home for an annual festival, apparently without success. In a supporting letter, his son Philonides hints at Kleon's fall from grace with the king:

> Nothing truly will be dearer to me than to protect you for the rest of your life
> in a manner worthy of you and of myself, and if the fate of mankind befalls you, to
> see that you enjoy all due honours; this will be my chief desire, honourably
> to protect you both while you live and when you have departed to the gods. If
> possible, then, make every effort to obtain your release for good, or if you see no
> chance of that, for at least the time of low Nile, at which season there is no danger
> and Theodoros can be left to take your place, in order that you may spend this
> season at least with us. (translation *Sel.Pap.* I 94)

Theodoros indeed succeeded Kleon as chief engineer and took over the latter's archive, including, surprisingly, the private letters. The archive is therefore known as the archive of *Kleon and Theodoros.

After their time in office, some officials took home documents that were important to them personally and intermingled them with their private correspondence and even their private library. *Apollonios, strategos of the Apollonopolite Heptakomias nome in Upper Egypt, maintained a regular correspondence with people from his hometown, Hermopolis, where his wife, Aline, his daughter Heraidous, and his mother, Eudaimonis, lived. When his archive was discovered in the Hermopolite, it became apparent that Apollonios had carried home several official and private papers after his term in office. A substantial number (almost 100 out of the 225 papyri) are deemed to belong to the private part of the archive.

Apollonios was in office at the time Hadrian succeeded Trajan as emperor (117 CE), when a revolt of the Jews was raging in several countries. Surprisingly, he even took part in a battle against the Jews at Memphis. No wonder that his dedicated wife was worried about him, expressing her feelings in one of her letters: "I take no pleasure in food and drink, but stay awake continually night and day with one worry, your safety" (*C.Pap.Jud.* II 436). Apollonios's mother, Eudaimonis, possessed a sharp tongue and advised her son to "do the same as the strategos here, who puts the burden on the notables" (*C.Pap.Jud.* II 437). In another letter she alludes to the risks Apollonios was taking: "Be sure that I shall pay no attention to the god [Hermes] until I get my son back safe." Although she also complains about receiving too little financial support from her family, she undoubtedly exaggerates: "I already have the vision of being naked when winter starts" (*C.Pap.Jud.* II 442). Apollonios may have been flattered by the letter from his female servant, Taus, who appears to have been very devoted to the strategos : "I beg you, my lord, if it please you, to send for me. Else, I die because I do not behold you daily. Would that I were able to fly and come to you and make obeisance to you..." (*Sel.Pap.* I 115). Unsurprisingly, Apollonios cherished these letters.

Personal and Family Archives of a Private Nature

Personal versus Family Archives

A personal archive is kept by a single person, whereas a family archive (*Familien-archive* in Seidl's terminology) must fulfill one of the following two conditions:

(a) The archive was put together by a family member who also kept papers for his wife or other close relatives, mostly parents, sisters, sisters-in-law, and daughters.

(b) The archive was inherited by the oldest son or daughter and was thus continued by the following generations.

In several cases both conditions are fulfilled. The family archive of *Philosarapis, for instance, had four successive archive holders, following the line of the first-born sons of the ancestor Maron to the last central figure, Philosarapis II. They kept documents for other relatives as well. Our knowledge of this family, one of the wealthiest in the Roman Fayyum, spans no less than 135 years.

When a family archive is passed from an older to a younger generation, it is best named after the last owner, as Seidl (1962, 16) strongly recommended, and this practice has sometimes been rigorously followed even when the last owner is unknown (compare the "archive of the Anonym," Pestman in *Pap.Lugd.Bat.* XXVII, p. 93). Nonetheless, for a number of reasons, especially when the last owner is unknown, the name of the central figure or of an ancestor may be used: Of the more than eighty texts of the Tebtynis archive of *Patron's descendants, Patron himself did not significantly contribute to it, whereas his three sons and some of his grandchildren did, but it is not clear who among the Patronids was the actual archive keeper. In view of the fact that several members of this wealthy family from the Fayyum exercised the highest civic magistracies of Ptolemais Euergetis, they may have lived in the city and maintained a second residence in the country, at Tebtynis, where they were rather absentee landlords assisted by a *phrontistes,* or manager (Bagnall 2000). One of these managers was named Laches (Clarysse and Gallazzi 1993); another, Turbo. This example brings us to the problem of the archives of wealthy families, who often appointed a manager or steward to maintain important records: The archive may thus have been kept by either the family or the managers.

Private versus Professional Papers

Archives of an individual or a family may comprise private papers, documents from the professional sphere, or both. When the latter are dominant, the name of the archive usually refers to the profession of the archive keeper, such as the goldsmith *Menches (about 195 BCE, Oxyrhyncha). Typical professional archives are the so-called business or bookkeeping archives ("Buchführungsarchiv"; Seidl 1962), which contain primarily correspondence and accounts.

The *Zenon archive is a standard example of a business archive kept by an individual. Apart from numerous accounts and letters written to him, this famous manager also collected letters addressed to his employees, agents, or partners, as well as letters that had been forwarded to him for his information or for further investigation. Amid this serious and sometimes boring correspondence, the following scribbled note catches the eye: "Horos to Zenon, greetings. By February 3 [252 BCE] there will be 130 arouras [ca. 36 hectares] sown with poppy. If you please, do come and see me so you can feast your eyes on the sight. Farewell" (*P.Cair.Zen.* II 59243; translation by Crawford 1973). Horos wrote this letter with an Egyptian brush and in poor Greek, but his enthusiasm for a large field full of white or light purple poppy flowers prevails. Poppy was a new oil crop that was being experimented with on the estate.

Zenon's papers constitute the largest papyrus archive known to date. Such an extensive assemblage may be subdivided into several subarchives or files, some of which led a life of their own for a while before ending up in Zenon's hands:

October/November 261–April 258 BCE. *Palestinian file.* Zenon started out as the commercial representative of the minister in Palestine and learned a great deal about the prospering slave trade. Meanwhile, the king granted Apollonios a large estate of 2,750 hectares located at the desert border of the Fayyum area.

April 258–April/May 256 BCE. *Alexandrian file.* At the threat of the second Syrian war, Zenon returned to Egypt and was promoted to the minister's private secretary. In this capacity he took over Apollonios's correspondence at Alexandria and accompanied his employer wherever necessary. Because Zenon endorsed the minister's letters, adding the name of the town where he opened the letters, scholars have been able to reconstruct the exact route that Apollonios's staff followed through the delta, where they inspected the collection of the taxes.

April/May 256–248/247 BCE. After a serious illness, Zenon had to lead a more sedentary life: He became the private manager of the large estate belonging to the minister in the Fayyum and supervised the urbanization of the neighboring town of Philadelphia. Zenon took over the archive of his predecessor, Panakestor, who had failed to develop the new estate in a timely fashion (Panakestor's file). During the first three years, Zenon was very much occupied with his managerial duties, and the minister kept close track of the developments, as shown by his abundant correspondence (Zenon's file of the estate). But the minister's interest gradually diminished, his letters became scarce, and Zenon was concentrating more and more on his own affairs (Zenon's personal file).

248/247–end 229 BCE. Between November 248 and early December 247 BCE Zenon was dismissed for an unknown reason. He was succeeded first by Eukles and later by Bion, both of whom were assisted by a secretary named Apollonios. The latter kept the estate's papers at that time (file of Apollonios, the secretary) but handed them over to Zenon when the estate was reclaimed by the new king, Ptolemy III. Meanwhile, Zenon lived in Philadelphia as a respected citizen and conducted his own business in a successful manner (Zenon's personal file, continued). After March 240 BCE he probably handed over his entire archive (which comprised all of the aforementioned files) to an anonymous person—possibly Apollonios, the estate's former secretary, and possibly one of Zenon's brothers. "Anonymous" continued the archive until the close of 229 BCE. By that time Zenon was no longer alive.

The largest business archive of Roman Egypt is that of *Heroninus, which is scattered among several collections and made up chiefly of letters (sometimes written on the backs of old literary texts) and accounts (253–306 CE). About 450 texts have thus far been published, but even more texts still await publication. The available evidence has been studied by Rathbone, who focuses on the structure of the estate, its personnel, and its management. Rathbone shows how the so-called archive of Heroninus is a "useful shorthand designation" in referring to a large, poorly defined group of texts. The core is formed by the papers of Heroninus himself, who was manager of a unit of the well-known estate of Appianus and of five further estates in the Fayyum; these estate papers form subarchives or files. A number of related texts, clearly of different origin but closely linked to Heroninus's papers, should not be considered as belonging to the archive *stricto sensu* (Rathbone 1991, 6–8, 410).

These two archives belonged to managers of large estates, but small businessmen, too, like the oil seller *Phanesis (233–223 BCE, Tebtynis), produced numerous papers. When *Dionysios, son of Kephalas, was a young man waiting to be recruited as an infantryman of the Ptolemaic garrison at Tenis-Akoris, he went into business in order to make a living, and the forty texts of his archive give us much information about these activities. After Dionysios joined the Ptolemaic army, the archive abruptly stops.

Some priestly functions similarly left their mark on private archives. Apart from their private papers, the choachytai, or libation pourers, collected professional documents such as records of the names of the mummies they looked after, payments of funerary taxes, transfer taxes on tombs, and disputes over professional affairs (e.g., the archive of *Teos and 'Thabis). Some also kept administrative documents of the association of choachytai, including a list of regulations (these informed members of the days of drinking and the expectation that they would be present at each other's embalming and funeral [*P.Choach.Survey* 61]).

Some professions, however, did not involve a mass of paperwork. Soldiers, at least those who were not in charge of a military camp, usually had a humble archive of private papers only. Conspicuously, they produced more documents before they were recruited (like the aforementioned *Dionysios, son of Kephalas) or after they retired. The Graeco-Latin archive of *Pompeius Niger contains only two texts from the twenty-four years in which he served as a soldier of the Legio XXII Deiotariana, but his next twenty years as a veteran are far better represented with thirteen documents (31–64 CE, Oxyrhyncha). The same is true of the archive of *Iulius Serenus, who retired with the rank of *decurio* (179–216 CE, Karanis).

Archives of Communities: Temples, Monasteries, Associations

Although the Ptolemaic administration took over several of their tasks, the Egyptian temples maintained an intensive administrative apparatus in Graeco-Roman times. Their archives comprise accounts, lists, letters, yearly reports to the government, oracle questions, or self-dedications to the god. All temple documents were as a rule written in demotic until well into the first century CE, when demotic disappeared for official and legal texts (see later discussion). The temple archive of *Soknobraisis at Bakchias in the Fayyum (116–212 CE), for instance, is exclusively Greek and includes yearly reports (accompanied by cover letters) to the government listing the sacred objects and declaring the number of priests. Sebbâkhîn put this archive up for sale on the antiquities market in the 1930s. Only at the end of the twentieth century was the actual temple of Soknobraisis identified; it faces the well-known sanctuary of his twin brother, Soknokonneus (Capasso 1996, 119; Davoli 2005, 29).

In addition to their archives, priests often collected literary texts, which were rarely written in Greek, as these temple libraries were "the last bastions of the native languages and scripts" (Depauw 1997, 160). The most illustrious library in Roman times was that in Tebtynis, which gathered for the last time the entire Egyptian literature of the past millennium: novellas such as the cycle of Pharaoh Inaros or of the sage and magician Setne; mythological, astronomical, and astrological treatises; and a collection of law texts and a herbal. One of the fragmentary papyri, which must have been more than ten meters long, was an encyclopedia of stars, rivers, villages, and gods written in hieratic with glosses in demotic and a few annotations in Greek characters (Ryholt 2005).

Several monasteries had similarly furnished (Graeco-Coptic) archives or libraries, such as that of Epiphanius *(P.Mon.Epiph.)* and the monastery of Phoibammon at

Deir el-Bahari. The latter produced a large number of ostraca and papyri and a few texts on parchment. Receipts of book loans and fragmentary inventories testify to the existence of a library; the monastery's archives consisted of documents related to its economic and administrative activities, short religious texts, the monks' "school" texts, and letters written by or to its bishop, Abraham (Godlewski 1986).

Archives of professional or cult associations are harder to detect. Their papers may have been kept by a member of the association among his personal papers or, in the case of cult guilds, by the temple.

Archives Comprising a Single Type of Document

Some archives contain a wide variety of documents, whereas others are rather monotonous, sometimes consisting of a single type of document and therefore named after it. The military correspondence of *Pates and Pachrates is a collection of Greek and demotic letters addressed to these officers and written by soldiers on campaign in the north of the country during the Judean-Syrian-Egyptian conflict of 103–101 BCE. The private correspondence of *Apollonios from Bakchias consists of fourteen letters written by and addressed to this estate manager active under the Flavian emperors. The tax lists kept by the *praktores argyrikon* of Soknopaiou Nesos are labeled "an early-third-century tax archive" by Lewis (1954).

COMPOSITION OF ARCHIVES

The composition of archives is here approached from two different angles.

Incoming versus Outgoing Documents

In this first approach I consider the archive holder as the central figure and evaluate his relationship to the documents (cf. Van Beek 2007). Some documents (mostly letters) are addressed to him; others (such as contracts or receipts) are drawn up for his benefit: All of these texts are part of the group of *incoming documents,* and one expects to find them in the archive of the key figure. Other texts, however, appear to be written by or in the name of the archive holder and are destined for other people: this group forms the *outgoing documents,* and their presence in the archive needs to be explained. Usually drafts or copies of these outgoing documents are involved. A special case is that of completed petitions: The original petition may be returned to the archive holder after a decision has been made and may contain a note by the official who dealt with the case. A standard example of an archive with both incoming and outgoing documents is that of *Apollinarios, strategos of the Panopolite nome, which consists of two administrative rolls: The first roll is a register containing copies of letters dispatched *by* the strategos in September 298 (outgoing); the second roll has some fifty letters written *to* the strategos by a superior in February 300 (incoming) (see figure 10.4).

The categories of incoming and outgoing documents do not cover all texts, however. Accounts, lists, and the like drafted by the archive holder for internal use and never meant to leave his dwelling, may fall under the heading of "internal documents." The terminology proposed here has been created by Clarysse for the Leuven project on archives.

Juridical versus Sentimental Value

This second approach tries to explain why the archive holder kept or cherished certain documents and not others. In case of official, business, and temple archives, the explanation is simply that the texts were of importance to the archive holder's office, business, or temple activities.

With regard to family and some personal archives, the answer is more complex and has been discussed by Pestman in a fine Dutch booklet on such archives. In general, family archives contain a rich variety of documents; hence, Pestman's enthusiasm: "Family archives are goldmines." He distinguishes between three groups of texts (Pestman 1989, 7–8), and to them I add a fourth group here:

(a) The first and most substantial group consists of *legal documents that could be submitted in case of a trial,* such as title deeds, loans, marriage contracts, wills, minutes of lawsuits, and tax receipts. Contracts concerning the purchase of real estate and even lease contracts might be presented in court to prove ownership. Loan contracts and acknowledgements of debt were put in the hands of the creditor, but when the loan was paid off, the creditor either returned them to the debtor or issued a receipt. Marriage and divorce contracts were safest in the archive of the wife's family.

Documents that were actually collected in antiquity in order to present them in court proceedings constitute a lawsuit archive or file. The so-called *Erbstreit archive deals exclusively with an inheritance dispute among three different parties within a single family, resulting in no fewer than five trials in a two-year period. Apart from the original demotic title deeds and their Greek translations, it includes copies of former lawsuits and even the original documents through which the final verdict of the judges (the *chrematistai*) is executed (186–133 BCE, Pathyris).

A number of family and personal archives contain a substantial lawsuit file. Ten out of the thirteen documents of the lector priest *Tefhapi from Siut are related to a trial concerning the inheritance of his father, who was married twice (186–169 BCE). Sixteen out of the twenty-two texts in the family archive of Gaius *Iulius Agrippinus concern the so-called Drusilla lawsuit. The widow Drusilla took legal action against

Figure 10.7. When returning this loan agreement to the debtor, the creditor canceled it by means of crosshatched lines (London, British Library inv. 1893; *P.Fam.Tebt.* 22; archive of Philosarapis).

the Roman veteran Agrippianus and, on his death, against his son Agrippinus. When the archive ends (103/117–148 CE, Karanis), the case remained unsettled.

(b) Of the second group of *odd notes without any juridical value and kept for sentimental reasons,* letters are a good example. Although correspondence was essential and often predominant in official, business, and temple archives, letters found in family and personal archives were meant to give a sign of life and were kept mainly for sentimental reasons. This second category includes texts other than letters, such as the demotic list of the birthdays of his five children, which *Amenothes, son of Horos, carefully drafted, starting with the oldest son born, on October 31, 150 BCE, and ending with the youngest scion, born on August 28, 129 (*P.Tor.Amen.* 3), or the school exercises written by Apollonios and kept by his older brother, Ptolemaios (*UPZ* I 147).

(c) *Literary works* were rarely kept by private persons, as the archive keeper had to have some interest in literature. Books might constitute the personal library of private persons. The recluses *Ptolemaios and his brother Apollonios, who devoted their lives to the god in the Memphite Serapeum (164–152 BCE), not only copied a fair number of extracts from literary texts and model letters but also borrowed terms and phrases found in them for their petitions and dream descriptions (Clarysse 1983, 57–60). When, however, only few literary works have been found, one can assume they were kept together with the remaining documentary papyri of the family archive (Clarysse 1983). The cavalry officer *Dryton, for instance, copied a play on the back of one of his old loans, known as the "Alexandrian erotic fragment," which tells the story of a woman who was abandoned by her lover (Bing in *P.Dryton* 50).

(d) However, people may have kept documents for various other reasons (perhaps practical in nature) that we do not yet understand. They may have kept outdated contracts that were no longer necessary for court cases but were useful as secondhand paper (e.g., *P.Dryton*, pp. 279–280; Clarysse 1983, 58–59 and n. 86).

GREEK, EGYPTIAN, AND BILINGUAL ARCHIVES

Spanning almost a thousand years, figure 10.8 shows the predominance of Greek archives and the lesser place occupied by Egyptian (that is, demotic and Coptic) archives. This should not surprise us: Greek was the language of the administration and of the upper class. In particular, the areas where many Greeks had settled (i.e., Lower Egypt, including the Fayyum area) furnished numerous Greek and Graeco-demotic archives even in the early Ptolemaic period.

Purely demotic archives are limited to the early Ptolemaic period and to the barely Hellenized southern part of the country, mainly Thebes. One of the oldest such archives is that of the Theban funerary priest *Teos and his wife, Thabis, which dates to the late fourth century BCE. Further demotic archives (dating through the end of the third century BCE) were found in Upper Egypt. These include the family archive of the herdsman and soldier *Pabachtis, son of Paleuis, who was living in Edfu and serving on the southern border until the great Upper Egyptian revolt in 206 BCE. Some title deeds in this archive have a Greek registration docket, which is not enough to classify them as bilingual archives. As several Upper Egyptians became Hellenized to a certain degree after the suppression of the revolt in 186 BCE, the purely demotic archives of the south gradually give way to bilingual archives. The government was supportive of this development and introduced among other things Greek notaries. In particular, Pathyris, some thirty kilometers south of Thebes, yielded numerous bilingual family archives of Egyptian soldiers who were serving in the Ptolemaic army and became partly Hellenized (Pestman 1965, Vandorpe 2008).

In the early Roman period, new registration requirements were introduced, and the first party of a contract was obliged to add an elaborate subscription in Greek. Consequently, demotic notary contracts disappeared by the late first century CE, though demotic was still used for other types of texts until the third century. The Upper Egyptian sites, formerly important suppliers of demotic and bilingual archives, no longer produced such records. Fayyum towns like Tebtynis and Soknopaiou Nesos, by contrast, still yield bilingual archives that date to the late first century (Depauw 2003).

Graeco-Latin archives constitute a minority, and even in these, Latin texts make up only a small percentage (see chapter 6; for an exception, see the Graeco-Latin archive of *Claudius Tiberianus). After his retirement, *Flavius Abinnaeus, a cavalry officer who commanded the military camp of Dionysias in the Fayyum, took part of his official archive home, probably to Philadelphia, and added it to his private documents and those of his wife, Nonna. Of the more than eighty texts, only two were written in Latin; these were kept for obvious reasons: a petition to the emperors Constantius and Constans in which Abinnaeus claims the command of the cavalry *ala* at Dionysias, and a sharp letter from the dux of Egypt dismissing the commander two years later (341–351 CE; *P.Abinn.*).

In the Byzantine period, the Greek language was still dominant in official and economic matters, but Coptic became popular for private documents. Several hundred texts constitute the well-known bilingual archive of a family from sixth-century Aphrodito, named after the landlord and notary Flavius *Dioscoros. Having been trained in both languages, Dioscoros developed two types of handwriting: uncial writing, which he used for his Greek literary and Coptic texts, and a cursive writing, found in his Greek documents. Most of the Coptic texts, which are in the minority in this archive, still await publication. Dioscoros's papers provide a wealth of information on the Christianized environment in which the family lived and more generally on the society and economy of sixth-century Egypt. Dioscoros's native language was Egyptian, and his belief was Christian, but he was also versed in the pagan Greek culture and had studied Roman law.

The archive can be divided into several, well-delineated periods. Some of the oldest documents are related to Dioscoros's father, Apollos, who moved the family into the upper classes of Aphrodito and was eventually accorded the honorific nomen "Flavius." In the last decade of his life, Apollos retired to a monastery that he had himself founded. Dioscoros received a higher education in Antinoopolis or Alexandria. Following in his father's footsteps, he became village headman and received numerous petitions. After acting as notary in the nome metropolis Antinoopolis for some years, he returned to Aphrodito sometime between 570 and 573. Having a great interest in Christian and pagan literatures, Dioscoros maintained a private library that included works by Homer and the comedy writer Menander. In his spare time he appears to have been an enthusiastic poet of wedding songs and the like, written in classical Greek meters.

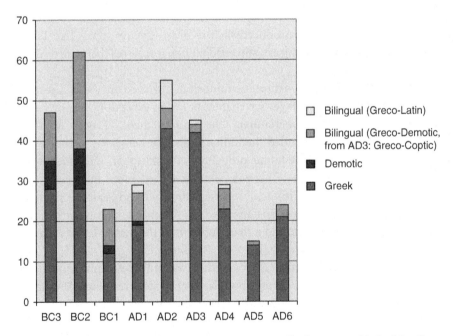

Figure 10.8. Language use in archives up to 600 CE. In all, about one third of the Graeco-Roman and Byzantine archives are bilingual (Greek, demotic, Latin, or Coptic): They may be "real" bilingual archives, which show a good balance between the two languages, or "limited" ones, in which one of the two languages is predominant. Graph: W. Clarysse.

CLASSIFYING ARCHIVAL PAPERS AND FILES

Archives are useful if they are easily accessible. Graeco-Roman Egypt organized its public records well, and especially for the Roman period we can describe in detail how these records were kept (Wolff 1978; Cockle 1984; Burkhalter 1990). Here I focus on visible traces of classification found among the preserved archives.

A very simple way to classify papers is to roll them up together and write a label on the strip of papyrus or linen used to tie up the package, such as "letters" (archive of *Peteharsemtheus, son of Panobchounis).

Several official and business archives of the third century BCE have a registration system for letters, which demonstrates that these papers were systematically arranged (e.g., the archive of the official *Tesenouphis and the business archive of *Zenon).

Beginning in the second century BCE, a more evolved system of classification was developed for official archives and eventually became the standard in the Roman administration. Documents were pasted together into a *tomos synkollesimos*. Usually documents of a single type were collected in chronological, topographical, or alphabetical order. This method of classification was applied to several types of documents, not least to declarations. The individual sheets were referred to by the number of the roll and that of the pasted sheet within the roll.

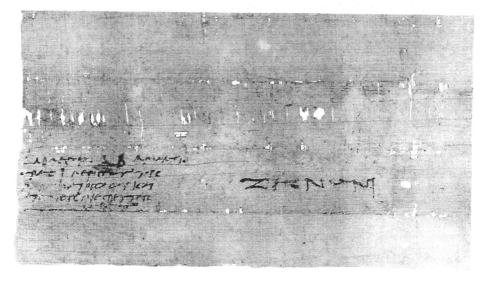

Figure 10.9. The estate manager Zenon usually endorsed letters he received with the place and date of receipt, as well as the subject. On the back of this letter from Apollonios, written in the minister's chancellery, Zenon made the unusual addition of the hour of receipt, as urgent matters were involved. The docket, written to the left of the address, reads: "Year 32, month of Mesore 2, at the 10th hour [that is, about 4 PM]. [Letter by] Apollonios about the animals for the envoys from Pairisades and Argos" (*P.Lond.* VII 1973 verso).

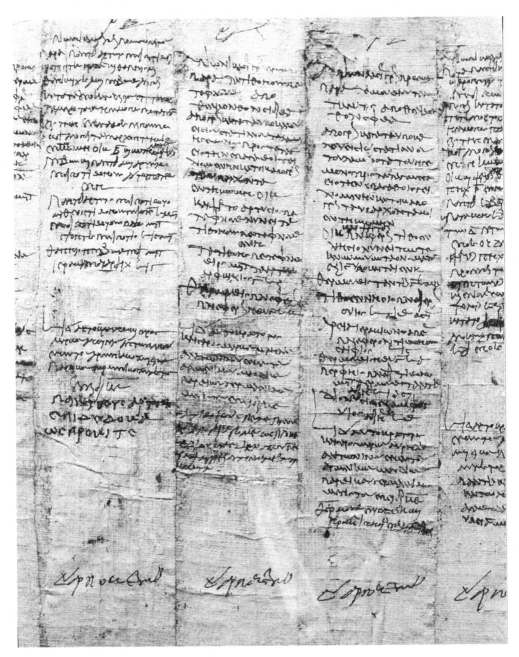

Figure 10.10. The Roman administration often collected individual documents by pasting them together into a *tomos synkollēsimos* ("pasted roll"). The sheets were numbered at the top: The photograph shows pages 102, 103, and 104 ($\rho\beta$, $\rho\gamma$, $\rho\delta$) (second century CE; Musées Royaux d'Art et d'Histoire, Brussels inv. E 7616). Reproduced courtesy of the Musées Royaux d'Art et d'Histoire, Brussels.

Pasted rolls of more than a hundred sheets were common (Clarysse 2003b). This classification system was rarely applied to private documents. *Asklepiades (alias Asklas), for instance, pasted his private and business letters for a seven-year period into one roll in chronological order by date of receipt, added at the top of the letter (29–23 BCE).

OSTRACA GROUPS: ARCHIVES *SUI GENERIS*

The bulk of the archives from Graeco-Roman Egypt are papyrus archives, but groups of interrelated documents also appear among the ostraca (and wooden tablets); these are usually small archives of tax receipts. It may be useful to distinguish between the "older" and the "younger" ostraca of buildings or towns. The older ones do not date from the last period of habitation and are usually found in rubbish dumps or the lower or older layers of buildings. The younger ostraca belong to the last period of habitation and are often kept in a niche or a corner of the taxpayers' dwellings. "Older" and "younger" are relative terms: "A group of ostraca can be sent to the dump very quickly, but this discarding may be the effect of the rehabilitation of a space cleaned after months or years" (*O.Claud.* I, p. 21). Ostraca have sometimes been found in the same building as papyrus archives but never in exactly the same spot. They are, as Montevecchi (1988, 248) has put it, rather archives *sui generis*.

Archives of younger ostraca may be reconstructed if they have been found during legal excavations. Few Ptolemaic ostraca were recovered under such conditions, as they usually do not belong to the last period of habitation. A large such archive is that of *Hor, who was attached to the sanctuary of the ibis in the Memphite Serapeum in the second century BCE. His drafts of dreams, oracles, and so on, mainly written in demotic, were discovered during excavations in 1965–1966 "while clearing the sand from a rough stone-built chapel adjoining the ibis-galleries at Saqqâra," where Hor was working (*O.Hor*). Roman-Byzantine houses have yielded more ostraca archives. In modern Aïn Waqfa in the oasis of Kharga, 82 Greek and 3 Coptic ostraca were discovered in and around two houses (called A and D). A group of 43 ostraca comes from one room of house D and is related to the farmer Poules (*O.Waqfa*).

Recent publications dealing with ostraca found during scientific excavations fortunately pay particular attention to the archaeological context (see chapter 2). The first volume of the Roman ostraca from Karanis in 1935 indicates the exact findspot of each ostracon: "Most of them were found in the ruins of ancient houses, among the rubbish of floors or cellar bins, or in wall niches where they had been carefully put aside. They were discovered singly or in groups" (*O.Mich.* I, p. IX;

the later editions follow the same system). The volume by Bingen and Clarysse (*O.Elkab*) of the Greek and demotic ostraca found in Elkab is a first-rate example of an edition of ostraca. The archaeological context and the findspots are given in detail, and the work is illustrated with surveyable maps.

If ostraca were acquired on the antiquities market or discovered in rubbish dumps, the original archives may be irretrievably lost. Most Greek and Latin ostraca from Mons Claudianus in the Eastern Desert, for instance, were found on a trash heap called the "southern sebakh," which lay south of the Roman fortress and east of the grain depot (*O.Claud.* I–III; see chapter 2). As the original archives cannot be reconstructed, the ostraca are published by type (e.g., "lettres privées") or by topic (e.g., "la mort et la maladie"). Some dossiers are put together, especially the correspondence of people like Petenophotes (*O.Claud.* II 243–254), Dioscoros and others (*O.Claud.* II 224–242); the editors stress that these letters are dossiers grouped together for prosopographical reasons (e.g., *O.Claud.* II, p. 43; Martin 1994, 572). Sometimes, however, ostraca archives may be reconstructed by using the various methods for the reconstruction of papyrus archives: the study of prosopographical data, museum archaeology, or reliance on the archaeological context; for instance, ostraca may be assembled into groups that were dumped together, as in the case of the Berenike ostraca (*O.Berenike*).

MOMENTS OF JOY

Archives may bring papyrologists moments of joy. The letters quoted here introduce us to a happy and an unhappy family, as their private correspondence illustrates.

On several occasions Paniskos, a soldier or a merchant engaged in the armor trade, asks his wife, *Ploutogeneia, to come to Koptos. In the first letter everything seems to be going well:

> First of all, I pray daily for your good health in the presence of all the gods. I would have you know then, that we have been staying in Koptos near your sister and her children, so that you may not be grieved about coming to Koptos.... So when you have received this letter of mine, make your preparations in order that you may come at once if I send for you. And when you come, bring ... six jars of olives, four jars of liquid honey, and my shield, the new one only, and my helmet.... If you find an opportunity, come here with good men.... When you come, bring your gold ornaments, but do not wear them on the boat. (translation *P.Mich.* III 214)

Ploutogeneia, however, has no intention of joining her husband at Koptos, thus infuriating Paniskos: "I have sent you three letters and you have not written me

even one. If you do not wish to come up to me, no one compels you. . . . The letter
carrier said to me when he came to me: 'When I was on the point of departing I said
to your wife and her mother "Give me a letter to take to Paniskos" and they did not
give it' " (translation *P.Mich.* III 217).

A totally different picture emerges from another archive of letters addressed
mostly to *Saturnila, mother of five sons. Her papers are referred to as the "happy
family archive" because of the "civilized and affectionate relationship between
mother and adult sons" (Bell 1950):

> Sempronius to his mother and lady Saturnila, very many greetings. Before ev-
> erything I pray for your good health and that also of my sweetest brothers, and at
> the same time I make daily supplication for you before the lord Serapis. Because
> I found someone who is coming to you upstream, I hurried to greet you by a letter.
> Do please, my lady, without delay write to me about your welfare, so that I may
> feel less anxiety. (translation *P.Mich.* XV 752)

But even this happy family had its moments of sadness, as, for instance, when
Saturnila's son Maximus mourned after his wife's death (Sijpesteijn 1976).

Historians who rely on guides or editions of papyrus archives need to be aware that
these studies are often the result of a long process of puzzling work. The major part
of the archives have not been found in their original depository. Even in antiquity
the individual items became mixed up in the wastepaper basket, on rubbish
dumps, in mummy cases, and in mummified crocodiles. In more recent times
native diggers carrying out illegal excavations split up archives and even individual
texts before putting them on the antiquities market. Papyrologists have several
methods at hand enabling them to rebuild the ancient archives in an iterative
process; they can avail themselves of published, as well as unedited, texts or
fragments spread all over the world. Although reconstructions represent a
fascinating aspect of papyrological research, they are never considered definitive
unless the papers have been found intact in their original setting.

The richness of archival research is reflected by the numerous types of archives,
by the variety of documents constituting them, and by the differences in duration:
Some archives are short lived, while others continue for several generations.
Although as a rule only papers with a juridical value were kept, several archive
holders were only acting like human beings when they filed letters and the like for
sentimental reasons, thereby allowing us to witness marital rifts or a mother's love
for her children.

The historian who gathers scattered clues from isolated texts may come to
similar conclusions as an archival researcher. But, whereas with isolated texts
interpreters are forced to make more speculative reconstructions since no immediate context is available, archives simply provide this context. They allow the
historian to reconstruct with a high degree of certainty an overall picture of the life

or career of an official, a businessman, or a family: Their papers may depict their cultural background and mother tongue, the class to which they belonged or were promoted to, their pagan or Christian belief, the land they possessed or leased, the house they lived in or the country house they owned, their job and ambitions, as well as their little worries and big problems and how they dealt with them. Archival research may create a microcosm of Graeco-Roman society and provide testing cases for models of social and economic behavior.

ARCHIVES MENTIONED IN THIS CHAPTER, LISTED ALPHABETICALLY

For each archive the entry gives the provenance, the range of attested dates (CE unless otherwise indicated), the principal edition, and information about the Leuven Homepage of Papyrus Collections (LHPC) record.

*Adamas, sitologos (199–197 BCE, Fayyum): *P.Tebt.* III 750–756, 941, 944–945; LHPC Clarysse 2003–2006; *Alopex, descendants of Alopex (308–355; Panopolis): *P.Panop.* and *P.Dubl.;* LHPC Geens 2003–2006; *Amenothes, son of Horos (171–116 BCE; Thebes): *P.Tor.Amen.;* Depauw 1997, 157; LHPC Clarysse 2003–2006; *Apollinarios, strategos of the Panopolite nome (298–300): Skeat 1961; *P.Panop.Beatty,* pp. XXI–XXV; LHPC Geens 2003–2006; *Apollonios from Bakchias (about 75–84): LHPC Smolders 2003–2006; Smolders 2004, 233–237; *Apollonios, strategos of the Apollonopolites Heptakomias (113–120; Hermopolis): *P.Giss.Apoll.;* Clarysse 1989; Rowlandson 1998, 118–124; Litinas 2001; Messeri 2001; *Apynchis, son of Tesenouphis (83; Soknopaiou Nesos): *BGU* XI 2095–2100; LHPC Geens 2003–2006; *Aristarchos, nomarches (250–238 BCE, Fayyum): Héral 1991, 1992; LHPC Van Beek 2003–2006; *Asklepiades alias Asklas (29–23 BCE; Herakleopolites): Olsson 1925, nos. 1–7; White 1986, nos. 63–65; LHPC Geens 2003–2006; *Aurelius Heras, *praepositus pagi* (316–318; Oxyrhynchus): Pruneti 1994; LHPC Geens 2003–2006; *Choachytai: Theban Choachytai Osoroeris and Panas: *P.Choach.Survey;* Depauw 1997, 157; *Claudius Tiberianus (100–120; Karanis): Pighi 1964; Adams 2003, 593–596; Strassi 2004; *Dionysios son of Kephalas (141–103 BCE; Tenis-Akoris): *Pap.Lugd.Bat.* XXII; Lewis 1986 (chapter 8.1); Pestman 1989, 71–74; Depauw 1997, 157–158; LHPC Van Beek 2003–2006; *Dioscoros (506–585; Aphrodito): Maltz 1957; MacCoull 1981 (on the Coptic papyri); Clarysse 1983, 55–57; Verbeeck 1989; Rowlandson 1998, 151–154; Fournet 1999, 2001; *Dryton, his wife, Apollonia, and their offspring (172–94 BCE; Pathyris): *P.Dryton;* Rowlandson 1998, 105–112; LHPC Vandorpe 2003–2006; *Erbstreit (186–133 BCE; Pathyris): *P.Erbstreit;* Ritner 1984;

LHPC Vandorpe 2003–2006; *Eutychides, son of Sarapion (Hermopolis): *P.Sarap.;* Kehoe 1992, 67–72; *Flavius Abinnaeus, *praefectus alae* (342–351; Dionysias–Philadelphia): *P.Abinn.;* Barnes 1985; Pestman 1989, 134–137; LHPC Geens 2003–2006; *Gaius Iulius Agrippinus (103/117–148; Karanis): Meyer 1906a, 1906b; Maehler 1970, 1982; Rupprecht 2001; LHPC Geens 2003–2007; *Heroninus (247–270; Theadelphia): Pintaudi 1976; Clarysse 1983, 47; Rathbone 1991; Kehoe 1992, 92–117; Ferro 1994; *Hor (168–151 BCE; Memphis): *O.Hor;* Depauw 1997, 158; *Horos, son of Nechouthes: *P.Adl.;* Pestman 1965, 47–48; Herrmann 1975; Messeri-Savorelli 1990; Depauw 1997, 155; LHPC Waebens 2008; *Isidoros, village scribe (161–164, Trikomia and Lagis): LHPC Smolders 2003–2006; *Iulius Serenus (179–216, Karanis): *P.Hamb.* 158–196; LHPC Clarysse 2003–2006; *Kleon and Theodoros: Lewis 1986 (chapter 2); Van Beek 2005; LHPC Van Beek 2003-2006; *Krokodilopolis, notarial office (?) (Fayyum): *P.Petr.*² I; *Kronion (second century; Tebtynis): *P.Kron.; P.Mil. Vogl.* II, III, VI; Rowlandson 1998, 125–133; Bagnall 2000; LHPC Smolders 2003–2006; *Melitian monks of Labla (511–513): McGing 1990; LHPC Clarysse 2003–2006; *Menches, goldsmith (ca. 195 BCE, Oxyrhyncha): *P.Mich.* XVIII 771–774; *Menches, village scribe: Crawford 1971; P. W. Pestman in *P.Rain.Cent.*, pp. 127–134; Lewis 1986 (chapter 7); Verhoogt 1998a, 1998b, 2005; LHPC Vandorpe 2003-2006; *Milon, *praktor* (225–222 BCE; Edfu): Depauw 1997, 159; Clarysse 2003a; LHPC Clarysse 2003–2006; *Oxyrhyncha, granary of (152–149 BCE): *P.Erasm.* I and II; *Pabachtis, son of Paleuis (265–208 BCE; Edfu): *P.Hausw.Spiegelberg; P.Hausw.Manning;* Depauw 1997, 155; LHPC Müller 2003; *Pakebkis, descendants of (126–162; Tebtynis): Melaerts 1991; Bagnall 2000; LHPC Smolders 2003–2006; *Pates and Pachrates, correspondence of Pates and Pachrates (103–101 BCE; Pathyris): *P.War of Scepters*, pp. 37–81; LHPC Clarysse 2003–2006; *Pathyris, *archeion* of (ca. 111–110 BCE): Vandorpe 2004, 166–167; *Patronids (formerly called the archive of Laches) (108–176; Tebtynis): Bagnall 1973; Clarysse and Gallazzi 1993; Bagnall 2000; LHPC Smolders 2003–2006; *Petaus, village scribe (182–187; Ptolemais Hormou): *P.Petaus;* *Peteharsemtheus, son of Panobchounis: Pestman 1965; Lewis 1986 (chapter 8.2); LHPC Waebens 2008; *Phanesis, oil seller (233–223 BCE, Tebtynis): Muhs, Grünewaldt, and Van den Berg-Onstwedder 2002–2003; LHPC Clarysse 2003–2006; *Philosarapis (89–224; Tebtynis): *P.Fam.Tebt.;* LHPC Smolders 2003–2006; *Ploutogeneia (296–298; Philadelphia): *P.Mich.* III 275–298; Schwartz 1968; Rowlandson 1998, 147–151; LHPC Smolders 2003–2006; *Pompeius Niger (31–64; Oxyrhynchus?): Whitehorne 1988; Rathbone 2001; LHPC Smolders 2003–2006; *Praktores argurikon* of Soknopaiou Nesos (an early third-century tax archive): Lewis 1954, 297–298; Nachtergael 2005, 232–235; *Ptolemaios and his brother, Apollonios, recluses in the Memphite Serapeum (164–152 BCE): *UPZ* I; Clarysse 1983, 57–60; Lewis 1986 (chapter 5); Clarysse 1986; Hoogendijk 1989; *Pyrrheia, granary of Pyrrheia: Clarysse and Hauben 1991; LHPC Clarysse 2003–2006; *Sarapias (165–264/270; Tebtynis): Verhoogt 1998a; Clarysse 2006; LHPC Smolders 2003–2006; *Saturnila (about 175–199; Karanis?): Bell 1950; Sijpesteijn 1976; Rowlandson 1998,

143–147; Barrenechea 2001; LHPC Van Beek 2003–2006; *Socrates, tax collector (106–171; Karanis): Van Minnen 1994, 237–244; Strassi 2001; *Soknobraisis, temple of Soknobraisis at Bakchias (116–212): Gilliam 1947; LHPC Clarysse 2003–2006; *Taienteus (315–274 BCE; Thebes): *P.Brit.Mus.* I; *P.Ryl.Dem.* 10–14; Pestman 1989, 14–24; Depauw 1997, 156; *Tefhapi from Siut (185–169 BCE; Lycopolites): *P.Siut;* Shore-Smith 1959; Vleeming 1989; Depauw 1997, 157; *Teos and his wife, Thabis: *P.Teos;* Depauw 1997, 156; LHPC Depauw 2003–2006; *Tesenouphis, toparches (224–217 BCE, Fayyum): *P.Sorb.* I 38–55; LHPC Clarysse 2003–2006; *Theogonis, grapheion of Theogonis: *CPR* XVIII; *Thmouis, record office in Thmouis (Mendesian nome): *P.Thmouis* 1–4; *Totoes: *P.Tor.Botti,* esp. 204–205; *PSI* IX 1014–1025; Pestman 1989, 24–29; Depauw 1997, 156; *Zenon (mid-third century BCE; Philadelphia, Fayyum): for bibliography see *Pap.Lugd.Bat.* XXI; Clarysse and Vandorpe 1995; Rowlandson 1998, 95–98.

BIBLIOGRAPHY

Adams, J. N. 2003. *Bilingualism and the Latin Language.* Cambridge: Cambridge University Press.

Bagnall, R. S. 1995. *Reading Papyri, Writing Ancient History.* London: Routledge.

——. 2000. "Village and Urban Elites in Roman Tebtunis." In Bancroft Library Gallery, Berkeley. http://tebtunis.berkeley.edu/ancientlives/bagnall.html.

Bagnall, W. S. 1973. "Some Prosopographical Observations on the Laches Archive." *BASP* 10: 65–70.

Barnes, T. D. 1985. "The Career of Abinnaeus." *Phoenix* 39: 368–374.

Barrenechea, F. 2001. "A New Letter from the Sempronius Dossier: A Letter from Maximus." *BASP* 38: 21–34.

Bell, H. I. 1950. "A Happy Family." In *Aus Antike und Orient: Festschrift Wilhelm Schubart zum 75. Geburtstag,* ed. S. Morenz and W. Schubart, 38–47. Leipzig: Harrassowitz.

Boussac, M.-F. 1993. "Archives personnelles à Délos". In *Comptes rendus des séances de l'Académie des Inscriptions et Belles-lettres (CRAI).* 677–693. Paris: Klincksieck.

Brosius, M., ed. 2003. *Archives and Archival Traditions: Concepts of Record-keeping in the Ancient World.* Oxford: Oxford University Press.

Burkhalter, F. 1990. "Archives locales et archives centrales en Égypte romaine." *Chiron* 20: 191–215.

Capasso, M. 1996. "Catalogo dei papiri di Bakchias, II: i PBakchias 101–133." In *Bakchias III: Rapporto preliminare della campagna di scavo del 1995,* ed. S. Pernigotti and M. Capasso, 119–147. Studi di egittologia e di antichità puniche. Monografie, series maior 3, Pisa: Giardini.

Clackson, S. J. 2004. "Museum Archaeology and Coptic Papyrology: The Bawit Papyri." In *Coptic Studies on the Threshold of a New Millennium: Proceedings of the Seventh International Congress of Coptic Studies. Leiden 27 August–2 Sept. 2000,* ed.

M. Immerzeel and J. van der Vliet, vol. 1, 477–490. Orientalia Lovaniensia Analecta 133. Leuven: Peeters.

Clarysse, W. 1983. "Literary Papyri in Documentary 'Archives.' " In *Egypt and the Hellenistic World,* ed. E. Van 't Dack et al., 43–61. Studia Hellenistica 27. Leuven: Peeters.

——. 1986. "UPZ I 60, a Reconstruction by Revillout." *Enchoria* 14: 43–49.

——. 1989. "Apollonios: Ambtenaar en familievader." In *Familiearchieven uit het land van Pharao,* ed. P. W. Pestman, 85–106. Zutphen, the Netherlands: Terra.

——. 2003a. "The Archive of the Praktor Milon." In *Edfu, an Egyptian Provincial Capital in the Ptolemaic Period, Handelingen Contactforum Brussels, 3 September 2001,* ed. K. Vandorpe and W. Clarysse, 17–27. Brussels: Koninklijke Vlaamse academie van België voor wetenschappen en kunsten.

——. 2003b. "Tomoi Synkollesimoi." In *Archives and Archival Traditions: Concepts of Record-keeping in the Ancient World,* ed. M. Brosius, 344–359. Oxford: Oxford University Press.

Clarysse, W., and C. Gallazzi. 1993. "Archivio dei discendenti di Laches o dei discendenti di Patron?" *AncSoc* 24: 63–68.

Clarysse, W., and H. Hauben. 1991. "Ten Ptolemaic Granary Receipts from Pyrrheia." *ZPE* 89: 47–68.

Clarysse, W., and K. Vandorpe. 1995. *Zénon, un homme d'affaires grec à l'ombre des pyramides (Ancorae: Steunpunten voor Studie en Onderwijs* 14). Leuven: Presses universitaires de Louvain.

Cockle, W. E. H. 1984. "State Archives in Graeco-Roman Egypt from 30 BC to the Reign of Septimius Severus." *JEA* 70: 106–122.

Crawford, D. J. 1971. *Kerkeosiris, an Egyptian village in the Ptolemaic period.* Cambridge: Cambridge University Press.

——. 1973. "The Opium Poppy. A Study in Ptolemaic Agriculture." In *Problèmes de la terre en Grèce ancienne,* ed. M. I. Finley, 223–251. Civilisations et Sociétés 33. Paris: Mouton.

Davoli, P. 1998. *L'archeologia urbana nel Fayyum di età ellenistica e romana.* Missione congiunta delle Università di Bologna e di Lecce in Egitto. Monografie 1 Athenaeum. Napoli: Procaccini.

——. 2005. *Oggetti in argilla dall'area templare di Bakchias (El-Fayyum, Egitto): Catalogo dei rinvenimenti delle Campagne di Scavo 1996–2002.* Biblioteca degli Studi di egittologia e di papirologia 3. Pisa: Giardini.

Depauw, M. 1997. *A Companion to Demotic Studies (Pap.Brux.* 28). Brussels: Fondation égyptologique Reine Elisabeth.

——. 2000. *The Archive of Teos and Thabis from Early Ptolemaic Thebes: P. Brux. Dem. Inv. E. 8252–8256.* Monographies Reine Elisabeth 8. Turnhout: Brepols.

——. 2003. "Autograph Confirmation in Demotic Private Contracts." *CdÉ* 78: 66–111.

Ferro, C. 1994. "I rendiconti dell'archivio di Heroneinos." *Analecta Papyrologica* 6: 37–51.

Fournet, J.-L. 1999. *Hellénisme dans l'Égypte du VIe siècle: La bibliothèque et l'œuvre de Dioscore d'Aphrodité* (MIFAO 115). Cairo: Institut français d'archéologie orientale.

——. 2001. "Du nouveau dans les archives de Dioscore d'Aphrodité." In *Atti del XXII Congresso Internazionale di Papirologia, Firenze, 23–29 agosto 1998,* ed. I. Andorlini, G. Bastianini and M. Manfredi, 475–485. Florence: Università di Firenze. Istituto papirologico G. Vitelli.

Gallazzi, C. 1990. "La 'Cantina dei Papiri' di Tebtynis e ciò che essa conteneva." *ZPE* 80: 283–288.

Gilliam, E. H. 1947. "The Archives of the Temple of Soknobraisis at Bacchias." *Yale Classical Studies* 10: 179–281.

Godlewski, W. 1986. *Deir el-Bahari V: Le monastère de St. Phoibammon.* Warsaw: PWN.

Hagedorn, D. 1970. "Papyri aus Panopolis in der Kölner Sammlung." In *Proceedings of the XIIth International Congress of Papyrology, Ann Arbor, August 13-17, 1968*, ed. D.H. Samuel, 207–211. Toronto: Hakkert.

Héral, S. 1991. *Les archives bilingues du nomarque Aristarchos d'après les papyrus de Ghôran.* Mémoire de D.E.A., Institut de Papyrologie, Université de Paris IV–Sorbonne.

——. 1992. "Les archives bilingues de nomarques dans les papyrus de Ghôran." In *Life in a Multi-cultural Society: Egypt from Cambyses to Constantine and Beyond,* ed. J. H. Johnson, 149–157. Studies in Ancient Oriental Civilization 51. Chicago: Oriental Institute.

Herrmann, J. 1975. "Sachteilung und Wertteilung bei Grundstücken: Zu den griechischen Kaufurkunden des Horus-Archivs." In *Festschrift für E. Seidl. Zum 70. Geburtstag,* ed. H. Hübner, 53–60. Cologne: Hanstein.

Hoogendijk, F. A. J. 1989. "Ptolemaios: Een Griek die leeft en droomt in een Egyptische tempel." In *Familiearchieven uit het land van Pharao,* ed. P. W. Pestman, 46–69. Zutphen: Terra.

Jördens, A. 2001. "Papyri und private Archive: Ein Diskussionsbeitrag zur papyrologischen Terminologie." In *Symposion 1997: Vorträge zur griechischen und hellenistischen Rechtsgeschichte (Altafiumara, 8–14 Sept. 1997),* ed. E. Cantarella and G. Thur, 253–267. Cologne: Böhlau.

Kehoe, D. P. 1992. *Management and Investment on Estates in Roman Egypt during the Early Empire.* Papyrologische Texte und Abhandlungen 40. Bonn: R. Habelt.

Leuven Homepage of Papyrus Collections (LHPC). Database-driven website containing a recent list and detailed descriptions of archives from Graeco-Roman and Byzantine Egypt. Contributions by W. Clarysse, M. Depauw, K. Geens, K. Müller, R. Smolders, B. Van Beek, K. Vandorpe and S. Waebens. Leuven 2003–2008. http://www.trismegistos.org/arch/index.php.

Lewis, N. 1954. "Miscellanea Papyrologica." *CdÉ* 29: 288–298.

——. 1986. *Greeks in Ptolemaic Egypt: Case Studies in the Social History of the Hellenistic World.* Oxford: Oxford University Press.

Litinas, N. 2001. "A Letter from the Strategos Apollonios Archive? *P.Lond.* inv. 1228." In *Atti del XXII Congresso Internazionale di Papirologia, Firenze, 23–29 agosto 1998,* ed. I. Andorlini, G. Bastianini and M. Manfredi, 805–812. Florence: Università di Firenze. Istituto papirologico G. Vitelli.

MacCoull, L. S. B. 1981. "The Coptic Archive of Dioscoros of Aphrodito." *CdÉ* 56: 185–193.

Maehler, H. 1970. "Neue Dokumente zum Drusilla-Prozess." In *Proceedings of the XIIth International Congress of Papyrology, Ann Arbor, August 13–17, 1968,* ed. D.H. Samuel, 263–271. American Studies in Papyrology 7. Toronto: Hakkert.

——. 1982. "Neues vom Prozess der Drusilla gegen Agrippinus." In *Symposion 1997: Vorträge zur griechischen und hellenistischen Rechtsgeschichte (Altafiumara, 8–14 Sept. 1997),* ed. E. Cantarella and G. Thur, 325–333. Cologne: Böhlau.

Maltz, G. 1957. "The Papyri of Dioscoros." In *Studi in onore di Aristide Calderini e Roberto Paribeni.* 2, 345–356. Milan: Ceschina.

Martin, A. 1994. "Archives privées et cachettes documentaires." In *Proceedings of the 20th International Congress of Papyrologists. Copenhagen, 23–29 August 1992*, ed. A. Bülow-Jacobsen, 569–577. Copenhagen: Museum Tusculanum.

McGing, B. C. 1990. "Melitian Monks at Labla." *Tyche* 5: 67–91.

Melaerts, H. 1991. "Autour du *P.Mil.Vogl.* II, 73." *CdÉ* 66: 266–278.

Messeri, G. 2001. "Suggestioni da PSI IV 308" *ZPE* 135: 165–168.

Messeri-Savorelli, G. 1990. "Un nuovo documento dell'archivio di Horos figlio di Nechutes." *Analecta Papyrologica* 2: 53–61.

Meyer, P. M. 1906a. "Papyrus Cattaoui. II: Kommentar." *APF* 3: 67–105.

——. 1906b. "Zum Drusilla-Prozess." *APF* 3: 247–248.

Montevecchi, O. 1988. *La Papirologia*, 2d ed. Milan: Vita e pensiero.

Muhs, B., A. Grünewaldt, and G. Van den Berg-Onstwedder. 2002–2003. "The Papyri of Phanesis, Son of Nechturis, Oil Merchant of Tebtunis, and the Ptolemaic Cloth Monopoly." *Enchoria* 28: 62–81.

Nachtergael, G. 2005. "Papyrologica II." *CdÉ* 80: 229–245.

Olsson, B. 1925. *Papyrusbriefe aus der frühesten Römerzeit*. Uppsala: Almqvist och Wiksell.

Orrieux, Cl. 1983. *Les papyrus de Zénon: l'horizon d'un grec en Egypte au IIIe siècle avant J. C.* Deucalion. Paris: Macula.

——. 1985. *Zénon de Caunos, parépidèmos, et le destin grec.* Annales littéraires de l'Université de Besançon 320. Paris: Belles Lettres.

Pantalacci, L. 2008. *La lettre d'archive: communication administrative et personelle dans l'antiquité proche-orientale et égyptienne*. Topoi: Orient-Occident. Supplément 9. Lyon: Maison de l'Orient et de la Méditerranée.

Pestman, P. W. 1965. "Les archives privées de Pathyris à l'époque ptolémaïque: La famille de Pétéharsemtheus, fils de Panebkhounis." In *Pap.Lugd.Bat.* XIV: 47–105.

——, ed. 1989. *Familiearchieven uit het land van Pharao*. Zutphen: Terra.

——. 1995. "A Family Archive Which Changes History." In *Hundred-gated Thebes: Acts of a Colloquium on Thebes and the Theban Area during the Graeco-Roman Period*, ed. S. P. Vleeming, 91–100. *Pap.Lugd.Bat* 27. Leiden: Brill.

Pighi, G. B. 1964. *Lettere latine di un soldato di Traiano (P.Mich. 467–472)*. Bologna: Zanichelli.

Pintaudi, R. 1976. "Papiri fiorentini dell'archivio di Heronas." *ZPE* 20: 233–248.

Pruneti, P. 1994. "L'archivio di Aurelius Heras praepositus pagi." *Aegyptus* 74: 33–36.

Rathbone, D. W. 1991. *Economic Rationalism and Rural Society in Third-century* A.D. *Egypt: The Heroninos Archive and the Appianus Estate.* Cambridge: Cambridge University Press.

——. 2001. "PSI XI 1183: Record of a Roman Census Declaration of A.D. 47/8." In *Essays and Texts in Honor of J. David Thomas*, ed. T. Gagos and R. S. Bagnall, 99–113. American Studies in Papyrology 42. Oakville, Conn.: American Society of Papyrologists.

Ritner, R. K. 1984. "Property Transfer." In *Grammata Demotika: Festschrift für E. Lüddeckens zum 15. Juni 1983*, ed. H.-J. Thissen and K.-Th. Zauzich, 171–187. Würzburg: Zauzich.

Rowlandson, J., ed. 1998. *Women and Society in Greek and Roman Egypt: A Sourcebook.* Cambridge: Cambridge University Press.

Rupprecht, H.-A. 2001. "Ein Verfahren ohne Ende: Der Prozess der Drusilla." In *Atti del XXII Congresso Internazionale di Papirologia, Firenze, 23–29 agosto 1998*, ed. I. Andorlini, G. Bastianini and M. Manfredi, 1135–1144. Florence: Università di Firenze. Istituto papirologico G. Vitelli.

Ryholt, K. 2005. "On the Contents and Nature of the Tebtunis Temple Library: A Status Report." In *Tebtynis und Soknopaiu Nesos: Leben im römerzeitlichen Fajum. Akten des Internationalen Symposions vom 11. bis 13. Dezember 2003 in Sommerhausen bei Würzburg*, ed. S. L. Lippert and M. Schentuleit, 141–170. Wiesbaden: Harrassowitz.

Schwartz, J. 1968. "Autour du dossier de Paniskos (*P.Mich.* 214–221)." *Aegyptus* 48: 110–115.

Seidl, E. 1962. *Ptolemäische Rechtsgeschichte*, 2d ed. Ägyptologische Forschungen 22. Glückstadt: J. J. Augustin.

Seidl, E. 1973. *Rechtsgeschichte Ägyptens als römischer Provinz. (Die Behauptung des ägyptischen Rechts neben dem römischen)*. Sankt Augustin: Richarz.

Shore, A. F., and H. S. Smith. 1959. "Two Unpublished Demotic Documents from the Asyut Archive." *JEA* 45: 52–60.

Sijpesteijn, P. J. 1976. "A Happy Family?" *ZPE* 21: 169–181.

Skeat, T. C. 1961. "Papyri from Panopolis in the Collection of Sir Chester Beatty." In *Proceedings of the IX International Congress of Papyrology, Oslo, 19–22 August 1958*, ed. L. Amundsen and V. Skånland, 194–199. Hertford: Norwegian Research Council for Science and the Humanities.

Smolders, R. 2004. "Two Archives from the Roman Arsinoites." *CdÉ* 79: 233–240.

Strassi, S. 2001. "Le carte di Sokrates Sarapionos, praktor argyrikon a Karanis nel II sec. d.c." In *Atti del XXII Congresso Internazionale di Papirologia, Firenze, 23–29 agosto 1998*, ed. I. Andorlini, G. Bastianini and M. Manfredi, 1215–1228. Florence: Università di Firenze, Istituto papirologico G. Vitelli.

———. 2004. "In margine all'archivio di Tiberianus e Terentianus: *P.Mich.* VIII 510." *ZPE* 148: 225–234.

Van Beek, B. 2005. "A Letter from Zenon to Kleon: A New Date for *P.Zen.Pestm.*, Suppl. B." *AncSoc* 35: 119–128.

———. 2007. "Ancient Archives and Modern Collections: The Leuven Homepage of Papyrus Archives and Collections." In *Proceedings of the XXIVth International Congress of Papyrology (Helsinki, 1–7 August 2004)*, ed. J. Frösén, T. Purola and E. Salmenkivi, 1033-1044. Helsinki: Societas Scientiarum Fennica.

Van Minnen, P. 1994. "House-to-House Enquiries: An Interdisciplinary Approach to Roman Karanis." *ZPE* 100: 227–251.

Vandorpe, K. 1994. "Museum Archaeology or How to Reconstruct Pathyris Archives." *EVO* 17: 289–300.

———. 2004. "A Greek Register from Pathyris' Notarial Office: Loans and Sales from the Pathyrite and Latopolite Nomes." *ZPE* 150: 161–186.

———. 2008. "Persians soldiers and Persians of the Epigone. Social Mobility of Soldiers-Herdsmen in Upper Egypt." *APF* 54: 87–108.

Verbeeck, B. 1989. "Dioskoros: Dorpshoofd, dichter en notaris." In *Familiearchieven uit het land van Pharao*, ed. P. W. Pestman, 138–162. Zutphen: Terra.

Verhoogt, A. M. F. W. 1998a. "Family Papers from Tebtunis: Unfolding a Bundle of Papyri." In *The Two Faces of Graeco-Roman Egypt: Greek and Demotic and Greek-Demotic Texts and Studies Presented to P.W. Pestman*, ed. S. P. Vleeming and A. M. F. W. Verhoogt, 141–154. *Pap.Lugd.Bat* 30. Leiden: Brill.

———. 1998b. *Menches, Komogrammateus of Kerkeosiris: The Doings and Dealings of a Village Scribe in the Late Ptolemaic Period (120–110 BC)*. (*Pap.Lugd.Bat.* 29). Leiden: Brill.

———. 2005. *Regaling Officials in Ptolemaic Egypt. A Dramatic Reading of Official Accounts from the Menches Papers.* (*Pap.Lugd.Bat.* 32). Leiden: Brill.

Vleeming, S. P. 1989. "Strijd om het erfdeel van Tefhapi." In *Familiearchieven uit het land van Pharao,* ed. P. W. Pestman, 30–45. Zutphen: Terra.

White, J. L. 1986. *Light from Ancient Letters.* Philadelphia: Fortress.

Whitehorne, J. E. G. 1988. "More about L. Pompeius Niger, Legionary Veteran." In *Proceedings of the XVIII International Congress of Papyrology,* ed. B. G. Mandilaras, vol. 2, 445–450. Athens: Greek Papyrological Society.

Wolff, H. J. 1978. *Das Recht der griechischen Papyri Ägyptens in der Zeit der Ptolemäer und des Prinzipats.* Vol. 2, *Organisation und Kontrolle des privaten Rechtsverkehrs.* Handbuch der Altertumswissenschaft 10.5.2/Rechtsgeschichte des Altertum 5.2. Munich: Beck.

CHAPTER 11

THE ANCIENT BOOK

WILLIAM A. JOHNSON

FROM the beginnings of Greek written literature until deep into the Roman era, a "book" was fashioned by taking a premanufactured papyrus roll, writing out the text, attaching additional fresh rolls as the length of text required, and, when finished, cutting off the blank remainder. Needed were the papyrus rolls, ink, pen, sponge, glue, and knife. This could have been a casual process. But, in fact, as the papyri show us, it was not. A lot follows from this fact—that literary texts were produced, in general, with strict attention rather than casually—and our first order of business is to understand clearly what constituted the ancient book.

THE BOOKROLL

Books on papyrus in the form of rolls ("bookrolls") were the norm from the beginnings through the early Roman era. The first Greek vase representation dates to the early fifth century, but the Egyptians had used papyrus bookrolls for at least two thousand years before that. Over the course of the second to the fourth centuries CE, the codex came to replace the bookroll (discussed later), but the bookroll was the dominant format for Greek and, later, Roman literary texts for about one thousand years. During that lengthy period, the look and feel of the bookroll varied in only relatively minor points of style. The appearance of the book-as-object is remarkably stable over time and place, and this fact allows us to advance some generalities.

The papyrus writing material was, as we have already seen (chapter 1), man-ufactured in two-layer sheets made from papyrus pith. The resulting sheets were not unlike paper today: somewhat thicker and certainly tougher but more or less in keeping with modern page size; for quality productions, typically 20–25 cm (8–10 in.) in width and 19–33 cm (7.5–13 in.) in height (Johnson 2004, 88–92). The sheets, however, were not sold separately, as paper is today but were joined together into rolls of a fixed number of sheets (typically twenty; Lewis 1974, 54–55; Skeat 1982, 169–72), pasted left over right so that the writing would flow easily—downhill, as it were—over the join. Manufactured papyrus rolls were of quality that varied widely, from wrapping paper to writing material. The elder Pliny (*HN* 13.74–78) gives us Latin terms for the grades, along with information on the criteria used for grading. Important were the color, the texture, and the width of the sheets: Better was white, thin, smooth, and wide sheeted (Johnson 1993). Use of the top grades appears to have been typical for the production of books. Despite heavy damage to most surviving papyri, one finds evidence of painstaking attention to detail in the manufacture of the rolls. Manufactured joins, for example, were often constructed in the manner of a rabbet in cabinet joinery, with a layer of one of the two-layered sheets meticulously stripped away so that the join itself comprised only three layers—thus both smoother and less prone to damage (J. Rea in Turner 1978, 20; Coles et al. 1985, 115). Locating the join can be nearly impossible on the back, where the vertical fibers run, but also sometimes surprisingly challenging on the front of the roll, where one would think the mismatch of horizontal fibers would make the join readily apparent. (The Arden papyrus, MP 1233, is a good example: See figure 11.1 and comments at Johnson 2004, 91*n*4.) Such was the care given to smoothing and joining in the manufacture of better-made rolls.

Once the scribe took the manufactured roll in the hand, attention to detail did not stop. The scribe's payment was based on the quality of the writing (*P. Lond.* inv. 2110 [Bell 1921]; Diocletian, *Edictum de pretiis rerum venalium*, col. 7.41–43). Books on papyrus are generally written in a "book hand," a style of writing in which the letters are kept wholly or mostly separated to improve legibility. A fair number, perhaps a third of the total, are written in a formal or semiformal script with at least pretension to elegance. Importantly, relatively few are written in cursive or otherwise substandard scripts.[1] Those written in book hands, whether calligraphic or nondescript, generally show signs of having been written by a trained scribe. Most telling is the layout, which tends to be exceedingly exact in several respects (see later discussion).

Bookrolls from our earliest direct witnesses (fourth century BCE) are laid out along the length of the roll in columns running left to right. (See figure 11.2.) Prose texts were written in columns that were narrow relative to their height, roughly analogous to a modern newspaper. Over time, the preferred style may change—wider (it seems) in Ptolemaic texts, narrower in the early Roman era, wider in the later empire—but the column width almost always falls within 4.5–9 cm (2–3.5 in.)

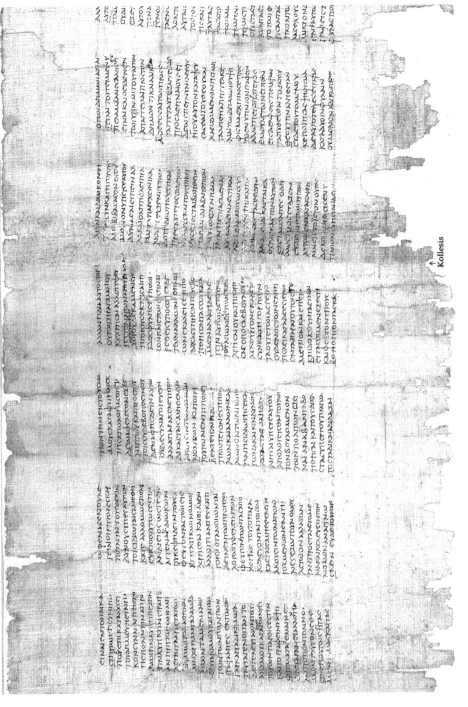

Figure 11.1. MP 1233 (*P.Lond.Lit.* 132). The Arden papyrus, cols. 29–34.

Kollesis

and usually within 4.5–7.5 cm (2–3 in.), a narrow range. The column height, by comparison, ranges broadly but tends to be at least twice that of the width—usually within 12–26 cm (5–10 in.), thus ensuring the general look of a tall, slender column.

Verse texts are different since the column width is simply a function of the script size and the verse length; for hexameters, the column was quite wide, and for trimeter texts somewhat less so (see table 11.1). Again, over time minor changes in style assert themselves: For example, Ptolemaic verse texts often evince a preference for as narrow a space as possible between the columns, to the extent that a long line from one column is allowed to run right up to the next, while Roman-era verse texts tend toward somewhat wider, more distinct intercolumnar spacing. Still, like prose texts, bookrolls that contain verse are generally stable in look and feel over time, stylistic particulars aside. Worth remark is that prose, with its narrow and (mostly) justified columns, is immediately distinguishable from poetry.[2]

As described, the layout is remarkably exact for a hand-produced item. The measurement from the left edge of one column to the next column stays *typically* within ± 1.5 mm as one ranges along the roll—the width of a broad pen stroke. Also typical are evenness in the straightness of the written line, rough evenness in spacing between lines, fairly exact alignment in the run of the left edge of the

Table 11.1. Typical Bookroll Dimensions (Johnson 2004)

Dimension	Normative Range
roll height	Ptolemaic: 19–25 cm Roman era: 25–33 cm
column height	class I: 12–16 cm class II: 16–21 cm class III: 21–27 cm
column width, prose	class I: 4.5–6 cm class II: 6–7.5 cm class III (rare): 8–9 cm
column width, verse	trimeter: ca. 8–11 cm hexameter: ca. 11–14 cm
intercolumn, prose	class I: ca. 1.5 cm (1.2–1.8) class II: ca. 2.0 cm (1.9–2.5)
upper margin	everyday ms: 3–4 cm deluxe ms: 3–6 cm
lower margin	everyday ms: 3–5 cm deluxe ms: 3–7 cm
letters per line	13–24 (at extremes 10–30)
lines per column	25–50 (at extremes 18–64)

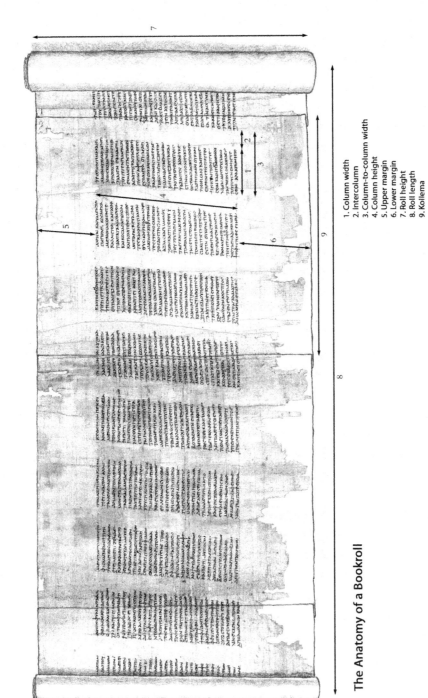

The Anatomy of a Bookroll

1. Column width
2. Intercolumn
3. Column-to-column width
4. Column height
5. Upper margin
6. Lower margin
7. Roll height
8. Roll length
9. Kollema

Figure 11.2. Anatomy of the bookroll.

column (and, by the Roman era, rough justification of the right), and the alignment of the top and bottom of the columns relative to the top and bottom of the roll. A telling detail is scribal attention to "Maas's law," named after the scholar (Paul Maas), who first drew attention to the phenomenon. In accordance with this "law," bookrolls often exhibit a forward tilt in the column, such that the left and right edges of the column move steadily to the left as the scribe works his way down to the bottom. (See figure 11.1.) This tilt becomes a regular feature in the early Roman era and dominates in the second and third centuries. That Maas's law is a deliberate feature (and not a product of scribal inattention) is confirmed both by its regularity—in a sample of 192 Oxyrhynchus papyri, 70 percent showed a distinct, measurable tilt forward, and only two a definite tilt in the other direction—and by the presence on several papyri of ruling dots set out as guides to keep the angle of the tilt consistent (Johnson 2004, 91–99).

The bookroll, here and elsewhere, shows distinct signs of deliberate design and attention to what is stylish, as well as exactness in execution involving both measurement and expert estimation. All of this is consistent—as a general picture—with the conclusion that bookrolls were generally the product of scribes trained for the task, that is, to an artisan apprentice trade. The trade clearly also involves a strong sense of the cultural demands on the product. The bookroll signaled culture and learning, but for a bookroll to qualify as such required a particular look and feel with well-defined traditions of detail. Counterexamples exist, of course, but—school texts of Homer to one side—it is important to stress how rare these are.

The writing itself, formed with a view to clarity, is laid out in continuous letters *(scriptio continua)*, that is, without spaces between words. It is sometimes said that ancient books lacked punctuation, but that is not strictly true; what is true is that in ancient books the punctuation was far less elaborated. Minor points of articulation or breath pauses, where we now place a comma or a colon, are left unpunctuated for the most part; when marked, raised dots are normally used, and these are often additions by a reader.[3] Punctuation is, however, routine for marking periods (i.e., at the end of a sentence), changes between speakers in drama and dialogue, and other major points of division, such as the poems within an epigram collection. Points of major division are most often signaled by the *paragraphos* (a horizontal line at the left edge of the column); where the division occurs in midline, the *paragraphos* is conjoined with a space (more usual in Ptolemaic texts) or a raised dot (·) at the appropriate point in the line of text. Changes of speaker, whether in drama or philosophical dialogue, are usually marked with a *dicolon* (:), in form like today's colon, to distinguish from the dots that mark the separation of sentences. Other sigla such as *diplê* (>) and *diplê obelismenê* (>—) appear but only sporadically (McNamee 1992). Little interferes, then, with the run of the text aside from the *paragraphoi*. For the reader, the *paragraphoi* naturally act as landing points for breath and mental pauses and as visual cues for returning to a passage when a reader looks up from the text (Johnson 1994). But the overall effect is (to us) of a radically unencumbered stream of letters.

A few other details of the written text are worth cataloguing as well. In all periods, rules for the division of words between lines were strictly observed.[4] Here again we find evidence of attention to detail and an apparently deliberate distinction from documentary texts, where such rules are routinely violated. Iota adscript was written in every period, though erratically applied by the Roman era; the literary papyri show here a clear desire to maintain traditional orthography even in the face of a significant shift in pronunciation (most documentary texts drop *iota mutum* wholesale in the Hellenistic era; Clarysse 1976). Also in every period, *scriptio plena* (e.g., unelided δέ before a vowel) was a normal if irregular feature for both poetic and prose texts, written even when not spoken so as to help with the parsing of the words. From the second century BCE on, an apostrophe, as in our texts today, was sometimes used to mark elision (e.g., δ'). In the early Roman era diaeresis came to be added over iota and upsilon at the beginning of a word (e.g., ἵνα, ὕιος) and in "organic" uses (e.g., Ἀϊδι), also apparently to help with word division. In the third century CE, the habit arose of placing an apostrophe between doubled mutes or liquids (e.g., τετ'τιγων, *P.Oxy.* VII 1016.232; cf. Turner and Parsons 1987, 11). Very occasionally there were other aids to reading, such as a sling underneath (the ancient *hyphen*), which indicated that the reader should take the letters together as part of the same word; or a diastole (in form like our comma), indicating the separation of a letter group. Also occasional was the addition of a breathing or an accent to help disambiguate a letter group. Except in school exercises, accents are common, however, only in the difficult dialectical terrain of Greek lyric texts; the same is true for marks of quantity. Common in documents but rare in bookrolls is the use of indentation *(eisthesis)* and reverse indentation *(ekthesis)*; in literary papyri these are normally used only to indicate verse groups or change in meter. In general, then, lectional aids were few, and little by way of help or intervention interrupted the flow of the letters. Thorough training was necessary for one to be able to read this *scriptio continua* readily and comfortably.

Note that the net effect is designed for clarity and beauty but not ease of use, much less mass readership. Importantly, this design is not one of primitivism or ignorance. The ancients knew perfectly well, for instance, the utility of word division—the Greek school texts on papyri (see chapter 14) bear eloquent testimony to the need for emerging readers to practice syllable and word division. Similarly, philhellenism in the early empire led to the adoption of *scriptio continua* in Latin literary texts, which earlier had used interpuncts (raised dots) to divide the words—that is, word division was *discarded* by the Romans in deference to Greek aesthetic and cultural traditions. As already mentioned, readers would sometimes add detailed punctuation to texts as a guide to syntax and breath pauses, yet the punctuation does not become more complex over time: In general the deliberate scribal practice was to copy only the bare-bones punctuation of major points of division even when detailed punctuation was available. Strict functionality, clearly, is not a priority in bookroll design. The bookroll seems, rather, an egregiously elite product intended in its stark beauty and difficulty of access to instantiate what it is to be educated. This comes as no surprise. Whatever the cost of papyrus (a topic of debate; see Skeat 1995), the *Edictum Diocletiani de pretiis rerum venalium*, col. 7.41–43, already mentioned, makes clear that the major cost of a book—the scribe's work—is fully 2–2½ times what it costs to have a scribe scribble out a contract: "To a scribe for best writing, 25 denarii per 100 lines; for second-quality writing, 20 denarii per 100 lines; to a notary for writing a petition or legal document, 10 denarii per 100 lines."

The documentary papyrologist will want to interpose the observation that there are many well-made documents, and that is certainly true. At the level of detail, documents rarely look *just* like a bookroll—the vertical spacing will be different, for instance, or the columns will be too wide. But a great many documents look bookish in one respect or another. A book hand may be employed, for example. Fine-grade papyrus stock may be used. The text may mimic contemporary literary habits of textual presentation like punctuation or the use of iota adscript. Conversely, literary texts written on rolls very rarely have any specifically documentary features. Still, one must be careful not to overstate the case. If a third of bookrolls were written with some elegance, more than half were written in fairly rapid, nondescript hands (mostly "second quality" in the terms of the Edict of Diocletian, one supposes). Nonetheless, these do not look like tax receipts. Even in the case of bookrolls written in nondescript hands, there is generally enough attention to detail of layout and text to support the iconography of the bookroll here delineated. A bookroll was not always a fully elegant product, then, yet also not cheap: Even a second-quality book hand was twice the expense of the hand typical of a legal document under Diocletian's Edict.

The bookroll itself also had traditional features that instantiate the need to preserve and endure, features that are, again, not regular or even usual for documentary texts. The margins above and below the columns tended to be quite wide: 3–5 cm was a typical measure for run-of-the-mill manuscripts, 3–7 cm for deluxe, with extreme examples ranging to 8 cm and more (Johnson 2004, 130–141).[5] Practicality is in play since the papyrus roll tended to fray at the edges, but a margin of 2 cm would have served to prevent this. There is surely something here of aesthetic display and even of conspicuous consumption. Typical bookrolls used only 40–70 percent of the front papyrus surface available for writing. The back was typically left blank, again to protect the text written on the inside. At the front edges of the finished roll was attached a blank sheet as protection against fraying and damage to the front of the written text, and we see such sheets (the *protokollon*) occasionally among the papyri. Among the carbonized rolls from Herculaneum are examples of the rods (*umbilici*) used to facilitate rolling and unrolling the papyrus without crushing the front and end of the roll (Capasso 1995, 73–98). Literary and artistic sources describe wrappers for fancy rolls (διφθέρα, *membrana*: Lucian, *Ind.* 16; Tibullus 3.1.9; Martial 1.66.11) and of cases for carrying them (τεῦχος, *capsa*, *scrinium*: Horace *Ep.* 2.1.268; Martial 1.2.4), but the papyri naturally do not provide direct evidence. Remains of bookrolls do, however, include a number of title tags, often on parchment, which stuck out from the rolled edged of the papyrus so as to provide a handy label when the papyrus was stored on a bookshelf or in a carrying case.

In general terms, we can assume that one work or one book of a work was equivalent to one roll, but complications and exceptions occur. In particular, we are uncertain of the incidence of rolls containing more than one work.[6] An Oxyrhynchus papyrus (*P.Oxy.* 1810) from the early second century probably contained the five early Philippic speeches of Demosthenes, for example; a book list in a third-century papyrus (*P.Laur.* inv. 19662v = *Corp.Pap.Fil.* 3) specifies one roll containing Plato's *Meno* and *Menexenus* and another containing the two *Hippias* dialogues and *Euthydemus;* a late Ptolemaic papyrus (*P.Berol.* inv. 16985 = MP 980) almost certainly contained books 19–22 of the *Iliad,* and several other papyri bear witness to the habit (more common early on) of putting two "books" of Homer in one bookroll. Still, the evidence seems limited to Homer and to short speeches and philosophical dialogues; there is no hint, for instance, that multiple plays were placed in a single bookroll.

From the length of dramas and other poetry books, we can with reasonable certainty infer that rolls as short as 3 meters (4 cm in diameter) were common. But how large could a roll be? Here, too, we encounter complications: A conceptual "book" was not always housed in a single bookroll. Pliny tells us of a work by his uncle divided into three "books" *(libri)* but written in six bookrolls *(volumina)* "on account of their size"; among the Herculaneum papyri, the fifth book of Philodemus's *On Poems* survives in two recensions, one in a single roll and the other (in a slightly more generous format) split into two rolls. Clearly, at some point a large "book" might, as a matter of convenience, be divided into two rolls. Judging from the example of *On Poems* 5, as well as statistical accumulations, that point was somewhere around 15 m, which translates into a nine-centimeter diameter (roughly equivalent to a two-liter bottle of Coca-Cola). Occasional rolls were even longer: The *Iliad* roll already mentioned (*P.Berol.* inv. 16985) seems to have been about 19 m long; and new evidence from Herculaneum suggests that Philodemus's *On Piety* was a single roll of about 23 m. In general terms, however, based on both specific examples and broad statistical data, a normative range of 3–15 meters seems reasonably certain for the ancient bookroll (Johnson 2004, 143–152).

The diameter and heft of the rolled-up bookroll could itself be an iconographic feature of design. At least by the Hellenistic era, the poetic bookroll was typically slim in diameter, a fact made programmatic and famous by Callimachus. Book divisions in the ancient novel, too, seem to have accommodated to this thin and lightweight model. Many historical texts, on the other hand, were different, probably in every period and certainly from the Hellenistic era on: a much longer roll, thus thicker and heavier in the hand, "monumental" in aspect, as well as content. (A book of poetry hardly ever contained more than sixteen hundred lines and rarely much more than a thousand; a book of history could contain the equivalent of well more than four thousand.)

Note that there is no "standard" or "average" length to which bookrolls tended, as some earlier researchers supposed. Since the roll end was determined by the stroke of a knife, there was no incentive to fill out the contents; to extend the book, the scribe simply glued on another blank roll. Note also how extreme the upper range is. It is hard for us to imagine routinely managing a "book" the size of a wine bottle (for a bookroll of ten meters) or a supersized Coke (fifteen meters), yet that, clearly, was what happened. This detail of voluminology corresponds with social attitudes toward the use of the bookroll, including, in particular, the use of lectors—yet another aspect of the elitism often associated with the ancient bookroll.

THE CODEX

Codex books—that is, the style of "book" we use today—come firmly into the historical record in the first century CE (Martial 1.2; 14.184–192; Roberts and Skeat 1983, 24–29; Harris 1991) and over the next three centuries came to supersede the bookroll for literary texts. Bookrolls were almost exclusively made of papyrus in every period (there is only scattered evidence for leather rolls), but parchment quickly came to be the usual material for the codex.[7] Early codices were nonetheless often made with papyrus and deserve brief remark here.

The first thing to notice is that for codices, too, one began with the papyrus roll, not (as we moderns might expect) with sheets. To produce a codex required sheets of the same height but twice the width of the desired page since the sheet was folded in the center to make up the leaves of the quire.[8] (For details of quire construction see chapter 25.) The roll, as indicated, was the standard way that papyrus was sold, and thus for an ancient Greek or Roman the natural procedure was to fashion the leaves by cutting off sheets of appropriate size from a manufactured roll. There is some contrary evidence: For a very few codices, it appears that sheets may have been manufactured to a special, large format so as to accommodate the codex manufacture. From what we can tell, however, that appears to be a rarity. In papyrus codices we commonly see the telltale glue join *(kollêsis)* that signals a roll as the ultimate source for the sheets that make up the quires. This is not to say that scribes were unaware of the point of *kollêsis:* The desire to avoid glue joins (or at least to avoid more than one join per sheet) contributed to the narrowness of the leaf in papyrus codices as compared to the relative squareness characteristic of codices made from parchment (Turner 1977, 49–51).

In the writing, scribes of Greek and Latin codices generally follow the same rules of word division, punctuation, and the like as for the bookroll. One might also expect the earliest papyrus codices to mimic the look of the roll, with (for prose) tall, narrow columns. This presumption has been so strong that an earlier generation of scholars thought to see a developmental pattern whereby codices with multiple columns were assumed to be early in date. Accumulation of evidence (and cogent analysis by Eric Turner) has shown the contrary, however: Papyrus codices in every period are mostly written in single columns, with only rare multiple-column examples—and those examples distributed over time (Turner 1977, 35–37).[9] From the earliest witnesses, that is, the codex—even while keeping in line with the conservative traditions of writing—seems to exhibit a somewhat different aesthetic in its pages. The basic look and feel are noticeably distinct from the roll since the individual (double) pages confront the reader rather than a continuous stream of written columns.

A different history accompanies this dissimilarity in aesthetic. The facts are these: (1) In the second century, when codices appear in any numbers, bookrolls still account for more than 90 percent of surviving books; by the fourth century, codices account for 80 percent of the total; by the sixth century, the changeover is complete (*Leuven Database of Ancient Books;* hereafter *LDAB*).[10] (2) Early codices (from the second or third century) in the main are more likely than bookrolls to be written in workaday hands (labeled "reformed documentary" in Roberts [1979, 12–15]; cf. Turner [1977, 36–37, 86]). Calligraphic and pretentious scripts are a rarity rather than the substantial percentage (ca. 30 percent) already noted for bookrolls. (3) Christian texts are almost always written in codex form. Only five of one hundred New Testament papyrus fragments listed in the *LDAB* are written on bookrolls, and Christian writings in the broader sense tend strongly to favor the codex form (in excess of 80 percent of all examples). Conversely, only a small percentage of classical texts are written in codex form in the early period (second or third century); pagan texts written in codex form come into their own only from the fourth century on. (4) Coincident to the changeover from roll to codex is a shift in book content from classical literature to Christian texts. Only a tiny percentage of surviving books are Christian in the second century; perhaps 10 percent in the third; about 40 percent in the fourth; and more than 50 percent by the fifth (*LDAB;* including codices on parchment). (5) Also coincident to the transition to the codex is a change of material from papyrus to parchment. As early as the fourth century, a quarter of the surviving witnesses are parchment; by the seventh, parchment predominates.

From these facts flow historical supposition. Christians appear to be instrumental in the adoption of the codex. In 1954 C. H. Roberts speculated that the codex format may reflect a desire to distinguish the Gospels iconographically from the rolls associated with Jewish scripture; T. C. Skeat (with support from an elderly Roberts [1983]) drew parallels to the use of tablets for writing the Jewish Mishnah and supposed that a "proto-Gospel" with the sayings and passion of Jesus may have been the source of Christian fondness for the codex form; H. Gamble (1995) has hypothesized as reason for the preference an early collection of Pauline epistles in codex form. Others have highlighted the ability of the codex to embrace in one package the whole of the developing Christian canon (probably wrongly: Early codices were not normally so bulky, and the Gospels continued to circulate individually). Scholars have also been quick to associate the workaday character of early codices with the working-class Christian community. However all this may be, it seems clear enough that up to the end of the second century the bookroll constituted the enduring image of what a classical literary text was meant to be; that early Christians deliberately adopted the different codex format for their scriptures; and that from the second through the fourth centuries, as Christianity grew more accepted and influential and as the codex format became better known and appreciated, the codex gradually supplanted the roll as the essential idea of the "book."

The shift in technology from roll to codex had important practical results. The codex had the following essential and consequential advantages: (1) Compass and compactness: Several bookrolls could be fashioned into a single codex (Turner [1977, 82] presents some statistics). The ability to collect corpora into one cover would have great consequence for the use and survival of classical literature. (2) Durability: The covers helped protect the content, and the codex was less prone to squashing, tearing, and other damage. (The constant rolling and unrolling of papyrus rolls led to frequent tears and other deterioration, as repairs on papyrus bookrolls attest.) The concomitant change to parchment results in a book of unprecedented durability, again a critical point for the survival of classical texts. Frequently cited as advantages of the codex (but probably red herrings) are also (3) ease of access and reference (*pace* Harris 1991, the assumption that a reader could mark and locate a passage more readily is based on exaggerated modern notions of the difficulty of using a bookroll) and (4) economy of material (less material was needed since both sides were used, but the use of ample margins, for instance, makes it unlikely that this was an important ancient consideration). In any case, the codex also had its disadvantages, principally that book production was more complicated since it involved the planning of the quires and the sewing of a binding and covers. Without implying direct cause and effect, we can see that medieval characteristics such as the rise of scriptoria, renewed encyclopedism, and the habit of extensive marginal annotation can be located within the series of changes we associate with the transition to codex form.

BOOKS AND THEIR CONTENT

Fragments of more than 3,000 bookrolls, 1,000 papyrus codices, and another 1,000 parchment codices survive from antiquity *(LDAB)*. As we expect, these books reflect a great diversity of content. Technical treatises of all types survive, including medical, astronomical, mathematical, musical, philosophical, and grammatical discourses; commentaries, lexica, mythographica, and other paraliterary texts also survive in "book" form (cf., e.g., *C.Pap.Med.*, *C.Pap.Fil.*, *C.Gramm.*, *C.Comm.Lex.*, and *CPP*; Rossum-Steenbeek 1998). But the great bulk of what a bookroll or literary codex comprises is not only literary—that, of course, is a consequence of the modern categorization—but high literary and, as we have seen, in a distinct, recognizable format.

I tabulate in table 11.2 the prevailing authors on papyrus bookrolls, about a third of what survives. I do not differentiate by date or provenience, but the huge majority are of the Roman era, and a disproportionate number are—as always for the literary papyri—from Oxyrhynchus. The most common authors are in aggregate the direct or indirect result of scholastic influence. We do not need the papyri to tell us of the great importance of Homer in Greek education and culture, but they certainly do so: To the hundreds published, we should add several hundred unpublished fragments of the *Iliad* and the *Odyssey* that languish in collections for the simple reason that there are many more significant papyri awaiting editorial attention (see chapter 27). Dozens of the Homeric papyri show the telltale marks of students as they practiced accentuation and scansion; Homer in any case is the text we most expect to find in a household interested in maintaining a sense of Greek identity. Hesiod is a similar case, though not nearly so common as Homer—perhaps something like finding a copy of Shakespeare next to a Bible in an English household. The remainder of the authors at the top of the list are determined by preference in the schools. Most of these do not surprise us: Demosthenes, Isocrates, and indeed Thucydides and (differently) Menander are what one expects as a result of the needs or tastes of rhetorical schools (especially of the Roman era); similarly for Plato and the philosophical schools. Euripides' overwhelming popularity is also at least in part of the schools' making: Lines by Euripides are common as writing practice on materials like ostraca, tablets, and cut sheets of papyrus. But there are unanticipated results as well. We would not, I think, have predicted the relative scarcity of Aristotle, Sophocles, or even Aeschylus.[11]

Significant is that what does survive is, in the main, pretty demanding. The canonical texts that survive in quantity were themselves not easy fare for Hellenistic- or Roman-era readers. When we think of authors that survive mostly or only through papyri, the list is decidedly highbrow: Sappho, Alcaeus, Alcman, Bacchylides, Hyperides, Herondas, Philodemus, Posidippus, and Timotheus. In contrast, the lighter literature of antiquity—the so-called ancient novel, for instance—is evident but relatively rare (Stephens and Winkler 1995). Uncontroversial but worth

Table 11.2. Common Authors in the Papyri (*LADB*)*

Author	Bookrolls	Papyrus codices
Homer–Iliad	363 (+100?)	95
Demosthenes	115 (+8?)	24
Homer–Odyssey	93 (+26?)	24
Euripides	84 (+27?)	22 (+1?)
Hesiod	76 (+26?)	10 (+3?)
Plato	64 (+12?)	4
Isocrates	61 (+9?)	14 (+1?)
Thucydides	56 (+15?)	2
Callimachus	45 (+9?)	16
Menander	43 (+34?)	14 (+4?)
Herodotus	33 (+5?)	0
Xenophon	30 (+3?)	2
Aeschines	28 (+13?)	3
Aeschylus	25 (+4?) (note: 22 of these are a matched set)	0
Apollonius Rhodius	23 (+6?)	5
Pindar	20 (+11?)	4 (+1?)
Sophocles	18 (+7?)	6
Aristophanes	16 (+7?)	26
Sappho	14 (+6?)	1?
Theocritus	11 (+4?)	5
Hippocrates	11 (+3?)	5
Archilochus	10 (+7?)	0
Aristotle	9 (+1?)	1

*Question mark indicates uncertainty about either attribution of author or book form.

repeating is the conclusion that the papyri give no evidence for mass readership of books. Rather, the ancient book is—not always, but in general—a product to be associated with the intellectual and social elite. These books are best situated within the general context of Greeks in a non-Greek land working to maintain their sense of Hellenic identity. In the high empire, where our papyrological evidence is most dense, the Graeco-Roman elite favored highbrow texts for personal attainment and recreation, as we see, for example, in the pages of Lucian, Gellius, and Athenaeus. The papyrological record is—again in broad stroke—a clear reflection of this kind of elite tendency.

BOOKS AND SOCIETY: THE "SCHOLARS" OF OXYRHYNCHUS

Much of the importance and wonder of papyrology is the ability to reach through the window of time to grasp details of the ancient world otherwise lost to us and to write through individual witnesses the sort of "thick" history that is more fully descriptive of ancient society. As we turn to questions of ownership and use of the papyri, we must steer away from generalities to address a specific time and place. I choose as a case study the second century and the evidence for a group of "scholars" in Oxyrhynchus. This "scholarly" group is more broadly representative of Graeco-Roman elite society than one might suppose and serves as an illustration of how the papyri can lead to a fresh understanding of the use of books and indeed of the very nature of reading in antiquity.

I begin with a well-known example. *P.Oxy.* XVIII 2192, a letter excavated in Oxyrhynchus and thus presumably (though not certainly) a letter sent to that city, is assigned to the second century of our era on the basis of the scripts. The letter is written in at least three (more probably four) hands. The body of the letter, mostly lost, is written in the flowing semiliterary hand of a practiced scribe. Following the body of the letter, as often with ancient letters, the sender adds a subscription in his own hand ("I hope you're well, my dear brother"). The same hand, that of the sender, adds a substantial postscript underneath the subscription. A second postscript, also substantial, follows the first in what is clearly a third hand (which we will call that of the sender's colleague). Following that the papyrus breaks off, but there are remains of what appears to be yet a third postscript, in what seems to be a fourth hand (apparently, a second colleague).

The postscripts deserve our close attention, for they combine to convey a vivid impression of one side of "scholarly" activity in second-century Oxyrhynchus. The first postscript, in the sender's hand, writes: "Have a copy made of books six and seven of Hypsicrates' *Men Who Appear in Comedies* and send it to me. Harpocration says that Pollio has them among his books, and probably others have it too. And he also has epitomes in prose of Thersagoras's *Myths of Tragedy.*"

A different hand—the sender's colleague—then adds another paragraph in postscript: "Demetrius the bookseller has them (that is, the two books of the *Men Who Appear in Comedies*), according to Harpocration. I have ordered Apollonides to send to me some of my own books—which ones you'll find out from him. And if you find any volumes of Seleucus's work on *Tenses/Metrics/Rhythms* that I don't own, have copies made and send them to me. Diodorus's circle also has some that I don't own." (Text as in Hatazilambrou 2007.)

Not every point is clear, but a number of inferences can be reasonably drawn. First, though the books are personally owned ("some of my own books," writes the colleague), we garner a strong impression of a group that shares books—and not just any books but those that are learned compilations of background information for classical drama, rather like a scholar's accumulation of reference works today. We sense the vigor with which this group of people pursues the collecting of such books and the serious interest in having some rather arcane knowledge available. Second, the sender's colleague seems to assume that the recipient will both recognize him by his hand (though it is possible that the lost beginning or final subscription to the letter identifies him) and know all about Seleucus as well as the contents of his own library ("collect the volumes that I don't already own"). The focus in the letter on reference books for tragedy and comedy seems to imply something akin to a scholarly project, or at least a circle of readers with focused attention for the moment on, it appears, classical drama. The colleague in any case seems eager to acquire all available books within a defined area of knowledge. The ease with which he orders the recipient to collect "whatever volumes [of Seleucus] I don't own" is also telling: We gain the impression of a man of some means. Third, the tightness of the network merits comment. Harpocration (whom Eric Turner [1952, 92] identified with the Alexandrian lexicographer)[12] appears to be the central node of the personal network, but both the sender and the sender's colleague give independent suggestions for either alternate books to be obtained or alternate sources for the books. One has the vivid sense of both a small, friendly community of those interested in books of this sort and of close connections between Oxyrhynchus and whatever town the request derives from. The alternate source suggested by the sender's colleague—οἱ περὶ Διόδωρ[ου]—leads to our final point, which is that this circle of book collectors and readers knows of another circle that seems in some sense an analogue to themselves—"Diodorus's circle"[13] is evidently also a group interested in (and perhaps defined by) its interest in books of a learned sort. One wonders, though it cannot be proven, whether those in "Diodorus's circle" might well have referred to these two writers and their compeers as "Harpocration's circle."

The details in this letter are echoed by other documents of similar period from Egypt. From second-century Alexandria, Theon (again identified by Turner as the grammarian of same name; Turner [1952, 93]) writes a letter to Heraclides in Oxyrhynchus, accompanied by six Stoic texts on self-improvement (*P.Mil.Vogl.* I 11). In elevated (indeed pompous) Greek, Theon writes, "Inasmuch as I take great pains to furnish you with useful books, especially those that contribute toward a better life, I think it behooves you not to be careless in the reading of them since the serviceableness that comes from these books is not trifling for those who take pains to acquire the advantage." Theon continues: "I am sending the books you requested via Achilles," and after the subscription he adds a list of the books. Another, very lacunose, second-century letter, *SB* XIV 11996 (=*Corp.Pap.Fil.* 5), contains similar verbiage about sending books, apparently among friends, via a courier. Written in the second century and (probably) from the Fayyum, *P.Lit.*

Lond. 97, a prose farce, has a note on the back that "Heraclides made the copy from the library of Praxias."

Several book lists (usually of somewhat obscure import) come down from antiquity, but at least a few from the second or third century CE are clearly either lists of *desiderata* or catalogues of existing bookrolls, and—of interest here—these book lists are *usually* rather abstruse materials like rare works, philosophical works, and commentaries.[14] Yet another second-century letter (*P.Petaus* 30), this time from Ptolemais Hormou, is written by a son to his father and reads: "When Deios was with us, he showed us the six parchments (μεμβράνας). We did not take any of these, but we made collations against eight others, for which I paid 100 drachmas on account." Apparently a traveling scribe or book dealer of some sort offers "parchments" (meaning parchment rolls? codices?) for sale but as an ancillary service provides an opportunity to collate texts in his collection. These various papyrus documents, though a thin stream, help to make vivid a second-century scene in which a small community of literate men in the regional capitals and perhaps also the towns of provincial Egypt (cf. van Minnen 1998) were actively searching for and sharing literary texts, commentaries, and works of reference, seeking to improve both the text and their knowledge of it.

With this understanding as background, let us return to *P.Oxy.* 2192, the first text we examined. What is particularly striking about this letter is the fact that the scholars pursue their interests as a *group* and that what the letter seems to imply is not so much the individual scholar busy with his studies but *a circle of readers with scholarly interests* and one with contacts in Oxyrhynchus, which, as the metropolis, has similar readers' circles, along with other resources of interest to "scholarly" readers.

This suggestion of scholarly activity as a group undertaking dovetails interestingly with another set of documentary evidence from the sands of Oxyrhynchus, namely, the actual artifacts of scholars' texts themselves—for, to anticipate, the marginal annotations in papyrus bookrolls that belong to scholars are also often the product of multiple people's work. I focus on a group of texts already collected as "scholar's texts" by a couple of earlier researchers (Turner 1956; McNamee 1981, 2007). These are annotated texts that contain textual remarks and variants and in which the textual variants are attributed to a person by name; that is, the marginal annotations read, for instance, "Thus was [the reading] in Theon's"; "So in Apion's"; and so forth. The interest in attribution—in applying a *name* to the variant reading—seems to mark an enterprise or an attitude toward the text that is fully consistent with our notion of a "scholars' text." The challenge is to define better the social context for these texts.

The number of such texts is not large, but it is also not small: nineteen in all. In the remarks that follow, I will restrict my remarks to the sixteen Oxyrhynchite texts that form the bulk of the evidence[15] since I wish to explore the possibility that these texts constitute a group of some sort. The Oxyrhynchite texts share a surprising number of uniformities:

(1) Almost all the bookrolls comprise noncanonical texts, and most are difficult works to read. Aside from *P.Oxy.* 445 (the *Iliad*), the texts fall, moreover, into two distinct types. First are a number of dramatic works, most of which are unusual plays: four plays by Sophocles (*Ichneutai, Eurypylos, Trachiniai, Theseus*) and several plays (it appears) by Epicharmus; all of these (except, of course, the bookroll of the *Trachiniai*) are unique surviving witnesses to their texts. Second are a number of lyric and elegiac texts that make up several bookrolls of Pindar, a couple of Stesichorus, a couple of Alcaeus, and one each of Alcman, Bacchylides, and Simonides.

(2) Rarely is the scribe involved in the annotation of textual variants, and when he is, there are always other annotators as well.

(3) It is unusual, however, to find only the scribe of the text and a single annotator, though that does happen three times. In thirteen of the sixteen examples, multiple annotators are in play, often as many as four, five, or six. Note that for many of these texts, the very fragmentary state of preservation tends to *understate* the number of annotators since only a few margins, at most, are likely to survive.

(4) Most of the texts (ten of the sixteen) show signs of substantial additions of readers' marks (such as added punctuation, word division, or elision markers), and almost all have at least some readers' marks (as is generally common in bookrolls, especially for difficult texts). Often multiple readers are involved.

(5) Most of the texts are also marked up with *chi* or other sigla in the left margin (again, ten of the sixteen, even though in some cases very little of the left margin survives). Such sigla have sometimes been taken as keys to commentaries, but, to follow McNamee (1992, 19–22), these are best understood as a variety of ways of signaling *nota bene;* that is, they are marks by readers that signal passages of interest or those that need further attention.

(6) A common remark by the editors of these texts is that the annotator's hand is "contemporary with the text," and my review of these manuscripts in photograph confirms that very few (no more than a couple) of the annotators here write with hands that are disconsonant with the time period of the scribal hand. Certainly palaeography is a crude measure of date, but it is interesting that the fact of multiple annotators, whatever the exact social context, does not seem to be the product of a book's passing from hand to hand over numerous generations.

(7) Two of the Sophocles bookrolls are written by the same scribe, and four others are also by scribes who are identified as having written other bookrolls among the Oxyrhynchus publications.[16] The fact that six of the sixteen texts here are written by identified scribes must be considered against the fact that, among many hundreds of published literary texts from Oxyrhynchus, only forty-five scribes in total have been identified as having written multiple bookrolls (Johnson 2004, 61–65). It is hard to know what exactly to make of the correspondence, but a reasonable inference is that the coincidence of scribal hands is the consequence of the disposal in the Oxyrhynchite town dump of a set of bookrolls by a single owner

or group (in the manner of the Hypsipyle archive; Cockle [1987, 21–22]; and see also Houston [2009]). If that is the case, then of interest is the fact that the other bookrolls by these identified scribes are also predominantly bookrolls of tragedy, lyric, and elegiac.

I do not mean to overstate the uniformities since there is certainly a great deal of variation in detail, such as the fact that a number of bookrolls are freely annotated by a number of hands, whereas others seem principally annotated by one hand with occasional additions by others. Yet for all that the uniformities remain remarkable. If I am seeing this at all clearly, we seem to be dealing not just with a random collection of examples but also with a *group* that in use and function represents a *type*. That is, the use and function of the manuscripts seem to reflect some rather specific sociocultural context that prevailed in second-century Oxyrhynchus. By that I do not mean to suggest that the use of the manuscripts can be localized to a particular set of contemporaries—the fact that the manuscripts are assigned all along the spectrum of more than a century defeats that hypothesis. Nor do I wish to draw too tight a line between the letter we examined earlier (*P.Oxy.* 2192), in which a group of scholars are collecting background data for the study of tragedy, and the prominence of bookrolls of tragedy in the group here. Nonetheless, I do find of great interest the fact that the group centers on a couple of genres in a manner similar to the "scholarly project" implied in *P.Oxy.* 2192. In general terms, what seems to me so fascinating about this group of manuscripts is what they may suggest about scholarly habitudes, that is, what sociocultural models of behavior we can find that account for the ways in which these papyri seem to have been used.

Noteworthy at once is that two standard models do not seem adequately to account for the consistencies here noted:

(1) The *diorthôtês* model. In this model one expects that once the scribe is finished copying, the bookroll is handed over to a "corrector" (the *diorthôtês*), who collates the text for errors—whether this happens at the instigation and under the control of the scribal shop or the owner is immaterial. This model does not seem adequately to account either for the style of annotation, in which the attributions are carefully named, or for the number of hands involved in annotating the text with variant readings and other "learned" data.

(2) The inheritance model. We know of bookrolls in antiquity that were passed along with an estate (Bagnall 1992; Clarysse 1983), which is hardly a surprise given the value of the artifact and, for exotic texts, the rareness of the product. In that case, the reuse of the bookroll from generation to generation might account for the presence of multiple annotators. But that model, which is frankly what I expected to find, does not obtain here. The hands for any given manuscript are too contemporary (and often too numerous) to allow it, whether by inheritance we mean from relative to relative (as, for example, parent to child) or from master to pupil.

Moreover, the list presents some surprises of detail. I draw attention in particular to Oxyrhynchus papyrus 2387 (Alcman's *Partheneia*). In the intercolumn to *P.*

Oxy. 2387 we find the usual syntax of attribution: μό(νον) Π(τολεμαίου) [fr. 3.ii.19: "only in Ptolemy's"], οὔ(τως) Π(τολεμαίου) [3.ii.22, "thus in Ptolemy's"]. Here, as always, the referent of the possessive is not entirely clear: Ptolemy's what? His commentary? His copy? In this case, however, we have more information, for the upper margin (2387, fr. 1) contains an extremely interesting note: π]αρενγρά(φεται) ἐν τοῖς ἀντιγρά(φοις) αὕτη | [καὶ ἐν τῶι] πέμπτωι· καὶ ἐν ἐκείνωι | [ἐν μὲν τῶι] Ἀρ(ιστο)νί(κου) περιεγέγρα(πτο), ἐν δὲ τῶι Πτολ(εμαίου) | ἀπερ[ί]γρα(πτος) ἦν ("This [passage] is wrongly inserted in copies [also in the] fifth (book), and in that book it was bracketed [in] Aristonicus's copy but was left unbracketed in Ptolemy's"). That is, the writer of the note claims not only that the passage is *generally* interpolated into copies of book five but also that, in two *specific* antigraphs (those belonging to Aristonicus and Ptolemy respectively), the interpolation is variously treated. Throughout the list of papyri with attributed annotations, as mentioned, one is confronted with the question of the referent for the possessive: "Thus it was in Theon's"; "Thus only in Ar( )'s" (whether the abbreviation "Ar" means Aristophanes or Aristarchus or someone else). Where the name may be taken to match that of a known grammarian, the impulse has been to take the possessive with the notion of an accompanying *hypomnema* (commentary): "Thus the reading was in Aristophanes' (or Aristarchus's or Theon's) commentary on Sophocles." And I suppose that this resolution is correct for at least some of these manuscripts. Nonetheless, in the case of *P.Oxy.* 2387, it seems, it is not Aristonicus's and Ptolemy's commentaries that are being collated but rather the copies that belong to these two people. Moreover, Aristonicus is very likely the Augustan-age grammarian of that name.[17]

In any case, the fact that the annotation in *P.Oxy.* 2387 witnesses a group of readers with access, whether directly or at a remove, to the unique Alcman copies used by Aristonicus and Ptolemy accords with other evidence in our list. For instance, in *P.Oxy.* 2452, the variant reading is attributed not simply to a scholar whose name begins Ari (again, the resolution of the abbreviation is uncertain), but the variant is specifically said to be ἐν ἐτέρῳ Ἀρι( ) ("in the second copy, that belonging to Ari(?)"). In several other cases, too, attributed variant readings are accompanied by remarks like "in the other (copy)," "in the first (copy)," and "in the antigraph," which makes clear that at least some of the general activity we seek to tease out of this body of evidence is certainly collation against actual copies as opposed to collation and annotation on the basis of commentaries. The heavy use of sigla like *chi* and ζή(τει) likewise helps to flesh out the picture since these are notes (always placed at the left of the column of text) that mark something that needs to be examined further or specially noted. That is, they are the skeletal markings of an active investigation into points of detail in the text.

What image then can we construct of the use to which these texts are put? In attempting to answer that question, I want to consider, by way of illustration, one last piece of evidence, again from the second century (ca. 170 CE) but this time from the literary tradition and—though written by a man who spent his later life in

Egypt—a text most likely written in Athens. The text is the *adversus Indoctum* of Lucian, a diatribe that in attacking an "uneducated" Syrian and his circle makes clear by contrast how an intellectual circle *should* work. The Syrian does everything wrong: He collects expensive antique books but does not know how to judge their textual value (*Ind.* 1); he does not know how to read the texts aloud so as to bring out the meaning (*Ind.* 2); he is not well educated in things literary (*Ind.* 3, cf. 26–27, where he is ridiculed for his ignorance of Plato, Antisthenes, Archilochus, Hipponax, Aeschines, and Eupolis); he collects a circle of friends who are not men of culture but flatterers or worse (*Ind.* 7; cf. 17, 20); his sham attempts at elite intellectual display and discussion thus devolve into drunken parties (*Ind.* 22–23). Several points of intense interest emerge from the scene Lucian paints: (1) The context for the use of high literary books is an intellectual circle; (2) for a true intellectual circle, elite education is assumed not just for the central figure but for the group as well; (3) education assumes (a) an ability to read performatively, with detailed, deep knowledge of the meaning, style, structure, and conventions, (b) a broad knowledge of rather arcane persons and works in the literary tradition, and (c) strikingly, the ability to judge the value and correctness of the *text* of a bookroll. Note, however, that Lucian does not present the Syrian as someone aspiring to be a leading scholastic or scholar. Rather, the Syrian seems simply to aspire to be among the elite but in a time period when the elite (under the "scholar emperor" Aurelius; cf. *Ind.* 22) particularly valued learning and when leading elites sought to achieve a strong sense of intellectual refinement among their ranks.

The portrait in Lucian interlocks with the papyrological evidence in some intriguing ways. For instance, readers' marks in the papyri (such as added punctuation) may of course be successive attempts to make sense of the text, but the prevalence of multiple readers' marks may also indicate that members of these intellectual groups repeatedly made performative readings of the text whether by way of entertainment or as a springboard for discussion. The annotations in the papyri of variant readings and other details from named antigraphs of previous scholars are in keeping with Lucian's hints of a strong interest in antique, autograph texts. A general interest in the correctness and the antiquity of the text and, importantly, the vesting of the judgment of the value of a particular copy of a text in the hands of "the educated" also seems quintessential to attitudes of the time. Most important, though, is the link between what we find in Lucian and what the multiple hands of the annotators and the evidence in papyrus letters seem to suggest about a social context for the creation of a "scholarly" product.

The combination of evidence does not, that is, seem to sit well with the dominant medieval and modern image of a scholar quietly sitting in his study, reading a difficult text together with a commentary and transferring notes from that commentary into the margins of his bookroll or collating a text side by side with its exemplar. Nor do the mechanics of reading in a precodex culture encourage that type of behavior, given the awkwardness of opening more than one bookroll at a time. Rather, the presence of textual variants in multiple hands seems likely to be, in some sense, the result of repeated group discussion and analysis of the text. As we have seen, that group work would itself include a variety of activities, including, of course, not only the reading of *hypomnemata* but also, it appears, collation against other copies of the text, especially any available copies of particular value; the reading of works that provided background or ancillary information, such as the *Men Who Appear in Comedy* and *Myths in Tragedy*, volumes sought from among Pollio's books in papyrus letter *P.Oxy.* 2192; and no doubt (to infer from Lucian) vigorous discussion of points of style, structure, convention, as well as (to infer from the papyrus annotations) discussion of the constitution of the text. This "scholarly" work may well have typically revolved around a central figure—think of Diodorus's circle and the references to Harpocration in that same Oxyrhynchus letter—but the scene is by no means necessarily professional or scholastic: The other men in the cubiculum and at dinner need hardly be "scholars" in any conventional sense.[18] Lucian and his Syrian remind us that the "scholarly" enterprise was, in the second century, at least as closely linked to a particular type of cultural elitism and indeed exclusionism, focused on Greek letters, as to professional "scholarship," and that those engaged in the criticism, interpretation, and constitution of canonical Greek texts probably went well beyond the group of grammarians and scholars usually cited.

NOTES

1. Most of the substandard scripts (about 15 percent of the total) are Homeric papyri. Some problems of editorial selection come into play here since many Homeric papyri remain unpublished. Percentages are derived from tables 3.1 and 3.2 in Johnson 2004, 162–184.

2. Lyric texts created before the colometric researches of early Alexandrian scholars were presumably written as prose, but these, too, were written in verse units from the third century BCE on. See Turner and Parsons (1987, 12).

3. Ancient grammarians speak of other punctuation dots (ἡ μέση στιγμή, ὑποστιγμή) that mark lesser pauses in a sentence, but of this the papyri show evidence that is sporadic and inconsistent—certainly not part of a generalized system used and understood by readers (Turner and Parsons 1987, 9; Johnson 1994).

4. "A syllable divides after its vowel: but division is permitted between doubled consonants or two consonants, the first of which was a liquid or a nasal or a sibilant; and after a single consonant, if that letter is part of a preposition forming a compound word" (Turner and Parsons 1987, 16–17).

5. Earlier scholars have seriously underestimated the typical size of margins.

6. Sometimes cited in this regard is a statement by Tzetzes (*Proleg. de comoedia Aristoph.*, Prooemium 2.10–11 Koster), ascribed to Callimachus, in which it is said that at the time of Ptolemy III the Library of Alexandria contained 400,000 "mixed" books and 90,000

"single and unmixed," but it is unclear whether "mixed" rolls refer to bookrolls containing multiple works.

7. There is considerable debate over whether the parchment codex or the papyrus codex came first; see Turner (1977, 35–42); Roberts and Skeat (1983, 29).

8. Large vellum skins and, of course, the large-format paper used for modern books can be folded both horizontally and vertically to make up quires of four, eight, or even sixteen sheets. The maximum height of papyrus (about thirty-five cm), as normally manufactured, precluded horizontal folding for all but very small books.

9. By contrast, the double column was a favored format for parchment codices of literary prose texts. Turner (1977, 35) has speculated that these later, parchment codices were deliberate imitations of high-class bookrolls.

10. Statistics from the *LDAB* in this chapter are based on its state as of January 2006.

11. The sample is, of course, largely restricted to towns and villages in Egypt, but that in effect gives a snapshot of the scene at the far reach of Hellenism—probably representative, that is, of the broad swath of the Hellenic population around the Mediterranean. With the exception of the Homeric texts, the problem of editorial selection in the publication of literary fragments (an important consideration for earlier analyses like Willis [1968]), is no longer a serious difficulty.

12. This remains only a probability, however, as does the identification of Pollio with lexicographer Valerius Pollio of Alexandria and of Diodorus (a common name) with Pollio's son, a second-century Alexandrian who was a member of the Alexandrian Museum (note that Pollio and Diodorus are not linked in the letter itself). Turner's suggestion that the Harpocration mentioned here is the Alexandrian has now been elevated to a fact in *Der neue Pauly.*

13. The *P.Oxy.* editor (Roberts) translates this as "Diodorus and his friends"; Radt (1997, 6) thinks it "more probable" that the phrase here, as commonly enough in classical and Hellenistic Greek, is simply a paraphrase for "Diodorus" (see LSJ s.v. περί, as well as the extensive treatment of the phrase in Radt [1980, 47–56]). Nonetheless, the use of this phrase for "Diodorus" seems characteristic of high literary rather than documentary Greek; the examples in Preisigke's lexicon of οἱ περὶ τὸν δεῖνα (2.288) in papyrus letters and other documents all seem consistent with the translation "X and intimate associates," whether family or friends. In any case, it is the focus on the man within the context of his (somewhat invisible) friends and followers that I seek to capture in the translation "Diodorus's circle."

14. Examples include *P.Oxy.* XLVII 3360, *P.Ross.Georg.* I 22 = *Corp.Pap.Fil.* 2, *P.Laur.* inv. 19662 = *Corp.Pap.Fil.* 3, *P.Vars.* 5 = *Corp.Pap.Fil.* 4, *P.Turner* 9, and *P. Lond.* inv. 2110 (Bell 1921); for a comprehensive collection of book lists on papyrus see Otranto (2000).

15. *P.Oxy.* 445 (*Iliad* 6), *P.Oxy.* 841 AB (Pindar, *Paeans*), *P.Oxy.* 1174 + 2081a + *Pap.Flor.* X (Sophocles, *Ichneutae*), *P.Oxy.* 1175 + 2081b (Sophocles, *Eurypylos*), *P.Oxy.* 1234 + 1360 + 2166 (Alcaeus), *P.Oxy.* 1361 (Bacchylides, *Scolia*), *P.Oxy.* 1805 + 3687 (Sophocles, *Trachiniae*), *P.Oxy.* 2295 (Alcaeus), *P.Oxy.* 2327 (Simonides), *P.Oxy.* 2387 (Alcman), *P.Oxy.* 2394 (Doric lyric, Alcman?), *P.Oxy.* 2427 (Epicharmus, various plays), *P.Oxy.* 2442 (Pindar), *P.Oxy.* 2452 (Sophocles, *Theseus*), *P.Oxy.* 2803 (Stesichorus), *P.Oxy.* 3876 (Stesichorus). Attributed textual annotations in papyri not from Oxyrhynchus: *P.Par.* 71 (Alcman, from Memphis), *P.Hawara* 24–28 (*Iliad* 1–2, from Hawara), *P.Lit.Lond.* 30 (*Od.* 3, said to come from Soknopaiou Nesos). List and analysis here are based in part on evidence assembled in McNamee (2007), kindly shared in manuscript; cf. also McNamee (1981).

16. Following the numeration in table 2.1 in Johnson (2004), Scribe #B1 (Sophocles: *P.Oxy.* 1174 + 2081a + *Pap.Flor.* X, *P.Oxy.* 1175), #A19 (*P.Oxy.* 2327), #A22 (*P.Oxy.* 2427), #A24 (*P.Oxy.* 2452), #A30 (*P.Oxy.* 2442).

17. Or at least it seems a telling coincidence that the rare ancient notices of Aristonicus cite both a son (Athen. 11.481d, *Iliad* scholia 4.423a[1] Erbse) and a father (*Suda* P 3036) named Ptolemy, both grammarians and teachers in Rome. McNamee (2007) points out that, even though a given abbreviation may be uncertain, *all* of the attributed names listed in the appendix seem plausibly to be names of known grammarians, or at least all of the abbreviated names can be so resolved.

18. For analogous circles of readers in Rome attached to private libraries (hence to prominent political and social figures), see Marshall (1976). The scene suggested here, where the social elite in Hellenic Egypt play at being intellectuals, may help explain why it was unnecessary for those appointed to the Alexandrian Museum in the Roman era to be scholars per se, though all seem to be members of the social elite. (For details on museum members who were not scholars see Lewis [1963] = Lewis [1995, 94–98]; Fraser [1972, 333–334]; Lewis [1981] = Lewis [1995, 257–274].)

BIBLIOGRAPHY

Abbreviations

CPP = Catalogue of Paraliterary Papyri, ed. Marc Huys. http://cpp.arts.kuleuven.be/.
LDAB = Leuven Database of Ancient Books, ed. W. Clarysse. http://ldab.kuleuven.be/.
Der neue Pauly = Der neue Pauly: Enzyklopädie der Antike, ed. C. von Hubert and
    H. Schneider. Stuttgart: J. B. Metzler, 1996–2003.

Bagnall, R. S. 1992. "An Owner of Literary Papyri." *Classical Philology* 87: 137–140.
Bell, H. I. 1921. "The 'Thyestes' of Sophocles and an Egyptian Scriptorium." *Aegyptus* 2: 281–288.
Capasso, M. 1995. *Volumen: Aspetti della tipologia del rotolo librario antico.* Naples:
    Procaccini.
Clarysse, W. 1976. "Notes on the Use of the Iota Adscript in the Third Century BC." *CdÉ*
    51: 150–166.
———. 1983. "Literary Papyri in Documentary 'Archives.' " In *Egypt and the Hellenistic World:*
    Proceedings of the International Colloquium, Leuven, 24–26 May 1982, ed. E. Van 't Dack,
    P. van Dessel, and W. van Gucht, 43–61. *Studia Hellenistica* 27. Leuven: Orientaliste.
Cockle, W. E. H. 1987. *Hypsipyle, Euripides: Text and Annotation Based on a Re-examination*
    of the Papyri. Rome: Ed. dell'Ateneo.
Coles, R. A., M. Manfredi, P. J. Sijpesteijn, and A. S. Brown. 1985. *The Harris Papyri,* vol. 2.
    Zutphen, the Netherlands: Terra.
Fraser, P. M. 1972. *Ptolemaic Alexandria.* Oxford: Clarendon.
Gamble, H. 1995. *Books and Readers in the Early Church: A History of Early Christian Texts.*
    New Haven, Conn.: Yale University Press.

Harris, W. V. 1991. "Why Did the Codex Supplant the Book-Roll?" In *Renaissance Society and Culture: Essays in Honor of Eugene F. Rice Jr.*, ed. J. Monfasani and R. G. Musto, 71–85. New York: Italica.

Hatzilambrou, R. 2007. "P. Oxy. XVIII 2192 revisited." In *Oxyrhynchus: A City and its Texts*, ed. A. K. Bowman et al. 282–286. Graeco-Roman Memoirs 93. London: Egypt Exploration Society.

Houston, G. 2009. " Papyrological Evidence for Book Collections and Libraries in the Roman Empire." In *Ancient Literacies: The Culture of Reading in Greece and Rome*, ed. W. A. Johnson and H. Parker. New York: Oxford University Press.

Johnson, W. A. 1993. "Pliny the Elder and Standardized Roll Heights in the Manufacture of Papyrus." *Classical Philology* 88: 46–50.

——. 1994. "The Function of the Paragraphus in Greek Literary Prose Texts." *ZPE* 100: 65–68.

——. 2004. *Bookrolls and Scribes in Oxyrhynchus*. Toronto: University of Toronto Press.

Lewis, N. 1963. "The Non-scholar Members of the Alexandrian Museum." *Mnemosyne* (ser. 4) 16: 257–261.

——. 1974. *Papyrus in Classical Antiquity*. Oxford: Clarendon.

——. 1981. "*Literati* in the Service of the Roman Emperors: Politics before Culture." In *Coins, Culture, and History in the Ancient World: Numismatic and Other Studies in Honor of Bluma L. Trell*, ed. L. Casson and M. Price, 149–166. Detroit: Wayne State University Press.

——. 1995. *On Government and Law in Roman Egypt: Collected Papers of Naphtali Lewis*. Atlanta: Scholars Press.

Marshall, P. 1976. "Library Resources and Creative Writing at Rome." *Phoenix* 30: 252–264.

McNamee, K. 1981. "Greek Literary Papyri Revised by Two or More Hands." In *Proc. XVI Int. Congr. Pap.*, ed. R. S. Bagnall et al., 79–91. Chico, Calif.: Scholars Press.

——. 1992. *Sigla and Select Marginalia in Greek Literary Papyri* (*Pap. Brux.* 26). Brussels: Fondation égyptologique Reine Élisabeth.

——. 2007. *Annotations in Greek and Latin Texts from Egypt*. American Studies in Papyrology. Oakville, Conn.: American Society of Papyrologists.

Otranto, R. 2000. *Antiche liste di libri su papiro* (*Sussidi eruditi* 49). Rome: Edizioni di Storia e Letteratura.

Radt, S. 1980. "Noch einmal Aischylos, Niobe Fr. 162 N. 2 (278 M.)." *ZPE* 38: 47–58.

——. 1997. "Zu P. Merton 19, 2 F. und P. Oxy. 2192, 43 F." *ZPE* 119: 6.

Roberts, C. H. 1954. "The Codex." *Proceedings of the British Academy* 40: 169–204.

——. 1979. *Manuscript, Society and Belief in Early Christian Egypt*. London: Oxford University Press.

——, and T. C. Skeat. 1983. *The Birth of the Codex*. London: Published for the British Academy by Oxford University Press.

Rossum-Steenbeek, M. van. 1998. *Greek Readers' Digests? Studies on a Selection of Subliterary Papyri*. Leiden: Brill.

Skeat, T. C. 1982. "The Length of the Standard Papyrus Roll and the Cost-Advantage of the Codex." *ZPE* 45: 169–175.

——. 1995. "Was Papyrus Regarded as 'Cheap' or 'Expensive' in the Ancient World?" *Aegyptus* 75: 75–93.

Stephens, S. A., and J. J. Winkler. 1995. *Ancient Greek Novels: The Fragments: Introduction, Text, Translation, and Commentary*. Princeton: Princeton University Press.

Turner, E. G. 1952. "Roman Oxyrhynchus." *JEA* 38: 78–93.

———. 1956. "Scribes and Scholars in Oxyrhynchus." In *Akten des VIII. Internationalen Kongresses für Papyrologie, Wien 1955,* ed. H. Gerstinger, 141–146. MPER, n.s., 5. Vienna: Rudolf M. Rohrer.

———. 1977. *The Typology of the Early Codex.* Philadelphia: University of Pennsylvania Press.

———. 1978. "The Terms Recto and Verso: The Anatomy of the Papyrus Roll (*Pap.Brux.* 16)." *Actes du XVe Congrès international de papyrologie, Bruxelles-Louvain, 29 août–3 septembre 1977,* pt. 1, ed. J. Bingen and G. Nachtergael. Brussels: Fondation égyptologique Reine Élisabeth.

———. 1980. *Greek Papyri: An Introduction,* 2d ed. Oxford: Clarendon Press.

———, and P. J. Parsons. 1987. *Greek Manuscripts of the Ancient World,* 2d ed. London: University of London, Institute of Classical Studies.

Van Minnen, P. 1998. "Boorish or Bookish? Literature in Egyptian Villages in the Fayum in the Graeco-Roman Period." *Journal of Juristic Papyrology* 28: 99–184.

Willis, W. H. 1968. "A Census of the Literary Papyri from Egypt." *GRBS* 9: 205–241.

CHAPTER 12

PAPYROLOGY AND ANCIENT LITERATURE

TIMOTHY RENNER

LITERARY AND SUBLITERARY PAPYRI

WHILE the vast majority of literary texts on papyrus, parchment, ostraca, or wood tablets are written in Greek, the texts inscribed on these materials are also our source for the longest and most important Egyptian literary compositions known from the Pharaonic and Hellenistic periods. Further, in spite of the overriding use of Greek as both an administrative language and a mark of elite culture in Egypt during the Roman period, a modest number of papyri shed light on the use or study of Latin literary texts in that province and on occasion make specific additions to the study of Latin literature more generally. Taken together, the varied contributions of papyri continue to bring new energy to the study of ancient literature and ensure that the boundaries of the texts that are the objects of its study shall not remain finite. Because as material objects they transmit works to us directly from their world, literary papyri (although often fragmentary and in need of much attention by modern editors to make them accessible to nonpapyrologists) bring the study of ancient literatures and their cultures alive with special immediacy.

The term *literary papyri* at first calls to mind texts of major genres such as epic, drama, lyric, history, and other types of prose narrative. However, papyrologists today, particularly those who study papyri written in Greek, usually include under "literary" several categories of "subliterary" or "paraliterary" papyri. These include papyri containing texts such as commentaries, lexica, and grammatical treatises, which are in some sense ancillary to the study of the major genres and have traditionally been so regarded. Further, the term *subliterary* is often used to refer to other types of technical works such as those on mathematics, science, and medicine, which in this book are treated in chapter 15.[1]

PAPYRI AND EGYPTIAN LITERATURE

If it were not for papyri and their decipherment and publication over the past two centuries, our familiarity with Egyptian literature today would be much reduced. Although literary texts of some length have been preserved by inscriptions on tombs and stelae, hieratic and demotic papyri, including wooden writing boards and ostraca, are responsible for our knowledge of most of the Egyptian texts that contain narrative tales and fables, instructions or precepts, and love poetry.[2] The most recent count of demotic literary papyri,[3] including some items not yet published, totals 539. The number of hieratic literary papyri, excluding funerary texts, is estimated to be substantially less than this. Although their numbers are small, the role of papyri in transmitting this ancient literature is very great by comparison with Greek or Latin literatures, which in the absence of the important additions that the papyri bring to them would still be available, to a great extent, through the medieval tradition had papyri never been known to moderns. Another basic difference between Graeco-Roman literary works and literary works in Egyptian is that the latter are usually anonymous, with the exception that some are pseudepigraphically attributed to pharaohs, sages, or other figures of past eras.

Here it is possible only to mention general categories of texts and to highlight a few details. The earliest hieratic literary compositions preserved on papyrus, ostraca, or wooden tablets are "instructions" that dispense advice on how best to live life. The earliest copies of the texts themselves date to the Middle Kingdom, although in the case of some of the most famous instructions the dramatic setting is the Fifth or the Sixth Dynasty. Texts composed during the Middle Kingdom and attested on papyrus include not only further instructions but also a wider variety of poetic and prose works. There are hymns to rulers and to the Nile. Especially, there is a wide range of prose tales such as the rather lengthy *Eloquent Peasant,* which mixes seriousness and irony in a demonstration of the value of rhetoric, or the *Story of Sinuhe,* detailing the life of a courtier sojourning in foreign lands. *The Story of the Shipwrecked Sailor* continues the fascination with biography or pseudobiography in the context of traveling and public service, while *Three Tales of Wonder* (with its dramatic setting in the Fourth Dynasty) touts the cleverness of lector-priests and glorifies the birth of a new pharaoh. Worthy of special mention in New Kingdom literature are a series of prayers used as school texts, love poems, further instructions (including some used in school), and a fascinating composition on the immortality of writers (Bresciani 1990; Lichtheim 1973–1974, vols. 1–2).

With the *Prophecies of Neferti,* a Middle Kingdom hieratic text preserved on ostraca and an Eighteenth Dynasty St. Petersburg papyrus (Lichtheim, vol. 1, 1973, 139–145), begins our record of a series of compositions that foretell the coming of evils upon Egypt through unrest or invasion, followed by the rise of a great king who brings peace. In a guise of this kind, such compositions glorify a regime in power or, in the case of works from the Persian period and later, serve to console Egyptians and express nationalistic fervor. With the theme of the conquest of Egypt by evil foreigners accentuated, these later works include the *Demotic Chronicle,* preserved in an early second-century BCE papyrus in Paris, and the *Oracle of the Lamb,* which survives in a demotic Vienna papyrus of the Augustan period and purports to have been spoken under Pharaoh Bocchoris of the Twenty-fourth Dynasty. The continuation of this tradition of prophecy into the Roman period as seen in the *Oracle of the Potter,* attested in Greek papyri of the second and third centuries CE, serves as a reminder that, even where literary texts are concerned, the divide between Egyptian and Greek is not always absolute (Koenen 1968). Demotic papyri of the Ptolemaic and Roman periods containing the adventures of Setne Khamwas, a New Kingdom prince, and tales entitled *Egyptians and Amazons* exemplify the interpenetration of Greek and Egyptian story elements, while the *Myth of the Eye of the Sun* is based more strictly on Egyptian elements (Lichtheim 1980, vol. 3).

Papyri and the Study of Greek Literature

The most spectacular and extensive finds of completely new Greek literature occurred for the most part at the end of the nineteenth century, when papyrology brought to light several entire ancient literary works that were previously known only as names (Turner 1968, 17–24). The body of ancient Greek literature continued to expand on the basis of papyrological evidence. By the early part of the twentieth century, more Greek authors or individual compositions had been "rediscovered," and many additions made to the existing corpora of several Greek authors, often forcing scholars to rethink their approaches to these writers' works. Indeed, the papyri had begun to substantially change the landscape of ancient Greek literature as it was known to the modern world (Powell and Barber 1921). Today, with approximately six thousand items published to date as listed in Mertens-Pack³ (see the list of selected electronic resources), texts containing Greek literature or subliterary texts make up some 87 percent of published literary papyri from Egypt up to the Arab conquest. These papyri include carefully produced, expensive bookrolls or codices, informal copies of literary works made by educated readers or students, and subliterary texts intended to accompany the reading of authors such as Homer. School copies and subliterary papyri ancillary to major works especially provide us with insights into the ways in which works of literature were used for schooling or individual study (see chapters 11 and 14). Indeed, most aspects of the study of ancient Greek literature and culture have been affected in some way by the recovery, study, and publication of papyri. Here there is space only to touch upon highlights.

Among Greek poetic texts, our acquaintance with archaic and classical lyric and elegy is heavily dependent on papyri, before the availability of which authors could be sampled only through quotations by other ancient writers. For instance, although a number of papyrological contributions to his varied compositions had been made earlier in the twentieth century, a more recently published Cologne fragment of an epode by Archilochus, with its passion and sexual explicitness, showed the poet in a new, if not wholly unexpected, light (Merkelbach and West 1974). About 60 percent of the poetry of Alcaeus known today derives from papyri, especially those of the Oxyrhynchus collection housed in Oxford. The passages of Alcaeus that are attested on papyrus, although many of their verses are fragmentary, are nearly always individually longer than those that were previously known through citation by authors such as Athenaeus and Strabo. Substantial portions of Sappho's surviving work, too, are known only on papyrus, and discoveries of her work continue: Thus, a striking new fragment of a poem alluding to the old age of Tithonus as a parallel to the writer's own graying hair came to light recently from mummy cartonnage in the Cologne collection, its early third-century BCE date in fact making it one of the earliest known of Sappho's texts (Gronewald and Daniel 2004). The several dozen existing quoted passages or tags from Alcman and with them our knowledge of archaic Spartan choral lyric were greatly enhanced by the publication in the later nineteenth century of a Louvre papyrus containing one hundred verses plus marginal notes, as well as by commentaries on the poet's works that were uncovered in the Oxyrhynchus collection during the twentieth. Bacchylides would be unknown except as a name were it not for the 1896 discovery in Upper Egypt of a papyrus roll containing several of his dithyrambs and odes. Pindar himself has become much more comprehensively understood by Hellenists today now that papyrology has brought to light parts of his paeans and dithyrambs to supplement the *Epinician Odes* preserved in medieval manuscript. The fragments of the elegiac poems of Simonides have increased fivefold (see the case study later on) as a result of papyrus discoveries, and the papyri have shed considerable new light on the "Homeric" qualities of Stesichorus while broadening our knowledge of his production overall. Finally, in the early days of papyrology, a good portion of the popular fourth-century BCE poet Timotheus's dithyramb *Persae* was discovered on a roll—itself one of the earliest Greek papyri, attributable to the late 300s—that had been disinterred from cartonnage.

In the area of hexameter verse, most of the surviving lines of the Hesiodic *Catalogue of Women* are still fragmentary. However, thanks to papyri, which are largely responsible for what we know of the work in detail, we are now in a much better position to assess the content, connectedness, and overall shape of the poem, as well as its relationship to the mythographical tradition (Merkelbach and West 1967, 1–120). A Strasbourg papyrus recognized during the 1990s as preserving some 130 verses of Empedocles' *On Nature* is noteworthy for demonstrating that a text of a Presocratic work was in circulation in Egypt in the first century CE and that the author combined a rationalizing approach to the physical world with a doctrine of reincarnation (Martin and Primavesi 1998; Janko 2004). A papyrological window into the biographical hexameters of Erinna, who may have written during the fourth century BCE, was opened by a papyrus in Florence containing more than fifty lines attributed to her poem *Distaff*, which may now be added to several epigrams by and about her that are known from the *Anthologia Palatina*. The skepticism of one prominent philologist over the likelihood of a self-identified wool worker from a small Aegean island having written sophisticated poetry in a unique combination of Aeolic and Doric should not detract from the excitement of recovering more of what may well be another all-too-rare female Greek literary voice (West 1977).

New discoveries on papyrus have enhanced the few works of Attic drama preserved in manuscript by giving us substantial fragments of additional plays, especially by Euripides and Aeschylus (Diggle 1998). In the case of the latter these include a large portion of a satyr play, the *Diktyoulkoi*, only the second such known to the modern world after Euripides' *Cyclops*. With respect to Euripides we are especially indebted to the papyri for substantial knowledge about such tragedies as *Hypsipyle* and *Cresphontes* (Bastianini and Casanova 2005, 1–9). Although the papyri have brought to light commentaries, summaries, and other subliterary accompaniments to classical authors too copious to detail here (see Bastianini et al. 2004–), a series of Roman-era prose *hypotheseis* (short summaries) has especially enhanced our knowledge of Euripides' lost or partially preserved tragedies (Luppe 2002). A general point worth noting with respect to ancient *hypotheseis* and summaries of classical works is that the origins, aims (whether for the purpose of accompanying the reading of a major work or for use in schools, for instance), and relationships of such texts to their main works, as well as to scholia, ancient commentaries, and mythographical texts, have in recent decades increasingly become the objects of specialized study (Rossum-Steenbeek 1998; cf. Cameron 1995, 119–127).

With respect to New Comedy, previously known largely through Latin adaptations by Plautus and Terence, papyrology has revolutionized our state of knowledge, especially by providing us first, nearly a century ago, with the Cairo codex containing multiscene portions of two of Menander's plays (plus parts of two others) and second, since the 1950s, with additional fragments of his plays, together with a complete play, the *Dyskolos*, via a series of third-century CE codices in the Bodmer collection in Geneva. Beginning in 1891 with the publication of a British Museum roll containing some seven hundred verses of the literary mimes of Herondas, an author known previously but only through testimonia and brief quotations (Kenyon 1891b, 1–39), the papyri have transformed our picture of Hellenistic poetry. During the late nineteenth and earlier twentieth centuries, before the publication of several dozen significant papyri, Callimachus was a poet known for his *Hymns* preserved in manuscript and as the author of numerous other poetic and scholarly works attested in quotations and references by ancient authors or in Byzantine compilations such as the Homeric scholia and the *Suda*. Extended passages of the *Aetia, Hecale,* and *Iambi* such as we have today were lacking. Although new discoveries continue, the publication in midcentury of a monumental edition collecting and annotating all of the known texts, on papyrus and from elsewhere, made possible a much fuller appreciation of Callimachus's pivotal role with respect to literary innovation (Pfeiffer 1949–1953; Cameron 1995). The role of the small, damaged, but informative group of papyri containing scholia and summaries, known as *Diegeseis,* of Callimachus's major poems should be highlighted here as an example of the contribution of subliterary texts to understanding and supplementing the fragmentary works themselves, as was mentioned earlier in connection with Euripides.[4] However, it is not only Hellenistic authors from Alexandria for whom papyri provide vital new texts and information. This is illustrated by the enormously rich assemblage of Hellenistic poetic fragments on papyrus attested by the standard, late-twentieth-century scholarly corpus (Lloyd-Jones and Parsons 1983; cf. Zetzel 1987).

Furthermore, a blockbuster discovery riveted the attention of Greek and Latin poetry specialists alike following reports during the 1990s of an extensive, late third-century BCE papyrus roll recovered from mummy cartonnage and containing more than one hundred epigrams attributable to Posidippus of Pella. Published in 2001, the "new Posidippus," with its thematic grouping of poems that center around divination, stones, dedications, and the like, has already generated hundreds of scholarly studies on topics ranging from the arrangement of ancient poetry books to the physical characteristics of bookrolls (Bastianini and Gallazzi 2001; Acosta-Hughes and Renner 2002). All of these papyrological discoveries both have affected our appreciation of Hellenistic poetry in its own right and have important consequences for students of Latin authors, many of whose Hellenistic Greek models or predecessors would otherwise remain but dimly known. For example, not only can a translation of a Hellenistic original such as Catullus's *Coma Berenices* poem (no. 66) now be directly compared with a substantial part of the corresponding passage in the *Aetia,* but our new grasp of the spirit and the innovative qualities of Callimachus's work as a whole also provides numerous opportunities to better appreciate the ways in which Roman poets utilized or reworked Callimachean approaches to poetry, in the process usually creating something uniquely Roman.

With regard to prose as well, the papyri have infused new texts into the body of available Greek literature. Probably the most critical single discovery of prose on papyrus for all of classical studies was revealed by the publication in 1891, by F. G. Kenyon of the British Museum, of a text written on a group of four first-century CE rolls obtained at an undetermined location in Upper Egypt and containing the nearly complete *Athenaion Politeia*, attributed to Aristotle (Kenyon 1891a). This "constitution," which traces the history of Athenian government from the Dark Age to the fourth century, was reported in ancient references to have formed part of a series of studies of different forms of polity by Aristotle and his pupils. Only a small part of the text had been known since 1880, on the basis of a papyrus fragment in Berlin. The *Athenaion Politeia* has become a fundamental source of information on Athenian history and one in the absence of which historians of ancient Greece today would scarcely recognize their own field of study.[5]

Our access to lost Attic prose was also enriched by the recovery in Egypt, between 1847 and the 1880s, of four papyrus rolls of Greek oratory ranging from the first century BCE to the second CE. They made it possible for the first time in the modern world to sample six speeches—one of them nearly complete, the others less so—of the fourth-century orator Hyperides alongside the remaining corpus of Attic orators transmitted to us in manuscript. Another event provided a new historical voice for our understanding of the concluding years of the Peloponnesian War and the period immediately following. This is the publication early in the twentieth century of a portion of the so-called *Hellenica Oxyrhynchia*, which has occasioned lively scholarly debate concerning its author's take on events and relationship to contemporary sources such as Xenophon and Diodorus. Prose from the classical period, too, is a papyrus text written in an "epigraphic" script attributable to as early as the mid-fourth century BCE and containing commentary on Orphic theogonic verses. Unique for the fact of its deriving not from Egypt but from an excavation in Greece (near Thessaloniki), the so-called Derveni papyrus is of great importance for Greek religion in the age of the Sophists. It also appears to be the oldest known perishable object carrying a Greek literary text (Janko 2002). To move somewhat later in time, what we know of the history and the subject-matter range of the ancient novel has changed considerably as a result of papyrus finds. Fragments of Chariton datable to the second and third centuries CE overturned the early twentieth-century assertion that this relatively early author of novels—and therefore the entire genre—was a product of the late Roman world. Further, the discovery of fragments of ancient Greek novels, such as the *Ninus Romance* or the *Phoinikika* of Lollianos, with its crime and violence—both of which were previously unknown except through the testimony of other authors—has shown that not all ancient Greek novels may be fitted into the traditionally recognized categories of ideal and rhetorical romance (Stephens and

Winkler 1995; Stephens 2003). Finally, in addition to the *hypotheseis* and summaries designed to accompany major authors that were discussed earlier, we ought to mention one other type of subliterary composition, the grammatical treatise. It would be fair to say that papyri have significantly changed the possibilities for the questions we might ask about the history of such texts. Whether focused on a special topic or aimed at covering schematically a series of standard points, as discussed in the case study later on, ancient grammatical works on papyrus provide an important supplement to treatises known from manuscript and allow us to begin to see what kinds of grammar summaries or studies were current in one Greek-speaking province, as well as how those texts might actually have been utilized.

Papyrology has also changed many of the ideas once firmly held about the textual history of Greek authors whose main works are fully preserved in the manuscript tradition and has often provided material for debate about the nature of that tradition. The discovery of early Hellenistic papyri of Homer was especially unsettling and provocative for textual critics because many such papyri contain so-called "plus verses," verses not found in the medieval manuscripts. The generally accepted solution is to attribute the elimination of most of these after the second century BCE to the influence of Aristarchus's editing and commenting. On the whole, the textual characteristics of *Iliad* and *Odyssey* papyri of the later Hellenistic and Roman periods do not differ greatly from those of the medieval manuscript traditions, which formed the basis of the first modern critical editions. Nevertheless, recent scholarship shows that even the Homeric papyri of the Roman period—which are so numerous as to make Homer the undisputed leader in terms of frequency of finds of literary papyri—need to be taken into account in assessing any Homeric verse if they provide evidence for it (Haslam 1997; Skafte Jensen 2005). Among classical authors, Homer is somewhat of an anomaly because of the oral aspects of his composition and because of modern scholars' intense interest in the earlier stages of transmission. However, a study of the papyri of nearly any poetic or prose author—papyri will often be distributed over time from the Hellenistic period to the Arab conquest—leads to new insights into the ways in which one may view the medieval manuscript tradition. Further, such an examination often impresses upon us the relative lack of adherence, by comparison with modern expectations, of ancient editions to a single received text (see for example Haslam 1978).[6]

PAPYRI AND LATIN LITERATURE

Papyri of Latin authors are relatively rare in Egypt. Totaling about two hundred known items at present, they consist mainly of several dozen fragments of known works of classical authors such as Terence, Cicero, Sallust, Vergil, Livy, Lucan, and Juvenal, as well as a number of legal texts. However, two especially noteworthy contributions of papyrology to Latin letters deserve mention here. The first is a papyrus fragment containing several new verses of Latin elegy that was discovered at Qasr Ibrim, in Egyptian Nubia about 150 miles south of Aswan, dated by archaeological, palaeographical, and historical evidence to between 50 BCE and 25 CE, and argued persuasively to be the work of the early Augustan poet and ill-starred military leader Cornelius Gallus (Anderson, Parsons, and Nisbet 1979). Although many of the twelve lines represented are fragmentary, the papyrus is of special interest to historians of Latin literature seeking to understand the basis for the flowering of Roman elegy in the Augustan world and hungry for even a scrap of new text which might shed light on the development of this genre between Catullus and Propertius. The second contribution is a Michigan papyrus (strictly speaking, it is a page of a vellum codex) containing about forty verses from Seneca's *Medea* which appears to preserve intact readings that became corrupt in the archetype of the medieval tradition. The papyrus's fourth-century CE date shows that Seneca's tragedies were read in the East during this relatively late period and seems to help confirm a surge in interest in learning Latin in Egypt at this time (Markus and Schwendner 1997).

RESOURCES FOR EDITING AND STUDYING LITERARY PAPYRI

Although Greek and Latin literary papyri share many commonalities with documentary papyri and are frequently published in volumes together with documents,[7] their study has often been seen as a separate branch of Graeco-Roman papyrology.[8] Indeed, a senior Hellenist and papyrologist who works on both literary and documentary Greek papyri once remarked that editing a literary papyrus is something that any Greek and Roman classicist ought to be able to do because many of the basic principles for establishing and criticizing the text are similar where both medieval manuscripts and literary papyri are concerned. However, editing literary texts that are recovered from papyrus requires a specific set of resources which overlap with but are not in all respects the same as those used by scholars who are concerned primarily with Greek and Roman literature known only through the medieval tradition. Obviously the editor or critic of a literary papyrus employs whatever part of the vast resources of classical philology are necessary. These include edited texts of authors, scholarly commentaries on works of literature, collections of fragments of writers in a particular genre, and lexica, whether in print or electronic form. Among the electronic tools developed by classical studies in general, the University of California–Irvine's online *Thesaurus Linguae Graecae* (*TLG*), which collects and presents all texts attributed to Greek authors from Homer to the fall of

Byzantium in searchable form, has become an essential tool for papyrologists seeking to identify newly found texts within the corpus of Greek literature or to locate parallel passages to new texts on papyrus.[9]

More specialized compilations that focus wholly or mainly on the papyri and are useful for literary papyrology consist of three groups. Those of the first are organized around types of literary or subliterary works and may include texts other than those on papyrus. A number of Greek literary texts, especially many of those that are revealed by papyri, are anonymous because the names of their authors are not preserved or on account of their subliterary nature. Thus, many are not contained in the *TLG*. Along with texts to which names of authors are attached, some categories of these unattributable texts have been included in printed corpora specific to their genres, notably collections of papyri containing philosophy, biography, ancient novels, and grammar (Adorno et al. 1989–1999; Gallo 1975–; Stephens and Winkler 1995; Wouters 1979). An additional tool, the *Catalogue of Paraliterary Papyri (CPP)*, currently an electronic data bank in process, contains descriptions of Greek papyri and other written materials which, because of their paraliterary, diverse, and anonymous character, cannot be found in the *TLG* and tend to be accessible only in scattered publications. Begun as a database of mythographical papyri, the *CPP* is currently adding papyri with all kinds of lists and catalogues. The *CPP's* stated goal is to include digital versions of full-text editions of the paraliterary papyri and to incorporate other materials such as grammatical papyri and commentaries, as well as medical and liturgical texts.

A second type of resource is organized primarily around papyri and other ancient books as physical objects in historical time and in space (both their places of origin, insofar as known, and their location in modern collections). The *Advanced Papyrological Information System (APIS)*, whose goal of providing online data and, where possible, images of all papyri in collections is approaching completion for North American centers of papyrological study, and has made substantial progress with respect to Europe. The *APIS* essentially treats literary papyri in the same way as it does the documentary texts that make up the majority of its entries. Another resource, one that focuses solely on literary texts, is the online *Leuven Database of Ancient Books (LDAB)*. Moreover, it covers not only literary papyri but also early books of other kinds, such as the great biblical codices of the late Roman period.[10] At present the *LDAB* comprises more than twelve thousand items that date from the fourth century BCE to 800 CE. The *LDAB's* data bank includes some thirty-seven hundred anonymous texts, most of which are on papyrus. The project uses the term *books* to mean "texts that were intended to reach the eyes of a reading public or at least possessed a more than ephemeral interest or usefulness."[11] The *LDAB* does not attempt to give a full bibliography for each item, whereas the institutional web pages that are linked to form *APIS* do.

Into a third category falls the single most useful organizational tool for studying literary papyri and one that is also essential for the scholar of Greek and Roman literature concerned with authors represented on papyrus: R. A. Pack's annotated catalogue of Greek and Latin literary papyri from Egypt. The second print edition, designated Pack² (Pack 1965), in which 3,026 literary and subliterary papyri are catalogued according to author, if known, and according to genre in the case of anonymous texts, is now forty years old. Its successor, created by the Centre de Documentation de Papyrologie Littéraire (CEDOPAL) of the Université de Liège and referred to as Mertens-Pack³, is based on the numbering system of Pack² but is now an online resource that is updated regularly. Like the earlier versions of Pack, it gives a full bibliography for each item.[12] To ascertain what papyri covering a particular genre of Greek or Latin literature have been published so far, their dates, locations, and other metadata, as well as what studies have been published concerning them, one goes first to Pack² and Mertens-Pack³.[13]

It is obvious that these various resources overlap to a greater or lesser extent in terms of coverage. Some are linked—for example, *LDAB* and *CPP*. There is not sufficient space here to discuss in detail the somewhat differing varieties of metadata that are given by each of these compilations and their arrangement in different database fields. For instance, compared with the *LDAB* and Mertens-Pack³, the *CPP* provides more detailed descriptions of the contents, as well as the state of preservation, hand, and lectional signs. The majority of these electronic tools do not provide actual texts or images; exceptions are the images provided on many of the institutional Web sites which make up *APIS* and the intention of the *CPP* to include online texts. Finally, ongoing bibliographical components of two long-established papyrological journals remain especially useful: (1) the systematic "Literarische Texte unter Ausschluss der Christlichen" sections which appear periodically in *Archiv für Papyrusforschung* and include summaries with brief evaluations of new texts; (2) the relevant parts of the thorough "Testi recentemente pubblicati" and "Bibliografia" sections in *Aegyptus*.

Electronic bibliographical tools and databases for Greek and Latin papyri are thus quite well developed. These items do not, however, include hieratic and demotic literary papyri, for which one must turn to the newly conceived Demotistische Literaturübersicht, housed at the Katholieke Universiteit in Leuven.

A Look at the "New Simonides": A Brief Case Study

The expansion of what we know about the elegiac compositions of Simonides' poetry as a result of papyrological discoveries is a good example of how new literary papyri can have far-reaching implications for classical studies not simply by winning additional lines of text for us to read but also by contributing to literary historical debates or provoking new ones. The publication of *P.Oxy.* LIX 3965 by P. Parsons in 1992, following up on suggestions made by E. Lobel, who in 1954 had published *P.Oxy.* XXII 2327, containing poetry by an unknown author, allowed the surviving text of the two rolls to be combined. This resulted in a more extensive group of lines comprising one or more elegiac poems by Simonides that center around events of the Persian Wars. The two rolls in question, each datable to the second century CE on the basis of their writing and each consisting of many fragments defined by a common hand and fabric, overlap at various points and may be different copies of the same collection of poetry although they were not written by the same person.[14] The identification of *P.Oxy.* LIX 3965 as Simonides is representative of how literary papyrologists make the most of their often scattered data. A few words of one scrap were shown to belong to a passage of Simonidean elegiac verses quoted by Stobaeus. Another tiny scrap, labeled Fr. (i.e., fragment) 5, bore bits of three lines of writing from the interior of a column and included only eight Greek letters that could be read without dispute. Two of these scanty lines overlap, however, with Simonidean verses quoted by Plutarch.

Let us take a closer look at the editing process for Fr. 5. As is customary for new literary texts in *P.Oxy.* volumes, the scrap was first represented in "diplomatic" transcript[15] accompanied by a critical apparatus describing the surviving ink of the uncertain letters in detail and in as objective terms as possible.[16]

Fr. 5

. . .

]. αιθερ[

]. δ .. [

]πολυ[

. . .

1] ., foot of upright with junction to left, ν acceptable.

2] . δ .. [, first, probably cross-bar and right-hand side of η; second, perhaps upper right-hand arc of small circle; third, short horizontal trace at upper level.

3] πολυ[, of π the top, part of the left-hand junction, and the right-hand side with a rather messy join (so rather than γ [or the like] ε Lobel); of υ the left-hand branch (ν Lobel, but the stroke extends too far to the left).

To this bare information let us add what we know from elsewhere. A previously known pair of fragments of Simonides' elegiacs, designated Fragments 10–11 in M. West's first edition of elegiac and iambic poets, consists of three couplets quoted successively almost in their entirety by Plutarch (*De Herodoti malignitate* 42, 872d), who attributes them to Simonides and cites them as evidence that the Corinthians stayed in their assigned position during the battle of Plataea and did not run away as Herodotus implies. The final two verses overlap with the first two fragmentary lines of the scrap (in West's second edition the passage was renumbered as Fragments 15–16; see West 1992, 121–122). Parsons's restored transcript of Fr. 5 of *P.Oxy.* 3965 uses halved square brackets (⌐⌐) to indicate the boundaries of the papyrus scrap within the text derived from Plutarch:

P.Oxy. 3965 Fr. 5 + frr. 10–11 (West)

μέccoιc δ' οἵ τ' Ἐφύρην πολυπίδακα ναιετάοντες,
παντοίηϲϲ ἀρετῆϲ ἴδριεϲ ἐν πολέμῳ,
οἵ τε πόλιν Γλαύκοιο Κορίνθιον ἄϲτυ νέμοντεϲ

Fr. 5

. . .   < > κάλλιϲτον μάρτυν ἔθεντο πόνων,
] αιθερ[χρυϲοῦ τιμήεντος ἐꟼν αἰθέρι⌐· καί ϲφιν ἀέξει
] δ . . [αὐτῶν τ' εὐρεῖαν κλꟼ⌐ηδόν⌐ꟾα καὶ πατέρων
]πολυ[   ]πολυ[

In itself Fr. 5 added only four letters—]πολυ[, two of which are in fact uncertain—to what was already known about Simonides' work. However, the identification of 3965 (and consequently 2327) as containing elegiacs by him enabled the more extensive parts of both rolls to be used to significantly enrich our knowledge of the poet's work. Prior to these developments, a comment in the Byzantine lexicon *Suda* that Simonides composed poems in elegiac meter on battles of the Persian Wars had been viewed skeptically. The number and nature of the separate poems that may be represented by the rolls, together with their relationship to possible public performance, to the historical sympathies of different Greek allies, and to the narrative of Herodotus, are still the subject of lively debate. However, the contents of the new papyri do indeed appear to include elegiac verses on several notable military actions such as Plataea and Artemisium, as well as a symposium scene that may be part of yet another elegiac composition.[17]

Perhaps most striking is the poem represented by a group of fragments which, it is plausibly argued, celebrates—probably for a public occasion within a year or two of the actual event—the battle of Plataea. This composition must have been one hundred or more verses in length, perhaps considerably more. As reconstructed by Parsons and commented upon by others, the earliest extant lines discuss the Trojan War and the death of Achilles, thereby setting up a presumed parallel between an ancient East-West conflict and the contemporary one with Persia. Invoking the Muse, the poet describes the departure of the Spartan army, accompanied by "the horse-taming sons of Zeus, the hero Tyndaridai, and mighty Menelaos," from home and its progress to Corinth, Megara, and Eleusis before arriving at Plataea (a catalogue of forces before the battle furnishes a plausible context for the praise of the Corinthians in Fr. 5, described earlier).

Little or nothing remains of the battle description. However, a measure of the attention that the contents of these two rolls have attracted among scholars of ancient literature is the flurry of publications that have been devoted to the "New Simonides," including a special edition of the classical periodical *Arethusa*, with articles by a wide range of Hellenists and, most recently, an edited volume exploring Simonides' elegiacs (Boedeker and Sider 1996, 2001). The extent to which Simonides in the Plataea poem provides an epic framework for recent events is striking. In many other respects as well, the labors of the *P.Oxy.* scholars over what would seem to many but philological minutiae have produced consequences that are far reaching for an understanding of the Greek poetic tradition, as well as the history and culture of the early fifth century BCE.

"OPEN" GRAMMATICAL TEXTS: A BRIEF CASE STUDY

To a greater or lesser degree, texts of major authors in ancient times often vary from copy to copy more than we may be used to seeing. After all, nineteenth- and twentieth-century classical philology has taught us to establish "the" text. Let us now look at a passage from a Greek grammatical fragment, *P.Mich.* inv. 30, which illustrates how certain types of subliterary texts are "open" to a much greater extent. The papyrus, of unknown provenance, arrived in Ann Arbor in 1930 after purchase on the antiquities market.[18] Its contents most resemble a *Technê Grammatikê*, a relatively brief but in a certain sense comprehensive treatise on Greek grammar that is typified by a composition preserved in manuscripts from the tenth century on, where it is attributed to Dionysius Thrax, a second-century BCE pupil of Aristarchus. A group of around two dozen papyrus fragments ranging in date from the first through the sixth century CE are close in character and content to Dionysius, albeit with numerous individual variations in detail (Wouters 1979, 33–210).[19]

By examining the discussion of adverbs (ἐπιρρήματα) in Column II of the Michigan papyrus, we can appreciate the fluidity of this grammatical tradition more fully. Written in a practiced but informal hand that shows fluctuation in the straightness of the lines as well as variant forms for several of the letters—utilitarian qualities that are quite common in subliterary papyri—it appears to be part of a leaf of a codex assignable to the third or fourth century CE on the basis of palaeography. After the text was initially written, additions—perhaps by the writer of the text, although they have a slightly more formal quality and appear to be in darker ink—were made above the line at various points. In line 8, someone has crossed out several letters with vigorous diagonal strokes. High stops were used from time to time, especially to separate words in a list of examples:

Col. II (Recto)

– – – – – – – – – –

ἐπίρρημά ἐστιν] λέξις [
κατὰ μίαν ἐκφορ]ὰν δηλουμ[ένη προτακτικὴ ἢ ὑποτακ]τικὴ ῥήματ[ος
      τῶν] δὲ ἐπιρημάτ[ων τὰ   4
            νῦν [
μέν ἐστιν ἁπλᾶ, ὡς] αὐτίκα. σύν[θετα
          ] α[
δὲ   ] ἀσ[ύ]νθετα σα.[
       ὄ]ντα μὲν παρονο-
μασμένα   ] [[3–4]]καλῶς ανα   8
      ]   οἷον
ἐπίρ]ρημα τηνικάδε
      ] οἷον
      ]ιν κάτω ἄνω
      ]. τῶν χρόνου
      ]κα ἐπιρήματα   12
      ] τούτοις ὑποτακτέ-
ου   π]αραστατικά
      ] ποιότητος ..[
ἐπ]ιρήματα .[16
      ].ναιμω[
      ]μας πύξ .[
      ]. λιγρυφίς [
      ]α διχῇ ὦ[δε   20
      ]. πρόχνυ . [
      margin

2. . : Part of horizontal in mid-line; alternatively, read]ανδηλ[.].μ[4. Read ἐπιρρημάτ[ων 5. αυτικα˙ pap. 6. . [: ι, ρ, φ, ψ 10. κατω˙ ανω˙ pap. 11.] . : α, ε, κ? 12. Read ἐπιρρήματα; next, possible space-filler ink 15. . [: φ or c, then high horizontal 16. ἐπι]ρρήματα seems less likely. . [: τ or υ? 17.] . : α or ω? 18.]μας˙ pap. . [: ν? 19. Read λικριφίς 20.]α˙ pap.

3. προ (or ὑπο-)τακ]τικὴ ῥήματ[ος, "placed before (or after) a verb."

4. After the basic definition of adverb, a distinction is made between those that are simple or uncompounded (ἁπλᾶ, ἀσύνθετα) and those that are compound (σύνθετα).

5. νῦν, added above the line, is perhaps intended as a second example (alongside αὐτίκα) of adverbs that are ἁπλᾶ.

6. Perhaps τὰ δὲ] ἀσ[ύ]νθετα σάφ[α, "and the uncompounded (adverbs): sapha...," with σάφα, "clearly," being the first example of this category cited.

7–9. Whether or not our suggested supplement in 7–8 is correct, in some way the writer mentions παρονομασία or some form of παρονομάζειν, a term that is not easily paralleled in *Technê*-type texts. Then something has been deleted,

followed by discussion involving at least two examples, καλῶς and τηνικάδε:
Perhaps the point is that these two adverbs are "derived," παρονομασμένα.

8. The deleted letters look somewhat like ρον.

9. Although τηνικάδε refers to time, it may be cited here because it is said to be "derived" like the words cited in 7–8. Adverbs of time seem to be discussed as a category in 11–12.

10.]ιν: It does not seem possible to read the expected οἷον, "for example." κάτω ἄνω should belong to the category of ἐπιρρήματα τοπικά, or directional adverbs.

11–12. In 11 the writer apparently turns again to adverbs of time: The word ἐπιρήματα in 12, together with the fragmentary adjective—perhaps δηλωτι]κά or τοπικά or παραστατι]κά (cf. 14), "expressive of"—might still be part of this discussion.

13–14. "Under these must be classified." The reference must be to the category of adverbs referred to in 12.

14. π]αραστατικά, "expressive of."

11. ἐ]κ τῶν χρόνου?

17. ναί μῶ[ν, as a pair of examples? As the comparanda (cf. below) show, the examples of adverbs given in 18–21 belong to the list of adverbs of ποιότης (or μεσότης) indicating manner.

18. Perhaps ν[ύξ = γνύξ, "with the knee."

19. λιγρυφίς = λικριφίς, a rare Homeric adverb meaning "sideways" or "aside" appears in Il. 14.463 and Od. 19.451. It is cited by Herodian four times in discussions of Homeric prosody. In the Technê papyrus P.Lit.Lond. 182, it is part of a long list of adverbs that are μεσότητος καά ποιότητος δηλωτικά, "expressive of state and quality."

21. σφόδρ]α? αἶψ]α? ἄμ]α?

The closest parallels to the Michigan text are provided by passages in Dionysius Thrax and in two Technê-type papyri of the first century CE and around 300, respectively. They are of great help in understanding the papyrus and in supplementing the missing sections—but none of them offers anything like a word-for-word correspondence:

Dionysius Thrax, Technê Grammatikê 19 (Grammatici Graeci I 1, 72–86)
Περὶ ἐπιρρήματος. Ἐπίρρημά ἐστι μέρος λόγου ἄκλιτον, κατὰ ῥήματος λεγόμενον ἢ ἐπιλεγόμενον ῥήματι. Τῶν δὲ ἐπιρρημάτων τὰ μέν ἐστιν ἁπλᾶ, τά δὲ σύνθετα· ἁπλᾶ μὲν ὡς πάλαι, σύνθετα δὲ ὡς πρόπαλαι. Τὰ δὲ χρόνου δηλωτικά, οἷον νῦν τότε αὖθις· τούτοις δὲ ὡς εἴδη ὑποτακτέον τὰ καιροῦ παραστατικά, οἷον σήμερον αὔριον τόφρα τέως πηνίκα. Τὰ δὲ μεσότητος, οἷον καλῶς σοφῶς. Τὰ δὲ ποιότητος, οἷον πύξ λάξ βοτρυδόν ἀγεληδόν. Τὰ δὲ ποσότητος, οἷον πολλάκις ὀλιγάκις. Τὰ δὲ ἀριθμοῦ δηλωτικά, οἷον δίς τρίς τετράκις. Τὰ δὲ τοπικά, οἷον ἄνω κάτω...

P.Yale 25.37–53 (I cent. CE, assigned) ἐπίρημα δ᾽ ἐστὶν λέξις κατὰ μίαν ἐκφορὰν δ[η]λουμένη προτακτικὴ ἢ ὑποτακτική, ῥήματος ἀσυν[θ]έτως σημαίνουσα ποσότητα ἢ ποιότητα ἢ χρόνον ἢ τόπον ἢ ἄρνησιν ἢ συγκατάθεσιν ἢ ἀπαγόρευσιν ἢ ἐπικέλευσιν ἢ

ἐρώτησιν ἢ εὐχὴ[ν] ἢ παραβολὴν ἢ διστα<σ>μόν. Ποσότητος μὲν οου (1. οὖν) ἐστιν
δηλωτικὰ τὰ τοιαῦτα· πολλάκις, ὀλιγάκις. Ποιότητος δέ, εὖ, καλῶς. Χρόνου δέ, νῦν,
ἐκθές, αὔριον. Τόπου δέ, ἐνθαῦθα, ἐκ<ε>ῖ, ἔξω. Ἀρνήσεος δέ, οὐ. Συγκαταθέσεος δέ,
ναί. Ἀπαγορεύσεος δέ, μή. Ἐπικελεύσεος δέ, τι, πάλιν. Ἐρωτήσεος δέ, ποῦ. Εὐχῆς δέ,
αἴθε. Παραβ[ο]λῆς δέ, ὡς. Δισ{σ}τασμοῦ δέ, σχεδόν, {ε}ἴσος.

P.Lit.Lond. 182.80–105 (ca. 300 CE, assigned) Ἐπίρρημα. Ἐπίρρημα τί ἐστιν; Λέξις
καθ᾽ ἕνα σχηματισμὸν ἐκφερομένη, προτακτικὴ καὶ ὑποτακτικὴ ῥήματος
ἀσυνθέτου, ἐν <πολλοῖς?> εἴδεσι θεωρουμένη. Τῶν δὲ ἐπιρρημάτων ἃ μέν ἐστι
μεσότητος καὶ ποιότητος δηλωτικά, οἷον καλῶς, σοφῶς, ἄρδην, ἀνέδην, βοτρυδόν,
ἀπριάτην, νύξ (1. πύξ?), γνύξ, λάξ, ὀδάξ, αννων (1. ἄφνω?), ἀκονιτί, σάφα, μάλα,
λικριφίς, ἀμοιβηδής, ἑλληνιστί, συριστί, καὶ ἔτι πλείονα. ἃ δὲ ποσότητος, οἷον δίς,
τρίς, πεντάκις καὶ ἔτι πλείο[να]. ἃ δὲ χρόνου, ἤδη, νῦν, αὖτις, πάλιν, ἐχθές, τηνίκα,
καὶ τὰ ὅμοια. ἃ δὲ εὐχῆς, οἷον αἴθε, εἴθε, βάλε, ἄβαλε. τινὰ δὲ ἀπαγορεύσεως, μή,
μηκέτι. τινὰ δὲ συγκαταθέσεως, ναί, ναίχι. τοῦ δ᾽ αὐτοῦ εἴδους κατωμοτικά, οἷον
νή ... τὸ μὰ κοινὸν τῆς ἀπωμόσεώς τε καὶ ἀπαιτή[σ]εως. ἃ δὲ ἐρωτήσεως, πίς,
ποῦ, πόθεν [± / 5] ταῦτα καὶ τοπικά ἐστιν. παρακελεύσεως δεῦτε, τὸ δ᾽ αὐτὸ καὶ
ῥῆμα γίνεται προστακτικόν. ὁμοιώσεως ἢ παραβολῆς ὡς. τὸ δ᾽ αὐτὸ καὶ πλείστας
ἔχει δυνάμεις. ἃ δὲ ἐπικελευστικά, ἅπερ οἱ μὲν ἐπιφθέγματα καλοῦσιν, οἱ δὲ
συνεμφάσεις, οἱ δὲ σχετλιασμούς, φεῦ, παπαῖ, ὤμοι. φασὶ δὲ κα[ὶ] εἰκασμοῦ τινα
εἶναι ἐπιρ<ρ>ήματα ὡς {τὸ} τυχόν, σχεδόν, ἴσως, τάχα. ἃ δὲ τάξεως, ἑξῆς, χωρίς.
ἐπίρρημα δὲ εἴρηται διὰ τὸ καθ᾽ ἑαυτὸ μὲν λεγόμενον μὴ ἀποτελεῖν διάνοιαν
ἐγγράμματον, προστασομέν<ου> δὲ ῥήματος, ζευγνύμενον ῥήματι κατὰ τὸ
πλεῖστον.

The surviving examples of adverbs in the Michigan papyrus show quite an impressive spectrum, from pedestrian καλῶς to the exotic Homeric λικριφίς (19), a word used in the *Iliad* to describe Polydamas's jumping aside to avoid Ajax's spear. Such an eclectic mixture of Homeric, Attic, and perhaps contemporary koinê items can, however, be paralleled in ancient grammatical literature, for example, in *P.Lit.Lond.* 182, which dates to the general period of the Michigan text. Our papyrus is obviously eclectic with respect to all of the other known *Technê* compositions—just as they themselves differ from one another.

As we struggle to understand and restore the fragmentary lines, we sometimes find ourselves returning to the same comparanda as "trots": for example, Dionysius or the London papyrus. These may themselves be separated in time by as many as five centuries: The London papyrus is assigned on palaeographical grounds to around 300 CE. The work attributed to Dionysius is purportedly from the second century BCE, although arguments have been advanced to place all or part of it as late as the fourth CE. However, even if Dionysius's *Technê* originated so late, it is clear that the Michigan papyrus regularly shares features of detail with the comparanda (both those cited earlier and others) ranging from the first through at least the fourth centuries CE. But the features are never the same if we look at the discussion of adverbs overall. Thus, categories of adverbs are never identical. In some texts, too, the classification system is more elaborate than in others. The examples that are given by these texts seem to draw from a common pool but never quite match, and the definitions of the adverb vary. Ancient grammatical treatises of this type, like several other categories of subliterary texts such as scholia, did not form a single tradition with one line of evolution in antiquity—as the papyri have been especially effective in demonstrating (Swiggers and Wouters 1995). In a sense, there can be as many different *Technai* as there are copies executed over several centuries. Each *grammatikos*, or other interested person who copies (or has copied) a *Technê* can potentially make additions to, or subtractions from, the prior text based on personal preference or on schoolroom needs. The *Technê*-type treatise is thus the ultimate "open" text. The Michigan papyrus, in spite of its fragmentary state, helps to reinforce these lessons and at the same time offers scholars who are used primarily to the philological study of standard Greek and Roman authors a new perspective on the transmission of texts.

NOTES

1. However, some of the electronic resources discussed in the present chapter include such texts. In addition, Christian texts are treated in chapter 25.

2. Under the category of literature written in Egyptian I here do not include funerary texts.

3. The preliminary online version of the Demotistische Literaturübersicht (*Enchoria*); see the section on resources for editing and studying literary papyri and the list of selected electronic resources.

4. An important set of scholia on *Aetia*, book 1, happens to have been written on one of the British Museum rolls containing the *Athenaion Politeia* rolls; see note 5.

5. For the mystery surrounding where and how the rolls were acquired in Egypt, see Bastianini (1996) and Manfredi (1992).

6. For considerable variation from the medieval text of Plato in a papyrus of the second or third century CE, see Adorno et al. 1991, I.1 (1999), pp. 212 ff. on *P.Mich.* inv. 5980.

7. From a cultural studies perspective it is interesting to note that, since the late nineteenth century, the canonical order of presentation in a "mixed" volume of edited papyri has been biblical texts first, then Greek and Latin literary texts, and finally documents.

8. Although the original motive for its creation was principally to assemble and standardize references to the very large number of volumes containing documentary papyri, the *Checklist* includes a number of entries for volumes that contain only literary or subliterary papyri (e.g., *P.Lond.Lit.*), although it does not claim thoroughness in this respect.

9. For full references to this and other web-based tools, see the selected list of electronic resources on page xv.

10. Included are all of the items in Lowe (1934–1966).

11. The *LDAB*, therefore, excludes papyrus documents quoting lines of Homer, questions to oracles, and magical texts other than those that are probably handbooks.

12. It is interesting as a measure of the increased publication of literary papyri during the past half century that the first edition of Pack, completed in 1952, listed only 2,369 published or otherwise noticed papyri, while Mertens-Pack[3] currently lists about 7,000.

Although Mertens-Pack[3] as a whole is an online tool, since 1981 P. Mertens, the initiator of the Liège project, and collaborators have published a number of separate articles that present current information about the papyri of classical and Hellenistic authors, as well as medical writers; see the Mertens-Pack[3] webpage for full details. In spite of the reference to "Greco-Roman Egypt" in the title, Pack[2] includes the literary papyri from Dura-Europos.

13. Note that the *LDAB* groups in a single entry multiple texts contained on a single roll if they were intended as parts of one book. This is especially the case for anthologies, which in Pack and Mertens-Pack[3] are split up among entries for the different authors quoted in them. However, the *LDAB* makes two entries when a literary papyrus is reused for another literary text and also follows this practice in the case of composite codices when the different works were originally written on individual quires.

14. Lobel had already suspected the Simonidean authorship of *P.Oxy.* XXII 2327. In 1981 in *P.Turner* 3, he succinctly set forth his criteria for naming Simonides as author of this and two other *P.Oxy.* rolls containing lyric verse. See also Parsons's introduction to *P.Oxy.* LIX 3965.

15. In addition to reflecting the fact that only one form of sigma was used in ancient texts, the use of lunate sigma in *P.Oxy.* is a long-standing practice intended, in the case of fragmentary texts, to maintain an initial stance of editorial neutrality with respect to whether the letter falls in the middle of a word or at the end.

16. The *P.Oxy.* series customarily gives more detailed descriptions of damaged or uncertain letters than do many publications of literary papyri. The practice of providing extensive descriptions of ink in the critical apparatus of a literary papyrus text serves as an additional kind of editor's commentary. It also stems from the fact that many literary texts do not lend themselves to restoration by close parallels from other texts in the way that documentary texts often do, and it reflects a long-established tendency among classical studies to treat papyri containing literature with greater ceremony and awe than the more numerous and, as traditionally viewed, more mundane documentary papyri.

17. Both of these papyri fall into a larger group of second-century CE Oxyrhynchus rolls that contain lyric and elegiac poetry from various archaic and early classical poets or commentaries on them.

18. The papyrus was first presented in a conference paper, "A New Michigan Grammatical Fragment and the Study of Greek Grammar in I–IV Century Egypt," at the XXIV International Congress of Papyrology, Helsinki, August 2004.

19. Wouters (1979) discusses sixteen *Technê*-type texts on papyrus; additional papyri have been published since or are being prepared by Wouters.

BIBLIOGRAPHY

Acosta-Hughes, B., and T. Renner. 2002. "Special Review Article." Review of Bastianini and Gallazzi 2001. *BASP* 39: 165–187.

Adorno, F., A. Carlini, F. Decleva Caizzi, M. S. Funghi, D. Manetti, M. Manfredi, and F. Montanari, eds. 1989–1999. *Corpus dei papiri filosofici greci e latini: Testi e lessico nei papiri di cultura greca e latina.* Florence: Leo S. Olschki.

Anderson, R. D., P. J. Parsons, and R. G. M. Nisbet. 1979. "Elegiacs by Gallus from Qasr Ibrim." *Journal of Roman Studies* 69: 125–155.

Bastianini, G. 1996. "Un luogo di ritrovamento fantasma." In *Atti del II convegno nazionale di egittologia e papirologia di Siracusa, 1–3 dicembre 1995*, 69–84. Syracuse: Istituto Internazionale del Papiro.

———, and A. Casanova, eds. 2005. *Euripide e i papiri: Atti del convegno internazionale di studi, Firenze, 10–11 giugno 2004* (Studi e Testi di Papirologia, n.s., 7). Florence: Istituto Papirologico "G. Vitelli."

———, and C. Galazzi, eds. 2001. *Papiri dell'Università degli Studi di Milano VIII: Posidippo di Pella: Epigrammi (P. Mil. Vogl. VIII 309)*. Università degli Studi di Milano, Pubblicazioni della Facoltà di Lettere e filosofia, CC. Con la collaborazione di Colin Austin. Milan: LED—Edizioni Universitarie di Lettere Economia Diritto.

Bastianini, G., M. Haslam, H. Maehler, F. Montanari, and C. Römer. 2004–. *Commentaria et lexica graeca in papyris reperta (CLGP), adiuvante Marco Stroppa*. Munich: Saur.

Boedeker, D., and D. Sider. 1996. "Fragments 1–22: Text and Apparatus Criticus." *Arethusa* 29(2): 155–166.

———. 2001. *The New Simonides: Contexts of Praise and Desire*. New York: Oxford University Press.

Bresciani, E. 1990. *Letteratura e poesia dell'antico Egitto*, 2d ed. Turin: Einaudi.

Cameron, A. 1995. *Callimachus and His Critics*. Princeton: Princeton University Press.

Diggle, J., ed. 1998. *Tragicorum Graecorum Fragmenta Selecta*. Oxford: Oxford University Press.

Gallo, I. 1975–. *Frammenti biografici da papiri*. Rome: Edizioni dell'Ateneo.

Gronewald, M., and R. W. Daniel. 2004. "Ein neuer Sappho-Papyrus." *ZPE* 147: 1–8.

Haslam, M. W. 1978. "Apollonius Rhodius and the Papyri." *Illinois Classical Studies* 3: 47–73.

———. 1994. "The Contribution of Papyrology to the Study of Greek Literature: Archaic and Hellenistic Poetry." In *Proceedings of the 20th International Congress of Papyrologists, Copenhagen 23–29 August 1992*, ed. A. Bülow-Jacobsen, 98–105. Copenhagen: Museum Tusculanum Press.

———. 1997. "Homeric Papyri and Transmission of the Text." In *A New Companion to Homer*, ed. I. Morris and B. Powell, 55–100. Leiden: Brill.

Janko, R. 2002. "The Derveni Papyrus: An Interim Text." *ZPE* 141: 1–62.

———. 2004. "Empedocles, *On Nature* I 233–364: A New Reconstruction of *P.Strasb.gr.* Inv. 1665–6." *ZPE* 150: 1–26.

Kenyon, F. G., ed. 1891a. *Aristotle on the Constitution of Athens*. London.

———, ed. 1891b. *Classical Texts from Papyri in the British Museum*. London.

Koenen, L. 1968. "The Oracle of the Potter." *ZPE* 2: 178–209.

Lichtheim, M. 1973–1980. *Ancient Egyptian Literature: A Book of Readings*. 3 vols. Berkeley: University of California Press.

Lloyd-Jones, H., and P. J. Parsons, eds. 1983. *Supplementum Hellenisticum*. Berlin: W. de Gruyter.

Lowe, E. A. 1934–1966. *Codices Latini Antiquiores: A Palaeographical Guide to Latin Manuscripts prior to the Ninth Century*. Oxford: Clarendon.

Luppe, W. 2002. "Scholia, Hypomnemata, und Hypotheseis zu griechischen Dramen auf Papyri." In *Der Kommentar in Antike und Mittelalter*, ed. W. Geerlings and C. Schulze, 55–77. Leiden: Brill.

Manfredi, M. 1992. "*L'Athenaion Politeia* di Aristotele e i papiri." In *Proceedings of the XIX International Congress of Papyrology, Cairo 2–9 September 1989*, ed. A. H. S. El-Mosallamy, vol. 1, 447–460. Cairo: Center for Papyrological Studies.

Markus, D., and G. Schwendner. 1997. "Seneca's *Medea* in Egypt (663–704)." *ZPE* 117: 73–84.

Martin, A., and O. Primavesi, eds. 1998. *L'Empédocle de Strasbourg*. Berlin: W. de Gruyter.

Merkelbach, R., and M. West, eds. 1967. *Fragmenta Hesiodea*. Oxford: Clarendon.

——. 1974. "The Cologne Epode of Archilochus." *ZPE* 14: 97–112.

Pack, R. A. 1965. *The Greek and Latin Literary Texts from Greco-Roman Egypt*, 2d ed. (=Pack²) Ann Arbor: University of Michigan Press.

Pfeiffer, R., ed. 1949–1953. *Callimachus*. 2 vols. Oxford: Clarendon.

Powell, J. U., and E. A. Barber, eds. 1921. *New Chapters in the History of Greek Literature: Recent Discoveries in Greek Poetry and Prose of the Fourth and Following Centuries* B.C. Oxford: Clarendon.

Quack, J. F. 2005. *Einführung in die altägyptische Literaturgeschichte III: Die demotische und gräko-ägyptische Literatur*. Vol. 3, *Einführung und Quellentexte zur Ägyptologie, Band III*. Münster: LIT Verlag.

Rossum-Steenbeek, M. van. 1998. *Greek Readers' Digests? Studies on a Selection of Subliterary Papyri* (Mnemosyne, suppl. 175). Leiden: Brill.

Skafte Jensen, M. 2005. Review of G. Nagy, *Homer's Text and Language* (Champaign, Ill. 2004). *Bryn Mawr Classical Review* 2005.04.0474:47.

Stephens, S. 2003. "Fragments of Lost Novels." In *The Novel in the Ancient World*, rev. ed., ed. G. Schmeling, 656–683. Leiden: Brill.

——, and J. Winkler, eds. 1995. *Ancient Greek Novels: The Fragments: Introduction, Text, Translation, and Commentary*. Princeton: Princeton University Press.

Swiggers, P., and A. Wouters. 1995. "*Techne* et *empeiria*: La dynamique de la grammaire grecque dans l'antiquité à la lumière des papyrus grammaticaux." *LALIES* 15: 83–100.

Turner, E. G. 1968. *Greek Papyri: An Introduction*. Oxford: Clarendon.

West, M. L. 1977. "Erinna." *ZPE* 25: 95–119.

——, ed. 1992. *Iambi et Elegi Graeci ante Alexandrum cantati*, 2d ed. Oxford: Oxford University Press.

Wouters, A. 1979. *The Grammatical Papyri from Graeco-Roman Egypt: Contributions to the Study of the "Ars Grammatica" in Antiquity*. Verhandelingen van de Koninklijke Academie voor Wetenschappen, Letteren, en Schone Kunsten van Belgie, Jaargang XLI, 92. Brussels: Academie voor Wetenschappen, Letteren, en Schone Kunsten van Belgie.

Zetzel, J. 1987. "Fragmentary Pleasures." *Classical Philology* 82: 347–362.

CHAPTER 13

....

THE SPECIAL CASE
OF HERCULANEUM

....

DAVID SIDER

PAPYROLOGISTS have many archives but only one Greek library; that is, only one findspot of literary texts that gives the appearance of having been assembled by one person, or at any rate by a like-minded group of people with the same literary (in this case, more specifically philosophical) interest. This library is the collection of rolls found in a richly endowed villa that had once been on the shore of the bay of Naples in Herculaneum, located between Naples itself and Pompeii.[1] The quantity and literary value of this one library alone would make it special; its particular history and the difficulty of reading its papyrus rolls make Herculaneum even more of a special case. For all that the architecture and sculpture of this villa are of extraordinary quality, it is noteworthy that this building is today known, indeed named, for its aesthetically far less appealing papyri: the Villa dei Papiri, this name having ousted the earlier designation, Villa dei Pisoni, even though most people are willing to accept the conclusion that the villa was built by L. Calpurnius Piso Caesoninus in the first century BCE and owned by his descendants until the eruption of Vesuvius in 79 CE.[2] As we shall see, almost without exception these books contain works of either Epicurus and his school or of Stoics, whom the Epicureans saw as rivals.

The modern recovery of Herculaneum began in 1709, when workers digging a well in the Italian town of Resina struck a theater many feet below the surface, containing statues and inscriptions, several of which presented honors to individuals by "the citizens of Herculaneum," *Herculanenses,* which immediately identified this buried and long-forgotten town. Archaeology may not have yet existed, but the robbing of ancient sites was well established. In this case, Prince d'Elboeuf of Austria, the ruling power at this time, took over from the well diggers in his eagerness to discover more statues with which to furnish his new villa in the nearby town of Portici (between Herculaneum and Naples); he thus became the first modern excavator of Herculaneum, but one more in line with miners interested in extracting only gems or ore and with no concern for their surrounding matrix. In d'Elboeuf's case, the gems were the statues; the matrix the buildings, which became riddled with tunnels until digging ceased when d'Elboeuf returned to Austria in 1716.

Although in the course of later excavations earlier tunnels were discovered, some of them perhaps dating to antiquity, it was this early eighteenth-century unearthing of treasures that brought knowledge of Herculaneum to the awareness of modern Europe. We can pass over the details of the fits and starts of further excavation (for which see Parslow [1995]; the story is vividly told for a popular audience by Deiss [1985]). The important facts are that the excavations came under the control of the Spanish, who expelled the Austrians in 1734 and whose king, Charles III, ordered the tunnels reopened in 1738, looking to the ancient town as a source of decoration for his own palace, located not far from that of d'Elboeuf in Portici. Charles asked Roque Joaquín de Alcubierre, an engineer in the Spanish army but no better trained than his immediate predecessors in archaeological fieldwork, to restart excavations. Since Charles was not interested in the many wall paintings, Alcubierre too felt free to break through walls in his quest for more portable treasures. He was famously described by Winckelmann as "this man, who (to use the Italian proverb) knew as much of antiquities as the moon does of lobsters, has been, through his want of capacity, the occasion of many antiquities being lost" (Winckelmann 1771, 22).

There was, however, a four-year suspension from 1741 to 1745 because Alcubierre and others were feeling ill from the air they were breathing under ground. This ailment was attributed to "mephitic" gases, a now archaic word derived from the Latin *mephitis*, "a noxious or pestilential emanation, esp. from the earth" (*Shorter Oxford English Dictionary*). This mephitis in fact led to the premature closing of the excavation tunnels in Herculaneum and the suspension later in the eighteenth century of further work under ground until well into the twentieth century. Where, however, the town has been opened to the air, there is no threat to archaeologists or tourists. Open-air excavations were carried on from 1828 to 1835 over most of Herculaneum, but sites still under ground, like the villa and the theater, remain a threat. (Only the small part of the villa that is exposed to the air is safe.) Although it was the malodorous gases, especially hydrogen sulfide, that drove people out, the air of underground Herculaneum also (still) contains odorless radon gas, a by-product of radium disintegration.[3]

In 1750 Alcubierre was transferred to Naples but not before supervising the initial exploration of what was to be the largest villa found in Herculaneum. Since it was set farther along the seashore from the main body of the town, it was found not by the extension of the tunnel system but rather by the drilling of yet another well, which indeed found water about 100 feet below the surface (water that is still seen today alongside the now partially excavated Villa dei Papiri)—and also a domestic dwelling. Two months later, in July of 1750, Alcubierre put the highly competent Karl Weber, a Swiss engineer, in charge of supervising the excavations. Tunnels were directed into the villa, and a second shaft was dug to allow for quicker entry and exit for the workers, as well as to facilitate the circulation of air and the removal of objects, most notably the bronze statues of family members, philosophers, dancers, and mythological characters that now grace the National Museum in Naples, where one may also see Weber's large architectural rendering of the villa, although not all of it had (or indeed has yet) been excavated.

THE DISCOVERY OF THE LIBRARY

Weber complained that working conditions were "dangerous and abhorrent, if not despicable";[4] nonetheless, statues, wall paintings, and floor mosaics could be recognized immediately for what they were. It is understandable that, working in the poor light and air in the narrow tunnels, the excavators did not immediately recognize that some of the blackened objects found in wooden cases and even underfoot were papyrus rolls. Thus, in the letter sent to King Charles in May just quoted, Weber tallied up the valuable objects found in the villa with reference to mosaic floors, marble and bronze statues, marble vases, bronze candelabras, and wall paintings; there was not a word about books. Yet just a few months later, Camillo Paderni—at this point only a royal draftsman hired to make sketches of wall paintings and other objects in preparation for the engravings that Bayardi was to publish in 1752[5]—reported for the first time the presence of books in the villa (although at the time Paderni was unaware that the many rooms under excavation in this part of Herculaneum were part of but one large structure) in a letter written to an English acquaintance dated November 18. This letter was later translated and published in the (London) *Philosophical Transactions*.[6] It reads in part (with original italics and archaic spelling):

> It is not a month ago,[7] that there have been found many volumes of *papyrus*, but turn'd to a sort of charcoal, so brittle, that, being touched, it falls readily into ashes. Nevertheless, by his Majesty's orders, I have made many trials to open them, butt all to no purpose; excepting some *words*, which I have picked out intire, where there are divers *bits*, by which it appears in what manner the whole was written. The form of the characters, made with a very black tincture,[8] that overcomes the darkness of the charcoal, I shall here, to oblige you, imitate two short lines; my fidelity to the king not permitting me to send you any more.

N . ALTERIUS . DVLC
DEM . CVRIS . CRVDE[9]

This is the size and shape of the characters. In this bit there are eight lines. There are other bits with many other words, which are all preserved in order for their publication.

"There have been found." This phrase conceals what Paderni reports in a later letter (of April 10, 1755) that at first the rolls were not recognized for what they were: "In a chamber[10] . . . there has been found a great quantity of rolls, about half a palm long, and round; which appeared like roots of wood, all black and seeming to be only of one piece. One of them falling on the ground, it broke in the middle, and many letters were observed, by which it was first known, that the rolls were of papyrus." Similar is the later report of John Hayter to his sponsor, the Prince of Wales (later King George IV):

> The manuscripts . . . which the Director [Paderni] and the equally ignorant, but clearly guiltless, labourers, mistook for pieces of charcoal, or burned timber, and which, in consequence, were removed, and applied by them, to the usual domestick purposes. In the course of their removal, however, some detached fragments happily fell from one, or two of these devoted volumes, and displayed upon their surfaces very distinguishable characters.[11]

That is, the dropped roll broke into (at least) two pieces, so that its interior columns, more protected from the heat than the surface, were visible.

The workers who broke open the roll showed their discovery to Alcubierre, but since Alcubierre's knowledge of Greek was no better than theirs, he took the rolls in turn to a local scholar, Canon Alessio Simmacho Mazzochi, who quickly took charge to the extent that he, along with Paderni, called for the careful and immediate removal of all the rolls to the royal museum at Portici. Numbers were assigned, but the total reached, about 1,800, includes all the "pieces" found, many of which were merely portions of rolls, so that often one original roll was (and still is) represented by several *P.Herc.* numbers. Thus, Philodemus's *On Poems*, book 1, has recently been edited from seven separate inventory items: *P.Herc.* 444, 460, 466, 1013, 1073, 1074, and 1081.[12] The villa has yielded 800–1,100 rolls, some of which are but parts ("books") of works too long for one roll. *On Poems,* for example, was in five books.

UNROLLING THE BOOKS

As Paderni noted in his letter of November 1752, the rolls now stored in Portici were dried and made brittle by the pyroclastic flow that filled the villa; their outer layers were usually blackened as well. Attempts to unroll them were unsuccessful, although their potential as a source of new classical texts was clear. Paderni, seeking royal support, as well as personal glory, and too impatient to wait until (as was soon to happen) a safe method of unrolling was devised, went before the king and queen with rolls and a broad-bladed knife and, "having opened one of the rolls (that is, he cut it with a knife) in their presence, made them conceive the value of the hidden treasure he had uncovered."[13] Paderni thus illustrated his initial plan for getting to the legible parts of the text; that is, he sliced many rolls vertically into two parts, a process that crushed into dust all the letters along and on either side of the cut. Unfortunately, many rolls were cut before inventory numbers were assigned, with the result that two halves of the same roll were given quite different numbers, and the close relationship of the two halves was forgotten or lost in the archives.

Any sheets (called husk or bark, *scorza*) that had escaped blackening could be peeled from the interior (the marrow, *midollo;* the process is called *scorzatura*), although not always easily, as moisture over the years would sometimes cause one layer to cling to the next.[14] Moreover, the act of peeling would often destroy the sheet. At this early stage, then, it was seen that draftsmen would be needed to copy the exposed text before it was removed from the half roll. The drawings *(disegni)* made by these draftsmen, all of whom were ignorant of Greek, thus became the only record of the text whenever the original was lost.[15]

Various other ways of opening the rolls were attempted. Raimondo di Sangro experimented with mercury, hoping that this heavy liquid would insinuate itself between the layers of a roll placed vertically in a box and force them apart. Instead, the large drops simply pulverized the constraining material. Undeterred, di Sangro completely immersed some rolls in mercury, with equal lack of success. Next, rosewater (for unfathomable reasons) was applied, but this proved to be almost as disastrous as the mercury treatment. More rolls were destroyed. The next experiment was to try to separate the layers with gas, which may have seemed like a reasonable course, but one wonders why the chemist in charge, Gaetano la Pira, chose a gas so smelly (hydrogen sulfide?) that it drove people from the royal palace, which would perhaps have been forgiven had it not atomized the papyri as efficiently as had the mercury treatment.

Yet another experiment took place: M. Mazzochi put a roll in a bell jar so that the sun would shine on it, in the hope that, as the heat evaporated the moisture in the roll, the layers would separate. There was, it seems, some separation, but the steamy atmosphere also caused the ink to run, rendering the letters so altered that the text was now taken (no doubt with some sense of excitement) to be Oscan.[16] Similar attempts with gas and steam were again attempted when twenty rolls were brought to England in 1802 and 1816 (to join the *disegni* that Hayter brought back). The English experimenters, among whom was the famous chemist Humphry Davy, essentially did little more than repeat the work done in Italy.[17]

It is extremely fortunate that King Charles at this point, in 1793, invited Father Antonio Piaggio to help with the unrolling. Piaggio, then employed by the Vatican library, was well known for his careful work in the transcribing of illegible texts.[18] It was natural that the skilled and scholarly Piaggio was repelled by the careless and destructive activities of Paderni and that this soon developed into a dislike of the man himself.[19]

Piaggio soon devised a more cautious and effective way of unrolling. Although the outer parts of many rolls were too friable ever to survive separation, somewhere in its interior the more flexible *midollo* seemed more promising. Piaggio realized that a small but constant pressure could safely separate the top layer from the one below. To apply this pressure he devised the first of his famous machines: The exposed edge of a *midollo* was attached to a thin animal membrane (bladder or gut) known as gold-beater's skin (since this membrane, when holding a thin layer of gold leaf, was pressed or beaten over a substance designed to receive a gold surface pattern), which in turn was attached to long ribbons or strings to be tied to a bar set over the roll, which was allowed to hang down. The papyrus, whose weight provided the main separative force, was attached to a roller that could be turned with a screw. As the roll opened to a width of several columns, pieces would be carefully cut off. This process was repeated until the *midollo* was opened to the subscriptio, at which point the work's identity would finally be revealed.[20] Such a slow process produced an obvious need to construct several of Piaggio's machines so that a number of rolls could be unrolled at the same time. The revealed columns were sent to the *disegnatori*.

Once again we have a vivid contemporary description of the process:

> It is incredible to imagine what this man [Piaggio] contrived and executed. He made a machine, with which (by the means of certain threads, which being gummed, stuck to the back part of the papyrus, where there was no writing), he begins, by degrees, to pull, while with a sort of ingraver's instrument he loosens one leaf from the other (which is the most difficult part of all), and then makes a sort of lining to the back of the papyrus, with exceeding thin leaves of onion [before he changed to animal membranes] (if I mistake not), and with some spirituous liquor, with which he wets the papyrus, by little and little he unfolds it. All this labor cannot be well compre-hended without seeing. With a patience superior to what a man can imagine, this good father has unrolled a pretty large piece of papyrus, the worst preserved, by way of trial. . . . Father Antonio, after he has loosened a piece, takes it off where there are no letters; and places it between two crystals for the better observation; and then, having an admirable talent in imitating characters, he copies it with all the lacunae, which are very numerous in this scorched papyrus. . . . The worst is, the work takes up so much time, that a small quantity of writing requires five or six days to unroll, so that a whole year is already consumed about half this roll.[21]

EARLY ATTEMPTS AT READING, EDITING, AND PUBLISHING

Success at last: The promise of an ancient library was to be revealed, a collection of manuscripts of an age "which outruns the date of any other Manuscripts upon earth" (Hayter 1811, 5). There was, however, a certain sense of disappointment when it soon became clear that the bulk of the books seemed to be not the hoped-for lost works of the famous poets and historians but the rather dry disquisitions written by Philodemus, known previously almost exclusively from his elegant epigrams preserved in the manuscripts of the *Greek Anthology*. The first four titles to be identified by their *subscriptiones* were Philodemus's *De Musica* IV, *Rhetorica* II, *Rhetorica* I, and *On Vices and Their Corresponding Virtues*. Winckelmann was only the first of many to express his disappointment in print and to put forward his own wish list of what he would have preferred to see recovered from the ashes. Who, he asked, needs another treatise on rhetoric and ethics when we already have Aristotle? Would it not be better to find lost historical works of Diodorus Siculus and Theopompus and some plays of Sophocles, Euripides, and Menander (reasonable enough choices), to say nothing of the lost "rules of symmetry composed by Pamphylius for the use of painters"?[22] This last odd choice reflects the personal desire of an art historian, as wish lists tend to do. The lyric poet William Wordsworth, for example, wanted more Pindar and Simonides. Note that almost all the names listed here (though not Pamphilus) have in fact been augmented by papyrological discoveries, although more from the sands of Egypt than from Herculaneum, where, however, Philodemus's quotations of classical authors occasionally provide new fragments or better readings of previously known lines (cf. Delattre 1996).

Although I have more to say about attempts to open and read the rolls from the late eighteenth century to the present, it is at this former point that publication of the papyri begins. Appropriately enough, the first roll to be opened was the first to be printed—in 1793: Philodemus's *De Musica* IV (=*P.Herc.* 1497), edited by Carlo Maria Rosini, the bishop of Pozzuoli, who provided a learned introduction to Philodemus. This treatise appeared in the first series of *Herculanensium Voluminum quae supersunt* (VH).[23] Each column was shown in a full-page engraving made from its *disegno*, facing a two-column page that comprised both a printed version of the Greek text (with the lavish touch of having restored letters printed in red to set them off from the more fully preserved letters) and a Latin translation. Dotted lines indicated lost lines of text. To meet the call for more rapid publication (a request made by, among others, Carolina Bonaparte, the wife of the then king of Naples), a second series began in 1862 (*VH²*). This *Collectio Altera* also consisted of eleven volumes and included the texts of sixteen rolls. Without the intensive editorial work done on the text of the first series, it contained little more than reproductions of the *disegni*. Publication ceased in 1876.[24]

After Piaggio died in 1796, work on the papyri slowed down and then had to cease completely during the political turmoil of these years. King Ferdinand IV of Naples (and III of Sicily) and his wife, Maria Carolina (daughter of Empress Maria Theresa of Austria), had done much to make Naples powerful and cultured, but, in opposing the overthrow of the monarchy in France, they sadly underestimated Napoleon's power and ambition. Although at peace with France since 1796, they hoped to take advantage of Napoleon's expedition in Egypt. Encouraged by his wife and with the help of Lord Nelson, Ferdinand invaded Rome but could not hold it for long.[25] Nor could they remain in Naples any longer. In 1798 work on the papyri was suspended completely when Ferdinand and Maria Carolina, as well as their entire court, fled to Palermo in Sicily in order to escape Napoleon's invading forces. Ferdinand and the queen left on one of Nelson's ships, taking with them all the papyri, which had been packed in sawdust.

Southy (1873, 213–214) describes the scene imaginatively:

> Lady Hamilton, like a heroine of modern romance, explored, with no little danger, a subterraneous passage, leading from the palace to the seaside: through this passage the royal treasures, the choicest pieces of painting and sculpture, and other property [including the papyri, too unglamorous to name here] ... were conveyed to the shore, and stowed safely on board the English ships. On the night of the 21st, at half-past eight, Nelson landed, brought out the whole royal family... and carried them safely, through a tremendous sea, to [his ship] the Vanguard.

The French arrived the next year, when they helped the republican class of Naples establish the short-lived Repubblica Partenopea, in memory of the land's early Greek name of Parthenope. The republicans, however, were unable to make a success of their new government. Ferdinand soon regained power and, having already sent the papyri (still cushioned by sawdust in their original packing crates) in 1802, was able to recall his court to Naples. In 1806 the court again fled to Palermo ahead of Napoleon's invading army. This time, though, the papyri stayed put, now housed in the Royal Museum in Portici.

As one can see, interest in the newly discovered papyri was such that accounts of them were published with some frequency in the London press,[26] and the famous art historian Winckelmann incorporated an extensive account of the papyri in his open letter of 1771. More scholarly interest is demonstrated by the works of Schütz (1795) and von Murr (1806), only the first of a long line of German scholars, who dominated Herculaneum studies well into the twentieth century.[27] For example, for decades the Bibliotheca Teubneriana published the only or the most thorough edition of *Rhetoric, De Ira, De Musica 4, On Vices 10, De Oeconomia, De Rege Bono secundum Homerum,* and *De Libertate Dicendi.* Similarly C. Jensen's edition of Philodemus's *On Poems* 5 (1923) and H. Diels's of Philodemus's *On Gods* 1 and 3 (1916, 1917) offered texts that influenced much later scholarship on these subjects.

After a period in which little was done on the papyri themselves, Marcello Gigante almost single-handedly revived interest in these texts when he actively invited scholars from every country to edit and reedit the papyri in the Officina dei Papiri, housed in the National Library in Naples, and began the still ongoing series La Scuola di Epicuro (1978–). Furthermore, the new journal he and others edited, *Cronache Ercolanesi* (see *CErc* in the bibliography), published many texts too small for book format, most notably fragments of Epicurus's own *On Nature.*

THE CONTENTS OF THE LIBRARY

As mentioned, the bulk of the discoveries proved to be Epicurean texts, and of these in turn the majority belong to Philodemus. With the most minor of exceptions, all the texts were previously lost; indeed, apart from Epicurus's *On Nature,* even their existence was unknown. With regard to Philodemus, only his epigrams were extant, and Cicero told of his acquaintance with Lucius Calpurnius Piso Caesoninus, consul in 58 BCE and the father-in-law of Julius Caesar. The only title ascribed to him in the scanty testimony is his *Syntaxis of Philosophers,* some parts of which have been found in the villa. A bare but comprehensive list of the Epicurean material includes the following, all, however exiguous, identified by *subscriptiones:*[28] Epicurus, *On Nature;*[29] Metrodorus, *On Wealth;* Carneiscus, *Philistas;* Colotes, *Against Plato's Euthydemus, Against Plato's Lysis;* Polystratus, *On Irrational Contempt [for Popular Opinion], On Philosophy;* Demetrius the Laconian, *On Geometry, On Poems, On Some of Epicurus' Opinions, On Some Investigations into Daily Living, Against the Problems of Polyaenus;* Philodemus, *On Lives(?) and Morals, On Epicurus, On Piety, On Death, On Gods, On Vices, On Flattery, On Music, On Conversation, On Anger, On Frankness of Speech, On Wealth, On Poems, On Rhetoric, On Signs, On the Good King according to Homer, Pragmateiai, On the Stoics, On Gratitude, Syntaxis of Philosophers.*

Some few Stoic works have also been found, as might be expected of a library that was formed by an Epicurean writer, who would want to be well informed of his philosophical rivals; indeed one wonders why more Stoic texts have not been found. Known so far are Chrysippus, *Logical Investigations, On Providence;* and Zeno, *Craterus.*[30]

A few Latin works have also been found. In addition to the epic verses on (at least in the preserved columns) the battle of Actium (see note 9), scraps of Lucretius and Ennius have recently been published, as well as *Money Lender* by the comic poet Caecilius Statius.

It is not easy within the limits of this chapter to assess the contribution this library has made to current knowledge of Hellenistic philosophy.[31] Surely, though, one of its principal contributions has been in the area of ancient literary theory, which in the past had to jump from Aristotle's *Poetics* and *Rhetoric* to Horace's *Ars Poetica.* With the eventual publication of several books of Philodemus's *On Poems* (largely with that of book 5 by Jensen [1923]), Philodemus's regular practice of rehearsing his opponents' theories before criticizing them laid bare an entirely new world of literary theories, much of which had been silently absorbed by Latin authors, such as Horace in his literary epistles.[32]

The relatively small number of Latin texts raises the question of the nature of the original collection. Was it primarily the working library of an Epicurean philosopher, most likely Philodemus himself, as suggested by the number of duplicated rolls?[33] Philodemus, however, died well over a century before the eruption of Mount Vesuvius, and this library was located in the largest villa in Herculaneum, which surely belonged to a Roman who would have had some favorite Latin readings handy, to say nothing of necessary household archives. More Latin papyri may yet be found among the still unopened rolls, but the laws of probability predict that the breakdown of these will reflect that of those already opened.

Two possibilities suggest themselves: first, that along with other portable goods the favorite books of the owner of the villa in 79 CE were removed before the pyroclastic flow arrived; second, that the so-called Latin library remains unexcavated in the villa. Supporting the first possibility is that the signs of hasty removal of objects includes even the books, some of which were found not in the rooms and shelves where others were found but in the nearby hallways. The owner or his major domo might well have engaged in a form of triage in which the books considered most valuable (the texts wished for by those people disappointed by Philodemus) were saved. The historical irony is that had they not been "saved," that is, taken away from Vesuvius, they would in fact have been saved by the tufa that has preserved the unique copies of the philosophy library.

Supporting the second possibility is that all the papyri were found quite close to a corner of the house that was never excavated. That is, Weber's famous plan shows an empty area along the upper right-hand corner of an atrium, where the books were found. Atria, however, are surrounded by rooms and thus cannot form the outer edge of the villa, as a careless glance at the plan might indicate. Moreover, recent excavations have revealed two previously unknown stories below the level on which the statuary and papyri were found. Here too there is the possibility of a Latin library, which Romans tended to keep separate from their Greek volumes. In this chapter it is appropriate to do no more than mention the current debate between those who favor further excavations (largely papyrologists) and those who argue for maintaining the current state of excavations, which are deteriorating from exposure to sunlight, air, and pollution. Indeed, one well-known archaeologist has been quoted as saying, "I am almost indifferent on the subject of the papyri." The battle will play itself out in the coming years.

Any future papyrus finds would also help define the nature of the villa's library. At the present, too many possibilities present themselves. The technical nature of these treatises, including annotated and duplicate copies, strongly suggests the working library of an Epicurean philosopher. The preponderance of works written by Philodemus further suggests that it was Philodemus's own library. How such a working library made its way from Philodemus's modest dwelling (as he himself describes it in an epigram) to the grandest building in Herculaneum is most easily answered if we accept the view that the villa was owned by a descendant of the Piso who has several secure links with Philodemus.[34] That is, leaving out the necessary provisos, Philodemus dies before Piso, who receives Philodemus's library into his villa (already decorated with busts of Epicurus and other philosophers, to say nothing of the famous jumping *porcellino* (famous enough to maintain this name, even though *porcellina* would be more accurate) with its inescapable Epicurean coloring. Piso's heirs add nothing to this philosophical library, which suggests that their interest did not match that of Piso Caesoninus.[35] They would, either out of piety or simple neglect, have held on to the collection during the several generations between Piso's death, ca. 40 BCE, and the eruption of Vesuvius in 79 CE.

The collection of Greek philosophical texts thus forms a well-defined library that was quite likely gathered by Philodemus. The palaeographical investigations of Guglielmo Cavallo (1983) have shown that it comprises rolls written as early as the late second century BCE (ibid., 51), which form Cavallo's "gruppo A," seven rolls (in nine *P.Herc.* numbers), each containing one or another book of Epicurus's *On Nature* (ibid., 28–29). If, as we have been imagining is the most likely case, they belonged to Philodemus, he would have obtained them in Athens during his study there and carried them along with him on his travels (which may have included Rhodes, Alexandria, and Himera) before arriving in Herculaneum. All in all Cavallo identifies seventeen groups (A–R [no J]), plus a number of "scritture varie," which do not fit easily into any of the groups. They are distinguished on palaeographical grounds and arranged in assumed chronological order. Cavallo further identifies thirty-four different scribes (Anonimi I–XXXIV). Since all the hands are professional, none can be the once-sought-for "mano di Filodemo." The last groups show the influence of Latin writing, not surprising in a society where Latin was the predominant language. Even group R, however, seems to date to the end of the first century BCE and the beginning of the next century, which is consistent with the picture painted earlier, that the philosophical library was essentially formed over the working life of Philodemus, whose death, on the basis of circumstantial evidence alone, is regularly placed in the neighborhood of 40 BCE, at about age seventy, although he may well have lived for another decade. Someone would have added a few works by other Epicureans (there are no works by Philodemus in group R), but essentially the collection was closed at the beginning of the millennium.

At present, no new rolls are subjected to any technique of unrolling, whether by machine, mercury, gas, or steam. Progress, however, is still being made on already opened texts, even those that have already been published. In part these advances are due to research in the archives that leads to the recognition that disparately numbered pieces were once part of the same roll, and in part, binocular microscopes have enabled us to make better readings. Far more impressive than the latter, however, are the readings made possible in recent years by the use of multispectral imaging (MSI), which can distinguish black letters from their almost equally black background when the sheets are photographed through filters in the infrared range. Thus, some sheets that are completely black to the eye in ordinary light, even through a microscope, can now be read as easily as uncharred papyri. (MSI has also proved of value in reading the charred Derveni and Petra papyri.)

The future holds even greater promise. Computer-assisted tomography, developed to view the interior details of living bodies, will be able virtually to unwind a roll by distinguishing each layer from its *sovro-* and *sottoposti,* with none of the physical loss inherent in almost all earlier unrolling and *scorzature.* However slowly this high-tech version of a Piaggio machine proceeds, we now expect that all eight hundred or so unopened rolls will be revealing their secrets. What texts can we expect? A well-known scholar in this field is anecdotally reported regularly to have asked the nonresponsive Epicurean gods for "non piu di Filodemo." His spirit is likely to be disappointed.

NOTES

1. These texts will be our exclusive concern. A documentary archive was found elsewhere in Herculaneum; cf. Camodeca and Del Mastro (2002). Other writing was preserved on wax tablets and in the form of graffiti; for the former see Capasso (1995), and for the latter see Gigante (1979b).

2. For the sculpture of the villa see Mattusch (2005); for its architecture see Wojcik (1986). A still useful volume on all aspects of the Villa, including the papyri is Comparetti and De Petra (1972). Note also McIlwaine (1988, 1990). The journal *Cronache Ercolanesi,* although devoted primarily to the subject of the papyri, remains a source of information about the site of ancient Herculaneum in general. The question of ownership of the villa need not be discussed here; cf. Capasso (1991, 43–64).

3. I am grateful to Valerio Papaccio, the architect at Pompeii and Herculaneum, for information on this matter. The Romans prayed to the personified *Mephitis* to avert pestilential exhalations of all sorts. The name Mephistopheles, invented for sixteenth-century tellings of the Faust legend, doubtless owes its origin to this Latin word.

4. Letter of May 22, 1752, Archivio di Stato, Napoli. Fondo Casa Reale Antica 1539, Inc., 44, translated by C. Parslow (1995, 91).

5. Later Paderni was to become the king's curator of antiquities and then, more formally, director of the Museum Herculanense, part of the royal palace in Portici, where the papyri and other antiquities were displayed. A number of these wall paintings are of interest here because they portray papyrus rolls (some of them with nonsense letters), inkwells, pens, *capsae,* and *sillyboi,* as well as people reading from papyrus rolls. For Paderni, see Comparetti and De Petra (1972, 238–250) and Mansi (1997). Today almost all the papyri, along with those *disegni* (see below) not taken to Oxford, are housed in the Officina dei Papiri as part of the Biblioteca Nazionale, located in the Palazzo Reale di Napoli. Napoleon took a few papyri to Paris (*P.Herc.Paris;* they have since been returned to Naples), others went to Oxford, and one piece is in Copenhagen *(P.Herc.Haun.).* Images of those Oxford papyri that were not destroyed by Sickler's attempt at unrolling (discussed later) are available online; see the introduction to the bibliography. Naples, therefore, has always been the chief place of study for these papyri, although modern imaging techniques now allow much valuable work to be done at a distance.

6. *Philosophical Transactions* 48(1) (1754) and subsequently reprinted in Comparetti and De Petra (1972, 238).

7. That is, October 19, 1752, for which date the contemporary excavation report reads: "mi fu consegnato n. 4 volumi di papiri, il tutto trovato al pozzo di Ceci"; cf. Comparetti and De Petra (1972, 155).

8. On the composition of the ink cf. Störmer (1990).

9. Interestingly, although the vast majority of the rolls found in the villa contain Greek texts, Paderni chose to quote from one of the few Latin papyri. Although this particular fragment has been lost, it can reasonably be identified as coming from the Latin epic poem that describes, at least in the extant remains, the battle of Actium, *P.Herc.* 817, first published in the second series of *Herculanensium Voluminum quae supersunt* (1809). If this is true, the dots here printed on the line represent the raised interpuncts of this papyrus. Cf. Garuti (1958, xv, 69). None of the various attempts to assign an author to this poem has won wide acceptance.

10. The findspots are discussed later.

11. Hayter (1811, 30). A modern papyrologist would find this early description of Greek papyri fascinating reading. Apart from its firsthand account of the ambitions and easily bruised egos (including Hayter's own) of the men charged with opening the papyri, there is also the attraction of reading of "chasms" in the papyri, which Hayter himself later experimentally calls "lacunae" (Hayter in fact puts quotation marks around the word). While Hayter consistently refers to the texts as "manuscripts," he does take note of the word the Italians used: "papiro."

12. See Janko (2000, 86–114, fig. 2). Similarly, note Obbink's account of the several of the inventoried pieces that he used to edit Philodemus's *On Piety* (Obbink 1996, 37–53), which also describes Obbink's discovery (made independently by Daniel Delattre while working on Philodemus's *De Musica*) that, since the layers had been numbered as they were removed (and drawn) from the inside of the roll outward, they were, after this procedure had been forgotten, thereafter *read* in this order, even though the layers closest to the middle are those at the conclusion of the text on any particular roll. The rereading of the papyri according to the original order has come to be known as the Obbink-Delattre method. The situation is made even worse when, as often happened, the papyrus roll had been cut down the middle by Paderni, so that the reconstruction of the text calls for alternating between two or more *P.Herc.* numbers.

13. Part of Piaggio's memoir, written between 1769 and 1771: Società Napoletana di Storia Patria Ms. 31-C-21. Cf. Parslow (1995, 103–106).

14. Modern scholarship in whatever language has maintained many of these now-technical terms such as *scorza* and *midollo;* others are given as appropriate.

15. Those that remain in Naples are designated N; those that (see later discussion) were removed to Oxford are designated O. Thus, N and O are treated in apparatus critici as primary witnesses. Furthermore, a new critical sign, a sublinear asterisk (ǫ), was introduced into edited Herculaneum texts to indicate those letters the editor believed had been misread by the *disegnatore*. Thus, for example, Obbink (1996, 184) on *De Pietate* 1133 prints τῶι where N has τῶν.

16. Winckelmann (1771, 111); Capasso (1986, 135–137).

17. See Drummond and Walpole (1810). Unfortunately many of these did not survive the "development" attempted by Friedrich Sickler, whose initial communications with the Englishman Thomas Tyrwhitt on the terms on which he would work are available in Sickler and Tyrwhitt (1817); see Comparetti and De Petra (1972, 80–81) for a somewhat horrified account of Sickler's "Dummheit."

18. On Piaggio, see Longo Auricchio and Capasso (1980).

19. His manuscript account of Paderni's activity is well described and quoted by Parslow (1995, 103–106).

20. *Subscriptiones* often contain column and/or line totals and occasionally *kollemata* counts as well.

21. Anonymous in Comparetti and De Petra (1972, 245–246), reprinted from the London *Philosophical Transactions* (1795), which credits the account to "a learned Gentleman of Naples." An even earlier and more detailed account of Piaggio's machine is too long to quote here: Winckelmann (1771, 112–114). Angeli (1994) describes all these early attempts at unrolling, as well as later ones.

22. Winckelmann (1771, 116–117). For writings on art by the fourth-century BCE Pamphilus, cf. *Suda* s.v. Πάμφιλος Ἀμφιπολίτης.

23. On Rosini, see Cerasuolo, Capasso, and D'Ambrosio (1986). Publication of this series reached volume eleven in 1855. (Volume seven was never published; volume five appeared in two parts).

24. *VH³, Collectio Tertia*, consisted of only one volume and was published in 1914, shortly before World War I.

25. Lord Nelson was actively engaged in warfare with Napoleon's forces throughout this entire period, much of the time in the Mediterranean, where he often gave support to the kingdom of Naples, indeed sometimes to an extent greater than that desired by the English crown, led as he was by his infatuation for Queen Maria Carolina (and for Emma Hamilton, who may have been encouraged in this affair by the queen).

26. Most notably in the *Gentleman's Magazine*, which between 1804 and 1820 published thirteen accounts of the new discoveries.

27. Note, among other things, the many *kleine Schriften* of Theodor Gomperz dedicated to these texts, only some of which were collected in Dorandi (1993). For a survey of more recent German scholarship, see Gigante (1988), supplemented by Gigante (2001).

28. For the *P.Herc.* numbers of each title, physical description, Greek titles, book numbers, and column and line numbers, see Gigante (1979a, 44–55), which also contains a complete bibliography of each, the last of which is supplemented by Capasso (1989) and Del Mastro (2000); see also Dorandi (2001). The following list does not include a number of substantially preserved works whose titles scholars have only (however reasonably) guessed at, such as *P.Herc.* 831, Demetrius *Peri Meteorismou*, or whose usual title in scholarly literature derives from the content rather than from the *subscriptio*, such as *P.Herc.* 1424, Philodemus *Oeconomicus*, where in fact the subscriptio has *On Vices and Their Corresponding Virtues*. Nor does this list correlate the various other titles that seem to belong to this last complex rubric, which in addition to *Oeconomicus* also comprises *Flattery, [Arrogance]*,and *[Greed]*.

29. Books 11, 14, 15, 25, 28, 34, and an unknown book (on time); on this work see Arrighetti (1971) and Sedley (1973, 1974).

30. In this general context one has to distinguish between Zeno of Citium (Philodemus's Epicurean teacher) and the Stoic Zeno of Sidon.

31. A brief overview appears in Gigante (1995, 15–48).

32. Jensen (1923) has been superseded by Mangoni (1993). Reconstructing the views of some of Philodemus's opponents are the articles by Asmis (1990, 1992a, 1992b). On Crates, see Broggiato (2001).

33. For example, Gaiser (1988) and Dorandi (1991) are each editions of *P.Herc.* 1021 and 164, parts of Philodemus's *Syntaxis of Philosophers,* which overlap somewhat where Plato's Academy is treated.

34. The links between Philodemus and Piso Caesoninus are (1) Cicero's blaming Piso's moral failings in large part on his weakness for the hedonism of Epicureanism, which he learned from Philodemus (*In Pis.* 68–72); (2) Philodemus's dedicating his *On the Good King according to Homer* to Piso; and (3) Philodemus's addressing Piso directly in one of his epigrams, in which he invites him to take part in an Epicurean celebration. See Sider (1997, 5–8). Nonetheless, despite what might have been expected, there is no literary, papyrological, or epigraphical evidence that associates any Piso with the town of Herculaneum.

35. This is not to suggest that they were any the less cultured; Piso Caesoninus's son L. Calpurnius Piso Frugi Pontifex and his two sons are the most likely dedicatees of Horace's *Ars Poetica.* On this reconstruction of the library's history, Piso may have simply inherited a library so technical that he himself did not read anything more than the *Good King,* which was dedicated to him (and is also relatively undemanding).

BIBLIOGRAPHY

The Herculaneum papyri are so extraordinarily well documented that even their bibliography needs an introductory paragraph. For a physical description of the papyri themselves, see note 28. A briefer but more up-to-date guide to current editions is given at http://www.herculaneum.ox.ac.uk/books, which also cites editions of passages gathered from the papyri under useful rubrics (e.g., Angeli's edition [1994] of Epicurus's fragmentary epistles). This site also has a link to the home page of the Herculaneum Society, which contains information about Web sites that depict both the papyri themselves and *disegni.* McIlwaine (1988, 2000) offers a bibliography that includes all aspects of Herculaneum. The most comprehensive and continuing source of new editions, as well as articles on the history of the collection, is *Cronache Ercolanesi* (*CErc*). Moreover, the back pages of *CErc* regularly publish work in progress, thus providing a guide to future bibliography on the papyri. The best overall introduction to both the papyri and their history is Capasso (1991), but much original work in the archives continues to be done, much of it by, alone and together, Blank and Longo Auricchio; see, for example, Blank and Longo Auricchio (2004). Other useful bibliographical aids are Dorandi (1989), an index to all the philosophers (and other thinkers) named in the papyri, and Delattre (1996).

Angeli, A. 1994. "Lo svolgimento dei papiri carbonizzati." In *Il Rotolo librario: Fabbrica-zione, restauro, organizzazione interna,* ed. M. Capasso, 37–103. Galatina: Congedo.

Arrighetti, G. 1971. "L'Opera *Sulla Natura* di Epicuro." *CErc* 1: 41–56.

Asmis, E. 1990. "The Poetic Theory of the Stoic 'Aristo.' " *Apeiron* 23: 147–201.

——. 1992a. "Crates on Poetic Criticism." *Phoenix* 46: 138–169.

——. 1992b. "Neoptolemus and the Classification of Poetry." *Classical Philology* 87: 206–231.

Bayardi, O. A. 1752. *Prodromo delle antichità d'Ercolano.* 5 vols. Naples: Stamperia Reale.

Blank, D., and F. Longo Auricchio. 2004. "Inventari antichi dei papiri ercolanesi." *CErc* 34: 39–152.

Broggiato, M. 2001. *Cratete di Mallo: I frammenti*. La Spezia, Italy: Agorà.

Camodeca, G., and G. Del Mastro. 2002. "I papiri documentari ercolanesi (*P.Herc. MAN*): Relazione preliminare." *CErc* 32: 281–296.

Capasso, M. 1986. "Carlo Maria Rosini e i papiri ercolanesi." In *Carlo Maria Rosini (1748–1836): Un umanista flegreo fra due secoli*, ed. S. Cerasuolo, M. Capasso, and A. D'Ambrosio, 129–192. Pozzuoli, Italy: Azienda autonoma di cura, soggiorno e turismo di Pozzuoli.

——. 1989. "Primo supplemento al Catalogo dei Papiri Ercolanesi." *CErc* 19: 193–264.

——. 1991. *Manuale di papirologia ercolanese*. Galatina, Italy: Congedo.

——, ed. 1994. *Il Rotolo librario: Fabbricazione, restauro, organizzazione interna*. Galatina, Italy: Congedo.

——, ed. 1995. "Le tavolette della villa ercolanese dei papiri." In his *Volumen: Aspetti della tipologia del rotolo librario antico*, 111–117. Naples: Procaccini.

——, ed. 1997. *Bicentenario della morte di Antonio Piaggio: Raccolta di Studi*. Papyrologica Lupiensia 5. Galatina, Italy: Congedo.

Cavallo, G. 1983. *Libri scritture scribi a Ercolano: Introduzione allo studio dei materiali greci*. *CErc* 13 (Suppl.). Naples: Gaetano Macchiaroli.

Cerasuolo, S., M. Capasso, and A. D'Ambrosio, eds. 1986. *Carlo Maria Rosini (1748–1836): Un umanista flegreo fra due secoli*. Pozzuoli, Italy: Azienda autonoma di cura, soggiorno e turismo di Pozzuoli.

Comparetti, D., and G. De Petra. 1972. *La Villa Ercolanese dei Pisoni: I suoi monumenti e la sua biblioteca*. Turin: E. Loescher, 1883; repr., Naples: Centro Internazionale per lo Studio dei Papiri Ercolanesi.

Deiss, J. J. 1985. *Herculaneum, Italy's Buried Treasure*, rev. and updated ed. New York: Harper & Row.

Del Mastro, G. 2000. "Secondo supplemento al Catalogo dei Papiri Ercolanesi." *CErc* 30: 157–242.

Delattre, D. 1996. "Les Mentions de titres d'œuvres dans les livres de Philodème." *CErc* 26: 143–168.

Diels, H. 1970. *Philodemos. Über die Götter: erstes und drittes Buch*. Berlin: Verlag der Königl. Akademie der Wissenschaften, 1916, 1917; repr. Leipzig: Zentralantiquariat der Deutschen Demokratischen Republik.

Dorandi, T. 1989. "Testimonianze ercolanesi." In *Corpus dei papiri filosofici greci e latini*, Parte 1, *Autori noti*. Vol. 1, 1–78. Florence: Leo S. Olschki.

——. 1991. *Filodemo, Storia dei Filosofi: Platone e l'academia (P.Herc. 1021 e 164)*. Naples: Bibliopolis.

——. 1993. *Theodor Gomperz: Eine Auswahl herkulanischer kleiner Schriften, 1864–1909*. Leiden: Brill.

——. 2001. "Supplemento ai Supplementi al Catalogo dei Papiri Ercolanesi." *ZPE* 135: 45–49.

Drummond, W., and R. Walpole. 1810. *Herculanensia*. London: T. Cadell & W. Davies.

Gaiser, K. 1988. *Philodems Academica: Die Berichte über Platon und die Alte Akademie in zwei herkulanensischen Papyri*. Stuttgart–Bad Cannstatt: Frommann-Holzboog.

Garuti, G. 1958. *C. Rabirius: Bellum Actiacum e papyro Herculanensi 817*. Bologna: N. Zanichelli.

Gigante, M. 1979a. *Catalogo dei papiri ercolanesi*. Naples: Bibliopolis.

———. 1979b. *Civiltà delle forme letterarie nell'antica Pompei.* Naples: Bibliopolis.

———. 1988. *La Germania e i papiri ercolanesi.* Heidelberg: Carl Winter Universitätsverlag.

———. 1995. *Philodemus in Italy: The Books from Herculaneum,* trans. D. Obbink. Ann Arbor: University of Michigan Press.

———. 2001. *Die deutsche Forschung über die herkulanensischen Papyri in den letzten drei Jahrzehnten.* Nachrichten der Akad. d. Wissenschaften in Göttingen. Philol.-hist. Kl. Nr. 11. Göttingen: Vandenhoeck & Ruprecht.

Hayter, J. 1811. *A Report upon the Herculaneum Manuscripts in a Second Letter, Addressed, by Permission, to His Royal Highness the Prince Regent.* London: Richard Phillips.

Janko, R. 2000. *Philodemus: On Poems, Book One.* Oxford: Oxford University Press.

Jensen, C. 1923. *Philodemos über die Gedichte, Fünftes Buch.* Berlin: Weidmann.

Longo Auricchio, F., and M. Capasso. 1980. "Nuove accessioni al dossier Piaggio." In *Contributi alla Storia della Officina dei Papiri Ercolanesi,* 17–59. Naples: Industria Tipografica Artistica.

Mangoni, C. 1993. *Filodemo: Il quinto libro della Poetica (P.Herc. 1425 e 1538).* Naples: Bibliopolis.

Mansi, M. G. 1997. "Per un profilo di Camillo Paderni." In *Bicentenario della morte di Antonio Piaggio: Raccolta di Studi.* Papyrologica Lupiensia 5, ed. M. Capasso, 77–108. Galatina, Italy: Congedo.

Mattusch, C. C. 2005. *The Villa dei Papiri at Herculaneum: Life and Afterlife of a Sculpture Collection.* Los Angeles: J. Paul Getty Museum.

McIlwaine, I. C. 1988. *Herculaneum: A Guide to Printed Sources.* 2 vols. Naples: Bibliopolis.

———. 1990. "Herculaneum: A Guide to Printed Sources: A Supplement." *CErc* 20: 87–128.

Murr, C. G. von. 1806. *Philodem von der Musik.* Berlin: H. Frölich.

Obbink, D. 1996. *Philodemus: On Piety.* Part 1: *Critical Text with Commentary.* Oxford: Oxford University Press.

Parslow, C. C. 1995. *Rediscovering Antiquity: Karl Weber and the Excavation of Herculaneum, Pompeii, and Stabiae.* Cambridge: Cambridge University Press.

Schütz, C. G. 1795. *Proposita in Philodemi Περὶ μουσικῆς librum IV.* Jena: Ex Officina Goepferdtii.

Sedley, D. 1973. "Epicurus, *On Nature,* Book XXVIII." *CErc* 3: 5–83.

———. 1974. "The Structure of Epicurus' *On Nature.*" *CErc* 4: 89–92.

Sickler, F., and T. Tyrwhitt. 1817. *Herculaneum Rolls: Correspondence relative to a Proposition made by Dr. Sickler of Hildburghausen, upon the Subject of their Development.* London: J. Barfield.

Sider, D. 1997. *The Epigrams of Philodemos: Introduction, Text, and Commentary.* New York: Oxford University Press.

Southey, R. 1873. *Life of Nelson.* London: G. Bell and Sons.

Störmer, F. C. et al. 1990. "Ink in Herculaneum." *CErc* 20: 183.

Winckelmann, J. J. 1771. *Critical Account of the Situation and Destruction by the First Eruptions of Mount Vesuvius of Herculaneum, Pompeii, and Stabia . . .* London: T. Carnan and F. Newbery.

Wojcik, M. R. 1986. *La Villa dei Papiri ad Ercolano: Contributo alla ricostruzione dell'ideologia della nobilitas tardorepubblicana.* Rome: L'Erma di Bretschneider.

CHAPTER 14

EDUCATION IN
THE PAPYRI

RAFFAELLA CRIBIORE

THE last twenty years have witnessed a renewed interest in literacy and education in
the Greek, Roman, and Byzantine worlds. Previously, H.-I. Marrou's history of
education (1975; first edition 1948) and the study of Roman education by S. Bonner
in 1977 were the authoritative works in this field. Both authors used the papyri to a
limited extent and only to confirm the ancient literary accounts of education. They
believed the evidence from Egypt reflected a pallid image of the highly literary
practices in Greece and Rome. In the past two and a half decades, some of the new
research, which has focused on the role of education and orality in classical Athens
(e.g., Thomas 1992) and on literacy in the ancient world (Harris 1989), has taken
the papyri into limited account. In 1996 Raffaella Cribiore produced a rigorous
study of school exercises in Hellenistic, Roman, and early Byzantine Egypt that
included a catalogue of exercises and extensive photographic documentation. The
book on education by Teresa Morgan (1998) was based on this body of material.[1]
Cribiore complemented her previous study with another, published in 2001, that
also took into account school texts and rhetorical exercises on papyrus.

In what follows, I focus on Greek education during the roughly ten centuries
between the conquest of Egypt by Alexander of Macedon and the Arab conquest. One
might question the legitimacy of covering this vast period as a continuum since it has
long been recognized that, from the socioeconomic point of view, Greek and Roman
Egypt differed significantly. Did education undergo any changes during these ten
centuries? Can one be indicted for adopting a methodology similar to that of earlier
scholars, who placed evidence into the neat categories derived from the literary

sources? Some changes did indeed occur, but they neither warrant a different periodization nor significantly affect the essentially "frozen" quality of education in Egypt as in other Roman provinces (Cribiore 2001b, 8–9).

While literary and anecdotal traditions alone reveal what we know of Greek education elsewhere, Egypt has offered a large quantity of educational material that permits us to glimpse the everyday, unexceptional practices of schooling and to observe certain details. The sands of Egypt have preserved school exercises written by students and teachers and some texts that were used in schools. This educational material is extant on papyrus, ostraca, wooden and waxed tablets, and, more rarely, parchment. In addition, information about ancient schools (and learning environments generally) emerges from the papyri and from findspots of exercises and other archaeological material (ibid., 15–44). When referring to "schools" in antiquity, we must be open to all scenarios because of the diversity and frequent lack of formality in schooling not only in villages but also in urban environments. While the papyri have transmitted the names of a considerable number of teachers who are identified only by their professional title (Cribiore 1996, 161–170), direct references to schools are more infrequent because of the lack of formal settings. Thus, the recent discovery in Alexandria of eighteen or more classrooms (*auditoria*) used in late antiquity for higher education is tantalizing. In this case, the literary tradition[2] converges with the archaeological findings to spotlight a formal school setting used by grammarians, sophists, and teachers of philosophy.

The literary sources indicate a strict division of levels of schooling. This remains largely valid, provided that one recalls that there were no fixed age limits for admission to (or graduation from) a certain level and that education at the primary level depended much on circumstances. The aims of the first stage were to teach basic reading, writing, and numeracy. The second-level teacher, the grammarian, trained students to read literary texts (particularly the poets) fluently, and reinforced grammatical and orthographical knowledge of the language. In schools of rhetoric, young men of the elite read prose (the orators and historians in particular), continued to study some poetry, and perfected their oral and written expression. These three stages formed what the ancients called the *enkyklios paideia*, that is, the "complete education," which enveloped those privileged young men who had access to it until the end.[3]

IDENTIFYING A SCHOOL EXERCISE

By "school exercise," I refer to students' work written in school or for school at any of the three educational levels and to teachers' preparations for their classes. In the category "school texts" I include works of literature and commentaries that appear to have been used in school contexts. Several factors often simultaneously contribute to identifying a school exercise: writing materials; features such as lines, decorations, punctuation, and lectional signs; and types of textual material. These characteristics might point to an exercise even in the absence of indications from palaeography, but one can reach virtual certainty when the hand is a clumsy "school hand" or an accomplished "teacher's hand."

Writing Materials Used in School

The writing materials of school exercises do not differ significantly from those generally used in Egypt (which are covered in chapter 1), but the ways students employed them show some peculiarities (Cribiore 1996, 57–74). Parchment was used sparingly, unlike papyrus, ostraca, and tablets. Both students and teachers wrote most of their exercises on papyrus. Students did not have much chance of getting large, unused papyrus of good quality. School papyri are often thick and rough and of mediocre if not altogether poor quality; they show marks of damage, such as missing fibers and clumsy attempts to repair them with patches. To have a papyrus for an exercise, a student might wash off writing or cut an unwritten part from a larger written piece. Students at elementary levels did not need much writing space and could make use of blank areas on previously used papyri. At higher levels of education, however, students wrote their work across the fibers on the back (*verso*) of papyri whose fronts (*recto*) already bore writing. Unlike beginning writers, they did not need to follow the horizontal fibers as guidelines and were able to write on a relatively less smooth surface.

Ostraca, both sherds of broken pottery and pieces of limestone, were ideal for short exercises. Convenience rather than cost per se dictated their use: They were so readily available that one could overcome the relative disadvantage of their uneven surface. Students used them more at elementary levels than in later stages, and teachers wrote on them model alphabets that could easily circulate in class. The visible correlation between the size of an ostracon and the length of an exercise indicates that schoolchildren selected them according to the writing space needed. Not all ostraca with literary texts necessarily originated in school contexts. In most cases, though, this material points to an exercise: Scholars had no problem getting hold of papyrus. In remote places such as the quarry settlement of Mons Claudianus and the Roman military *praesidia* along the road of Myos Hormos, ostraca were the principal writing material used for education and everyday matters. The good, literary level of the school ostraca found in the former fort prompted their editor to posit the existence of a schoolmaster who instructed children of military personnel (*O.Claud.* I 179–189, and II 409–416). Ostraca found in Krokodilô and Maximianon also testify to some kind of basic instruction, but their level is below that attested in Mons Claudianus (Cuvigny 2003). It is impossible to know whether those who wrote them were children or illiterate adults and whether the instruction was imparted by a schoolmaster or by another adult with some education.

In comparison to other materials, tablets, which were made of wood, were considerably more expensive because wood was scarce in Egypt. No tablets from the Ptolemaic period are extant, and more tablets survive from the early Byzantine period than from the Roman age. Both wooden tablets and waxed tablets were used for educational purposes, either as individual pieces or joined together (up to ten tablets) to form "notebooks." Students used pen and ink to write on the wooden tablets, which could be covered with a coating that made the surface smoother and allowed the writing to be washed off to some extent. Waxed tablets were hollowed out, leaving a narrow rim around the edges. This concavity was filled with wax, which was inscribed with a pointed stylus and erased with its spatula-shaped back. Since they could easily be reused, these tablets were popular at elementary levels, where the need to erase was frequent. Teachers and more experienced students wrote calligraphic exercises and grammar on wooden tablets.

Other Distinguishing Features

Special features such as lines, borders, and decorations of various kinds help identify a school exercise (Cribiore 1996, 75–96). Some of these had the practical purpose of dividing or highlighting sections, but others served only to embellish schoolwork. The common practice of writing words without separation (*scriptio continua*) made it necessary to employ reading and writing aids in the form of spaces, dots, and oblique strokes that divided syllables and/or words. Words in lists were often divided into syllables, and these same divisions are visible in passages of authors that still offered learners a challenge. Teachers found these divisions useful in the passages they wrote out for their classes. Models of this kind (e.g., ibid., nos. 292, 296, and 342) were most often written on tablets that might have been hung or circulated in the classroom. Since exercises, particularly in the Roman and Byzantine periods, presented poetic texts in continuous lines, without respecting colometry (superficially indistinguishable from prose), marks were often used to separate verses (Cribiore 1992). Finally, mistakes provide a strong argument for identifying a particular document as schoolwork. Slips of the pen and phonetic mistakes are also present in professional copies but often abound in exercises. Morphological errors in grammatical exercises distinguish them from copies written by grammarians, and syntactic mistakes indicate students' compositions.

School Hands and Teachers' Hands

The vast majority of "school hands," that is, the writing of learners, display obvious features caused by low speed and immaturity of handwriting (Cribiore 1996, 102–118). Large size, irregular alignment and margins, varying inclination of letters, and clumsy letter forms are evident to the palaeographer. It is possible to isolate four different types of hand according to their writing experience: the "zero-grade hand" is that of the complete novice; the "alphabetic hand" can be trusted for not more than alphabets and is unable to bear the burden of longer texts; the "evolving hand" does a good amount of writing and is moderately fluent but still displays a coarse and uneven look; finally, the "rapid hand" is that of the older student and cannot identify an exercise in the absence of other characteristics.

Teachers' hands may exhibit the large size that is characteristic of students' hands (indeed, they may be even larger) but show fluency, regularity, strength, and excellent legibility (ibid., 97–102, 121–128). They are not as rigid and formal as "book hands" but display a considerable degree of beauty, that is, an attractive evenness and precision of the strokes. "Teachers write letters of great beauty for the children to imitate," wrote John Chrysostom in the fourth century CE (*MPG* 59.385.56). The hands of models from Graeco-Roman Egypt are graceful and elegant even though their style is often informal. Models are attested in both literary and visual sources. In the absence of erasable blackboards and schoolbooks with words separated, they were of great help both at the elementary and the grammatical levels. Students could easily handle small ostraca with models of alphabets without much risk of damaging them, but large and heavy ostraca inscribed by teachers might have been displayed in the classroom (e.g., Cribiore 1996, 319; *O.Claud.* II 415).

Types of Textual Material

Some examples point directly to schoolwork, but the papyrologist must also use other criteria of distinction, particularly for textual materials at advanced levels of education. Alphabets and the repetition of individual letters can represent teachers' models and students' and apprentice scribes' practice. Much is still unknown about the education of scribes, such as whether they followed a regular course of study for some time or enrolled in scribal schools from the beginning (for scribes of Christian texts, see Haines-Eitzen 2000). Scribes needed to have specialized training at a certain point to learn different styles of writing and acquire the complex terminology used in legal and bureaucratic documents.[4] Since knowing the proper letter sequence was presumably a prerequisite for their specialized training, exercises that reinforced that ability were assigned to pupils at elementary levels. Combining letters into syllables and mastering syllabaries was the next hurdle for these learners. Syllabaries were more or less complete and elaborate combinations of consonants and vowels; they exist in the form of teachers' models and students' exercises, full of mistakes and imprecision. They were important in the teaching of reading and writing (see Cribiore 1996, nos. 78–97). Authors such as Quintilian (1.1.30) and Plato (*Polit.* 278b) emphasized the necessity of mastering all of the combinations because they enabled a learner to proceed to words, phrases such as maxims, sayings and single verses, short passages, and, finally, long passages of authors.[5]

Lists of words also exist as models and students' exercises.[6] The vast majority display words either divided into syllables or arranged in groups according to the number of syllables and were intended to teach reading and writing. Word lists, however, do not necessarily pertain to an elementary level of learning or automatically indicate school contexts, and the papyrologist needs to distinguish carefully. Some lists arranged by theme, such as mythological and heroic genealogies taken from literary works, belong to more advanced levels of education (e.g., Cribiore 1996, no. 390). When students were ready to go beyond single words, their writing assignments started with limited amounts of prose and verse and evolved progressively into extensive passages of authors. Elementary students wrote maxims, sayings of famous men, and short excerpts from poetry. Students of grammarians copied or wrote (from dictation) long passages, mostly from the poets. An important caveat: Identifying an exercise at this point becomes more problematic since advanced students usually possessed a trained (rapid) hand that is virtually undistinguishable from that of other educated people and scholars.

Knowledge of textual materials can still help us to identify schoolwork at higher levels of education. Compositions with mistakes of morphology and syntax unmistakably belong to school contexts. When they contain paraphrases and summaries of Homeric episodes and books, however, we must take into account other distinguishing characteristics in order to tell them apart from professional copies (ibid., nos. 344–357). The same is true in the case of *scholia minora*, Homeric commentaries that consist of lists of words taken from the Homeric text *(lemmata)* and accompanied by the corresponding words in a more current form of Greek (glosses). In the past these commentaries were automatically considered the products of school activity, but the general educated public also needed such "translations." Thus *scholia minora* circulated as private copies and professionally produced books written in formal hands. While the exercises Cribiore included (ibid., nos. 325–343) seem to have originated in school settings, and undoubtedly many more copies were used in educational contexts, it is impossible to tell them apart from those consulted by the general public. Grammar was also a prominent subject in secondary education. Students read and copied parts of grammatical handbooks *(technai)* and engaged in morphological exercises of declension and conjugation (ibid., nos. 358–378).

When a young man entered a school of rhetoric, his hand was fairly trained, his spelling more secure, and as a rule he indulged less in decorations of any sort, so that it is more difficult to recognize students' work at this stage than before.[7] In addition, since the teaching of rhetoric was preeminent in Alexandria but only a limited number of papyri from there have been preserved, the body of rhetorical exercises at the papyrologist's disposal is limited. Textual material greatly helps us to understand how rhetoric was generally taught and practiced in Egypt, but one is hard put to distinguish the work of students and teachers from that of amateurish practitioners of rhetoric. Nevertheless, a substantial number of rhetorical exercises—different from professional texts and orations actually delivered—are extant. They range from preliminary exercises *(progymnasmata)* to whole declamations *(meletai)*.

BOOKS USED IN SCHOOL

The teachers' models functioned as books for copying and consultation leading up to the initial studies under the grammarian, when a student still needed help in decoding words. The fourth-century Christian writer Basil of Caesarea (*Homilia dicta tempore famis et siccitatis* 67c) mentions some students breaking in anger the tablets that belonged to their teacher. It is reasonable to suppose that many of the tablets found in Egypt were the property of teachers who lent them to students. One might conjure up a scenario in which the ownership of tablets and some degree of literacy were the simple prerequisites for a primary teacher to set up a school. Yet, papyrus books *(biblia)* that presented material in simplified ways also existed. The literary and papyrological sources indicate that students used books at higher levels of education. A few letters on papyrus are illuminating in this respect since they casually allude to schoolbooks of various kinds (*P.Giss.* 85; *SB* III 7268; *P.Oxy.* III 531). Identifying such texts, however, is not easy. Even though there was not a large market for books with special features (because the models adequately covered those needs), some exceptions exist (Cribiore 2001b, 137–143). In a few papyri the written text shows spaces between words and a very legible handwriting (e.g., *P.Ryl.* III 486). In another papyrus with a text on the labors of Heracles written with gaps between the words, colorful illustrations indicate that it probably addressed a young audience (*P.Oxy.* XXII 2331). Since Homer was heavily present in ancient education, most examples of school texts can be found among Homeric papyri that exhibit dots or vertical dashes to separate the words (e.g., *MPER* n.s. III 3) and/or an unusual wealth of accents and other lectional signs. This is particularly true when the accents were added, sometimes clumsily, by the hand of a student who was doing an exercise in accentuation (*P.Lond.Lit.* 28). As noted earlier, texts with *scholia minora* and grammatical handbooks were in use in the grammarian's classroom.

LEARNING ACCORDING TO THE PAPYRI

Approaching Literacy

The school exercises and the few school texts from Graeco-Roman Egypt are little more than precious outlines of what went on in an ancient classroom. Education was largely oral and thus is mostly out of our reach. Yet, starting from the extant remains and taking into account a few vivid papyrus letters written by parents and students, archaeological findings, and the information that the ancient writers handed down, we can hope to fill in the picture to a large extent. In considering

teaching methods, we must keep in mind that bilingualism (or diglossia) constituted a hurdle for students at every level of education. In Egypt, as in other
provinces of the empire, many individuals, who in their daily lives functioned in
the indigenous language, learned Greek in school. Those who were exposed to
Greek at home were in a privileged condition for learning but had to confront the
fact that the koinê Greek of their daily life differed significantly from the Attic Greek
they encountered in school. Learning methods and teaching aids had to take this
reality into account and remedy the lack of books that could easily be consulted, as
well as the absence of tables of contents, indices, library catalogues, and the like.

One way to cope with these disadvantages was to enforce an extremely
thorough mastery of the alphabet, which became as flexible as the numerical
order and was used as both a mnemonic device and an organizational tool.
Teachers discouraged rote memory of the alphabet and made up exercises that
consisted of following other alphabetical sequences: skipping a fixed number of
letters, proceeding from the bottom up, and pronouncing tongue twisters made up
of alphabets in scrambled order. In addition, the maxims that served as copying
exercises sometimes formed alphabetical acrostics; the syllabaries inculcated ways
to combine letters; and words were listed in alphabetical order, which was used as a
mnemonic device. Strengthening the memory was a constant concern. More
advanced students not only memorized texts word for word but also practiced
mnemotechniques in rhetorical school (Blum 1969; Small 1997).

The papyri contain examples of the rigid teaching method attested by the
literary sources that taught reading and writing by means of building blocks (letters,
syllables, words, sentences, and passages). Yet the school exercises from Egypt
indicate that this sequence was not universally followed. In order for students to
practice handwriting, teachers made them write their names and copy verses and
texts of very limited extent as soon as they learned their letters (e.g., Cribiore 1996,
nos. 136, 160, 202, 383, 403). These students could not read what they had copied but
proceeded blindly, committing every sort of mistake and omission (Cribiore 2001b,
167–172). This copying method apparently became more popular in the late Roman
and Byzantine periods and sometimes coexisted with the traditional method. It was
particularly useful to those who were in school for only a short time because they
could thus acquire a limited literacy that enabled them to perform in a society in
which most people were somewhat familiar with reading and writing (Hanson 1991;
Bowman 1991). The painfully written subscriptions of the so-called slow writers and
an example such as that of Petaus, a town clerk who could not read but passed
himself off as literate, are eye-openers (Youtie 1966).

The cultural content of an elementary education was very limited: Some
maxims and sayings (sometimes by Isocrates and Menander) and a few verses of
Homer and Euripides were powerful symbols of literacy. The elementary package
also included numerical literacy. Since the letters of the alphabet, with the addition
of three more signs, functioned as numbers, it was always assumed that numerical

operations were part of the first phases of instruction. The mathematical exercises found in Egypt, however, allow us to make a few distinctions (Cribiore 2001b, 180–183). Students rarely wrote down additions, which they might have recited aloud, and engaged in written multiplications and fractions only when their handwriting was fairly proficient. Many tables of fractions exist, but most of them are capably written and were either hung in offices to facilitate computation or used as teachers' models. Elementary students mostly learned mathematical operations by memorizing these tables. Extensive and advanced mathematical work was part of the teaching of specialized schools.[8]

Christian education was closely modeled on pagan Greek formation and progressed through the same stages. Besides studying the traditional classic authors, however, students also copied and learned by heart the *Psalms* and passages from the Scriptures (e.g., Cribiore 1996, no. 403). From the third century CE on, Coptic schooling also used religious texts for practice and, like Greek education, entirely ignored Pharaonic culture (Cribiore 1999). Students likely learned the Greek and Coptic alphabets at the same time, but it is difficult to ascertain whether the teaching of the two languages proceeded simultaneously as the student advanced. A characteristic of Coptic education was to teach beginners to write the opening and formulaic parts of letters, therefore addressing practical needs. Epistolary texts were not used as copybooks in Greek school contexts. Since there are no evident remains of advanced Coptic exercises, the highly rhetorical style of authors such as Shenoute and Besa in all probability originated from their exposure to patristic literature and Greek rhetorical education.

I have referred so far to "students" and "teachers" generically, but education was open not only to males. Girls also had access to primary instruction, but boys were the vast majority. The disproportion became more pronounced in grammar schools, though a number of girls of the upper class also attended, as certain papyrus letters sent by women attest (Cribiore 2001b, 74–101; Bagnall and Cribiore 2006). Rhetorical training, the last stage of the *enkyklios paideia,* was in any case closed to female students because it was envisioned as preparation for public and political life. Low-level teaching was not entirely in the hands of male teachers. The literary sources disclose little about women teachers and completely disregard female primary teachers, but the papyri indicate the existence of a few of them. Even though, like their male counterparts, these teachers appear by their title (*deskalos* or *deskalê*) in documents that do not reveal anything about their didactic activity (e.g., *P.Mich.* VIII 464; *P.Mich.* II 123; and *BGU* I 332), their presence per se is a significant testimony that education in antiquity was not entirely out of women's reach.

Strengthening the Language

Students who entered the grammarian's class developed and amplified knowledge previously acquired. This common educational principle reached paradoxical proportions in the ancient world. The grammarian's students already knew that the elements of knowledge fitted precisely into a grid and were tightly connected like the links of a chain, and they soon realized that multiple connections existed with the previous level. With their divisions and lectional signs, the teachers' models provided necessary help to the inexperienced student who read slowly, by syllables and words. They formed a transition to the texts in general circulation, which were less "user friendly." Education proceeded in a circular fashion, so that the more advanced students revisited texts they had previously encountered. Their reading now was more fluent, and the questions they had to answer about a text were more thorough and diverse, but most of the authors they dealt with were those they had met before.

On the whole, the school papyri agree with the literary sources with regard to the authors studied under the grammarian, but they are less helpful in identifying the reading list of an advanced student whose hand was experienced (Cribiore 2001b, 192–204). This, for instance, is the reason that Hesiod does not frequently appear among the school papyri, although the educational writers attest to his presence in the schoolroom, and the extant papyri that preserve his works are quite numerous.[9] Homer was the author that students came to know in detail, and the thousand or so extant Homeric papyri confirm his popularity among the cultivated public. Both students and the general public vastly preferred the *Iliad* to the *Odyssey*. The grammarians read the first six books of the *Iliad* in detail, and their more advanced students went through the whole work.[10] Ancient teachers always concentrated on the beginning of an author's work; thus, the first two books in particular were the subject of a meticulous analysis. Euripides was a major presence in education, whereas other tragedians were overlooked. He was linguistically more accessible, and his most rhetorical plays (*Phoenissae, Orestes, Hecuba, Medea,* and *Alcestis*) continued to occupy students in a school of rhetoric. The popularity of *Phoenissae* was uncontested from the time pupils wrote maxims to improve their penmanship until they engaged in composition exercises (Cribiore 2001a). The maxims of Menander also accompanied students from the beginning to the end, up to the time when they learned to develop them with the rhetor, and Menander's plays, copied with many mistakes and corruptions by students and teachers alike, appear among the *P.Bodmer*. Menander's *monostichoi* continued to enjoy a vast popularity in the Byzantine period, but his comedies lost favor. Teachers at advanced levels preferred Aristophanes, who was more interesting linguistically. Thus Zuntz (1975) has shown that marginal notes in late papyri of Aristophanes derive from schoolbooks (e.g., *P.Oxy.* VI 856). The presence of other poets in the schoolroom is more difficult to verify. Some works by Callimachus, Theognis, Sappho, Hipponax, and Pindar surface but very sporadically because of the usual difficulties in identifying advanced schoolwork.[11]

Did the grammarians concentrate exclusively on poetry? Undoubtedly this was their traditional area of expertise, but they also taught reading, writing, and grammar with the aid of fables and some Isocrates. One again sees the wide application of the educational principle of making a pupil revisit the same texts at subsequent levels. Present at all stages of education, fables were the basis of the first rhetorical exercises. Likewise, elementary students copied short excerpts from the *Cyprian Orations* of Isocrates *(Ad Demonicum, Ad Nicoclem, Nicocles);* read more extensive passages under the grammarian with the help of professionally produced books; and, with the rhetor, developed maxims from these orations. A book of tablets containing these three speeches, summaries, and lexical notes squeezed into the margins is the product of the grammarian's schoolroom (Worp and Rijksbaron 1997).

Isocrates remained enormously popular at all times. Among seven Byzantine school tablets, which date mostly from the seventh century and preserve Greek and Coptic texts, one tablet dated to 470 CE displays a model and a copy from the *Ad Demonicum* and a list of months (Duttenhöfer 1997). Before writing down the model, the teacher exhorted the pupil, "Pay attention. I wrote in nice letters." Likewise, a passage from *Nicocles,* written from dictation in the sixth century on the back of a protocol, testifies to the continuous attraction Isocrates exercised (Lundon and Messeri 2000). Because of the heavily gnomic (that is, moralistic and didactic) content of these three orations, they were also very well liked by the general public: They make up about half of the papyri of Isocrates. While ancient authors suggest that students at this stage paid more attention to reading literature than to writing, the papyrological sources indicate that they practiced epistolary writing (as some letters sent to families show) and later perfected their skills with the rhetor (Cribiore 2001b, 215–219).

The papyri allow us to enter the grammarian's schoolroom and glance at all aspects of its activity. Since Homer was the author par excellence, let us follow the grammarian's teaching by focusing on some of the Homeric exercises. As I have already said, metrics was an area of fundamental interest, so students had to do exercises in accentuation. In a Roman papyrus, a student wrote down only the first half of each line of *Odyssey* 9.122–150, producing two crowded columns separated by a thick, rough line. In an exercise that probably also involved memorization, the student used the papyrus very economically to show his knowledge of the lines up to the caesura (Cribiore 1996, no. 291).[12] A grammarian had to elucidate all of the words in the Homeric text, thereby producing "historical notes" *(historiai),* that is, details on the mythological matters, persons, places, and events mentioned. Two fragments from a third-century papyrus preserve a student's exercise: names of Achaean heroes from the *Iliad,* together with their fathers and mothers and a list of gods with their genealogy (*P.Oxy.* LXV 4460). The content, the evolving hand, the decorated title, and the long lines that separate the sections mark this as a product of the grammarian's schoolroom.

Another evolving hand wrote on the verso of a Roman account (*P.Oxy.* LVI 3829). The student in question committed several mistakes and corrected some of his clumsy letters by rewriting them above the line. This papyrus spotlights a series of school activities. It contains the end of a catechism (questions and answers) that listed the characters of the *Iliad;* a narrative concerning the events leading to the Trojan War (including the judgment of Paris); *Iliad* 1.1; and a summary of that book. The first section with *erôtêmata* allows us to perceive the oral side of the grammarian's teaching. A student had to demonstrate his knowledge by answering various questions, such as on the identity of Hector's advisers or on the seers who appear in the *Iliad*. The question-and-answer format was extremely popular in late antiquity and in the Middle Ages to systematize knowledge in various fields, such as medicine and grammar, into easily assimilated parcels. It seems to have originated as a pedagogical tool in the Roman schoolroom.

The grammarian's practice of explaining all historical and geographical details often went to extremes. His students learned much information that bordered on the useless and paid attention to the minutiae in a text rather than to the meaning and themes of the whole. But in one area the grammarian's pedantic focus on details was necessary. The linguistic background of the students made elucidation of unfamiliar Homeric vocabulary imperative. Students who already had trouble with the Attic Greek they encountered in school needed more help in decoding Homeric terminology. *Scholia minora* to Homer provided an elementary commentary that they had to consult and copy. It is not surprising that these are more numerous for the *Iliad* than for the *Odyssey* since teachers and the general public were more interested in the former. The grammarian focused on the first book of the *Iliad*, for which he provided glosses that covered the text almost in its entirety. An exercise with *scholia minora* to a few lines of book one carries us into the midst of the classroom and shows how students at every level read according to syllables and not to whole words (Cribiore 1996, no. 339). A student apparently first copied the whole column of the *lemmata* and then the glosses in a parallel column. He was following a model and wrote down only the first syllable of each gloss and interrupted his work after five lines.

Once the class had assimilated the vocabulary of the first book of the *Iliad*, the grammarian could zero in on other difficult terms in a variety of books, thereby providing a sparser commentary. Consider, for example, a fragment of a roll with *Iliad* 5.24 written by a teacher: The glosses accompany a text reproduced in its entirety and provide an easily consulted Homeric dictionary (ibid., no. 330). In compiling their vocabularies to Homer, grammarians used glossographical material that had an ancient, scholarly origin, but the erudite *scholia vetera* that appear in some Homeric manuscripts have a different scope and tone. Grammarians felt free to modify and integrate that ancient exegesis; as a result, the *scholia* found in Egypt also provide their personal contributions. This elementary glossographical material was assimilated into a Byzantine compilation, the so-called *D-scholia*, which offered every kind of Homeric exegesis, such as paraphrases and summaries of Homeric books, mythographical material, and inquiries *(zêtêmata)* into certain questions. Mythographical notes are found in a number of school papyri (e.g., ibid., no. 183). Montanari (1995) has shown that teachers consulted an ancient commentary on mythological subjects, usually called *Mythographus Homericus*, which circulated in scholarly and scholastic circles.

The technical aspect of grammar had very likely always been a part of the grammarian's teaching, but the fact that no grammatical exercises and texts have survived from the Hellenistic period cannot be only the result of chance. The Alexandrian scholars worked on systematization of parts of grammar, but only from the beginning of the Roman period did grammar become codified into a body of knowledge that was transmitted separately. It is not a coincidence that texts containing *scholia minora* appeared in the same period and not before. Until then the need to classify grammatical terms and forms was not felt with the same urgency, and the understanding of the Homeric text was less deficient. Linguistic tools were increasingly more necessary to approach the ancient authors and grasp the nuances of poetry. Grammatical manuals that treated the parts of speech started to circulate (Wouters 1979), but their influence on schoolwork seems to have been limited. Up to the fourth century, the papyri that preserve parts of handbooks used in school differ from the *Technê* of Dionysius Thrax, a grammarian who wrote around 100 BCE (see, e.g., Cribiore 1996, nos. 358, 359, 362, 368, 371, 373). The authenticity and dating of the body of this text as it was transmitted are still under scrutiny (e.g., Law and Sluiter 1995), but it is clear that it became the standard school text only from the fifth century on. In the previous period, grammarians had to rely on the work of their predecessors and adapt it to their pedagogical needs. A papyrus from the first century, which provides definitions of genders, numbers, and types of nouns, well exemplifies this trend (*PSI* inv. 505; Di Benedetto 1957). This manual was either a cheap professional copy or a copy made by a teacher and follows the question-and-answer format throughout.

Learning Rhetoric

The training of a young man of the elite who entered a school of rhetoric relied heavily on what he had learned with the grammarian. Knowledge at this stage was organized according to the customary inflexible order in links of progressive difficulty, each connected to the one before and to the next (Cribiore 2001b, 220–244). Thus *progymnasmata* expanded the knowledge of poetry already acquired and concentrated on Homer and the *Iliad* in particular.[13] In practicing exercises such as those of praise (*encomium*), blame (*psogos*), impersonation (*êthopoiia*), and description (*ekphrasis*), a student improved his skill in writing, expression, and observation. At a higher level of expertise, he could incorporate some *progymnasmata* into the composition of declamations (*meletai*) on deliberative and forensic subjects. Theon of Alexandria composed a handbook of preliminary exercises in the first century (Patillon 1997), and in fourth-century Antioch, the sophist Libanius wrote *progymnasmata* as models for his students (Foerster 1963, vol. 8).

While most of the exercises in these and later collections correspond to those found in the papyri, students in Egypt practiced especially *êthopoiiai* and *encomia*. It is important to note, however, that most of the exercises on papyrus are in verse (epic hexameters and iambics) even though the various literary collections contain examples only in prose as preparation for rhetorical discourse. It seems that rhetorical training not only was based upon previous knowledge of the poets but also reinforced and expanded students' poetic skills. The student who wrote an exercise of impersonation followed the text of a certain author but lingered on a mythological or literary figure's reaction to a specific event, reporting, for instance, the words of Phoinix reproaching Achilles or those of the latter at the point of death.[14] An *êthopoiia* did not require much originality, but it was very useful to practice the *êthos* of several characters, a skill a student needed because he would never appear in his own persona in historical and argumentative declamations.

Encomia found in Egypt are very similar to those that appear in rhetorical textbooks and did not focus only on mythological subjects. Consider, for example, the encomium of the fig, which was supposedly the favorite fruit of Hermes, the god of rhetoric, and sports a heavily decorated title (*P.Oxy.* XVII 2084), or the praise of the horse in another papyrus also found at Oxyrhynchos (*P.Oxy.* LXVIII 4647). Praise of various persons and gods was a traditional subject. A Roman exercise preserves an encomium of Dionysus that extols him on the occasion of a certain celebration. Its irregular, rapid hand and the general presentation point to a teacher's model rather than to the composition of a rhetor that was actually delivered (*P.Köln* VII 286). As Libanius shows (e.g., *Ep.* 63), speeches of praise were useful to the student who stopped at this level of rhetorical education and could use this skill to compose panegyrics of officials. Rhetors and poet-grammarians often engaged in similar exercises and competed in public contests and festivities (e.g., *P.Oxy.* VII 1015).

Young men who continued in their education faced rigorous training. The theory of "issue" (*stasis*), which governed the composition of declamations, was a formidable, demanding system. In the preliminary exercises, a student had used building blocks to construct relatively short pieces, but now he had to follow painstakingly detailed instructions to learn to construct arguments and cases. In spite of limitations, this system helped develop verbal skills and the capability of analyzing the pros and cons of a case. The traditional Roman division of declamations into *suasoriae* (on imaginative, deliberative themes) and *controversiae* (fictitious legal cases) was not followed in Greek education, where declamations were distinguished as either historical or fictive. In Egypt, in any case, historical declamations were much more common, and examples of fictive *meletai* are rare.[15] The random chance of survival and the preservation of only a few Alexandrian papyri might be responsible for that, but one should not rule out the possibility that sophists in Egypt taught rhetoric mainly through literary texts (historical and orator-ical) and avoided fictitious legal themes. A young man who wished to practice law could learn on the job or go to a school of Roman law either in Alexandria or abroad, particularly to the renowned school of Berytus (Beirut).

In the late Roman period, a change in the training of the advocates occurred, and the education acquired in a school of rhetoric became increasingly insufficient. Most young men who aspired to jobs in the administration opted to learn Roman law. A knowledge of some Latin, therefore, became mandatory, and the so-called Latin school exercises found in Egypt are evidence of this. They consist of bilingual glossaries and bilingual lists of authors. Most of the glossaries are transliterated; that is, they are written entirely with the Greek script (Kramer 1983, 2001). The vast majority of the bilingual word lists are from the *Aeneid* and show either the whole text or isolated words rendered in Greek.[16] A few bilingual books also contain texts of Cicero, Juvenal, Sallust, and Terence.[17] The script of these glossaries and lists consists of either fluent, cursive hands (those of teachers perhaps or of lesser *scriptoria*) or the formal hands of professionally produced books (Cribiore 2003–04). It seems, therefore, that these were not exercises written by students but were more or less formally produced books on which they practiced their reading skills. It is likely that a veneer of Latin was sufficient to enter a school of Roman law.

In conclusion, the contributions of the papyri to our knowledge of education are many. They beautifully illustrate what the ancient educational writers have handed down regarding the methods and stages of teaching and at the same time allow us to glimpse real students and teachers whose actual work was preserved. They are evidence that iron rules systematized knowledge and a strict curriculum governed the various stages of education; when its traces are faint, it is only because of the difficulty of identifying the work of advanced students. But the papyri also provide important correctives to the literary sources. They show that elementary training served both the student who was going to continue his schooling and the one who dropped out and that education, for all its rigidity, never lost touch with reality. Likewise, it appears that grammatical education not only exposed students to the poets and rules of grammar but also gave them the ability to express themselves in letters sent to family members, a skill that they perfected at later stages. While modern educational theorists have maintained that poetry was exclusively the province of the grammarian and that the rhetor taught only prose (e.g., Marrou 1975, 296), the papyri provide a more nuanced view of the transition between the two levels and prove that poetry continued to interest the student of rhetoric. The numerous rhetorical exercises in verse point neither to an eccentric phenomenon nor to the exclusive predilection of the Egyptians for poetry but confirm that poetry was cultivated everywhere at high levels of education, particu-larly in late antiquity, though only the sands of Egypt offer us remnants of actual school contexts.[18]

NOTES

1. Morgan (1998) needs to be used with some caution, especially for matters concerning higher education. In what follows, I identify exercises by the numbers included in Cribiore (1996) and refer to full bibliographic references only for items that have appeared subsequently.

2. Especially Zacharias Scholasticus and Damascius; see Kugener (1903) and Zintzen (1967).

3. I cover neither philosophy, which was outside this circle, nor specialized areas of knowledge such as higher mathematics, geometry, and astronomy.

4. Apprentice scribes did most of the exercises in copying parts of personal and official letters that are included in *MPER* n.s. XV. For scribal practice at a higher level, see, for example, *P.Köln* VII 298, and *P.Oxy.* LXVIII 4668.

5. In describing the steps involved in the teaching of reading and writing , modern historians rigidly follow the accounts of ancient authors such as Augustine, *De ordine* 2.7 (24); Ambrose, *De Abraham* 1.30; Manilius, *Astronomica* 2.755–764; Jerome, *Ep.* 107.4 and 128.1; and Gregory of Nyssa, *De beneficentia* 5–13.

6. To the lists in Cribiore (1996, nos. 98–128), add Di Bitonto–Kasser (1998), a model that was reused for cartonnage.

7. Cribiore (1996), whose main interest was to show the various stages in learning to write, included only a few exercises at this level that showed a deficient hand. Morgan (1998) relied only on these; consequently, her treatment of rhetoric in Egypt is incomplete. Cribiore (2001b, 220–244) covered rhetoric more fully.

8. Apprentice scribes practiced multiplications and fractions extensively, as many exercises in *MPER* n.s. XV show. They also wrote down tables of weights, measures, and the like; see, for example, *P.Köln* VIII 352.

9. On his presence in school, see Cribiore (1996, no. 386) (Hesiod as copybook), ibid., no. 390 (in a list of words), and *P.Oxy.* LXI 4099 (mythographic lists). See also *P.Oxy.* XXIII 2355, a school text. According to the *LDAB*, the papyri of Hesiod number 155.

10. See two recently published school papyri with *Iliad* 24, *BASP* 41 (2004): 46–50.

11. See Cribiore (1996, nos. 303, 379, 590, 234, 235, 237, 247) and McNamee (1994).

12. See a similar exercise on *Iliad* 24, *BASP* 41 (2004): 46–50, and on mythological hexameters with dots for metrics, *P.Köln* VIII 328.

13. See Cribiore (1996, 344–357). See also, for example, *PSI* XIII 1303; *P.Harr.* I 4; *P.Ryl.* III 487; *O.Bodl.* II 2171; *P.Köln* VII 286; and *P.Oxy.* LXVIII 4647.

14. Cf. G. A. Gerhard and O. Crusius, *Mélanges Nicole* (Geneva 1905), 615–624, and *P.Cair.Masp.* III 67316v.

15. On rhetorical treatises found in Egypt see, for example, *P.Oxy.* III 410; LIII 3708; and *P.Yale* II 106. Examples of historical declamations are *BKT* VII 4–13; *P.Oxy.* XXIV 2400; VI 858; II 216; XV 1799; XLV 3235 and 3236; *P.Yale* II 105; *P.Lond.Lit.* 139; and *P.Hib.* I 15. Examples of fictive declamations are *P.Lond.Lit.* 138; *P.Oxy.* III 471; and *P.Hamb.* III 163 (in Latin). The themes of the historical declamations found in Egypt are largely from Athenian history in the period of Demosthenes and following the death of Alexander.

16. Gaebel (1970). See *Aeneid LDAB* 4146, 4149, 4154, 4155, 4156, 4160, 4146, and 4162; and *LDAB* 4159 (*Georgics*).

17. Cicero is represented in four papyri, *LDAB* 554, 556, 559 (passages from orations *in Catilinam*), and 558 (*Divinatio in Q. Caecilium*). See also *LDAB* 2559 (Juvenal); 3875 and 3877 (Sallust); 3982 and 3983 (Terence).

18. Cf. Eunapius, *VS* 10.7.10–13, 493. See Cameron (1965, 2004).

BIBLIOGRAPHY

Abbenes, J. G. J., S. R. Slings, and I. Sluiter, eds. 1995. *Greek Literary Theory after Aristotle: A Collection of Papers in Honour of D. M. Schenkeveld.* Amsterdam: VU University Press.

Bagnall, R. S., and R. Cribiore 2006. *Women's Letters from Ancient Egypt, 300 BC–AD 800.* Ann Arbor: University of Michigan Press.

Blum, H. 1969. *Die antike Mnemotechnik.* Hildesheim: Georg Olms.

Bonner, S. F. 1977. *Education in Ancient Rome: From the Elder Cato to the Younger Pliny.* Berkeley: University of California Press.

Bowman, A. K. 1991. "Literacy in the Roman Empire: Mass and Mode." In *Literacy in the Roman World,* 119–131. Ann Arbor: Journal of Roman Archaeology.

Cameron, Alan. 1965. "Wandering Poets: A Literary Movement in Byzantine Egypt." *Historia* 14: 470–509.

——. 2004. "Poetry and Literary Culture in Late Antiquity." In *Approaching Late Antiquity: The Transformation from Early to Late Empire,* ed. S. Swain and M. Edwards, 327–354. Oxford: Oxford University Press.

Cribiore, R. 1992. "The Happy Farmer: A Student Composition from Roman Egypt." *GRBS* 33: 247–263.

——. 1996. *Writing, Teachers, and Students in Graeco-Roman Egypt.* Atlanta: Scholars Press.

——. 1999. "Greek and Coptic Education in Late Antique Egypt." In *Ägypten und Nubien in spätantiker und christlicher Zeit,* ed. S. Emmel et al., 279–286. Wiesbaden: Reichert.

——. 2001a. "The Grammarian's Choice: The Popularity of Euripides' *Phoenissae* in Hellenistic and Roman Education." In *Education in Greek and Roman Antiquity,* ed. Y. L. Too, 241–259. Leiden: Brill.

——. 2001b. *Gymnastics of the Mind: Greek Education in Hellenistic and Roman Egypt.* Princeton: Princeton University Press.

——. 2003/04 "Latin Literacy in Egypt." *KODAI: Journal of Ancient History* 13/14 (2003/04) [2008]: 111–118.

Cuvigny, H., ed. 2003. *La route de Myos Hormos: L'armée romaine dans le désert oriental d'Égypte.* 2 vols. Cairo: Institut français d'archéologie orientale.

Di Benedetto, V. 1957. "Frammento grammaticale." *Annali Pisa* 2(26): 180–185.

Di Bitonto–Kasser, A. 1998. "*P.Bodmer* LI recto: Esercizio di divisione sillabica." *Museum Helveticum* 55: 112–118.

Duttenhöfer, R. 1997. "Schultexte auf byzantinischen Holztafeln: Isokrates, Pros Demonikon §17." *Akten 21. Papyrologenkongresses,* 244–250. Stuttgart: Teubner.

Emmel, S., M. Krause, S. G. Richter, and S. Schaten, eds. 1999. *Ägypten und Nubien in spätantiker und christlicher Zeit.* Wiesbaden: Reichert.

Foerster, R. 1963. *Libanius, Opera.* 12 vols. 1903–1927; repr. Hildesheim: Olms.

Gaebel, R. E. 1970. "The Greek Word-Lists to Vergil and Cicero." *Bulletin of the John Rylands Library* (Manchester): 284–325.

Haines-Eitzen, K. 2000. *Guardians of Letters: Literacy, Power, and the Transmitters of Early Christian Literature.* New York: Oxford University Press.

Hanson, A. E. 1991. "Ancient Illiteracy." In *Literacy in the Roman World,* 159–198. Ann Arbor: Journal of Roman Archaeology.

Harris, W. V. 1989. *Ancient Literacy.* Cambridge, Mass.: Harvard University Press.

Kramer, J. 1983. *Glossaria bilinguia in papyris et membranis reperta.* Bonn: Pap. Texte Abh. 30. Bonn: R. Habelt.

———. 2001. *Glossaria bilinguia altera.* Munich: K.G. Saur.

Kugener, M.A., ed. 1903. *Zacharias Scholasticus, Vita Severi. Patrologia Orientalis* II, fasc. 1. Turnhout: Brepols.

Law, V., and I. Sluiter, eds. 1995. *Dionysius Thrax and the Techne Grammatike.* Münster: Nodus Publikationen.

Leuven Database of Ancient Books (LDAB). http://ldab.arts.kuleuven.ac.be/.

Lundon, J. 2004. "The Scholia Minora in Homerum: An alphabetical List." http://www.uni-koeln.de/phil-fak/ifa/NRWakademie/Lundon/ScholiaMinora.htm.

———, and G. Messeri. 2000. "A Passage of Isocrates on the Back of a Protocol (*P.Vindob G* 39977)." *ZPE* 132: 125–131.

Marrou, H.-I. 1975. *Histoire de l'éducation dans l'antiquité,* 7th ed. Paris: Seuil.

McNamee, K. 1994. "School Notes." In *Proceedings of the Twentieth International Congress of Papyrologists,* ed. A. Bülow-Jacobsen, 177–182. Copenhagen: Museum Tusculanum Press.

Montanari, F. 1995. "The *Mythographus Homericus.*" In *Greek Literary Theory after Aristotle: A Collection of Papers in Honour of D.M. Schenkeveld,* ed. J. Abbenes, S. Slings, and I. Sluiter, 135–172. Amsterdam: VU University Press.

Morgan, T. 1998. *Literate Education in the Hellenistic and Roman Worlds.* Cambridge: Cambridge University Press.

Patillon, M. 1997. *Aelius Théon: Progymnasmata.* Paris: Les Belles Lettres.

Small, J. P. 1997. *Waxed Tablets of the Mind: Cognitive Studies of Memory and Literacy in Classical Antiquity.* New York: Routledge.

Swain, S., and M. Edwards, eds. 2004. *Approaching Late Antiquity: The Transformation from Early to Late Empire.* Oxford: Oxford University Press.

Thomas, R. 1992. *Literacy and Orality in Ancient Greece.* Cambridge: Cambridge University Press.

Too, Y. L., ed. 2001. *Education in Greek and Roman Antiquity.* Leiden: Brill.

Worp, K. A., and A. Rijksbaron. 1997. *The Kellis Isocrates Codex.* Oxford: Oxbow.

Wouters, A. 1979. *The Grammatical Papyri from Graeco-Roman Egypt: Contributions to the Study of the "Ars Grammatica" in Antiquity.* Brussels: Koninklijke Academie voor Wetenschappen, Letteren en Schone Kunsten van België, Klasse der Letteren.

Youtie, H. C. 1966. "Pétaus, fils de Pétaus, ou le scribe qui ne savait pas écrire." *CdÉ* 41: 127–143 = *Scriptiunculae* II (Amsterdam 1973), 677–695.

Zintzen, C. 1967. *Damascii vitae Isidori reliquiae.* Hildesheim: Olms.

Zuntz, G. 1975. *Die Aristophanes-Scholien der Papyri.* Berlin: Seitz.

CHAPTER 15

MATHEMATICS, SCIENCE, AND MEDICINE IN THE PAPYRI

ALEXANDER JONES

THE contribution of papyrology to our present understanding of ancient science is large but very unevenly distributed. First of all, in antiquity no overarching concept existed of a field of study coextensive with the common modern meaning of "science." When we speak of science in antiquity, we generally mean two different things: first, a handful of more or less autonomous traditions or disciplines that dealt with healing, time reckoning, the interpretation of ominous astronomical phenomena, and so on in both the Near Eastern and classical civilizations; and second, a range of subjects—meteorology and zoology are examples—that did not become established as disciplines but were usually subsumed by Graeco-Roman authors within the broad heading of natural philosophy. In this chapter we are concerned only with the scientific disciplines that were recognized as such in antiquity.

Perhaps the first lesson that the papyri can teach us about ancient science comes from realizing that the areas where they fall silent are not entirely accidental. Thus, optics (the study of visual appearances), harmonic theory, and theoretical mechanics are scarcely present in the papyri, although each of these sciences had an abundant literature in Hellenistic and Roman times and was well represented in the medieval transmission of Greek scientific texts. This fact probably indicates that these were academic specialties studied almost exclusively for their own sake in a few intellectual centers (Alexandria, for instance, but not Oxyrhynchus). In many fields the community of research scientists and advanced students equipped to understand their work was always small; thus, according to one plausible estimate, the number of creative mathematicians in the Graeco-Roman world was never so much as a hundred (Netz 2002, 202–205).

The sciences that are significantly attested among the papyri are mathematics, medicine, astronomy, and astrology. Again we can see why this should be so. Medicine and astrology were professions with numerous practitioners who possessed collections of reference texts and whose activity involved producing written documents. Astronomy, though not a profession in its own right, had a central role in weather prediction, calendrics, and, above all, astrology. Mathematics, too, had its uses in calculation and mensuration, and applied and theoretical mathematics were often components of technical and liberal education, respectively. In other words, these were all subjects that were cultivated for external ends at least as much as for pure intellectual satisfaction. The most obvious difference between the evidence of the medieval textual tradition, which was heavily influenced by the intellectual elite of the later Roman and Byzantine periods, and that of the papyri is that much of the papyrological record has a direct bearing on practice and applications.

MATHEMATICS

Scribal Mathematics

Two broad styles of doing mathematics can be distinguished in the ancient world. One was concerned with finding numerical values of quantities or magnitudes in set situations, usually (although not always) expressed in terms of real-world objects; the other, with finding and proving properties of mathematical entities such as whole numbers or circles, usually (but not always) treating them as abstractions. We customarily associate the label "Greek mathematics" with the latter style while associating the former with Egypt and Mesopotamia, but both were in fact practiced side by side in the Graeco-Roman world, and there was a certain amount of sharing of methods and results between them. To take a single instance, the theorem that the surface of a sphere has four times the area of its largest circular section, which Archimedes discovered and proved rigorously in *On the Sphere and Cylinder*, could subsequently appear without demonstration as a mensurational formula in practically oriented texts such as Hero's *Metrica*. The appropriate distinction to make is thus not between Greek and Near Eastern but between academic and scribal mathematics.

The medieval manuscript tradition was highly selective. It favored the abstract, proof-oriented academic style through the survival of writings by a small number of authors, most notably Euclid, Archimedes, and Apollonius, who were active in the third and early second centuries BCE, along with a few rather less eminent figures such as Pappus, who lived in late antiquity. Such texts in the quantity-oriented scribal style as were transmitted (e.g., the *Arithmetica* of Diophantus and some of the works attributed to Hero of Alexandria) belonged to the more literary part of this tradition most closely related to the proof-oriented style. By contrast, the papyri confront us repeatedly with its more practical side, the kind of mathematics that was useful—or thought to be so—for everyday purposes. For pre-Hellenistic Egypt, moreover, papyri are our principal source of information on mathematics.

Numbers in Greek papyri were almost always written in the Ionian (alphabetic) notation, which used ten as its base but was not a place value notation; thus, having learned that B plus E equals Z ($2 + 5 = 7$) does not make it immediately obvious that K plus N equals O ($20 + 50 = 70$). Egyptian scripts used an analogous non-place-value decimal notation, though the individual symbols were not alphabetic. A component of scribal training in all periods was to learn how to perform arithmetical operations on numbers written in these notations. Numerical tables were extensively used in both the teaching and practice of arithmetic (Fowler 1999, 234–240, and see 268–276 for an inventory of papyri).

The most basic task was to learn the sums and products of pairs of units, tens, and hundreds. We have about twenty specimens from the Graeco-Roman period—on papyrus, as well as on wooden or waxed tablets—of addition and multiplication tables. A multiplication table for the number 7, for example, might give the results of multiplying 7 by 1, 2, 3, ... 9, 10, 20, 30, ... 90, 100, 200, 300, ... 900, 1,000, 2,000, 3,000, ... 9,000, and 10,000. Performing arithmetical operations by means of tables would, of course, have been slower and more cumbersome than relying on memory; one was probably expected to memorize these tables rather than retain them as ready reference.

Division presented problems that were more vexatious for the scribe (though more interesting for the modern mathematician) because of the way that fractions were expressed, which was different from both our modern fractions, like 3/5, and our modern decimals, like 0.6. This notation, which was originally Egyptian but later adapted to the Greek Ionic numerals, required any fraction to be broken down into the sum of a series of distinct, so-called unit fractions, that is, ½, ⅓, ¼ ... (but a special symbol for ⅔ was also available). Thus, the result of dividing three by five, or six by ten, would be written as a symbol representing a half followed by the numeral for 10 (I), both marked as fractions by a raised stroke, because $3/5 = 1/2 + 1/10$. Because it is by no means a trivial problem to find a set of unit fractions that add up to a given quotient, tables were made that listed the results of dividing, say, 10 into 1, 2, 3, ... 9, 10, 20, 30, ... 90 (and so forth). Such tables are about twice as common as addition and multiplication tables not because one had to do division more often than the other operations but probably because the appropriate combinations of unit fractions were harder to commit to memory.

Aside from tables, the commonest form that mathematical texts take in the papyri is as collections of problems. In Egypt a tradition of problem texts can be traced back to a half dozen or so mathematical texts preserved from the first half of the second millennium BCE, among which are two substantial and important hieratic rolls known as the Moscow and Rhind mathematical papyri (Gillings 1972; Chace et al. 1927–1929; Struve 1930). Following these, there is a long gap in the documentation, after which it resumes in the Hellenistic period and continues to the Byzantine. A regular feature of problem texts, whether early or late and regardless of the language in which they are expressed, is that they illustrate methods of solution by specific numerical examples rather than prescribing procedures in general terms, and no argument is provided to justify the procedures. The simplest problems and, one surmises, the most practically useful are metrological conversions and the calculation of rectangular areas and volumes, where the handling of the chaotic systems of units of measure (see chapter 8) is again as much a part of the lesson as the principle that area or volume is the product of the linear dimensions.

The problem texts are algorithmic: a step-by-step procedure is carried out on a particular set of data so that the student can learn the pattern and apply the same steps to different data. Texts practically never present a method in general terms and say, for instance, "to get the area of any rectangle, you multiply the length by the width"; instead, one might have a series of problems that deal with specific rectangular fields with stated numbers for the length and width. (Much of elementary mathematics is still learned this way.) Complex problems are distinguished from simple ones only by the number of steps to be performed. Geometrical problem texts are accompanied—intermittently in the Pharaonic papyri, regularly in the Graeco-Roman—by diagrams that schematically display a particular situation and are often labeled with numerals that represent the various dimensions.

As an illustration of a problem text we may take an early specimen, Problem 44 of the Rhind papyrus, which asks the reader to calculate the volume of grain in a cubical box, the length, width, and depth of which are all 10 cubits. The text instructs us to multiply 10 by 10, getting 100, and then to multiply this by 10, getting 1,000. Then we are told to add half again of this result, getting 1,500, which, the text says, is the capacity of the box in a unit called *khar*. Finally, we are told to take a twentieth of this figure, that is, 75, and this is the capacity of the box in a unit called a quadruple *hekat*. Here the strictly geometrical aspect of the problem—finding the number of cubic cubits the box contains—is dealt with in the first two multiplications, followed by the metrological aspect of expressing this quantity in conventional units of capacity. Essentially the same procedure is followed for Problem 41, which asks for the volume of grain in a cylindrical container with a diameter of 9 and a height of 10, except that the different shape requires a different formula for the volume in cubic cubits: One subtracts a ninth from the diameter, multiplies this first by itself and then by the height. Typically for this genre of text, no indication is given that the formula is an approximation. The style of writing is in general very terse; much of the explaining must have been oral.

Alongside such practically useful formulae, one finds throughout the tradition problems that, although expressed in terms of real-world objects, can only be regarded as puzzles or exercises since one could not easily imagine analogous situations arising outside of the classroom. Thus in the Rhind papyrus the genuinely practical Problem 63 (to divide seven hundred loaves among four workers according to specified pay scales) immediately follows a puzzle in which one is asked to determine the quantities of gold, silver, and lead in a bag from the price paid for it, all of this subject to certain unreal conditions that give just the right information to make the problem soluble. In later papyri, where the repertoire of mathematical techniques is enlarged relative to the pharaonic texts, probably under Babylonian or Greek influence, the new methods give rise to more and more unreal situations. A third-century-BCE demotic papyrus, *P. Cairo* J.E. 89127–30 + 89137–43 (Parker 1972, 41), contains a problem (no. 33) in which a square piece of land of known area is miraculously rearranged as a circle, and we are asked to find its diameter: The solution is in part an exercise in finding an approximate square root, a technique probably borrowed from Mesopotamia. A Greek papyrus from the first or second century CE, *P.Chic.* 3 (Goodspeed 1898), consists of problems in which one has to find the areas of irregularly shaped plots of land that (conveniently) can always be broken down into a few right-angled triangles so that the solution is obtainable through the theorem of Pythagoras. One could cite comparable instances from many manuscripts. The emphasis on impractical problems in the mathematical papyri raises interesting questions about the goals and rationale of the mathematical education of scribes in antiquity.

It goes without saying that documentary papyri contain immense quantities of numerical data, some of which resulted from calculations. Recent studies of pharaonic Egyptian mathematics (Imhausen 2003a, 2003b) have for the first time brought such evidence to bear on the interpretation of "administrative mathematics" as found in the problem texts, showing how extensively the framework of the problems is determined by the professional practice of scribes and accountants. The Graeco-Roman material deserves to be subjected to this kind of analysis.

Academic Mathematics

Compared to the problem texts, the known papyri that contain Greek mathematics in the proof-oriented tradition are very few indeed. Most attention to date has been given to the papyri that include parts of the most famous of all Greek mathematical treatises, Euclid's *Elements*. Four have been published so far, and more certainly lurk in the major collections (Fowler 1999, 209–217). All the known papyri of the *Elements* date from the interval between the late first and the third centuries CE, thus at least three centuries after Euclid's time. By itself this fact would be dangerous as a basis for hypotheses, but it turns out that the earliest definite references to Euclid's *Elements* in Graeco-Roman authors are from about the same time as the earliest of the papyri, so it seems likely that the book's adoption as a standard school text was, surprisingly, this late. It was likely part of the process whereby deductive geometry became a curricular subject taught more widely if also more superficially than it had been in the Hellenistic period. Three of the four Euclidean papyri certainly do not derive from complete copies but present excerpts, apparently intended for some didactic purpose. The fourth, *P.Fay.* 9, might have belonged to a full text but presents significant variants—including the omission or displacement of an entire theorem—with respect to the medieval textual tradition. We are still far from knowing how faithfully the *Elements* as it has come down to us represents what Euclid wrote and how much our text owes to editors of the Roman period and late antiquity.

Deductive mathematical treatises discussed a small range of objects (e.g., points, lines, circles) in a highly standardized idiom, but their arguments develop on a large scale. While the distinctive terminology should make it easy in principle to identify a small fragment of a manuscript as belonging to this genre, one would generally need a substantial amount of text to take the identification further. Still, it is remarkable that no papyrus fragment has yet been shown to belong to any identifiable work of the Greek mathematicians except the *Elements,* not even a scrap of the most renowned of them, Archimedes. This is in strong contrast to the prominence of the mathematical literature among the secular texts preserved in Byzantine manuscripts or translated into Arabic around the ninth century. Again we seem to be seeing evidence that serious study of academic mathematics was concentrated in just a few centers. Perversely, the most advanced mathematics preserved in a contemporary document from antiquity is a series of geometrical theorems, with accompanying diagrams, written on a set of ostraca found at the distinctly remote site of Elephantine (Mau and Müller 1960). These texts were written in the third century BCE, that is, roughly contemporary with or barely later than Euclid himself, and they concern the construction of the regular polyhedra inside a sphere, which is the subject matter of the culminating book 13 of the *Elements.*

ASTRONOMY AND ASTROLOGY

The Hellenistic Period

Leaving aside a few brief or incidental references to astronomical phenomena, chiefly of calendrical interest, no astronomical texts survive on Egyptian papyri older than the Hellenistic period. For that matter, few astronomical papyri in any language are preserved from the beginning of Greek rule until the second half of the first century BCE, but they include some of exceptional importance. One reason for this is that our documentation of early Greek astronomy consists largely of reports and adaptations in texts of a later period. It is unlikely that it will ever be possible to write a history of ancient astronomy that depends entirely on contemporary sources, but by their help one can get some sense of the infidelities, selectiveness, and biases of the later testimony. The Hellenistic astronomical papyri are quite diverse in genre and content, though certain themes recur, notably an emphasis on annually recurring phenomena of the sun and stars, the relationships between the sun and moon, and the regulation of calendars. Another notable feature is the presence, side by side, of specifically Egyptian elements with others that were typical of the generality of Greek astronomy.

One early witness to this fusion of Greek and Egyptian material is *P.Hib.* I 27, which on internal and external grounds can be dated with certainty to about 300 BCE. The main body of the text is a weather *parapêgma*, a variety of document highly characteristic of Greek astronomy. A *parapêgma* is a list of dates of astronomical events that recur at intervals of one solar year and dates of weather patterns that were also believed to recur annually. The astronomical events included the solstices and equinoxes, and the dates when stars and constellations were first seen to rise or set before dawn or after dusk; apparently, these were believed to be signs, perhaps even causes, of the more regular weather changes. Since they attempted to delineate a connection between the heavens and certain aspects of the immediate human environment, the *parapêgmata* came to be subsumed under the category of astrology by certain Roman-period writers such as Ptolemy.

It is commonly supposed that astronomers as early as the fifth century BCE produced *parapêgmata,* but the Hibeh *parapêgma* is the oldest one extant. It is also the earliest datable Greek text that clearly refers to the signs of the zodiac (i.e., the division of the zodiac into equal twelfths as distinct from the zodiacal constellations). Unlike the later Hellenistic examples preserved through the manuscript tradition or as inscriptions, the Hibeh *parapêgma* incorporates the dates of many religious festivals—both Greek and Egyptian, some local to Sais—and stages of the Nile's flood cycle, and all the dates are specified according to the Egyptian calendar, which in the short term (on the order of a decade or two) could function as an ersatz solar calendar. A prefatory letter purports that the contents of the papyrus were taught to the author, a man who had lived in the Saite nome for five years, by a "wise man in Sais," who apparently was an Egyptian, but the presence of phrases that are repeated verbatim in the "Eudoxus" papyrus (discussed later) suggests that this claimed pedigree is fictitious.

The Egyptian calendar proved to be Egypt's most important and enduring contribution to the development of astronomy; its strictly uniform months and years had obvious advantages over the Greek lunar calendars for accurate time-reckoning. Early Greek efforts to coordinate the two kinds of calendar are reflected in *P.Ryl.* IV 589, an early second-century-BCE account of debts to which has been appended a list of Egyptian calendar dates that correspond to the first days of lunar months. The months in question are according to the Egyptian reckoning, beginning with the morning disappearance of the waning moon rather than the evening appearance of the new moon crescent, and the twenty-five-year cycle by which the dates were determined also seems to have been known in Egypt before the Ptolemaic period. A small scrap of text from third-century-BCE Gurob, *P.Petrie* III 134, attests to Greek interest in the *decans,* constellations traditionally used in Egypt for time-reckoning at night, and the problem of correlating the *decans* with the Egyptian calendar.

The most famous of all astronomical papyri, *P.Par.* 1 (first half of second century BCE), is commonly known as the "Eudoxus papyrus," or *Ars Eudoxi* (Blass 1887). This is a rendering of the words *EYΔΟΞΟΥ TEXNH*, "art of Eudoxus," which are spelled out by the initial letters of an acrostic iambic poem on the back of the roll and which may or may not have been composed by the same individual as the text on the front. The lengths of the poem's twelve lines also manage to encode the structure of the Egyptian calendar year's months and days. The name "Eudoxus" here stands as a metonym for astronomy—the great contemporary of Plato had nothing to do with the composition of the papyrus, although he is one of several authorities cited in it.

The preserved part of the roll, almost two meters long, contains on its front the final twenty-four columns of an astronomical treatise with interspersed figures; not counting geometrical diagrams, this is the oldest known illustrated Greek manuscript. The figures, which are obscure and for the most part have little or no relation to the text, combine features of Greek cosmology (circles that represent a spherical earth, sun, and moon and the zodiac) and Egyptian imagery (scarab, Horus, scorpion). Though laid out as prose, the treatise was originally composed at least partly in verse. The purported author is identified in the final column as one Leptines. A wide range of topics is discussed at an elementary level: the most obvious periodicities of the sun, moon, and planets; the risings and settings of the fixed stars; an eight-year cycle for a lunar calendar (but not the more accurate nineteen-year cycle, though this was certainly familiar in the Hellenistic period); a crude geocentric cosmology; the causes of the moon's phases and eclipses; and the relative sizes of the sun, moon, and earth. As a whole the work does not seem to be an adequate index of what astronomers were doing in the early second century, but it is probably a fair portrayal of what an educated layperson knew about the subject.

An early first-century-BCE papyrus from Abusir al Melek, *P.Berl.* 13146 + 13147, is the first known witness to the kind of astronomy that would become predominant in the papyri—and indeed in the Graeco-Roman world—during the Roman period (Neugebauer, Parker, and Zauzich 1981). Unlike the foregoing texts, it is in demotic Egyptian, though there are indications that it was adapted from a fuller model in Greek. The back has a text that describes a procedure for determining Egyptian calendar dates of solstices and equinoxes, but the important text is on the front, a list of predictions of the dates and circumstances of lunar eclipses during the years 85–74 BCE. (The papyrus was actually written after these dates and incorporates some details apparently derived from observations.) These are older than any other extant Greek or Egyptian predictions of complex astronomical phenomena. The papyrus does not reveal the purpose of the eclipse predictions, but almost certainly they were connected with the—ultimately Mesopotamian— tradition of interpreting eclipses as astrologically ominous events, so this may also be the oldest astronomical papyrus motivated by astrology.

The Roman Period

Astrology, as a coherent theory that systematically describes the effects of the instantaneous state of the heavens on human lives and characters seems to have come into existence about 100 BCE, probably in Egypt (Pingree 1997). It spread rapidly throughout the Graeco-Roman world during the following century, thereby creating a demand for astronomical data and in particular the locations of the heavenly bodies relative to the zodiac and to the local horizon at any given date and time. The abundance of Roman-period astrological and astronomical papyri implies that astrologers existed in large numbers throughout Egypt; yet curiously they are almost invisible in documentary texts. A passing mention of a "one-eyed astrologer [*astrologos*]" in *P.Oxy.* LXI 4126 appears to be unique.

The most common manifestation of the bond between astrology and astronomy was the personal horoscope, a document that states the birthdate of an individual and lists the zodiacal locations of the sun, the moon, and the five planets known in antiquity, as well as the point of the zodiac that was rising on the horizon at the date and time of birth. Horoscopes were obviously astrological in purpose— pronouncements about the life of the individual were based on it—but purely astronomical in content. Astrologers used the astronomical data in a horoscope as the basis for making forecasts about the individual whose birth was recorded in it, but this interpretation was never put into writing.

The authors of treatises on astrology sometimes incorporated genuine horoscopes in their works to illustrate techniques of interpretation. One second-century textbook that survived through the medieval tradition, the *Anthologies* of Vettius Valens, contains about a hundred horoscopes from the author's files, but most works limited themselves to one or two, relying for the remaining part on contrived textbook examples. Horoscopes on papyrus, by way of contrast, are authentic records from consultations with astrologers. They are among the more frequently encountered personal documents. When O. Neugebauer and H. B. van

Hoesen published the first comprehensive collection of Greek horoscopes from all sources (Neugebauer and van Hoesen 1959), they included roughly fifty horoscopic papyri and ostraca. The number of extant specimens—mostly Greek, a handful demotic—is now approaching two hundred (see especially Baccani 1992 and *P.Oxy. Astron.* 4236–4300a in Jones 1999a). They were evidently produced by numerous horoscope casters working in many localities over a long period and hence give a more reliable picture of the activity of astrologers (valid at least for Egypt, if not for the whole Roman Empire) than the "literary" sources.

The format of most horoscopes from all periods is highly standardized; *P.Oxy. Astron.* 4264 (Jones 1999a, 2.402–403), for an unnamed individual born on the morning of April 18, 300 CE, is a typical example:

> Good fortune. Nativity.
> Year 16 of Diocletian,
> Pharmouthi 23, hour 4 of day.
> Ascendant and Mars in Gemini.
> Saturn in Leo.
> Moon in Virgo.
> Jupiter in Capricorn.
> Sun, Mercury, and Venus in Aries.
> Good luck!

Thus we have, in order, a brief introductory formula (optional), the name of the individual (optional, and omitted in this example), the person's birthdate and time of birth, a list of the seven heavenly bodies and the ascendant point *(hôroskopos)* with their positions in the zodiac at the time of birth, and a brief closing formula (optional). For the positions most horoscopes, like this one, give only the name of the relevant sign of the zodiac. Occasionally one finds more precise locations in degrees or degrees and minutes counted from the beginning of the sign (each sign is thirty degrees long). The typical medium was a scrap or ticket of papyrus, perhaps reused, and there is considerable variation in the quality of hands and standard of orthography. A few horoscopes are more elaborate, stretching out the information by means of a formulaic text that provides a full paragraph for each heavenly body, and such horoscopes—surely reserved for the wealthier customers—are written out in bookhands on rolls that must have been two to three meters long when complete.

The papyrus horoscopes always gave the birthdate of the person in question in this form: regnal year, Egyptian month and day, and hour of day or night. Even when the date formula is damaged or lost, it can usually be reconstructed from the astronomical data. This is not because the stated positions of the heavenly bodies are usually very accurate (they are typically correct only to within five or ten degrees, and larger errors are not uncommon). Rather, because each planet has a different periodicity for its revolution around the zodiac, the combined information derived from a set of individually imprecise positions can suffice to narrow down the possible dates within the historically and palaeographically admissible interval to a unique dating accurate to within one day (Jones 1999a, 1.47–52).

The document itself might have been produced anywhere from within days of the birthdate (supposing it was obtained on behalf of a newborn child) to at most several decades later since only in theoretical writings would there be an interest in finding the horoscopes of deceased people. The earliest known horoscope, a demotic ostracon, is for someone born in 38 BCE, and the latest, a Greek papyrus, is for someone born in 508 CE. In between, the numbers of horoscopes peak between 150 and 300, although this pattern probably reflects only the relatively high survival rate of papyri of all kinds during that period. The general impression is that, once horoscopic astrology became established in Egypt in the second half of the first century BCE, it remained steadily popular until the end of the fourth century, when a marked decline began (ibid., 1.5–6).

In the ancient debates about the validity of astrology, one sometimes encounters a caricature of a horoscope caster as someone who watches the sky, waiting to record the places of the heavenly bodies at the instant when he hears a signal that a child has been born. The reality as exposed in the papyri is not at all like that. The astronomical information in horoscopes and other astrologically oriented documents was not obtained by observation but rather by calculation from various kinds of theory. The majority of the astrologers likely knew little technical astronomy, but they had written resources, especially tables, that supplied the data they needed.

Many fragments of astrologers' tables are extant (in addition to *P.Oxy.Astron.* 4148–4235 in ibid., see 1.301–307 for a checklist of astronomical papyri published elsewhere, among which are nearly fifty tables). The tables consist mostly of numbers, sometimes accompanied by names of the signs of the zodiac (when the information consists of the positions of a heavenly body) or names of months (when the information consists of dates), but both zodiacal signs and months are also sometimes coded as numbers running from one to twelve. All these data are often laid out in a tabular grid of black or red lines. In many tables the successive rows represent steps of progressing time (e.g., successive days or years), while the various columns contain different categories of data associated with those dates. One of the techniques for identifying and analyzing astronomical tables is to look for mathematical patterns in the numbers as one reads down a column or set of columns, for example, determining whether the numbers increase or decrease by constant or roughly constant amounts and, if so, by how much. Each of the heavenly bodies has characteristic patterns of motion that manifest themselves in such numerical patterns.

The tables also tend to conform to certain established formats (Jones 1999b). The most frequently attested variety of astronomical table, the sign-entry almanac, is a table of the dates when, according to computation, each planet crosses from one sign of the zodiac to a neighboring sign. We have examples of sign-entry almanacs covering intervals from as early as the late first century BCE and as late as the fourth century CE. Such a table, which could extend over several decades of planetary motion, would make it trivially easy to find the zodiacal signs occupied by each planet on a given date, though it would be of no use for obtaining more precise positions in degrees. Another common type of table, the ephemeris, gives computed positions for all seven heavenly bodies for every single day in a succession of months and years. The known examples are spread over an even wider temporal span, from the first century BCE to the fifth century CE. The principal application of ephemerides was probably not in casting horoscopes, however, but in the so-called catarchic branch of astrology, which professed to determine whether any particular day was auspicious or inauspicious for different activities. Two or three other standardized formats of almanac are attested, in which computed planetary positions are given at regular intervals. With the sole exception of the ephemerides, which are mentioned in a few astrological texts dating from late antiquity, none of these varieties of table is preserved or discussed in the literature preserved through the medieval manuscript tradition.

The first questions that naturally occur to a historian of astronomy are, how were these almanacs and ephemerides calculated, and what kind of theories of planetary motion underlie them? Unfortunately, it is generally difficult or impossible to work backward from the computed results in such tables to the methods of computation, especially given the fragmentary condition of the papyri. On the other hand, we know of other varieties of tables (and a few instructional texts that describe how to make or use them) that have a closer connection to the astronomical theories. These are analogous in function to the astronomical tables preserved by the medieval tradition, which are chiefly those incorporated in two second-century-CE works by Ptolemy: his treatise *Mathematical Syntaxis* (now usually called by its medieval nickname, the *Almagest*), and the *Handy Tables*. Like Ptolemy's tables, the ones on papyrus would have been employed only by the more technically competent and sophisticated astrologers to find precise positions of the heavenly bodies, the kind of data recorded in the more elaborate horoscopes. The discovery of these "primary" tables is among the most important developments in the study of ancient science in the last generation; it has cast light on a part of Greek astronomy, the existence of which is scarcely hinted at in the medieval tradition.

Before such tables were encountered, what we knew about the theories of motion of the heavenly bodies current during the Roman period was practically limited to the works of Ptolemy. It was assumed that Ptolemy's approach in the *Almagest* was representative of his contemporaries and predecessors, at least as far back as Hipparchus (second century BCE). Ptolemy's astronomy is geocentric, and its basic principle is that the heavenly bodies move around a stationary earth along geometrical paths compounded out of circular motions. For example, a planet might be assumed to revolve with uniform speed around a relatively small circle called an epicycle, which itself revolves uniformly around the earth, thereby making it appear that the planet varies in speed and even periodically reverses the direction of its motion through the zodiac. The object of the theory was to establish the sizes, speeds, and positions of the various revolutions consistent with observations. Tables based on such geometrical theories or models use what we would now call trigonometrical functions to represent the way that an observer on earth sees these circular motions. Largely through the *Almagest*'s influence, Islamic, Byzantine, and western European astronomy continued along similar lines until the seventeenth century.

Soon after the decipherment of Mesopotamian cuneiform script in the late nineteenth century, it was discovered that astronomers in Babylonia during the last four centuries BCE had developed planetary theories that operated on entirely different principles. Babylonian astronomy employed sophisticated combinations built up from simple arithmetical sequences but without trigonometry to reproduce the observed patterns of astronomical phenomena. Babylonia turned out to be the source of certain conventions of Greek astronomy, such as the division of the zodiac into twelve signs of thirty degrees each; the representation of fractions as sixtieths ("minutes"), sixtieths of sixtieths ("seconds"), and so forth; and a handful of specific significant numbers such as a highly accurate estimate of the average length of the lunar month. Nonetheless, the dependence of the Greek tradition on the Babylonian did not appear likely to extend beyond these important but elementary borrowings (Neugebauer 1975, 2.601–607).

Since the 1980s, about twenty Greek papyri have come to light that reveal that, from the first through the fourth centuries CE, a substantial part of the most complex Babylonian arithmetical theories were used in Egypt in forms adapted to accommodate the Egyptian calendar instead of the Babylonian lunar calendar but otherwise practically unchanged. The first of these "Graeco-Babylonian" papyri (and still perhaps the most astonishing) turned up in a private collection and was first published by Neugebauer, who fully recognized its revolutionary significance (Neugebauer 1988; see also Jones 1997). It is a fragment of a very elaborate kind of computation of the circumstances of new or full moons, familiar from cuneiform tablets of the last three centuries BCE and known as "system B." Other tables found among the Oxyrhynchus papyri proved to be computations of dates and zodiacal positions of planetary phenomena, such as first visibilities and stationary points, in which the same methods of calculation were used that we find in the cuneiform tablets; the majority of the Babylonian planetary models are now identifiable in Greek papyri (*P.Oxy.Astron.* 4152–4161 in Jones 1999a). The Babylonian methods seem in fact to have been more widely employed than methods based on theories of circular motion until the third century CE. After that time, Ptolemy's astronomical tables began to compete vigorously with them, as is attested by several fragments of papyrus manuscripts of his *Handy Tables*, but the Babylonian methods seem to disappear from the record only after the fourth century—yet there is scarcely a hint of knowledge of them in any of the literature from the medieval tradition. Historians are only beginning to explore the consequences of this new picture of rival traditions and to speculate about the channels of transmission.

In comparison to the mass of known astronomical tables and texts related to prediction and astrological applications (now approaching two hundred papyri), the papyri that contain genuine theoretical texts constitute a mere handful (Jones 2003). For the most part, the astrologers of Roman Egypt did not devote much space in their libraries to astronomical theory; it is noteworthy that no fragment even of the *Almagest*, the work in which Ptolemy presented the empirical reasoning behind his predictive tables, has shown up on papyrus. Nonetheless, we do possess two disconnected passages from a treatise comparable to Ptolemy's but written a generation earlier, about 105 CE, in *P.Oxy.Astron.* 4133 and *PSI* XV 1490, but these, though of enormous historical interest, are altogether exceptional in the papyrus record. The passage in *P.Oxy.Astron.* 4133 discusses an analysis of a pair of observations of the position of Jupiter relative to certain stars in the constellation Cancer, one made by unidentified astronomers in 241 BCE and the other by the author himself in 105 CE. These are the only known dated astronomical observations preserved in a Greek source earlier than Ptolemy. The other passage concerns the construction of tables for calculating the sun's zodiacal position on the basis of a theory of the sun's motion around the earth that was geometrical but significantly different from Ptolemy's.

Paralleling the situation with the horoscopes, Egyptian-language astronomical papyri are vastly outnumbered by those in Greek, but a few demotic specimens are known of both the "almanac" and "primary" varieties of table. Horoscope casting is documented in the ostraca from the temple at Medinet Madi, in both Greek and demotic, and more circumstantial evidence exists that astrology was practiced in a bilingual temple setting at Tebtynis (Jones 1994). The Egyptian scribal traditions of the Roman period also preserved texts relating to the older, nonmathematical and nonastrological astronomy of the pharaonic period, most impressively in *P.Carlsberg* 1, an extensive commentary on astronomical texts and pictures that independently survive in some New Kingdom royal tombs (Neugebauer and Parker 1969).

Many strictly astrological papyri other than horoscopes have been published, and more await study in the major collections (checklist in Baccani 1992, 32–34). They have not as yet altered our understanding of the evolution of Graeco-Roman astrology as much as the astronomical papyri have affected the historiography of astronomy—perhaps reflecting the fact that the study of ancient astrology still is more preoccupied with the discovery and editing of texts than with historical analysis of their contents. Yet the potential of the papyri for improving our understanding of the early development of astrology is considerable since very little of the medievally transmitted literature is older than the second century CE. A large portion of the astrological papyri derive from handbooks on the interpretation of horoscopes, similar in character to much of the astrological literature that survives through the medieval manuscript tradition, though specific textual overlaps are rare. Several of the popular astrological handbooks, especially in the earliest period, were written in verse, and papyri have made substantial contributions to the known corpus of astrological verse, including notably several fragments in elegiac meter attributable to the first-century author Anubio (Obbink 2004).

Special interest attaches to a small number of papyri, both Greek and demotic, that relate to so-called general astrology. While horoscopic astrology focused on the individual, general astrology attempted forecasts of events and circumstances pertaining to entire peoples and countries, for example, by interpreting the appearance of eclipses or the positions of the planets at the annual first rising of Sirius. Several texts help to trace a historical connection between this branch of astrology and the much older Mesopotamian tradition of astral omens, documented in cuneiform texts as early as the Old Babylonian period (early second millennium BCE). Most impressively, the Roman-period demotic papyrus *P.Vind.* 6278+ preserves Egyptian eclipse omen texts of a distinctly Babylonian flavor that can be dated to approximately 500 BCE, which suggests that Egypt was an important intermediary in the transmission of this lore even before the Hellenistic period (Parker 1959). The permeability of the language barrier between Egyptian and Greek is shown by textual coincidences between omen interpretations based on the rising of Sirius in the demotic *P.Cairo* 31222 (Hughes 1951) and the Greek *P.Oxy.* LXV 4471.

MEDICINE

The Egyptian Tradition

One can draw obvious parallels between the role of papyri in the historiography of ancient medicine and in that of ancient mathematics. From the second millennium BCE we have parts of several (mostly) hieratic medical manuscripts, including two substantial rolls, and these are our principal sources of knowledge of Egyptian medicine (Westendorf 1999, 1.6–79). The Graeco-Roman period is represented by a few demotic medical manuscripts and considerably more written in Greek, and we also have a generous literature in Greek and Latin transmitted through the medieval tradition. However, whereas the demotic and Greek mathematical problem texts contain essentially the same style of mathematics, the language divide was more significant in medicine; thus, the demotic medical papyri appear as a continuation of older Egyptian medicine operating in parallel but scarcely inter- acting with the Greek medicine that was imported to Egypt during the Hellenistic period. Moreover, Greek medical authors and texts identifiable from the medieval tradition are much better represented in the papyri than the mathematical authors.

The dozen extant medical manuscripts from the second millennium are all instructional or reference texts. None has a known author, and most can be shown on textual grounds to be copies rather than autographs. Each is composed as a collection of shorter and more or less independent sections (cf. again the mathe- matical problem texts) that tend to follow standardized patterns according to their purpose. In particular, there was an established way of prescribing a diagnosis and treatment, which in its full form comprised a descriptive title ("treatment for such- and-such affliction"), a second-person conditional that described details of the case ("If you investigate a man with such-and-such affliction..."), a diagnosis ("this is a case of..."), a verdict ("Then you will say: an affliction with which I will struggle"), and a course of treatment. Such texts, as well as the structurally simpler directions for medicines, account for the majority of the material in the papyri. Large sections of a manuscript or perhaps an entire roll may be dedicated to a specialized subject. Thus, one of the oldest of the medical papyri, Ramesseum V (Twelfth Dynasty, nineteenth century BCE), contains recipes for illnesses of the "vessels" (a term that describes various stringlike or tubular entities, e.g., muscles), while the roughly contemporary Kahun papyrus is devoted to women's afflictions. Other manuscripts have more eclectic contents.

The Edwin Smith and Ebers papyri, which are the largest and most historically significant of the extant Egyptian medical manuscripts, may serve as illustrations of the varieties of instructional text that a physician might possess or have access to. They both date from the early New Kingdom (sixteenth century BCE); both were purchased at Luxor by the American collector Edwin Smith in or before 1862, along with fragments of the Rhind mathematical papyrus; it is possible that all three manuscripts were discovered in a single library or archive. The Ebers papyrus is a calligraphic and massive roll, some twenty meters long, containing nearly nine hundred text sections in a hundred columns of text on the front side and a further eight columns on the back. It is an eclectic collection comprising blocks of varying numbers of texts that share a common format and subject matter; for example, one section consists of about a hundred recipes for ailments of the belly, though most of the sections are much briefer. There are comparatively few of the formal diagnosis-and-treatment texts. A remarkable feature, unique to this papyrus, is a theoretical section describing the connections that exist between the heart and the "vessels." The Smith papyrus is considerably shorter (not quite five meters long), and the seventeen columns of text on its front are devoted to a collection of diagnosis-and-treatment texts unified by their subject matter—the surgical treat- ment of wounds—and by a principle of organization according to the part of the body affected, beginning with the head and progressing downward. On the back, the same hand has written a short collection of spells against epidemics and a few medical and cosmetic recipes.

The pharaonic medical papyri exhibit a broader chronological spread than the mathematical papyri, and although there is again a documentary gap between the second-millennium Egyptian texts and those of the Graeco-Roman period, it is much shorter, extending only about seven centuries and centered on the first half of the first millennium BCE. (The oldest of the late manuscripts may in fact belong to the end of the Persian period.) The most obvious questions raised by the Hellenistic- and Roman-period texts are, how much continuity do they show with the pharaonic texts, and do they give any signs of interaction between the indigenous medical knowledge and foreign (Near Eastern, then Greek) medicines? At the present state of scholarship it appears that, at least as a literary tradition (and that is primarily what the papyri give evidence of), Hellenistic-Egyptian medicine followed much the same lines as in the second millennium, adhering to the same forms of expression for procedures and recipes. The corpus of texts is still small and fragmentary, however, and one would not be surprised if in due course incontrovertible instances came to light of material transmitted from Greek to Egyptian or vice versa, paralleling what we know happened in mathematics, astronomy, and astral divination.

The Graeco-Roman Tradition

Between two and three hundred Greek papyri with medical contents are currently known (Andorlini 1993). The projected *Corpus dei Papiri Greci di Medicina* will include editions or reeditions of all this material (Andorlini 1997, 2001, 2004). Additionally, documentary papyri occasionally refer to subjects related in varying degrees to the practice of medicine, and a number of papyri mention individual physicians (Sudhoff 1909, 254–275). Physicians were thus much more publicly visible than astrologers; the comparatively abundant epigraphical documentation of physicians tells much the same story for the Mediterranean world as a whole.

Ephemeral medical documents, which are of course entirely missing from the corpus of medical literature in the medieval tradition, abound in the form of small papyrus and parchment fragments and ostraca. They are predominantly artifacts of the pharmacological aspect of medical practice: labels of medicaments (the surviving specimens are all from late antiquity), catalogues of products, prescriptions, and single recipes. While some of these documents were surely issued to patients to deal with specific ailments, we also find collections of recipes, typically grouped by the class of affliction or affected part of the body, and these evidently served as reference texts. Most of these practically oriented collections would not have been authorial, published treatises but rather personal and traditional compilations.

Physicians apparently did possess manuscripts of the medical authorities of the past, and their tastes were not radically different from those of the scholars whose libraries fed into the medieval manuscript tradition. Among the roughly thirty known papyri that represent fragments of works that have otherwise survived, nearly two thirds are from works in the Hippocratic corpus. In view of the fact that these include several manuscripts of the *Epidemics* and the *Letters,* texts that can have had little practical application, we can infer an interest in the scholarship of the profession detached from everyday utility. Galen is the next most popular author, though lagging far behind Hippocrates, and it is an interesting measure of how soon his fame spread to Egypt that we find a copy of his *De Placitis* from Hermopolis, *P.Münch.* II 43 + *BKT* IX 42, dated palaeographically to the beginning of the third century, thus remarkably close to the author's lifetime (Hanson 1985).

More interest naturally adheres to texts that did not survive the medieval transmission. Considering the mere quantity of text in them, what the papyri add to the body of "literary" medical treatises available to us is proportionately very small, but this is no adequate measure of their historical value. A major problem that the selectivity of the medieval manuscript tradition presents us is the complete absence of original medical writings from the Hellenistic period (except, probably, for one or two late items included in the Hippocratic corpus). For what knowledge we have of the revolutionary anatomical and physiological research programs carried out by Herophilus and Erasistratus in the third century BCE, the subsequent rise of the medical sects, and the conflict between the empiricists and their dogmatic opponents, we are heavily dependent on later reports, above all in Galen's works. But Galen, though generous with his discussions and criticisms of his predecessors, is perhaps not a wholly objective reporter.

Two examples suffice to illustrate the direct contribution of papyri to our evidence for Hellenistic medical theory. A third-century BCE manuscript, fragments of which are now in four different collections (*P.Grenf.* II 7b + *P.Ryl.* I 39 + *P. Heid.* inv. 401 + *P.Hib.* II 190), contains a treatise on the physiology of vision that clearly reflects physical speculations current at the time, for example, in the assumption of "pores" through which visual rays emanate from the eye (Marganne 1994, 37–96); its authorship is disputed, but some connection with the school of Erasistratus is plausible. In addition, *P.Iand.* V 82, from the first century BCE, preserves parts of a treatise discussing the nomenclature of the female and male reproductive organs, which again seems likely to have been composed by a member of the Erasistratean school (Azzarello 2004).

The single most informative medical papyrus extant, however, known as the *Anonymus Londinensis* (*P.Lit.Lond.* 165), is from the early Roman period, probably the first century CE (Diels 1893; Manetti 1999). In part the importance of this manuscript is due to its exceptional preservation: Approximately 3½ meters of the roll, with thirty-nine columns of text, survive more or less intact, together with smaller fragments. However, the treatise, which according to current supposition is a draft autograph in an uncompleted state, is also of exceptional intrinsic interest both as a source for early Greek medical theory and as an exercise in scientific doxography. One long section, digesting a lost work ascribed to Aristotle, reviews and systematizes theories of the causes of disease attributed to a number of named medical and philosophical authorities of the fifth and fourth centuries BCE; this is followed by an inquiry into more specific physiological questions that bring Hellenistic theories into play and attack the opinions of Erasistratus and his school.

BIBLIOGRAPHY

Andorlini, I. 1993. "L'apporto dei papiri alla conoscenza della scienza medica antica." *Aufstieg und Niedergang der Römischen Welt: Geschichte und Kultur Roms im Spiegel der neueren Forschung*, ed. H. Temporini. Vol. 2.37.1, 458–562. New York: W. de Gruyter.

——, ed. 1997. *"Specimina" per il Corpus dei Papiri Greci di Medicina: Atti dell'Incontro di studio, Firenze, 28–29 marzo 1996*. Florence: Istituto papirologico G. Vitelli.

——, ed. 2001. *Greek Medical Papyri*. Vol. 1. Florence: Istituto papirologico G. Vitelli.

——, ed. 2004. *Testi medici su papiro: Atti del Seminario di studio, Firenze, 3–4 giugno 2002*. Florence: Istituto papirologico G. Vitelli.

Azzarello, G. 2004. "PIand V 82: Trattato sull'apparato genitale e renale (?)." In *Testi medici su papiro: Atti del Seminario di studio, Firenze, 3–4 giugno 2002*, ed. I. Andorlini, 237–256. Florence: Istituto papirologico G. Vitelli.

Baccani, D. 1992. *Oroscopi greci: Documentazione papirologica*. Messina, Italy: Sicania.

Blass, F. 1887. *Eudoxi Ars Astronomica qualis in charta Aegyptiaca superest*. Kiel; repr. in *ZPE* 115: 79–101.

Chace, A. B., L. Bull, H. P. Manning, and R. C. Archibald, eds. 1927–1929. *The Rhind Mathematical Papyrus: British Museum 10057 and 10058*. 2 vols. Oberlin, Ohio: Mathematical Association of America.

Diels, H. 1893. *Anonymi Londinensis ex Aristotelicis Iatricis Menoniis et aliis medicis eclogae*. Supplementum Aristotelicum 3.1. Berlin.

Fowler, D. 1999. *The Mathematics of Plato's Academy: A New Reconstruction*, 2d ed. Oxford: Clarendon Press.

Gillings, R. J. 1972. *Mathematics in the Time of the Pharaohs*. Cambridge, Mass.: MIT Press.

Goodspeed, E. J. 1898. "The Ayer Papyrus: A Mathematical Fragment." *American Journal of Philology* 19: 25–39.

Hanson, A. E. 1985. "Papyri of Medical Content." *Yale Classical Studies* 27: 25–47.

Hughes, G. R. 1951. "A Demotic Astrological Text." *Journal of Near Eastern Studies* 10: 256–261 and pl. x.

Imhausen, A. 2003a. *Ägyptische Algorithmen: Eine Untersuchung zu den mittelägyptischen mathematischen Aufgabentexten*. Wiesbaden: Harrassowitz.

——. 2003b. "Egyptian Mathematical Texts and Their Contexts." *Science in Context* 16: 367–389.

Jones, A. 1994. "The Place of Astronomy in Roman Egypt." In *The Sciences in Greco-Roman Society*, ed. T. D. Barnes, 25–51. Edmonton: Academic Printing and Publishing.

———. 1997. "A Greek Papyrus Containing Babylonian Lunar Theory." *ZPE* 119: 167–172.

———. 1999a. *Astronomical Papyri from Oxyrhynchus.* 2 vols. in 1. Philadelphia: American Philosophical Society.

———. 1999b. "A Classification of Astronomical Tables on Papyrus." In *Ancient Astronomy and Celestial Divination,* ed. N. M. Swerdlow, 299–340. Cambridge, Mass.: MIT Press.

———. 2003. "A Posy of Almagest Scholia." *Centaurus* 45: 69–78.

Manetti, D. 1999. " 'Aristotle' and the Role of Doxography in the Anonymus Londiniensis (*P.Br.Libr.* inv. 137)." In *Ancient Histories of Medicine: Essays in Medical Doxography and Historiography in Classical Antiquity,* ed. P. J. van der Eijk, 95–141. Leiden: Brill.

Marganne, M.-H. 1994. *L'ophtalmologie dans l'Égypte gréco-romaine d'après les papyrus littéraires grecs.* Leiden: Brill.

Mau, J., and W. Müller. 1960. "Mathematische ostraka aus der Berliner Sammlung." *Archiv für Papyrusforschung* 17: 1–10.

Netz, R. 2002. "Greek Mathematicians: A Group Picture." In *Science and Mathematics in Ancient Greek Culture,* ed. C. J. Tuplin and T. E. Rihll, 196–216. New York: Oxford University Press.

Neugebauer, O. 1975. *A History of Ancient Mathematical Astronomy.* 3 vols. New York: Springer.

———. 1988. "A Babylonian Lunar Ephemeris from Roman Egypt." In *A Scientific Humanist: Studies in Memory of Abraham Sachs,* ed. E. Leichty, M. deJ. Ellis, and P. Gerardi, 301–304. Philadelphia: Samuel Noah Kramer Fund, University Museum.

———, and R. A. Parker. 1969. *Egyptian Astronomical Texts.* Vol. 3, *Decans, Planets, Constellations, and Zodiacs.* Providence, R.I.: Published for Brown University Press by L. Humphries, London.

Neugebauer, O., R. A. Parker, and K.-T. Zauzich. 1981. "A Demotic Lunar Eclipse Text of the First Century B.C." *Proceedings of the American Philosophical Society* 125: 312–327.

Neugebauer, O., and H. B. van Hoesen. 1959. *Greek Horoscopes.* Philadelphia: American Philosophical Society.

Obbink, D. 2004. *Anubio: Carmen astrologicum elegiacum.* Leipzig: Saur.

Parker, R. A. 1959. *A Vienna Demotic Papyrus on Eclipse- and Lunar-Omina.* Providence, R.I.: Brown University Press.

———. 1972. *Demotic Mathematical Papyri.* Providence, R.I.: Brown University Press.

Pingree, D. 1997. *From Astral Omens to Astrology: From Babylon to Bikāner.* Rome: Istituto italiano per l'Africa e l'Oriente.

Struve, W. W. 1930. "Mathematischer Papyrus des Staatlichen Museums der Schönen Künste in Moskau." *Quellen und Studien zur Geschichte der Mathematik, Astronomie, und Physik.* Ser. A Vol. 1. Berlin: Springer.

Sudhoff, K. 1909. *Ärztliches aus griechischen Papyrus-Urkunden: Bausteine zu einer medizinischen Kulturgeschichte des Hellenismus.* Leipzig: J. A. Barth.

Westendorf, W. 1999. *Handbuch der altägyptischen Medizin.* Vol. 1. Leiden: Brill.

CHAPTER 16

THE RANGE OF DOCUMENTARY TEXTS: TYPES AND CATEGORIES

BERNHARD PALME

WHY SOME THINGS ARE DOCUMENTED AND OTHERS ARE NOT

The diversity of texts and types of documents can easily create the impression that papyrological evidence offers a representative view on almost all aspects of life in antiquity. But even in Egypt the geographical and chronological distribution of preserved papyri is very uneven, concentrated on a few sites on the edges of ancient settlement. Much of the material surviving from the Ptolemaic and Roman periods was produced and found in villages, while nearly all of the papyri from the Byzantine period come from cities, mainly the metropoleis of the nomes.

Equally uneven is the spreading of preserved papyri over the centuries.[1] The number of Greek texts fluctuates from the beginning of papyrological documentation (about 300 BCE) until Greek was replaced first by Coptic (after 700 CE) and later on by Arabic as the main language of Egypt (after 800 CE). The comparatively small number of papyri, wooden panels, and ostraca preserved from other parts of the Graeco-Roman world are methodologically highly important because they allow us to compare and sometimes to correct our views based on the evidence from Egypt.[2] Unfortunately, because they are few and come from a handful of places, papyri from outside Egypt offer hardly more than some selective spotlights (cf. chapter 20).

Besides the physical and climatic conditions of preservation, the preferences of papyrologists have a strong influence on the available material. The present state of editions differs greatly among linguistic groups. Compared to the roughly 650 volumes of Greek papyri published so far, other languages are poorly represented with barely 35 volumes with Coptic documents, although extensive collections of Coptic texts remain unpublished. The small circle of specialists in demotic and Arabic papyri have edited only about four thousand fragments of demotic and around three thousand Arabic papyri.

Even with Greek papyri, editors tend to publish documents that offer numerous parallels, and they have favored literary texts over documents, so that while the proportion of edited literary to documentary papyri is about 1:5, the actual proportion of preserved papyri is probably closer to 1:50. Papyri from archives and dossiers (see chapter 10) are also more likely to be edited than isolated texts.

Written Documents and Illiterate People

Even on an optimistic assessment, only a small percentage of the population of Graeco-Roman Egypt was able to write and read, even among those who helped govern the villages. On the other hand, a considerable number of papyri and ostraca document efforts to learn to write (see chapter 14). A large part of transactions and communications was done orally and did not find any written expression. Even such far-reaching agreements as marriages very often happened without any written contract. Whole areas of life were never documented. For a document to be put into writing there must have been a need to secure and memorialize information. As a consequence, written documentation in antique cultures very often dealt with matters concerning power, wealth, or dependence. The majority of the papyrological evidence is thus connected with the justification and securing of material rights or responsibilities between private people or between the state and the individual.

The difficulty in giving a systematic overview of the documentary papyri is a product of their extreme textual diversity. Compared to the Ptolemaic period, the spectrum of papyri continually and considerably widened during the Roman period. It is hard to say whether this tendency reflects a change in the common writing traditions or (probably) whether it was the consequence of a more elaborated administration and changes in the legal system.

Every classification of the documentary papyri becomes complex, as the model of Orsolina Montevecchi, with thirteen main categories and dozens of minor categories, shows.[3] However, this complexity may be anachronistic in trying to understand ancient documents. Furthermore, the categories change depending on the choice of historic, juristical, or technical-formal features. Finally, different languages created different written forms. The "papyrological habit" explained in the following pages primarily describes the practices displayed in Greek documents, largely applicable to Coptic as well. Other categories might be useful for demotic or Arabic documents.[4]

Lost Documentation

It is impossible to determine the loss of private correspondence or accounts, but we may estimate what was lost in the sector of official administration. Throughout the entire "papyrological millennium" Alexandria was the capital of Egypt. As residence of the Ptolemaic kings and seat of the highest officials, Alexandria accommodated not only the famous library but also the central archives of the court and headquarters of administration. Here converged the accounts of the tax and finance administration, as well as the papers of legal affairs and the records of diplomatic affairs. During the principate, Alexandria was the seat of the governor and several financial procurators. In late antiquity it continued to be the capital of the diocese. At all times it housed the archives of those governors, where the papers of the individual office-holders were collected. Presumably since Claudius but at the latest since the middle of the second century CE, the core of the archive consisted of the official diaries (*commentarii*), which listed all of the activities of the prefects. Perhaps also since the first century CE the extensive books containing copies of all of the prefects' correspondence might have been stored there as well. Since the reign of Marcus Aurelius or at the latest since the Severan emperors numerous petitions have also been added to the archives. *P. Yale* I 61 tells us that, during a three-day period at a *conventus* of the prefect Subatianus Aquila in 210 CE, more than 1804 petitions were handed in. This may hint at the amount of the paperwork in the governor's headquarters. Furthermore, the judicial decisions of the governors and other judges, notifications of birth from Roman citizens, *epikrisis* records, and of course official correspondence with the central government in Rome were collected as well.[5]

Almost all of this is lost, save for a few documents that returned to the *chôra*. If we had just a small fraction of the contents of these archives, our knowledge of the Ptolemaic, Roman, and early Byzantine administration, government, and diplomacy would have quite a different base.

Similar archives were also kept in the offices of the local administration in the roughly fifty districts (nomes), described in chapter 22.[6] Not a single find has been made of a nome archive that could give us a representative selection of all of the archival materials collected there for centuries; only fragments remain. Occasionally old records were thrown away or their blank reverse sides used as cheap paper for private use. To such reuse we owe the survival of one example (*P.Panop.Beatty* 1–2) of the incoming and outgoing correspondence of a *strategos*.

After the *mêtropoleis* received a city council during the reign of Septimius Severus, the volume of public documentation increased still further, including the records of council meetings. Once more, the surviving texts represent a very small fragment of the original quantity.

Types of Documents

Conventionally the documentary papyri (and ostraca) are divided into private and public. On the basis of historical and formal features, private documents can be classified into private communications, records of private legal transactions, accounts, and finances, and documents of piety and worship. The second group contains documents concerning the interaction between the state and individuals and pronouncements of the government and administration. Only the last group was meant for public dissemination. The formal subdivisions should not be taken too strictly, as overlaps occur.

Private Documents

Private Communications

In a quite mobile society, written communication played an important role. Hundreds of letters and reports survive, but their chronological distribution is unbalanced: About 550 letters from the Ptolemaic period have been edited, but half of these originate from the Zenon archive. By contrast, about 1900 have been published from the first three centuries of Roman rule. Whether there was less letter writing in the Ptolemaic period or the hazards of survival are responsible for this situation, we do not know. The following categories can be classifed by contents:

Among the oldest Greek papyri, letters between private persons appear as a genre that followed particular formal conventions. Every papyrological anthology contains a certain number of *private letters* touching the modern reader through their immediacy and realism.[7] Remarkably, quite a few letters were written by women and even by children or teenagers.[8] Also in social terms, it seems as if a wide spectrum is represented. Although most of the private correspondence comes as expected from the upper classes such as the *metropolitai* or landowners and (later) in the better-educated parts of the Christian clergy, it seems as if at least occasionally simple farmers and day laborers sent letters, too. It often remains unclear whether the sender wrote the letters with his own hand or dictated them to a professional scribe.

In most cases the letter reports that the sender is in good health. Sometimes letters speak of small daily concerns, for instance, requests to send particular items. Some, however, were written in extraordinary situations like some letters from recruits in the Roman fleet in Misenum reporting home to their families[9] or communications about the death of a relative (*P.Fouad* 75). The exterior design of private letters usually exhibits fixed patterns. From the third century BCE to the fourth century CE, private letters used a stylized phrasing, either "X to Y, greetings" or "To X from Y, greetings." Additionally, a whole series of stereotyped phrases was used, in particular in the introduction and the final greetings. Dozens of private letters start with the phrase "Above all I wish you to be healthy" and finish with the usual *formula valetudinis:* "I pray that you will be well for many years." Among the stereotyped elements we very often find greetings directed to other members of the household and wishes that the children of the house will not be touched by the "evil eye." At least the final formula of greetings should be written with the sender's own hand if that person is literate. Because of the widespread clichés only a few really emotional comments appear.[10] Any search, for instance, for a love letter among the papyri would be in vain. Reference to peculiar situations, events, and people make private letters often difficult to understand for the present-day reader. From the fourth century CE onward the habit developed of omitting the correspondent's name at the beginning of the letter and instead writing the postal address on the reverse side.

A second category is *business correspondence.* The majority of these letters contain reports to a superior or colleague or orders to a subordinate. Most of these are connected with the management of large estates. The extensive correspondence of the Zenon and Heroninos archives belongs largely to this category. As parts of more extensive archives (which ideally also contain accounts and legal contracts), business letters can offer various insights into forms of cultivation, structures of organization, labor systems, and economic circumstances of estates. It is likely characteristic of the general economic and productive structures in Egypt that records and correspondence regarding commercial enterprises did not survive to a comparable extent.

Among the private letters stand out two groups that follow their own design and form and come close to the literary genre of "open letters": More than 100 *letters of recommendation* survive in Greek and a couple in Latin.[11] They range from the third century BCE to the sixth century CE; 55 of them come from the Ptolemaic period, and no fewer than 49 of these from the Zenon archive. In contrast, only a dozen *letters of condolence* survive, dating from the first to the sixth or seventh century CE.[12] It can hardly be a coincidence that the *consolatio* established itself as a literary genre during just this period. Not a single example survives from the Ptolemaic period. Surprisingly, perhaps, all of the condolence letters express only moderate sorrow, sympathy, and encouragement. Their stereotyped style of writing also explains why there is no significant difference between the pagan and the Christian letters of condolence.

Standardized formulas are also evident in the two dozen written *invitations* for dinner,[13] which belong mainly to the second and third centuries CE. These are small in size (ca. 5 × 5 cm) and are formulated in short words following this pattern: name of the host—the person invited—invitation to dinner—occasion of the invitation—place of the party—hour and date. Because they were delivered personally, they do not mention any address. Birthdays, weddings, *epikriseis,* or the awarding of honorary posts were occasions for such dinners. From time to time they had a religious character, for instance, invitations to the "*klinê* of Anoubis" (*SB* XX 14503) or Sarapis that was to take place in a private house or a holy shrine. In the formulation of *SB* X 10496 (third century CE), even the god himself supposedly issues the dinner invitation. Similar invitations occur also for Christian feasts (*SB* XVI 12980).

Finally, there is the large but heterogeneous group of *private notes, lists, and memoranda.* Concerning their content, the spectrum reaches from short messages to the listing of various ordinary, daily items (such as laundry lists) and records of income or expenses (such as for a feast). Among these, lists of objects for dowries stand out. Very often only various items are listed, without a heading informing us of the purpose.

Private Legal Documents

A very large part of the texts written on papyrus serve to secure certain rights and claims. At all times legal transactions were set down in writing to be protected from later alterations. These documents of juridical relevance follow specific formulas and patterns, the fundamentals of which are generally uniform, although they sometimes surprise us with local (often nome-specific) particularities. Legal documents were usually composed by professional scribes who had to know the correct terminology and the appropriate clauses. Their work might have been made easier with sample texts like *SB* XX 15027. Indispensable components of such legal documents were, in a strict sense, the fixing of the business and its resulting obligation, the precise naming of the parties to the contract (including the father's name, the origin of each party, and, during Roman times, also a physical description), and the date and place of writing. Written contracts or agreements had value as evidence in court, but for the legal force of a transaction, only the parties' agreement was decisive. The establishment of a written document was not legally necessary.

The evolution of the processes for drawing up contracts is discussed in detail in chapter 23. In general, we may suppose that copies remained in the hands of the contracting parties, but in some procedures a copy was also placed in a trusted repository. In the Ptolemaic period this was often the "contract keeper" (*syngraphophylax),* but another possibility existed, having contracts drawn up and registered by the professional notaries *(agoranomoi)*. From the third century BCE until at least the third century CE the state notary's office offered contracting parties the option to register publicly their private legal contracts. This was common and indeed compulsory after 146 BCE for demotic records also (*P.Par.* 65).

Another form of official recording of private legal business developed from banking transactions. While in Ptolemaic times such *diagraphai* were considered as additional evidence for otherwise recorded business, beginning with Augustus (*BGU* IV 1184, 27 BCE), "independent" diagraphai were valid "bank-notarial" documentation of the underlying legal business as well. Bank diagraphai disappear before the end of the third century CE (the latest independent *diagraphê* is *SPP* XX 74 from 276; the latest dependent one is *M.Chr.* 171, col. II, from 293).

The participation of state authorities and especially the entry of the contract into an official register gave the agreement additional security and, from our point of view, created another type of surviving documentary record. Such *grapheion registers* survive for the Arsinoite villages Theogenis (*CPR* XIII, second century BCE), Kerkesoucha Orous, and Tebtynis (*P.Mich.* II 121–128; *P.Mich.* V 238, first century CE). These registers were organized as the office's *journal d'entrée* and recorded every contract in chronological order. They usually give detailed descriptions of the type of business, the parties, the object of contract, and the monetary value. One of them lists the 247 contracts (which came in within four months) and summarizes their title and content: 136 *homologiai* (contracts generally, sometimes specified as contract of sale or contract of dowry), fifty leases, twenty-seven loans, seventeen employment contracts, and so on.

During the first century of Roman rule every nome had appropriate archives where private and public papers were stored. In 72 CE at the latest (*BGU* I 184 = *M. Chr.* 202) the archives were divided into a depository of public records (*bibliothêkê dêmosiôn logôn*) and a depository of property records (*bibliothêkê enktêseôn*), where the records of ownership for land and real property (and slaves?) were kept. The central archives in Alexandria—we do not know a lot about them—were further extended by Hadrian's time. The Roman administration encouraged registration by declaring that nonnotarial contracts would be accepted at the court only after an expensive "disclosure." By the end of the third century CE the official *syngraphai* (by state notaries), the bank *diagraphai,* and all other types of legal documents except the *cheirographon* and the *hypomnema* disappeared. In the next 150 years the state did not offer citizens any official authority to certify and secure their private legal contracts. Only the emerging of private notary offices at the beginning of the fifth century CE brought about a basic change. From now on the *tabellio,* who was appointed by the state but acted as a trusted private person, composed the documents.[14] Such contracts note as usual the date and place of conclusion, the parties of contract, the type of business, processing features, and the sum in question. Beginning with the Severan emperors, additionally, the stipulation clause found its way into Greek contracts. Below this agreement first the witnesses and then the *tabellio* sign.

LEGAL CONTRACTS

Specific types of contracts (e.g., marriages, sales, leases) required a set of specific regulations. They remained similar over the whole papyrological timespan. But individual purposes and local variations produce significant diversity in detail. Shifting conceptions of the law reflect changes of mentality and of social and economic conditions. For this reason each document should be studied in the context of the whole corpus of the parallel texts.

Records of legal acts usually follow stereotyped forms. One must make a clear distinction between the type of legal transaction and its written form in a specific style of record (see the preceding section). Some styles of records were used mainly for specific types of transactions, but there was no strict and universal correspondence. Every systematic classification of the legal documents is in danger of anachronism, as modern legal points of view differ from those of the ancients. For this reason we distingush only two large categories (although further juristic differentiation would be possible): legal transactions that concern people and those concerning things.

Contracts Regarding Persons   In a society that consisted of strictly separated groups of different ethnic, legal, and fiscal status, as Egypt was particularly down to the third century CE, the ascertainment and proof of personal status was of central significance for every individual. The society of Graeco-Roman Egypt was always divided between freemen and slaves. The legal (and fiscal) status of freeborn individuals was defined through the state. Although slaves formed a small minority of the population (and terms for slaves in informal contexts are sometimes ambiguous), in legal contexts clarity was essential. Cases absolutely free of doubt can be found in about 170 edited *sales of a slave*.[15] Only 15 of them date from Ptolemaic times, while most survive from the Roman period. Christianity did not stop either slavery or the keeping of records on sales of slaves, the majority of whom were female. Often they were unwanted children who had been exposed and then were picked up to be raised as slaves. Some records of slave sales written outside Egypt show that a certain importation of slaves was carried on at all times. Moreover, a few *emancipations* of slaves (mostly authenticated in public by an *agoranomos*) are found throughout the papyrological millennium.[16] There were different legal types of emancipations such as those connected with a specific legal act (*P.Oxy.* I 48–50) or with a *donatio mortis causa* (*P.Stras.* II 122) or issued by public proclamation through a herald (*Jur.Pap.* 7). Besides deeds of sale and emancipations, there exist many other types of documents that occasionally illuminate topics such as the escape of slaves, their scope of work activity, and their education (*C.Ptol.Sklav.* 53–255).

For freeborn persons, their legal and fiscal status was defined by birth. Under certain circumstances there was a need for additional arrangements, laid down in a great variety of documents. Underaged children were subordinate to the authority of the father, only rarely to their mother's authority. Orphans had to be placed under the care of a guardian. *Requests for a guardian* give us a good sense of the detailed prescribed steps that had to be undertaken (e.g., *P.Harr.* I 68; *M.Chr.* 325). *Appointments of guardians* (*P.Ryl.* II 120) and oaths on assuming guardianship (*SB* VI 9049) are the results of these procedures. Comparable proceedings can be found in *requests for tutors* of women *(kyrioi).*[17] According to Greek law, women were capable of owning property but did not enjoy any legal capacity to act independently (in Egyptian law they did). Normally there was no need for a record dealing with the assumption of a guardianship for a woman. But if no husband or other male relative existed, an application for the *appointment* of a *kyrios* had to be adressed to the *strategos, exegetes,* or prefect. Some applications of this kind survive in the original, and many others are embedded as copies in other business documents.[18] Under Roman law, women could act on the basis of the "right of three children" even without a guardian, but for the confirmation of that right they had to send an application to the prefect, too (e.g., *P.Oxy.* XII 1467).

Occasionally other cases of acts concerning family affairs and status appear: Both Ptolemaic and Roman papyri mention adoptions, but actual *acts of adoption* are not known before late antiquity.[19] Single documents also give us an idea about exceptional measures, such as the emancipation of a daughter from the *patria potestas* (*ChLA* XII 521) or disownment (*apokêryxis*) by a family (*P.Cair.Masp.* I 67097 verso D; III 67353; *Jur.Pap.* 11, all sixth century CE).

A vast number of *marriage contracts* survive, although marriages without any written record were fully valid and obviously common; some were later documented in writing (e.g., *SB* VI 9264). More than 140 marriage contracts survive from the fourth century BCE to the fourth century CE. In keeping with general patterns of preservation, half of these date to the second century CE.[20] The legal form and the design of the written record vary greatly down to the Byzantine period, when only one type remained in use. Until the fourth century CE a marriage was formed either by the act of *ekdosis* ("handing over" the bride), recorded in a document called "a contract of living together," or by the act of furnishing a dowry. But other types can also be found. The oldest marriage contract (*P.Eleph.* 1, 310 BCE)—which is at the same time the oldest dated Greek papyrus overall—was concluded in front of six witnesses who sealed the document. The bride and the bridegroom both descended from different Greek *poleis,* and the bridegroom and the bride's father are given the right to decide where the couple would live. This was a private agreement which has neither been registered in any official way nor corresponded to the legal norms of any state. A final clause establishes in particular that the contract is supposed to be valid in every city. Intention was a decisive point for the choice of a certain type of record and the legal framework. In 128 CE *P.Yadin* I 18 was drawn up in Maoza in the district of Petra (province of Arabia) for a Jewish couple. It basically followed Greek legal traditions and was written in the Greek language because this made it possible to present the record in front of a Roman court and secured the woman more property rights. Just a few years earlier (122–125 CE), a contract for the second marriage of the widow Babatha was drawn up at the same place but was in Aramaic and in the form of a Jewish *ketubba* (*P.Yadin* II 10).[21]

Deeds of divorce were concluded individually or by mutual agreement and were also shaped in various written forms according to local traditions. Second-century CE contracts of divorce from the Arsinoite nome show extensive stereotyped formulas (*P.Corn.* 52). In addition to the confirmation of separation, such contracts contain clauses about the return of the dowry and permission to remarry.[22] In an indirect way these acts show us underlying conceptions of marriage and female rights, as well as general moral values.

One matter that needed written form was the settlement of succession other than by intestacy. The following types of written arrangements often appear in papyri:[23] Greek *wills* (*diathêkê*) are formulated as one-sided statements intended to take effect in the event of death and follow a stereotyped formula with few, mostly local, variations. Typically they begin with these words: "(So and so) made the following dispositions in good mental health." Some special forms are joint declarations of husband and wife (e.g., *M.Chr.* 307), parental division *inter liberos* upon death (e.g., *P.Mich.* V 321, 322a), and agreements concerning succession made between husband and wife in marriage contracts.

The *meriteia* (often called *donatio mortis causa* by scholars) may have developed from Egyptian traditions. Nevertheless, it was also popular among the Greek elements of the population. Apparently standard Greek wills were more common in metropoleis, *meriteiai* in villages. We also have thirty Roman wills dating from the late first century to the early fourth century CE. At first these were written in Latin, but beginning around the time of Alexander Severus they appear also in Greek.[24] Women use the same legal instruments as men in this domain. Public recording of wills was common during the Ptolemaic period and obligatory in the Roman. The opening of a testament had to follow certain rules (*BGU* XIII 2244). It was not unusual to update a testament several times, but a written revocation was necessary to make previous wills ineffective.[25]

Contracts Concerning Property Documents that deal with property, its acquisition, and various activities of related business number in the thousands. In terms of quantity, this group represents the majority not just in legal documents in a wider sense but also in documentary papyri in general. These data are not biased: The wish to establish rights or obligations in writing was the decisive reason for an extensive production of such texts. This section describes only some of the basic types, each one of which could be subdivided into a series of subtypes of acts arranged by content, form, and temporal (and often local) character.

It is hardly surprising that sales are one of the best represented transactions in papyri. The seller transfers the property and the full right to a specific thing to the buyer and confirms the receipt of the purchase price. The *contracts of sale* are formulated as records of already settled transactions. During the Ptolemaic period the objective formula "he sold" (seller)—"he bought" (buyer) was the most frequent, while later on the subjective homology ("I acknowledge that I have sold and received the price") was more common. Objects of purchase are chiefly real estate, movable property, animals (mainly donkeys), and slaves, who are occasionally described in detail. There had to be an official registration *(katagraphê)* of the purchase of real estate and slaves. Many questions concerning legal-historical or social and economic-historical areas (for instance, liability for defects, status of business partners, development of prices) can be addressed to the records of sales. A transfer of rights (similar to a sale) could be effectuated also by a *deed of gift*, although this was less common (cf. *P.Neph.* 31, introduction). Furthermore, houses, estates, and movable property, too, were objects of *division contracts*, which were made mainly between relatives. Deeds of gift and divisions often contain clauses of revocation. The preserved samples come mainly from Roman times.

Besides sales and gifts, other forms of assignment of rights existed. Although similar in purpose, they differ strictly in terminology and legal concepts, as, for instance, does the cession *(parachôrêsis)* of katoikic ("settler's") land. Originally given by the Ptolemaic kings to their soldiers on revocable tenure, katoikic land was still a special category of real estate during the Roman period. Legally it was not seen as true private property, although it was heritable and even transferable to women from the second century BCE on. Such parcels of land *(klêroi)*, like military accommodations, could not be sold, but it was possible to transfer them for monetary "compensation."

From Roman and increasingly from Byzantine times we have records of transactions that straddle the boundary between sale and loan. Normally they deal with agricultural products (often wine) or products of craftsmanship. In a *sale on delivery* or loan of money with repayment in kind the vendor receives his money immediately, although the product is to be delivered at a set date in the future.[26] Sometimes a precise statement of price or the amount of the sold product is missing, which creates the impression that the sale on delivery hides a loan with excessive interest. The fact that the majority of the almost two hundred actual known sales on delivery date from the sixth and seventh centuries CE and involve a dependent rural population points in the same direction. But many times prepurchase of a product of the harvest might also account for these transactions. The *sale on credit* is a similar transaction but is organized the other way around, as the product is going to be paid for later but is delivered immediately after the sale. Nevertheless, the purchase price is stated as "received," and a contract of loan that deals with the relevant sum was set up.[27]

In every century of the "papyrological millennium" the most numerous preserved contracts are *loans*.[28] The delivery of money or other valuables, as well as the fixing of interest and (normally) a deadline for repayment, demanded a written security—and records of loan were carefully preserved. Formally, loan contracts show both subjectively and objectively styled types, and their content can be separated into two basic groups: loans of money and loans in kind. The latter often deal with seeds borrowed from a state-owned granary, which normally had to be given back after the harvest with an additional 50 percent. Loans in money legally bore 24 percent interest during the Ptolemaic period and 12 percent during the Roman. Numerous loans of money declare themselves as interest-free loans, but they probably already included the interest in the capital sum. Fictitious loans also appear, hiding other transactions. The duration of loans varied considerably (from a few weeks to many years). In the Byzantine period the term of repayment often is not fixed but depends on the creditor's preference. This of course further weakened the debtor's position. Loan contracts were usually made invalid after repayment by simply crossing them out, but repayment receipts were also common.

Contracts of deposit were another method of securing property rights. A custodian confirms that he has taken over certain objects (sometimes even people). He can use the objects but is obliged to give them back on the owner's demand. Some contracts of deposit arouse the suspicion that other transactions are involved (e.g., a dowry for illegal marriages of soldiers).[29]

Another extensive group is that of legal documents connected to gainful employment, like lease, rent, work, and related business contracts. In antiquity, contracts of this kind were uniformly called misthôsis in Greek. Contracts of lease dealing with agricultural estates have survived by the hundreds, reflecting an important agricultural reality. Others involve workshops, shops, and stores or parts of them.[30] The contracts often describe in detail the location and the condition of the piece of land, the work and tax obligations, the payment of the rent, and clauses of penalty. Some common characteristics are evident in the various styles of lease contracts. During the Ptolemaic period, leases were almost always designed as an objective statement: "(So and so) has leased to (so and so)." In the third century BCE the six-witness act predominated, while in the second century contracts were ratified by an agoranomos and later the objective homology ("acknowledges that he has leased"). In the Roman period two different types developed. One is a contract form that appeared either in narrative style ("has leased") as an objective homologia or as a private written cheirographon ("I have leased to you"), a form very common in the Arsinoite nome. The second type was expressed as an offer of lease ("I wish to lease"), even though the deal had already been settled. In the Byzantine period the subjective homology ("I acknowledge that I have leased") prevailed, but one can observe a remarkably uneven local distribution of the lease contracts, which might reflect different agrarian conditions in various parts of the country. The records of leases concentrate heavily on the Arsinoite, with many fewer appearing from the Oxyrhynchite and Hermopolite nomes. The duration of leases was usually short (often until the next harvest, e.g., one year), but a special form of hereditary leasehold, the emphyteusis, appeared in Byzantine times. The emphyteusis created a long-term lease, often for a lifetime and even for several generations. In particular, churches and monasteries often handed their plots over on this basis.[31] In general, rental agreements follow the same patterns as leases. The only difference is that rental agreements deal with houses, rooms, or parts of them.[32]

Other contracts involving labor were also called *misthôsis*. Thus, contracts of employment and work, apprenticeship, and transport, as well as the renting of animals, were designed in a formal and terminological style similar to contracts of leases. A *work contract* centers on the production of a certain object or performance of services, and payment of all or part of the wage is sometimes made in advance. *Contracts of apprenticeship* spell out the manner and skills of the job (most commonly weaving).[33] *Nursing contracts* concern the nursing and care of infants, who were often rescued from exposure (*C.Pap.Gr.* I). In some contracts a remarkable condition requires the nurse to procure a new infant if one dies. *Contracts of transport* deal with the use of an animal or a ship and include detailed arrangements about loads, delivery dates, and destinations. Furthermore, numerous *shipping contracts* are preserved, especially from Roman and Byzantine Egypt. They contain the shipowner's acknowledgments of reception of cargo and arrangements for transport, often for the shipping of tax grain.[34] Most surviving contracts of transport deal with trips within Egypt. However, the remarkable examples of a maritime loan for a commercial journey to Somalia (*SB* III 7169, second century BCE) and another one to India (*SB* XVIII 13167, second century CE) show that comparable arrangements also existed for transport across the sea.

Eventually *misthôseis* were also linked to other legal transactions, especially loans. Most common was the *antichrêsis*, a credit transaction in which capital and/or interest were not paid back but paid off through work or the use of an item. The latter mainly concerns a house or an apartment (or a part of it), a garden, and so on that the creditor could use in lieu of repayment. Such contracts do not necessarily reflect desperate debtors.[35]

Accounts

Another extensive group of private documents, described broadly as economic texts, includes accounts of all kinds, receipts, orders for payment, proofs of banking, lists of incoming or outgoing money or goods, transport lists, and much more. No strict "types of records" developed; rather, a huge variety of texts exists. The content and form of these documents were determined by individual habits and requirements.

As we expect in an agricultural economy, farm accounts are prominent in every century. Usually these are lists that, with luck, have a heading giving their purpose and date. In isolation they often seem unremarkable, but in groups and properly approached they can inform us of the size and structure of both smaller and bigger estates, as well as the methods of cultivation and management. An outstanding example is the Kellis agricultural account book (*P.Kell.* IV 96). Unsurprisingly, such accounts originate in particular from large estates (e.g. *P.Oxy.* XVI 1911 and LV 3804 from the Apions). Small farmers had neither the necessity nor the skill for doing such systematic accounts. Most of these accounts are, in any case, mere lists of income and expenses that did not require more sophisticated analysis.

In the area of trade and handicraft production we find particularly short receipts and lists. Although the single documents—often written on ostraca—are again stereotyped, they offer very valuable historical evidence because of their volume. The following examples illustrate the broad textual spectrum that is evident in lists, calculations, bills, and so on: information about the affairs of private households, like a list of expenses for food and fuel from the third century BCE (*UPZ* II 158 A, cols. 1–2) or the monthly calculations by a cook in 185 or 215 CE (*P.Oxy.* I 108, cols. 1–2). Several inventories of books are of cultural-historical significance (*C.Liste Libri*). A list of clothing belonging to Zenon gives us an interesting insight into the wardrobe of a wealthy man (*P.Cair.Zen.* I 59092), especially if compared to the list of clothes that the *scholasticus* Theophanes took with him on his journey to Antioch nearly six hundred years later (*P.Ryl.* IV 627, cols. 1–2). Theophanes also left highly informative notes about the stops and expenses incurred on his journey (Matthews 2006). An inventory of church property (*Sel.Pap.* I 192) from the fifth or sixth century offers welcome information on the equipment used in early Christian worship.

Small daily purchases were paid for in cash without any written record. Especially in Roman times, however, it was also common to pay larger sums through written *banker's orders.* Clearing and transfer involved both money and grain. The banker transferred sums of money from one account to another; grain was transferred by the *sitologoi,* tax officials who were also responsible for the state granaries, where private grain accounts were kept as well. Tax payments in grain or payments to other private people could be transferred with written (and sealed) orders.

Belief and Superstition

Documentary papyri join the literary and semiliterary sources as important evidence of religion and cult. The diversity of the textual evidence in this area does not easily fit into a system.[36] A series of Ptolemaic and Roman records directly concern temples, pagan priesthood, and cult, such as a list of Egyptian temples in Kerkeosiris, which was written by a village scribe in 115/114 BCE (*P.Tebt.* I 88); applications for the purchase of priestly offices (e.g., *P.Tebt.* II 294 and 296); prohibitions against disturbing divine services; texts for the sealing of sacrificial animals (*BGU* I 356), and much more. Tellingly, most Greek texts concern the contact of priests with state authorities, while matters of cult and belief or the temples' internal affairs are nearly absent in the Greek papyrological documentation; demotic texts fill part of that gap.

On the other hand, documents that reflect private piety, especially those connected with cults surrounding death, are numerous. Mummification of various grades was practiced until Christian late antiquity, and several documents deal with sending mummies to the family grave (*Sel.Pap.* I 104; *C.Pap.Hengstl* 59); many receipts record the transport of mummies, often by ship (*P.Hamb.* I 74). So called *mummy labels* were used to identify the bodies; these labels are small wooden tablets with the name and age of the deceased, as well as occasionally destination and notes on charges paid. Thousands of such mummy tablets survive and provide information especially on onomastics and demography.[37] A remarkable tabulation of funeral expenses appears in *SPP* XXII 56.

Papyri are also welcome testimonies of popular piety and widespread superstition. Besides magical texts and prayers (which belong to the semiliterary area), extensive magical textbooks (like *PGM* I 1–15), instructions in religious methods (*PGM* II 13.234–244), and numerous amulets (e.g., *P.Princ.* III 159, against fever) are found. The biggest homogeneous group in this domain are *oracle questions*. More than seventy examples, chronologically spread over all centuries, have been published, and many more remain unedited.[38] Oracles occasionally have a political connection, like the oracle of Hermes Trismegistos, which dealt with the suppression of a revolt in the Thebaid under Ptolemy VI (*O.Hor*, pp. 1–6). From time to time oracles were also used in the search for justice.[39] But mostly they concern private matters, chiefly reflecting distress or difficult decisions. Many such documents, especially of the first two centuries CE, are preserved from Oxyrhynchus and Soknopaiou Nesos, where the local god, Soknopaios, was worshiped (*SB* XVIII 14043–14050). The question concerning a marriage in *W.Chr.* 122 is an instructive, maybe even typical example. Another prominent group includes some 140 *horoscopes*, most of them dating from the second and third centuries CE. Christianity did not end people's faith in magical methods; both amulets and oracular questions continue down to the seventh century.[40]

Public Life

Political History

Documents with a direct reference to political events are relatively rare. No original records of diplomatic correspondence or historical events survive. Nevertheless, some types of papyri deal with historical situations and sometimes also with events of impact on world history. All of them are purely accidental discoveries.

An official war report about an operation by the Ptolemaic fleet along the Cilician coast in 246 BCE (*W.Chr.* 1) provides a concrete episode from the Third Syrian War, between Ptolemy III and the Seleucid empire, which is otherwise known only from anecdotal evidence. A multilingual dossier highlights the Jewish-Syrian-Egyptian conflict, also called the "war of scepters," which lasted from 103 to 101 BCE (*C.Jud. Syr.Eg.*). A private letter (*P.Köln* IV 186) refers to combat during (probably) the Sixth Syrian War, and a whole series of letters and official documents also shows the dynastic and regional conflicts within Egypt during the rule of the later Ptolemies (e.g., *W.Chr.* 9–12). A piece of official correspondence between subaltern officials shows arrangements for the visit of a Roman senator to Egyptian sanctuaries with holy crocodiles in 112 BCE, long before Egypt was actually annexed to the Roman Empire (*P.Tebt.* I 33). An *epistula* of Claudius to the Alexandrians from November 41

CE shows the unstable situation in the capital of Egypt (*C.Pap.Jud.* II 153). At the same time, this famous letter offers remarkable evidence for the style of Roman government. Hadrian's accession to the throne is announced in *P.Oxy.* LV 3781, dated August 117, and *P.Giss.* I 3 contains an invitation for the related celebration. Such documents are preserved because they were copied and sent to the nomes as official announcements. In one instance, *CPR* XXIII 24, which is an official announcement of news about imperial victories, sheds light on these procedures.

Among the "historical papyri" only the *certificates of pagan sacrifices* from the period of the Decian persecution of Christians form a salient type of document. Decius enacted an edict in September 249 that obligated all citizens of the empire to make sacrifice for the gods. Forty-five original certificates from the year 250/251 CE have been published so far,[41] half from a single findspot (Theadelphia). As becomes obvious from their stereotyped formula, these certificates were indeed styled as requests (*libelli*) to a local commission for confirmation of a food and drink sacrifice. One (*W.Chr.* 125) was issued for a female priest serving the cult of the crocodile god Petesouchos; not even pagan priests were excluded from the obligation. Apart from this extraordinary group the papyri tell us next to nothing about universal measures like Diocletian's persecution of Christians, for which one might expect massive effects, including written documentation in Egypt. A sample of what once existed comes from *P.Oxy.* XXXIII 2673 (304 CE), in which a lector makes a sworn statement that his church does not own any property.

More concrete are administrative regulations. The reforms of the Tetrarchs, for example, are elucidated by several important sources. The edict of the prefect Aristius Optatus from March 297 (*P.Cair.Isid.* 1) enforces a collateral measure for the introduction of a new tax system. In addition, *CPR* XXIII 20 (298) preserves a fragmentary copy of Diocletian's edict ordering a general census, and *P.Panop. Beatty* 1 and 2 (298 and 300) provide unique testimony for Diocletian's campaign to the southern border of Egypt. On various occasions historical events of far-reaching consequences are reflected in papyri amazingly quickly, at least in an indirect way. For example, the profound change in the recruiting system that occurred in 376 CE is visible in the papyri of the following year.[42] The disastrous plague of 542, which killed about a third of the population of Constantinople, has been credited with a 20 percent decline in tax rates in the Upper Egyptian village of Aphrodito in the year 544 CE.[43]

Pronouncements of Government and Administration

Records of government administration and public life may nearly match private legal documents in their bulk. But those records and their types depend much more on the political arrangements, the structures of administration, and the systems of taxation than contracts do. All administrative documents were supposed to be stored in official archives.

Legislative, judicial, and administrative announcements issued by rulers themselves survive in significant quantity. They express the intention of the government and therefore are excellent historical sources, even if many of them deal with matters of subordinate importance. More than one hundred such regulations, *prostagmata*, by the Ptolemaic kings are known *(C.Ord.Ptol.)*, and a similarly impressive number of various orders (epistles, edicts, rescripts, etc.) of the Roman emperors from Augustus to Gallienus are preserved.[44] Among the latter, the decrees of Caracalla *(P.Giss.* I 40) and the *apokrimata* (legal decisions) of Septimius Severus *(P.Col.* VI 123) are especially important. In late antiquity there are fewer imperial orders, although some extensive texts exist, for instance, Justinian's rescript of the year 551 in *P.Cair.Masp.* I 67024. Also remarkable is a fragmentary papyrus that carries some lines of Justinian's edict XIII, promulgated in 539 CE *(P.Oxy.* LXIII 4400 and addendum). These imperial decrees are, of course, not original documents but copies, whether public or private.

Edicts and orders *(epistalmata)* of high officials, in particular of the prefects, appear in fair numbers.[45] They contain mainly administrative regulations (such as Mettius Rufus's edict on the archives, *M.Chr.* 192) or judicial decisions. Such sentences (in full or in abstracts) were also quoted as a legal basis in later petitions. For instance, *P.Vind.Tandem* 1, a copy of a letter by Ptolemy II (285–246 BCE) written in the middle of the third century CE, demonstrates how long some legal decisions might be remembered and cited.

Compilations of legal instructions, made for official use, were probably supposed to provide a quick orientation to laws or to serve as a guideline for decisions. The interval between the original and the copy could again be considerable: The so-called (Egyptian) law book of Hermopolis, the demotic original of which goes back to the third century BCE, was still copied in a Greek translation in the second half of the second century CE *(P.Oxy.* XLVI 3285). A passage of the tax law *SB* XVIII 13315 of 89 CE relates to a decree of Tiberius. The so-called *Gnomon of the Idios Logos* is the famous collection of legal canons and regulations for that procurator. In its opening the author (probably an earlier holder of that office) indicates his intention to catalogue all relevant instructions since Augustus. An extensive copy of the *Gnomon* in *BGU* V 1210 dates after 149 CE, but another, fragmentary copy in *P.Oxy.* XLII 3014 was written in the first century and therefore proves the older age of the *Gnomon.*

Minutes and Proceedings

Apparently all civil service departments were told to keep official diaries in which every action was written down.[46] Extracts from these *hypomnêmatismoi* are frequently mentioned. Many original examples also survive, such as *W.Chr.* 41, a journal of a *strategos* of the Ombite nome. Written by secretaries, they were published by public notice and later put into archives.

Similarly, officials had to compile *copybooks* containing duplicates of their correspondence. Even the smallest departments generated paperwork, as is demonstrated by two dozen journals written on potsherds at the small outpost called Krokodilô in the middle of the Eastern Desert (*O.Krok.* 1–5, 7, 24–40). An outstanding example is *P.Panop.Beatty* 1, containing the outgoing letters of the Panopolite *strategos*, which are virtually complete for September 298 CE. The text is of particular interest because at this precise time preparations were being made for the arrival of Diocletian and his army. There are sometimes as many as seventeen outgoing letters a day, produced by six writers, concerning correspondence with the president of the local town council, with the head of the provincial financial administration, with *strategoi* of neighboring districts, with military persons, and so on. Its counterpart, *P.Panop.Beatty* 2, lists the incoming official correspondence of January and February 300. The largest number of letters was sent by the procurator of the Lower Thebaid (fifty letters in two months), and often his communications arrived on the same day in Panopolis, although the headquarters of the procurator was about 120 miles away. Account books of the postal station at Takona, north of Oxyrhynchus, give insight into the logistical efforts involved (*P.Oxy.* LX 4087 and 4088). These stations compiled records of the number and ranks of traveling officials and messengers, as well as of the number of horses and the expenses for their food. The postal service of the Ptolemaic kings was also well organized, as a journal of an intermediate posting station shows (*Sel. Pap.* II 397).

After Septimius Severus granted councils to Alexandria and the metropoleis, their administrative duties (and financial accountability) for the nomes continuously increased. Each *boulê* kept the minutes of its meetings. Snatches of these detailed acts survive from Oxyrhynchus and Hermopolis.[47] Not only resolutions but also discussions, motions, comments, and acclamations were recorded verbatim and therefore present an insight into the routine meetings and business of the city councils, which consisted mainly of the installation of (liturgical) officials and financial administration. *Proceedings* of this kind were widespread, for *P.Yadin* I 12 contains extracts from council minutes of Petra as early as 124 CE.

Official Correspondence

Many papyri contain correspondence between officials. Higher authorities transmit orders and instructions to lower levels, which had to report in turn to their superiors. Sometimes very detailed information about specific official issues was communicated, such as that in the carbonized papyrus *P.Bub.* II 5, in which the *eklogistes* of the Boubastite nome in the Nile delta posed questions to his *strategoi* concerning financial matters (tax debts?). Another type of correspondence dealt with official inquiries, such as *P.Oxy.* XXXIII 2665: Two *bibliophylakes* and *bouleutai* from Oxyrhynchus report that a condemned person whose property is supposed to be confiscated actually has no property in their district. The official correspondence of the village clerk Petaus provides a good impression of the content of such exchanges of letters (*P.Petaus* 10–25). The extent of paperwork seems to have been huge in view of the fact that written communications were required even between officials who worked in the same metropolis—maybe even next door. Formalism made it necessary to file every single official act. An instructive instance came to light in the correspondence of the *basilikos grammateus* Hephaistion (alias Ammonios), who in the year 194 CE also administered the vacant post of *strategos* of his district. Hephaistion, acting as vice *strategos*, sent to himself in his position as *basilikos grammateus* letters and instructions, correctly using the polite phrases and other elements of official correspondence (*SB* XVIII 13175).

Even to illiterate people a document from an official chancery was recognizable because of its layout and the use of a special, stylized handwriting distinct from the usual business script. Only a few complete originals from chancelleries of the Ptolemaic kings or Roman governors have survived. We have an imposing order with the personal handwriting of Ptolemy X Alexander I (*UPZ* I 106), perhaps one signed by Cleopatra VII (*P.Bingen* 45), one of the prefect Subatianus Aquila (*SB* I 4639), and a letter of the Emperor Theodosius II (*ChLA* XLVI 1392). Most instructive is a comparison of the order of Aquila in the year 209 with a letter of Fl. Iulius Ausonius, *praeses Augustamnicae*, in the year 342.[48] The letters show remarkable palaeographic and formal similarities despite their considerable chronological distance and their composition in different offices: the design of the greeting, the position of the date and place of issue on the left margin, as well as the dating by consuls at the bottom of the document. An additional feature for the authenticity of official documents was the seal, which, however, is usually lost today. "I have sealed" became the standard expression of approval under official and private letters of business, accounts, and tax receipts of all kinds.

The Administration of Justice

Relatively few normative sources for law have survived, apart from enactments of law by the kings, emperors, and prefects. For instance, the *dikaiômata* of Alexandria (*P.Hal.* 1, after 259 BCE) provide information on the laws of the Greek poleis. The coexistence and blending of different legal systems with their separate juridical institutions becomes manifest in a vast quantity of documents that were produced in the administration of justice.[49] During the Ptolemaic period summonses (like *P.Hib.* I 30), official reports of summons (*BGU* VIII 1773–1778), statements of witness (*P.Heid.* VIII 413–416 with a list of comparable documents on p. 45 f.), and court proceedings (*P.Petr.* III 22a–g) inform us of the procedures followed in courts of law. In particular, the *reports of proceedings* stand out as a specific category of text: About thirty examples are extant from the Ptolemaic period, and more than two hundred from the Roman period until about 300 CE.[50]

Stenographers recorded trials verbatim in shorthand. Afterward they made a clean copy and filed it after the head of the court had checked it. Because copies of official proceedings were often used as evidence in court, the archived files were accessible to the public. Until Diocletian's time, reports of proceedings were always written in Greek; afterward they sometimes had a framework of introductory formulas in Latin. More than fifty such bilingual reports of proceedings from late antiquity are known.[51] Whatever their origin, they show almost identical layout and the deliberate utilization of different sizes and characters of handwriting, even in the military courts.[52]

Often connected to the preparations for trials are the so-called *orders to arrest*. Standardized in formulation, these documents sometimes concern official inquiries after one or more people for an institution or a court; sometimes they are practically arrest warrants. The nearly twenty examples from the Ptolemaic period were produced by various officials (*P.Paramone* 9, introd., 104–106); the more than forty orders to arrest from the Roman period show a much stronger standardization in wording and the authorities involved. Until nearly the mid-third century, when substantial administrative reforms took place, almost all of the orders are produced by *strategoi* and address the *archephodoi* of a village. The approximately twenty orders from the next four centuries are mostly sent by centurions, *beneficiarii* or *praepositi pagi*. The recipients are village officials such as *eirenarchai* or *komarchai*.[53]

Interaction between State and Individual

Another extensive category of official documents comprises texts arising from contact between the authorities and the general population. All incoming declarations, petitions, and so on (often in multiple copies) went into the state archives. Each record had a stipulated format, and those received were pasted together into a roll and numbered. Any item could thus be identified by box, roll, and column. About 330 CE these *tomoi synkollêsimoi* disappear, a fact that indicates profound changes in the organization of the public offices.[54]

PETITIONS TO AUTHORITIES

It may be significant that petitions to officials are the commonest type of record except tax receipts. More than a thousand survive from the entire "papyrological millennium." The petitions sought redress for abuses or help against injustice. Often they inaugurated a lawsuit.

The *enteuxis* is the classical Ptolemaic form of petition. In the third century BCE the *enteuxeis* addressed the king directly (e.g., *P.Enteux.; M.Chr.* 8–16). The structure of the petitions is constant: After the opening, in the usual letter form—"to king X...from NN (+title)"—followed a description of the injustice suffered and the request for concrete measures to correct it. The entry ended with the formulaic greeting *eutuchei* ("farewell"), which was used only for the king.

Administrative orders (*BGU* III 1011, II 5 ff.) explicitly urged the petitioners to make the petitions as short as possible. Nevertheless, it is hard to imagine that all *enteuxeis* were handed over personally to the king. As a copy went to the *strategos*, petitions likely went through several levels before the king—in the best case—agreed and added written instructions. The petitioner himself had to ensure that the instructions were carried out. Petitions to officials (*strategoi*, *epistrategoi*), called *hypomnêmata*, differed from the *enteuxeis* more in linguistic details than anything else. From the second century BCE on, the differences diminish.

Besides petitions, people handed in notifications (*prosangelmata*) to civil and military officials and tried to obtain protection without a judicial decision. People did not hope for a judgment with formal legal force but for the realization of justice through an official authority. This "bureaucratic justice" also appears on the local level, as shown by the applications to the garrison commander Dioskourides in the years 154–145 BCE (*P.Phrour.Diosk.* 1–12).

During the Roman period petitions were addressed to all levels of the provincial administration, from the local police officer through the *exegetes* at the urban level and the *strategos*, as well as the *basilikos grammateus* at the district level, to the procurators of equestrian rank (e.g., *epistrategoi*, *iuridicus*) and the prefect himself. At the annual *conventus* there was a possibility of reaching the prefect also outside Alexandria. All judgments were accessible to the public because they were required to be posted in Alexandria and the relevant metropolis, which also made it possible to obtain private copies. This practice is best shown in the example of the *Apokrimata* (*P.Col.* VI 123), a copy of the judicial decisions of Septimius Severus concerning eleven petitions. During the Roman period a separate group of petitions was addressed to centurions, decurions, and *beneficiarii*. So far more than fifty texts of this kind have been published.[55] The military appears in similar roles in epigraphical and papyrological evidence for other parts of the empire, especially the *beneficiarii*.

After Diocletian's reform, petitions had to be addressed to the governors of the subprovinces, or *duces*. In addition, from the fifth century on, local dignitaries (urban authorities, *officiales* of the governor's staff, owners of large estates) increasingly appear as recipients. During every period petitions followed stereotyped formulas.[56] They give extensive insight into legal transactions and conceptions of law because of their detailed narrations of disputes and the requests for concrete measures of relief.

Almost thirty papyri dealing with the *medical inspection* of sick or injured persons are known. These records date from the late first to the fourth century CE. The doctors who wrote such reports were called "official doctor" from the late second century on and were commissioned by the municipality (*P.Oxy.* LVIII 3926). A private person who wanted an official medical inspection had to apply to the *strategos* or (later) to the *ekdikos* or *nyktostrategos* (e.g., *P.Oxy.* LI 3620).

Reports on the examination of corpses show that in Roman Egypt an autopsy was required in cases of violent death (*P.Oxy.* I 51; *P.Rein.* II 92).

ROUTINE DECLARATIONS TO AUTHORITIES

The Roman administration of Egypt, with its strict hierarchy and precisely pre-scribed official procedures, developed a series of very specific documents. The tightening and standardization of administrative channels, the compulsory public service that was established and expanded from the mid-first century CE on, and the efforts to control the population, personal status, financial circumstances, and place of residence at the same time enforced the formalization of official paper-work. Many specific types of documents have in common the fact that they developed during the first century and disappeared in the second half of the third century. Uniformity in wording, layout, and (often) size is remarkable, as most of these documents were drafted by private individuals and handed in to officials on certain occasions. Their skilled handwriting reveals that documents that were addressed to the authorities were normally written by professional scribes, who were also trained in the layout and wording of declarations and contracts.

Of essential significance for all inhabitants of Graeco-Roman Egypt (and the whole empire) was their legal and fiscal status. Especially for the privileged classes it must have been a major concern that their status be officially documented and thus easily transferred to the next generation. Taxes and services were distributed in different ways among the various, more legally than ethnically defined groups—Romans, Alexandrians, Hellenes, *Aigyptioi*. The worries about status and an appropriate registration in the files of the fiscal authorities lie behind many declarations and applications. It may have been helpful for preservation that such documents were carefully treated and handed down over the generations—like present personal documents. A Latin certificate of birth (*testatio*) that was drawn up for the soldier M. Lucretius Clemens in 127 on behalf of his son Serenus was kept by his descendants for at least a century (*P.Diog.* 1).

Notifications of Birth   Nearly all of the approximately forty notifications of birth come from the privileged sectors of the population, the *metropolitai*, citizens of Antinoopolis and Roman citizens.[57] The earliest examples are from the period of the Julian-Claudian emperors, the latest from the beginning of the fourth century; more than half were found in Oxyrhynchus. In most cases the father, sometimes together with the mother (but in the Oxyrhynchite also the house owner), announced to the village or metropolis secretary in the form of a *hypomnema* the birth of a son or (occasionally) a daughter. Often two, three, or more years passed between birth and declaration, but this had no significance because tax liability started at fourteen. The small number of birth notifications indicates that they can hardly have been obligatory. Things were different only in Antinoopolis, where the announcement had to be made within thirty days in order to gain special privileges. Moreover, declaration within this period was obligatory for the legitimate children of Roman citizens and had to be made in Alexandria, where it was registered and posted in public, while the father received a certificate on a wax tablet. So far thirteen such declarations are known, dating from 62 (*CPLat.* 148) to 242 CE (*CPLat.* 163). For illegitimate offspring (e.g., children of soldiers before Septimius Severus), instead of such a declaration, a private-law declaration had to be made in front of seven witnesses and recorded on a wax tablet.

Epikrisis   As another bureaucratic procedure to define legal status, the *epikrisis* of boys who had completed their thirteenth year produced extensive papyrological documentation. This check of personal and fiscal status determined who would enjoy Roman or Alexandrian citizenship and was therefore exempted from the poll tax. It also clarified who belonged to the privileged population of the metropoleis and had to pay only half the rate, as well as who was Egyptian and had to pay the full amount.[58] For the *epikrisis* of the native population the district authorities (*strategoi* and *basilikoi grammateis*) were responsible; for the *epikrisis* of the local Roman citizens and their households (as well as, up to the middle of the second century, of Alexandrians), the prefect.[59] In general, the status of an individual followed that of the parents, but a certain degree of social mobility was possible, for instance, with the attainment of Roman citizenship through military service. Status was verified by the presentation of older *epikrisis* documents or census declarations. It is not uncommon at the beginning of the third century to find among the documents presented *epikrisis* papers from ancestors written half a century earlier. Various types of records inform us of these developments: *epikrisis* declarations (e.g., *P.Oxy.* XII 1452), *epikrisis* registers, and excerpts from *epikrisis* files (e.g., *Doc.Eser.Rom.* 93).

Hellenes and Priests   Certain social groups with special status had their own required status documents and processes for scrutiny. Among the Hellenes, the more exclusive class of "those from the gymnasium" stood out, especially in Oxyrhynchus. They underwent additional selective training and examination. For instance, *P.Mich.* XIV 676, from 272 CE, shows a particularly remarkable application for *epikrisis* for the gymnasial class. Here the presented genealogy goes back six generations on the paternal side and eight on the maternal. Also mentioned is a maternal ancestor who had passed the (gymnasial) *epikrisis* under Nero—more than two hundred years earlier. Similar arguments occur in *P.Oxy.* XLVI 3279.

A second exclusive group comprised the Egyptian priestly families. If someone wanted to obtain a priesthood, he was required to be circumcised, in addition to meeting certain genealogical and physical conditions. Corresponding *applications for circumcision* had to be made to the *strategos*, at least from the middle of the second century CE on; this may indicate the Roman government's increased control of temples. The disappearance of the applications for circumcision (latest example: *PSI* V 454 from the year 320 CE) marks the decline of the Egyptian cults.[60]

Census Declarations   Registration of the inhabitants and their property was the most important precondition for a counting of both the fiscal objects and the fiscal subjects. Under the Ptolemies this took place through annual self-declaration; in Roman times through the "house-to-house-declaration," adapting the model of the census of Roman citizens. Every head of a household, who was typically also the home owner, male or female, had to submit a written *census declaration* to the district authorities every fourteen years. An enormous bureaucratic effort from both the officials and the general population was required because all household heads had to present themselves to the authorities of their home area. Orders to conduct a census generally came from the prefect and were obligatory for all peregrine inhabitants. Augustus introduced a seven-year cycle in 11/10 BCE, but in 19/20 CE this was changed to a fourteen-year cycle, still sufficient for collecting the data needed for the poll tax. There must have been millions of declarations, as the census in this form was carried out until 257/258 CE. More than three hundred edited census declarations show not only how consistently documentary patterns were maintained for decades but also how local peculiarities of formula developed.[61]

Before the registration began, the administration routinely ordered people to return to their registered homes. The approximately one dozen copies of so-called *reintegration edicts* (or references to such) that survive threatened to impose sanctions against those who disobeyed and remained in the cities, particularly Alexandria.[62] The unstated objective is the recovery of tax fugitives. Some reintegration edicts seem to have been precipitated by urban disturbances. For instance, *P.Giss.* I 40, col. 2, is probably the edict mentioned by Cassius Dio 77, 23, 2 in connection with the massacre that Caracalla carried out in Alexandria in 215 CE.

Notifications of Death   The almost one hundred notifications of death of a male relative edited so far also had a fiscal purpose.[63] Formally, these so-called notifications are applications made by relatives to the local officials of the metropolis or the villages to list the deceased person in the register of the departed and delete him from the roll of taxpayers. The declarant received a duplicate with the official subscriptions as evidence, while the original was—often in form of a *tomos synkollêsimos*—put into the archive. Notifications of death were imposed under Augustus (*C.Pap.Gr.* II 1, 2/3 CE) in connection with the poll tax. At the beginning of the fourth century this type of record disappears. Surviving examples show again the haphazard distribution of papyrological evidence: Although notifications of death must have been required everywhere, about sixty exemplars come from the Arsinoite and twenty-six from the Oxyrhynchite nome, while from other nomes only two or three have survived.

SERVICES FOR THE STATE

Egypt's punctual and complete payment of taxes was vital to every government. Consequently, papyri show a highly elaborate system of fiscal administration but provide much more information about the local levels than about the higher, central offices.[64] For every period the papyrological evidence offers rich information about numerous officials concerned with assessing and collecting the taxes payable in kind or in money, the settlement of accounts, control and forwarding of taxes, recovery of outstanding debts, and much more. With many thousand relevant texts, the fiscal administration is as central in papyrological sources as it was in the people's lives.

Taxes   Most significant were the duties on land, which generally had to be paid in wheat. Under both Ptolemaic and Roman rule they were largely calculated on the basis of the yield of the land. The tax wheat was directly transferred from the threshing floor to the state granary. Here the *sitologoi* recorded the entry and acknowledged receipt;[65] moreover, they reported to the *strategos* both daily and monthly (*P.Vind.Worp* 4, introd., pp. 39–42; *P.Dub.* 4, introd., p. 20). Under the Ptolemies, vineyards and gardens were also burdened by a special tax payable in money. Other taxes were levied on animals, slaves, and various occupations. State-controlled banks received the taxes for the government's account.[66]

Innumerable tax receipts document the poll taxes, which under Ptolemaic rule were called *syntaxis* and salt tax and had to be paid by male Egyptians. The Romans imposed the *laographia* on all male inhabitants between fourteen and sixty-five years of age, except Romans and citizens of the Greek poleis. From the late first century CE on, tax collection was carried out mainly by liturgical officials, with tax farming used only for indirect taxes. In Diocletian's fiscal reform, Egypt was subjected to the general system of *capitatio-iugatio,* which imposed a unified tax assessment that embraced both land and people. In actuality, however, the taxes were collected mostly on the basis of landholdings, still largely in grain but also partly in cash. Again, numerous tax receipts document payments for the *annona militaris,* intended to feed the army and the civil servants, as well as for the grain collected for Rome and later Constantinople (*embolē*). According to Justinian's edict XIII 8 (539 CE), eight million artabas (approximately 312 million liters) of wheat left Egypt each year for Constantinople. Many transportation contracts with shipowners and some extensive records concerning the office of the *praefectus annonae Alexandriae* (*P.Ryl.* IV 652, *P.Turner* 45, *SB* XXIV 16261) illuminate the complicated control and accounting system.

The specific taxes, fees, customs dues, and other duties were collected by different officials, with their own types of tax receipts, which vary also by locality. Within each type, however, the uniformity of formula for several decades is remarkable. Absolutely essential components of each tax receipt are the taxpayer's name, the tax, the year of tax assessment, the amount paid, and the tax collector's name and title. Tax receipts were usually written on the cheapest material available—very often potsherds, on which they survive by the thousands.[67] Tax receipts on ostraca have been found throughout Egypt and elsewhere.[68]

Customs and Tolls   Large numbers of receipts for customs duties testify to the intensive movement of goods across provincial boundaries but even more to traffic across internal barriers, where various tolls (mostly 1–2 percent) had to be paid.[69] Like tax receipts, those for customs duties are brief, stereotyped texts, often on ostraca. Hundreds of toll receipts written in the villages on the periphery of the Fayyum (e.g., Soknopaiou Nesos, Karanis, Philadelphia) for the caravan drivers record their imports and exports between the oases of the Western Desert and the Nile valley. The transport animals (donkeys, camels), the goods, and their loads are mentioned briefly.[70] There was also a charge for security, the "desert guard." Toll receipts appear during the early first century and disappear soon after 260 CE as a result of changes in the customs system.

Control of Property   Also well documented are measures to control the objects of taxation. Taxpayers' declarations would be checked by official "visit" (*episkepsis*). Many texts dealing with land survey and some tax lists of enormous length (e.g., *P.Col.* II), compiled on the local level, have survived. Particularly impressive are the long tax rolls of the Ptolemaic and Roman periods from Kerkeosiris, Karanis, Philadelphia, and Theadelphia.[71] Fiscal obligations were recorded in registers such as *P.Thmouis* 1 (Mendesian nome, 170/171 CE). From Byzantine times we have accounting vouchers issued on the basis of the general register, especially from the tax office of Hermopolis (*CPR* XXIV, p. 45n30), as well as extensive records of tax payments. Apparently officials by that time preferred to keep the records not in rolls but in codices.[72]

Also related to the fiscal administration are registers of landowners and lists of taxpayers, some of which are extensive. Such documents occasionally reflect social and economic peculiarities such as the extensive rural exodus from Philadelphia under Nero, which became obvious from a register of missing tax debtors (*P.Ryl.* IV 595 from 57 CE), or the social structure of landowners in the Hermopolite nome around the middle of the fourth century CE by means of a land register (*P.Herm. Landl.* 1–3). From the period of Justinian we have the "cadastre of Aphrodito" (*SB* XX 14669), which lists the property of urban landowners, along with a tax register from the same village,[73] which records one year's tax payments in gold and copper coins, and a "budget" for the nome capital Antaiopolis (*SB* XX 14494).

Owners of real property were required to report it by written *property returns*. Under Ptolemaic rule, private land was mainly building plots and garden land (e.g., olive and palm groves, vineyards). Real property declarations, known from the third century BCE, then disappear (*W.Chr.* 221–224, and the list in *P.Heid.* VII, pp. 36 f.). In the second and first centuries BCE, a notary had to document transactions involving land and to record the contract in a register. The state could thus keep track of private real property and ensure payment of the sales tax.

Individual property returns were periodically revised and supplemented by general declarations, their volume increasing with the spread of private property under the empire. State-owned land that was leased out also generated paperwork, and unattractive parcels could be assigned for compulsory cultivation.[74] In case of crop failure or if the area had not been flooded by the Nile, the administration granted a reduction in taxes. This required a written *declaration of uninundated land;* some seventy examples of this type of document from the period from 158 to 245 CE show that requests for tax reduction were not uncommon.[75]

One also was required to declare any animals that one possessed, especially camels, sheep, and goats, which were taxed. These declarations make us realize once again what a small fraction of the immense volume of paperwork has come into our hands. So far forty-three *declarations concerning camels* are known,[76] all of them from the Arsinoite and dated to the period between 122 and 217 CE. A single example from the year 330 CE (*P.Col.* X 288), however, shows that, much later, similar declarations were also demanded from time to time. *Registrations of livestock* were thought to have appeared only from the second century CE on, until *BGU* XVI 2578–2587 proved their existence since the beginning of Roman rule.[77] More than seventy registrations of sheep and goats survive from various nomes, dating from Augustus to the third century.

All of these types of declarations were gathered in the offices of the *strategos* and *basilikos grammateus* and stored in the archives. The declarations, reports, and accounts of the taxation system also had to be forwarded to the central archive in Alexandria. Official diaries of the *strategos* clearly show that the original documents went to Alexandria, while the copies remained in the locality.

Irrigation Work Since pharaonic times the Egyptians were required to do compulsory work to maintain the irrigation system. In the papyri, work on dikes and ditches is well documented, especially after an early Roman reorganization. Every man of "Egyptian" status was obligated to work five days a year on the irrigation and drainage canals and received a certificate afterward. More than 170 of such *penthemeros certificates* remain from different villages of the Arsinoite nome, dating from the reign of Claudius to that of Elagabalus.[78] Several other documents (for instance, an order to compile lists of workers [*SB* VIII 9925] or reports by *sitologoi* on dike work [*BGU* XIII 2273–2275]) confirm our impression of a tight organization. In other nomes comparable service was required with local variations; for example, in the Oxyrhynchite nome this service was called the "five naubion," reflecting the quantity of earth (the *naubion*) each man had to remove from the canals. Irrigation works were checked by "visits" and reports.[79] The disappearance of work certificates after about 221 clearly indicates that the jobs were administered differently, because the irrigation system still had to be cared for.

Liturgies   In the course of the first century CE the population of Egypt was increasingly burdened with compulsory services ("liturgies," Greek *leitourgiai*). Virtually all public jobs below the level of the *strategos* and *basilikos grammateus* (e.g., collection of taxes, security services) had to be done for a certain period (up to three years) without payment by those deemed able to afford the service. Liturgies were assigned proportionally according to property. From the second to the fourth century the liturgical service was an elaborate system,which yielded its own specific types of files and documents (e.g., *P.Leit.* 1–14). In special nominations to liturgy, various officials were required to present candidates and argue for their nomination.[80] Those officials who were responsible for nominations, like the *komogrammateus* and the *strategos,* informed themselves about the property of the chosen candidate at the *bibliothêkê enktêseôn* (*P.Petaus* 10 and 11, *P.Flor.* II 206–207). After such a check, the liturgists were usually nominated by the *strategos.* Sometimes high-ranking *procuratores* like an *epistrategos* or even the *idios logos* were also involved in nominations (*P.Oxy.* XLIX 3508, for a dike overseer). The governors' guidelines for the criteria for liturgical service were collected (*SB* VI 9050), and inadequate candidates were refused.[81] If necessary, a substitute had to be nominated.[82] The liturgical official had to swear an oath at his assumption of office.[83] Many nominees tried to avoid liturgical service, and protests against nomination or requests for exemption refer to disqualifying reasons such as advanced age, insufficient property, double burden through other liturgies, or membership in an exempt group of people.[84] Repeatedly the governors took strict steps against the flight of liturgists, like Petronius Mamertinus in 138 CE (*P.Oslo* III 79). Papyri from the second and third centuries show that in several cases the proposed candidates preferred to relinquish their property rather than accept a liturgical office (*W.Chr.* 402; *SB* XXVI 16526). Especially in the fourth century it seemed necessary to guarantee liturgical services with sureties for the officeholders (e.g., *PSI* I 86). During the fifth century the system obviously underwent some significant changes, including the option for a nominated liturgist to pay somebody else to perform the service (*CPR* X 17–20).

Military

Military history is probably the area that benefits most from the documentary texts found outside of Egypt: Latin ostraca from a camp in Libya provide military reports (*O.BuNjem*); the wood panels from Vindolanda at Hadrian's Wall (*T.Vindol.* I–III) and similar ones from Vindonissa (*T.Vindon.*) come from military bases and shed light on the official and private agenda of soldiers (and their relatives); papyri from Dura Europos written in the *scriptorium* of the *cohors XX Palmyrenorum* represent the most extensive textual assemblage from the army's internal administration. (See chapter 20 for a description of the Dura papyri and other finds from the Near East.)

The Dura papyri are our richest source of rosters like the *Feriale Duranum* (*Rom.Mil.Rec.* 117); but the Egyptian papyri also provide similar documents. A comparison of the duty roster of legio III Cyrenaica in *Rom.Mil.Rec.* 9 (90–96 CE) with the roster on *O.Claud.* II 308 (150 CE) reveals that in different units the files followed exactly the same patterns. Ostraca—in particular those from the Eastern Desert—offer various examples of the daily, official correspondence, the circulars, and the reports that had to be prepared by every commander of even the smallest guardpost (*praesidium*).[85] Besides testimonies for the routine guard duties and receipts for food and wine, some exceptional documents exist, such as the report about an attack by barbarian raiders on a small outpost (*O.Krok.* 87).

Numerous documents deal with the interactions between the army and local society or describe the feeding of the army. From the first until the third century, supplies were acquired mainly by purchase and requisition. On such occasions the military issued receipts in Greek. Particularly impressive is the long series of such receipts issued by horsemen to the *summus curator* for money they received against their hay allowance (*P.Hamb.* I 39). Occasionally papyri transmit not only complaints about requisitions by soldiers but also complaints by soldiers about the lack of food supplies. In addition to the petitions to soldiers or officers mentioned earlier, papyri describe soldiers' civil duties and their rôle as judges in lawsuits.[86]

Changes

Late antiquity saw a series of profound social and economic changes that manifest themselves importantly in the papyrological documentation. The Roman system of control of fiscal objects and subjects gradually faded away, together with its documents, starting in the mid-third century. Many offices changed name or definition. The old land categories and the katoikic land also disappeared or lost meaning in the fourth century, while bureaucratic control of property changed in the course of Diocletian's reforms. Papyri show the *censitor* at work in Egypt, surveying the arable land for the new fiscal system (*P.Cair.Isid.* 2). Many of the long-term developments can be traced in papyri, such as the decline of the council and the bouleutic class, the expansion of the large estates, the growth of patronage, the ascension of several families into the aristocracy of the empire through imperial service, and the increasing interweaving of state and private spheres. The papyrological documentation of the Byzantine period is dominated by large archives more than in any other era.

As we have seen, from the fifth century on, contracts were drawn up by a *tabellio*. New formulas are found in Byzantine contracts of lease, purchase, and loans, even where the content remains much the same as earlier. Certain clauses mirror the changed historical conditions; for example, landlords take over the payment of taxes on leased land. Poor peasants and tenants depend more on the landlord for capital equipment, like spare parts for the water wheels. With *deeds of surety* the semipublic Great Houses tried to counter tendencies to flight. While in earlier centuries deeds of surety were common in connection with lawsuits, they were now used as a measure against *anachorêsis*. More than 180 sureties dating from the fourth to the seventh century have been edited.[87] More than the half of these belong to the sixth century. A substantial number were also undertaken in order to release an arrested debtor or fugitive. This tradition continued later with Coptic sureties.[88]

Another type of document prominent in Byzantine times is the record of private arbitration. In a *compromise*, two parties agreed to submit a dispute to one or more arbiters. If they solved their case by mutual agreement—before filing a lawsuit—they drew up a written settlement of the dispute (*dialysis*).[89] So far approximately thirty compromises and fifty settlements have been published. Most of them explain in detail the history of the conflict (e.g., *P.Münch.* I 1, 7, 14; *P.Mich.Aphrod.*). The increasing number of these documents in the sixth century shows that people preferred to solve legal disputes privately and to avoid litigation. The strange coincidence that about 530 CE bilingual judicial proceedings from state courts disappear has been interpreted as indicating that formal litigation was absent and private arbitration paramount for the settlement of civil disputes. Although the conclusion that the Egyptian courts disappeared after Justinian has been refuted, a good explanation for the disappearance of proceedings has not yet been found.

Papyri offer ample information about early Christianity and its institutions (churches, monasteries, and clergy) starting in the fourth century but little before.[90] An archive consisting mainly of letters and contracts gives a colorful impression of the activities in a fourth-century Melitian monastery in Middle Egypt and its abbot, Nepheros, a "holy man" respected for his spirituality (*P.Neph.*). Documents shed light on various events of Christian lives such as the priest's role as a mediator between individual and state authority, requesting mercy for a deserter (*P.Abinn.* 32), contracts that deal with the sale of a hermitage (*P.Dub.* 32–34), and the economic activities of the church as landowner (e.g., *CPR* X 1–16), but there is no repertory of "Christian documents" as such.

Every survey that describes the range of documentary papyri is necessarily subjective and selective. The diversity of texts written on papyrus is greater than any overview can demonstrate. As authentic testimonies of societies in which only a tiny elite was able to read and write, papyri in all their variety witness the authority and ubiquity of the written word.

NOTES

1. Habermann (1998, 144–160).
2. For the spread of papyrus in the ancient world, see Lewis (1974, 84–94); cf. chapter 20 for papyri written outside Egypt.

3. Montevecchi (1972, 86–89); compare the "Sachübersicht" in *SB* XXVI pp. V–XI with ten main categories and many more subcategories.

4. Masterly surveys of the papyrological evidence are Turner (1980, 127–153); Bagnall (1995, 9–31); and Hagedorn (1997, 59–71).

5. Haensch (1992, 209–317).

6. Cockle (1984, 106–122); much is said on archives by Wolff (1978) and Burkhalter (1990, 191–215).

7. For collections of papyrus letters cf. the references in *Checklist* (chapter 3) by Oates et al. (2001); all of the anthologies contain numerous private letters as well.

8. Bagnall and Cribiore (2006).

9. For example, the letters of Apion (alias Antonius Maximus) (*Sel.Pap.* I 112; *BGU* II 632), Apollinaris (*P.Mich.* VIII 490, 491), and Claudius Terentianus (*P.Mich.* VIII 468, 476), all from the second century CE.

10. Famous examples are Hilarion's letter to his wife (*P.Oxy.* IV 744) and complaints by the boy Theon (*P.Oxy.* I 119).

11. Cotton (1981); Kim (1972); Treu (1973, 629–636).

12. Collected in Chapa (1998). For observations on the genre, see Worp (1995, 149–154).

13. Cf. *P.Oxy.* LII 3693, introduction, with references and literature.

14. Wolff (1961, 115–154); A. Jördens, *P.Heid.* V, pp. 371–373.

15. Straus (2004, 345–349).

16. *C.Ptol.Sklav.* 28–37; Biezuńska-Małowist (1966, 433–443).

17. *M.Chr.* 320 in Greek; *ChLA* V 290 and IV 269 in Latin.

18. For procedure and documents see Rupprecht (1986, 95–102); supplements in *P.Hamb.* IV 270, introduction.

19. For example, see *Jur.Pap.* 10; *M.Chr.* 363; *P.Oxy.* XVI 1895; *P.Köln* VII 321.

20. Yiftach-Firanko (2003), with the sources on pp. 9–39. For well-preserved marriage contracts see *Sel.Pap.* I 2–5.

21. Katzoff (1996, 223–234).

22. For divorce agreements see Erdmann (1941, 44–57); Yiftach (2001, vol. 2, 1331–1339).

23. Well over 220 examples survive; cf. Yiftach (2002, 149–164). The basic literature is still Kreller (1919).

24. Migliardi Zingale (1997).

25. The cavalry officer Dryton drew up at least three testaments—in 164, 150, and 126 BCE: *P.Dryton* 1, 2, 3, and 4, a copy. On the revocation of a will see *Sel.Pap.* II 424; *P.Oxy.* I 107; *SB* VIII 9766; and *P.Oxy.* XXXVI 2759.

26. Listed in Jördens, *P.Heid.* V, pp. 296–301, and Kruit (1992, 167–84, supplement). On the problem of hidden loans see Bagnall (1977, 85–96).

27. For example, see *M.Chr.* 226, *SB* XXII 15703; cf. Jördens (1993, 263–282).

28. Ptolemaic: Rupprecht (1967); Roman: Kühnert (1965); Byzantine: Preissner (1956). The *HGV* lists almost two thousand loans and related documents.

29. Explicitly stated in *Jur.Pap.* 22a, col. 1, 9–12. *M.Chr.* 334 and 335 may be "deposits" of this kind.

30. Herrmann (1958, 247–288) compiled an impressive list of 42 Ptolemaic, 228 Roman, and 198 Byzantine land leases. Since then the numbers have increased significantly.

31. Simon (1982, 365–422).

32. Müller (1985, 345–361).

33. Hengstl (1972); Jördens, *P.Heid.* V, pp. 125–375.

34. Meyer-Termeer (1978, 88–104); supplements in *P.Wash.Univ.* II 82, introd.

35. Sources and discussion in Rupprecht (1992, vol. 2, 271–289).

36. A quick impression may be obtained from *W.Chr.* 65–135, *Sel.Pap.* I 193–200, and *C.Pap.Hengstl* 56–71.

37. Representative collections: *C.Étiq.Mom.*; *SB* III 7037–7125; *SB* V 7697–7736.

38. Valbelle and Husson (1998, vol. 2, 1055–1071).

39. Anagnostou-Canas (1998, 1–16).

40. *SB* XIV 11658; *SB* XXVI 16703; *SB* XVIII 13250; Husson (1997, vol. 1, 482–489).

41. J. R. Rea, *P.Oxy.* LVIII 3929 introd., and R. Duttenhöfer, *P.Lips.* II 152 introd., both with further references.

42. Zuckerman (1998, 79–139).

43. Zuckerman (2004, 189–212).

44. Collected by Oliver (1989), together with the epigraphical evidence.

45. For surveys on edicts see Katzoff (1980, 807–44) and Chalon (1964, 251–256).

46. Early examples are *P.Petr.* II 27 (2); *BGU* VIII 1767, 1768; late examples are *P.Oxy.* LX 4075; *CPR* XVIIA 18.

47. Oxyrhynchus: *P.Oxy.* XII 1413–1419; XXVII 2475–2477; Hermopolis: *SPP* V contains an extensive set of proceedings from the council (mid-third century CE); cf. Bowman (1971, 32–34).

48. Compare the photo of *SB* I 4639 in Schubart (1911, pl. 35) with that of *ChLA* XLVII 1421.

49. For a representative selection see *M.Chr.* 20–33, 50–55, and 79–97.

50. Coles (1966, 55–63).

51. Catalogued in Thomas (1998, 132–134); supplements in D. and U. Hagedorn, *P.Thomas*, p. 217m.

52. *P.Oxy.* LXIII 4381; *P.Acad.* 56/1 + 2 + 57/1; and *ChLA* XLVII 1437.

53. *P.Mich.* X 589–591, introd.; Hagedorn (1979, 61n2); Drexhage (1989, 102–118).

54. Clarysse (2003, 344–359). An instructive picture of a *tomos synkollêsimos* is *Pap. Lugd.Bat.* V, pl. 1, in which eighteen declarations from 174 CE are pasted together.

55. Whitehorne (2004, 161–169).

56. Montevecchi (1972, 189–192) and Fournet and Gascou (2004, 141–196).

57. *P.Bingen* 105, introduction. Well-preseved examples are *P.Fay.* 28; *P.Gen.* I² 33; *P.Petaus* 1 and 2 contain two copies of a birth notification for an eight-year-old girl; *Pap. Lugd.Bat.* VI 33 for an Antinoopolite.

58. Nelson (1979, 3–40); Kruse (2002, vol. 1, 252–271; vol. 2, 638–640).

59. Haensch (1992, 313–317, app. 4); on the *epikrisis* papers of Roman citizens see *P.Diog.* 6 and 7; on those of illegitimate children see *SB* I 5217, *P.Oxy.* XII 1451, *BGU* IV 1032; on those of slaves see *PSI* IV 447.

60. Approximately twenty applications for circumcision have been edited; cf. Kruse (2002, vol. 2, 728–733).

61. Bagnall and Frier (1994, 179–312) (list of documents).

62. Examples are *P.Lond.* III 904; *SB* XX 14662; *P.Fay.* 24.

63. See *C.Pap.Gr.* II; Kruse (2002, vol. 1, 139–168; updated list on page 143n256).

64. Normative sources are few; the most famous is perhaps *P.Rev.*, a collection of tax regulations.

65. Hundreds of receipts of *sitologoi* demonstrate this procedure from the mid-third century BCE to the mid-fourth century CE.

66. A most impressive example is the extensive roll *P.Col.* II 1 R 4 + *BGU* XIII 2270 + 2271 + *P.Berl.Frisk* 1 + *P.Graux* III 30 + *SB* XVI 13060 (verso: *P.Col.* V 1, verso 4; *P.Graux* IV 31), Arsinoite nome, 155 CE.

67. Thousands of tax receipts appear in *O.Amst., O.Amst.Shelt., O.CairoGPW, O.Wilck., O.Bodl.* I–II, *O.Elkab, O.Heid.,* and *O.Ont.Mus.* I–II, among others.

68. Eastern Desert: *O.Claud.* I–IV, *O.Krok.;* Western Desert: *O.Douch.* I–V, *O.Kellis.* Tax receipts from outside Egypt are similar to those in Egypt (e.g., *P.Petra* I 7–10).

69. Sijpesteijn (1987, 23–25).

70. For lists of such receipts see Drexhage (1982, 61–84); Sijpesteijn (1987, 102–143, nos. 1–919).

71. *P.Count* I 22–44; *P.Tebt.* I; *P.Mich.* IV; *BGU* IX 1891–1989; *P.Col.* V 1, verso.

72. Tax codices: *CPR* V 26; *P.Sorb.* II 69; *MPER* IX 44–53 + 56 + *SB* XXII 15711.

73. See Zuckerman (2004, 248–271).

74. Kruse (2002, vol. 1, 559–609).

75. Habermann (1997, 223–226); Kruse (2002, vol. 1, 235–250).

76. Kruse (2002, vol. 1, 181n361–364).

77. Habermann (2001, 77–100, esp. 89 ff).

78. The earliest known penthemeros certificate is *P.Fay.* 286 (41–54 CE); the latest, *P.Fouad* I 62 (221 CE). For a list of documents see *P.Mich.* XVI 141–147.

79. For example, see *P.Köln* VIII 341 verso; *P.Tebt.* III.1 725; *W.Chr.* 389.

80. Nominations for liturgy are listed in Lewis (1997, 110 f). Cf. also *Sel.Pap.* II 342–345 (second–fourth centuries CE) and the catalogue of liturgies in *P.Petaus* 88.

81. For example, see *P.Wisc.* II 81: The prefect reproves a *komogrammateus* because he has nominated an unqualified person; *CPR* XXIII 27: A *strategos/exactor* refers an inadmissible nomination back to the *boulê.*

82. For example, see *P.Louvre* II 114; *P.Gen.* I² 37.

83. See *P.Iand.* III 33; *P.Leit.* 12; *P.Oxy.* XLIII 3097, 3098.

84. Just a few examples: *W.Chr.* 396; *W.Chr.* 29; *SB* XIV 11980; and *SB* XII 10797.

85. *O.Claud.* I–III, *O.Krok., O.Florida,* and *O.Douch* I–V.

86. *M.Chr.* II 84; *P.Mich.* III 159; *P.Gen.* I² 74; *P.Oxy.* XIV 1637.

87. Listed in B. Kramer, *P.Heid.* IV, pp. 118–125 (fourth cent.); G. Bastianini, *Misc.Pap.* I 25–27 (fifth–seventh centuries); *P.Vind.Sijp.* 17–21 (deeds of sureties for liturgists), and Fikhman (1981, 469–477).

88. Till (1958, 165–226); *CPR* IV 102–112.

89. Compromises: Rupprecht (1997, 267–268); settlements: Gagos and van Minnen (1994, 121–127).

90. Papyrological sources are collected in *NewDocs* I–IX. For anthologies of Christian letters see Ghedini (1923); Naldini (1998).

BIBLIOGRAPHY

Anagnostou-Canas, B. 1998. "'Justice' oraculaire dans l'Égypte hellénistique et romaine." *Revue historique de droit français et étranger* 76: 1–16.

Baccani, D. 1992. *Oroscopi greci: Documentazione papirologica* (Ricerca Papirologica 1). Messina: Sicania.

Bagnall, R. S. 1977. "Price in 'Sales on Delivery.'" *GRBS* 18: 85–96.

———. 1995. *Reading Papyri, Writing Ancient History.* London: Routledge.

———, and R. Cribiore. 2006. *Women's Letters from Ancient Egypt, 300 BC–AD 800.* Ann Arbor: University of Michigan Press.

Bagnall, R. S., and B. W. Frier. 1994. *The Demography of Roman Egypt.* Cambridge: Cambridge University Press.

Bieżuńska-Małowist, I. 1966. "Les affranchis dans les papyrus de l'époque ptolémaïque et romaine." In *PapCongr. XI*, ed. O. Montevecchi, 433–443. Milan: Istituto Lombardo di Scienze e Lettere.

Bowman, A. K. 1971. *The Town Councils of Roman Egypt* (American Studies in Papyrology XI). Toronto: Hakkert.

Burkhalter, F. 1990. "Archives locales et archives centrales en Égypte romaine." *Chiron* 20: 191–215.

Chalon, G. 1964. *L'édit de Tiberius Julius Alexander: Étude historique et exégétique.* Lausanne: Urs Graf.

Chapa, J. 1998. *Letters of Condolence in Greek Papyri* (Pap.Flor. XXIX). Florence: Gonnelli.

Clarysse, W. 2003. "Tomoi Synkollesimoi." In *Ancient Archives and Archival Traditions: Concepts of Record-Keeping in the Ancient World*, ed. M. Brosius, 344–359. Oxford: Oxford University Press.

Cockle, W. E. H. 1984. "State Archives in Graeco-Roman Egypt from 30 BC to the Reign of Septimius Severus." *JEA* 70: 106–122.

Coles, R. A. 1966. *Reports of Proceedings in Papyri* (Pap.Brux. IV). Brussels: Fondation égyptologique Reine Élisabeth.

Cotton, H. M. 1981. *Documentary Letters of Recommendation in Latin from the Roman Empire.* Königstein: Hain.

———, W. E. H. Cockle, and F. G. B. Millar. 1995. "The Papyrology of the Roman Near East: A Survey." *JRS* 85: 214–235.

Drexhage, H.-J. 1982. "Beitrag zum Binnenhandel im römischen Ägypten aufgrund der Torzollquittungen und Zollhausabrechnungen des Faijum." *MBAH* 1: 61–84.

———. 1989. "Zu den Überstellungsbefehlen aus dem römischen Ägypten (1.–3. Jahrhundert n. Chr.)." In *Migratio et Commutatio: Studien zur Alten Geschichte und deren Nachleben Thomas Pekáry dargebracht*, ed. H.-J. Drexhage and J. Sünskes, 102–118. St. Katharinen: Scripta Mercaturae Verlag.

Erdmann, W. 1941. "Die Ehescheidung im Rechte der graeco-ägyptischen Papyri." *ZSav* 61: 44–57.

Fikhman, I. F. 1981. "Les cautionnements pour les coloni adscripticii." In *PapCongr. XVI*, ed. R. S. Bagnall, G. M. Browne, A. E. Hanson, and L. Koenen, 469–477. Chico, Calif.: Scholars Press.

Fournet, J.-L. 1999. *Hellénisme dans l'Égypte du VIe siècle: La bibliothèque et l'œuvre de Dioscore d'Aphrodité.* Cairo: Institut français d'archéologie orientale.

———, and J. Gascou. 2004. "Liste des pétitions sur papyrus des Ve–VIIe siècles." In *La pétition à Byzance*, ed. D. Feissel and J. Gascou, 141–196. Paris: Association des amis du Centre d'histoire et civilisation de Byzance.

Gagos, T., and P. van Minnen. 1994. *Settling a Dispute: Toward a Legal Anthropology of Late Antique Egypt.* Ann Arbor: University of Michigan Press.

Ghedini, G. 1923. *Lettere cristiane dai papiri greci del III e IV secolo.* Milan: Pubblicazioni della Università Cattolica del Sacro Cuore.

Habermann, W. 1997. "Aspekte des Bewässerungswesens im kaiserzeitlichen Ägypten I: Die 'Erklärungen für nicht überflutetes Land' (Abrochia-Deklarationen)." In *Miscellanea Oeconomica: Festschrift Harald Winkel* (Pharos 9), ed. B. Tenger and K. Ruffing, 223–226. St. Katharinen: Scripta Mercaturae Verlag.

——. 1998. "Zur chronologischen Verteilung der papyrologischen Zeugnisse." *ZPE* 122: 144–160.

——. 2001. "Die Deklarationen von Kleinvieh (Schafe und Ziegen) im römischen Ägypten: Quantitative Aspekte." In *Landwirtschaft im Imperium Romanum*, ed. P. Herz and G. Waldherr, 77–100. St. Katharinen: Scripta Mercaturae Verlag.

Haensch, R. 1992. "Das Statthalterarchiv." *ZSav* 109: 209–317.

Hagedorn, D. 1997. "Papyrologie." In *Einleitung in die griechische Philologie*, ed. H.-G. Nesselrath, 59–71. Stuttgart: Teubner.

Hagedorn, U. 1979. "Das Formular der Überstellungsbefehle im römischen Ägypten." *BASP* 16: 61–74.

Hengstl, J. 1972. *Private Arbeitsverhältnisse freier Personen in den hellenistischen Papyri bis Diokletian*. Bonn: Habelt.

Herrmann, J. 1958. *Studien zur Bodenpacht im Recht der graeco-aegyptischen Papyri* (Münch. Beitr. 41). Munich: Beck.

Husson, G. 1997. "Les questions oraculaires chrétiennes d'Égypte: Continuités et changements." In *PapCongr. XXI*, vol. 1, ed. B. Kramer, W. Luppe, H. Maehler, and G. Poethke, 482–489. Stuttgart and Leipzig: Teubner.

Jördens, A. 1993. "Kaufpreisstundungen (Sales on Credit)." *ZPE* 98: 263–282.

Katzoff, R. 1996. "Greek and Jewish Marriage Formulas." In *Classical Studies in Honor of David Sohlberg*, ed. R. Katzoff, 223–234. Ramat Gan: Bar-Ilan University Press.

——. 1980. "Sources of Law in Roman Egypt: The Role of the Prefect." *ANRW* 2(13): 807–844.

Kim, C.-H. 1972. *Form and Structure of the Familiar Greek Letter of Recommendation*. Missoula, Mont.: Society of Biblical Literature for the Seminar on Paul.

Kreller, H. 1919. *Erbrechtliche Untersuchungen auf Grund der graeco-aegyptischen Papyrusurkunden*. Leipzig: Teubner.

Kruse, Th. 2002. *Der königliche Schreiber und die Gauverwaltung: Untersuchungen zur Verwaltungsgeschichte Ägyptens in der Zeit von Augustus bis Philippus Arabs (30 v. Chr.–245 n. Chr.)* (APF Beih. 11). Munich: Saur.

Kühnert, H. 1965. *Zum Kreditgeschäft in den hellenistischen Papyri Ägyptens bis Diokletian*. Diss. Freiburg.

Lewis, N. 1974. *Papyrus in Classical Antiquity*. Oxford: Clarendon.

——. 1997. *The Compulsory Public Services of Roman Egypt*, 2d ed. (*Pap.Flor.* XXVIII). Florence: Gonnelli.

MacCoull, L. S. B. 1988. *Dioscorus of Aphrodito: His Work and His World*. Berkeley: University of California Press.

Matthews, J. 2006. *The Journey of Theophanes: Travel, Business, and Daily Life in the Roman East*. New Haven, Conn.: Yale University Press.

Mazza, R. 1998. "*P.Oxy.* XVI 1911 e i conti annuali dei pronoetai." *ZPE* 122: 161–172.

——. 2001. *L'archivio degli Apioni: Terra, lavoro, e proprietà senatoria nell'Egitto tardoantico*. Bari: Edipuglia.

Meyer-Termeer, A. J. M. 1978. *Die Haftung der Schiffer im griechischen und römischen Recht* (Stud.Amst. XIII). Zutphen, the Netherlands: Terra.

Migliardi Zingale, L. 1997. *I testamenti romani nei papiri e nelle tavolette d'Egitto. Silloge di documenti dal I al IV secolo d.C.*, 3d ed. Turin: Giappichelli.

Montevecchi, O. 1972. *La papirologia.* Milan: Società editrice internazionale.

Müller, H. 1985. *Untersuchungen zur "misthosis" von Gebäuden im Recht der gräko-ägyptischen Papyri.* Cologne: Heymann.

Naldini, M. 1998. *Il Cristianesimo in Egitto: Lettere private nei papiri dei secoli II–IV,* 2d ed. Fiesole: Nardini.

Nelson, C. A. 1979. *Status Declarations in Roman Egypt* (American Studies in Papyrology 19). Amsterdam: Hakkert.

Oates, J. F., R. S. Bagnall, S. J. Clackson, A. A. O'Brien, J. D. Sosin, T. G. Wilfong, and K. A. Worp. 2001. *Checklist of Editions of Greek, Latin, Demotic, and Coptic Papyri, Ostraca, and Tablets,* 5th ed. (BASP Suppl. 9). Oakville, Conn.: American Society of Papyrologists.

Oliver, J. H. 1989. *Greek Constitutions of Early Roman Emperors from Inscriptions and Papyri.* Philadelphia: American Philosophical Society.

Pestman P. W., W. Clarysse, M. Korver, M. Muszynski, A. L. Schutgens, W. J. Tait, J. K. Winnicki. 1981. *A Guide to the Zenon Archive* (*Pap.Lugd.Bat.* 21). Leiden: Brill.

Preissner, H. 1956. "Das verzinsliche und das zinslose Darlehen in den byzantinischen Papyri." Diss. Erlangen.

Rupprecht, H.-A. 1967. *Untersuchungen zum Darlehen im Recht der graeco-aegyptischen Papyri der Ptolemäerzeit* (Münch. Beitr. 51). Munich: Beck.

———. 1986. "Zur Frage der Frauentutel im römischen Ägypten." In *Festschrift für Arnold Kränzlein: Beiträge zur antiken Rechtsgeschichte,* ed. G. Wesener, 95–102. Graz: Leykam.

———. 1992. "Zur Antichrese in den griechischen Papyri bis Diokletian." In *Pap.Congr. XIX,* ed. A. H. S. El-Mosallamy, vol. 2, 271–289. Cairo: Center for Papyrological Studies.

Sijpesteijn, P. J. 1987. *Custom Duties in Graeco-Roman Egypt* (Stud.Amst. 17). Zutphen, the Netherlands: Terra.

Simon, D. 1982. "Das frühbyzantinische Emphyteuserecht." In *Symposion 1977: Vorträge zur griechischen und hellenistischen Rechtsgeschichte (Chantilly, 1.–4. Juni 1977)* (Akten der Gesellschaft für griechische und hellenistische Rechtsgeschichte 3), ed. J. Modrzejewski and D. Liebs, 365–422. Köln/Wien: Böhlau.

Straus, J. A. 2004. *L'achat et la vente des esclaves dans l'Égypte romaine.* Munich: Saur.

Thomas, J. D. 1998. "*P.Ryl.* IV 654: The Latin Heading." *CdÉ* 73: 125–134.

Till, W. C. 1958. "Die koptischen Bürgschaftsurkunden." *BSAC* 14: 165–226.

Treu, K. 1973. "Christliche Empfehlungs-Schemabriefe auf Papyrus." In *Zetesis: Bijdragen op het gebied van de klassieke Filologie, Filosofie, Byzantinistiek, Patrologie, en Theologie, aangeboden aan Prof. Dr. Émile de Strijcker,* 629–636. Antwerpen/Utrecht: De Nederlandsche Boekhandel.

Turner, E. G. 1980. *Greek Papyri: An Introduction,* 2d ed. Oxford: Clarendon Press.

Valbelle, D., and G. Husson. 1998. "Les questions oraculaires: Histoire de la recherche, nouveautés et perspectives." In *Egyptian Religion: The Last Thousand Years. Studies Dedicated to the Memory of J. Quaegebeur,* ed. W. Clarysse, A. Schoors, and H. Willems, vol. 2, 1055–1071. Leuven: Peeters.

Van Minnen, P. 2000. "An Official Act of Cleopatra (with a Subscription in Her Own Hand)." *AncSoc* 30: 29–34.

Whitehorne, J. 2004. "Petitions to the Centurion." *BASP* 41: 161–169.

Wolff, H. J. 1961. "Der byzantinische Urkundenstil Ägyptens im Lichte der Funde von Nessana und Dura." *RIDA* 8: 115–154.

——. 1974. "Zur Geschichte der Sechszeugen-Doppelurkunde." In *PapCongr XIII*, ed. E. Kiessling and H.-A. Rupprecht, 469–479. Munich: Beck.

——. 1978. *Das Recht der griechischen Papyri Aegyptens in der Zeit der Ptolemäer und des Prinzipats*, vol. 2 : *Organisation und Kontrolle des privaten Rechtsverkehrs*. Munich: Beck.

Worp, K. A. 1995. "Letters of Condolence in the Greek Papyri." *Analecta Papyrologica* 7: 149–154.

Yiftach, U. 2001. "Was There a "Divorce Procedure" among Greeks in Early Roman Egypt?" In *PapCongr. XXII*, ed. I. Andorlini, G. Bastianini, M. Manfredi, and G. Menci, vol. 2, 1331–1339: Florence: Istituto Papirologico "G. Vitelli."

——. 2002. "Deeds of Last Will in Graeco-Roman Egypt: A Case Study in Regionalism." *BASP* 39: 149–164.

Yiftach-Firanko, U. 2003. *Marriage and Marital Arrangements: A History of the Greek Marriage Document in Egypt, Fourth Century* BCE–*Fourth Century* CE (Münch. Beitr. 93). Munich: Beck.

Zuckerman, C. 1998. "Two Reforms of the 370s: Recruiting Soldiers and Senators in the Divided Empire." *REB* 56: 79–139.

——. 2004. *Du village à l'Empire: Autour du registre fiscal d'Aphroditô (525/526)*. Paris: Association des Amis du Centre d'Histoire et Civilisation de Byzance.

CHAPTER 17

THE MULTILINGUAL ENVIRONMENT OF PERSIAN AND PTOLEMAIC EGYPT: EGYPTIAN, ARAMAIC, AND GREEK DOCUMENTATION

DOROTHY J. THOMPSON

INTRODUCTION

When in 525 BCE Cambyses, the great king of Persia, captured Egypt and initiated a new dynasty, he was represented in this new province of the Persian empire by his satrap, and Aramaic became the main language of the administration. Around half a millennium later, with the death of Cleopatra VII and the capture of Alexandria by the Roman general Octavian in 30 BCE, yet another new dynasty of absentee pharaohs was established, and Egypt was incorporated into the Roman empire. This time, however, the language of the administration remained Greek, as it had been under the intervening Ptolemaic dynasty. During the Persian period (525–404 and 343–332 BCE), Aramaic, as the language of rule, was just one of the different languages in use in Egypt. Similarly, during the period of Ptolemaic rule (332–30 BCE), which followed Alexander of Macedon's conquest of Egypt, though Greek was the main non-Egyptian language employed, it was not the only one.

This chapter is concerned with the extent to which the surviving documentation from the five-hundred-year period from Cambyses to Cleopatra allows us to investigate and reconstruct the changing contexts of language use and linguistic practices. The main languages of the papyrological documentation treated here are Egyptian (primarily in the demotic script), Aramaic, and Greek, but Phoenician, Carian, Latin, and other languages also make an appearance. Who used which language and in what contexts, how widespread bilingualism may have been in different periods of non-Egyptian rule, how far Aramaic under the Persians and later, following Alexander's conquest, Greek took on the role of prestige languages, and, in contrast, which areas were linguistically unaffected by foreign conquest are all questions worth consideration. In addition, the limits to the evidence of the papyri and the need to look elsewhere—at epigraphy, for instance, or material culture—must enter the broader historical picture (Vittmann 2003). And if in the end some questions remain still unanswered, this simply reflects some of the limitations of papyrological evidence. For in addition to the hazard of the uneven survival of documentation, there is also the inherent problem of arguing from literate to oral practice, from the written, that is, to the spoken word. In any noncontemporary society a gap remains here that is hard to bridge. The concentration, therefore, in what follows on the social context of multilingualism is probably unavoidable (Adams and Swain 2002, 11).

THE PERSIAN PERIOD

The key areas for investigation in the Persian period, as indeed later under the Ptolemies, are the central administration and the different local communities in their official and their private dealings, both in urban centers and in the countryside of the Nile valley, the Delta, and the western oases. We need to consider both who produced the written record that survives and how far we can move from this to actual language choice in these various areas. In the absence of information on the scale of immigration or the extent of new settlement in Egypt in this period, we cannot assess the resulting changes in linguistic practices in anything other than the most general manner. Nevertheless, as is clear from surviving texts, the population of Egypt under Persian control was a mixed one with many different peoples who spoke (and often also wrote) a range of languages. Some groups were already well established when the Persians came: the Ionian, Carian, and Jewish troops employed and settled under the preceding Saite dynasty. Phoenician settlers, too, who were often involved in shipping and commercial ventures, may be traced back even further; an additional military role is suggested by the name of the Phoenician quarter at Memphis—the "Tyrian Camp" (Herodotus 2.112.2). With the Persian conquest, a new influx into Egypt of administrators, garrison troops, and settlers may be documented. Living in the southern fortress settlement at Elephantine, for instance, were Babylonians, Bactrians, Caspians, Chorasmians, Medes, Persians, Aramaeans, and Jews (Porten et al. 1996, 18). At the important religious center of Abydos, graffiti were written in Aramaic, Phoenician, and Carian in this period, as well as in Greek in the Cypriot syllabary. Now written also in the demotic script, Egyptian, of course, remained the main language of the country. Demotic was also used in parts of the administration, as, for instance, on ostraca recording water rights at Manâwir in the Kharga oasis (*O.Douch.dem.* and *O.Man.*, forthcoming).

The main non-Egyptian documentation of the Persian period is that in Aramaic, which served as the administrative language throughout the Persian empire. After Egyptian, Aramaic was the most widespread language employed in this period, and the main editions of Aramaic texts (not included in the *Checklist*) are those of Cowley (1923), Aimé-Giron (1931), Kraeling (1953), Driver (1957), Bresciani and Kamil (1966), and Segal (1983), with a selection of translated texts in Grelot (1972) and Porten et al. (1996, for Elephantine); Porten and Yardeni (1986, 1989, 1993, 1999) have republished these, adding some new material. To judge from the smaller number of surviving texts, Phoenician was a minority language (Segal 1983, 5, 9–10, 139–145, from Elephantine and Memphis; Vittmann 2003, 44–83, more generally), along with Carian, Nubian, and other tongues (Ray 1994, 51).

From Elephantine and Syene (modern Aswan), both garrisons on the southern border, from Hermopolis and Memphis in Middle Egypt, and to a lesser degree from elsewhere, texts have survived from licit and illicit excavations (Vittmann 2003, 84–119). Groups of letters like those from Hermopolis, which originated in Memphis (Bresciani and Kamil 1966; *Pap.Eleph.Eng.* B1–7; Vittmann 2003, 90–91), family papers, official rulings and correspondence, together with economic documents, all help to illustrate the life of these communities of foreign settlers. Language plays a complex role in cultural variation, and other forms of evidence may supplement the papyri. From Edfu, for instance, in the fourth century BCE, Aramaic tombstones imply a Semitic community in the city (Kornfeld 1973). Edfu may be the origin, too, of *Papyrus Amherst* 63, a long Aramaic religious text actually penned in Egyptian script. The demotic writing of this intriguing text implies both a scribe and a reader more familiar with the script of the land they lived in than with that of the text in question (Vleeming and Wesselius 1985). As illustrated further below, the phenomenon of nonmatching language and script is a feature of multilingual societies.

From Memphis, the papyrological documentation is complemented by Herodotus's fifth-century-BCE account of this capital city (2.112). Moreover, since Jews were among the Semitic settlers of Late-Period Egypt, the Old Testament joins the surviving documentation in illustrating the mixed society of the times (Porten 1968, 3–27). The prophet Jeremiah (44.1), for instance, mentions four Jewish communities already established in Egypt before the Persian conquest at Migdol (Pelousion), Tahpanhes (Daphnae), Noph (Memphis), and Pathros (the south), presumably centered on Elephantine, where a Jewish temple was founded before Cambyses' invasion (*Pap.Eleph.Eng.* B19.13–14, from 407 BCE). The key border towns of Elephantine and Syene are the source of the most extensive papyrological documentation for this period (Porten 1968; Porten et al. 1996). From these and other papyri, the balder accounts of the literary sources are filled in, and the picture takes on life.

Much of the Aramaic documentation from the Persian period is of a private nature, deriving from a limited number of areas, where groups of family documents were preserved in pots or other containers. One set of texts, however, is written on skins, described by Herodotus (5.58.3) as the standard writing material of Ionia, and preserved together with a leather bag. An Egyptian origin seems likely since these texts, which date from a period when the satrap Arsames was out of the country (ca. 410 BCE), contain correspondence about his Egyptian interests, including revenues from his land (Driver 1957; Grelot 1972, nos. 63–74). Just as later members of the high administration—the *dioikêtês* Apollonios (under Ptolemy II), for instance—received gift estates in the Egyptian countryside, so under the Persians it is clear that this satrap, related as he was to the Achaemenid royal house, had acquired extensive landed interests in the province. And in Arsames' close circle of associates and senior administrative officials we meet one Neḥtihôr, who was in charge of the satrap's Egyptian estates. His name suggests an Egyptian. We may assume that, like Udjaḥorresnet from Sais, who some generations before served at the court of Cambyses and then at that of Darius (Lloyd 1982; Briant 2002, 57–59), Neḥtihôr was fluent in the conqueror's language, in this case Aramaic, which he used in correspondence with the satrap. Reflecting the advantages that come with the acquisition of the rulers' tongue, such high-level Egyptian cooperation—collaboration, even—is not at all surprising. It recurs under the Ptolemies and was probably more widespread than a simple consideration of names might suggest since, unlike Neḥtihôr, many Egyptians opted for Greek nomenclature and language as being those of the new ruling class.

Names, therefore, are not entirely reliable as an indicator of an individual's ethnic origin. Nonetheless, especially on a group basis, they may serve as an introduction to the composition of a particular society. The Aramaic texts from Memphis, for instance, contain Babylonian, Aramaean, Sidonian, Jewish, and even Moabite names; they also make reference to Ionians, Carians, a Cretan slave and his daughter, a Hyrcanian, a (possible) Lydian, and Arabs as well (Segal 1983, 8). How many different languages were involved is unclear, but Memphis was a cosmopolitan city with a thriving Nile port and dockyards. Official accounts were kept in Aramaic, and many scribes were apparently involved in the work; one Memphite shipyard journal, for instance, records members of Persian military units and adds a Caspian to the list of non-Egyptians in the city (Porten and Yardeni 1993, C3.8, from 473 BCE). Texts like this or the ten-month-long customs account, later reused for a copy of the "Romance of Aḥiqar" (ibid., C3.7, from 475 BCE; cf. C1.1, with Briant 2002, 385), perhaps again from Memphis, are the product of a well-embedded administration that utilized Aramaic speakers and scribes up and down the Nile and at the major guardhouses. Fragments of household listings (Porten and Yardeni 1993, C9–10) and records of land registration (ibid., C20–24) imply a thorough control of both population and land throughout the country. The scale of the bureaucracy involved can only be imagined, but to judge from Ptolemaic practice it must have been significant.

Yet throughout the period of both Persian and Ptolemaic rule, the language of the majority remained Egyptian. Demotic was the main script employed in legal documents, letters, accounts, and other texts. With demotic, more than any other of the written languages and scripts, we face the problem of how far the written text signifies the spoken language. Put simply, once Egyptian begins to be written in Coptic, the language appears to be full of Greek words taken over into Egyptian, up to 20 percent on one calculation (Fewster 2002, 228). Of this there is little sign at an earlier date, when few Greek words are found in demotic (Clarysse 1987), at least in legal, literary, and religious texts. Moreover, if, as J. D. Ray has argued (1994, 53–54), demotic was originally developed as a stylized version of hieratic to serve the needs of a central administration in a reunification of Egypt under Saite rule, then it is likely that this form of the Egyptian language was deliberately preserved in a relatively uncontaminated state. The written script will have differed from the spoken language, and the degree to which Aramaic and, later, Greek vocabulary or figures of speech were incorporated into Late Period Egyptian is unknowable through demotic.

THE PTOLEMAIC PERIOD

When Alexander of Macedon invaded Egypt in 332 BCE and captured this Persian satrapy, the Persian administration and Aramaic-based bureaucracy speedily disappeared to be replaced by Greeks and Greek. Some of the earlier foreign communities remained, though the degree of continuation or of new immigration that this involved cannot be determined. Thus, when an Aramaic tax receipt is found from the Theban area issued by one Joseph to a certain Simeon in 252 BCE, some eighty years after the conquest, we cannot tell whether the taxpayer was a descendant of earlier settlers or belonged to a new wave of immigrants under Ptolemy II (Porten and Yardeni 1999, D8.13, cf. 2004/5). In some centers, there is good evidence for the continued use of Aramaic in both spoken and written form (Clarysse 2002, 8, in Thebes, Edfu, and Tebtynis). On the whole, however, the Ptolemaic administration increasingly functioned in Greek. As the papyri indicate, Greek was now by far the most common non-Egyptian language of the period.

Along with this change in the language of rule came a change in mortuary practices that has significant effects on our evidence. An innovation in the manufacture of mummy casing under Ptolemy II involved the recycling of waste papyrus, mainly from scribal offices, in a form of *papier mâché* or "cartonnage" (see chapter 4). This new source of papyrological texts is responsible for the bureaucratic slant of Ptolemaic documentation. Numerous administrative texts, official rulings, and reports now join the private letters, family archives, and the stray or collected texts that have been found in excavation. The apparent growth in bureaucracy under the Ptolemies may in part be a feature of this new practice. Furthermore, the increase in administrative documentation makes it possible to analyze the population in ways not feasible before. Land surveys and tax registers allow the historian to quantify, at least to some degree, the mixed population of the period and the main economic basis of society. Only when we have a sense of the major groups within the population can we place the role of the more minor ethnic communities in context.

So what do we know of the make-up of the population of Ptolemaic Egypt? How widespread were the new Greeks, who came as members of the army, as officials in the new administration, as merchants, freebooters, adventurers, or as craftsmen to settle in Egypt? What other non-Greek immigrants of long-standing and more recent origin had their homes there, what roles did they play, and how readily were they accepted or assimilated? Finally, to what extent can the papyri help answer our questions?

As noted already for Persian-period Egypt, one cannot expect to find a consistent pattern. The newcomers settled in certain areas, especially, of course, the capital. In the earlier capital of Memphis, the strange group of Greek poets and philosophers and the Dionysiac sculpture of the main temple avenue to the Serapeum imply a strong Greek presence (Lauer 1976, plates 1–5, 8–9). Under Ptolemy I, the capital was moved to Alexandria, which was now developed as a strong center of Greek culture. Here, in the context of the Museum and the Library, the story of the translation of the Septuagint and the circulation in Greek of translations from Egyptian (the Dream of Nectanebo, for instance; see *UPZ* I 81; LDAB 6863) suggest a culture of bilingualism. Unlike the situation elsewhere in the country, in Alexandria Greeks most probably formed a majority, but the damper climate of the coastal region means that the only papyri to have survived from this city are those found upcountry. For the same reason, the situation in the

Delta is also virtually unknown in this period, apart from a few inscriptions and gravestones.

The second main center of Greek settlement that we know of was the Fayyum, a marshy area drained early in the Ptolemaic period, where the survival of carton-nage texts from a necklace of surrounding cemeteries allows us to document the local population with its heavily immigrant element. This area (renamed the Arsinoite nome under Ptolemy II) was primarily used for the settlement of soldiers, as cleruchs with plots of land sufficient to provide a living for themselves and their families. Where the military went, others followed, and Greeks here are documen-ted as teachers and doctors, wine producers or wine merchants, as well as actors and artists, working in a whole range of businesses and official capacities. Overall in this nome, in the mid-third century BCE, Greeks accounted for around 18 percent of the civilian population, and when the military element is added, the figure for Greeks rises to more than 30 percent of a total of approximately eighty-five thousand (Clarysse and Thompson 2006, 2: 94–95, 154–157). Some of these "Greeks" may not themselves have been from families that originated in Greek lands, since the term Hellene under the early Ptolemies came to represent a tax category for a privileged group among the population, one that might include Egyptians. Nevertheless, such Egyptians counted as Greek and, by functioning in Greek in various positions within the Greek sphere, to all intents and purposes they were Greek.

Under the Ptolemies, primarily as a result of cleruchic settlement but also of other opportunities in this flourishing kingdom, Greeks were to be found through-out the country (see, for example, Clarysse [1995] on Thebes). The degree, however, of Greek settlement in the Arsinoite nome was certainly exceptional. In the Apollonopolite, or Edfu nome, to the south, a land survey from 119/118 BCE records just 3 percent of all land as held by cleruchs (P.Haun. inv. 407, ed. Christensen 2002), an interesting contrast to the 33 percent of cleruchic land recorded for the Arsinoite village of Kerkeosiris in the same year (Crawford 1971, 44). And since cleruchic plots were significantly larger than average, Greek landholders in the Apollonopolite must have represented a very small proportion of the nome's total population. Figures for the country as a whole are lacking. Overall, however, we may surmise that Greeks are unlikely ever to have represented more than 15 percent of the total and that this was probably a higher figure than that for immigrant settlers in the preceding Persian period, for these two empires differed in their military requirements. Both needed garrisons within their country to ensure their hold on their respective countries, but under the Ptolemies a strong national army was additionally required to protect and extend their kingdom in a world of competing Hellenistic powers. The Great King faced no such competition.

How Greek did Ptolemaic settler Greeks remain, and to what extent were they assimilated within the population? Education, the legal system, and the use of Greek (though not exclusively so) within the administration, the army, and social institutions like the gymnasium all helped to endorse Greek status (Goudriaan 1988; Thompson 2001). Nevertheless, certain countervailing tendencies (intermarriage, for instance) and local ways, especially local religion, played a part in the progressive Egyptianization of the Greeks of Ptolemaic Egypt. Finally, when the Romans came and instituted their rule, those Greeks who were not citizens of the three Greek cities of Alexandria, Naucratis, and Ptolemais were now all counted together under the heading of "Egyptians." These different processes are known primarily from the papyrological record. In what follows, and particularly in the case studies at the end of this chapter, only some aspects of the social and linguistic context can be examined.

The recognition of different ethnic groups is normally made on the basis of names. Yet, as already indicated, these are sometimes problematic. The same individual may use different names in different contexts, and in Ptolemaic Egypt the use of double names—names in both Greek and Egyptian—is a complicating factor (Clarysse 1985, 1992). Two examples will illustrate the problem we face—the impossibility of ascribing identity according to an individual's name.

In an Arsinoite salt-tax register from 229 BCE, two sons of Nehemsesis are listed living next door to one another (*P.Count* 4.113–116). The first, Petoys, is a police-man; for his brother, no occupation is given, but the lower tax dues recorded under his name indicate a Hellenic tax status, which is corroborated by his Greek name, Pasikles. We do not know at what stage Pasikles acquired a Greek name, but he clearly belonged to that bilingual sector of society which moved with ease between the two worlds, Egyptian and Greek. Policemen, too, like his brother, Petoys, formed part of the Greek side of society; from the second century BCE on, such men might be included in cleruchic allotments. Living most probably in the capital of the nome, the two sons of Nehemsesis belonged to a group of Egyptians who played an important role in the success of the Ptolemaic regime. It seems safe to assume that they were bilingual, though we have no direct evidence of this.

My second example is the *dioikêtês* Dioskourides, an official from the top echelons of the Ptolemaic administration in the mid-second century BCE, well known from the papyri (see *UPZ* I 14). Philippe Collombert's study of a stone anthropoid sarcophagus with long hieroglyphic inscriptions brings surprising new information on this high official (Collombert 2000; cf. Coulon 2002). Identified not only by his name and position (*snty* is the Egyptian for Greek *dioikêtês*), Dioskourides is also given his court title of *archisômatophylax*, hesitantly transliterated into Egyptian as *mꜣrkysmṯpyrks*. His mother's name was Tetosiris, but his father is not named. The most interesting feature of this sarcophagus, however, is that a high official in the administration, the son perhaps of a mixed marriage, chose to be buried according to his mother's ethnicity. This man, who spent his career in Greek officialdom, where the language of the administration was primarily Greek, would have moved with equal facility and confidence in the Egyptian circles from which (at least) his mother came. Furthermore, in the case of Dioskourides, it is material culture—his sarcophagus—which adds interest to the papyrological record. Not everything is what it seems to be at first. Both Pasikles and Dioskourides may be added to the ranks of those bilinguals who regularly moved between two worlds. Like their ethnicity, our evidence is context specific.

In attempting to quantify the extent of intermarriage in Ptolemaic Egypt, we again rely on names. A database of 427 adult households, derived from the texts of *P.Count* from the mid-third century BCE, yields some interesting information. Wives are recorded in 75 out of 85 households in which the name of the household head is Greek. Of these wives, the names of all but six are also Greek. On this evidence, therefore, 92 percent of Greek males married women who were Greek. Among the far larger number of couples where the husband has an Egyptian name, not a single one is registered with a Greek-named wife. According to this third-century evidence, then, intermarriage would seem to have occurred in only one direction. The data of these households are found to need a little modification when data from all of the *P.Count* tax-paying couples from the third and second century are considered together. Out of a total of 685 couples in which the name of both husband and wife is known, 105 Greek-named husbands (74.5 percent) were married to wives with Greek names, and 36 (25.5 percent) to women with Egyptian names. Of those 544 husbands with Egyptian names, 536 (98.5 percent) had wives with Egyptian names, while the wives of just 8 (1.5 percent) had Greek names; furthermore, most of this last group were from the second century BCE (Clarysse and Thompson 2006, 2: 297, 327–328). An important feature of papyrological documentation is that it allows this form of quantification; once again, more data add complexity to the linguistic picture.

Differences in the Greek and the Egyptian sectors of the population as identified by their names and documented in their marriage patterns are evident in other areas as well. As already noted, land surveys bear witness to the Greeks' more extensive land holdings. They also had larger households. In the database of 427 tax-paying households of *P.Count*, no Egyptian household numbers more than eight, whereas one Greek household consisted of twenty-two adults. A significant lack of daughters is also apparent in Greek households; this is not characteristic of Egyptian families. Various explanations may be considered, including the exposure of new-born girls by only the Greek side of the population. Slaveholding is also a distinctive feature of the Greek households (ibid., 2: 226–317). We can only imagine what all of this meant in terms of the languages used in various contexts, but it seems likely that at least some used different languages at home and at work.

The Greek immigrants' diverse geographical backgrounds may be illustrated by the range of ethnic designations in use during the Ptolemaic period. A recent collection of these contains more than 250 different ethnic terms, the majority from different areas of the Greek-speaking world (La'da 2002). And while such ethnic denominations do not necessarily indicate a specific individual's actual origin (some were also used in an extended sense with other meanings; the label "Persian of the *epigonê*," for instance, came to function as a status term for those under obligation in a legal context, Pestman [1990, 91]), their geographical range nevertheless provides a measure of the diverse origins of immigrants to Ptolemaic Egypt.

Not all immigrant groups, of course, were new. We have already met the Ionians and Carians, who, according to Herodotus (2.152–154), were brought to Egypt as mercenaries by Psammetichus I, who settled them in the Delta. Moved to Memphis by pharaoh Amasis in the sixth century, they remained in that city, where they became known respectively as Hellenomemphites and Caromemphites and enjoyed their own ethnic quarters (the Hellenion and the Karikon) and representatives (Thompson 1988, 82–88). A record of the major dike of the city of Memphis (*PSI* V 488, from 257 BCE) allows us to locate these different ethnic neighborhoods. The Hellenion and the Karikon lay to the northwest, and the Syro-Persikon quarter was situated southwest of the city. According to Strabo (17.1.32), who wrote in the late first century BCE, the population of Memphis was a mixed one. The papyri, supported by excavation and inscriptions, show just how mixed it was both linguistically and culturally.

The Carian grave stelae reused in the fourth century BCE in the building of the sacred animal necropolis on the headland of North Saqqara must have come from this community at an earlier date (Masson 1978), and it is these texts that allowed the decipherment of the Carian language (Ray 1981, 1998). Because some of the owners of these gravestones had Egyptian names, the picture is of a mixed Egyptian-Carian community in the Persian period, when Carian soldiers served the Persian rulers as mercenaries, and some ran barges on the Nile (Vittmann 2003, 155–179). The dispersal of their gravestones and the lack of Carian texts from the Ptolemaic period suggest that, linguistically, Carians had become assimilated by the time of Alexander. Nevertheless, their quarter remained distinct, as were the privileges of their temple. For when, in the mid-third century BCE, the Astarte priests of those known as the Phoenico-Egyptians in Memphis wrote (in Greek) to Zenon, a man of importance in the area, asking for a contribution of oil for their temple, they requested the same "as is granted to the temples in Memphis of the Carians and Hellenomemphites.... For the temple of Astarte," they explained, "is similar to those of the Carians and the Hellenomemphites" (*PSI* V 531). One detects a competitive element among these different ethnic communities.

The Ionians of Memphis may be traced in the archaeological and the papyrological record of both Persian and Ptolemaic periods. Like the Ionians at Naucratis, the only Greek city in Egypt before Alexandria, the Hellenomemphites possessed their own representatives, known as *timouchoi;* they are mentioned in a late third-century-BCE shipping account (*UPZ* I 149.16). This connection with shipping already in the fifth century is found in the long Aramaic customs account from the Persian period (Porten and Yardeni 1993, C3.7, from 475 BCE); together with Carians, some Ionians are labeled "rascals" in one Aramaic text from the city (Segal 1983, no. 26). Their necropolis lay a little to the north of the city near Abusir;

the text of Timotheus's play, *The Persians,* came from here (van Minnen 1997). The "Curse of Artemisia," one of the earliest Greek papyrus texts from Egypt, written in a mixture of Ionic and Doric dialects, also derives from this Hellenomemphite milieu; the spoken Greek of the city appears to have left its mark on this text, the content of which has a strong Egyptian flavor (*UPZ* I 1 = Rowlandson 1998, no. 37, from the late fourth century BCE). Artemisia, daughter of Amasis, calls on Oserapis (the deified Apis bull, soon to be adopted in its Hellenized form as the Greek god Sarapis) and the gods who sit in Poserapis (the Egyptian "House of Osiris-Apis," transliterated here in Greek) to curse the father of her daughter, who has failed to provide the proper burial rites for their child. Some of the Hellenomemphites, it is clear from this text, were already well assimilated into Egyptian culture by the time Alexander's army arrived.

One key difference between the Hellenomemphites and the Caromemphites or the Phoenico-Egyptians of the city is that, whereas the Hellenomemphites kept their own language (Ionic Greek), the other immigrant groups gradually abandoned theirs. During the Ptolemaic period, the only use of Phoenician known in Memphis is preserved not on papyrus but on a stone dedication, on top of which was placed a stele of Horus standing on crocodiles (Vittmann 2003, 76, Abb. 36). The face of the stele is covered in hieroglyphs with magical spells against snakes, scorpions, and other such dangers; the spells were to be "read" by anyone who drank the water, which, when poured over them, flowed into a surrounding rivulet and collected in a basin at the front. The Phoenician military visitor from Thebes who made this dedication, probably in the second century BCE, appears to be well aware of the problems encountered by those unfamiliar with foreign scripts. Other dedications and texts penned by Phoenicians under the Ptolemies were written in Greek. Like the Jews of Ptolemaic Egypt, Phoenician immigrants were by now generally Hellenized, at least in the language they used.

Other immigrants to Ptolemaic Egypt are known from the papyri, but of their linguistic practices little is known. The military group of Idumaeans, who settled as a *politeuma* in Memphis in the late second century BCE, had their own whitewashed temple dedicated to Qos, who in Greek is called Apollo (*OGIS* II 737). A similar army contingent was quartered at Hermopolis, where, along with other Semitic names, Qos/Apollo figures strikingly in the nomenclature of the earliest generation recorded. Within three generations, however, in nomenclature the Idumaeans of Hermopolis had Hellenized almost entirely. It therefore comes as somewhat of a surprise (and a salutary reminder of how dangerous it is to draw conclusions from what patchy evidence remains) that some three hundred years later the singing of hymns in a foreign language (*xenikê glôssa,* presumably Edomite) and the unusual sacrifice of sheep (?) and goats are recorded as still in use among this same Hermopolite community (*P.Giss.* 99.9–13). Yet, as with other liturgies (Latin, for example, in parts of the Roman Catholic church or Coptic in the Coptic church today), the continuation of a language in such a context does not necessarily imply more widespread familiarity or understanding; this "foreign tongue" may well represent a "fossil language." In the case of the Jewish *politeuma* in neighboring Herakleopolis, where Jewish laws and practices are recorded in second-century-BCE texts but where all recorded dealings are in Greek (*P.Polit.Jud.*, with Thompson 2009), it is equally possible that Hebrew was used in liturgical contexts. This is not, however, recorded in the papyri.

Arabs formed a further ethnic group in Ptolemaic Egypt, but in this case, to judge from the contexts where they are found and their nomenclature, assimilation for Arabs was with the majority population. Under Ptolemy II, Arabs joined Persians and Hellenes with a tax privilege (*P.Count* 30.63, from 254–231 BCE), but their names are consistently Egyptian. One Greek appeal, which possibly involves an Arab, highlights the problems we face in understanding how these different groups within the mixed population of Ptolemaic Egypt may have perceived themselves and, in turn, have been perceived by those around them. A camel driver sent to Syria complains to Zenon, as manager of the *dioikêtês'* interests, that Zenon's representative has mistreated him: he has not been properly paid and has been given only poor-quality wine to drink (*P.Col. Zen.* II 66, from 256/255 BCE). The reason the writer gives for this treatment is that he is a *barbaros* who cannot speak Greek *(hellenizein);* his suffering is such, he claims, that he is in danger of starvation. Self-description as a barbarian represents a fairly extreme adoption of the language and outlook of the ruling power, though we should not forget the probable intervention of the scribe who translated the complaint— whatever its original language—into what he considered suitable expression for such an appeal. Nevertheless, the claim as it stands is a striking one, implying a strong awareness of discrimination that Zenon was expected to respond to.

Other linguistic groups recorded from the Ptolemaic period include the Nabataeans, who in 39/38 BCE dedicated a shrine to their local god on the road between Giza and Memphis (Huss 2001, 750n8), and a Roman or Italian, Gaius Acutius, who left a record in Latin (but his name written in Greek) recording his visit to the Isis temple at Philae in 116 BCE (*SEG* XXVIII 1485). In *OGIS* I 129, in contrast, a reinscribed Ptolemaic royal order to protect a synagogue ends with a Latin summary. It is on the more durable medium of stone rather than papyrus that these particular records survive. Choice of writing material must join language choice as a variable in the picture.

As earlier under the Persians, however, the main language of Egypt must have remained Egyptian. For the fact that this is not immediately apparent in the written record, two features are responsible: the primacy of Greek in administrative texts from mummy cartonnage and the better record of publication of Greek texts than of the more difficult texts in demotic. Nevertheless, both in texts from the Egyptian side of the population—from cartonnage, excavation, or family collections of legal texts—and in the preponderance of Egyptian names found in the papyri, we may still approach the majority language through the written record.

From Text to Speech and Back Again

To move from the written to the spoken word demands a leap of the imagination. How far was the vocabulary employed by scribes that of everyday speech? How many of those with literate skills were familiar with more than one language, and to what extent is it possible to recapture the degree of multilingualism in a society? The papyri present just a few hints.

The language of the papyri is affected by many factors, sometimes clear and sometimes obscure. The peculiarity of Egyptian demotic with its apparent distance from the everyday vocabulary in the Egyptian villages has already been noted. Other influences are reflected in the vocabulary of the administration. In the Persian period, some Iranian and Semitic technical terms—for "document," "land measurement," "lawsuit," "judge," and so on—are found in the Aramaic texts; at the same time, some Egyptian terms—for an Egyptian form of "marriage endowment," for instance, for "castor oil," "natron," and "barley"—were simply transliterated into Aramaic (Segal 1983, 10–11). One key term introduced in this period—"artaba," the capacity measure used for cereals—passed into regular usage and was taken over by the Greeks. Though it is always interesting to compare the contexts and different linguistic influences over time, how widely these terms were adopted into everyday speech is generally unknown.

In Greek, the formal, often standardized, language of the bureaucracy appears to be the product of scribal training, just as the occasional introduction of literary vocabulary into documentary texts seems likely to reflect the literary education of Greek schools. Again, the use of specialized vocabulary sometimes represents the adoption of Egyptian institutions in transliterated form (*pheritob*, for instance, as the title of a temple official) or the translation of specialist terms into Greek, like those for land at various stages of irrigation: "waterlogged" (*embrochos*), "not reached by the water" (*abrochos*), *hypologos* ("unproductive"), and so forth. This is a phenomenon also found in the broader context; transliteration and translation are alternatives in the process of language contact. The choice of script is a further variable (as noted earlier). From the mid-Ptolemaic period (201/200 BCE), one of the rebel kings of Thebes (*Porô Yr Gonafor* = pharaoh Haronnophris) is recorded in an Egyptian graffito at Abydos that is actually written in Greek script (*P.Recueil* 11; cf. *P.Recueil* 12).

The language of the texts themselves can sometimes show linguistic features that may be transferred from text to speech. Dialect is one such aspect. The impact of Doric dialect forms has been observed, especially in the nomenclature of the elite families of Alexandria, as representing Macedonian influence in the highest social circles of the Ptolemaic court and in the capital (Clarysse 1998).

Bilingualism is a further subject that one may approach through the texts. Both bilingual texts and bilingual archives survive; their survival, however, is easier to note than to interpret. Bilingual texts have implications for both writer and reader, and in the case of administrative texts, the bilinguality of the early generations of scribes, now retooled in Greek as the new administrative language, may on occasion be traced through the technology of writing itself. Whereas Greek was normally written with a sharpened reed *(kalamos)*, for Egyptian demotic a frayed rush was used (Tait 1988) and different ink. Greek written with a rush thus implies a biliterate but lazy scribe, who has not bothered to switch the implement with which he is writing. This occurs quite frequently in the third century BCE (Clarysse 1993, 186–195). At the same time, the Greek of such texts sometimes shows the influence of Egyptian vocabulary and syntax (Clarysse 1990; 1993, 197–200).

The same phenomenon suggested by this practice is reinforced by the language of the texts themselves, though whose language choice was involved remains a question. Some sets of administrative data switch language within the same operation, at least at the lower levels. The salt-tax register of *P.Count* 2 + 3 (229 BCE), for instance, written on one papyrus, switches from a village register compiled person by person in demotic to a Greek tax-district record recorded village by village, and back again to summary tax-area totals, now registered in demotic. It was only at nome level and above that Greek became the rule, and many scribes, it seems, moved with ease between the two main languages of the time (Clarysse and Thompson 2006, 2: 6–7, 70). Within the Ptolemaic bureaucracy, especially in the third century BCE, bilinguality was an everyday occurrence. Both the languages of the texts produced and the technology used to write them imply a bilingual flexibility in speech, as well as in writing.

A similar mix of languages appears in receipts that the tax collectors issued, sometimes in Greek, sometimes in demotic, and sometimes in both. We may speculate whether the taxpayer's language played any part in the scribe's choice of language. When the taxpayer's name appears written in larger and clearer demotic, an awareness of the receipt's purpose may explain the particular language choice. The verbal interchanges preceding such transactions can only be imagined. More often language choice may reflect the prime identity of the scribes, or the demands of the office they worked in. Thus, the increased use of Greek for tax receipts in the Thebaid starting in 165 BCE has been interpreted as resulting from the reestablishment of central control on the south, when Egyptian officials were downgraded following the great revolt some years before (Vandorpe 2000, 177). By the second half of the second century BCE bilingual offices were perhaps less common than before; the growing use of the rulers' language was a sign of changing times.

Bilingual archives (archives, that is, in the broader papyrological sense; see chapter 10) have already been mentioned. Taking many forms, in terms of language use they indicate those areas of society in which bilingualism was present at least to a limited degree. So, for instance, in the Zenon archive in both official and private dealings, texts in different languages reflect the language choice of different correspondents. With a handful of demotic texts *(P.Zen.dem.)* and a few bilingual receipts *(P.Zen.Pestm.* 1–13) among the overwhelming majority of documents in

Greek, the composition of this archive represents the language environment of Zenon and his circle (Orrieux 1983, 146–150).

In family archives made up of demotic legal contracts, another process is apparent. Over time Greek-language use began to affect even a predominantly Egyptian practice. In part this followed a government initiative. From 145 BCE on, in order to have legal validity, demotic contracts had to be registered in Greek at a registry office (see chapter 23). From this date on, Greek dockets are found appended to demotic contracts, which in translated form might then be used in a Greek court of law. Among the mortuary priests of Hawara or of Memphis and Thebes, texts written in both Greek and Egyptian are thus found in later family archives (Thompson 1988, 186–189). Demotic contracts with Greek summaries of their contents represent a limited form of bilingual text. They tell us little of the owner's bilingualism—perhaps more of the scribe's—but the gradual move to Greek legal practices seems likely to mirror a more general, ongoing process at least at the institutional level, with concomitant bilingual activities. Thus, by the time the Romans came, any Egyptian legal forms that survived (for marriage contracts, for instance) were generally expressed in Greek.

SOME MIXED CONTEXTS

One way in which to investigate the multilingual environment of Persian and Ptolemaic Egypt is to highlight some of the areas where the different peoples who lived together in Egypt came into contact with one another. There are sufficient similarities between our two main periods for us to consider them in tandem. The following case studies are very selective in coverage and made simply *exempli gratia*, but they involve mixed-language environments, bilingual archives, and several typical situations of the time.

The guardposts of Persian Egypt at Syene, Elephantine, and elsewhere have already been introduced. From among the Jewish and Aramaean military settlers of the south, a number of family archives illustrate a variety of interethnic contacts on an everyday basis. Particular individuals stand out. Mibtahiah is one (*Pap.Eleph. Eng.* B23–33, mid-fifth century BCE). Daughter of Mahseiah, son of Jedaniah, Mibtahiah was first married to Jezaniah, son of Uriah, who served together with her father. The couple was well endowed with a house and the parcel of land it was built on. Jezaniah may have predeceased his wife since Mibtahiah was later married to Eshor, son of Djeho, a royal builder by whom she had two children. From later contracts drawn up after the death of her second husband, it is known that Eshor was also known by the Jewish name Nathan (*Pap.Eleph.Eng.* B32.8–9, cf. p. 196n6, from 416 BCE; B33.2, from 410 BCE). In this Aramaic-speaking context, where in the

Elephantine fortress families lived close to one another and where the local governor and troop commander, both Persians, might oversee their contracts (B31.4–5), an Egyptian incoming husband had joined the Jewish community and changed his name. In dealings with another Egyptian builder, Peu, son of Paḥe, Mibtahiah might meanwhile swear by Sati, the local Egyptian goddess (*Pap. Eleph. Eng.* B30.4–5, from 440 BCE). Ethnic (like language) lines were forever being crossed, and identities changed.

A further case of mixed marriage in the same community is documented in the contracts of Ananiah, son of Azariah, who married Tamut, the Egyptian slave of his neighbor Meshullam, son of Zaccur. Meshullam is described as an Aramaean from Syene and a member of the detachment of (the Persian) Varyazata, whereas the groom, who pays a bride price (or *mohar*) to Meshullam, is a servant of Yahweh in the Elephantine fortress. At the time of their marriage contract (*Pap. Eleph. Eng.* B36, from 449 BCE), Tamut already had a son, Palṭî, who came along with her; like his mother, however, he remained Meshullam's property. Ananiah and Tamut then had a daughter, Jehoishma. About twenty years later Tamut's owner, Meshullam, drew up a contract offering manumission to her and her daughter on his death—on the condition that they continue to serve him during his lifetime and then that of his son, Zaccur (*Pap. Eleph. Eng.* B39, from 427 BCE); this, indeed, they did. Finally, when the daughter, Jehoishma, married, Meshullam's son, Zaccur, provided her dowry, and in that contract she is called his "sister" (B41, from 420 BCE).

The cultural mix and unusual human situations of these texts are hard to match. The Egyptian-named and probably Egyptian slave girl Tamut, "she of (the goddess) Mut," formed part of a social institution—slavery—that was not native to Egypt but came with the settlers. Despite her married status, until she acquired her conditional freedom, Tamut remained the property of her original owner, as did her daughter and son. We do not know at what age she was enslaved or whether indeed she was born a slave, but in her family life Egyptian is unlikely to have been her first language. It is striking, if not surprising, that her children were given Semitic names. On the other hand, the world of the texts preserves just one side of the experience, and this may sometimes be deceptive.

As with Aramaic in the country's guardposts under the Persians, so later under the Ptolemies the army provided a context in which Macedonians and Greeks predominated and the Greek language flourished. Troops, however, need wives, and, as we have seen, local marriages often followed. The army thus provided a standard context for contact with the majority Egyptian population.

Not all contact was so peaceable, however. The billeting of troops on a local population is likely to cause problems. However much the authorities attempted to control the process—and try they did (e.g., *C. Ord. Ptol.* 1, 5–10, 24, all under Ptolemy II)—disruption and ensuing difficulties were probably inevitable (Lewis 1986, 21–24). One bilingual group of texts (in Greek and demotic) from the second century BCE tells the tale of a certain Sennesis, daughter of Patepnebteus, who was first married to an Egyptian named Petosiris and later lived with her son, Esoroeris, and his wife. When a Cyrenean soldier, Neoptolemos, son of Neoptolemos, was billeted on the family, trouble ensued. Sennesis took up with Neoptolemos and later married him. In subsequent legal proceedings Esoroeris claimed he had been beaten up and driven from his home by Neoptolemos, who lived upstairs. A counterclaim was filed, but eventually Sennesis, now known by her Greek name of Isias, together with her husband, Neoptolemos, came to a settlement with her son (*Pap.Eleph.Eng.* C33, from 198 BCE; D8–10, from 137/136 BCE). The language mix of these texts once again seems likely to reflect that of this sector of society, where the wife of a Greek army man had something of an advantage.

A less agreeable outcome resulted from another case, at an earlier date, when a Greek soldier intruded on an Egyptian marriage. Among a collection of texts from the Memphite Serapeum, there survives a petition presented to the king and the queen by the Egyptian twin sisters Taous and Thaues, daughters of Nephoris and Argynoutis (?), who played the parts of the goddesses Isis and Nephthys in the mourning ceremonies for the Apis bull that died in 164 BCE. Their complaints are directed against their mother, who had left their father for Philippos, son of Sogenes, a Greek soldier who was serving in the area. Philippos—they claim—had plotted the death of their father, who had escaped Philippos's dagger only by plunging into the Nile and swimming to a nearby island, where he took a boat to Herakleopolis. There he died of grief and, at the time of writing, still lay unburied. Nephoris and her son, Panchrates, are now accused of stealing the oil allowance that belonged to the twins. Taous and Thaues enlisted a friend of their father who was resident in the Serapeum, Ptolemaios, son of Glaukias, to write for them in Greek (*UPZ* I 18). Bilingualism runs through the story—Greek soldier, Egyptian wife, her two Egyptian daughters who impersonate the twin goddesses in a key religious ceremony—but when it came to writing complaints, then a Greek like Ptolemaios was required. Personal scenarios like these, with liaisons crossing the ethnic divide, are of the essence of papyrological documentation.

A third example of the mixed world of the military appears in the archive of the Cretan cavalry officer Dryton, of his second wife, Apollonia, also known as Senmonthis, and of their daughter, Apollonia, also known as Senmouthis, together with her husband, Kaies (*P.Dryton*). As suggested by the women's double names, Dryton, a citizen of Ptolemais in Upper Egypt, and his family moved in a very mixed world. The archive itself comes from Pathyris, a garrison town loyal to the crown, which was entirely destroyed during the great revolt in Upper Egypt in 88 BCE. Almost equal numbers of Greek and demotic texts survive in this archive (29 Greek and 25 demotic), as well as five bilingual texts. Dryton came from a Cretan family; the validity of his ethnic designation, which could have been that of his army unit, is confirmed by the particularly Cretan names of Dryton himself and of his son (by a previous wife), called Esthladas. Apollonia, his second wife, is labeled a Cyrenean, but her strongly Egyptianized family would appear to have been in

Egypt for some generations. In her many business dealings, she—or perhaps her scribe—tended to use Egyptian (Vandorpe 2002), and all of her five daughters (like their mother) had double names: Apollonia-Senmouthis, Aristo-Senmonthis, Nikarion-Thermouthis, Apollonia the younger-Senapathis and Aphrodisia-Tachratis. The practice continued into the next generation, which, to judge from those whose documents survive, increasingly moved over to the Egyptian side. Apollonia-Senmouthis married an Egyptian soldier, Kaies, and none of their three daughters has a Greek name recorded. The second half of the archive contains more demotic than Greek texts. Through the study of family archives, like that of Dryton's descendants or those of other military families (Lewis 1986, 124–152), we may enter the mixed military and civilian environments of the second half of the Ptolemaic period.

A second area where we may tease out the input of different ethnic groups and their multilingual activities is along the Nile, the country's main artery, which linked Upper and Lower Egypt in both geographical and economic terms. Nile barges carried the agricultural wealth of the south to the markets of the capital cities—to Memphis and later Alexandria. On the whole, as a big business that involved capital investment and large returns, shipping tended to be under immigrant control. Persians and later Greeks, especially upper-class Alexandrians, and even Ptolemaic queens owned the great Nile barges that carried the grain, while these were made, mended, and sailed by local Egyptians (Porten et al. 1996, 15, 77; Thompson 1983). Carians, too, were involved in shipping (*Pap.Eleph.Eng.* 11.3, from 411 BCE; Segal 1983, no. 26, together with Ionians), as indeed were other immigrants. In mid-first-century-BCE Memphis, for instance, the shipping company of the *nauklêroi Hippodromitai* appears to have been the preserve of Phoenicians (Thompson 1988, 60–1). Nowhere is the immigrant presence clearer than in the long Aramaic customs account of the fifth century BCE, where the ships carrying wine, oil, empty jars, hardwood (for building), and other products for the king's storehouse are regularly specified as those of Greek ("Ionian") shipowners (Porten and Yardeni 1993, C3.7). When, under the Ptolemies, patterns of landholding are documented from different areas of the country, it becomes clear that the Greek settlers (and especially the soldiers who were settled with plots of cleruchic land by way of a retainer or pension) enjoyed the larger estates, where they cultivated Egypt's cash crops and reared their flocks of sheep. Agriculture was by far the most important sphere of production, and, in this potentially profitable area, social standing was matched by economic power. So, too, in shipping and other productive spheres, the immigrants' economic strength is documented in the papyri. Aramaic, Greek, Carian, and Phoenician all joined Egyptian as languages in use along the Nile during these five hundred years of foreign rule.

Examples of similar mixed contexts could well be multiplied. Religion is another obvious area (see chapter 24). Here one brief example may suffice. Life in the Memphite Serapeum in the mid-Ptolemaic period is, as already noted,

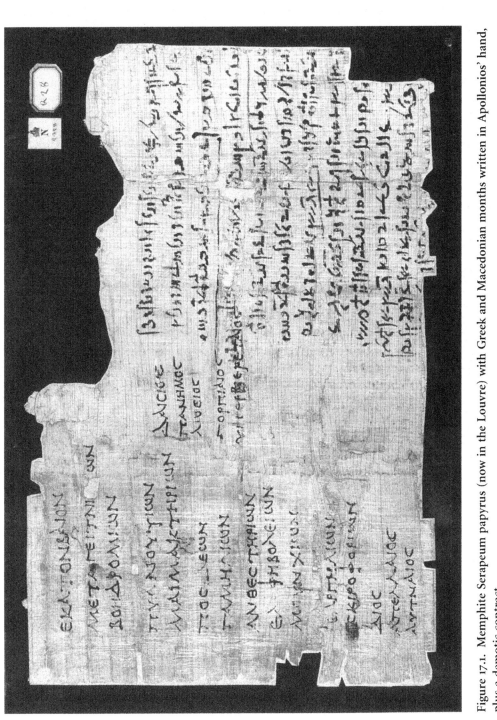

Figure 17.1. Memphite Serapeum papyrus (now in the Louvre) with Greek and Macedonian months written in Apollonios' hand, plus a demotic contract.

known from the papyri of the two sons of Glaukias. The peculiar position of Ptolemaios and briefly of his younger brother Apollonios as detainees (*katochoi*) in the temple enclosure of Sarapis is certainly of interest. Of more relevance here, however, the mix of Greek and demotic in the archive, as in the lives of the brothers and their circle, takes the reader into a complex and fluid environment between two worlds where, in the temple's protected environment, Greeks and Egyptians lived their lives together and interacted. Ptolemaios copied down Greek literature and wrote quite passable Greek; they also owned some demotic wisdom literature (see figure 17.1). Apollonios, who often ran his brother's errands and led a troubled life, dreamed bilingually in Greek and Egyptian (at least his dreams are recorded in the two languages). Both brothers, it is clear, were bilingual, as indeed was the multicultural world in which they lived (Thompson 1988, 212–265).

Up above the city of Memphis on the desert headland of North Saqqara, the Apis bull—Sarapis now for the Greeks—had a nonexclusive following among the different peoples of Ptolemaic Egypt. Here, in the Serapeum, Egyptian might be transcribed into Greek, as in the account of Nektembes' dream (*UPZ* I 79.4–5, from 159 BCE). Alternatively, Egyptian sentiments and prayers were translated into Greek, as when Petesis, son of Chonouphis, mummifier in chief of the Apis and Mnevis bulls, appealed to the king and queen for protection for his house, which was constantly under attack. He asked for the protection of a royal order, written (presumably in ink) on a whitened board outside the house in both Greek and native letters (*UPZ* 107.30, from 99 BCE). And before he made his request, he called on the gods whom he served to grant the royal couple "health, victory, power, strength, and lordship over the lands below heaven" (*UPZ* I 106.13–14, from 99 BCE). The wording and the sentiment come straight from the world of Egypt, here translated into Greek. Eventually his request was granted, but despite the bilingualism of the royal order, Petesis gained no respite from his attackers, and, finally, he resorted to legal means. In this interplay of language, culture, law, and religion, the complex nature of life for yet another sector of Ptolemaic society comes to life through the papyri.

BIBLIOGRAPHY

Adams, J. N., M. Janse, and S. Swain, eds. 2002. *Bilingualism in Ancient Society: Language Contact and the Written Text*. Oxford: Oxford University Press.

Adams, J. N., and S. Swain. 2002. "Introduction." In *Bilingualism in Ancient Society: Language Contact and the Written Text*, ed. J. N. Adams, M. Janse, and S. Swain, 1–20. Oxford: Oxford University Press.

Aimé-Giron, N. 1931. *Textes araméens d'Égypte*. Cairo: Service des Antiquités de l'Égypte.

Bowman, A. K., and G. Woolf, eds. 1994. *Literacy and Power in the Ancient World*. Cambridge: Cambridge University Press.

Bresciani, E., and M. Kamil. 1966. "Le lettere aramaiche di Hermopoli." In *Atti della Accademia Nazionale dei Lincei. Memorie della classe di scienze morali, storiche e filologiche* 8 ser. 12.5: 357–428.

Briant, P. 2002. *From Cyrus to Alexander: A History of the Persian Empire.* Trans. P. T. Daniels. Winona Lake, Ind.: Eisenbrauns.

Christensen, T. 2002. "The Edfu Nome Surveyed: *P.Haun.* inv. 407 (119–118 BCE)." Diss. University of Cambridge.

Clarysse, W. 1985. "Greeks and Egyptians in the Ptolemaic Army and Administration." *Aegyptus* 65: 57–66.

——. 1987. "Greek Loan-words in Demotic." In *Aspects of Demotic Lexicography: Acts of the Second International Conference for Demotic Studies, Leiden, 19–21 September 1984,* ed. S. P. Vleeming, 9–33. Studia Demotica 1. Leuven: Peeters.

——. 1990. "An Epistolary Formula." *CdÉ* 65: 103–106.

——. 1992. "Some Greeks in Egypt." In *Life in a Multi-cultural Society: Egypt from Cambyses to Constantine and Beyond,* ed. J. H. Johnson, 51–56. Studies in Ancient Oriental Civilization 51. Chicago: Oriental Institute.

——. 1993. "Egyptian Scribes Writing Greek." *CdÉ* 68: 186–201.

——. 1995. "Greeks in Ptolemaic Thebes." In *Hundred-gated Thebes: Acts of a Colloquium on Thebes and the Theban Area in the Graeco-Roman Period,* ed. S. P. Vleeming, 1–19. Papyrologica Lugduno-Batava 27. Leiden: Brill.

——. 1998. "Ethnic Diversity and Dialect among the Greeks of Hellenistic Egypt." In *The Two Faces of Graeco-Roman Egypt: Greek and Demotic and Greek-Demotic Texts and Studies Presented to P. W. Pestman,* ed. A. M. F. W. Verhoogt and S. P. Vleeming, 1–13. Papyrologica Lugduno-Batava 30. Leiden: Brill.

——. 2002. "A Jewish Family in Ptolemaic Thebes." *Journal of Juristic Papyrology* 32: 7–9.

Clarysse W., and D. J. Thompson. 2006. *Counting the People in Hellenistic Egypt,* 2 vols. Cambridge: Cambridge University Press.

Collombert, Ph. 2000. "Religion égyptienne et culture grecque: L'exemple de Διοσκουρίδης." *CdÉ* 75: 47–63.

Coulon, L. 2002. "Quand Amon parle à Platon (la statuaire Caire JE 38033)." *Revue d'Égyptologie* 52: 85–112.

Cowley, A. 1923. *Aramaic Papyri of the Fifth Century* B.C. Oxford: Clarendon Press.

Crawford, D. J. 1971. *Kerkeosiris: An Egyptian Village in the Ptolemaic Period.* Cambridge Classical Studies. Cambridge: Cambridge University Press.

Driver, G. R. 1957. *Aramaic Documents.* Oxford: Clarendon Press.

Fewster, P. 2002. "Bilingualism in Roman Egypt." In *Bilingualism in Ancient Society: Language Contact and the Written Text,* ed. J. N. Adams, M. Janse, and S. Swain, 220–245. Oxford: Oxford University Press.

Goudriaan, K. 1988. *Ethnicity in Ptolemaic Egypt.* Dutch Monographs on Ancient History and Archaeology 5. Amsterdam: Gieben.

Grelot, P. 1972. *Documents araméens d'Égypte.* Paris: Éditions du Cerf.

Huss, W. 2001. *Ägypten in Hellenistischer Zeit 332–30 v. Chr.* Munich: Beck.

Johnson, J. H., ed. 1992. *Life in a Multi-cultural Society: Egypt from Cambyses to Constantine and Beyond.* Studies in Ancient Oriental Civilization 51. Chicago: Oriental Institute.

Kornfeld, W. 1973. "Jüdisch-aramäische Grabinschriften aus Edfu." *Anzeiger der Oesterreichischen Akademie der Wissenschaften in Wien, Philos.-Hist.Klasse* 110: 123–137.

Kraeling, E. G. 1953. *The Brooklyn Museum Aramaic Papyri: New Documents of the Fifth Century B.C. from the Jewish Colony at Elephantine*. New Haven, Conn.: Yale University Press.

La'da, C. A. 2002. *Foreign Ethnics in Hellenistic Egypt*. Prosopographia Ptolemaica 10. Leuven: Peeters.

Lauer, J.-Ph. 1976. *Saqqara the Royal Cemetery of Memphis. Excavations and Discoveries since 1850*. London: Thames and Hudson.

Lewis, N. 1986. *Greeks in Ptolemaic Egypt: Case Studies in the Social History of the Hellenistic World*. Oxford: Clarendon Press.

Lloyd, A. B. 1982. "The Inscription of Udjaḥorresnet: A Collaborator's Testament." *JEA* 68: 166–180.

Masson, O. 1978. *Carian Inscriptions from North Saqqâra and Buhen*. Texts from Excavations, Memoir 5. London: Egypt Exploration Society.

Matthews, R., and C. Roemer, eds. 2003. *Ancient Perspectives on Ancient Egypt*. Encounters with Ancient Egypt. London: UCL Press, Institute of Archaeology.

Melaerts, H., and L. Mooren, eds. 2002. *Le rôle et le statut de la femme en Égypte hellénistique, romaine, et byzantine: Actes du colloque international, Bruxelles–Leuven 27–29 novembre 1997*. Leuven: Peeters.

Orrieux, Cl. 1983. *Les papyrus de Zenon. L'horizon d'un grec en Égypte au IIIe siècle avant J.C.* Paris: Macula.

Pestman, P. W. 1990. *The New Papyrological Primer*. Leiden: Brill.

Porten, B. 1968. *Archives from Elephantine: The Life of an Ancient Jewish Military Colony*. Berkeley: University of California Press.

Porten, B., J. J. Farber, C. J. Martin, G. Vittmann, L. S. B. MacCoull, S. Clackson, S. Hopkins, and R. Katzoff. 1996. *The Elephantine Papyri in English: Three Millennia of Cross-cultural Continuity and Change*. Leiden: Brill.

Porten, B., and A. Yardeni. 1986. *Textbook of Aramaic Documents from Ancient Egypt*. Vol. 1, *Letters*. Winona Lake, Ind.: Eisenbrauns.

———. 1989. *Textbook of Aramaic Documents from Ancient Egypt*. Vol. 2. *Contracts*. Winona Lake, Ind.: Eisenbrauns.

———. 1993. *Textbook of Aramaic Documents from Ancient Egypt*. Vol. 3, *Literature, Accounts, Lists*. Winona Lake, Ind.: Eisenbrauns.

———. 1999. *Textbook of Aramaic Documents from Ancient Egypt*. Vol. 4, *Ostraca*. Winona Lake, Ind.: Eisenbrauns.

Porten, B., and A. Yardeni, 2004/5. "Two Aramaic Salt-tax Receipts by the Scribe Joseph." *Enchoria* 29: 55–59.

Ray, J. D. 1981. "An Approach to the Carian Script." *Kadmos* 20: 150–162.

———. 1994. "Literacy and Language in Egypt in the Late and Persian Periods." In *Literacy and Power in the Ancient World*, ed. A. K. Bowman and G. Woolf, 51–66. Cambridge: Cambridge University Press.

———. 1998. "Aegypto-Carica." *Kadmos* 37: 125–136.

Rowlandson, J., ed. 1998. *Women and Society in Greek and Roman Egypt: A Sourcebook*. Cambridge: Cambridge University Press.

Rutherford, I. 2003. "Pilgrimage in Greco-Roman Egypt: New Perspectives on Graffiti from the Memnonion at Abydos." In *Ancient Perspectives on Egypt*, ed. R. Matthews and C. Roemer, 171–189. Encounters with Ancient Egypt. London: UCL Press, Institute of Archaeology.

Segal, J. B. 1983. With contributions by H. S. Smith. *Aramaic Texts from North Saqqâra with Some Fragments in Phoenician.* Texts from Excavations, Memoir 6. London: Egypt Exploration Society.

Tait, W. J. 1988. "Rush and Reed: The Pens of Egyptian and Greek Scribes." *Proceedings of the XVIII International Congress of Papyrology,* ed. B. G. Mandilaras, vol. 2, 477–481. Athens: Greek Papyrological Society.

Thompson, D. J. (Crawford). 1983. "Nile Grain Transport under the Ptolemies." In *Trade in the Ancient Economy,* ed. P. Garnsey, K. Hopkins, and C. R. Whittaker, 64–75. Berkeley: University of California Press.

Thompson, D. J. 1988. *Memphis under the Ptolemies.* Princeton: Princeton University Press.

—— . 2001. "Hellenistic Hellenes: The Case of Ptolemaic Egypt." In *Ancient Perceptions of Greek Ethnicity,* ed. I. Malkin, 301–322. Cambridge, Mass.: Harvard University Press.

—— . 2009. "Ethnic Minorities in Hellenistic Egypt." In *The Political Culture of the Greek City after the Classical Age,* ed. R. Alston and O. M. van Nijf, Groningen-Royal Holloway Studies on the Greek City after the Classical Age, vol. 2. Leuven: Peeters.

Van Minnen, P. 1997. "The Performance and Readership of the *Persai* of Timotheus." *APF* 43: 246–260.

Vandorpe, K. 2000. "The Ptolemaic Epigraphe or Harvest Tax *(shemu)*." *APF* 46: 169–232.

—— . 2002. "Apollonia, a Businesswoman in a Multicultural Society (Pathyris, 2nd–1st Centuries B.C.)." In *Le rôle et le statut de la femme en Égypte hellénistique, romaine, et byzantine: Actes du colloque international, Bruxelles–Leuven 27–29 novembre 1997,* ed. H. Melaerts and L. Mooren, 325–336. Leuven: Peeters.

Vittmann, G. 2003. *Ägypten und die Fremden im ersten vorchristlichen Jahrtausend.* Mainz am Rhein: Verlag Ph. von Zabern.

Vleeming, S. P., ed. 1995. *Hundred-gated Thebes: Acts of a Colloquium on Thebes and the Theban Area in the Graeco-Roman Period.* Papyrologica Lugduno-Batava 27. Leiden: Brill.

—— , and J. W. Wesselius. 1985. *Studies in Papyrus Amherst 63: Essays on the Aramaic Texts in Aramaic/demotic.* Amsterdam: Juda Palache Instituut.

CHAPTER 18

THE MULTILINGUAL ENVIRONMENT OF LATE ANTIQUE EGYPT: GREEK, LATIN, COPTIC, AND PERSIAN DOCUMENTATION

JEAN-LUC FOURNET

DID the multilingual environment of late antique Egypt change fundamentally compared to earlier periods? The linguistic situation of the fourth to seventh centuries does not at first seem much different from that of the past: As in the Ptolemaic period and under Roman rule, we find the same coexistence of an Egyptian substrate and a Greek-speaking population, plus, since the Roman conquest, a Latin-speaking element with a fairly marginal place. But over the centuries the relationships between these three languages evolved, and, leaving to one side some isolated cases (Armenian and Syriac), late antiquity witnessed two important changes: (1) the Sassanid occupation, which produced documentation in Pehlevi, and (2) the emergence of a new script intended to record the contemporary vernacular language, Coptic. I limit myself here to these three languages—Coptic, Latin, and Pehlevi, all of which were widely spoken and written in Egypt in the fourth to seventh centuries, analyzing their use and interaction with Greek, which remained the official language and is by far the most abundantly documented. Each of these languages poses in a distinctive way the problem of multilingualism or—for our documentation is only written—of multiliteracy and presents a nuanced picture, ranging from a nearly total and deliberate absence of bilingualism to a deep bilingualism (where the relationship between the languages tends to reverse itself), passing by way of diglossia.[1]

PEHLEVI: LANGUAGES IN CONTACT WITHOUT INTERACTION

One language makes a sudden appearance in Egypt's papyrological documentation: Pehlevi, or Middle Persian. The Pehlevi texts of Egypt are limited to the decade of the Sassanian conquest (619–629),[2] begun by Xusrō (Chosroes) II Parwēz. They total nearly 950—a remarkably large number for such a short time-span.They are written on papyrus, parchment, skin, and linen and come mainly from the Fayyum (figure 18.1). Except for unpublished papyri in Vienna, which vanished after World War II and have only recently been rediscovered, these have been published or republished by Dieter Weber in two volumes of the *Corpus Inscriptionum Iranicarum* (*CII*).

The Pehlevi documentation is actually rather disappointing. The texts, almost all fragmentary, are very hard to read because of the extremely cursive and stylized script. The commentary in the editions is also excessively focused on philological matters, making it difficult to draw out its full historical value (Huyse 1995).

All the Pehlevi texts are documentary and secular, above all of a military character (orders, lists of provisions for soldiers, itineraries). Some are connected to commerce, but even there a link with the army exists. Private documents are very rare: a number of private letters (e.g., *CII*, P. 18, a letter from a Persian to his sister, showing that the Persian population in Egypt was not entirely male but that some families had followed the soldiers) and three sale contracts (Weber 1992a, 501–502).

It is difficult to draw conclusions from these documents about the impact of the Persian conquest on the inhabitants of Egypt and the linguistic relationship between conquerors and conquered. The same is true of the few contemporary

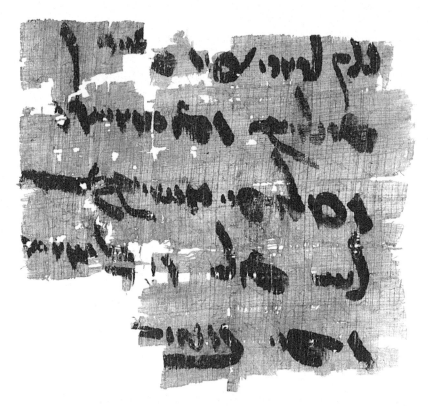

Figure 18.1. An example of a complete Pehlevi document: an order for delivery (*CII*, P. 69 = *P.Heid. Pahl.* 9). Photo courtesy of the Institut für Papyrologie, University of Heidelberg.

Greek and Coptic texts (Butler and Fraser 1978, xlvi–xlix; MacCoull 1986; Altheim-Stiehl 1992a; Huyse 1995, 358). The impermeable character of each body of evidence is striking. The Greek and Coptic texts rarely refer to the Persians and do not characterize the nature of relations between them and the Greek-Egyptian population. The Pehlevi texts are focused on military problems (notably on supply), and the local population is nearly absent from them. One good indication is that no Greek, Coptic, or even Latin personal name appears in them, only Persian names, except for Abraam (*CII*, P. 136) and Samuel, a Jewish merchant, perhaps from Elephantine (Weber 1992b, 341; *CII*, P. 137). Egyptian place names are far more visible (*CII*, P. 55, 148), but for purely military reasons. In short, there are few connections between the two bodies of documents, with the notable exception of the case of Šahrālānyōzān, a high official who appears in some Greek papyri in the form Σαραλανεοζαν (*CII*, P. 81; Weber 1991; Sänger 2008).

The papyrological sources give no sign of any bilingualism, however limited, in the population of Egypt. The total absence of bilingual documents is noteworthy,[3] as is that of Pehlevi texts written by Graeco-Egyptians. Certainly there were oral or written contacts. For instance, in *P.MoscowCopt.* 37–38 the reader Menas says, "I asked the Persians to..."; *P.Oxy.* LI 3637 says that the recipient had "also had written instructions about this matter from our master the all-praiseworthy Saralaneozan"; *CPR* IV 48 is a contract for the delivery of linen between the inhabitants of Pousire (Hermopolite nome) and "their master," Perês Kôsrôi (Pērōz-Xusrō), in which the only instance of an oath "by the safety of the King of Kings" occurs. All these texts show very formal contacts that were carried out through interpreters on the Persian side or by means of networks or institutions already in place and used by the Persians. If any effort at linguistic adaptation was made, it was on the part of the Persians that we must look for it. Thus, the Persians Rasbanas and Remê wrote letters in Greek to the *scholasticus* Marinus (*P.Oxy.* LI 3637, XVI 1862–1863; cf. Foss 2002, 170–171).

A few rare points of interference between the two languages, which show that these ten years of conquest, despite everything, did leave various linguistic traces, may nonetheless be noted: The name of the Persian office *salār* ("official") passed into Greek in the form σελλάριος and appears in several Greek and Coptic documents of this period, particularly in the archive of Theopemptos and Zacharias (Foss 2002). In the reverse direction, the Persians borrowed from Egyptian Greek the words *lṭl'* (λίτρα, "pound") and *lagānag* (λάγυνος, a liquid measure).[4] These points of contact are, however, limited to borrowings of an institutional nature (title, measures), which can occur even with the most superficial contact.

Several reasons account for this superficiality: indifference, even rejection of the Persians on the part of the Graeco-Egyptians, who did not wish to be friendly with the invader, and most of all the impression that this conquest changed the internal situation in Egypt very little not only because of its short duration but above all because the Persians limited themselves to a military presence and relied for the rest on existing institutions. It is true that our knowledge of this period is still imperfect and would benefit from a fuller study bringing together the Greek, Coptic, and Pehlevi documentation.

Latin: Diglossia with Limited or Imperfect Bilingualism

Latin in Egypt and Imperial Policy

The situation of Latin in late antique Egypt is paradoxical: Of around 565 papyrological documents partly or entirely in Latin, those of the fourth to seventh century amount to a mere 140.[5] To put it another way, the Latin documentation of this period is three times less abundant than of the principate (first–third centuries). And yet it is a well-known fact that the reforms of Diocletian and the policies of Constantine brought, along with Romanization at the institutional level, a Latinization of the administration of the eastern provinces, to which Egypt belonged (e.g., Rochette 1997, 116–126). The reforms of Diocletian, by imposing Latin as an official administrative language, undeniably had an effect: Of the 140 papyri in question, about 90 date precisely to the fourth century. The Alexandrian Claudian, as comfortable in Greek as in Latin and official poet at the western court, is one of the best examples of the success of this policy. But the efficacy of this Latinization has long been questioned (Turner 1961; Adams 2003, 635–637, 758). From the end of the fourth century, moreover, imperial policy tended to reaffirm the position of Greek: In 397, judicial decisions were allowed to be rendered in Greek, as well as in Latin; in 439, Theodosius II allowed anyone to make a will in Greek; the prefect Cyrus (439–441) abolished the official use of Latin in the pretorian prefecture of the east; in 450, Latin lost its privileged status at the court of Constantinople; and even Justinian (529–565), who considered Latin his *patria lingua*, pragmatically issued his *Novels* in Greek for the eastern provinces and authorized a Greek translation of the legislative collections issued by his government so that the Greek-speaking population might understand them. These

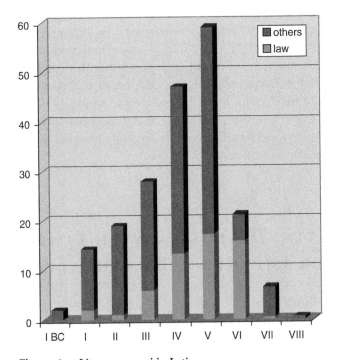

Figure 18.2. Literary papyri in Latin.

decisions help to explain the continued dominance of Greek reflected in the Egyptian documents. In any event, although Latin documents are scarce compared to those of the principate (a characteristic in which they are no different from the papyrological documentation as a whole), the high proportion of Latin literary texts for late antiquity is all the more striking (see figure 18.2). This paradox raises questions about the use of Latin in Egypt.

Conditions of the Use of Latin: Superficial Bilingualism or Diglossia

The Decline of Bilingualism

Latin-Greek bilingualism is less well attested in the late antique papyri than in those of the Roman period. The reasons for this situation are several: (1) Latin, once obligatory for status documents (like birth certificates) among the very limited body of Roman citizens, was no longer closely tied to Roman citizenship, particularly after that had been granted on all of the subjects of the empire by the *Constitutio Antoniniana* (212); (2) the growing recruitment of Graeco-Egyptian auxiliaries for the army led to the disappearance of Latin private letters, which are a good indicator of true bilingualism practiced in Latin-speaking circles and are found in quantity at military sites from the principate (e.g., *O.Claud., O. Krok., O.Max., O.Fawâkhir*).[6] Nor are there for the fourth to the seventh centuries any archives like those of Claudius Tiberianus and his son, Claudius Terentianus (mainly *P.Mich.* VIII 467–481, found at Karanis in the Fayyum, 100–120; cf. Adams 2003, 593–596), which illustrate the bilingualism of a family of veterans who settled in the Egyptian *chôra*.

The only bilingual archive from a military milieu is that of Flavius Abinnaeus (Arsinoite, 341–351).[7] Of the eighty-five texts known, two are in Latin. The first is *P. Abinn.* 1 (340–342), a petition by Abinnaeus, asking the emperors to confirm his nomination as *praefectus alae Quintae Praelectorum*, which the *dux Aegypti* Valacius was refusing him. The second, *P.Abinn.* 2 (344), is a letter in which Valacius removes Abinnaeus from his position. The use of Latin in these two cases can be explained by the two individuals' knowledge of the language because of their military status. Considering that the rest of the archive is entirely in Greek, however, another explanation is more compelling: Valacius uses Latin to give his letter an official character that might impress Abinnaeus. Similarly, the latter uses Latin to address the empire's highest authorities. Here Latin plays the role of "language of power." "On the evidence of this archive, then, Greek was in regular use as an official, formal language, but Latin was available as a sort of 'super-high' language which could be employed either to make obvious the location of supreme power, or in appeal to a supreme authority" (Adams 2003, 557).[8]

Latin as Language and Display of Power

It is striking to observe the disappearance of private letters in Latin. The Latin letters from fourth-to-seventh-century Egypt, as far as we can identify their authors, are almost entirely official letters sent by very high officials: thus, *P.Ryl.* IV 623 and *Ch.L.A.* XIX 687 (Hermopolis, 317–324; figure 18.3), letters of recommendation of *rationalis* (a high finance official) Vitalis to Delphinius and to Achillius, the governor of Phoenicia, on behalf of Theophanes (and coming from the only Graeco-Latin archive of the period besides that of Abinnaeus; cf. Moscadi 1970); *P.Abinn.* 2 (cf. above); *P.Ryl.* IV 609 (Hermopolis, 505), *epistula probatoria* of the *comes rei militaris Thebaici limitis*. Latin thus remained the prerogative of the highest officials of the military and civil administrations, on the model of texts coming directly from the chancery of the pretorian prefect[9] or issued by the emperor (constitutions, edicts, rescripts).[10]

This use of Latin is visible during this period mainly in the bilingual minutes of legal hearings—probably the type of document that most accurately reveals the Greek-Latin "bilingualism" of late antique Egypt, showing the direct influence of imperial policy with regard to Latin, as well as its limits. Despite some earlier examples, it is with Diocletian that such transcripts of hearings before high magistrates, mixing Latin and Greek, develop (figure 18.4).[11] Their particularity lies in the back-and-forth between languages ("code switching"; cf. Adams 2003, 383–390): The formal structure (date, place, formulas introducing interventions) is in Latin; the words of the judge are sometimes in Greek (when he speaks to the defense), sometimes in Latin (when he addresses his *officium*), while those of the advocates, the accused, or the witnesses are in Greek; the judge's sentence is in either Latin or Greek. "The use of Greek reflects the need for comprehensibility, that of Latin or mixed-language utterance, the exclusion of some hearers for a moment from the proceedings, and a desire on the part of the officials to present themselves symbolically as representatives of Rome and as an exclusive group" (Adams 2003, 386).

One might ask whether the Latin in these texts was not a fictitious representation of what actually happened. Such doubts would be exaggerated for the fourth century. But a comparison between the use of languages in the transcripts of the fourth century and those of the fifth and sixth (Rochette 1997, 119–20) shows that the colloquy and sentence were only in Greek from the fifth century on. The increasingly local recruitment of high officials may explain the gradual loss of adequate competence in Latin. In any case, however, the formal framework remains in Latin, showing that the language played, even if artificially, the role of a language of power. In other documents, only the date or a validation formula (e.g., *legi, proponatur*) is enough. Rather than bilingualism, we must speak of diglossia, even if superficial.

This required use of Latin, moreover, increasingly stereotyped and distant from natural usage, betrays itself in the Latin documents by various symptoms like the faulty insertion of Greek letters, a failure to respect the rules of Latin spelling, and morphological confusions.[12]

Latin as a Language of Law

The use of Latin in transcripts of trials is also tied to the fact that Latin was the language par excellence of law. Roman law, the only valid system at this period, was obviously expressed in Latin, and after the Antonine Constitution many officials needed to know it. Diocletian certainly encouraged the study of law, granting privileges to officials who studied it and creating new professorships of Latin in the east. Alexandria became an important center for the study of legal Latin, competing with or complementing the famous law school of Beirut. This spread

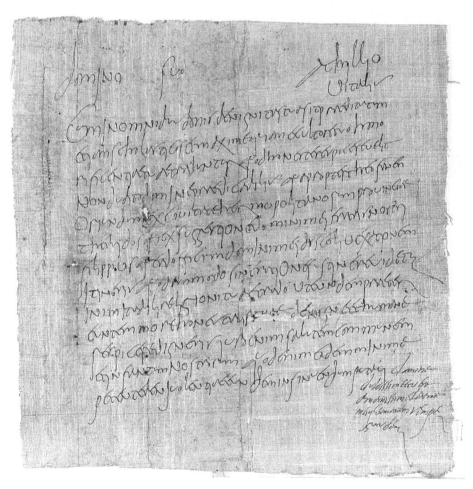

Figure 18.3. Letter of recommendation from the *rationalis* Vitalis to the governor of Phoenicia on behalf of Theophanes of Hermopolis (*Ch.L.A.* XIX 687, 317–324 = *P.Stras.* inv. L1). Photo and collection of the Bibliothèque Nationale et Universitaire de Strasbourg.

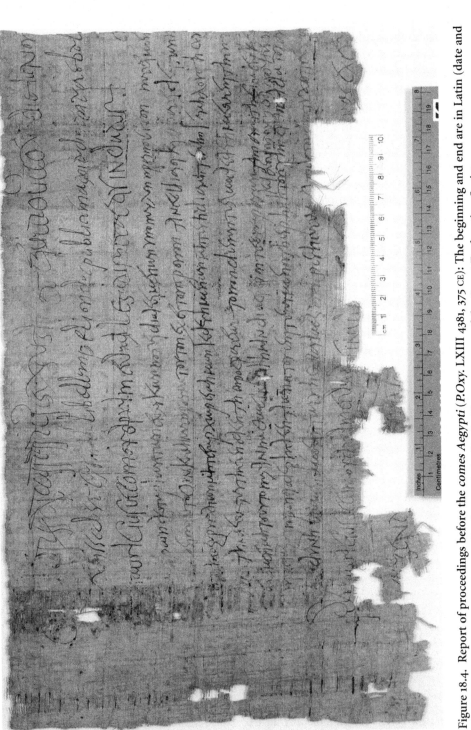

Figure 18.4. Report of proceedings before the comes Aegypti (*POxy.* LXIII 4381, 375 CE): The beginning and end are in Latin (date and dialogue between judge and his staff); the rest is in Greek. Photo courtesy of the Egypt Exploration Society.

Figure 18.5. Completion of the lawyer Justus in Greek and Latin letters (*P.Oxy.* LXIII 4397, 244–245). Photo courtesy of the Egypt Exploration Society.

of Roman law produced an intense activity of collecting jurisdictional documents and jurisprudential corpora and of copying legal books, all of which has left traces in the Egyptian papyri. A nontrivial part of the Latin literary papyri of Egypt is juristic (fifty-six out of about two hundred texts), reaching a peak in the fourth to sixth centuries, a period framed by Diocletian, a promoter of Latin language and Roman law, and Justinian, whose great activity in legislation and the creation of legal corpora is well known (figure 18.2).[13]

The fact that Latin was perceived above all as a language of law had an impact on documentary practice:

- The notaries (*nomikoi,* literally "men of law") might be led to include Latin words in their documents to refer to legal ideas. This is what Dioscoros of Aphroditê does several times during a will (*P.Cair.Masp.* II 67152, Antinoopolis, 570), for example in lines 64–66: τὴν ἰδίαν δύναμιν καὶ βεβαίωσιν ἔχειν ὡς *confirmateumenous* ἐν τῇ παρούσᾳ τελευταίᾳ βουλήσει, "(I wish these codicils) to have their own force and validity as 'confirmed' in the present will." These words are transliterations into Latin letters of Greek versions of Latin words (here, *confirmo* becomes *confirmateuo,* transliterated into Latin with a Greek participial ending).
- From the fifth to the seventh century the notaries of the Arsinoite, Oxyrhynchite, and Herakleopolite nomes write their signatures at the end of the documents in Latin transliteration.[14] For example, *P.Oxy.* LXIII 4397 (545): δι' ἐμοῦ Ἰούστου ὑποδιακ(όνου) συμβολαιογράφ(ου) ἐτελειώθη | *di' em(u) Iust(u) upodiacon(u) sumbolai(ografu) eteliothh,* "completed by me, Justus, subdeacon and notary" (figure 18.5). This artifice, which sometimes produces its share of blunders (*P.Oxy.* VII 1042.34: *di emu Serηnu etelioth*), gave legal prestige to the document. This is the best example of a very imperfect diglossia—I should say digraphia—denuded of all bilingualism.

Latin Literary Papyri: The Needs of a New Class

The development of Latin as a language of power and law, however marginal or superficial, led to the emergence of a new class of civil and military officials and of lawyers (*scholastikoi*) who had to acquire at least a rudimentary knowledge of Latin. This learning process is well documented by the Latin literary papyri found in Egypt. The graph of these papyri is highly significant when compared to that of Greek literary papyri, which reaches its peak in the second century; it rises abruptly in the fourth century and reaches a peak in the fifth before falling again (figure 18.2). The Latin papyri attest various phases of learning, ranging from elementary teaching to a higher level (Rochette 1997, 165–210; Adams 2003, 623–630): (1) Latin alphabets with equivalents of Greek letters, sometimes with the names of Latin letters in Greek; (2) writing exercises; (3) Latin or Graeco-Latin grammars; (4) Graeco-Latin glossaries (where Latin is often transliterated into Greek) of several types:[15] alphabetic or thematic glossaries or glossaries of Latin authors (Rochette 1990, 1996; *C.Gloss.Biling.* II pp. 5–8); (5) conversation manuals; (6) collections of model letters (just one case, from the third–fourth century, *P.Bon.* 5, which gives letters with a strongly legal character as examples); (7) Latin authors (Mertens 1987), above all Cicero and Vergil but also Juvenal, Livy, Lucan, Sallust, Seneca, Terence, anonymous works like the Montserrat *Alcestis* (Mertens-Pack³ 2998.1, fourth century), or the *Psalmus Responsorius* in the same codex (van Haelst 1210) and legal authors (e.g., Gaius, Papinianus, Ulpian, Codex Theodosianus).

Various indications, like transliteration into Greek (Kramer 1984, 1378–1379; Rochette 1999) and the use of administrative vocabulary in the glossaries, show that these papyri were composed mainly for Greek speakers, who were less interested in the glories of Roman culture than in the necessity—more and more pressing from Diocletian on—to learn Latin quickly for practical reasons.

Latin in Christian Milieus

The Latin-Greek-Coptic conversation manual (Mertens-Pack³ 3009 = *P.Rain. Unterricht kopt.* 270, *C.Gloss.Biling.* I 15, sixth century), given its Coptic element and the religious coloration of its lexicon, seems to have been intended for Christian (perhaps monastic) circles. It poses the problem of the connections between Latin and Christian milieus (Cavenaile 1987). A number of Latinized monastic circles existed in Egypt, but these were very marginal: It was for Latin-speaking monks of the Pachomian congregation that Jerome translated Pachomius's rule into Latin (404). Apollô directed a community near Hermopolis where several monks, we are told, were "versed in Greek, Latin, and Egyptian" (*Historia Monachorum in Aegypto* 8.62). More interesting is the presence of Latin in the Montserrat codex mentioned earlier, part no doubt of an ancient collection of Christian books in Greek and Coptic from the region of Nag Hammadi, to which a Greek-Latin lexicon of the Pauline epistles also belonged (Wouters 1988). This library, the setting of which is still controversial, may have belonged to a religious community (perhaps sectarian) of Upper Egypt (Agosti 2002, 80–87), and these texts demonstrate that its members needed instruction in Latin, as well as Greek and Coptic. Similarly, among the Manichaeans of Kellis, the need to learn Latin was felt around the same time (*P.Kellis* V C. 20.24–26: "The Great Teacher let him travel with him, so that he might learn Latin"), perhaps for missionary purposes.

Other Latin papyri from a Christian setting are rare and hard to interpret because we know little about their precise context: *P.Lond.* V 1792 (fifth–sixth century), a Latin letter addressed by an *epitropos* to an ecclesiastic, and the curious cluster of Greek letters introduced by a Latin sentence of biblical inspiration, with Latin docket (*P.Oxy.* XVIII 2193–2194 and *P.Köln* IV 200, fifth–sixth century). Other than those already mentioned, Christian literary papyri in Latin are the products of schools: *PSI* XIII 1306 (fourth–fifth century), Ephesians in Latin and Greek; *P.Rain. Unterricht* 184 (sixth–seventh century; with regard to the date, cf. *P.Thomas,* pp. 19–23), Latin Lord's Prayer with transliteration into Greek.

The data are scant and difficult to use. Despite everything, Latin remained marginal: Greek was the official language of the church, Coptic its natural language and that more customary in monastic milieus.

Consequences of Latino-Greek Bilingualism or Diglossia

It is not always easy to distinguish between the results of Romanization and those of Latinization. The most obvious result of the latter is the penetration of numerous Latin words into the Greek of Egypt, a phenomenon visible already under the principate but limited essentially to military milieus and certain semantic fields (cf. Ghiretti 1996) and much more evident from Diocletian on. These words, collected earlier by Daris (1991), are now the object of a specialized dictionary based on Greek and Coptic sources, *Lex.Lat.Lehnw.,* which will provide a solid base for a complete study of the impact of Latin on the Greek of Egypt. For the moment, we may simply recall that Latin words were obviously introduced in the domain of civil and military institutions and of taxation as a result of imperial reforms (sometimes going so far as to duplicate Greek words, like δηφήνσωρ < *defensor,* next to ἔκδικος). More revealing are numerous Latin words that concern artisanry (names of trades and products, especially textiles and foodstuffs). The impact of Latinization is also visible in the degree of adaptation by the borrowing language. We see, indeed, many hybrid words (Daris 1991, introduction): verbs with Greek suffixes (ἀμβιτεύω < *ambio;* ἐξπελλεύω < *expello*), sometimes without any Latin equivalent (ἀδνουμενεύω < *ad nomen*); nouns created from two Latin words (δελματικομαφόριον < *dalmatica* and *maforte*) or from a Latin plus a Greek word (σύγκελλος < σύν + *cella;* παγάρχης < *pagus* + -άρχης); abstract nouns with no Latin equivalent (ἐξακτορία < *exactor;* ῥιπαρία < *riparius*). Such formations show

how perfectly Latin words were integrated into the borrowing language. The influence of Latin is also apparent at the level of handwriting, especially in the development of the so-called Graeco-Latin graphic koinê (see chapter 5). Finally, as far as bibliology is concerned, Roman juristic practice, which privileged the codex, was certainly one of the influences (along with Christian books) in the eventual triumph of the codex over the bookroll and its adoption not only for accounting and recordkeeping but also for literary authors (Gascou 2000, 289–291). Greek *paideia*, so resistant to Latin influence, finally bowed before Roman pragmatism, but here we move into the complex domain of Romanization and leave the realm of language for the broader world of culture.

COPTIC: DIGLOSSIA WITH REAL BILINGUALISM

The relationship of Greek and Coptic is richer, better documented, and more complex. The population of late antique Egypt mostly spoke its vernacular language, Coptic, or more exactly "Egyptian," as the papyri say, but in some circumstances it had to use Greek, the language common to the entire east. The problem, more fundamentally, is one of the relationship of a population with its administration and elites—relationships in which the phenomena of multilingualism and diglossia are most clearly observable. There is much in this area we still do not know, above all because Coptic papyrology has advanced less rapidly than Greek. Recent discoveries (Kellis) are in the process of shedding new light, but the moment for a full synthesis has not yet arrived. In short, Coptic papyrology is a domain in the midst of change and expansion (Clackson 2004).[16]

The Birth of Coptic

The first three centuries of Roman domination witnessed the decline of the vernacular scripts: The hieroglyphs, no longer used except as an artificial script in monumental inscriptions, disappear after 393/394 (Philae); hieratic, also tied to temple culture, starts becoming incomprehensible even to priests starting in the second century, as the *Onomasticon* of Tebtynis shows, with its marginal glosses in demotic and Old Coptic (Osing 1998, papyrus I). Starting in the middle of the first century, even demotic, the only script in current use to represent the spoken Egyptian language, declines along with the temples where it was taught, and it vanishes almost completely in the third century, even though it is attested as late as a graffito at Philae in 452/453 (Bagnall 1993, 237; Lewis 1993; Fournet 2003a, 429–430). The Egyptians thus found themselves without a script for communication among themselves and were obliged, if they could, to use Greek—a point important for the decline in the quality of written Greek, visible in many papyri of the second to the fourth centuries.

Furthermore, it was to the convenient, alphabetic Greek that they turned to try to create a new script. Apart from some transliterations of names, it is only in the first–second century that the first attempts at creating a coherent graphic system are found, one that used the Greek alphabet augmented by some demotic signs denoting phonemes absent in Greek: This is what is called Old Coptic (Quagebeur 1982, modified by Bagnall 2005), born in a pagan milieu intent on preserving traditional learning and allowing the recording of texts tied to cult practices such as magic and astrology. The school ostraca of the temple of Narmouthis (Fayyum), which date to the second to third century, in which hieratic words are transliterated into Old Coptic (*O.Narm.Dem.* II 34–41), offer a good example of the context in which these experiments in Old Coptic were conducted (figure 18.6).

Among the varied experiments in Old Coptic, it is probably in the third century that one took hold, was diffused by pathways still obscure to us, and led to the birth of Coptic properly speaking (Bagnall 2005, 18). This, unlike Old Coptic, was certainly a deliberate creation that resulted from Christian initiative in well-off, Greek-speaking Egyptian circles—hence the large quantity of Greek words in Coptic (about 20 percent), not only concrete ones but also auxiliary words like conjunctions and prepositions.[17] Coptic is thus the offspring of Greek-Egyptian bilingualism, designed above all for the translation of the scriptures into a vernacular tongue—a need evident already in the third century in the Coptic glosses to the Greek text of Isaiah in *P.Chester Beatty* VII or the minor prophets in a codex in the Freer Collection (van Haelst 293, 284). In the following century, Coptic expanded dramatically not only as a literary medium but also for ordinary use, still in Christian circles. The Egyptian population, which became mainly Christian in this period, had from this point on its own means of writing, which allowed it to communicate in its own language. The expansion of Coptic had consequences for Greek: With those only uneasily bilingual now able to communicate in Coptic, the quality of the language in Greek letters recovers something of its higher level seen in the Hellenistic period.

Despite the rapidity of the spread of Coptic and the homogeneity of its users, from a linguistic standpoint it was highly diverse: It was made up of several dialects identifiable in their phonological and graphic variation. These are mainly, from north to south, Bohairic (B), Fayyumic (F), Mesokemic (M), Akhmimic (A), sub-Akhmimic or Lykopolitan (A² or L), and Sahidic (S).[18] Sahidic ("southern dialect") was the standard Coptic literary dialect until its displacement by Bohairic ("northern dialect") in the tenth century, probably because of the settling of the Coptic patriarchate in Wadi Natrun (west delta).

Figure 18.6. A school exercise in hieratic writing with translation in Old Coptic (*O.Narm.Dem.* II 38, second–third century CE), facsimile. Courtesy of Paolo Gallo.

Coptic versus Greek

Characterizing the relationship between the use of Coptic and the use of Greek and, on the basis of that, describing the Egyptian-speaking community are difficult problems that have been approached through various methods.

A Complex Problem: Inadequate Criteria

(1) ETHNICITY

This is difficult to perceive. Legal categories are useless because the terms "Egyptian" and "Greek," as the Romans used them, did not correspond to any ethnic realities, only to legal and fiscal distinctions (thus, the Greeks of the *chôra* were classified as "Egyptians"); moreover, these were obsolete by late antiquity. Only with the coming of the Arabs would a new term arise, "Copt" (a deformation of the Greek word *Aigyptios*, "Egyptian"), which designated the Egyptians—all Christians—in opposition to the Muslim Arabs.

Nor are naming practices able to reveal ethnicity from the fourth century on. The onomastic repertory was Christianized, thereby partly erasing the differences between Greek and Egyptian names. We see, moreover, particularly in the fourth century, a fashion for certain Greek names even among the Copts; and, finally, some Graeco-Egyptian names (and even Latin ones) are of indeterminate character. The names of the authors of fourth-century Coptic letters found at Kellis (*P.Kell.* V) are sufficient proof: Egyptian names, to be sure (Psemnouthes, That, Shamoun), but also Graeco-Egyptian (Horion), Christian (Matthaios, Makarios), Greek (Lysimachos), and Latin (Valens) names.

In a class by itself was Alexandria, a profoundly Greek city that had no very visible Egyptian-speaking population, as the absence of Coptic inscriptions and graffiti shows.

(2) RELIGION

Although this is more solid, it is complicated to handle. Pagan (or paganizing) Hellenism has often been set up against a Coptic Christian culture. This distinction, always too schematic, becomes unworkable after Christianity becomes the state religion under Constantine. Another schematic opposition, between anti-Chalcedonian Christians who spoke Coptic and Chalcedonian Christians who spoke Greek,[19] depends on a nationalistic vision that has been strongly criticized of late (Wipszycka 1992, esp. 122–125). This opposition is all the more futile in that the Chalcedonian/anti-Chalcedonian split is almost entirely absent from the papyrological documentation and does not seem to have been a criterion of linguistic differentiation. The language of the church of Egypt remained Greek as long as possible. It was the liturgical language and the language of communication between the patriarch of Alexandria and his bishops. The festal letters, veritable treatises with doctrinal and disciplinary content sent by the patriarch to the bishops of Egypt each year to announce the date of Easter, were still written in Greek well after the Arab conquest (*BKT* VI 5 = van Haelst 621, from 713 or 719). Greek was the language of Christian public space, as, for example, in the monumental inscriptions in Egyptian churches (see the inscription of the Muʿallaqa, the "Hanging Church" from 735; Fournet 1993).

This inadequate dichotomy has given way to a more legitimate opposition: Greek was the language of the church, but Coptic was spoken by most of the monks. Monks and anchorites could get by without Greek and use the maternal language of the majority, whether by deliberate rejection of Greek, by indifference toward the Greek *paideia* so ubiquitous in the world, or by cutting themselves off from public life, where Greek remained indispensable. In fact, the majority of Coptic papyri from the fourth to the seventh centuries come from monastic settings or from sectarian religious communities like the Gnostics or Manichaeans. But Egyptian monasticism was more diverse than is often thought: Besides the Latin speakers mentioned earlier, it included a Greek or Greek-speaking component (Wipszycka

1992, 115–116) and even to some extent encouraged Greek, which was necessary for managing the monasteries' economic activities. Moreover, in early Egyptian monasticism, those monks and anchorites, who acted as intermediaries between the population and the authorities, needed Greek. We see this from the bilingual fourth-century archives of the Melitian monastery of Hathor and of Apa Johannes (mentioned later), which contradict the ideological vision transmitted by hagiographic literature (van Minnen 1994).

At the same time, it was quite possible for important church positions to be occupied by Copts who did not speak Greek (Wipszycka 1992, 110): Kalosiris, bishop of Arsinoe, needed an interpreter at the Council of Ephesos (*ACO* II/1/1, p. 185, 90); the bishops Abraham of Hermonthis and Pisenthios of Coptos (sixth–seventh century) did not know Greek.

This connection between Coptic and the monks (supposedly poor and rejecting the city) has led scholars to propose a third criterion.

(3) SOCIAL AND ECONOMIC STATUS

Urban communities, because they were more affluent and cultivated, would on this view have spoken mainly Greek, while village populations (less rich, uneducated) spoke Coptic. This schematization is partly valid (especially for the urban elites involved in municipal duties), but the use of the two languages was actually less simply divided. Centuries of cohabitation had led Greeks to learn Egyptian, particularly in the course of managing agricultural estates—a point on which the papyri do not inform us adequately. In return, some categories of villagers needed Greek in order to manage their businesses and carry on village duties, as well as in relations with the pagarch and the metropolis. A kind of natural bilingualism thus developed. In the fourth century, the villagers of Kellis, even if they have Egyptian names, write both Greek and Coptic. In the sixth century, the archives of the village of Aphroditê are almost entirely in Greek, and one of its inhabitants, Dioscoros, not only was capable of drawing up Greek legal documents as a notary in the capital of his province, the Thebaid, but could also write poems in Greek. In short, this criterion also gives only an imperfect account of spoken bilingualism and simultaneously fails to explain the distribution of the written documentation between Greek and Coptic.

The best explanation of the evidence is that the two languages were complementary, depending on the context of usage; in other words, there was a functional link between language and type of written document, which evolved over time. Bilingualism combines with a clear diglossia, the contours of which gradually change.

The Complementarity of the Two Languages by Genre

The number of Coptic documents follows an upward curve (figure 18.7), almost the reverse of that of Greek documents.[20] These two curves clearly illustrate that the conditions of use and complementarity of Greek and Coptic evolved between

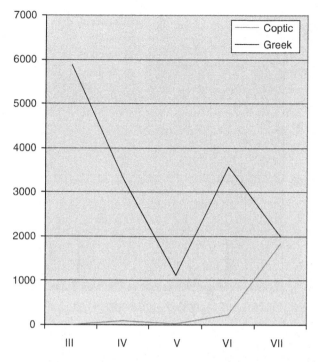

Figure 18.7. Quantitative comparison of Greek and Coptic documents.

the fourth and seventh centuries—to the benefit of Coptic, which would replace Greek in its major domain, legal documents, after the Arab conquest, which marked the end of Byzantine rule in Egypt (Richter 2002, 16–27). Three phases can be distinguished, which we will treat by looking at the bilingual archives of each period; these demonstrate the relationship between Greek and Coptic and its evolution, as shown in figure 18.8, which classes the Coptic documents according to three types (letters, accounts/lists, others).[21]

(1) FOURTH CENTURY TO ABOUT 570: THE DEVELOPMENT OF COPTIC

For this period, we have two Graeco-Coptic archives:

- The archives of the Melitian monastery of Hathor (Kynopolite nome), made up of that of its abbot Apa Paieous (334–340)[22] and that of one of his successors, Nepheros (350–360).[23] Paieous, with his Egyptian name, knew both Greek and Coptic; he signed in Greek on a contract (*P.Lond.* VI 1913.18), giving his name a Hellenized form, Pageus; he also received numerous letters in Greek and at the same time wrote (?) and received letters in Coptic (*P.Lond.* VI 1920–1922). The same is true of Nepheros. Coptic is used only for letters in these archives, while other documents (contracts, receipts,

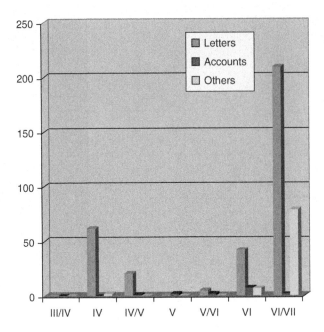

Figure 18.8. The Coptic documents from the beginning up
to the Arab conquest.

accounts) are in Greek. It is worth noting also that the three Coptic letters in
the dossier of Paieous concern very down-to-earth subjects (making clothes,
sending provisions), in contrast to some of the Greek letters, which deal with
important subjects like the relations between the Melitian congregation and
the bishop of Alexandria (*P.Lond.* VI 1914). Moreover, the editor of *P.Lond.*
VI 1914 regarded the writer as a Copt (because of the errors he made); as a
result, the choice of Greek would have been linked to the nature and
importance of this letter, a kind of official report.

- The archive of the anchorite Apa Johannes (Lykopolis, ca. 375–400).[24] This
  dossier is made up of letters in Greek and in Coptic, addressed by monks,
  churchmen, soldiers, officials, and private individuals to Apa Johannes, who is
  identified with the famous John of Lykopolis, a "holy man" known from the
  literary sources (Zuckerman 1995, 188–194).[25] These persons ask John to pray
  for them or to intercede in their favor with the authorities. It is difficult to
  assess the reasons for the choice of language, particularly when the senders do
  not give their identity. Some of the authors of Coptic letters, however, are
  certainly monks (*P.Ryl.Copt.* 268, 269, 271, 313). Even this, however, is not so
  simple: One of supplicants, Psoïs, writes to Apa Johannes in Greek, even
  though the poor quality of his Greek shows that he was a Coptic-speaking
  Egyptian (*P.Herm.* 7). It is thus all the more surprising to find Psoïs writing in
  Greek to a Copt who is said not to have known Greek. We have in fact a letter by

Apa Johannes himself, written in Greek, but only its signature is in his own hand, and that is in Coptic (*P.Amh.* II 145; figure 18.9). To put it another way, Apa Johannes must not have known Greek (information confirmed by Palladius) and, in order to deal with the numerous requests he received, used a "secretariat," which translated those in Greek for him and drew up at his request letters that he needed to send in Greek. The letter of Psoïs shows that a Copt could feel himself obliged to write in Greek to another Copt.

To these two archives we may add, besides the papyri from the Nag Hammadi cartonnage, those from Kellis (Dakhla Oasis), which, although they do not form an archive properly speaking, are of the greatest interest:

- The texts from Kellis (ca. 350–370) come from a Manichaean circle.[26] Apart from a number of accounts, the Coptic texts are private letters, while the Greek papyri include, besides private and business letters, petitions, receipts, and a variety of official and legal documents (e.g., prefectural edict, loans, sales, manumission). Apart from this clear partition, one is struck by the perfect bilingualism of some of the main figures. Thus, Tithoes writes a Coptic letter to his son, Samoun (*P.Kell.* V C. 12), while the latter writes a letter in Greek to his father (*P.Kell.* I 12). Moreover, Tithoes and Samoun receive letters in Greek from Ammonios (*P.Kell.* I 10 and 11). A woman named That goes from Coptic to Greek within a single letter without an obvious reason (*P.Kell.* V C. 43). The bilingual character of this community is well summed up in Makarios's recommendation to his "son," Matheos: "Study [your] psalms, whether Greek or Coptic" (*P.Kell.* V C. 19.13–14).

These three groups very clearly show a division between private documents written in Coptic and legal documents written exclusively in Greek. Apart from some private accounts, Coptic is reserved for private letters. Nonetheless, these remain strongly marked by Greek in that they borrow structure and formulary from Greek letters; in some cases, the address (prescript), the final salutation, and the endorsement are written in Greek. All of this presents a picture of a population more bilingual than one might have expected, one that, except the particular case of legal documents, moved from one language to the other according to criteria that are not always evident to us and are not based on belonging to a monastic community or on not knowing Greek. The case of Psoïs plainly shows that, in the fourth century, a permeability between the two languages continued to exist, made possible by widespread bilingualism even if sometimes imperfect. The nationalist conception of the use of languages is clearly untenable.

(2) CIRCA 570–642: A PERIOD OF TRANSITION

This was a hinge period, during which Coptic began to be used, rather timidly, for legal documents (included in "Others" in figure 18.8). Four archives date to this period and illustrate this phenomenon well:

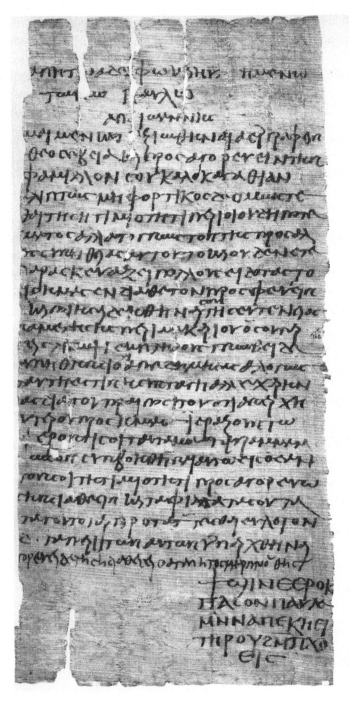

Figure 18.9. A Greek letter of anchorite Apa Johannes, signed by
him in Coptic (*P.Amh.* II 145, end of the fourth century CE).

- The archive of Dioscoros of Aphroditê (506–585)[27] is the largest group of Byzantine papyri, the Coptic part of which is still poorly known and partly unpublished. Its protagonist, Dioscoros, a notable of the village whose business affairs he managed, a small landowner, a notary, and curator of the monastery founded by his father, knew both Coptic (his native language) and Greek (which he mastered sufficiently to write poetry; see *P.Aphrod.Lit.* IV). In contrast to the Greek texts (petitions, contracts and other notarial texts, administrative letters, tax receipts, private and official accounts), the majority of the Coptic texts are letters, either private or concerned with his father's monastery (MacCoull 1991, 1992, 1993). But we also find here, for the first time in Coptic, texts of another sort: two arbitrations drawn up by Dioscoros (569 and ca. 570),[28] the first between monks (figure 18.10), the second between laity.
- The archive of Pathermouthis, son of Menas (Syene, 574–613),[29] contains primarily Greek documents concerning the properties of Patermouthis and his wife, Kako (sales of houses and boats, cessions) and settlements of the disputes that these provoked among members of the family. The few Coptic documents have a characteristic profile: We find at least one letter (*SB Kopt.* III 1293), a legal settlement (*P.Lond.Copt.* I 446), and a debt settlement (*SB Kopt.* III 1395). Moreover, the only documents of the archive in which Kako acts without her husband are in Coptic (*SB Kopt.* III 1394, 1395), which may link the use of Coptic to an inability, more widespread among women, to express oneself in Greek (Clackson 2004, 29).
- The archive of Abraham, bishop of Hermonthis (Thebes, ca. 600),[30] is an important group written almost entirely in Coptic. It contains a number of letters concerning Abraham's pastoral activity. More original is, for the first time, a coherent body of texts of a juridical nature. These are mostly sureties, but we find also orders, work contracts, and loans. They are sometimes described using the Greek technical terms *asphaleia* ("guarantee") or *homologia* ("acknowledgement"). They close with the signature of the con-tracting party and sometimes with a witness (using the Greek verb *stoikhei,* "I agree"). Still, we must underline the fact that these apparently legal texts come from an ecclesiastical context. On the other hand, while he is abbot of the monastery of Phoibammon (Thebes), Abraham has his will written (as was legally obligatory) in Greek (*P.Lond.* I 77—the only Greek document of his archive). Some thirty years later (634), Abraham's successor as head of the same monastery, Apa Victor, made his will in Coptic (*P.KRU* 77). This development shows the advance of Coptic.
- The small archive of Pachymios, purple-seller (Panopolis, 592–616),[31] contains various types of contracts in Greek (house sales, property division, loans, work contract) and offers the first dated example of a contract in Coptic, a betrothal agreement (*CPR* IV 23, 608), drawn up at This by the

Figure 18.10. The first dated Coptic text: a settlement drafted by Dioscoros of Aphroditê (*P.Alex.* inv. 689, 569 CE). Photo by Alain Lecler (IFAO), courtesy Graeco-Roman Museum, Alexandria.

bilingual notary Paul, to whom we owe other contracts in Greek (*SB* I 4503–4505; cf. MacCoull 1995, 347–350).

These archives illustrate the same polarization between the private sphere, in which Coptic is ever more extensively used (letters), and the public sphere, where Greek is needed (legal texts). To be sure, the dossier of Bishop Abraham, who did not know Greek, shows how the church of Upper Egypt, by pragmatism and necessity, sought to develop legal texts in Coptic in imitation of public usage, but these concern only clergy and monks, who were mainly Coptic-speaking.

The first Coptic texts of a legal nature, drawn up by bilingual notaries, begin appearing in 569/570: arbitrations (Fournet forthcoming). But these texts display above all the parties' desire not to involve themselves in legal process (petition, trials in which Greek was required) and to resolve their controversies amiably and in their own language. They open up a kind of parallel track, which anticipates the development of Coptic legal texts in open competition with Greek. The list of those more or less precisely dated before the Arab conquest is short: *CPR* IV 90 (Hermopolite, 596), sale on delivery (the first Coptic text with notarial sub-scription); *CPR* IV 23 (Panopolite, 608), betrothal contract; *CPR* IV 48 (Hermopolite, 625), sale on delivery; *O.CrumST* 436 (Panopolite, 619 or 634), acknowledgement of debt; *P.Vat.Copt.* 2 and 3 (Antaiopolite, 624/625 or 654/655), division of house property and undetermined contract; *P.Vat.Copt.* 1 and 5 (Antaiopolite, 625/626 or 655/656), sales; *P.CrumST* 48 (Thebes, 625 or 640), receipt for a deed; *O.CrumVC* 5 (Edfou, 627), joint declaration concerning an inheritance; *P.KRU* 77 (Thebes, 634), will.[32] How are we to explain the appearance of these texts, which pose the thorny problem of the legal status of the Coptic language? It is true that we cannot judge a priori the legal validity of these documents even if they likely were valid. They come only from the Thebaid; does this reflect regional distinctiveness among the notaries? Or the weaker influence of Byzantine power and of Romanization? Or perhaps a deterioration of the judicial system? Should we connect it with the development of jurisdictional power in the church, some of whose bishops in the Thebaid did not speak Greek because they came from monastic circles to which they remained closely tied? In any event, it is noticeable that the acts with the most significant legal implications (sales or exchanges of property) date either to the Persian period (619–629) or to the Arab period (after 642), that is, to times of the weakness or disappearance of Byzantine power.

(3) AFTER 642: THE RISE OF COPTIC IN ALL TYPES OF WRITING

With the end of Byzantine domination as a result of the Arab conquest, Greek lost its exclusive status for legal documents, the number of which in Coptic rapidly increases at the expense of Greek, until Arabization in turn drives Coptic into disuse. Greek nonetheless continued in use until the eighth century (Worp 1984). It must, however, be stressed that, until that point, Coptic legal documents, which in any case owed much of their phraseology to their Greek counterparts, often continued to be preceded (after a Graeco-Arabic protocol) by an invocation and a dating formula in Greek, or at least concluded with a Greek notarial subscription (figure 18.11). This "fossilized" Greek plays, mutatis mutandis, the same role that Latin occupies in a number of documents of an earlier period, giving them an official tone.

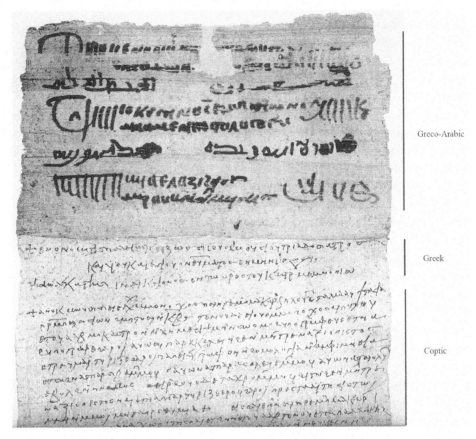

Greco-Arabic

Greek

Coptic

Figure 18.11. The beginning of a Coptic legal text (a release) with a Graeco-Arabic protocol, a Greek invocation, and a dating formula (*P.CLT* 1, 698 CE; Metropolitan Museum of Art, Accession Numbers 24.2.3a–c). Image copyrighted by the Metropolitan Museum of Art.

Some Aspects of Coptic Literacy in Greek

The historical circumstances of late antique Egypt made Greek indispensable in the administrative sphere, the business world, and the liturgy. The Copts were thus pushed toward bilingualism, that is, acquiring some Greek literacy.

Bilingual Education

"Coptic, which was born in bilingual milieus, in its beginning stages was probably taught in conjunction with Greek" (Cribiore 1996, 4). The papyrological documentation has produced numerous witnesses to the combined teaching of Greek and Coptic or to the teaching of Greek in Coptic milieus, at least down to the seventh century (Cribiore 1999).

There is one Graeco-Coptic school text as old as from the end of the third century (Cribiore 1996, no. 388): a codex of tablets containing, in Greek, among other items, a paraphrase of the *Iliad,* and, in Coptic, Psalm 46:3–10, as well as writing exercises. Whether the library constituted by the codices now in the Bodmer, Chester Beatty, and Montserrat (formerly Barcelona) collections and found not far from Nag Hammadi belonged to a schoolteacher or to a religious body (Fournet 1992, 253; Schubert 2002; Agosti 2002, 80–87), it attests the teaching of Greek and Coptic, along with Latin, in the fourth century. In the same period, in Kellis, the young Matheos was learning the Psalms in both Greek and Coptic (*P.Kell.* V C. 19.13–14). In the following centuries, papyrological evidence becomes more plentiful. Thus, we find the *Sententiae* of Menander, written in Greek and in Coptic (*P.Rain. Unterricht. kopt.* 268, seventh century, and 269, fifth–seventh centuries). The

Figure 18.12. An example of the difference in graphic style between Coptic and Greek in the same document (*O.BawitIFAO* 49, transport order, VII/VIII CE). The framed area is in Greek (cursive with ligatured letters); the rest of the text is written by the same hand in Coptic (capitals without ligatures). Reproduced by permission of the Institut français d'archéologie orientale, Cairo.

monasteries, which attracted people of all ages, varying backgrounds, and unequal literacy, have provided many examples of this double education; thus, in the Theban region, that of Phoibammon (Cribiore 1996, no. 19) or that of Epiphanius (*P.Mon.Epiph.* II 611–620).

To these we must add the lexica, glossaries, and Graeco-Coptic conversation manuals, notably *P.Rain.Unterricht. kopt.* 270 (=*C.Gloss.Biling.* I 15), a Latin-Greek-Coptic manual of the sixth century; the Greek-Coptic lexicon of Dioscoros of Aphroditê (*P.Rain.Unterricht. kopt.* 256, sixth century); and an Old Testament glossary (*P.Rain.Unterricht. kopt.* 257a, third–fourth centuries).

Fluent Literacy

Besides the bilingual letter writers of Kellis, I have already mentioned the bilingual notaries (e.g., Dioscoros of Aphroditê; Paul of This). These notaries were proficient in not merely two languages but two scripts as well: They were in effect capable of switching from one language to the other, fluently employing the writing style appropriate to each (from the fifth–sixth century on, Greek was more cursive than Coptic) (figure 18.12). In addition, when they drew up a contract in Greek they were aware of the problems of bilingualism and its possible limits in their clients. To avoid misunderstanding, they did not hesitate to translate certain Greek technical terms, glossing them with the appropriate Coptic word, introduced by ἤτοι "that is" (e.g., *P.Münch.* I 11.27: τοῦ ὑποπεσ‹σ›ίου ἤτοι χρηρε, "the cubbyhole under the staircase, or *khrere*"; cf. Sijpesteijn 1992, 242; Torallas Tovar 2004, 170).

Deficient Literacy

Coptophone writers frequently betray themselves by their handwriting (e.g., in unligatured uncials), their Copticization of personal or Egyptian geographical names, introducing Coptic letters, or replacing Greek terminations (–ος by –ε, for example), their untimely insertions of Coptic words, and their phonetic mistakes such as the confusion of consonants (e.g., mixing voiceless and voiced consonants, replacing ρ with λ in the Fayyum) or of vowels (e.g., ignorance of Greek quantities, variation in the use of vowels because of the tendency of the Coptic system accent to change vowel qualities).[33] Sometimes deficient syntax is the clue. Cases of Copticisms are more doubtful or difficult to distinguish (see, e.g., *P.Ross.Georg.* IV, appendix, p. 99, a letter full of Copticisms, or, in literature, Torallas Tovar 2004, 172).

Illiteracy

As in the Roman period, those illiterate in Greek could avail themselves of various solutions: asking a literate person to write a letter for them or, in the case of legal documents, to subscribe on their behalf with the usual formula: "I, so and so, wrote on his behalf because he does not know how to write."

Translation must have played a more important role than our documentation allows us to see. In contracts where the main party did not know Greek, the text was translated for him by the notary. We know only two examples in which such a phenomenon is expressly signaled:

- *P.Münch.* I 13.71 (Syene, 594), a sale contract entered into by two women with Egyptian names (Tsônê and Tseure), who declare at the end that they agree with the text "after it had been read to us and translated into Egyptian."
- *P.Lond.* I 77.69 (p. 231) (Hermonthis, ca. 600), the will of Bishop Abraham, mentioned earlier, which ends with the statement that "everything was translated into Egyptian for me by the notary named below."

It is obvious that in most cases this formula was omitted even though translation had occurred. That went without saying.

Public offices also needed translation in order to publicize certain texts. Thus, an order by the duke of the Thebaid on payments to officials had to be "translated into the vernacular language and posted" (*P.Cair.Masp.* I 67031.16, sixth century). Here we see the administration taking account of the linguistic limitations of its population, something that contradicts the popular image of a haughty imperial power that despised the vernacular languages.

One methodological conclusion is unavoidable: Egypt, because of the quantity of its preserved written documentation, is an ideal setting in which to observe the phenomenon of multilingualism. This cannot be understood without taking into account the totality of the written sources in the various languages, each of which illumines a different and complementary facet of its history. The era of a Hellenocentric papyrology has passed, and the papyrologist or historian of Egypt today must dismantle the barriers between the various bodies of material in order to let them converse with one another.

NOTES

1. *Diglossia* means here the coexistence in a single society of two languages distinguished by their *function*—a phenomenon not identical to bilingualism. For the application and development of this concept see Adams (2003, 537–541).

2. For the dates see Altheim-Stiehl (1991, 1992a, 1992b).

3. The few papyri with both Greek and Pehlevi are actually reuses of Greek documents by the Persians.

4. For the first, cf. *CII*, P. 149; for the second, *CII*, P. 140 (with commentary on pp. 23–24).

5. The Latin papyri have been collected in the following corpora: *C.Pap.Lat.* gathered documents and literary texts; *C.Epist.Lat.* is devoted to letters; finally and most important, *Ch.L.A.* assembles texts that contain Latin, whether published or not, by the country of collection. The numbers that I give here are based on the *Heidelberger Gesamt-verzeichnis der griechischen Papyrusurkunden Ägyptens* (http://www.rzuser.uni-heidelberg.de/~gvo/gvz.html): They exclude about 430 texts that are undated or of non-Egyptian provenance (like the papyri of Dura on the Middle Euphrates or the ostraca of Bu Njem in Libya).

6. See Fournet (2003a, 431–446).

7. *P.Abinn.*, *SB* XIV 11380, and perhaps *P.Gen.* I 80, *SB* VI 9605, X 10755, and XX 14954.

8. Here Adams modifies the opposition developed by C. A. Ferguson in his definition of diglossia between low language and high language (Adams 2003, 538). Adams rightly prefers to see Latin as a "super-high" language and Greek as a high language.

9. *SB* XX 14726 (Arsinoite, 399), letter of the pretorian prefect to the governor of Arcadia (accompanying an order in Greek).

10. For example, *PSI* I 112 (316), *P.Lips.* I 44 (324–337), *Ch.L.A.* XVII 657 (436–450), *SB* XX 14606 (425–450), with the end of a rescript that concludes with the autograph signature of Theodosius II.

11. A list of these texts is given in *P.Oxy.* LI, pp. 47–48 and Thomas (1998, 132–134). See also Rochette (1997, 119–120).

12. For example, in *Ch.L.A.* XVIII 660, a list of soldiers of the *ala III Assuriorum* (326 or 329), we read in II 2: *prigceps I turmηs* in place of *princeps I turmae* (cf. Adams 2003, 618–621).

13. The graph is based on the *Leuven Database of Ancient Books*, http://ldab.arts.kuleuven.be/ldab_text.php.

14. Byzantine notarial signatures are collected by Diethart and Worp (1986). Kramer (1984, 1382) studies those in Latin letters briefly.

15. Collected in *C.Gloss.Biling.*

16. The volumes of Coptic documentary papyri are included in the *Checklist* (http://scriptorium.lib.duke.edu/papyrus/texts/clist.html). There is also now the *Banque de don-nées des textes coptes documentaires* by Alain Delattre (http://dev.ulb.ac.be/philo/bad/copte/base.php?page=accueil.php). The Leuven Database of Ancient Books now includes Coptic literary papyri. For Coptic literature see Krause (1980) and Orlandi (1998). An electronic corpus of Coptic manuscripts is being developed under the direction of T. Orlandi (http://rmcisadu.let.uniroma1.it/~cmcl/).

17. Greek words in Coptic documentary texts have been collected by Förster (2002; 914 pages).

18. In parentheses I give the abbreviations used in the dictionary of Crum (1939).

19. The ecumenical council of Chalcedon (451), by condemning the theological positions of Dioscoros, the bishop of Alexandria, created a schism between partisans of the Chalcedonian creed (supported by the emperor) and those of Dioscoros (anti-Chalcedonians or monophysites).

20. The graphs are based, for the Greek documents, on Habermann (1998, 147) and, for the Coptic, on the *Banque de données des textes coptes documentaires* of Alain Delattre (see note 16).

21. The data in this graph should be considered with some reservation: Many papyri have only approximate dates. Thus, I have interpreted "III/IV" as "third or fourth" rather

than "end of the third, beginning of the fourth." Moreover, many documents were published with no title or only a vague one.

22. Greek texts: *P.Lond.* VI 1913–1919; Coptic: *P.Lond.* VI 1920–1922, and Crum (1927).

23. Greek texts: *P.Neph.* 1–14, 17–42; Coptic: *P.Neph.* 15, 16.

24. Greek texts: *P.Herm.* 7–10, 17, *P.Amh.* II 145 (with signature in Coptic), *P.Lond.* III 981 (p. 241); *SB* XVIII 13612; Coptic texts: *P.Ryl.Copt.* 268–274, 276, and perhaps 275, 292, 301, 310–314, 396, *P.Lond.Copt.* I 1123. On this archive see Zuckerman (1995) and Clackson (2004, 24–25).

25. Palladius, *Historia Lausiaca,* 35, and *Historia monachorum in Aegypto,* 1.

26. Greek texts: *P.Kell.* I (documents and subliterary texts), III (Isocrates), IV (account book), *O.Kellis* (documents), and some literary texts in vol. II (G. 91–94); Coptic texts: *P. Kell.* II and VI (literary), V (documents). It should be noted that some of these texts, although found at Kellis, were sent from the Nile valley.

27. Greek texts: principally *P.Cair.Masp.* I–III, *P.Flor.* I 93, III 279–298, 342, *P.Lond.* V 1660–1718; Coptic texts: see a provisional list in Fournet 2003b, 170–175. For a complete list of the texts composing this archive and the other archives related to it, see Fournet (2008, 307–343). On the Coptic archive of Dioscoros, see Clackson (2004, 25–28).

28. *P.Cair.Masp.* III 67353 recto, copy of the document edited by MacCoull (1985), the first dated Coptic text (569), and *P.Lond.* V 1709. About these texts (and another still unpublished) see Fournet (forthcoming). On the arbitrations, cf. *P.Mich.Aphrod.*

29. This archive also includes an older group (493–557/558), which is indirectly connected to it. Greek texts: *P.Lond.* V 1719–1737, 1846–1850, 1852–1859, 1861, *P.Münch.* I 1–16; Coptic texts: *O.CrumST* 439, *SB Kopt.* III 1293, 1394, 1395, 1666, and perhaps *P.Lond.Copt.* I 446 and *O.CrumST* 116, 423. On the Coptic side of this archive, see Clackson (2004, 28–29).

30. Coptic texts: Krause (1956); Greek text: *P.Lond.* I 77 (p. 231).

31. Greek texts: *P.Par.* 20; 21; 21bis; 21ter, *SB* I 4503–4505; 5285–5287; Coptic texts: *CPR* IV 23; perhaps 83.

32. For the dates of *P.Vat.Copt.,* still unpublished except the first one (Förster and Mitthof 2004), see Bagnall and Worp (2004). On some of these texts, see MacCoull (1997). *P.CrumST* 48 and *O.CrumVC* 5 can be dated owing to their link with *SB* I 5112.

33. See Gignac (1976, 332–333).

BIBLIOGRAPHY

CII = D. Weber, *Ostraca, Papyri, und Pergamente: Textband.* Corpus Inscriptionum Iranicarum. Part 3. Pahlavi Inscriptions. Volume 4. Ostraca and Papyri. Texts I. London 1992; D. Weber, *Berliner Papyri, Pergamente und Leinenfragmente in mittelpersischer Sprache.* Corpus Inscriptionum Iranicarum. Part 3. Pahlavi Inscriptions. Volume 4, Ostraca, and vol. 5, Papyri. London 2003 (photos in J. de Menasce, *Ostraca and Papyri.* Corpus Inscriptionum Iranicarum. Part 3. Pahlavi Inscriptions. Volume 4–5. Ostraca and Papyri. Portfolio I. London 1957).

Mertens-Pack[3] + number = *Catalogue des papyrus littéraires grecs et latins.* http://promethee.philo.ulg.ac.be/cedopal/index.htm.

Van Haelst + number = Van Haelst, J. 1976. *Catalogue des papyrus littéraires juifs et chrétiens*. Paris: Publications de la Sorbonne.

Adams, J. N. 2003. *Bilingualism and the Latin Language*. Cambridge: Cambridge University Press.

Agosti, G. 2002. "Il poemetti del Codice Bodmer e il loro ruolo nella storia della poesia tardoantica." In *Le Codex des Visions*, ed. A. Hurst and J. Rudhardt, 73–114. Geneva: Librairie Droz.

Altheim-Stiehl, R. 1991. "Wurde Alexandreia im Juni 619 n. Chr. durch die Perser erobert? Bemerkungen zur zeitlichen Bestimmung der sāsānidischen Besetzung Ägyptens unter Chosrau II. Parwēz." *Tyche* 6: 3–16.

———. 1992a. "The Sasanians in Egypt: Some Evidence of Historical Interest." *BSAC* 31: 87–96.

———. 1992b. "Zur zeitlichen Bestimmung der sāsānidischen Eroberung Ägyptens: Ein neuer *terminus ante quem* für Oxyrhynchos ist nachzutragen." In *ΜΟΥΣΙΚΟΣ ΑΝΗΡ: Festschrift für Max Wegner zum 90. Geburtstag*, ed. O. Brehm and S. Klie, 5–8. Antiquitas, Reihe 3. Bonn: Habelt.

Bagnall, R. S. 1993. *Egypt in Late Antiquity*. Princeton: Princeton University Press.

———. 2005. "Linguistic Change and Religious Change: Thinking about the Temples of the Fayoum in the Roman Period." In *Christianity and Monasticism in the Fayoum Oasis*, ed. G. Gabra, 11–19. Cairo: American University in Cairo Press.

———, and K. A. Worp. 2004. "Dating the Coptic Legal Document from Aphrodite." *ZPE* 148: 247–252.

Butler, A. J., and P. M. Fraser. 1978. *The Arab Conquest of Egypt and the Last Thirty Years of the Roman Dominion*, 2d ed. Oxford: Clarendon.

Cavenaile, R. 1987. "Le latin dans les milieux chrétiens d'Égypte." *Miscel·lània Papirològica Ramon Roca-Puig*, 103–110. Barcelona.

Clackson, S. J. 2004. "Papyrology and the Utilization of Coptic Sources." In *Papyrology and the History of Early Islamic Egypt*, ed. P. M. Sijpesteijn and L. Sundelin, 21–44. Leiden: Brill.

Cribiore, R. 1996. *Writing, Teachers, and Students in Graeco-Roman Egypt*. American Studies in Papyrology 36. Atlanta: Scholars Press.

———. 1999. "Greek and Coptic Education in Late Antique Egypt." In *Ägypten und Nubien in spätantiker und christlicher Zeit*, ed. S. Emmel, M. Krause, S. G. Richter, and S. Schaten. Vol. 2, 279–286. Wiesbaden: Reichert.

Crum, W. E. 1927. "Some Further Melitian Documents." *JEA* 13: 21–25.

———. 1939. *A Coptic Dictionary*. Oxford: Clarendon.

Daris, S. 1991. *Il lessico latino nel greco d'Egitto*, 2d ed. Estudis de Papirologia i Filologia bíblica 2. Barcelona: Institut de Teologia Fonamental.

Diethart, J. M., and K. A. Worp. 1986. *Notarsunterschriften im byzantinischen Ägypten*, MPER N.S. 16. Vienna: Hollinek.

Förster, H. 2002. *Wörterbuch der griechischen Wörter in den koptischen dokumentarischen Texten*, TU 148. Berlin: De Gruyter.

Förster, H., and F. Mitthof. 2004. "Ein koptischer Kaufvertrag über Anteile an einem Wagen. Edition von P.Vat.Copt. Doresse 1," *Aegyptus* 84: 217–242.

Foss, C. 2002. "The *Sellarioi* and the Other Officers of Persian Egypt." *ZPE* 138: 169–172.

Fournet, J.-L. 1992. "Une éthopée de Caïn dans le *Codex des Visions* de la Fondation Bodmer." *ZPE* 92: 253–256.

——. 1993. "L'inscription grecque de l'église Al-Mu'allaqa." *Bulletin de l'Institut français d'Archéologie Orientale* 93: 237–244.

——. 2003a. "Langues, écritures, et culture dans les *praesidia.*" In *La Route de Myos Hormos: L'armée dans le désert Oriental d'Égypte,* ed. H. Cuvigny, 427–500. Fouilles de L'IFAO 48. Cairo: Institut français d'archéologie orientale.

——. 2003b. "Une lettre copte d'Aphrodité? (Révision de *SB Kopt.* I 290)." In *Études coptes VIII,* ed. C. Cannuyer, 163–175. Lille-Paris: Association francophone de coptologie.

——. 2008. "Liste des papyrus édités de l'Aphrodité byzantine." In *Les archives de Dioscore d'Aphrodité cent ans après leur découverte. Histoire et culture dans l'Égypte byzantine,* ed. J.-L. Fournet, 307–343. Études d'archéologie et d'histoire ancienne. Paris: de Boccard.

——. forthcoming. "Sur les premiers documents juridiques coptes." In *Études coptes XI, Treizième journée d'études (Marseille, 7–9 juin 2007),* ed. A. Boud'hors and C. Louis. Cahiers de la Bibliothèque copte 17. Paris: de Boccard.

Gascou, J. 2000. "Fragment d'un codex juridique du Bas-Empire (P.Strasb. L 9)." In *La codification des lois dans l'Antiquité,* ed. E. Lévy, 285–291. Travaux du CERPEOGA 16. Paris: de Boccard.

Ghiretti, E. 1996. "Note sul bilinguismo greco-latino dell'Egitto romano." *Aevum* 9: 275–298.

Gignac, F. T. 1976. *A Grammar of the Greek Papyri of the Roman and Byzantine Periods.* Vol. 1, *Phonology.* Milan: Istituto editoriale Cisalpino-La Goliardica.

Grohmann, A. 1952. *From the World of Arabic Papyri.* Cairo: Al-Maaref Press.

Habermann, W. 1998. "Zur chronologischen Verteilung der papyrologischen Zeugnisse." *ZPE* 122: 144–160.

Huyse, Ph. 1995. "Die mittelpersische Papyrologie: Fortschritte und Ziel einer jungen Wissenschaft." *Indo-Iranian Journal* 38: 357–367.

Kramer, J. 1984. "Testi greci scritti nell'alfabeto latino e testi latini scritti nell'alfabeto greco: un caso di bilinguismo imperfetto." In *Atti del XVII Congresso Internazionale di Papirologia,* vol. 3, 1377–1384. Naples: Centro internazionale per lo studio dei papiri ercolanesi.

Krause, M. 1956. "Apa Abraham von Hermonthis: Ein oberägyptischer Bischof um 600." Ph.D. Diss., University of Berlin.

——. 1980. "Koptische Literatur." In *Lexikon der Ägyptologie,* vol. 3, 694–728. Wiesbaden: Harrassowitz.

Lewis, N. 1993. "The Demise of the Demotic Document: When and Why." *JEA* 79: 276–281.

MacCoull, L. S. B. 1985. "A Coptic Cession of Land by Dioscorus of Aphrodito: Alexandria meets Cairo." In *Acts of the Second International Congress of Coptic Study,* ed. T. Orlandi and F. Wisse, vol. 7, 159–166. Rome: CIM (=L. S. B. MacCoull, *Coptic Perspectives on Late Antiquity* [Aldershot: Variorum, 1993], no. VII).

——. 1986. "Coptic Egypt during the Persian Occupation: The Papyrological Evidence." *Studi Classici e Orientali* 36: 307–313 (=L. S. B. MacCoull, *Coptic Perspectives on Late Antiquity* [Aldershot: Variorum, 1993], no. XII).

——. 1991. "A Coptic Monastic Letter to Dioscorus of Aphrodito." *Enchoria* 18: 23–25.

——. 1992. "More Missing Pieces of the Dioscorus Archive." In *Actes du IVe Congrès copte,* ed. M. Rassart-Debergh and J. Ries, 104–112. Publications de l'Institut orientaliste de Louvain 41. Louvain-la-Neuve: Université catholique de Louvain, Institut orientaliste.

——. 1993. "The Apa Apollos Monastery of Pharoou (Aphrodito) and Its Papyrus Archive." *Le Muséon* 106: 21–64.

——. 1995. "Further Notes on Interrelated Greek and Coptic Documents of the Sixth and Seventh Centuries." *Cd'É* 70: 341–353.

——. 1997. " Dated and Datable Coptic Documentary Hands before A.D. 700." *Le Muséon* 110: 349–366.

Mertens, P. 1987. "Les papyrus littéraires latins d'auteurs classiques durant les deux dernières décennies." *Miscel·lània Papirològica Ramon Roca-Puig*, 189–204. Barcelona.

Moscadi, A. 1970. "Le lettere dell'archivio di Teofane." *Aegyptus* 50: 88–154.

Orlandi, T. 1998. "Koptische Literatur." In *Ägypten in spätantik-christlicher Zeit: Einführung in die koptische Kultur*, ed. M. Krause, 117–147. Wiesbaden: Reichert.

Osing, J. 1998. *Hieratische Papyri aus Tebtynis*, vol. 1. Copenhagen: Carsten Niebuhr Institute.

Quagebeur, J. 1982. "De la préhistoire de l'écriture copte." *Orientalia Lovaniensia Periodica* 13: 125–136.

Richter, T. S. 2002. *Rechtsemantik und forensische Rhetorik: Untersuchung zu Wortschatz, Stil, und Grammatik der Sprache koptischer Rechtsurkunden*. Kanobos 3. Leipzig: Wodtke und Stegbauer. Reprinted with a new introduction, Wiesbaden: Harrassowitz, 2008.

Rochette, B. 1990. "Les traductions grecques de l'*Énéide* sur papyrus: Une contribution à l'étude du bilinguisme gréco-romain au Bas-Empire." *Études Classiques* 58: 333–346.

——. 1996. "Papyrologica bilinguia Graeco-latina." *Aegyptus* 76: 57–79.

——. 1997. *Le latin dans le monde grec: Recherches sur la diffusion de la langue et des lettres latines dans les provinces hellénophones de l'Empire romain*. Collection Latomus 233. Brussels: *Latomus*.

——. 1999. "Écrire en deux langues: Remarques sur le mixage des écritures grecque et latine d'après les papyrus littéraires bilingues d'auteurs classiques." *Scriptorium* 53: 325–334.

Sänger, P. 2008. "Saralaneozan und die Verwaltung Ägyptens unter den Sassaniden." *ZPE* 164: 191–208.

Schubert, P. 2002. "Contribution à une mise en contexte du *Codex des Visions*." In *Le Codex des Visions*, ed. A. Hurst and J. Rudhardt, 19–25. Geneva: Librairie Droz.

Sijpesteijn, P. J. 1992. "The Meanings of ἤτοι in the Papyri." *ZPE* 90: 241–250.

Thomas, J. D. 1998. "P.Ryl. IV 654: the Latin Heading," *Cd'É* 73: 125–134.

Torallas Tovar, S. 2004. "Egyptian Lexical Interference in the Greek of Byzantine and Early Islamic Egypt." In *Papyrology and the History of Early Islamic Egypt*, ed. P. M. Sijpesteijn and L. Sundelin, 163–198. Leiden: Brill.

Turner, E. G. 1961. "Latin versus Greek as a Universal Language: The Attitude of Diocletian." In *Language and Society: Essays Presented to Arthur M. Jensen on His Seventieth Birthday*, 165–168. Copenhagen: Berlingske.

Van Minnen, P. 1994. "The Roots of Egyptian Christianity." *APF* 40: 71–85.

Weber, D. 1991. "Ein bisher unbekannter Titel aus spätsassanidischer Zeit?" In *Corolla Iranica: Papers in Honour of Prof. Dr. David Neil MacKenzie on the Occasion of His 65th Birthday*, ed. R. E. Emmerick and D. Weber, 228–236. New York: P. Lang.

——. 1992a. "Pahlavi Papyri Revisited." In *Proceedings of the XIXth International Congress of Papyrology*, vol. 2, 493–508. Cairo: Ain Shams University.

——. 1992b and 2003. cf. *CII*.

Wipszycka, E. 1992. "Le nationalisme a-t-il existé dans l'Égypte byzantine?" *Journal of Juristic Papyrology* 22: 83–128 (=E. Wipszycka, *Études sur le christianisme dans l'Égypte de l'Antiquité tardive*. Studia Ephemeridis Augustinianum 52. Rome: Studia Ephemeridis Augustinianum, 1996, I.1).

Worp, K. A. 1984. "Studien zu spätgriechischen, koptischen und arabischen Papyri." *Bulletin de la Société d'Archéologie Copte* 26: 99–107.

Wouters, A. 1988. *The Chester Beatty Codex Ac. 1499: A Graeco-Latin Lexicon on the Pauline Epistles and a Greek Grammar.* Leuven-Paris: Peeters.

Zuckerman, C. 1995. "The Hapless Recruit Psois and the Mighty Anchorite, Apa John." *BASP* 32: 183–194.

CHAPTER 19

ARABIC PAPYRI AND ISLAMIC EGYPT

PETRA M. SIJPESTEIJN

INTRODUCTION: A HISTORY OF ARABIC PAPYROLOGY

Although they borrowed their words for it from the Greek—*bardī, abardī, fāfīr,* and *chartis* (transformed into *qirṭās*)—the Arabs enjoyed a long-standing acquaintance with papyrus and its singular benefits. As references in the Qur'ān (Q 6:7, 91) and in pre-Islamic and early Arab poetry show, papyrus (presumably imported from Egypt) and other traditional media, such as ostraca, leather, parchment, textiles, stone, and bone, were already fully in use on the Arabian Peninsula in pre-Islamic times. Among the sheets and other writing material used to record God's words as revealed to Muḥammad, later to become the Qur'ān, were certainly also papyri,[1] but none of this material has survived.

Papyrus cultivation and use were unaffected by the Muslim conquest, and Egypt's new rulers even continued to export it to the Byzantine territories and to Italy. Indeed, production was expanded in the ninth century, when plantations were developed in Sicily and Iraq, the latter presumably to feed the ever-expanding bureaucratic appetite of the Abbasid chancellery in the caliphal capital, Baghdad.[2] And just as the Muslims adopted pre-Islamic administrative habits, so they also took on pre-Islamic languages: Not only did papyrus itself continue to be used as before, but Greek was maintained in both the official and the private spheres at least until the end of the eighth century and Coptic until the eleventh (*CPR* XXII, introduction).[3]

The first two known Arabic papyri date to a mere twenty-two years after Muḥammad's *hijra* from Mecca to Medina in 622 CE; written during the conquest of Egypt, they record deliveries of matériel to the conquering Arab armies.[4] From that moment on, Arabic papyri appear in steadily larger numbers and span the same wide topical range that we know from Greek and Coptic documents.

Not until the introduction of paper making, which was allegedly brought about by the capture of Chinese paper makers at the battle of Talāz in 751 (Bloom 2001, 42–45), did the ascendancy of papyrus face a significant challenge. By the early tenth century, although papyrus continued to be used in Iraq, paper began to supersede it, as paper mills began springing up in Damascus, Tiberias, and Tripoli; by the twelfth century, they had spread to Morocco and Spain as well (Grohmann 1952, 53). The first paper documents found in Egypt date between 796 and 816,[5] but here the papyrus industry continued into the second half of the eleventh century, when the last dated papyri were written.[6] The last papyri preserved in Italy are from the same period.[7]

Although Arabic papyri are well represented in papyrus collections around the world, the study of Arabic papyrology is younger and less well developed than that of its Graeco-Roman counterparts, having been launched only in 1824, when a small sealed jar containing three Arabic papyrus texts was found near the Saqqāra pyramid by a team of French excavators. With the publication of two of these papyri a year later by Silvestre de Sacy (1758–1838), the discipline of Arabic papyrology was born (1825, 1831).

Even though no archaeological missions were dispatched solely to search for Arabic papyri, like those that resulted in the great discoveries of Greek papyri at the end of the nineteenth and the beginning of the twentieth century, Arabic papyri nonetheless found their way into most of the world's major papyrus collections, and today there are some exclusively *Arabic* papyrus collections (Sijpesteijn 2003, 2006; Grohmann 1952). Altogether an estimated 150,000 are extant today (including parchment and paper documents that in some cases date into the modern period), and more are being unearthed every year (Sijpesteijn 2006; Rāghib 1996, 2). The major caches, however, have come from only a handful of sites in Egypt (e.g., the Fayyum, Ihnās (Herakleopolis), Ashmūnayn (Hermopolis), Akhmīm (Panopolis), Edfu (Apollonopolis Magna), and Ishqaw (Aphrodito)), while some Arabic papyri and ostraca have also come to light in Fusṭāṭ. Outside Egypt, significant finds have been made in the Negev desert (*P.Ness.* III) and in Khirbet Mird near the Dead Sea (*P.Mird*), as well as outside Damascus and in Samarrāʾ in Iraq (Grohmann 1952, 11).

After the 1824 texts, Silvestre de Sacy published two more Arabic papyri (1833), but thereafter no substantial work was conducted for some fifty years, until the arrival of two of Arabic papyrology's greatest practitioners: Joseph Karabacek (1845–1918) and Adolf Grohmann (1887–1967). Karabacek's name is connected in particular with the papyrus collection of Archduke Rainer at Vienna, of which he served as director. Grohmann edited Arabic papyri from many collections in Europe and Egypt and also wrote several Arabic papyrological handbooks (e.g. *P.Cair.Arab.* I–VI, 1952, 1966). Other names of note from this "golden age" include C. H. Becker (1876–1933), who published some important early papyri from the correspondence of the governor Qurra b. Sharīk (in office 709–715), and several historical studies based on these texts (*P.Heid.Arab.* I, 1902–1903, 1906, 1911). In England, another important name from this period is that of D. S. Margoliouth (1858–1940), who worked mostly with manuscripts and published an edition of the Arabic papyri preserved at the Manchester University library (*P.Ryl.Arab.*). These "founding fathers," however, left few successors, and the discipline had to wait until the 1950s before their legacy bore fruit in the work of, most notably, Claude Cahen (1909–1991), Albrecht Dietrich (1912–), G. Levi Della Vida (1886–1967), and Nabia Abbott (1897–1981).

Again around thirty years passed before a third generation of Arabic papyrologists emerged to pick up the torch. Although continuing to focus on texts, this third wave has been characterized by two new developments: the systematic use of Arabic papyri for linguistic studies and the gathering of texts according to themes, which had been done to some extent before, especially to reaggregate archives, but on a much less ambitious scale. With the work of Gladys Frantz-Murphy (1944–) (*CPR* XXI), Werner Diem (1944–) (*P.Vindob.Arab.* I–V; *CPR* XVI), Geoffrey Khan (1958–) (1990, 1994), Raif Georges Khoury (1936–), and Yūsuf Rāghib (1941–) (*P.Marchands* I, II, III, V/1; *P.Vente*), Arabic papyrology in the early twenty-first century seems finally to have achieved sustainable momentum.

The issue of training for Arabic papyrologists is also receiving welcome attention. With the founding of the International Society for Arabic Papyrology (ISAP) in 2001, the conferences and workshops it organizes, and the initiatives it supports, progress has been made in setting Arabic papyrology on the road to becoming an established and recognized discipline (http://www.ori.unizh.ch/isap.html). The ISAP has organized Arabic papyrology workshops in Europe, and online Arabic papyrological training is offered at the University of Zurich's Arabic papyrology school (http://orientx.unizh.ch:8080/aps_test_2/home/index.jsp). The multilingual diversity of the early Islamic world is also being addressed through cross-disciplinary initiatives and studies as Arabic papyrology builds bridges to other fields and scholars become increasingly alert to the advantages of studying contemporary documents together, even if written in different languages.

The incorporation of documents written on paper, parchment, leather, and other materials makes the chronological boundaries of Arabic papyrology difficult to draw. While acknowledging the specific skills involved and the knowledge necessary to read papyri (as opposed, for example, to Mamlūk paper documents), all documents—from Andalusia to Khurasan—written before the arrival of the Ottomans in Egypt in 1517 are generally considered to belong to the field of Arabic papyrology.[8] The *Checklist of Arabic Documents* (http://www.ori.unizh.ch/isap/isapchecklist.html) accordingly reflects the wider chronological and geographical limits of the Arabic documents. For practical purposes, however, I have concentrated on papyrus documents from Egypt.

READING AND PUBLISHING ARABIC TEXTS

Besides the problems well known to papyrologists of all times and places—the damaged, fragmentary state of the papyri and the lack of archaeological and historical context for most documents—Arabic papyrology has labored under additional challenges.

First are philological peculiarities that demand special technical attention. Arabic papyri and paper documents do not use diacritical dots in the same systematic manner as do printed texts, thereby making decipherment often extremely difficult. Vowel signs are also absent, and the letter *hamza* is generally not written, coinciding with the manuscript tradition. Most orthographic and linguistic peculiarities of the Arabic papyri have been described by Hopkins in his grammar (1984). On top of this, Arabic papyrology still lacks most of the basic hermeneutic tools—such as dictionaries, lexicographical works, and onomastica— that papyrologists rely on in other languages. A crucially important tool for the editing of documents is the expanding Arabic papyrology database, a searchable online database of edited Arabic papyri (http://orientx.unizh.ch:9080/apd/project. jsp), which will be accompanied by a dictionary of terms that appear in the papyri.

The publication of Arabic papyri editions generally follows the "Leiden method" in the use of brackets. Uncertainly read letters cannot be indicated by dots underneath them as is done in Greek papyrology, and even though it has been suggested that horizontal superstrokes be used for this purpose, no generally accepted alternative has been developed as of yet.

Arabic papyrus texts, following late Byzantine practice, are generally written first on the side with vertical fibers, and then on the side with horizontal ones. The text on early Arabic papyri is generally very spaciously arrayed, with large, elongated letters and large spaces between the letters, which sometimes results in words being broken off at the end of the line and continued on the next. From the ninth century on, the script becomes smaller and more cursive and, especially in private letters, can spill over into the upper and side margins, with lines being written perpendicular or even upside down relative to the main text. In later paper documents the lines often curve upward at the end of the page as a result of changed aesthetic conventions. The implications of this evolving layout and the other physical features of the Arabic documents still await full scholarly treatment.

The convention of folding and sealing Arabic papyrus letters continues pre-Islamic practice: The names of the sender and addressee appear on the back side of the written text (or in the top margin of the main text), on the right and left side of the papyrus respectively, with a space in between to allow a string and clay seal to be attached. The layout of the address is continued in later paper letters, when the practice of sealing has been abandoned but when letters still seem to be folded in the same manner. The order of the sender and addressee can be reversed when the addressee is of a higher rank than the sender. The addresses are often accompanied by instructions for delivery of the letter and may mention mosques, churches, markets, and streets by name, as well as houses and shops located in them, thereby providing unique information on the urban structure of towns and villages.

ARABIC LITERARY AND SUBLITERARY PAPYRI

Largely because most Arabic papyrologists have come to the field as historians or linguists, Arabic literary papyri have tended not to receive the same level of attention as documentary texts. Following the pioneering work of Abbott, who edited a wide variety of literary fragments from the Oriental Institute collection at the University of Chicago, David-Weill (1939) and Khoury (1972, 1986) have published some important manuscripts in their entirety. Nevertheless, the number of literary papyri that remain unedited and unstudied is significant, including many that antedate or are completely unknown from the manuscript tradition.[9]

For the Qur'ān, the earliest surviving papyrus fragments come from the eighth–ninth centuries and are datable on the basis of their palaeography to more than a century after the third caliph, 'Uthmān (r. 644–656), compiled the standard-version Qur'ān, according to the Islamic narrative tradition.[10] The absence of any securely datable *maṣḥaf* (copy of the Qur'ān) or fragment thereof from this early period has fuelled discussion about both the date and place of the Qur'ān's formation (Hawting and Shareef 1993), as well as the degree of linguistic and orthographic variation among its early redactions. Qur'ānic verses also appear on amulets and in prayers for private use and are quoted in letters on papyrus and paper, but these are generally difficult to date.

The papyri also preserve other well-known texts, such as the earliest version of a fragment from the *maghāzī rasūl* (the prophet's campaigns) and the *ḥadīth Dāwūd* (actions and words of David), dating to the ninth century.[11] Of the numerous prophetic *ḥadīth* fragments that survive, few have been edited, and many even remain unidentified. Two large early *ḥadīth* collections—those of the Egyptian *ḥadīth* scholars 'Abd Allāh b. Laḥī'a (d. 790) (Khoury 1986) and Ibn Wahb (d. 812) (David-Weill 1939)—have been preserved on a ninth-century papyrus roll and codex, respectively. In these early versions, one can trace the development of *isnāds* (chains of transmitters) and the structure of the stories told in them, especially where it is possible to compare these with later sources. The processes of ordering and categorizing traditions, the formation of the canonical *ḥadīth* collections, and especially the process by which certain *ḥadīths* were excluded can all be traced through the papyri and suggest promising lines of inquiry.

Other important literary survivals are the earliest fragment of the *Thousand and One Nights* on paper (Abbott 1949) and the earliest preserved Arabic astronomical text on a ninth-century papyrus.[12] Poetry is represented by a large unedited panegyric for the prophet's son-in-law and nephew, the fourth caliph, 'Alī (r. 656–61), and verses from an ode by Dhū al-Rummah (d. 735–736), now housed in the University of Michigan and Oriental Institute (Abbott 1972, doc. 7). Significant fragments of historical, grammatical, and legal works have also been preserved on papyrus (Abbott 1957, 1967, 1972).

Of the many scribal exercises preserved in papyrus collections, only a few have so far been published (e.g., *CPR* XVI 35), despite the rich potential of these documents to provide important insights into the school systems of the time, the levels of literacy prevalent, and the kinds of texts deemed culturally valuable or educationally suitable. Of a related nature, we also have what seem to be aides-mémoire for public presentations or notes written down at lectures, offering an interesting insight into how the Islamic emphasis on mnemonic retention and oral transmission was adapted for practicability.

In addition, literary fragments, along with autograph manuscripts, through their deletions, repetitions, and corrections, often open a valuable window onto the processes of writerly practice, as well as the time and circumstances of composition. Scribal mistakes, such as the accidental loss of identical adjacent syllables (haplology), erroneous repetition of a word, phrase, or combination of letters (dittography), and writing once what should be written twice (haplography), all shed light on the process of copying manuscripts, while marginal notes and corrections offer hints about collocation with earlier manuscripts or verification by an authoritative teacher or author.

Also well represented in papyrus collections, amulets and private prayers are another genre of texts that is still in need of proper scholarly attention.[13] A detailed study of amulets could tell us much about chronological changes in the popularity of certain religious customs, as well as the interaction between so-called popular cults and official rites and between the three monotheistic faiths. Medical recipes and requests for medicines similarly offer insights into medical practice (e.g., *CPR* XVI 24; Dietrich 1954).

When studied together, literary texts have much to offer on textual production and consumption, as well as issues of literacy and the circulation of literary works. And even small fragments can be useful here by offering clues, mapping their finding places to regional preferences, and supplying evidence on the relationship between codices and rolls as media for literary production—topics about which hardly anything is known from the Islamic period (Grohmann 1966, 65–67).

THE ISLAMIC NARRATIVE TRADITION

Medieval Islam is blessed with an exceptionally deep and well-developed store of narrative sources—the countless Arabic chronicles, legal, religious, and literary works that have long shaped our view of this period. It is the interplay and exchange with this parallel body of material, as well as the potential it creates for the Arabic papyri to provide a check or control on its evidence, that gives Arabic papyrology much of its vitality. But to understand how papyri can complement and enrich the evidence of the Islamic narrative tradition, we need first to consider some of the specific historiographical problems inherent in that tradition.

The canonical Islamic historical works, while based on earlier oral and written traditions, make their appearance only at the end of the eighth and the beginning of the ninth century—that is, *two hundred years* after the rise and formation of Islam. This extended time lapse, combined with a cultural emphasis on the oral transmission of historical information, necessarily left its mark on how ideas and events were conceived of and presented. Even more important, by the time these texts were written, notions about the origins and formation of Islam had become formalized and standardized, resulting in a historical orthodoxy that makes alternative narratives very difficult to retrieve.

This process of standardization was further compounded by the homogeneity of historiography's practitioners. Almost exclusively urban, bourgeois, and male, most of them also lived and worked under Islam's second dynasty, the Abbasids. Not only did they absorb and propagate the Abbasid anti-Umayyad prejudice (the Abbasids had seized power from the Umayyads in 750 and moved the caliphal capital from Damascus in Syria to Baghdad in Iraq), but their focus tends to be on the eastern part of the Islamic empire, where most of them were active.

How then can the papyri correct or adjust the view these sources offer?

ARABIC DOCUMENTARY PAPYRI

Historical Events

The clearest cases occur where an historical event described ambiguously in the narrative sources can be checked or corrected against the papyri. The battle of Badr, to take but one example, to which the narrative sources have ascribed contradictory dates, may now be securely placed in Jumāda II of the second year of the hijra (November 623), thanks to a seventh-century papyrus from Palestine (*P.Mird* 71; Cook and Crone 1977, 160n56). Additionally, the papyri can also help us to reassess impressions or perceptions and even wholesale interpretations. For example, papyrological evidence of the diligence and conscientiousness of his administration allows us to revisit the (mostly Abbasid) narrative tradition of the Umayyad governor Qurra b. Sharīk as an unjust tyrant (Sundelin 2004, 8, where earlier references can be found).

Language and Script

Despite the attempts of early papyrologists to link them, the writing of the papyri does not fit the canon of seven well-balanced scripts famously ascribed to Ibn Muqla (d. 990); while parallels between the script of the papyri and that used for chancellery documents and bookhands can be determined in individual cases, the palaeography of the documents in general follows its own path, and a detailed and well-chronicled study of Arabic palaeography in the documents is still lacking.[14] Nevertheless, thanks to the probings into Arabic orthography of Simon Hopkins (1950–) (1984) and Werner Diem (1979–1981), among others, we now have a fairly detailed picture of the papyri's "Middle Arabic" and, through its mistakes and hypercorrections, some idea of the spoken language of the time (Hopkins 1984).[15]

Language in a more general sense and in particular multilingualism also help us to understand the process of Arabization. The continued use of Greek and Coptic in the administration (discussed later) contradicts the assertion in the Arabic narrative sources that the Caliph ʿAbd al-Malik (r. 685–705) imposed the exclusive use of Arabic on the chancellery in the year 700 (Balādhurī, *Futūḥ al-buldān*, 193), an order said to have been implemented in Egypt by his governor, ʿAbd Allāh (in office 705–709) in 706 (Kindī, *Kitāb al-Wulāt*, 58–59). The first known Arabic documents are all related to the administration and appear in bilingual papyri together with Greek translations. They also continue the Byzantine practice of having each papyrus roll start with a thicker sheet that gives the names of the reigning emperor, the governor, and sometimes the financial director under whom the roll was produced, as well as the date of manufacture and name of the papyrus mill. The earliest bilingual Arabic-Greek document of this type was found in Nessana and mentions (in place of the emperor) Caliph Muʿāwiya (r. 661–680); the first entirely Arabic protocols do not appear until 732.[16] Again, the continued use of Greek in protocols runs counter to the tradition preserved in Arabic narrative sources that ʿAbd al-Malik, angered over the "Coptic" practice (not, incidentally, corroborated by the papyri) of putting a cross and the name of Christ at the top of protocols, replaced these with Arabic religious phrases (Balādhurī, *Futūḥ al-buldān*, 240). Other bilingual administrative documents include a receipt written in 643 for sixty-five sheep delivered to an Arab army unit; the late seventh-century demand notes for oil and wheat found in Nessana; and demand notes for workers, food, and other products for the Muslim rulers from the governorship of Qurra b. Sharīk (in office 709–715).[17]

Entirely Arabic documents increase in number from the first quarter of the eighth century on. Even though Greek and Coptic documents continued to be produced in large quantities, as discussed earlier, the tenth-century apocalypse of Samuel of Qalamūn (Ziadeh 1915–1917) provides evidence that an increased use of Arabic was considered a threat to the native Egyptian language. Just what influence Arabic writings had on the use of Greek and Coptic is, however, not clear. In some tenth-century legal documents from Tebtynis in the Fayyum, one of the parties to the transaction has the contents "explained in the foreign language," presumably Coptic.[18] The last datable Coptic documents are a series of legal documents, letters, and lists of the eleventh century.[19] While Coptic continued to be used as a liturgical language, Christian literary production, including the Bible, switched to Arabic from the tenth century on.

Arabization can also be traced through the phenomenon of *linguistic interference*. The use of Arabic loanwords and expressions in Coptic texts is attested in documents from the seventh century on but was insignificant until the ninth century and remained mostly limited to technical administrative and medicinal terms (Richter 2004, 107–112). Arabic, by contrast, shows a steady development from the importation of Greek words (often via Coptic immediately following the conquest) to the introduction of Persian words in the Abbasid period, when Persian officials arrived in Egypt.[20] In the Islamic period certain pre-Islamic Greek honorifics continued to be used for Christian and even Muslim officials, though whether this indicates Muslim appropriation or assimilation or perhaps an uninterrupted Greek scribal tradition is unclear. As for place names, at least in the early stages, Greek forms persisted in Arabic texts, though from the eighth century on they began to be replaced by their Coptic variants, which frequently referred to an ancient Egyptian toponym (Grohmann 1959). What these changes from Greek to Coptic/ Egyptian and/or Arabic place names signify deserves to be examined in more depth.

Significant interference is also apparent in the borrowing of Greek terms for Arabic technical, administrative, and managerial concepts, a practice that forces us to ask what this meant for the Egyptian perception of these newly introduced concepts and functions and what this tells us about Arabic rule.[21] The introduction into Arabic of Greek and Latin terms that had been out of use for several centuries in Egypt or had never been part of the *Egyptian* Byzantine vocabulary raises further questions about the provenance of Islamic administrative practice.[22]

An Arabic Legal Tradition

The early evolution of Islamic law is notoriously difficult to reconstruct from the Arabic literary sources, where it remains overshadowed by the "classical system" presumed by later jurists to have existed from Islam's beginning. The development of Islamic law and its relation to its predecessors, however, is not totally lost; it can be traced to some extent through the development of Arabic legal terminology.

Ignored by the narrative sources, this subject touches upon topics of integration, conversion, Arabization, immigration, and authority.

The earliest Arabic papyri reflect a legal system different from indigenous Egyptian practice (Khan 1994, 2005). A similar distinction between the local and newly introduced Arab legal tradition can be observed in Umayyad and early Abbasid documents found in the eastern Islamic empire in Sogdia and Bactria (Khan 1994, 2007). In bilingual Greek-Arabic documents, the Arabic is not a translation of the Greek portion, but has instead its own features and traditions, and a different scribe is named at the end of the Greek and the Arabic texts. In the ninth century, however, Arabic papyri begin to exhibit influences from the local, Greek/Coptic legal practice, with expressions and words originating in the eastern Islamic Empire, and witnessed there in earlier documents, starting to find their way into the documents (Khan 2005).

Behind these issues lies the larger question of the relationship between legal theory and practice, for which the documents again offer uniquely useful evidence. In Islamic law, for example, documents do not constitute evidence (cf. Q 2: 282), but as their ubiquity shows, they were obviously an essential force in day-to-day business and transactions of all sorts. This raises questions about how documents acquired contractual force in an environment of minimal enforceability, how written records functioned in a largely oral society, and how those with low levels of literacy interacted with the judicial and bureaucratic system. Other documents reveal how certain legal prohibitions, such as the ban on usury, were circumvented by permissible legal transactions, such as future sale (*CPR* XXVI 17, introduction).

For a later period, Christian and Jewish legal documents written in (Judeo-) Arabic use the same formulas as Islamic ones, even though they are sometimes drawn up according to different legal principles (cf. Abbott 1941). This process of reciprocal influence on the formulas of the papyrus documents needs to be examined in more detail, as it does for extralegal documents, such as official and private letters, and tied in with what we know about historical events and circumstances.[23]

Administrative History

One of the most vexing questions about early Islamic administration is the degree of bureaucratic and administrative sophistication and experience that the Arabs brought to their empire and, by extension, the degree of continuity and change in the conquered provinces. Straightforward numerical insufficiency on the conquerors' part ruled out a top-to-bottom restaffing of the Byzantine administration and meant that only the highest central offices were at least initially taken over by Muslims. The continuity in administrative personnel at the lower levels of the administration, necessary to ensure the uninterrupted collection of tax revenues, also accounts for the overwhelming sense of continuity in the daily life of the indigenous population that comes through in the documents. Nevertheless, this continuity should not be allowed to conceal certain important changes that also took place.

Not only were the administrative districts reorganized (Sijpesteijn 2007b), but within a generation of their takeover, the Arab conquerors imposed the collection of a poll tax, an adaptation of the Qur'ānic *jizya* (Q 9: 29) but framed according to the new Greek term *andrismos* (*CPR* XXII 1). We should probably view this melding of selective change and underlying continuity not as an Arab failure to offer an alternative to the Byzantine system but rather as an intentional and focused adaptation of the system to the conquerors' own needs and traditions (Sijpesteijn 2007a, 2007b, forthcoming-a). Bureaucracy, indeed, seems to have been an area of special interest to the Arabs, as the net increase in administrative documents that resulted from the conquest amply testifies.

The documentary legacy of the Arab army is thinner than for prior armies that came through Egypt, though perhaps much has been lost beneath Fusṭāṭ, the Muslim-founded garrison town where it was initially stationed (south of the center of modern Cairo). Greek and bilingual Arabic-Greek papyri list the special deliveries of fodder, food, clothes, horses, and other supplies to units moving up the Nile or stationed in the Egyptian countryside (*CPR* VIII; *SB* VII 9748–9760). Other Arabic documents indicate how the system of soldiers' payments was organized (Morimoto 1994). Seniority in Islam and experience in battle determined the ranking on the *dīwān* (register of state pensions), which specified the payments to soldiers and their families, a system seemingly new to the Byzantine and Sassanian regions. Records of the soldiers and their families who were eligible for a stipend were kept by officials sent to the garrisons to keep track of births, deaths, and the arrivals of newcomers (Maqrīzī, *Khiṭaṭ*, 1, 252; Kindī, *Kitāb al-Wulāt*, 86). One seventh-to-eighth-century list of houses in Fusṭāṭ and the individuals living in them might be related to the *dīwān* recordkeeping (Sijpesteijn 2008b). From Qurra b. Sharīk's letters to the pagarch of Ishqaw/Aphrodito, which date to the early eighth century, we know much more about how Egyptian communities contributed supplies, labor, and technical skills to the Muslim army and fleet, as well as the other public activities of the caliph in Damascus and the governor in Fusṭāṭ (*P.Lond.* IV; *P.Heid.Arab.* I).

These letters originate, however, fifty years after the conquest, when economic and ideological factors had effected profound changes in the Islamic social and administrative structure in Egypt. From the end of the seventh and the beginning of the eighth century, Christian officials started being replaced by Muslims at the level of the pagarchy, whereas at the village level indigenous Christians retained their authority. At the same time, the Muslim authorities in Egypt initiated several large-scale land surveys and censuses aimed at improving their knowledge of the country's landholdings and increasing their tax take as recorded in the papyri (Abbott 1965; *CPR* XXI 55). These developments were part of an empirewide program to increase the Muslim presence in the administration and to Islamicize the administration (Sijpesteijn 2007b; forthcoming-a). We have some indication of the reaction this caused from a papyrus that bears witness to the first Christian uprising (Bell 1945); another late seventh-century letter encourages the inhabitants of Nessana to organize a tax protest against the new Muslim rulers in the area (*P.Nessana* III 75).

Later documents are equally important for examining the day-to-day functioning of Muslim rule in Egypt and the development of the administrative structures that underlay it. Petitions show the channels open to citizens for redress against corrupt officials and rulers (Khan 1990; *P.Khalili* I 16), hence the many threats of punishment that the Umayyad governor Qurra b. Sharīk addresses to lower officials who were abusing taxpayers or allowing others to do so (*P.Qurra; P.Heid. Arab.* II).

Conversion and Religious Practice

The relationship between Arabization and conversion is another issue for which the papyri can be very helpful. Onomastics has been used to trace the process of acculturation in pre-Islamic Egypt and for Islamization in medieval Iraq and could also be used for similar research on Islamic Egypt.[24] The differences between Arabic and Islamic names, between Christian and Muslim Arabic variants of the same name (e.g., Yaḥyā and Yuḥannis), and the presence of Muslims with non-Muslim parental names can all be drawn upon in this regard. Some caution, however, is required, as it is not clear how consciously names were chosen and whether an Arabic or even a Muslim name signifies a sense of Arab or Muslim identity or whether it represents merely an attempt to join the new ruling class. These problems are well illustrated by a Coptic letter written between two correspondents with Muslim names and contemporary Arabic letters written or received by men bearing Christian names.[25] A related problem involves the privileges that were associated with conversion in this early period. The literary sources are not conclusive about the degree to which converts in practice enjoyed the rewards that the law prescribed for conversion: release from the poll tax, a lower agricultural tax rate, and inclusion on the *dīwān*. The papyri add to the complexity, but unlike the narrative sources, they have the potential, through their anchoring in time and place, to give more detailed information.

Islamic religious practice (as well as the practice of other religions), the celebration of festivals, and the expression of religious duties are all generously illuminated by the papyri. From the earliest Arabic dated document, in which the sheep received from the town of Ihnās are described as "fifty for slaughtering and fifteen other sheep" (*SB* VI 9576) to the ninth-century letter in which the sender asks the addressee to buy a sacrificial animal for the Great Offering Feast after Ramaḍān (Rāghib 1980, no. 19), we learn about the practicalities of daily religious life. In a late seventh-century letter, the addressee is invited to join the sender on the caliph's pilgrimage caravan and urged to bring camels for the trip.[26] Other documents written during the pilgrimage give background information and contemporary color to the travel accounts preserved in narrative sources.

We can also see from the papyri how Islam's religious and legal institutions interacted with local practices and historical conditions from the everyday experience of the Christians, Muslims, and Jews living under its rule. Unlike the narrative sources, moreover, the papyri have the special advantage of being relatively free of moralizing judgments in their treatment of minority behaviors. In a ninth–tenth century complaint to the governor about a prayer leader who has introduced innovations in the prayer and has even brought a bottle of date wine into the mosque, the writer asks the governor to take his responsibility as supervisor of religious morals seriously and replace the wrongdoer (Rāghib 1978, no. 5).

Information about how the execution of the Muslim religious duty of giving alms could range from a state-collected and -distributed tax to a personal expression of piety is an especially useful illustration of Islam's evolution and adaptability (Sijpesteijn 2007c). Petitions from prisoners beseeching the sender's intercession or from a "poor man who has nothing, not little nor much," as well as lists of widows, orphans, and poor people receiving alms, all help to show us how the duty to distribute alms functioned in practice (e.g., Jahn 1937, no. 7; *P.Khalili* I 1).

The papyri also tell us about the process of Muslim appropriation of local religious practices, cultic places, and religious ideas—in short, about the Islamization of the Egyptian landscape. A late seventh-century letter records the visit of a number of Muslims at Saint Catherine's monastery in the Sinai (*P.Ness.* III 72, 73, dated 683 or 684?).

Commerce and Production

While the papyri generally have a rather narrow geographical scope, citing mostly Egyptian place names, the earliest Arabic commercial letter was written from somewhere in North Africa to a town in Upper Egypt (Rāghib 1991). Other documents add to our understanding of how Egypt engaged the Mediterranean economic system and how commercial contacts with East Asia via the larger Islamic empire increased after the Arab conquest (Sijpesteijn 2004a). Thus, while Alexandria's status as the primary city in Egypt is generally believed to have declined dramatically after the Muslim conquest, an early eighth-century letter indicates that it was still an important focus of activity for Fayyum merchants, presumably because it was connected to overseas markets, as was also the case in the medieval period (Sijpesteijn 2004b; Udovitch 1996).

While a detailed study of prices for transport, goods, and services has been written on the basis of the later medieval Geniza documents (Ashtor 1969), nothing comparable exists for the earlier period, although various documents contain a wealth of information on this topic. The well-developed commercial structures that greased the wheels of economic life, such as checks and bills of credit (*suftaja, ṣaḥīfa*), legal institutions such as partnerships, and transport networks are well known from narrative sources. But it is the documents that tell us how these worked "on the ground"—their safety, effectiveness, and availability—and portray the importance of trading on credit versus a money economy (Udovitch 1970).

Two mercantile archives demonstrate the potential of this material. The first consists of about one hundred letters and legal documents related to a ninth-century family of textile merchants situated in the Fayyum and their partners in Fusṭāṭ (*P.Marchands* I–III).[27] The letters show us how cloth was ordered piecemeal from different weavers in the Fayyum, how clothes and textiles were traded and sold in Fusṭāṭ, and how new orders were filled. Other letters give insights into the private lives of these merchant families when they mention requests for financial support from distant family members, the illness or death of relatives, or exchanges between a mother and her son.

The second archive, which comprises at least thirty letters, remains largely unpublished (*P.Berl.Arab.* II 38–43).[28] Also from the ninth century, they deal with trade in wool, soap, textiles, and other household goods. The large amounts of money involved and the extensive commercial network within which these traders operated point to considerable sophistication in terms of both volume and value.

It is from documents such as these that we are also able to see two social groups that played an essential role in medieval economic life but which remain largely invisible in the narrative record. Women, sometimes writing their own documents and sometimes using (female) scribes to do so (*P.Khalili* I 17), appear in a wide range of economic activities from traditional female occupations, such as the domestic textile industry (Rapoport 2005), to commercial partnerships (*P.Khalili* I 21). Their relative freedom, depending on their social and marital status (unmarried, married, widowed), and the way in which their legal and social position changed over time and differed across religious communities all come through in the documents.

The second group is slaves. Slave sale and manumission contracts and inheritance documents show how human property was transferred and traded, by whom, and for what purposes (*P.Vente*; *P.Cair.Arab.* I 37). Contracts that record partnerships in which slaves play a role show their active involvement in the commercial sphere, and the frequent appearance of domestic slaves in documents of all sorts can be contrasted with the overwhelming impression given in the literary sources that all slaves were either musicians or dancing girls.

Rural History

Since most of the Arabic papyri have been found in the Egyptian countryside as opposed to permanently occupied towns, one would expect them to give us an especially good vista onto the organization of the countryside and the nature of rural life.

The reliance on the yearly inundation cycle of the Nile did not diminish under the Muslims, and the papyri contain much information on the organization and maintenance of irrigation systems, such as who was responsible for them (state officials or landowners) and how they were financed (from taxes, private monies, or corvée labor). These lead us directly into one of the central questions of this period: the distribution of power in the countryside—that is, whether the large landowners continued to play the important role they had played in late antique Egypt, how the appearance of Muslim landowners was related to conversion and Arab settlement, and how (or whether) Muslim landholders differed from their Christian counterparts (cf. Banaji 2001, 141–170). A related issue is the determination of who represented and carried out the wishes of the Muslim authorities in the countryside in their attempts to maximize agricultural fiscal income through land surveys, the development of "dead lands," and the supervision of peasants' movements. The fluctuating effectiveness of revenue-raising measures and the different methods applied by the authorities to collect agricultural taxes have been studied by Frantz-Murphy in her collection of agricultural leases and receipts (*CPR* XXI).

Historical events and processes, which might be difficult to trace in the narrative sources, colored as they often are by later discussions, have left a fertile residue in the papyri. The later legal debates about the fiscal status of conquered lands, for example, which supposedly depended on the circumstances of their capture, are difficult to disentangle from the economic and political concerns by which they were obviously influenced (Noth 1973). A change in Egypt's fiscal status effected in the early eighth century is, however, reflected in the agricultural leases and receipts (*CPR* XXI), thereby allowing us to understand the narrative sources better.

The agricultural revolution presumed to have followed in the wake of the Arab conquerors has to be studied in more detail with the aid of the many documents that show us the kinds of produce that grew in Egyptian fields and how this changed in the course of time. The degree to which agricultural production was specialized and what infrastructure and investment was required for such specialization are questions to which the papyri hold the answers. The abundance of material related to the medieval flax and textile trade, for example, would make an exceptionally good case study.

The history of the early Islamic Egyptian countryside is but one topic for which papyri can offer us invaluable new insights. While the importance of papyrological evidence and the light it shines on almost every aspect of life under medieval Islam is now widely acknowledged, the actual use of papyri as a historical source has been slower to take hold. With the development of new tools and infrastructure, however, many of the barriers that hinder students from entering this field are being broken down, and the road is opening on a new level of Islamic historical research.

ACKNOWLEDGMENT

For this chapter I have made extensive use of the following overviews on the study of Arabic papyrology: Sundelin (2004), Grohmann (1952, 1966), and Rāghib (1996).

NOTES

1. The tradition mentions sheets *(riqāʿ)*, shoulder blades *(aktāf)*, and palm branches *(ʿusub)* (Bukhārī, *Ṣaḥīḥ* III 257). The conqueror and first governor of Egypt, ʿAmr b. al-ʿĀṣ (d. 664), allegedly sent papyrus and wheat from Egypt to Medina (Yaʿqūbī, *Taʾrīkh*, vol. 2, 177).

2. The caliph al-Muʿtaṣim (r. 833–842) built a papyrus mill in Samarrāʾ in 836 (Yaʿqūbī, *Tarʾīkh*, II, 577; *Kitāb al-buldān*, 39). Pliny reported that papyrus grew at the Euphrates near Babylon (*NH* 13.11.73). For papyrus growth in Sicily, see Ibn Ḥawqal, *Kitāb ṣūrat al-arḍ*. Cf. Grohmann 1952, 19–21.

3. After the conquest, the use of Coptic as an administrative language actually increased in Upper Egypt, where Greek had never made much of an impact.

4. The first one, *SB* VI 9576, is mentioned later in the chapter; the second is a demand note for taxes paid in coin, of which only a photograph has so far been published (P.Berol. inv. 15002, depicted in Grohmann (1966, Tafel II).

5. A Inv. Chart. Ar. 7161.

6. The last known Arabic papyrus is dated A.H. 480 (1087 CE) and is kept in the John Rylands collection in Manchester (*P.Ryl.Arab.* X no. 10).

7. The latest is a papal bull dated 1057, which is preserved in the Vatican.

8. For the distribution of medieval Arabic leather and paper documents and parchments throughout the Islamic empire, see Khan 2005; Petrosyan et al. 1995, 122–123 (Central Asia); al-Akwaʿ 1985 (Yemen); and Zomeño 2003 (Andalusia).

9. See also the list of early ninth-century literary works preserved in manuscript form on parchment (Rāghib 1996, 3–4).

10. Like Qurʾānic paper and parchment codices (parchment seems to have been the preferred material), these Qurʾāns were also written on pages wider than they are high, a reverse of the later custom (Déroche 1983, 19; 1992).

11. The first two, published by Khoury (1972), are ascribed to *Wahb b. Munabbih* (d. 728) and are currently kept in the Heidelberg papyrus collection.

12. This ninth-century astronomical papyrus, part of a Dutch private collection, remains unpublished.

13. For published amulets on papyrus see Bilabel and Grohmann (1934). For handwritten paper amulets see, for example, Hanafi (2004), and for block-printed ones, see Schaefer (2002).

14. Abbott, Karabacek, Silvestre de Sacy, and Becker are reported as having tried to do so by Khan, who emphasizes the problems of such a method and instead gives a detailed description of the features of the papyrus scripts (*P.Khalili* I, pp. 27–46, esp. 44–46 and note 71).

But see the recent work by Alain George, who has identified a number of papyri that follow chancellery characteristics (2006). For a description of the palaeography of documents, see also Sijpesteijn (2008a).

15. For palaeographical albums see, for example, Moritz (1905); Gruendler (1993); Grohmann (1967, 1971).

16. Grohmann (1960); *CPR* III 1/2, nos. 109–112.

17. *SB* VI 9576; *P.Nessana* III; *P.Heid.Arab.* I; *P.Lond.* IV.

18. Frantz-Murphy (1994).

19. For this so-called Teschlot archive, see Richter (2000).

20. *CPR* XXI; Frantz-Murphy (2007); Rāghib (1991, 8).

21. For example, the terms *symboulos* and *protosymboulos* for governor and caliph, respectively. *P.Lond.* IV 1335.2, commentary.

22. For example, *veredarius* ("fast messenger") reappears in the Islamic period after an absence from the papyrological record for about four centuries (*CPR* XIV 33.2, commentary). See also, for example, the words *cursus* and *andrismos,* which have no Egyptian precedents; cf. Grohmann (1932).

23. See Khan's study of the historical development of petition formulae (1990).

24. For pre-Islamic Egypt, see Bagnall (1982); for Iraq, Bulliet (1994).

25. *CPR* II 228; e.g., *P.Khalili* I 14; Jahn (1937, no. 12).

26. Sijpesteijn (forthcoming-b).

27. *P.Marchands* IV contains twenty-two letters from three ninth-century textile agents.

28. The unpublished material can be found in the University of Michigan and University of Chicago collections. It is being prepared for publication by Yūsuf Rāghib and Petra Sijpesteijn.

BIBLIOGRAPHY

Abbott, N. 1941. "Arabic Marriage Contracts among Copts." *Zeitschrift der Deutschen morgenländischen Gesellschaft* 95: 59–81.

——. 1949. "A Ninth-century Fragment of the *Thousand Nights:* New Light on the Early History of the Arabian Nights." *Journal of Near Eastern Studies* 8: 129–164.

——. 1957. *Studies in Arabic Literary Papyri.* Vol. 1, *Historical Texts.* Chicago: University of Chicago Press.

——. 1965. "A New Papyrus and a Review of the Administration of 'Ubaid Allāh b. al-Ḥabḥ āb." In *Arabic and Islamic Studies in Honor of Hamilton A. R. Gibb,* ed. George Makdisi, 21–35. Leiden: Brill.

——. 1967. *Studies in Arabic Literary Papyri.* Vol. 2, *Qur'ānic Commentary and Traditions.* Chicago: University of Chicago Press.

——. 1972. *Studies in Arabic Literary Papyri.* Vol. 3, *Language and Literature.* Chicago: University of Chicago Press.

Al-Akwā', I. 'A. 1985. "Jāmi' Ṣan'ā' abraz ma'ālim al-ḥaḍāra al-islāmiyya fī al-Yaman." In *Maṣāḥif Ṣan'ā',* ed. Ḥuṣṣa al-Ṣabāḥ. Kuwait: Dār al-āthār al-Islāmiyya.

Ashtor, E. 1969. *Histoire des prix et des salaires dans l'Orient médiéval.* Paris: SEVPEN.

Bagnall, R. 1982. "Religious Conversion and Onomastic Change in Early Byzantine Egypt." *BASP* 19: 105–124.

Balādhurī. (d. 892). *Futūḥ al-buldān*, ed. M. J. de Goeje. 1866; repr., 1992, Leiden. In *The Origins of the Islamic State*, trans. P. K. Hitti and F. Murgotten. 1916; repr., Piscataway, N.J.: Gorgias Press, 2002.

Banaji, J. 2001. *Agrarian Change in Late Antiquity: Gold, Labour, and Aristocratic Dominance.* Oxford: Oxford University Press.

Becker, C. H. 1902–1903. *Beiträge zur Geschichte Ägyptens unter dem Islam.* Strassburg: K. J. Trübner.

——. 1906. "Arabische Papyri des Aphroditofundes." *Zeitschrift für Assyriologie und verwandte Gebiete* 20: 68–104.

——. 1911. "Neue arabische Papyri des Aphroditofundes." *Der Islam* 2: 245–268.

Bell, H. I. 1945. "An Official Circular Letter of the Arab Period." *JEA* 31: 75–84.

Bilabel, F., and A. Grohmann. 1934. *Griechische, koptische und arabische Texte zur Religion und religiösen Literatur in Ägyptens Spätzeit.* Veröffentlichungen aus den badischen Papyrussammlungen 5. 2 vols. Heidelberg: Verlag der Universitätsbibliothek.

Bloom, J. M. 2001. *Paper before Print: The History and Impact of Paper in the Islamic World.* New Haven, Conn.: Yale University Press.

Bukhārī. 1862–1908. (d. 870). *Ṣaḥīḥ*, ed. L. Krehl. Leiden: Brill.

Bulliet, R. W. 1994. *Islam: The View from the Edge.* New York: Columbia University Press.

Cook, M., and P. Crone. 1977. *Hagarism: The Making of the Islamic World.* Cambridge: Cambridge University Press.

David-Weill, J. 1939. *Le Djāmīʿ dʾ Ibn Wahb.* Textes arabes 3. Cairo: Imprimerie de l'Institut français d'archéologie orientale.

Déroche, F. 1983. *Les manuscrits du Coran: Aux origines de la calligraphie coranique.* Bibliothèque nationale, département des manuscrits, catalogue des manuscrits arabes 2, 1. Paris.

——. 1992. *The Abbasid Tradition: Qurʾāns of the 8th to 10th Centuries* A.D. Nasser D. Khalili Collection of Islamic Art 1. Oxford: Oxford University Press.

Diem, W. 1979–1981. "Untersuchungen zur frühen Geschichte der arabischen Orthographie." *Orientalia* 48: 207–257; 49: 67–106; 50: 332–383; 52: 257–404.

Dietrich, A. 1954. *Zum Drogenhandel im islamischen Ägypten : eine Studie über die arabische Handschrift nr. 912 der Heidelberger Papyrus-Sammlung.* Heidelberg: Carl Winter.

Frantz-Murphy, G. 1994. "Papyrus Agricultural Contracts in the Oriental Institute Museum from Third/Ninth Century Egypt." *Itinéraires d'Orient: Hommages à Claude Cahen, Res Orientalis* 6: 119–131.

——. 2007. "The Economics of State Formation in Early Islamic Egypt." In *From al-Andalus to Khurasan: Documents from the Medieval Islamic World,* ed. P. M. Sijpesteijn, L. Sundelin, S. Torallas Tovar, and A. Zomeño, 101–114. Leiden: Brill.

George, A. 2006. "The Geometry of Early Islamic Calligraphy." Diss. Oxford University.

Grohmann, A. 1932. "Griechische und lateinische Verwaltungstermini im arabischen Aegypten." *CdÉ* 7: 275–284.

——. 1952. *From the World of Arabic Papyri.* Cairo: Al-Maaref Press.

——. 1959. *Studien zur historischen Geographie und Verwaltung des frühmittelalterlichen Ägypten.* Österreichische Akademie der Wissenschaften, Philosophisch-historische Klasse. Denkschriften, 77, 2. Vienna: In Kommission bei R. M. Rohrer.

———. 1960. "Zum Papyrusprotokoll in früharabischer Zeit." *Jahrbuch Österreichische Byzantinische Gesellschaft* 9: 1–19.

———. 1966. *Handbuch der Orientalistik.* Vol. 1, *Arabische Chronologie.* Vol. 2, *Arabische Papyruskunde.* Leiden: Brill.

———. 1967–1971. *Arabische Paläographie.* Österreichische Akademie der Wissenschaften. Philosophisch-historische Klasse. Denkschriften 94.1. 2 vols. Vienna: Verlag der Österreichischen Akademie der Wissenschaften.

Gruendler, B. 1993. *The Development of the Arabic Scripts: From the Nabatean Era to the First Islamic Century according to Dated Texts.* Harvard Semitic Studies 43. Atlanta: Scholars Press.

Hanafi, A. 2004. "Two Unpublished Paper Documents and a Papyrus." In *Papyrology and the History of Early Islamic Egypt,* ed. P. M. Sijpesteijn and L. Sundelin, 45–62. Leiden: Brill.

Hawting, G., and A.-K. A. Shareef, eds. 1993. *Approaches to the Qur'ān.* London: Routledge.

Hopkins, S. 1984. *Studies in the Grammar of Early Arabic, Based upon Papyri Datable to before 300 A.H./912 A.D.* London Oriental Series 37. Oxford: Oxford University Press.

Ibn Ḥawqal. (d. after 973). *Kitāb ṣūrat al-arḍ,* ed. J. H. Kramers. Bibliotheca Geographorum Arabicorum II. Leiden: Brill, 1967.

Jahn, K. 1937. "Vom frühislamischen Briefwesen." *Archiv Orientální* 9: 153–200.

Khan, G. 1990. "The Historical Development of the Structure of Medieval Arabic Petitions." *Bulletin of the School of Oriental and African Studies* 53: 8–30.

———. 1994. "The Pre-Islamic Background of Muslim Legal Formularies." *ARAM* 6: 193–224.

———. 2005. *Arabic Documents from Early Islamic Khurasan.* London: Nour Foundation in association with Azimuth Editions.

———. 2007. "Newly Discovered Arabic Documents from Early Abbasid Khurasan." In *From al-Andalus to Khurasan: Documents from the Medieval Islamic World,* ed. P. M. Sijpesteijn, L. Sundelin, S. Torallas Tovar, and A. Zomeño, 201–215. Leiden: Brill.

Khoury, R. G. 1972. *Wahb b. Munabbih.* Wiesbaden: Harrassowitz.

———. 1986. *'Abd Allāh ibn Laḥīya (97–174/715–790), juge et grand maître de l'Ecole égyptienne: Avec édition critique de l'unique rouleau de papyrus arabe conservé à Heidelberg.* Wiesbaden: Harrassowitz.

Kindī. (d. 961). *Kitāb al-wulāt wa-kitāb al-quḍāt,* ed. R. Guest. In *The Governors and Judges of Egypt.* Leiden: Brill, 1912.

Maqrīzī. (d. 1442). *Al-Mawā'iẓ wa-'l-i'tibār fī dhikr al-khiṭaṭ wa-'l-āthār,* ed. A. F. Sayyid. London: Al-Furqān Islamic Heritage Foundation, 2002–2003.

Morimoto, K. 1994. "The Dīwāns as Registers of the Arab Stipendiaries in Early Islamic Egypt." *Res Orientalis* 6: 353–366.

Moritz, B. 1905. *Arabic Palaeography: A Collection of Arabic Texts from the First Century of the Hidjra till the Year 1000.* Cairo: Publications of the Khedival Library 16.

Noth, A. 1973. "Zum Verhältnis von kalifaler Zentralgewalt und Provinzen in umayyadischer Zeit: Die Ṣulḥ-'Anwa-Traditionen für Ägypten und den Iraq." *Die Welt des Islams* 14: 150–162.

Petrosyan, Y. A., and M. L. Swietochowski. 1995. *Pages of Perfection: Islamic Paintings and Calligraphy from the Russian Academy of Sciences, St. Petersburg.* Milan: Electa.

Rāghib, Y. 1978. "Lettres arabes (I)." *Annales Islamologiques* 14: 15–35.

———. 1980. "Lettres arabes (II)." *Annales Islamologiques* 16: 1–29.

———. 1991. "La plus ancienne lettre arabe de marchand." In *Documents de l'islam médiéval: Nouvelles perspectives de recherche,* ed. Y. Rāghib, 1–9. Cairo: Imprimerie de l'Institut français d'archéologie orientale.

———. 1996. "Les plus anciens papyrus arabes." *Annales Islamologiques* 30: 1–19.

Rapoport, Y. 2005. *Marriage, Money, and Divorce in Medieval Islamic Society.* Cambridge: Cambridge University Press.

Richter, T. S. 2000. "Spätkoptische Rechtsurkunden neu bearbeitet (II): Die Rechtsurkunden des Teschlot-Archivs." *Journal of Juristic Papyrology* 30: 95–148.

———. 2004. "*O.Crum* Ad. 15 and the Emergence of Arabic Words in Coptic Legal Documents." In *Papyrology and the History of Early Islamic Egypt,* ed. P. M. Sijpesteijn and L. Sundelin, 97–114. Leiden: Brill.

Schaefer, K. 2002. "Arabic Printing before Gutenberg: Block Printed Arabic Amulets." In *Middle Eastern Languages and the Print Revolution: A Cross-cultural Encounter. A Catalogue and Companion to the Exhibition,* ed. E. Hanebutt-Benz, D. Glass, and G. Roper, 123–128. Westhofen, Germany: WVA-Verlag Skulima.

Sijpesteijn, P. M. 2003. "North American Papyrus Collections Revisited." *Al-Bardiyyat* 1: 5–18.

———. 2004a. "A Request to Buy Silk from Early Islamic Egypt." In *Gedenkschrift Ulrike Horak,* ed. H. Harrauer and R. Pintaudi, 255–272. Papyrologica Florentina 34. Florence: Gonnelli.

———. 2004b. "Travel and Trade on the River." In *Papyrology and the History of Early Islamic Egypt,* ed. P. M. Sijpesteijn and L. Sundelin, 115–152. Leiden: Brill.

———. 2006. "Arabic Papyri from Current Excavations in Egypt." *Al-Bardiyyat* 2: 10–23.

———. 2007a. "The Muslim Conquest and the First Fifty Years of Muslim Rule in Egypt." In *Egypt in the Byzantine World, 300–700,* ed. R. S. Bagnall, 437–459. Cambridge: Cambridge University Press.

———. 2007b. "New Rule over Old Structures: Egypt after the Muslim Conquest." In *Regime Change in the Ancient Near East and Egypt: From Sargon of Agade to Saddam Hussein,* ed. H. Crawford, 183–202. Oxford : Oxford University Press for the British Academy.

———.2007c. "Creating a Muslim State: The Collection and Meaning of Sadaqa." In *Akten des 23. Internationalen Papyrologenkongresses, Wien, 22.–28. Juli 2001,* ed. B. Palme, 661–673. Vienna: Verlag der Österreichischen Akademie der Wissenschaften.

———. 2008a. "Arabic Palaeography." In *Encyclopedia of Arabic Language and Linguistics,* ed. C. Versteegh. Vol. 3, 513–524. Leiden: Brill.

———.2008b. "A Seventh-Eighth-Century List" In *Sixty-Five Papyrological Texts Presented to Klaas A. Worp on the Occasion of his 65th Birthday,* eds. F.A.J. Hoogendijk and B. Muhs. Papyrologica Lugduno-Batava 33, Leiden: Brill, 2008, 369–377.

———. Forthcoming-a. *Shaping A Muslim State: The World of a Mid-Eighth-Century Egyptian Official.* Oxford: Oxford University Press.

———. Forthcoming-b. "An Invitation to Join the Caliph's Pilgrim's Caravan." *Journal of Near Eastern Studies.*

Silvestre de Sacy, A. I. 1825. "Mémoire sur papyrus écrits en arabe et récemment découverts en Égypte." *Journal des Savants:* 462–473.

———. 1831. "Mémoire sur papyrus écrits en arabe et récemment découverts en Égypte." *Mémoires de l'Institut Royal de France, Académie des Inscriptions et Belles-Lettres* 9: 66–85.

———. 1833. "Mémoire sur deux papyrus, écrits en langue arabe, appartenant à la collection du Roi." *Mémoires de l'Institut Royal de France, Académie des Inscriptions et Belles-Lettres* 10: 65–88.

Sundelin, L. 2004. "Introduction: Papyrology and the Study of Early Islamic Egypt." In *Papyrology and the History of Early Islamic Egypt,* ed. P. M. Sijpesteijn and L. Sundelin, 1–19. Leiden: Brill.

Udovitch, A. L. 1970. *Partnership and Profit in Medieval Islam.* Princeton: Princeton University Press.

——. 1996. "Medieval Alexandria: Some Evidence from the Cairo Genizah Documents." In *Alexandria and Alexandrianism: Papers Delivered at a Symposium Organized by the J. Paul Getty Museum and the Getty Center for the History of Art and the Humanities and Held at the Museum, April 22–25, 1993,* 273–283. Malibu: J. Paul Getty Museum.

Ya'qūbī. (d. 284/897). *Kitāb al-buldān,* ed. M. J. de Goeje. Bibliotheca Geographorum Arabicorum 7. Leiden: Brill, 1892.

——. *Ta'rīkh,* ed. M. T. Houtsma. Leiden: Brill, 1883.

Ziadeh, J. 1915–1917. "L'apocalypse de Samuel, supérieur de Deir-el-Qalamoun: Texte arabe édité et traduit en français." *Revue de l'orient chrétien* 20: 374–407.

Zomeño, A. 2003. "Del escritorio al tribunal: Estudio de los documentos notariales en la Granada nazarí." In *Grapheîon: Códices, manuscritos, e imágines: Estudios filológicos e históricos,* ed. J. P. Monferrer Sala and M. Marcos Aldón, 75–98. Cordoba: Universidad de Granada.

CHAPTER 20

THE PAPYROLOGY
OF THE NEAR EAST

JEAN GASCOU

THE written documentation of the Hellenized Orient has already been inventoried and discussed.[1] Most of the writing materials, both flexible and rigid, attested in Egypt are also represented in the Near East: tablets, ostraca,[2] and, to be sure, papyrus, but writing in oriental languages is part of papyrology only by assimilation. When the Greeks and Macedonians destroyed the Achaemenid monarchy and opened the East and central Asia to Greek, they encountered in Asia Minor and on the Mediterranean coast peoples who already used papyrus. Farther to the East, in contrast, they found the custom of writing literary and religious works and public and private legal documents on skin (*diphthera* or *membrana*) well entrenched, whether this was finished as leather or as parchment.[3] Although the Seleucids introduced papyrus into countries like Babylonia, the use of skin remained dominant in north Syria, Mesopotamia, and central Asia under the Greek and non-Greek monarchies that emerged from the dissolution of Alexander's empire and under the Romans. We have direct testimony of this practice in the Parthian "parchments" from Avroman in Iranian Kurdistan,[4] a Graeco-Bactrian receipt for a tax on a transaction,[5] a substantial late antique dossier in the Bactrian language transcribed into the Greek alphabet,[6] and the texts of Dura and Beth Phouraia/Appadana on the Middle Euphrates.[7] Indirect testimony comes from the impressions left by writing materials on the Hellenistic and Roman sealings found in Mesopotamia, Palmyra, and other cities.[8] Numerous skins also appear in the finds from the Dead Sea, mainly for Jewish theological and liturgical works but also for legal documents. Only with the Roman conquest of inland areas does papyrus begin to compete with or supplant skins for some types of acts, often in military contexts, like the archives of units, or administrative settings, as with petitions.

A similar situation prevails with languages, for even if the Greeks and Macedonians promoted Greek as far east as central Asia and the borders of India, the Semitic languages of the Near East continued to be written. From a linguistic point of view the Roman conquest had contrasting and even paradoxical effects. Under the Romans, Greek gains ground in writing and is introduced even into countries where it was not customary. The most striking case is that of the Arabo-Nabataean zone, where Nabataean writing rapidly disappeared in favor of Greek after the creation of the province of Arabia in 106. Similarly, the final disappearance of the kingdom of Oshroene under Gordian III was accompanied by the replacement of Syriac by Greek at Marcopolis.[9] Edessa, however, the former capital of the Abgarids, forms an exception of great historical significance because, like Palmyra until its capture by Aurelian, this city kept its national language alongside Greek.[10] Hebrew experienced a nonliturgical resurgence, particularly between 132 and 135, during the Bar Kokhba revolt.[11]

THE DISCOVERIES

Near Eastern Texts from Egypt

Some papyri written in the Near East by local persons or by people from Egypt living in or visiting the Near East, especially soldiers, have been found in Egypt. These include letters,[12] title deeds for slaves,[13] and public[14] and private[15] documents. Some of these papyri belong to travel files. The archive of Zenon contains several accounts, letters, and documents from the years 261–252, collected by Zenon himself while on business trips to northern Palestine, southern Syria (the Hauran), the Ammanitis, and Idumaea (ca. 261–259).[16] Several centuries later, around 318 CE, the Hermopolite *scholastikos* Theophanes, a high official in the prefecture of Egypt, went to Antioch and brought back from this five-month trip his expense accounts, itineraries, and other papers.[17] Other texts come from Zenon's correspondents and those of his employer, the dioiketes Apollonios. They testify in their own way, during a period of conflict with the Seleucids, to the Ptolemaic domination over these areas. Several of them inform us about Toubias, a Transjordanian aristocrat in Ptolemaic service and a member of a family famous in Jewish history.

For good measure, we may add that the finds from the Near East include a number of "traveling" texts written at Edessa,[18] Marcopolis,[19] Carrhai,[20] Antioch,[21] Gaza,[22] and other localities where so far no papyri have been found.

Discoveries in the Near East

So far only about 600 Greek and Latin papyri from the Near East (including those found in Egypt) have come to light. That is far more than just fifty years ago, when the texts of Dura and Nessana had not yet been made fully available, but this is hardly anything compared to the roughly 50,000 Greek and Latin papyri of Egyptian provenance published so far. In some parts of the Near East, as in the area of Palmyra, the middle and lower Euphrates valley, and the Arabo-Nabataean zone, the climate is almost as arid as that of Egypt. But far more than Egypt, these countries experienced rebellions, wars, invasions, natural catastrophes, and other forms of devastation in antiquity, all unfavorable to the survival of texts. Vast stores of archives must have vanished in the destructions of Seleucia on the Tigris by the Parthians and then by Trajan, as well as in the sacking of Palmyra by Aurelian.[23] In other regions, excessive rainfall or the continuity of human occupation from antiquity to the present have destroyed or made the written materials inaccessible.

Indirect Discoveries

Some of our information is indirect in nature. Earlier I mentioned the sealings of Syro-Mesopotamian cities. Careful study of these, like that carried out by H. Seyrig for several Syrian cities, can inform us not only about the writing materials used but also about the format of the vanished documents and thus, to some degree, their content.

More eloquent, one might say, are the impressions of literary texts left by their ink on the mud bricks of one room at the Hellenistic site of Aï Khanoum in Afghanistan.[24]

Direct Discoveries

Fortunately for scholarship, most of the papyri of the Near East have been discovered during regular excavations and in known archaeological contexts. This is the case with Dura, Nessana, Petra, Khirbet Mird, and Aï Khanoum. As in Egypt, however, some of the finds have been clandestine. Before reaching the hands of editors, they have been the object of transactions, sometimes accompanied by false or doubtful information and sometimes dismembered into homogeneous batches. We are therefore still ignorant of the origin and environment of a dossier of such prime importance for the history of Roman Syria as that of the Middle Euphrates. The same obscurity afflicts two papyri said to come from Bostra.[25] In the case of the Dead Sea caves, the situation is mixed: Irregular discoveries have been intermingled with texts brought to light by archaeological missions. As a result, their editors and interpreters spent more time than they would wish in checking information and reassembling dossiers.[26] In consequence, the publications are rather disorderly and present difficulties to those who use these catalogues. Such is the case with the Jericho papyri (P.Jud.Des.Misc.), where a number of provenances other than Jericho and its environs are mixed in (e.g., Nahal Hever).

In general it is notable that, even taking into account texts written in the vernacular languages, most of our finds come from the Byzantine period (Nessana, Petra) and above all the Roman period (Dead Sea, Dura, Middle Euphrates); they tell us little about earlier states, particularly about the Seleucid monarchy. Moreover, they are distributed in two extended and discontinuous zones, namely the eastern edges of the Roman province of Syria (Dura, Beth Phouraïa/Appadana) and the Judaean and Arabo-Nabataean region (Dead Sea, Nessana, Petra, Bostra).

Within these zones, urban sites, the ancient "cities," are poorly represented except for Dura and Petra. (It is by no means certain that the papyri said to belong to Bostra actually come from Bostra itself.) The papyri discovered at Palmyra are insignificant and consist of some sixty unpublished fragments of Greek and Palmyrene papyri from the tomb of Kitot (40 CE), as well as one book of school tablets.[27] The twenty-one pieces from the Middle Euphrates may come from Appadana, a site in the Lower Khabour Valley that had just been promoted to the rank of city and given the name of Neapolis, but they were probably brought there by villagers from Beth Phouraia. Nessana and its neighbor, Sobata,[28] were only villages, and Khirbat Mird was just a small monastic establishment.[29] As to the discoveries from the Dead Sea, these were mainly items from various provenances and were hidden or discarded in caves.

The case of the grottoes and ravines of the Dead Sea leads to the positing of another characteristic useful to keep in mind in considering these dossiers. There are internal reasons (notably the narrowness of the chronological spread), sometimes reinforced by archaeological observations, to consider some of the finds deliberate deposits connected to specific crises of urgency or distress.

Such an interpretation seems nearly certain with the roughly forty Aramaic papyri from a cave in the Wadi Daliyeh, fourteen kilometers northwest of Jericho, which, considering the period covered (375–335 BCE) and the large quantity of human remains connected with them, must record in their own way the last episode of the Samaritan revolt under Alexander, in 331.[30] An analogous case appears to be attested at Jericho, this time in connection with the capture of the city by Ptolemy I in 312 BCE.[31] Similarly, the last secure dates found at Qumran place those finds in the period of the Jewish war of 66–73 CE. The contemporary pieces of the famous Simeon bar Kokhba, the "prince of Israel" who directed the Jewish revolt of 132–135 CE, provide a link among the finds of Murabba'at, Wadi Sdeir, and Nahal Hever. It is quite possible that the Judaeo-Nabataean women Babatha (daughter of Simon) and Salome Komaïse, the centers of many of the papyri from Nahal Hever, wanted to shelter their papers and their persons in the caves of this valley. At Masada it is also possible to see how, after the Roman capture of the site, the papers of the defeated Jews were discarded in various places.

The Middle Euphrates dossier must have been put together under analogous circumstances. A number of villagers from Beth Phouraia, worried about the Sassanid invasion of the years 253–256 (which actually led to the destruction of Dura), sought to preserve the documents connected with their legal proceedings and their property titles, hoping to recover them when things returned to normal.

THE FIVE MAIN DOSSIERS

The Near Eastern papyri form five principal bodies: Dura, the Middle Euphrates, Nahal Hever, Petra, and Nessana. Some description of each follows.

Dura

Dura-Europos is an ancient stronghold on the right bank of the Middle Euphrates, extensively altered by the Seleucids. From the beginning, they provided it with urban structures, including an archives (*chreophylakeion*) that functioned for centuries, particularly for the registration of legal documents (see *P.Dura* 15, 17, 28). Even in the third century of our era, Hellenistic law remained in use at Dura (*P.Dura* 12). Two texts are datable to the Seleucid period (*P.Dura* 15 and 34). Dura then came under Parthian rule (113 BCE) and eventually Roman control (166 CE) and even became a Roman colony in 211. The city, which was at that time part of the Roman province of Syria Coele, was occupied, then depopulated and destroyed between 253 and 256 by the Sassanids. This succession of governments is visible, among other ways, in the variety of languages represented at Dura: Greek and Latin, but also Palmyrene and Iranian. The published textual corpus amounts to 154 documents (45 on skin and 109 on papyrus), found in various parts of the site, along with some ostraca, mainly of the Parthian or Roman period.[32] The pre-Roman documents are written on skin, and those of the Roman period are to a large extent on papyrus, particularly in the military context. Most of the Dura texts that record private transactions are drawn up as double documents.[33]

The papers of the third-century Roman garrison deserve particular notice. They are largely in Latin and tell us in detail about the organization of the unit (the *cohors XX Palmyrenorum*), its festivals (in the famous *P.Dura* 60, the *feriale duranum*), its relationships, and its litigation.[34]

The written documentation of Dura can and must be studied in its archaeological context, which is well preserved and extensively (although not yet completely) published.[35] Fruitful excavations have resumed after a long hiatus under the direction of P. Leriche. This context includes the site's monumental inscriptions and above all its numerous and rich graffiti, which, in matters of the economy and accounting, display types of text and handwriting that one would have thought limited to papyrological texts. This epigraphy, however, is still incompletely published and scattered in the preliminary reports.[36]

The Middle Euphrates

This homogeneous and well-preserved ensemble of nineteen Greek and two Syriac items arrived in Europe in 1988 through the antiquities trade and is associated with several small objects of daily life that have not yet been published.[37] The place of discovery is still not entirely certain; the editors judge that it was fairly close to Dura, perhaps the Syrian village of Beth Phouraia on the Euphrates (where many of the people mentioned in the dossier lived) or, perhaps more likely, Appadana/Neapolis, the administrative center on which Beth Phouraia depended. Appadana, already known from the documents of Dura, is not well localized, but its name seems to survive in the present-day toponym, Tell Fudayn, on the Lower Khabour, the ancient Aboras, an eastern tributary of the Euphrates.

The nineteen publishable texts, datable to the years 232 to 252 and consisting of petitions, private legal documents, and letters, have all been published.[38] Even before their publication, Fergus Millar pointed out their unusual historical interest.[39] They do indeed help us to better understand the government of Roman Mesopotamia, the frontiers of Syria (which must now be pushed beyond the Euphrates along the Khabour), law, local authorities,[40] the army, and the municipal and religious institutions of cities like Nisibis, Marcopolis, and Carrhai. They illumine the end of the Abgarid monarchy at Edessa (*P.Euphr.* 19, 20). The petition *P.Euphr.* 1 is addressed to a historical figure, the prefect of Mesopotamia and consular governor of Syria, Julius Priscus, brother of the emperor Philip. The contribution of these texts to onomastic studies and to Syro-Mesopotamian historical geography is also noteworthy and received particular attention from the editors. So far, however, the Euphrates texts have not evoked quite the same degree of interest as those from Nahal Hever (discussed later), as one can see by comparing the modest scholarly bibliography the former have generated to the mass of writing on the latter.[41]

Nahal Hever

Hellenistic and Roman Judaea and Samaria have furnished numerous texts, most often found in the caves of the wadis emptying toward the Dead Sea. It is difficult to describe here all of these discoveries, some of which, like those of Qumran, are not directly connected to papyrology.[42] Some of these sites have already been mentioned,[43] including Wadi Daliyeh and other places in the vicinity of Jericho,[44] Khirbet Mird, Murabba'at,[45] and Masada.[46] Still-unpublished texts from Wadis Nar and Ghweir are known, and some Greek texts from the caves of Engadi have recently been published.[47] The texts from Nahal Hever, south of Engadi, form a discrete body both in their number and in their archival coherence. They come both from chance finds and from regular excavations carried out in 1960 and 1961 by an Israeli team in the cave called the "cave of horror" because of the human remains and especially in the "cave of the letters," by far the richer of the two. These have yielded biblical fragments[48] and documents in Greek, Hebrew, Aramaic, and Aramaic-Nabataean, belonging to three dossiers, the "archive" of Babatha and that of Salome Komaïse, as well as a packet of fifteen letters addressed by Bar Kokhba between 132 and 135 to his lieutenants at Engadi.[49] This dossier of "Simon Choseba" includes at least two letters written in Greek,[50] with the balance in Hebrew (a linguistic revival corresponding to the messianic spirit of the revolt) and in Aramaic. There is also one tablet in Aramaic.[51] The whole witnesses to the prince's ability to create a political structure and to rally around him non-Jewish elements of the population. The two other groups (sale contracts, a donation, petitions, property declarations, receipts, mortgage loans, marriage contracts) concern two Jewish women of Arab-Nabataean origin (from the village of Mahoza, "the port," on the south of the Dead Sea, in the territory of Petra) but who had interests in Judaea in the region of Engadi. These dossiers are linked at several points and break off in 131/132, that is, at the moment of the Bar Kokhba revolt, during which these women, after having hidden their papers, lost their lives or were otherwise unable to recover their documents.

Salome Komaïse (daughter of Levi and of Salome alias Groptê) (date range, January 125 to August 131) was married twice and kept papers that belonged to her first husband (*P.Hever* 12, 60–65), including two census declarations subscribed at Rabbath-Moab in Arabia (*P.Hever* 61 and 62) and the interested party's dowry receipt (*P.Hever* 65).

The much richer dossier of Babatha, daughter of Simon, covers the years 94 to August 132 and straddles a major historical change, the disappearance of the Nabataean kingdom and the creation in 106 of the Roman province of Arabia. Of the 35 pieces, 17 are in Greek, 9 bilingual, and the remainder in Aramaic-Nabataean and Aramaic. They are connected with Babatha's economic struggles with her second husband's first wife. One piece that is particularly interesting from the point of view of public procedure is a census declaration subscribed at Petra (*P.Yadin* I 16). Another, no. 10, Babatha's Aramaic marriage contract, is an excellent piece for jurists studying the position of the Jews.

The documents from Nahal Hever have aroused sustained interest, considering the critical period in the history of ancient Judaism that they span and the light they throw on the situation of Jews in a Hellenized and Romanized non-Jewish environment.[52] From them we now have a better understanding of the institutions and political structures of Judaea and of the province of Arabia. The literature concerning these documents has become extensive, particularly the numerous works of Hannah Cotton.[53]

Petra

"Mute" until 1993, the Arabo-Nabataean site of Petra produced a large cache of carbonized fragments discovered in the ruins of a serving room of the principal church. Their publication is still in progress, slowed by the extreme difficulties of consolidating, placing, and mounting the fragments, but already a considerable amount of material is available in two volumes.[54] About fifty pieces ranging in date from 537 to 593 have been identified; thus, they are contemporary with the Byzantine portion of the Nessana dossier, with which the Petra papyri have similarities from the point of view of diplomatics and onomastics; for these two sites, both of which were part of the Byzantine province of Palestine III during this period, shared the same Arabo-Nabataean heritage. Even the situations of the finds are analogous. The Petra dossier is in large part centered on the family of Theodoros, son of Obodianos (a distinctive Nabataean patronymic), a member of the local clergy (another point of similarity with the Nessana papyri). The papyri reveal not the commercial milieu of a caravan city but a settled, civic world of landowners and clergy living on the revenues from their landholdings. The documents have close parallels in the diplomatics of contemporary Egyptian material (settlements, or *dialuseis*,[55] as well as requests for corrections in land registers, or *epistalmata tou somatismou*). Tax receipts conform to Justinian's laws in specifying the number of assessment units *(juga)* and the status of parcels of land. A settlement document comes from Gaza in Palestine I (*P.Petra* I 2). As at Nessana, the local place names are largely of Arabic derivation, and one of the editors has shown that several place names in *P.Petra* have survived to the present.[56] They may even go back to the Nabataeans, who are considered an Arabophone people who were writing in Aramaic. Their role and place in the Arab conquest of the years 635/642 deserve a fresh examination.

Nessana

If Byzantinists have been slow to take into account the Egyptian papyri of late antiquity, they have been quicker to take an interest in those of Nessana.[57] This Byzantine and Umayyad corpus (spanning the years from 500 to 700) was discovered in 1935 at el-Auja, on the frontier between the Sinai and the Negev, in the ruins of the village of Nessana, which, like Petra, was part of the Byzantine province of Palestine III, a product of the breakup of the old province of Arabia. The Nabataean cultural and linguistic base is still visible, notably in personal names. These papyri were probably discarded, but, instead of being destroyed, they were kept in rooms attached to religious establishments. These texts are essentially Greek, but some are bilingual Greek-Arabic or entirely Arabic. Not all of them were published,[58] and the approximately two hundred literary and documentary pieces available in two volumes would benefit from revision.

The literary dossier is of great cultural interest because it includes a glossary of the *Aeneid* and fragments of the epic, works one would not have expected in the sixth century. Two fragments of a codex concerning the law of succession deserve further attention from legal historians (*P.Ness.* 11 and 12). The Byzantine portion of the documentary material consists of papers of soldiers who belonged to the *numerus* of the *devotissimi Theodosiaci*, attested from 505 to 596. A certain Sergius, who came from this milieu, became the head *(hegoumenos)* of the local martyrion of saints Sergius and Bacchus at the end of the sixth century. This role passed afterward to his son, Patrikios, and indeed to further descendants down to the end of the seventh century. Under the Arabs, Georgios, the next to the last representative of this family, became the civil and financial administrator of Nessana, with the result that Greek, bilingual, and Arabic administrative and fiscal documents became intermixed with the family papers. The archive is thus particularly precious for the history of the institutions and finances of Palestine under the Umayyads. As is the case at Dura, interpretation of the Nessana papyri also demands attention to the Greek and Nabataean epigraphic texts from the site, in which some of the *hegoumenoi* of the papyri reappear.[59]

PALAEOGRAPHY

This aspect of the subject, which requires mastery of many variables and a good knowledge of the Egyptian texts, has been treated by E. Crisci with prudence, perspicacity, and originality, approaching the subject as a cultural and social phenomenon.[60] The handwritings of the early Hellenistic period, offspring of the bilinear classical majuscule, are not very differentiated.[61] With later political fragmentation, however, regional tendencies emerge, as in the Parthian documents from Avroman.[62] In the Roman period, the Near East witnessed the development of its own style, which, earlier than in Egypt, tends to exaggerate the contrasts between letters, announcing in this fashion the quadrilinearity that characterizes Byzantine handwriting.[63] Regional differences blur under the Arabs: Egypt and the East use the same quadrilinear, high-contrast cursive, and, for fiscal texts, a form of minuscule.

FORMATS AND DIPLOMATICS

One of the oldest, most durable, and most constant traits of Near Eastern documents is their production in a double copy, the so-called diploma. The full and outwardly visible copy of a document *(scriptura exterior)* was headed, in a more limited space, by a cursive, compact, and often abridged version. This copy was then folded, sewn, and sometimes sealed, a process that has given it the designation of *scriptura interior*. The *scriptura interior* provided an authoritative copy in case of dispute over any aspect of the *scriptura exterior*.[64]

According to the allusions to this format in the Roman papyri of Egypt, like the registration of a slave sale that had taken place at Bostra,[65] its technical name was *diplôma hellênikon* ("Greek double document"). The ancients thus took a position in favor of a Greek origin for this format, whereas modern papyrologists do not exclude an encounter between Greek tradition and Roman customs or even practices of Semitic origin. The *diplôma* of Bostra must have been on papyrus because, to judge particularly from the finds of Nahal Hever, most of the *diplômata* that have come from the Arabo-Nabataean zone adopted this writing material. The writing is in this case parallel to the height of the original roll *(transversa charta)*, in the format that papyrologists call *rotulus*.[66] In the Syro-Mesopotamian zone, as we may deduce from the sealings of Palmyra and as we see in documents from Dura, the Middle Euphrates, Avroman, and Bactria, the *diplôma* is generally written on *rotuli* of skin.

The double document has other characteristics as well, such as the number of points at which the *scriptura interior* is closed, which varies from five to seven,[67] and these points are often validated on the back by the subscriptions of witnesses.

The Roman calendar is universally used in the Near East (*P.Hever*, pp. 146–149), with the consular formula and Macedonian or Roman months, supplemented by local or regional eras (e.g., era of Arabia, Seleucid era, era of Gaza). Regnal years are given much less regularly.

LANGUAGE

The Greek of the Near Eastern papyri is part of the common Greek dialect called koinê. Although there have been many attempts to explain its distinctive characteristics by a Semitic substrate,[68] the editors of *P.Euphr.*, in keeping with contemporary scholarly trends, have preferred to connect linguistic anomalies to the general trends of the common Greek speech of the Roman and Byzantine periods.

They also mention the influence of administrative Latin not only in the vocabulary but also in syntax. Moreover, this Greek contains words and expressions (e.g., idioms of an undefined origin) not used in the Greek of Egypt. Naphtali Lewis made many observations in the introduction to *P.Yadin* I (notably on the verb καθαροποιέω, in connection with guarantees against eviction), and Hannah Cotton has called attention to the use of χειροχρήστης for ὑπογραφεύς in *P.Hever* 64 v°). Peculiarities of the same sort have been observed in the dossier of Beth Phouraia/Appadana, for example, in connection with the term συγκωμήτης (*P.Euphr.* 1 and 4), found only in the Near East and seemingly a calque of the Latin *convicanus*.

Was koinê a living language? In the Jewish context, Greek seems linked to Roman domination and perhaps has a somewhat superficial character (*P.Hever,* p. 146). In Arabia, similarly, Greek was not adopted until after the disappearance of the Nabataean kingdom in 106 CE. Moreover, local languages were far from being eliminated, as the Semitic subscriptions to Greek documents from Nahal Hever and the Middle Euphrates demonstrate. In as important a center as Edessa, Syriac kept its status as the official language under Roman rule (*P.Dura* 28), a privilege that helps to explain the city's later distinction in Syriac literature. In the late texts of Petra and Nessana, Arabic surfaces in personal and place names.

LAW

Few scholars would deny the early advance of Roman norms in the domain of provincial and municipal institutions, as well as public law, well before the Antonine Constitution of 212.[69] The study of private law—of areas like marriage contracts, sales, and gifts—is by contrast dominated by the theme of the interaction of local legal systems, Hellenistic and Semitic, with Roman law, often with mixed results.[70] This approach is logical enough for the Judeo-Nabataean archives of the second century, given the diversity of the languages attested in this body of about a hundred documents. According to a recent scholarly workshop,[71] it seems that the juridical concepts used depended on the place and period in which documents were drawn up,[72] as well as on the language. Acts drawn up in Greek or written in the Roman province of Arabia diverge the most from the legal prescriptions of the Jewish sources, most notably in matters concerning the legal situation of women. Thus, in the documents from Nahal Hever, the woman is accompanied by an *epitropos* in documents drawn up under the Roman legal system but not in Hebrew, Nabataean, and Aramaic texts drawn up outside the Roman empire (i.e., in the Nabataean kingdom or under the Bar Kokhba regime).

So far as the diffusion of Roman law itself goes, the editors of *P. Yadin* I, like those of *P.Euphr.*, have noticed the conformity of these private documents to Roman legal prescriptions: thus, the formula of *stipulatio*, characteristic of Roman legal acts (ἐπερωτηθεὶς ὡμολόγησα, *interrogatus spopondi*), the reference to bona fides, and the role of notaries (*librarii*, νομικοί) in the drawing up of documents. In addition, *P. Yadin* I 28–30 provide three copies of the Greek formula for a procedural action concerning guardianship, in conformity with the formula for the *actio tutelae* in the praetor's edict. *P.Euphr.* 1 and 2, for their part, appear to refer, in the editors' view, to the interdicts of the praetorian edict *(unde vi, uti possidetis)*. This interpretation has not been challenged to date.

NEAR EASTERN PAPYROLOGY
AND EGYPTIAN PAPYROLOGY

We have no basis for a systematic comparison of the Hellenistic papyri of Egypt and those from the Near East, the latter having nothing on the scale of the compact but voluminous archives of Zenon (for the third century BCE) or those of the agoranomoi of Pathyris (for the second–first century). It is only for the Roman and Byzantine periods that serious comparison is possible. For some decades now there has been a consensus that Egypt after Augustus was fundamentally a Roman imperial province, even if it retained—more in form than in substance—some characteristics of the preceding Ptolemaic monarchy.[73] This province had a special status, created by Augustus, at first sight somewhat reduced by the near-total absence of civic institutions, but recent research has suggested that a sort of unofficial municipal life was already in place in Egypt by the second century CE.

Although this view is largely based on the information provided by the papyri, it is concerned with problems of a historical rather than strictly papyrological nature because papyrologists are in general more interested in studying the formal character of the texts than their content. For such formal questions, the written documentation from the Roman Near East is now sufficient in quantity and coherence to allow comparisons with the Egyptian papyri. This is what the editors of *P. Yadin* I and *P.Euphr.* have attempted in seeking to bring out the distinctive characteristics of each corpus and, to the extent that the written documents reflect their society of origin, regional particularisms. Indeed, the Near Eastern documentation—which still has many gaps, as, for example, with accounts, compared to the Egyptian papyri—does not offer a homogeneous typology but numerous variations of format and diplomatics in different times and places.

"Rome is the same everywhere," said the editors of *P.Euphr.* (66). This assertion is valid particularly for public documents such as petitions to governors and police officers, the phraseology and diplomatic format of which (the *hypomnêma*) are much the same in Egypt, Syria, and Arabia. Military archives, too, are relatively standardized.

In the domain of private law, however, the differences are more distinctive and, as we shall see, more significant. Like the rest of the Near East, Hellenistic Egypt used the double document,[74] but this format disappeared in Egyptian practice after the Roman conquest (see the section titled "Formats and Diplomatics"). Where they still occur, one can almost always show that the "diploma" was drawn up outside Egypt or comes from milieus with their own legal systems, like the military and Roman citizens. Some scholars see in these a transposition from the tablet diptychs normally used for Roman wills and call these Roman double documents.[75] Similarly, in the case of sale contracts, the diplomatics of the bilateral record of oral proceedings found in *P.Euphr.* 6–10 and known at Dura is unknown in Egyptian documents after the Hellenistic period, even though the formulas concerning eviction present in all of the texts do not appear in Egypt until the Byzantine period.[76] The Roman stipulation, present already in the second century in Arabia, does not become common in Egypt until after the Antonine Constitution of 212. Notarial subscriptions are unknown in Egypt until the Byzantine period, while *tabelliones,* called *librarii* or *nomikoi,* are involved in the drawing up of legal documents in the Roman Near East, again as early as the second century. Equally significant differences appear in dating practices: Consular formulas are rare in Egypt before the tetrarchy, while regnal years served as the standard dating system under the principate.

Some internal matters also deserve mention. The denarius is universally used as the unit of currency in Near Eastern documents, while in Egypt the drachma remains the standard unit until 296. This is only an example of the many details that would lead us to the conclusion that in the sphere of private law Egypt was Romanized more slowly than the rest of the Near East. Although it was a Roman imperial province, it was in some respects insular.

From the papyrological point of view, the Byzantine period offers a reversed perspective. From the fourth century on we see a kind of meeting of the two cultures, each apparently borrowing traits from the other: Handwriting is unified around a system foreshadowing the minuscule script; the double document disappears in the Near East except in areas outside Roman control (e.g., central Asia); Egypt adopts the *transversa charta* document format; legal vocabulary from the Near East turns up in Egypt (thus the verb καθαροποιεῖν, which appears only in the sixth century); the notariat is introduced there as well; denarii and myriads of denarii appear in papyri next to drachmas and talents; and consular dates are used next to regnal dating and then, after that vanishes, next to the indiction year.[77] This set of changes undoubtedly has much to do with the integration of Egypt into the large regional diocese of Oriens, itself under the authority of the praetorian prefect of the East, which would have led it increasingly to share the same institutions and the same civil and administrative law as Syria and the Arabo-Palestinian provinces. Some differences remained, certainly. For example, to judge from the Petra papyri, the introduction of the regnal year as the principal dating criterion came about there soon after the legislation on the subject promulgated in 537 (Nov. Just. 44), while Egypt lagged by a couple of years. The Petra papyri help to highlight a number of other Egyptian peculiarities, such as in the taxation of land, where although Egypt shared fundamental principles with the rest of the East (taxation by rate rather than by partition), it did not apply them in the same manner and with the same terminology (Egypt knew nothing of the *iugum*). It is possible that the administrative separation of Egypt and the Near East, which occurred in 380, when the diocese of Egypt was created, brought on a new wave of local particularisms.

NOTES

1. Cotton, Cockle, and Millar (1995, 214–235). These authors take account of texts assignable to non-Roman states; they register unpublished texts, documents of uncertain origin, and Near Eastern texts found in Egypt. For an update to this fundamental work see Mitthof and Papathomas (2004, 401–424, especially their notes 1–3).

2. Ostraca are less numerous than in Egypt, even though editors often include among them jar inscriptions that papyrologists would class among the *instrumenta*. An uncommon rigid material, unknown at least in Egypt but widespread under the Umayyads, is marble found in the ruins of ancient monuments and containing Arabic and Greek texts sometimes of a very everyday nature. These have been found at Nessana, in the Negev (published in *I.Ness.* 9–11), at Khirbat al-Mafjar near Jericho (Schwabe 1945), at Qasr al-Hayr al-Gharbi, and Andarin in Syria (partly unpublished). This practice existed in the Roman period but was probably rare; an example with a Greek letter was found at Izmir.

3. See Reed (1972). Editors use the words *parchment* and *leather* without technical study. For the widespread use of skins in the Persian Empire see Lewis (1974, 8–9). But papyrus was not entirely lacking before the arrival of the Greeks in regions near Egypt (Phoenicia and Palestine).

4. Minns (1915, 22–65). These are *rotuli* dated respectively to 88/87 and 22/21 BCE, registering sales of land (vineyards) and using Greek law. They were accompanied by a sale of a vineyard in Pehlevi in 13/12 BCE or 53 CE, depending on interpretation of the era date (Cowley 1919, 147–154). See Nyberg (1923) and Edmonds (1952).

5. The text, attributable to 167 or 181 BCE, comes from Sangcharak, southwest of Aï Khanoum, according to Bernard and Rapin (1994); see also Rea, Senior, and Hollis (1994), with the addendum of Hollis (1996), and Rapin (1996). Two Hellenistic texts from Afghanistan were published by Clarysse and Thompson (2007). One of the literary manuscripts from Aï Khanoum was also on "parchment."

6. Sims-Williams (1996); he describes a body of documents and letters on skin from northern Afghanistan. Their chronological range is 342 to 781. A number of these

are double documents with five holes closing the *scriptura interior* as in much earlier texts from Syria, Palestine, and Nabataean Arabia (see below the section titled Formats and Diplomatics).

7. See below the section titled The Five Main Dossiers.

8. See, particularly for Palmyra, Alexandretta, and Dolichê, Seyrig (1985).

9. Compare *P.Euphr.* 19 and 20 and *P.Euphr.* 6–7.

10. For this continuation of Syriac, see *P.Dura* 28. The official bilingualism of Palmyra is attested mainly by inscribed monuments, but it can hardly be doubted that Palmyrene written production had a similar pattern.

11. See the section titled The Five Main Dossiers.

12. Letters of Toubias, Hellenistic letters from Caria (*P.Cair.Zen.* I 59036 and 59056, of 257 BCE); letters from soldiers of the Legio III Cyrenaïca recently relocated to Bostra (*P.Mich.* VIII 466 [107] and 465 [108]); Roman letter from a military milieu written at Antioch (*BGU* III 794, with an allusion to vows before the Tyche of Antioch); letter of a woman to her aunt, written at Apamea (*P.Bour.* 25, fifth century).

13. *P.Cair.Zen.* I 59003 = *CPtol.Sklav.* 37 (Ammanitis, 259 BCE); *BGU* I 316 = *MChr.* 271 = *FIRA* III 135 (Ascalon, 359). Several slave sales found in Egypt were drawn up in Asia Minor: in Rhodes (*P.Oxy.* L 3593 [238–244]), Myra (*BGU* III 913 [206]), Side (*P.Turner* 22 [142], *BGU* III 887 = *MChr* 272 = *FIRA* III 133 = *CPJ* III 490 [151]), Seleucia in Pieria (*JurPap* 37 = *FIRA* III 132 = *ChLA* III 200 = *CPL* 120 [in Latin, 166]). These pieces provide valuable information about the institutions and law of the cities in question.

14. *SB* XII 11043, found in the Fayyum and dating to 152, is a report of proceedings before the procurator of Palestine. An order for payment of *annonai* and of *capita*, dated to 293, in Latin with a Greek subscription, mentions Caesarea (of Palestine?). It is not certain that it was written in Egypt (*SB* XVIII 13851). In addition, *P.Lips.* 34, a Hermopolite receipt for *vestis militaris*, mentions a payment made around 375 in Hierapolis in Syria. There is a circular of the *comes Orientis* on the movement of recruits, written at Antioch around 380 (*W.Chr.* 469).

15. For instance, *BGU* III 895 is a succession agreement from a Syrian milieu. Also worth mentioning is a Byzantine petition or letter from Aphrodisias (end of the sixth or start of the seventh century), with an account in grain on the verso (see Mitthof and Papathomas 2004), and *P.Münch.* III 43, a contract of Bithynian origin dated to 248.

16. Clarysse and Vandorpe (1995, 24–25, 90–92). See the collection of Durand (1997) with the review by Reekmans (1998).

17. Cadell (1989); Drexhage (1998).

18. *P.Dura* 28.

19. *P.Euphr.* 6–7.

20. *P.Euphr.* 10.

21. *P.Euphr.* 1.

22. *P.Petra* I 2.

23. The extent of our loss can be measured for Seleucia on the Tigris, where Italian excavations found more than 25,000 seals in the archives building, which was burned after 155/154 BCE, when Babylonia passed from Seleucid to Arsacid control. Most of these concern a salt tax *(halikê)*. Invernizzi (1996, 133) mentions papyrus and parchment, but he describes neither the proportions nor how the material was observed. The rescue excavations at Zeugma have led to the discovery of 65,000 imprints of Hellenistic seals, a deposit appropriate to this center's importance as a customs house. One may compare the

16,000 seals found in a house on Delos that was burned in 69 BCE (Auda and Boussac 1996, 511).

24. Hadot and Rapin (1987). A fragment of papyrus and two fragments of "parchment" (mid-third to early second century). The first is a philosophical dialogue on ideas, the second (in two fragments), iambic trimeters from some dramatic genre. The philosophical dialogue has been attributed to Aristotle or to Aristotelian circles. See the discussion and bibliographic update by Lerner (2003). It is not easy to determine whether the philosophical manuscript on papyrus was imported or comes from a local school (an analogous problem is raised by the celebrated papyrus containing the *Persians* of Timotheos).

25. One, a petition from 260, has received preliminary publication in Gascou (1999). The second is a badly damaged marriage contract in two fragments.

26. An example of these fruitful, but long and costly, efforts is provided by the reattribution to Nahal Hever of a part of the texts assigned to Cave 4 at Qumran (*P.Hever*, pp. 283–284, introd. to *P.Hever* 342–361).

27. A codex of seven literary tablets of the third century supposed to come from Palmyra (fables of Babrios; Hesiod) was published by Hesseling (1893) (Pack² 174, 491).

28. Youtie (1973), receipts of the sixth century connected to work on a *kisterna* (*SB* V 8073–8076).

29. Khirbet Mird, a toponym preserving its ancient name, Mar(d)os, is located in the Judaean desert, about twenty kilometers south of Jericho and near the laura of Saint Sabas. The Greek dossier has Arabic intermixed (Grohmann 1963), as well as Christian Palestinian (Perrot 1963). The Greek part includes letters, biblical and liturgical fragments, and a school text that span the period from the fifth–sixth century to the eighth–ninth and also a manuscript from the fifth–sixth century. See van Haelst (1991). The first two texts, letters, are reprinted as *SB* XX 14188–14189. The first letter seems to express hope for the recipient's renewed health, reading at the start of line 2 ὑμετέρας ἰάσ[ε]ως instead of [.]μετερα ιϵ[.]ως.

30. *P.Daliyeh*.

31. *P.Jud.Des.Misc.*, 11–12.

32. These texts come from excavations carried out between 1922 and 1924 for the Académie des Inscriptions et Belles-Lettres and continued from 1928 to 1937 in collaboration with Yale University. See Cumont (1926) and *P.Dura*. Besides flexible materials, several ostraca in Greek and four in Iranian were found (*YClSt* 14: 169, 195–209), along with a wax tablet and a cuneiform tablet of the second millennium BCE (Stephens 1937).

33. See the section titled Formats and Diplomatics.

34. These were republished by Fink (1971). The Latin texts from Dura were also reedited by R. Marichal, *ChLA* VI–IX. On the military unit see Pollard (1996) and Kennedy (1994).

35. A good example of exegesis of the Dura texts, using all of the available documentation, is offered by Saliou (1992).

36. For a bibliography, see Bérard et al., eds. (2000), *Guide de l'épigraphiste*, nos. 372–374, 2025, 2185–2186.

37. Feissel and Gascou (1989).

38. *P.Euphr.* 1–5 (*SB* XXII 15496–15500); *P.Euphr.* 6–10 (*SB* XXIV 16167–16171); *P.Euphr.* 11–17 (*SB* XXVI 16654–16660). The publication of the two Syriac pieces (*P.Euphr.* 19 and 20) is the work of Teixidor (1990, 1991); see the remarks of Brock (1991).

39. Millar (1993, 129–131, 155–156, 478–481).

40. Gascou (1999, 61–73).

41. For the institutions of the kingdom of Osrhoene and of Roman Mesopotamia, see Gnoli (2000). For their legal systems, see Stolte (2001).

42. See generally Tov and Pfann (1993). The some 920–930 Hebrew and Aramaic texts from Qumrân (current information kindly provided by M. Bélis) discovered in eleven caves (especially that called 4Q), from before the first Jewish revolt of 66/73 (more precisely, April/June 68), are essentially religious and liturgical in content (see the summary by Guglielmo 2003).

43. For further information see Schiffman and VanderKam (2000) and especially Tov (2002).

44. *P.Jud.Des.Misc.* Although half of this catalogue is devoted to the finds from Ketef Jericho (northwest of Jericho) (1–19), some of the Dead Sea sites are also represented: Wadi Sdeir, Nahal Hever, Nahal Mishmar, and Nahal Se'elim (Wadi Seiyal). The provenance of one text is unknown. The finds from the caves of Jericho include early documents in Aramaic (fourth century BCE). The balance (Aramaic and Greek) can be assigned to the Flavians, Hadrian, and the revolt of Bar Kokhba. On no. 16 see Haensch (2001). Further-more, no. 18 seems to me to be the registration of a copy of a marriage deed (γαμικῆς, 1.1, instead of ταμικῆς). Line 2 is the subscription of the agent who received or registered the copy (perhaps the individual mentioned at the start of line 1, where I would read ὁ δεῖνα χρε]οφύλαξ).

45. *P.Murabba'at.* The Greek pieces (nos. 89–157) are partly reprinted in *SB* X 10300–10307. For a historical perspective see Cotton and Eck (2002).

46. For the documentation of this site, some ten kilometers south of Nahal Hever, see *P.Masada* I; for the Graeco-Latin part, see *P.Masada* II. For a reedition of *P.Masada* II 741, see *SB* XXIV 15988.

47. Cohen (2006). The editor places them in the same chronological range as the texts of Nahal Hever. One element of support is provided by coins of Bar Kokhba. The first text supposedly mentions arouras, which is not credible in this context. Cohen (2007) publishes two fragmentary Greek texts from the same area.

48. Tov (1990). This text comes from the "cave of horror." For other biblical pieces from Nahal Hever see *P.Jud.Des.Misc.*, pp. 133–200.

49. Most of the Greek documents are in *P.Yadin* I; for the documents in languages other than Greek, see *P.Yadin* II, a catalogue in which the texts are arranged in a fashion that differs from what is announced in *P.Yadin* I and which, despite everything, includes some important Greek pieces (nos. 52 and 59). *P.Hever* has some additional Greek pieces; see especially pp. 131–279 by H. Cotton and the palaeographical study by J. D. Thomas, which is devoted to Greek documents. This section includes an introduction to the archive of Salome Komaïse, daughter of Levi.

50. *P.Yadin* II 52 and 59. The first of these invokes the scribe's inability to write in "Hebrew." For an analysis of the prince's dossier see Cotton (2003).

51. The tablet seems to be still unpublished. *P.Murabba'at* also contains pieces in Hebrew and Aramaic connected to the period of the "freedom of Israel," including letters by the prince himself (nos. 43 and 44).

52. See Katzoff and Schaps (2005).

53. See the excellent historical synthesis in *P.Hever*, pp. 133–165, and Cotton (1999).

54. *P. Petra* I and III. *P.Petra* I has generated substantial reviews, particularly Fournet (2003) and Kruit (2004). The stimulating introduction to the Petra papyri by Koenen (1996) is still worth reading.

55. It seems that at the end of the Byzantine period, the Palestinians, like the Egyptians, preferred to settle disputes by arbitration rather than by lawsuits in the civil courts, which consequently become rarer in our sources.

56. Daniel (2001).

57. See *P.Nessana* I (thirteen texts, including a glossary of the *Aeneid* and a fragment of the poem); *P.Nessana* II.

58. Thus, *P.Ness.* II 77 v, which is of great interest for the status of non-Muslims in an Islamic land.

59. See *I.Ness.* (particularly pp. 131–210, by G. E. Kirk, C. B. Welles, and F. Rosenthal).

60. Crisci (1996). See Otranto (1998).

61. In fact, J. Rea, in Rea, Senior, and Hollis (1994, 262), did not find anything in the receipt from Bactria that is not also found, for example, in Egypt; see also the remarks of Crisci (1996) on the ostracon from Qala-i Sam, in Seistan (Iran/Afghanistan border), pp. 157–158, and on the manuscripts of Aï Khanoum, pp. 162–167.

62. Crisci (1996, 160–161) doubts the stylistic influence of Aramaic handwriting.

63. The stylistic separation from Egypt is, however, less marked in those countries in direct contact with it (i.e., the Judaean and the Nabataean regions).

64. *Pauli sententiae* 5, 25, 6: *ut exteriori scripturae fidem interior servet.*

65. See *P.Oxy.* XLII 3054.9–10; the same expression occurs for a sale at Tripolis in Phoenicia (*P.Oxy.* XLII 3053.12) and for a "foreign" sale (*P.Vind.Bosw.* 7.17).

66. This direction is that of the slave sale *PSI Congr.XX* 15 and is one of the reasons the editor posited a non-Egyptian origin for this contract (see the bibliography given in the introduction). Considering its rather compressed formula, it could be a fragment of a *scriptura interior.*

67. There is an astonishing survival of this custom in Bactria.

68. See *P.Yadin* I 13–16.

69. Some nuances are added by Gascou (1999), who notes that on the edges of Syria the pre-Roman administrative territorial divisions were kept and municipalization was slow and late.

70. See the clear summary article by Migliardi Zingale (1999); the study by Hengstl (2002), despite its title, takes into account the totality of the juridical problems of the Near Eastern papyri.

71. See Katzoff and Schaps (2005).

72. The documents drawn up in the brief reign of Bar Kokhba are in Hebrew and thus in conformity with halachic law, in agreement with the political and ideological program of this prince.

73. See Lewis (1970), Bowman (1976), and Geraci (1983).

74. With particularisms, as in the archives of Pathyris, which do not adopt the *transversa charta* direction and present the various parts of the document in columns along the fibers.

75. See D. Rathbone, *P.Thomas* 6, pp. 99–113.

76. In their commentaries, the editors of *P.Euphr.* refer several times to Egyptian papyri of the sixth century.

77. Regnal years are no longer attested in Egypt after 384/385 until their reappearance in the reign of Justinian.

BIBLIOGRAPHY

Auda, Y., and M.-F. Boussac. 1996. "Étude statistique d'un dépôt d'archives à Délos." In *Archives et sceaux du monde hellénistique: Archivi e sigilli nel mondo ellenistico*, ed. M.-F. Boussac and A. Invernizzi, 511–523. Paris: De Boccard.

Bérard, F., D. Feissel, P. Petitmengin, D. Rousset, and M. Sève. 2000. *Guide de l'épigraphiste: Bibliographie choisie des épigraphies antiques et médiévales*, 3d ed. Paris: Éditions Rue d'Ulm.

Bernard, P., and C. Rapin. 1994. "Un parchemin gréco-bactrien d'une collection privée." *CRAI*: 261–294.

Bowman, A. K. 1976. "Papyri and Roman Imperial History, 1960–1975." *JRS* 66: 153–173.

Brock, S. 1991. "Remarks on *P.Euphr.* 20." *Aram* 3: 259.

Cadell, H. 1989. "Les archives de Théophanès d'Hermoupolis: Documents pour l'histoire." In *Egitto e storia antica: Atti del Colloquio internazionale, Bologna, 31.8–2.9.1987*, ed. L. Criscuolo and G. Geraci, 315–323. Bologna: Cooperativa Libraria Universitaria Bologna.

Clarysse, W., and D. Thompson. 2007. "Two Greek Texts on Skin from Hellenistic Bactria." *ZPE* 159: 273–279.

Clarysse, W., and K. Vandorpe. 1995. *Zénon, un homme d'affaires grec à l'ombre des pyramides*. Leuven: Universitaire Pers Leuven.

Cohen, N. 2006. "New Greek Papyri from a Cave in the Vicinity of Ein Gedi." *SCI* 25: 87–95.

Cohen, N. 2007. "New Greek Papyri from a Cave in Mount Yishai, near Ein-Gedi." In J. Frösén, T. Purola, E. Salmenkivi eds., *Proceedings of the 24th International Congress of Papyrology Helsinki, 1-7 August, 2004*, vol 1: 191–197, with plate V of vol. 2. Commentationes Humanarum Litterarum 122:1. Helsinki: Societas Scientiarum Fennica.

Cotton, H. M. 1999. "Some Aspects of the Roman Administration of Judaea/Syria-Palaestina." In *Lokale Autonomie und römische Ordnungsmacht in den kaiserzeitlichen Provinzen vom 1. bis 3. Jahrhundert*, ed. W. Eck and E. Müller-Luckner, 75–91. Schriften des Historischen Kollegs, Kolloquien, 42. Munich: R. Oldenbourg Verlag.

———. 2003. "The Bar Kokhba Revolt and the Documents from the Judaean Desert: Nabataean Participation in the Revolt (*P. Yadin* 52)." In *The Bar Kokhba War Reconsidered: New Perspectives on the Second Jewish Revolt against Rome*, ed. P. Schäfer, 133–152. Tübingen: Mohr.

———, W. E. H. Cockle, and F. G. B. Millar. 1995. "The Papyrology of the Roman Near East: A Survey." *JRS* 85: 214–235.

Cotton, H. M., and W. Eck. 2002. "*P. Murabba'at* 114 und die Anwesenheit römischer Truppen in den Höhlen des Wadi Murabba'at nach dem Bar Kochba Aufstand." *ZPE* 138: 173–183.

Cowley, A. 1919. "The Pahlavi Document from Avroman." *JRAS*, n.s., 51: 147–154.

Crisci, E. 1996. *Scrivere greco fuori d'Egitto: Ricerche sui manoscritti greco-orientali di origine non egiziana dal IV secolo a.c. all'VIII d.c.* Papyrologica Florentina 27. Florence: Edizioni Gonnelli.

Cumont, F. 1926. *Les fouilles de Doura-Europos, 1922–1924.* Paris: Librairie orientaliste Paul Geuthner.

Daniel, R. W. 2001. "*P. Petra* Inv. 10 and Its Arabic." In *Atti del XXII Congresso Internazionale di Papirologia,* ed. I. Andorlini, G. Bastianini, M. Manfredi, and G. Menci, vol. 1, 331–341. Florence: Istituto Papirologico "G. Vitelli".

Drexhage, H.-J. 1998. "Ein Monat in Antiochia: Lebenshaltungskosten und Ernährungs-verhalten des Theophanes im Payni (26. Mai–24. Juni) ca. 318 n." *MBAH* 17: 1–10.

Durand, X. 1997. *Des Grecs en Palestine au IIIe siècle avant Jésus-Christ: Le dossier syrien des archives de Zénon de Caunos (261–252).* Paris: Gabalda.

Edmonds, C. J. 1952. "The Place-names of the Avroman Parchments." *BSOAS* 14: 478–482.

Feissel, D., and J. Gascou. 1989. "Documents d'archives romains inédits du Moyen Euphrate (IIIe siècle après J.-C.)." *CRAI:* 535–561.

Fink, R. O. 1971. *Roman Military Records on Papyrus.* American Philological Association Monograph 26. Cleveland: Case Western Reserve University Press.

Fournet, J.-L. 2003. Review of *P.Petra* I. *AnTard* 11: 398–404.

Gascou, J. 1999. "Unités administratives locales et fonctionnaires romains: Les données des nouveaux papyrus du Moyen Euphrate et d'Arabie." In *Lokale Autonomie und römische Ordnungsmacht in den kaiserzeitlichen Provinzen vom 1. bis 3. Jahrhundert,* ed. W. Eck and E. Müller-Luckner, 61–73. Schriften des Historischen Kollegs, Kolloquien, 42. Munich: R. Oldenbourg Verlag.

Geraci, G. 1983. *Genesi della provincia romana d'Egitto.* Bologna: Cooperativa Libraria Universitaria Editrice Bologna.

Gnoli, T. 2000. *Roma, Edessa, e Palmira nel III sec. d.c.: Problemi istituzionali: Uno studio sui papiri dell'Eufrate.* Biblioteca di Mediterraneo Antico 1, Pisa-Rome: Istituti Editoriali e Poligrafici Internazionali.

Grohmann, A. 1963. *Arabic Papyri from Hirbet el-Mird.* Leuven: Publications universitaires.

Guglielmo, L. 2003. "*Micae Qumranicae,* I manoscritti di Qumran a quasi sessant'anni dalla scoperta." *Papyrologica Lupiensia* 12: 99–114.

Hadot, P., and C. Rapin. 1987. "Les textes littéraires grecs de la Trésorerie d'Aï Khanoum." *BCH* 111: 225–266.

Haensch, R. 2001. "Zum Verständnis von P. Jericho 16 gr." *SCI* 20: 155–167.

Hengstl, J. 2002. "Die byzantinischen Papyri aus Petra: Stand der Bearbeitung und Bitte um Unterstützung." *RIDA* 3e s. 49: 341–357.

Hesseling, D. C. 1893. "Tabulae ceratae assendelftianae." *JHS* 13: 293–314.

Hollis, A. S. 1996. Addendum to Rea, Senior, and Hollis 1994. *ZPE* 110: 164.

Invernizzi, A. 1996. "Gli archivi pubblici di Seleucia sul Tigri." In *Archives et sceaux du monde hellénistique: Archivi e sigilli nel mondo ellenistico,* ed. M.-F. Boussac and A. Invernizzi, 131–143. Paris: De Boccard.

Katzoff, R., and D. Schaps. 2005. *Law in the Documents of the Judaean Desert.* Leiden: Brill.

Kennedy, D. L. 1994. "The Cohors XX Palmyrenorum at Dura Europos." In *The Roman and Byzantine Army in the East: Proceedings of a Colloquium Held at the Jagiellonian University, Krakow in September 1992,* ed. E. Dabrowa, 89–98. Cracow: Uniwersytet Jagiellonskiego.

Koenen, L. 1996. "The Carbonized Archive from Petra." *JRA* 9: 177–188.

Kruit, N. 2004. Review of *P.Petra* I. *BibO* 61: 98–106.

Lerner, J. D. 2003. "The Aï Khanoum Philosophical Papyrus." *ZPE* 142: 45–51.

Lewis, N. 1970. "'Graeco-Roman Egypt': Fact or Fiction?" In *Proceedings of the Twelfth International Congress of Papyrology*, 3–14. Am.Stud.Pap. VII. Toronto: A.M. Hakkert.

———. 1974. *Papyrus in Classical Antiquity.* Oxford: Clarendon.

Migliardi Zingale, L. 1999. "Diritto romano e diritti locali nei documenti del Vicino Oriente." *SDHI* 65: 217–231.

Millar, F. 1993. *The Roman Near East, 31 BC–AD 337.* Cambridge, Mass.: Harvard University Press.

Minns, E. H. 1915. "Parchments from the Parthian Period from Avroman in Kurdistan." *JHS* 35: 22–65.

Mitthof, F., and A. Papathomas. 2004. "Ein Papyruszeugnis aus dem spätantiken Karien." *Chiron* 34: 401–424.

Nyberg, H. S. 1923. "The Pahlavi Documents from Avroman." *Le Monde Oriental* 17: 182–230.

Otranto, R. 1998. Review of Crisci 1996. *QS* 24: 197–206.

Perrot, C. 1963. "Un fragment christo-palestinien découvert à Khirbet Mird." *RBi* 70: 506–555.

Pollard, N. 1996. "The Roman Army as 'Total Institution' in the Near East? Dura-Europos as a Case Study." In *The Roman Army in the East,* ed. D. L. Kennedy, 211–227. JRA Supplementary Series 18. Ann Arbor: Journal of Roman Archaeology.

Rapin, C. 1996. "Nouvelles observations sur le parchemin gréco-bactrien d'Asangôrna." *Topoi* 6: 458–469.

Rea, J. R., R. C. Senior, and A. S. Hollis. 1994. "A Tax Receipt from Hellenistic Bactria." *ZPE* 104: 261–280.

Reed, R. 1972. *Ancient Skins, Parchments, and Leathers.* New York: Seminar Press.

Reekmans, T. 1998. Review of Durand 1997. *Cd'E* 73: 144–158.

Saliou, C. 1992. "Les quatre fils de Polémocratès (*P. Dura* 19): Texte et archéologie." *Syria* 69: 65–100.

Schiffman, L. H., and J. C. VanderKam, eds. 2000. *Encyclopedia of the Dead Sea Scrolls.* 2 vols. New York: Oxford University Press.

Schwabe, M. 1945. "Khirbat Mafjar, Greek Inscribed Fragments." *QDAP* 12: 20–30.

Seyrig, H. 1985. "Cachets d'archives publiques de quelques villes de la Syrie romaine." In *Scripta varia: Mélanges d'archéologie et d'histoire*, 417–441. Paris: Librairie orientaliste Paul Geuthner; reprinted from *Mélanges de l'Université Saint-Joseph* 23 (1940) 85–107.

Sims-Williams, N. 1996. "Nouveaux documents sur l'histoire et la langue de la Bactriane." *CRAI*: 633–654.

Stephens, F. J. 1937. "A Cuneiform Tablet from Dura-Europos." *RAssyr*: 183–189.

Stolte, B. H. 2001. "The Impact of Roman Law in Egypt and the Near East in the Third Century A.D.: The Documentary Evidence. Some Considerations in the Margin of the Euphrates Papyri *(P. Euphr.)*." In *Administration, Prosopography, and Appointment Policies in the Roman Empire: Proceedings of the First Workshop of the International Network Impact of Empire (Roman Empire, 27 B.C.–A.D. 406)*, ed. L. de Blois, 167–179. Amsterdam: J. C. Gieben.

Teixidor, J. 1990. "Deux documents syriaques du IIIe siècle après J.C., provenant du Moyen Euphrate." *CRAI*: 144–146.

———. 1991. "Un document de fermage de 242 après J.C." *Semitica* 41–42: 195–208.

Tov, E. 1990. *The Greek Minor Prophets Scroll from Nahal Hever (8HevXIIgr). Seiyâl Collection,* vol. 1, with R. A. Kraft and P. J. Parsons. Oxford: Clarendon Press.

——. 2002. "The Discoveries in the Judaean Desert Series: History and System of Presentation." In E. Tov, M. Abegg, Jr. et al., *The Texts from the Judaean Desert: Indices and an Introduction to the Discoveries in the Judaean Desert Series.* Oxford: Clarendon Press.

——, and S. Pfann. 1993. *The Dead Sea Scrolls on Microfiche: A Comprehensive Facsimile Edition of the Texts from the Judean Desert.* Leiden: Brill.

van Haelst, J. 1991. "Cinq textes grecs provenant de Khirbet Mird." *AncSoc* 22: 297–317.

Youtie, H. C. 1973. "Ostraca from Sbeitah." *Scriptiunculae,* vol. 2, 982–988. Amsterdam: A. M. Hakkert (reproduced from *AJA* 40 [1936] 452–459).

Sources not included in the *Checklist*

I.Ness. = H. D. Colt Jr. et al., *Excavations at Nessana,* vol. 1, 131–210 (by G. E. Kirk, C. B. Welles, and F. Rosenthal). London 1962: British School of Archaeology in Jerusalem.

P.Daliyeh = D. Gropp, *Wadi Daliyeh.* Vol. 2, *The Samaria Papyri from Wadi Daliyeh,* ed. E. Schuller et al., in consultation with J. VanderKam and M. Brady, Qumran Cave 4. XXVIII: Miscellanea, Part 2. Oxford: Clarendon, 2001.

CHAPTER 21

WRITING HISTORIES FROM THE PAPYRI

TODD M. HICKEY

This was neither more nor less than the queer extension of her experience, the double life that, in the cage, she grew at last to lead. As the weeks went on there she lived more and more into the world of whiffs and glimpses, she found her divinations work faster and stretch further. It was a prodigious view as the pressure heightened, a panorama fed with facts and figures, flushed with a torrent of colour and accompanied with wondrous world-music. What it mainly came to at this period was a picture of how London could amuse itself; and that, with the running commentary of a witness so exclusively a witness, turned for the most part to a hardening of the heart.

—Henry James, "In the Cage" (1898)

Because the papyrologist is an artisan working often with intractable material, because his texts and the inferences he draws from them are presented to the substantive disciplines as dependable facts, he cannot afford to remain unaware of the basic assumptions that he uses. He is necessarily concerned

also with such rules as have been devised for the detection of
error. Unless he operates within this framework, however
flexible, of principles and rules, he can give no guarantee of
his competence as a maker of facts.

—Herbert Youtie, "The Papyrologist: Artificer of Fact"
(1963)

There is no history, there are only historians.

—Lucien Febvre, as quoted in Paul Ricoeur, *The Contribution of French Historiography to the Theory of History* (1980)

Many students' first encounter with papyrological "method" comes through the
writings of the great editor Herbert Youtie, in the texts that "have established
themselves as 'the papyrologist's Bible.'"[1] Though none will deny that we can learn
much from these works, some will surely be repelled by the proposition that
papyrology should serve as handmaiden for the "substantive disciplines."[2] Being
an "artificer" of someone else's "facts" will have little appeal; much more
intriguing—they will readily understand how James's telegraphist was drawn
in—will be the thought of "divining" narratives from the "whiffs and glimpses"
of others' lives.[3]

Academic backgrounds doubtless play a pivotal role in the reaction. In an
influential article published in 1988, Deborah Hobson probed her generation of
papyrologists, noting:

> Thus we decipher papyri not because we want to find out about the history of
> Egypt but because we enjoy working with the Greek language; indeed our aca-
> demic training for this discipline is primarily in Greek philology and palaeogra-
> phy, not usually in historiography. In order to justify what we do as a legitimate
> part of classical scholarship, we are trained to view Egyptian Greek documents as
> manifestations of Greek or Roman language and culture more than as evidence for
> life in Egypt itself. (353)

But what if someone comes to papyrology from history, not philology? For certain
kinds of ancient historians, the papyri have an obvious appeal; of all the sources
available, they seem best suited to answer the kinds of questions and tell the kinds
of stories that interest them.[4] The texts themselves may well be secondary—
stimulating, even "seductive" (thus Hobson 1988, 362), means to an end more
than ends in themselves.[5]

In fact, papyrology has a long tradition of broader inquiry and historical
synthesis that extends all the way back to the days of Wilcken.[6] Nor has the process
itself of writing history from the papyri altogether escaped inquiry and discussion,
with Peter van Minnen (1993) and Roger Bagnall (1995) making the most important contributions in recent years.[7] Though the present chapter cannot retrace the
arguments in these works, it has been written in conscious dialogue with their

criticisms, prescriptions, and conclusions. Like Bagnall, I have drawn examples from the research (including my own) that is best known to me; as a result, my coverage of the field (and its problems and possibilities) is uneven. In light of the purpose of this volume—that is, lest this contribution become dated too quickly— I have privileged contemporary work of quality. Younger scholars also have an important place, for it is they who are doing some of the most interesting and challenging research.

Looking into the Mirror,
Opening Up the Closet

For the last decade of his life, Lucien Febvre's mantra was reported to be "History, science of the past, science of the present."[8] History's best practitioners do not need to be reminded that "the essence of the historical" is "a return of the past in the present discourse" (Certeau 1986, 214); they write self-consciously, acutely aware of their own "situatedness," of their ideologies and limitations. Thus, we find Jacques Revel counseling, "[H]e [the historian] knows that his information represents a choice in reality, upon which he superimposes other choices. He can at least attempt to measure the consequences of them and to take advantage of them" (1989, xvi), while Gadamer (influential in historical circles) advised, "The important thing is to be aware of one's own bias, so that the text can present itself in all its otherness and thus assert its own truth against one's own fore-meanings [*Vorurteile*]" (1989, 269). Self-reflection, however, has never been a hallmark of papyrology (cf. Bagnall 1995, 1), and this aspect of its disciplinary culture, I would argue, has been a significant impediment for *intra*disciplinary historical writing. Manifestations of this lack of reflection are readily discernable: Despite being in the vanguard of ancient studies in its application of technology, papyrology remains *in some senses* a nineteenth-century discipline.[9] The most unfortunate testimonium of this is the field's long failure to address the illicit trade in papyri,[10] which continues to this day—in contravention of Egyptian antiquities law and the 1970 UNESCO Convention on the Means of Prohibiting and Preventing the Illicit Import, Export, and Transfer of Ownership of Cultural Property.[11] Yet even when acquisitions have (or appear to have) fulfilled the letter of the law, there remain cases that leave one wondering how far removed we are from Belzoni's declaration, so jarring to the twenty-first-century ear: "The purpose of my researches was to rob the Egyptians of their papyri" (1820, 157). Consider, for example, the Milan Posidippus. The fact that "tomb robbers" (or the like—note our rhetorical proximity to "Indiana Jones") were its ultimate source was widely reported in the press, yet scholarly comment on the legal and ethical issues of the papyrus has been virtually nonexistent (despite the appearance of well more than one hundred publications concerning other aspects of the epigrams). I can only point to Dirk Obbink's forthright comments, reported in Wilford (2002): "I don't think anyone knows the details of what happened, or if they do, they're not talking.... The Egyptians have laws against looting and might demand the return of the papyrus." At the very least, ambiguous acquisitions and kindred acts (or *inactions*) imply the perpetuation of colonial sentiments, of paternalism and the notion that the West is the true heir to the ancient Mediterranean world.[12] This matters because these sentiments can subvert the writing of even those with the best intentions. Thus, Hobson, in an important critique of the "hellenocentricity" of papyrology, could nonetheless still write the following (1988, 355–356):

> When one gets out into the [Egyptian] countryside away from the major centres, one feels that one has been transported back to the world of the papyri. The mudbrick houses clustered together, topped by dovecotes, oxen pulling the water wheel, Egyptians riding into the desert on camels, even toll stations set up along the main road, all attest to a life for the peasant which must have remained remarkably unchanged from the earliest times to the present.[13]

In short, Phiroze Vasunia's prescription for mainstream classics is equally relevant for papyrology: "What matters is...that they [students of antiquity] genuinely think through what it means for them to profess and teach the past in the present historical moment, when the legacy of empire continues to do its work openly or in secret" (2003, 95).

That said, how can one expect critical engagement with present practice if the past remains unexamined? When it has been written, the history of papyrology itself has verged on hagiography: These are the giants upon whose shoulders we stand.[14] While the achievements of pioneers like Grenfell and Hunt remain remarkable and certainly merit acknowledgment, there seems ample room for the "rest of the story": for criticisms of method, to be sure, but also for the contextualization (or, if one prefers, deconstruction) of scholarship,[15] which should include readings of politics and even private lives.[16] Some may cry foul or call it gossip, but where does one draw the line between public and private,[17] and who is charged with holding the pen? Much more energy needs to be devoted to the creation and dissemination of disciplinary archives, and the purging of "objectionable" material from such assemblages (by those other than the principals) should be viewed in the harshest light. "Archivization produces as much as it records the event"—something of which those who work with archives of papyri should already be acutely aware.[18]

For those "on the outside" who wish to use the papyri to write history, there are additional impediments. Some of these (e.g., the need to learn technical skills to control the evidence) are obvious,[19] but a serious one, another nineteenth-century holdover, has received inadequate consideration. This is the gold standard for presenting papyrological texts, which has changed little since 1898, the year in which Grenfell and Hunt published the first volume of *The Oxyrhynchus Papyri*.[20] Although their "Oxyrhynchus model" was clearly superior to the alternatives of the day,[21] it does a great disservice to the papyri by excessively alienating them from the infrastructures that they reference and in which they functioned. Publication is a second excavation; like the archaeologist's brush, it sweeps away ancient traces, and through it, papyri partake ever more of the "circuit of activities characteristic of the present" and become ever more removed from the "sequence of operations to which they belonged."[22]

One of an editor's objectives should be to mitigate or remediate this process. Under the "Oxyrhynchus model," however, Greek literature and Christian texts receive pride of place at the front of the volume,[23] while the documents found with them (to say nothing of other artifacts) are relegated to the back, sometimes without translations or even complete transcriptions.[24] This method of organization is specious, for a literary "work is situated in history in a way that gives it documentary dimensions, and the document has worklike aspects.... [B]oth the 'document' and the 'work' are texts involving an interaction between documentary and worklike components" (LaCapra 1983, 30–31; cf. also 1995, 805; Chartier 1982, 39–40). Non-Greek texts, moreover, almost never appear.[25] Philology and "high" (i.e., Athens-Jerusalem) texts (in the traditional sense) are privileged over the social and cultural matrix of the papyrus itself—an irony, of course, since papyri *are* objects, often refuse[26]—and, in the interest of "objectivity" and "facts," speculation—the lifeblood of history—is avoided. The scholarly fashions of the day should not sully the papyrus, for which the goal is nothing short of monumentalization (although its text may be damaged, illegible, and subject to revision).[27] The final product, although touted for its ease of use (principally because translations are included), can be rough going for nonspecialists and students: "Context," however one chooses to define it, is a first principle of accessibility.

This is not to imply that editorial practice has been monolithic in the years since *P.Oxy.* I appeared. For decades the Dutch and Flemish, for example, have tended to construct their editions around archives, dossiers, and other kinds of clusters of related texts;[28] Katelijn Vandorpe's edition of the "Dryton archive" (*P.Dryton*), with its combination of the literary and the documentary, the Greek and the Egyptian, texts on various media (papyri, ostraca, even graffiti), and a healthy dose of interpretation, is an excellent representative of this alternative editorial paradigm.[29] Momentum for the contextualized study of "texts" and "objects" has also grown in the last decade or so,[30] and in 2005 a call for an integrated approach to the publication of papyri and other archaeological material was made at a panel during the annual meeting of Archaeological Institute of America.[31]

While such programs of scholarship certainly deserve encouragement, it is clear that more can be done. What is especially striking is the simplicity of some of the possible improvements; they would not require papyrologists to make a significant investment in new approaches to their texts (though novel approaches could certainly play a role). For example, accessibility—which papyrologists should prize out of self-interest if for no other reason (cf. Bagnall 1995, 113)—could easily be enhanced by the inclusion of broader synthetic studies within the text volume itself; these essays, which might be written by the editor or outsiders (or both in collaboration), could try to answer fundamental questions like "Why should a nonspecialist reader care about these texts?" or "Why are these papyri important?"[32] Moreover, while addressing the infrastructure of texts is desirable, it does not suffice to provide a list of artifacts without interpretation.[33] Papyrologists' general lack of interest in the visual also needs remedying.[34] The intersections of papyri with the "Fayyum" portraits (and their mummies)—indeed, with funerary art in general—with Ptolemaic royal sculpture, and with the hard-stone heads of priests (to give just three examples) furnish opportunities too rich to leave unexploited.[35]

THREE MODES: INTEGRATION, SCALE, VOICE

Integration

If the reassimilation of text and infrastructure has been a source of disappointment, the integration of papyri into the history of the ancient Mediterranean world has proceeded apace. Though rejections of papyrological (and other) evidence on the basis of Egypt's alterity or *Sonderstellung* continue to be made (and certain omissions of Egyptian material continue to baffle; cf., e.g., Horden and Purcell 2000), these seem to be more a function of "old habits dying hard" than anything else.[36] In 1995, Bagnall could point to multiple works that undermined these notions (see, e.g., pp. 61–68), and the list would be much longer today. More important, the validity of Egyptian evidence seems to have become less of an issue in this scholarship; in other words, papyrologists and ancient historians are moving from a defensive (or an offensive) posture toward one of assumption of relevance. In Cribiore's excellent survey (2001) of Greek education in the Hellenistic and Roman worlds,[37] for example, the validity of the Egyptian evidence is addressed in a few sentences in the introduction to the volume; her presentation seems almost matter-of-fact when compared to earlier treatments of the issue.[38]

A recent and rather ambitious attempt at integration is Constantin Zuckerman's *Du village à l'Empire* (2004).[39] Here, as the title suggests, there is no question about the relevance of the Aphroditê papyri with which Zuckerman is working for the broader stream of history: "This Egyptian village [i.e., Aphroditê] proves to be an accurate sample of imperial society, a microcosm in which problems that have been among the most debated of the economic and social history of the Byzantine Empire have left their imprint and, perhaps, the key to their solution" (12).[40] Zuckerman employs his texts, principally a fiscal register dating to 526/527, to posit additional Justinianic reforms in Egypt (beyond the famous Edict XIII; see 52–56); to document the impact of the bubonic plague on Constantinople (207–219); and to argue that fiscal practice in Aphroditê prefigures that in the Middle Byzantine Empire (238–240). Though parts of the book fail to convince (e.g., the discussion of the "minus carats" system [cf. 66 ff.] and, more important, the village social structure proposed [221 ff.]), and while the author's explicit hostility toward models and apparent reticence about experimenting with his data (cf. 234) cannot be encouraged (see further below), his confident injection of the papyri into mainstream debates is refreshing, as is the combination of serious historical discussion with an edition of a text critical for the author's arguments.

Written with similar assumptions about the relevance of the papyri (and comparable bravado) and also concerned with the society and economy of late antiquity is Banaji (2001).[41] There the resemblance ends, however: Banaji's scope is much larger in that he covers the whole of the Mediterranean (with an eastern emphasis) from the third to the seventh century, and—far from being averse to models—his materialist paradigm radiates from the pages. Banaji's ideology aside, his is one of the more important volumes on late antiquity to have appeared in the last two decades; the breadth of learning on display is remarkable, and the exposition provokes in a manner that recalls Peter Brown's œuvre. The combination, moreover, of literary and documentary evidence, archaeology, numismatics, and comparative data is unparalleled elsewhere in the field. Banaji is surely correct about the fourth-century rise of a new elite that had its origins in the military and bureaucracy and about the ever-increasing concentration of resources in the hands of these grandees. Other arguments—for example, his assertion that wage labor expanded dramatically on the "great estates"—are, however, more problematic. There is an irony in these cases: Despite the blinding array of references to primary sources, Banaji's work might be described as he has portrayed Weber's: "antithetical to historical detail" (ibid., 31). Not all detail, to be sure, but detail that does not suit the author's model of agricultural capitalism. It is the model that has preeminence here.[42]

This does not mean that models should be avoided (as Zuckerman has done), only that their heuristic or catalytic function cannot be forgotten; the cart must not come before the horse. Models from the social sciences have been used with particular effectiveness by the "Stanford School" of ancient history.[43] In Manning (2003), for example, the traditional ("Polybius," i.e., post-Raphia) model of Ptolemaic decline is overthrown by arguments based on the sources—an approach, of course, that even the most committed positivist would find appealing. The novelties in

Manning's work are the inclusion of Egyptian sources (not only papyri but also incised material—the Edfu temple donation text is particularly important) and, more critically, the substitution of an alternate, institutions-based ("neoclassical") model of the state.[44] Manning acknowledges that his own construction might itself be overturned (or need modification) with the advent of new texts, but he believes "that such risks are important. For in order to understand any document . . . one must have a conception of the historical context as well an idea of the structure of the state" (xi). Two points deserve emphasis here: One is that Manning's model, like all good models, is flexible, even expendable; the other—even more important—is that risk and experimentation should always trump the fear of making a mistake in historical writing. This can pose challenges for the papyrologist, who, in the editorial role, has been trained to produce accurate texts (and probably to refrain from "excessive" speculation).

Given the wealth of numerical data that the papyri contain, it is no surprise that papyrologists have long engaged in quantitative research. Generally speaking, however, these analyses have lacked sophistication, while the data themselves have tended to escape close scrutiny or (just as bad) conjecture—nothing ventured, nothing gained.[45] The simplest calculations can be fruitful if one is willing to experiment with the data; although precise "answers" may not result, the benchmarks or parameters established are often just as useful.[46] Yet computer-aided modeling is where the possibility of real advances is greatest. Anyone reading a book like Townsend (1993), an argument for the complementarity of historical data and the abstract modeling of (neoclassical) economics, cannot help but think that such models might be profitably applied to data from the papyri. The hitch is the mathematics, which are likely to be beyond the abilities of all but a few editors and ancient historians; collaboration would need to occur much more often than not. Some younger scholars have demonstrated, however, that one person can wear both hats: Ruffini (2004), for example, applies social network theory—and includes an admirable explanation of it—to the communities of "pagan" scholars in Athens, Alexandria, and Upper Egypt (or, more precisely, to the *Vita Isidori* of Damascius). This enables him to conclude that the Alexandrians were linked more closely to the Athenians than to their counterparts elsewhere in Egypt, and to posit alternative explanations for the collapse of the Alexandrian community in the 480s. More striking is the broad applicability plausibly proposed for the method: "The amount of data is nearly limitless. We could use this approach on Oxyrhynchite landholders, the civic [*sic*] elite of Aphrodito, or the desert fathers of Nitria or Scetis"—to give but three examples.[47]

The promise of these quantitative methods for historical research is echoed by another young practitioner, Katja Mueller, whose work has focused on the geography of the Fayyum.[48] A few caveats, however, seem in order. It is rather easy to be wowed by the complicated modeling employed in these methods and to attribute greater accuracy to them by virtue of this complexity (and because mathematics seems absolute), when, in fact, their difficulty likely makes them more susceptible to error than research conducted using traditional methods. Mueller, for example, dutifully provides her data, but who has checked them (or will do so)? Since most of her publications have appeared in unrefereed journals intended for papyrologists and ancient historians, this seems a valid question.[49] Then there is the matter of the continued viability of some of these methods. Mueller, again, uses the rank-size rule (Mueller 2002), but the discipline of geography has largely abandoned such techniques for methods informed by theories that integrate the spatial and the social (Lefèbvre, Foucault, Latour, et al.).[50] This does not mean that Mueller should not have created her model, only that its consumers should be aware that her method has fallen out of favor in its primary discipline.

Yet a problematic engagement is better than no engagement at all (cf. the remarks of Bynum 1991, 21, concerning American medievalists). Although this certainly holds true with respect to quantitative modeling, it is also valid for methods from cultural studies, a collection of disciplines for which Graeco-Roman Egypt—multicultural, quotidian, ruled by foreigners, and so on—seems a perfect fit. In Bagnall's words, "Within the world of the ancient Mediterranean, no society offers the array of evidence for the workings of cultural interaction in the lives of a wide spectrum of individuals that the Egypt of the papyri does.... Historians working with papyri thus have an opening to many of the liveliest areas of contemporary thought" (1995, 117). To be sure, others have also recognized this promise,[51] but I am struck by the compelling (and exciting) possibilities that remain. An ongoing project of my own has benefited considerably from readings in postcolonial and globalization theory, to such an extent that an extended description seems justified.[52] Though similar approaches have been utilized for Ptolemaic Egypt,[53] I would suggest that the Roman occupation furnishes a more suitable application.

Excursus: The Priests of Soknebtynis

> The vanquished always want to imitate the victor in his distinctive characteristics, his dress, his occupation, and all his other conditions and customs.
>
> —Ibn Khaldūn, *al-Muqaddima* (trans. Franz Rosenthal)

Kronion and Isidora were deputy prophet and prophetess, respectively, in the Tebtynis temple during the final quarter of the second century CE.[54] The eighty-odd texts in their dossier document eight generations of their family (cf. figure 21.1) from the second half of the first century CE into the third.[55] The dossier is scattered around the globe: Components of it ended up in Berkeley, Cairo, Copenhagen, Florence, Heidelberg, Milan, Lund, New Haven, and Oxford. "Thick" documentation of a group of individuals over such a lengthy period is unparalleled in the corpus of Roman papyri,[56] but more remarkable is the fact that the dossier includes literature in Greek, in addition to documentary texts, and that we also possess four hundred or so Egyptian literary papyri that these priests were using.[57]

This bilingual corpus reveals an apparent paradox: Scholarship has tended to view village priests as insular—a notion that is supported by the marriage practices attested in these texts—but this particular family was manifestly engaged with "Greek" culture.[58] I must emphasize that this engagement, which occurred through reading and writing (and presumably conversation) was not a casual one.[59] The handwriting of some family members is quite accomplished, even professional.[60] Moreover, while one might have anticipated priests having an interest in the Greek astronomical and astrological texts, for example, in the dossier, they clearly were also reading literature that would seem more at home in an elite "Hellenic" context (like the Hesiodic *Catalogue of Women*).[61]

On a more general (i.e., village) level, this phenomenon has already been noted in Van Minnen (1998), but the explanation he gives there (in an otherwise impressive piece of scholarship) is unsatisfying. Van Minnen's account is both teleological (i.e., Greek culture is seen as progressive) and without a satisfactory model of agency (culture is imagined as simply acting upon the priests). In addition, the notion of exchange or negotiation is lacking (the priests are assumed merely to be recipients); nor is there any acknowledgment that the process would have been individualized and uneven (the presence of "microcultures").[62] The papyri are well suited to provide the necessary nuance, but even unparalleled detail is of limited value without a theoretical framework.

"Strategies of power" and resistance, that is, "an experience that constructs and reconstructs the identity of subjects" (Gupta and Ferguson 1997, 19), are compelling concepts to place at the center of such a framework. The Roman conquest of Egypt in 30 BCE was a watershed event for Egyptian priests because they became subject to new strategies of power; the Empire would organize Egypt's differences in ways that varied significantly from those of the Ptolemies. Most notably, Roman rule led to the rupture of priestly and royal codependency and to the upheaval of Ptolemaic social structure:[63] With the exception of the citizens of a few "Greek" cities, the Empire's new subjects all became mere "Egyptians."[64] Yet (as elsewhere) the realities of rule led the Romans to make certain distinctions within this subaltern mass. Well known is the Roman *construction* of the "Hellenic" metropolite and gymnasial "classes."[65] Membership in both of these groups (the latter was actually an elite subset of the former) had a hereditary basis (in theory, at least), and the ruling power established an administrative apparatus or, rather, system of examination, the *epikrisis*, to control access to them.[66] Their members received various privileges (e.g., lower poll tax), while the gymnasial class, in conformity to the Roman belief that the wealthy and educated were best suited to rule, had access to civic power. The membership controls and privileges for both groups naturally

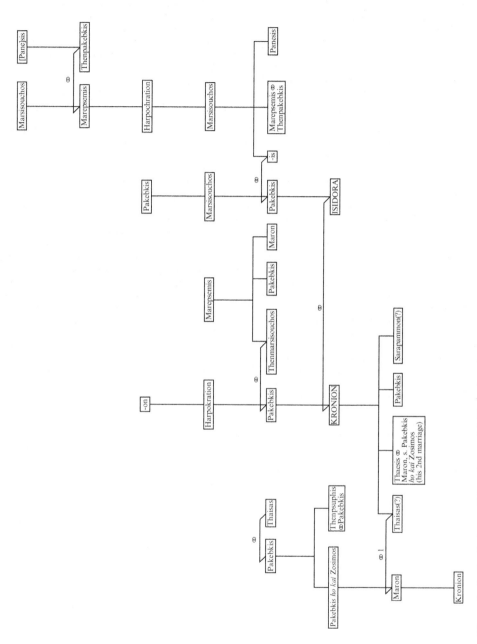

Figure 21.1. The principal relatives of Kronion and Isidora (working stemma).

contributed to endogamy and, in one part of Egypt at least, to extraordinarily high rates of sibling marriage (cf. Bagnall and Frier 1994, 130).

Less recognized is the fact that the Romans treated the priests in much the same way. They clearly saw value in the Egyptian cults and viewed their personnel as an important component of the social and administrative machinery.[67] The Romans did not need to create a hereditary priesthood, but they controlled access to the existing body through examinations comparable to those used for the elites in the *métropoleis* (cf. Capponi 2005, 94). Commentators have traditionally viewed these regulations as oppressive and ignored the obvious preference being shown.[68] The priests also enjoyed privileges comparable to or better than those of the urban elites, and, as already noted, they too practiced endogamy. This tendency predated the Romans, but Roman policy certainly did nothing to discourage the behavior.

Based on these kinds of similarities between the priests and the metropolite-gymnasial class, we might anticipate contact between the two groups.[69] Though much work remains to be done on this question, links did exist between the family of Kronion and Isidora and the descendants of Patron, a wealthy gymnasial clan that owned substantial property in the *meris* of Polemon (the division of the Arsinoite nome in which Tebtynis was located). Though the attested connections are what sociologists call "weak ties," they are nonetheless significant; it is a widely accepted principle of network theory that links of this sort provide access to social capital otherwise unavailable in one's own group.[70] Such connections also suggest that priestly interaction with metropolite networks played a role—an important one, possibly—in cultural exchange.

The papyri provide explicit testimony that cultural exchange occurred, but why it occurred is another question. That Greek medical and scientific texts were valued by the priests as "advances" is obviously unsatisfactory (i.e., teleological) and does not, in any case, account for the other Greek bookrolls that they were reading. Looking to the pragmatics of power, to culture as a signifier—to resistance—is helpful. "Practices that are resistant to a particular strategy of power are . . . never innocent of or outside power, for they are always capable of being tactically appropriated and redeployed within another strategy of power" (Gupta and Ferguson 1997, 18–19). Thus, one may argue that the same liminal position that enabled priests to represent legitimate (divinely sanctioned) power to a subject population also made them susceptible to Roman inducements and desirous of signs that would further distinguish them from the mass of *ananthrôpoi* ("inhuman") Egyptians.[71]

Yet one must take care to avoid oversimplifying what would have been a complex and shifting situation. Emulation surely does not imply wholesale adoption. On the contrary, adoption would have been selective, not to mention mutating and inverting,[72] and the priests' traditional constituencies and power bases would not have been ignored. The indigenous (written) language of the priests remained remarkably resistant to Greek loanwords (e.g., Clarysse 1987); John Ray speaks of demotic as "purified and filtered" (1994, 264). At the same time, the substantial Egyptian literary activity at Tebtynis has tended to be associated with preserving the past.[73] Both phenomena constitute resistance, but perhaps not in the manner that one might think at first glance. Some Egyptologists view priestly literary activity as a continuation of (implicitly or explicitly "pure") pharaonic traditions (e.g., Hoffmann 2000, 196–197), but the imperial context requires us to pay more and careful attention to the language and content of the Roman-period texts, which are not identical to earlier versions.[74] Then there is the case of the god Soknebtynis: Curiously, he was not syncretized with a Greek deity (Kronos) until after the Roman conquest.[75] Typically it is the conqueror who identifies his gods with those of the subject (*interpretatio*; cf. Webster 1995), but on this occasion, indigenous tradition seems to have "reached out" to authority.[76] Or did it? To what extent is this an act of conciliation, since it usurps the conqueror's traditional prerogative? Strikingly, the priests of Tebtynis overwhelmingly "endorsed" the syncretization with a practice at the heart of identity: the choice of their own names.[77]

Scale and Voice

"[F]oxes or hedgehogs, butterflies or mole catchers, parachutists or truffle hunters..." So goes Le Roy Ladurie's taxonomy of historians of literature (1998),[78] but the same might be said of those writing history from the papyri. Yet, despite the references to Braudel—when papyrologists have engaged with historical theory, the point of engagement has often been the *Annales* school (cf. Bagnall 1995, 112 ff.)—or the patently "macro" research of "parachutists" like Manning or Mueller,[79] papyrology has greater affinities with *microhistoria*; the evidence itself demands this.[80] A good deal of the writing that has drawn on the papyri is microhistory—of a sort; what is typically lacking is the theoretical framework, the crucial possibility of engaging the larger scales. This seems a missed opportunity. Microhistory, when done properly, is hardly anecdotal:[81] "Structures" may be put at risk by individuals.[82] "To the degree that a presupposition of submission by social agents goes with a macrohistorical choice of scale, the microhistorical choice leads to the opposite expectation, that of random strategies in which conflicts and negotiations take precedence under the sign of uncertainty" (Ricoeur 2004, 219). This is one of the benefits of reducing the scale of inquiry: Working "level with the ground" (*au ras du sol*) reveals "not just familiar objects in miniature but different configurations of the social" (Revel 1995a, 46; cf. Levi 1991, 97).

Objections that microhistory is dated reveal an ignorance of the approach; as is the case with the *Annales,* microhistory continues to be reformulated, and it readily accepts grafts from other methods.[83] Graeco-Roman Egypt is without doubt the theater of the ancient Mediterranean world that is best suited for serious trials (and refinements) of its practices. At the very least, microhistory's concept of the "normal exception" (*eccezione normale*) could help focus research energies on dissonant cultural fragments or, in other words, on the texts (sensu lato) that "certain forces have attempted to melt down into the anonymous mass of an unrecognizable culture" (the words of Derrida 1989, 821); these present our best opportunities to challenge existing conceptions.[84]

Closely connected to microhistory is the use of narrative,[85] which historians have adopted for a number of reasons: to emphasize the subjectivity of the historical process, to highlight the contradictions and heteroglossia of fragmentary sources (and representations of these sources in the historical present), or because the "contingent and discontinuous facts of the past become intelligible only when woven together as stories" (Lowenthal 1985, 218). Once again, the evidence from Graeco-Roman Egypt seems eminently suited for exploration,[86] yet initiative has been lacking: Only the work of James Keenan stands out for its narrative (and microhistorical) sensibilities.[87] While a papyrological Alabi's World is beyond our evidence—even the "multivocal" katochoi archive—and we lack "thick" enough documentation to support a Stories of Scottsboro, a Death of Woman Wang (with Aphroditê and environs in place of the T'an-ch'eng district, and the poet/notary Dioscoros taking the roles of both the author P'u Sung-ling and the magistrate Huang Liu-hung?) might be possible.[88] Less controversially—Woman Wang was criticized for its "fictions"—an examination of storytelling in Graeco-Roman Egypt along the lines of Fiction in the Archives could certainly be written; our petitions are not that far removed from the lettres de rémission that Natalie Zemon Davis employed in that volume (1987).[89] This is not to suggest that papyrologists ape these outside paradigms but to encourage them to extend the boundaries of their reading and to allow the fruits of this reading to inform their work. This is one trait of Keenan's research, and it also characterizes Sebastian Richter's recent study of the corpus of Coptic child-donation contracts. As one might expect (given the unusual content of these texts), this is well-trodden ground, but Richter's readings in cultural studies (in particular narratology) have led him to a novel and compelling conclusion: that the children involved were troublesome cases (for medical or other reasons) and that they were donated by overburdened parents who were in "a complex dilemma of emotional, social, and religious components." The stereotypical narrationes in these texts, "group autobiographies" owing to the many voices involved, bore the "therapeutic energy" of coherent narrative; they allowed those involved "to make sense out of nonsense. The interaction and communication between the monastery [receiving the children] and the issuers of child donation documents, resulting in the child donation narratio, would have been a medium providing the parents themselves and their community" with a means of coping with "disturbing, isolating experiences."[90]

The objective of this short contribution has not been to prescribe but to encourage and illuminate possibilities. Those who work with the material remains of Graeco-Roman Egypt are in a unique position among scholars of antiquity: Our evidence is such that a much wider range of methods and approaches is available to us. By virtue of this, we ought to be the pioneers in our departments—and innovation is certainly the best argument for our continued existence. Embracing our opportunities and having the courage to experiment (and speculate) boldly need not (and should not) require any dilution of the technical rigor that has characterized papyrology from its earliest days.[91] At the same time, we are obliged to begin working much more self-consciously—if philosophers are not always papyrologists, it would be desirable, at least, that papyrologists be philoso-phers[92]—and we must do so with the same scrupulousness that Youtie advised for editing. It is only through looking carefully in the mirror (and opening up our closet) that growth will occur, that our histories will merit the gifts that time, climate, and chance have bequeathed us.

Acknowledgments

This chapter assumes some familiarity with the fundamental texts and schools of historiography. For a good survey of these (written by a historian of late antiquity, no less), see Clark (2004).

I thank James Keenan, Leslie Kurke, Joe Manning, Elisabeth O'Connell, and the participants of the Columbia Summer Seminar in Papyrology for their remarks on earlier versions of this chapter; the deficiencies that remain are my own. I am responsible for all unattributed translations. I offer this chapter to the memory of Jock Weintraub in gratitude for those occasions when I was able to sit at his table.

NOTES

1. Keenan, this volume, chapter 3, on Youtie (1963, 1974).

2. Cf. the criticism in Van Minnen (1993, 12): "Papyrology is not an ancillary discipline, a view often erroneously held even by papyrologists. Papyrology is a primary discipline."

3. I owe the "In the Cage" metaphor (but not its application to papyrology) to Levi (1991, 106). Admittedly, the response of the papyrologist–historian to these narratives is more likely to be one of wonder, not a "hardened heart."

4. Cf. Bagnall (1995, vii): "Because the papyri are by far our best ancient source for many aspects of these areas of history [i.e., social and economic history]."

5. Cf. Bynum (1991, 15): "Behind whatever smooth surface they [i.e., her essays] may present to the modern reader lies the hard grappling with the texts—reading them, dating them, ascribing them—that is the *ordinary* work of the medievalist" (emphasis added).

6. See Keenan, this volume, chapter 3.

7. I would be remiss if I did not also mention Bowman (2002), a thoughtful essay.

8. Reported in Braudel (1969, 61); cf. also Wallerstein (1995). For this issue, see, for example, Gadamer (1987).

9. For the heyday of papyrological discovery, the Victorian Age, see Keenan, this volume, chapter 3.

10. Cf. already the remarks of Morelli (2002, 313). (I thank Fabian Reiter for bringing this review to my attention.)

11. The UNESCO Convention is available at http://portal.unesco.org/en/ev. php-URL_ID=13039&URL_DO=DO_TOPIC&URL_SECTION=201.html (accessed September 29, 2008). For an English translation of Egyptian law 117 of 1983 see http:// unesdoc.unesco.org/images/0006/000666/066629eo.pdf (accessed September 29, 1983). Since this chapter was written there have been welcome developments. In June 2007, the American Society of Papyrologists (ASP) overwhelmingly approved a resolution concerning the illicit trade in papyri. Two months later the leadership of the Association Internationale de Papyrologues (AIP) took up the issue at the International Congress of Papyrology in Ann Arbor; they sponsored an educational plenary session and created an ad-hoc committee to study the commerce further.

12. Cf. Reid (2002) on Western domination and control of Egypt's antiquities during the "long nineteenth century." The sequel to this volume will cover the years up to Nasser.

13. Contrast, for example, Abu-Lughod (1991, 154) ("homogeneity, coherence, and timelessness").

14. "Shoulders of giants" is a reference to R. K. Merton's celebrated work (1965) concerning "Newton's" aphorism. Merton's argument that a unified consensus (or meta-narrative) is being built through scholarship is (unconsciously) central to current papyrological method.

15. "Criticism of method": Van Minnen (1993) gives us a good model. "Contextualization of scholarship": Hombert (1933) (discussed by Keenan in chapter three of this volume) makes for ironic reading if one has any familiarity with the history of the Belgian Congo; one wonders whether parts of it could have been written without the "benefit" of the First World War; cf. Hochschild (1998, 292–306).

16. The Italian interest in the history of the discipline is admirably exceptional, and in some cases, "difficult" issues have been addressed; see, for example, Fabre (2002–2003) (on Medea Norsa's "racial" identity under Mussolini) and now Canfora (2005), kindly brought to my attention by my colleagues at the Istituto Papirologico "G. Vitelli." Cf. also Gigante (1986) (a reference I owe to James Keenan).

17. Papyrologists are confronted with the same problem in their ancient texts; see, for example, Franko (1988).

18. The quote is from Derrida (1995, 34) (speaking of the transformations of "technical structures"—fax machines, e-mail, etc.—but equally relevant to human agency).

19. For such "formidable entry fees," cf. Bagnall (1995, 110–111).

20. What follows should in no way be considered an indictment of the *quality* of the scholarship in the series *The Oxyrhynchus Papyri*.

21. Cf. Keenan (1993, 142–143) and chapter three of this volume (more critically).

22. I borrow the words of Certeau (1995, 444). For comparable observations, see Gagos, Gates, and Wilburn (2005); I thank the authors for sharing a draft of their publication. Note as well Van Minnen (1993, 12), observing Von Wilamowitz-Moellendorff's ability to see the "big picture" despite the volumes' organization.

23. Cf. Van Minnen (1993, 11) on literary papyrology: "New literary papyri are as a rule studied in splendid isolation from the culture that produced them."

24. The typology employed in a recent volume: "New Literary Texts (a. Tragedy and Comedy; b. Prose)," "Known Literary Texts," "Subliterary Texts (a. Scribal Practice and Draft; b. Magic)," "Documentary Texts." On occasion, the ancients' own attitudes seem to stand in stark contrast; cf. *P.Mich.* VI 390.

25. For the non-Greek material from Oxyrhynchus, cf. Bowman (2002, 218).

26. I do not mean to suggest that Grenfell and Hunt completely ignored material contexts (even in volumes besides *P.Fay.*). For the exploitation of the information that they do provide, see, for example, Verhoogt (1998). O'Connell (2007) shows how much can be done with the limited records that have been preserved.

27. In the preface to *P.Oxy.* L, the general editors write of their late colleague Edgar Lobel: "At the same time he inherited and continued a particular style: no parade of scholarship, no clutter of bibliography; no shrinking from 'I,' when the pronoun properly represented the subjective limitations of eyesight and intuition; an insistence on fact and precision, a distaste for easy solutions and grandiose speculations. This is a tradition of which we are proud; we hope that our next fifty volumes will maintain it."

"Subject to revision": There are currently eleven *volumes* of corrections to documentary texts alone!

28. For the distinction between archives and dossiers, cf. Martin (1994).

29. Although not every text is translated, and some pieces (through no fault of Vandorpe) appear as *descripta*, I have used this volume successfully with freshmen (i.e., it is accessible).

30. In papyrological circles, Van Minnen (1994) led the way, relying on data from the reasonably well-documented Michigan excavations at Karanis. In the wake of more recent "scientific" excavations, the possibilities have expanded. For the opportunities afforded by the excavations that occurred before World War I, cf. note 26 above.

31. Gagos, Gates, and Wilburn (2005) derives from this panel.

32. Such essays will be included in three of the new volumes of *The Tebtunis Papyri* (VII–IX). The practice, however, has precedents; cf. Rea on the Oxyrhynchite "corn dole" (*sitêresion*) in *P.Oxy.* XL and even (as James Keenan reminds me) Rostovtzeff's commentary on *P.Tebt.* III.1 703. Cf. also Zuckerman (2004) (though I would have preferred a text that was better annotated).

33. As I did in *P.Zauzich* 13–14. Yet not all houses "work" as well as that of Sokrates at Karanis (cf. Van Minnen 1994 and note 84 below).

34. In his sensitivity to the visual, Montserrat (cf. 1996) was unique among those who have edited papyri.

35. "Fayyum portraits": The connection to the gymnasial "class" (cf., e.g., Walker 1997) has not been adequately explored. "Funerary art in general": Riggs (2005) should reveal opportunities for those working with texts; the Soter tomb in Western Thebes (see most recently Herbin 2002 and Riggs 2005, 182 ff.) in particular cries out for an integrated approach, though not all of the papyri from the tomb have been published. Stanwick (2002) provides a fine synthetic ("text"-"object") treatment of Ptolemaic royal sculpture but is not the last word. Cf. also Baines (2004, esp. p. 35), excellent on elite self-presentation during the Ptolemaic period. One might also note the central position of the visual in the Egyptian religio-cultural system. (I thank Chris Hallett for bringing the works by Stanwick and Baines to my attention.)

36. *Sonderstellung:* The notion goes back to Tac. *Hist.* 1.11. "Old habits": There were always exceptions, of which Jones (1964) is a prominent one.

37. Her subtitle, *Greek Education in Hellenistic and Roman Egypt,* belies the real breadth of the book.

38. Contrast Rathbone (1989), a classic assault on the historiography of the ancient economy.

39. My understanding of this work has been enhanced by discussions with Roger Bagnall and James Keenan.

40. The *Sonderstellung Ägyptens* has always been less of a factor in the historiography of late antiquity, yet it certainly is present: "One is nevertheless hesitant to extend the generalization [about landholding in late antique Egypt] to other parts of the Empire. Egypt was always a special case" (Grantham 2004).

41. Zuckerman's failure to engage Banaji in any significant fashion is thus puzzling. Kulikowski (2005) speaks of a "Banaji effect": Banaji's work is ignored because his "sociology and his economics are monuments of opacity, painfully inaccessible to non-specialists." I do not share this opinion.

42. See further Hickey (2001, 106–107).

43. "Stanford School": The term is my coinage. Not all of the members have published on Graeco-Roman Egypt (e.g., Ian Morris), nor are they all at Stanford (e.g., Dennis Kehoe). Nor are they a monolith: Scheidel (cf. 2001), for example, is more pessimistic about ancient sources than Manning (cf. 2003).

44. Drawn from the work of economist Douglass C. North; see Manning (2003, 10–11) for elaboration and references.

45. Cf. Bagnall (1995, 73–75). He provides, incidentally, one of the exceptions to the rule in, for example, Bagnall (1992).

46. Cf. Hickey (2001, 78 ff). For the "power of estimates," see also Clarysse and Vandorpe (1997) and the seminal Rathbone (1990).

47. Ruffini (2004, 245). Ruffini himself addresses the Oxyrhynchite landholders and the village elite of Aphroditê in his doctoral dissertation (Ruffini 2005).

48. See, for example, Mueller (2003, 250; 2005b, 121) for statements concerning the applicability of her methods.

49. Mueller (2005a) was certainly refereed. Mueller and Lee (2005) may have been refereed since the *Journal of Archaeological Science* asks contributors to name five possible referees. (After this chapter was completed, two informaticians published a critique of Mueller's methods: P. Hoffman and B. Klin, "Careful with That Computer," *Journal of Juristic Papyrology* 36 [2006] 67–90.)

50. For criticism of the rank-size rule and central place theory in a work of ancient history, cf. Horden and Purcell (2000, 102–105), who claim, curiously, that these methods are "of increasing interest to historians as well as to geographers and economists."

51. See, for example, Wilfong (2007), a vade mecum for the study of gender in late antique Egypt; Dieleman (2005) on the sociocultural milieux of two bilingual papyri from the "Theban magical library" at the various stages of their existence (composition, compilation, use, and reuse); and Stephens (2003) on the bicultural poetics of Ptolemaic Alexandria (a "classics" book that displays knowledge of the nonliterary evidence).

52. I must caution the reader that I have not annotated this description as I would have a fully developed (and freestanding) work.

53. Cf. Will (1985) (with the criticisms of Bagnall, e.g., 1995, 101). Cf. also Stephens (2003, ch. 4) and Baines (2004, 34).

54. See Colin (2002) for indigenous priestesses in the Hellenistic and Roman periods.

55. I do not give a precise number because new texts continue to be discovered (and the relationship of certain papyri to the dossier is still being researched). In this sketch, I have not counted (or considered) some sixty papyri that recently came to light in Florence, Lund, New Haven, and Oxford and which have not yet received sufficient study. Last treatment of the dossier: Hanson (2001, 602–604).

56. The somewhat later Oxyrhynchite dossier of Sarapion aka Apollonianos (also eight generations) comes to mind, but it (at least as presented in Moioli 1987) cannot compare to the Tebtynis assemblage in either quantity or, more important, richness. If the literary material from Kôm Gamman could be connected to Sarapion, it might be another story.

57. If the structure in which the dossier (or at least the bulk of it) was found was used for wastepaper or served as a geniza (or as the temple library), only the scale or granularity, not the critical mass, of the argument here is (potentially) impacted.

58. "Insular": Cf., for example, Dieleman (2005, 208). Frankfurter (1998, 222), however, distinguishes the "culture … of the large Sobek priesthoods in the Fayyum" from that of priests in other villages. Marriage: The family of Kronion and Isidora was narrowly endogamous; only individuals from the priesthood (frequently the top levels of the hierarchy) were admitted. "Greek": I have set this in quotation marks because a serious definition of the culture in question is well beyond the scope of this discussion.

59. Pace Tait (1992, 310): "not cut off from Greek culture, but their concern with it was curiously limited."

60. The hands of Kronion and Isidora (et al.) are extant (the former being more accomplished than the latter), as are letters in Greek from both. For Roman-period letters from Tebtynis priests "in an artificial literary demotic hand," see Tait (1992, 307 and n. 20).

61. Note also Begg (1998, 190): "a page of Homer" (perhaps indicative of a pedagogical context, as indeed might the *Catalogue* be).

62. Cf. Van Minnen (1998, 112–113, 169).

63. I agree with the argument in Manning (2003) that the displacement of the temples as economic institutions began under the Ptolemies; I am thinking of the realia behind ideology.

64. For example, Capponi (2005, 92) and Baines (2004, 34): "By contrast, the Roman conquest was followed by a reduction in local autonomy and increased discrimination against those who were culturally non Greco-Roman [sic]." As opposed to the old regime: "In Ptolemaic Egypt people changed their ethnic affiliation by changing their clothes (almost)" (Van Minnen 2002, 348). Of course, the Roman transformations were a process, not an overnight development.

65. For example, Capponi (2005, 92), Bowman and Rathbone (1992, 120 ff.). Needless to say, the "Greek" ancestry of these populations was "diluted."

66. The last three sentences of this paragraph are distilled from Bowman and Rathbone (1992, 120 ff.). Van Minnen (2002) has some value for this topic, but I do not accept his revisionist claims: that the gymnasial class was not an elite, that it was not more privileged or less numerous than the metropolite class, and so on. I cannot address these arguments here. Ruffini (2006) critiques other issues; I thank him for sharing his work in advance of publication.

67. Cf. Glare (1993). I thank the author for allowing me access to her doctoral dissertation. Now also see *P.Dime* II, pp. 9–14, for administrative involvement.

68. "Preference shown": cf. Glare (1993). For the traditional view, cf. Dieleman (2005, 208–211).

69. Cf. http://tebtunis.berkeley.edu/ancientlives/bagnall.html (September 22, 2008).

70. Granovetter (1973) is the foundational text.

71. To borrow the expression of the Ammonios responsible for *P.Oxy.* XIV 1681.5–7 (third century CE): βάρβαρόν τινα ἢ Αἰγύπτιον ἀνάνθρωπον, "a barbarian or an inhuman Egyptian."

72. Cf. Appadurai (1996, 89–113), a classic text.

73. E.g., Tait (1994, 190, also 191): "The object of an education in Demotic (and Hieratic) must have been the maintenance of the native literate culture, both religious and secular." Priests' antiquarian interests (and literature as history): *P.Carlsb.* VI, p. 18. One must be cautious not to make the priests too prescient...

74. See, for example, the Tebtynis "Onch-Sheshonqy" in *P.Carlsb.* III.

75. Stated with the caveat that a lot of Tebtynis material remains inaccessible to me. Also see note 76.

76. Cf. Colin (2003, 278): "From 37 CE... all the official documents issued by the clergy of the god Soknebtynis (Fayum) identify this divinity with the Greek Kronos; it is tempting to think, in this case, that the sudden novelty was the product of a decision by the Council of the temple."

77. There is an explosion of Kronos and Geb names in the documentation from Roman Tebtynis that seems unlikely to be a fluke; for the family of Kronion and Isidora, see figure 21.1. (Note that Geb was typically assimilated with Kronos; therefore, "Pakebkis," i.e., "The one belonging to Geb," and "Kronion" are equivalents of a sort.) Holm (1936, 70) notes that the priests favored the indigenous Geb names.

78. I assume that Le Roy Ladurie derived his first pair (which goes back to Archilochus, fr. 201, of course) from Isaiah Berlin's well-known essay on Tolstoy.

79. Though, as noted earlier, Manning is certainly cognizant of the potential impact of "the micro."

80. That papyri are *fragmentary* is also relevant; cf. Ginzburg (1988).

81. "Anecdotal": Against this charge, cf. Ricoeur (2004, 213); see also Levi (1991, 96, 109) and Revel (1989, xiii; 1995b, 501). Sewell (2005, 75–77) finds such arguments problematic. For a general account of the criticisms of microhistory, see Grafton (2006, 63–67).

82. A classic formulation of Sahlins (cf. 1985, 136 ff.); see Sewell (2005, 197 ff.) for discussion and modification. Cf. also Revel (1995b, 500). These at-risk structures include those of the historical present, for instance, our own categories of analysis; cf. Feierman (1999, 206).

83. Not even quantitative methods (a favorite tool of macrohistorians) are incompatible.

84. *Eccezione normale:* Grendi (1972), though it is not entirely clear what he meant; cf. Revel (1989, xxx–xxxi). I concur with Levi (1991, 109); for another interpretation see Ricoeur (2004, 216). Again, these conceptions may be methodological (e.g.: I cannot prove it, but the house of Sokrates at Karanis [see Van Minnen 1994] strikes me as an *eccezione normale;* i.e., I wonder whether the finds from other Karanis houses would have impacted the way that papyrologists view archaeological material).

85. Cf. Ruggiero (1993, 18–20) as well as Stone (1979, 3–4).

86. Bagnall (1995, 38) seems too pessimistic.

87. See Keenan (1992), one of the most important papyrological articles ever published (in general, Keenan's scholarship—often ahead of the curve—has not received the attention that it merits); cf. also Keenan (1995). See also Schubert (2000, 9–13) ("Une histoire pour commencer"), which I typically translate during the first meeting of my undergraduate courses on Graeco-Roman Egypt.

88. *Alabi:* Price (1990); *katochoi* archive: See the excellent synthesis in Thompson (1988, ch. 7); *Scottsboro:* Goodman (1994); *Woman Wang:* Spence (1978).

89. For the petitions of late antiquity, a start has been made; cf. Fournet (2004). James Keenan informs me that the Catalan "memorials of complaint" (cf. Bisson 1998) are a better fit than Davis's documents.

90. Richter 2005, 260–261. I thank the author for giving me access to his work in advance of publication.

91. Cf. the emphasis on texts in Bynum (1991, 22).

92. Thus Gibbon (1814, 66), but of *historiens* (since he was writing in French).

BIBLIOGRAPHY

Abu-Lughod, L. 1991. "Writing against Culture." In *Recapturing Anthropology: Working in the Present,* ed. R. G. Fox, 137–162. Santa Fe, N.M.: School of American Research Press.

Appadurai, A. 1996. *Modernity at Large: Cultural Dimensions of Globalization.* Minneapolis: University of Minnesota Press.

Bagnall, R. S. 1992. "Landholding in Late Roman Egypt: The Distribution of Wealth." *JRS* 82: 128–149.

———. 1995. *Reading Papyri, Writing Ancient History.* London: Routledge.

———, and B. W. Frier. 1994. *The Demography of Roman Egypt.* Cambridge: Cambridge University Press.

Baines, J. 2004. "Egyptian Elite Self-Presentation in the Context of Ptolemaic Rule." In *Ancient Alexandria between Egypt and Greece,* ed. W. V. Harris and G. Ruffini, 33–61. Leiden: Brill.

Banaji, J. 2001. *Agrarian Change in Late Antiquity: Gold, Labour, and Aristocratic Dominance.* Oxford: Oxford University Press.

Begg, D. J. I. 1998. " 'It Was Wonderful, Our Return in the Darkness with . . . the Baskets of Papyri!' Papyrus Finds at Tebtunis from the Bagnani Archives, 1931–1936." *BASP* 35: 185–210.

Belzoni, G. B. 1820. *Narrative of the Operations and Recent Discoveries within the Pyramids, Temples, Tombs, and Excavations in Egypt and Nubia; and of a Journey to the Coast of the Red Sea in Search of the Ancient Berenice, and of Another to the Oasis of Jupiter Ammon.* London: John Murray.

Bisson, T. N. 1998. *Tormented Voices: Power, Crisis, and Humanity in Rural Catalonia, 1140–1200.* Cambridge, Mass.: Harvard University Press.

Bowman, A. K. 2002. "Recolonising Egypt." In *Classics in Progress: Essays on Ancient Greece and Rome,* ed. T. P. Wiseman, 193–223. Oxford: Published for the British Academy by Oxford University Press.

——, and D. W. Rathbone. 1992. "Cities and Administration in Roman Egypt." *JRS* 82: 107–127.

Braudel, F. 1969. *Écrits sur l'histoire*. Paris: Flammarion.

Bynum, C. W. 1991. *Fragmentation and Redemption: Essays on Gender and the Human Body in Medieval Religion*. New York: Zone Books.

Canfora, L. 2005. *Il papiro di Dongo*. Milan: Adelphi.

Capponi, L. 2005. *Augustan Egypt: The Creation of a Roman Province*. London: Routledge.

Certeau, M. de. 1986. *Heterologies: Discourse on the Other*, trans. Brian Massumi. Minneapolis: University of Minnesota Press.

——. 1995. "History and Mysticism." In *Histories: French Constructions of the Past*, ed. J. Revel and L. Hunt; trans. A. Goldhammer et al., 437–447. New York: New Press.

Chartier, R. 1982. "Intellectual History or Sociocultural History? The French Trajectories." In *Modern European Intellectual History: Reappraisals and New Perspectives*, ed. D. LaCapra and S. L. Kaplan, 13–46. Ithaca, N.Y.: Cornell University Press.

Clark, E. 2004. *History, Theory, Text: Historians and the Linguistic Turn*. Cambridge, Mass.: Harvard University Press.

Clarysse, W. 1987. "Greek Loan-Words in Demotic." In *Aspects of Demotic Lexicography: Acts of the Second International Conference for Demotic Studies*, ed. S. P. Vleeming, 9–33. Leuven: Peeters.

——, and K. Vandorpe. 1997. "Viticulture and Wine Consumption in the Arsinoite Nome." *Ancient Society* 28: 67–73.

Colin, F. 2002. "Les prêtresses indigènes dans l'Égypte hellénistique et romaine: Une question à la croisée des sources grecques et égyptiennes." In *Le rôle et le statut de la femme en Égypte hellénistique, romaine, et byzantine: Actes du colloque international, Bruxelles-Leuven, 27–29 novembre 1997*, ed. H. Melaerts and L. Mooren, 41–122. Leuven: Peeters.

——. 2003. "La documentation plurilingue de l'Égypte hellénistique: Un laboratoire des interactions linguistiques et culturelles." In *L'Orient méditerranéen de la mort d'Alexandre au Ier siècle avant notre ère: Anatolie, Chypre, Égypte, Syrie*, ed. M.-T. Le Dinahet, 257–280. Nantes: Éditions du Temps.

Cribiore, R. 2001. *Gymnastics of the Mind: Greek Education in Hellenistic and Roman Egypt*. Princeton: Princeton University Press.

Davis, N. Z. 1987. *Fiction in the Archives: Pardon Tales and Their Tellers in Sixteenth-Century France*. Stanford: Stanford University Press.

Derrida, J. 1989. "Biodegradables: Seven Diary Fragments." Trans. Peggy Kamuf. *Critical Inquiry* 15(4): 812–873.

——. 1995. *Mal d'archive: Une impression freudienne*. Paris: Galilée.

Dieleman, J. 2005. *Priests, Tongues, and Rites: The London-Leiden Magical Manuscripts and Translation in Egyptian Ritual (100–300 CE)*. Leiden: Brill.

Fabre, G. 2002–2003. "Medea Norsa ebrea?" *Analecta Papyrologica* 14–15: 337–350.

Feierman, S. 1999. "Colonizers, Scholars, and the Creation of Invisible Histories." In *Beyond the Cultural Turn: New Directions in the Study of Society and Culture*, ed. V. E. Bonnell and L. Hunt, 182–216. Berkeley: University of California Press.

Fournet, J.-L. 2004. "Entre document et littérature: La pétition dans l'Antiquité tardive." In *La pétition à Byzance*, ed. D. Feissel et J. Gascou, 61–74. Paris: Association des amis du Centre d'histoire et civilisation de Byzance.

Frankfurter, D. 1998. *Religion in Roman Egypt: Assimilation and Resistance*. Princeton: Princeton University Press.

Franko, G. F. 1988. "*Sitometria* in the Zenon Archive: Identifying Zenon's Personal Documents." *BASP* 25: 13–98.

Gadamer, H.-G. 1987. "The Problem of Historical Consciousness," trans. J. L. Close. In *Interpretative Social Science: A Second Look*, ed. P. Rabinow and W. Sullivan, 82–140. Berkeley: University of California Press.

———. 1989. *Truth and Method*, 2d rev. ed., trans. J. Weinsheimer and D. G. Marshall. New York: Crossroad.

Gagos, T., J. E. Gates, and A. T. Wilburn. 2005. "Material Culture and Texts of Graeco-Roman Egypt: Creating Context, Debating Meaning." *BASP* 42: 171–188.

Gibbon, E. 1814. *The Miscellaneous Works of Edward Gibbon, Esq., with Memoirs of His Life and Writings*, vol. 4. London: John Murray.

Gigante, M. 1986. *Girolamo Vitelli e la nuova filologia*. Santa Croce del Sannio: Istituto storico Giuseppe Maria Galanti.

Ginzburg, C. 1988. "Clues: Roots of an Evidential Paradigm." In *Clues, Myths, and the Historical Method*, trans. J. and A. Tedeschi, 96–125. Baltimore: Johns Hopkins University Press.

Glare (now Fewster), P. 1993. "The Temples of Egypt: The Impact of Rome." Ph.D. diss., Cambridge University.

Goodman, J. 1994. *Stories of Scottsboro*. New York: Pantheon.

Grafton, A. 2006. "History's Postmodern Fates." *Daedalus* 135(2): 54–69.

Granovetter, M. S. 1973. "The Strength of Weak Ties." *American Journal of Sociology* 78: 1360–1380.

Grantham, G. 2004. Review of Banaji 2001. http://www.eh.net/bookreviews/library/0784. shtml (accessed September 22, 2008).

Grendi, E. 1972. "Microanalisi e storia sociale." *Quaderni Storici* 7: 506–520.

Gupta, A., and J. Ferguson. 1997. "Culture, Power, Place: Ethnography at the End of an Era." In *Culture, Power, Place: Explorations in Critical Anthropology*, ed. A. Gupta and J. Ferguson, 1–29. Durham, N.C.: Duke University Press.

Hanson, A. E. 2001. "Text and Context for the Illustrated Herbal from Tebtunis." *Atti del XXII Congresso Internazionale di Papirologia*, ed. I. Andorlini, G. Bastianini, M. Manfredi, and G. Menci, 585–604. Florence: Istituto Papirologico G. Vitelli.

Herbin, F.-R. 2002. *Padiimenipet, fils de Sôter: Histoire d'une famille dans l'Égypte romaine*. Paris: Réunion des musées nationaux/Louvre.

Hickey, T. M. 2001. "A 'Public House' but Closed: 'Fiscal Participation' and Economic Decision Making on the Oxyrhynchite Estate of the Flavii Apiones." Ph.D. diss., University of Chicago.

Hobson, D. 1988. "Towards a Broader Context for the Study of Greco-Roman Egypt." *Échos du monde classique* 32, n.s., 7: 353–363.

Hochschild, A. 1998. *King Leopold's Ghost: A Story of Greed, Terror, and Heroism in Colonial Africa*. New York: Houghton Mifflin.

Hoffmann, F. 2000. *Ägypten: Kultur und Lebenswelt in griechisch-römischer Zeit: Eine Darstellung nach den demotischen Quellen*. Berlin: Akademie Verlag.

Holm, C. E. 1936. *Griechisch-ägyptische Namenstudien*. Göteborg: Wettergren & Kerbergs.

Hombert, M. 1933. "Le commerce des papyrus en Égypte." *Chronique d'Égypte* 15: 148–154.

Horden, P., and N. Purcell. 2000. *The Corrupting Sea: A Study of Mediterranean History*. Oxford: Blackwell.

Jones, A. H. M. 1964. *The Later Roman Empire, 284–602: A Social, Economic, and Administrative Survey.* Norman: University of Oklahoma Press.

Keenan, J. G. 1992. "A Constantinople Loan, A.D. 541." *BASP* 29: 175–182.

———. 1993. "Papyrology and Byzantine Historiography." *BASP* 30: 137–144.

———. 1995. "The Aphrodito Murder Mystery: A Return to the Scene of the Crimes." *BASP* 32: 57–63.

Kulikowski, M. 2005. Review of C. Kelly, *Ruling the Later Roman Empire.* http://ccat.sas. upenn.edu/bmcr/2005/2005-02-12.html (accessed September 25, 2008).

LaCapra, D. 1983. *Rethinking Intellectual History: Texts, Contexts, Language.* Ithaca, N.Y.: Cornell University Press.

———. 1995. "History, Language, and Reading: Waiting for Crillon." *American Historical Review* 100(3): 799–828.

Le Roy Ladurie, E. 1998. "Michelet: Le poète de l'histoire." *Le Figaro littéraire* (June 25).

Levi, G. 1991. "On Microhistory." In *New Perspectives on Historical Writing,* ed. P. Burke, 93–113. University Park, Penn.: Pennsylvania State University Press.

Lowenthal, D. 1985. *The Past Is a Foreign Country.* Cambridge: Cambridge University Press.

Manning, J. G. 2003. *Land and Power in Ptolemaic Egypt: The Structure of Land Tenure.* Cambridge: Cambridge University Press.

Martin, A. 1994. "Archives privées et cachettes documentaires." *Proceedings of the 20th International Congress of Papyrologists,* ed. A. Bülow-Jacobsen, 569–577. Copenhagen: Museum Tusculanum Press.

Merton, R. K. 1965. *On the Shoulders of Giants: A Shandean Postscript.* New York: Free Press.

Moioli, M. L. 1987. "La famiglia di Sarapion alias Apollonianus, stratego dei nomi Arsinoites ed Hermopolites." *Acme* 40: 123–146.

Montserrat, D. 1996. *Sex and Society in Graeco-Roman Egypt.* London: Kegan Paul International.

Morelli, F. 2002. "La raccolta dei *P.Bingen.*" *Chronique d'Égypte* 77: 312–321.

Mueller, K. 2002. "Ptolemaic Settlements in Space: Settlement Size and Hierarchy in the Fayum." *Archiv für Papyrusforschung* 48: 107–125.

———. 2003. "Mastering Matrices and Clusters: Locating Graeco-Roman Settlements in the *meris* of Herakleides (Fayum/Egypt) by Monte-Carlo-Simulation." *Archiv für Papyrusforschung* 49: 218–254.

———. 2005a. "Geographical Information Systems (GIS) in Papyrology: Mapping Fragmentation and Migration Flow to Hellenistic Egypt." *BASP* 42: 63–92.

———. 2005b. "Redistricting the Ptolemaic Fayum, Egypt: From Nomarchies and Toparchies to Weighted Voronoi Tessellation." *Archiv für Papyrusforschung* 51: 112–126.

———, and W. Lee. 2005. "From Mess to Matrix and Beyond: Estimating the Size of Settlements in the Ptolemaic Fayum/Egypt." *Journal of Archaeological Science* 32: 59–67.

O'Connell, E. 2007. "Recontextualizing Berkeley's Tebtunis Papyri." In *Proceedings of the 24th International Congress of Papyrologists,* ed. J. Frösén, T. Purola, and E. Salmenkivi, 807–826. Helsinki: Societas scientiarum Fennica.

Price, R. 1990. *Alabi's World.* Baltimore: Johns Hopkins University Press.

Rathbone, D. W. 1989. "The Ancient Economy and Graeco-Roman Egypt." In *Egitto e storia antica dall'ellenismo all'età araba: Bilancio di un confronto. Atti del colloquio internazionale,* ed. L. Criscuolo and G. Geraci, 159–176. Bologna: Cooperativa Libraria Universitaria Editrice Bologna.

——. 1990. "Villages, Land, and Population in Graeco-Roman Egypt." *Proceedings of the Cambridge Philological Society* 216, n.s., 36: 103–142.

Ray, J. D. 1994. "How Demotic Is Demotic?" *Egitto e Vicino Oriente* 17: 251–264.

Reid, D. M. 2002. *Whose Pharaohs? Archaeology, Museums, and Egyptian National Identity from Napoleon to World War I.* Berkeley: University of California Press.

Revel, J. 1989. "L'histoire au ras du sol." In *Le pouvoir au village: Histoire d'un exorciste dans le Piémont du XVIIe siècle*, G. Levi; trans. M. Aymard, i–xxxiii. Paris: Gallimard NRF.

——. 1995a. "Introduction." In *Histories: French Constructions of the Past*, ed. J. Revel and L. Hunt; trans. A. Goldhammer et al., 1–63. New York: New Press.

——. 1995b. "Microanalysis and the Construction of the Social." In *Histories: French Constructions of the Past*, ed. J. Revel and L. Hunt; trans. A. Goldhammer et al., 492–502. New York: New Press.

Richter, T. S. 2005. "What's in a Story? Cultural Narratology and Coptic Child Donation Documents." *Journal of Juristic Papyrology* 35: 237–264.

Ricoeur, P. 2004. *Memory, History, Forgetting*, trans. K. Blamey and D. Pellauer. Chicago: University of Chicago Press.

Riggs, C. 2005. *The Beautiful Burial in Roman Egypt: Art, Identity, and Funerary Religion.* Oxford: Oxford University Press.

Ruffini, G. 2004. "Late Antique Pagan Networks from Athens to the Thebaid." In *Ancient Alexandria between Egypt and Greece*, ed. W. V. Harris and G. Ruffini, 241–257. Leiden: Brill.

——. 2005. "Social Networks in Byzantine Egypt." Ph.D. diss., Columbia University.

——. 2006. "Genealogy and the Gymnasium." *BASP* 43: 71–99.

Ruggiero, G. 1993. *Binding Passions: Tales of Magic, Marriage, and Power at the End of the Renaissance.* Oxford: Oxford University Press.

Sahlins, M. D. 1985. *Islands of History.* Chicago: University of Chicago Press.

Scheidel, W. 2001. "Progress and Problems in Roman Demography." In *Debating Roman Demography*, ed. W. Scheidel, 1–81. Leiden: Brill.

Schubert, P. 2000. *Vivre en Égypte gréco-romaine: Une sélection de papyrus.* Vevey, Switzerland: Éditions de l'Aire.

Sewell, W. H., Jr. 1999. "The Concept(s) of Culture." In *Beyond the Cultural Turn: New Directions in the Study of Society and Culture*, ed. V. E. Bonnell and L. Hunt, 35–61. Berkeley: University of California Press.

——. 2005. *Logics of History: Social Theory and Social Transformation.* Chicago: University of Chicago Press.

Spence, J. D. 1978. *The Death of Woman Wang.* New York: Viking.

Stanwick, P. E. 2002. *Portraits of the Ptolemies: Greek Kings as Egyptian Pharaohs.* Austin: University of Texas Press.

Stephens, S. A. 2003. *Seeing Double: Intercultural Poetics in Ptolemaic Alexandria.* Berkeley: University of California Press.

Stone, L. 1979. "The Revival of Narrative: Reflections on a New Old History." *Past and Present* 85: 3–24.

Tait, W. J. 1992. "Demotic Literature and Egyptian Society." In *Life in a Multi-Cultural Society: Egypt from Cambyses to Constantine and Beyond*, ed. J. H. Johnson, 303–310. Chicago: Oriental Institute of the University of Chicago.

——. 1994. "Some Notes on Demotic Scribal Training in the Roman Period." *Proceedings of the 20th International Congress of Papyrologists*, ed. A. Bülow-Jacobsen, 188–192. Copenhagen: Museum Tusculanum Press.

Thompson, D. J. 1988. *Memphis under the Ptolemies*. Princeton: Princeton University Press.

Townsend, R. M. 1993. *The Medieval Village Economy: A Study of the Pareto Mapping in General Equilibrium Models*. Princeton: Princeton University Press..

van Minnen, P. 1993. "The Century of Papyrology (1892–1992)." *BASP* 30: 5–18. http://scriptorium.lib.duke.edu/papyrus/texts/history.html (September 21, 2008).

——. 1994. "House-to-House Enquiries: An Interdisciplinary Approach to Roman Karanis." *ZPE* 100: 227–251.

——. 1998. "Boorish or Bookish? Literature in Egyptian Villages in the Fayum in the Graeco-Roman Period." *Journal of Juristic Papyrology* 28: 99–184.

——. 2002. "αἱ ἀπὸ γυμνασίου: 'Greek' Women and the Greek 'Elite' in the *Metropoleis* of Roman Egypt." In *Le rôle et le statut de la femme en Égypte hellénistique, romaine et byzantine: Actes du colloque international, Bruxelles-Leuven, 27–29 novembre 1997*, ed. H. Melaerts and L. Mooren, 337–353. Leuven: Peeters.

Vasunia, P. 2003. "Hellenism and Empire: Reading Edward Said." *Parallax* 9: 88–97.

Verhoogt, A. M. F. W. 1998. "Family Papers from Tebtunis: Unfolding a Bundle of Papyri." In *The Two Faces of Graeco-Roman Egypt: Greek and Demotic and Greek-Demotic Texts and Studies Presented to P. W. Pestman by Alumni of the Papyrological Institute*, ed. A. M. F. W. Verhoogt and S. P. Vleeming, 141–154. Leiden: Brill.

Walker, S. E. C. 1997. "Mummy Portraits in their Roman Context." In *Portraits and Masks: Burial Customs in Roman Egypt*, ed. M. L. Bierbrier, 1–6. London: British Museum Press.

Wallerstein, I. 1995. "*Annales* as Resistance." In *Histories: French Constructions of the Past*, ed. J. Revel and L. Hunt; trans. A. Goldhammer et al., 367–370. New York: New Press.

Webster, J. 1995. "'Interpretatio': Roman Word Power and the Celtic Gods." *Britannia* 26: 153–161.

Wilfong, T. G. 2007. "Gender and Society in Byzantine Egypt." In *Egypt in the Byzantine World, 300–700*, ed. R. S. Bagnall, 309–327. Cambridge: Cambridge University Press.

Wilford, J. N. 2002. "A Mummy's Bequest: Poems from a Master." *New York Times* (November 26).

Will, E. 1985. "Pour une 'anthropologie coloniale' du monde hellénistique." In *The Craft of the Ancient Historian: Essays in Honor of Chester G. Starr*, ed. J. W. Eadie and J. Ober, 273–301. Lanham, Md.: University Press of America.

Youtie, H. 1963. "The Papyrologist: Artificer of Fact." *Greek, Roman and Byzantine Studies* 4: 19–32.

——. 1974. *The Textual Criticism of Documentary Papyri*, 2d rev. ed. London: Institute of Classical Studies.

Zuckerman, C. 2004. *Du village à l'Empire: Autour du registre fiscal d'Aphroditô (525/526)*. Paris: Association des amis du Centre d'histoire et civilisation de Byzance.

CHAPTER 22

GEOGRAPHY AND ADMINISTRATION IN EGYPT (332 BCE–642 CE)

MARIA ROSARIA FALIVENE

THIS chapter outlines the administrative geography of Egypt under the Graeco-Macedonian regime and as it evolved over the next millennium. This information comes from papyri and ostraca—sources that obviously differ from the material evidence of archaeological finds yet are not so distant from these as literary evidence often is.[1] What makes papyrological texts so informative is their being

---

1. Many topics foundational to this chapter are not treated here. I refer the reader to *Egypt from Alexander to the Copts: An Archaeological and Historical Guide* (Bagnall and Rathbone 2004) for an introduction to what modern Egyptian landscape can still tell us about the appearance of the country and its ways of life in the millennium that passed between Alexander's invasion (332 BCE) and the Arab conquest (642 CE). Bowman (1986) offers a narrative synthesis of the same period. In a longer historical perspective, the *Cultural Atlas of Ancient Egypt* (Baines and Málek 2000) is also very useful. More on the geographical side (in greater detail, too, and on a larger scale), the relevant maps of the *Barrington Atlas* (Talbert 2000, maps 74–80) and the *Tübinger Atlas des Vorderen Orients* (Heinen, Schlömer, and Pohlmann 1989; see also Gomaà, Hannig, and Pohlmann 1991), besides the *Dizionario dei nomi geografici* (Calderini and Daris 1935–2007) provide essential reference tools. All of these are best used in combination with information available on the Internet, particularly at the sites of the *Duke Databank of Documentary Papyri* and the *Heidelberger Gesamtverzeichnis der griechischen Papyrusurkunden Ägyptens*.

on the same timescale as the actors involved: their speaking, as it were, in everyday words. As invariably happens with qualities, this one also has its downside, which was described as follows by a pioneer of papyrological studies: "For in all such documents, the most necessary assumptions are those which every contemporary reader took for granted as obvious, whereas we have to infer or detect them from stray and casual allusions" (Mahaffy 1896, xxxvii). Mahaffy's observation applies most aptly to the difficulties one encounters when trying to reconstruct the administrative framework of Graeco-Roman Egypt and having to deal with the intricacies of a territory and its management as it evolved (conforming to long-established, seemingly timeless patterns) over time and under changing regimes (in the millennium that concerns us here: Ptolemaic, Roman, and Byzantine).

GEOGRAPHY

Following pharaonic tradition, Egypt under the Ptolemies was divided into an upper (northern) and lower (southern) country (*anô* and *katô chôra*, as they were called with reference to the south-north course of the Nile), and these in turn were partitioned into an approximately equal number of districts, or nomes (*nomoi*, demotic *tš*: Müller-Wollermann 1992, 243–244), their total number fluctuating over time around an average of forty. These districts also varied in size and importance; on the whole, however, and in view of the very long span of time concerned, they remained remarkably stable both as administrative units (until the early Byzantine period) and (even longer) as cultural systems (Kees 1961; Helck 1974; Bagnall 1993, 333–335). At its core, each district had a temple dedicated to the principal local divinity (e.g., Arsaphes/Herakles in the Herakleopolite) and a totemic animal of its own, as illustrated in the seventeenth book of Strabo's *Geography* (Strab. 17.1.39–40; see also 17.2.4, and Yoyotte and Charvet 1997, 152–154). Strabo devoted this entire book to Egypt; he was an expert witness, having lived and traveled in Egypt in the 20s BCE in the entourage of the first (Cornelius Gallus) and second (Petronius) Roman prefects.

As a rule, the Greeks named the districts and their capitals (*mêtropoleis*) after either the respective presiding deities or their totemic animals, thereby performing an act of *interpretatio graeca*, as well as an administrative one: The Herakleopolite district, for instance, was thus named on the basis of an equation between the Egyptian Somthous/Arsaphes (a god of youthful vigor, or *andreia*) and Herakles, while the neighboring Kynopolite received its Greek name from the canine god Anoubis (cf. Strabo 17.1.40). The Fayyum derives its modern name from ancient

Egyptian *Piom* or *Phiom* ("the lake"), which was translated as ἡ λίμνη in Greek, but under first Graeco-Macedonian and then Roman rule it was also called Arsinoe's district *(Arsinoites)* or *Krokodilopolites,* from the (Graecized) name of its metropolis, "the city of the Crocodiles" (the Leuven *Fayyum Villages Project* now offers a wealth of information on the geography of this district: see http://www.trismegistos.org). This renaming procedure, however, went little further than nome capitals. Villages (*kômai,* the smallest administrative unit in the land) usually kept their Egyptian names, which in the Greek documents were simply transliterated and adapted to Greek case endings, with the exception of new settlements and a few other places that for some reason (e.g., their good "connectivity degree": Mueller 2003a, 2003b; Ruffini 2007) acquired importance to newcomers.

Water was brought into the Fayyum by the Bahr Yusuf, a side branch diverging from the Nile more than three hundred kilometers to the south, on the border with the Thebaid (the southernmost part of Egypt, which comprised several nomes). Here Ptolemy I founded and named a city after himself: Ptolemais, as Alexandria was named after the Macedonian conqueror of Egypt. Just as Alexandria (founded early in 331 BCE on a site the Egyptians called Rhakotis: Fraser 1972, 3–7; Depauw 2000) was to counterbalance Memphis in the lower country, Ptolemais could be seen as the Graeco-Macedonian counterpart to Thebes (the ancient capital of Upper Egypt and later on a center of stubborn resistance against the foreign rulers). The Nile and the Bahr Yusuf ran approximately parallel through several nomes: Proceeding downstream, the best attested in papyri include Panopolite, Lykopolite, Hermopolite, Oxyrhynchite, Kynopolite, and Herakleopolite; the Antinoopolite district (a small area carved out of the Hermopolite) deserves special mention because Antinoopolis was the (enduring) creation of Hadrian in memory of Antinoos, who drowned in the Nile during the Roman emperor's visit to Egypt (130 CE). In the Roman period this part of Egypt was called "the Seven Nomes," as attested in both documentary (*BGU* II 646 and *P.Oxy.* XXXIV 2705: two letters from *praefecti* to the *strategoi* of the "Seven Nomes and the Arsinoite," dating from, respectively, 193 and ca. 225) and literary sources from around the same time: Claudius Ptolemaeus, the well-known mathematician, musicologist, astronomer, and geographer (born in Ptolemais), writes in his *Geography* that "the regions to the South of the Great Delta and of the Northern country are called *the Seven Nomes,* or *Heptanomis*" (4, 5, 55).

As the Bahr Yusuf flowed into the Fayyumic depression, the Nile followed its northward course across the Aphroditopolite and the Memphite and on to the Delta region, which was also divided into several nomes. East and west of the cultivable land (the *chôra,* as it was called in Greek) was the desert. Oases in the western desert (called Libya) were also inhabited: Strabo records that three of these were adjacent to Egypt and pertained administratively to it (17.1.5). The eastern desert bore the name of Arabia.

A list of the nomes of Egypt in the early Ptolemaic period is found (twice, with some variation) in the *Revenue Laws* papyrus, a collection of documents providing guidelines for the farming out of taxes, finally revised against the originals of the *dioiketes* Apollonios on September 1, 259 BCE, the twenty-seventh year of Ptolemy II (*P.Rev.* 38, 1; first edition: Grenfell 1896; new edition: Bingen 1952, and see Bingen 1978). Besides the eastern and western desert areas (respectively, Arabia and Libya), this list details the nomes of the delta region and then, starting with the Memphite, those in between the delta and the Thebaid, which is a collective name for all of the districts of southern Egypt (the *anô chôra*; see Bagnall 1993, 333–335, for a list of the districts that compose this region). There is a remarkable degree of coincidence between the *P.Rev.* list and the information provided by Strabo (*Geogr.* 17, 1, 18–50; see Grenfell 1896, 50–51) Pliny (*Naturalis Historia* 5, 49–50), Claudius Ptolemaeus (*Geogr.* 4, 38–73), and the itinerary given in *P.Oxy.* XI 1380 (invocation of Isis, second century CE).

THE ADMINISTRATIVE GEOGRAPHY
OF PTOLEMAIC EGYPT

The process by which the foundations of the Ptolemaic administration of Egypt were marked out on a geographical grid was not a straightforward one: It developed gradually and not at the same time even within the same nome. Particularly in the earliest phase of the Ptolemaic regime, different grids applied to the same territory, depending on the special interests of the administrators, who operated in different spheres: This may perplex modern interpreters of the relevant papyrological material. An administrative bilingualism took time to develop and refine, and this may well explain some apparent confusion, which is perhaps a reflection of misleading translations from Egyptian (the language in which certain functions and titles had been originally conceived) into Greek rather than an aspect (or problem) of the actual administrative practice in early Ptolemaic Egypt. Much of the managing and writing—including, one suspects, the invention of appropriate Greek titles for traditionally Egyptian functions—had to be entrusted to a class, or rather a caste (*ethnos* in Greek: Thompson 2001, 1261), of "Hellenes." These included the *Hellenizing* segment of the Egyptian population: Trained according to a Greek system of education (best exemplified by a third-century-BCE schoolbook from the Fayyum: Guéraud and Jouguet 1938), they would be able to speak and write both Egyptian and Greek; their willingness to cooperate was crucial especially in the first decades of Ptolemaic rule, when much of the administration was in fact recorded in demotic or bilingual documents. By learning the language of the new pharaoh, while at the same time mastering the mother tongue of the native population, this caste (or perhaps we should call it a lobby) clung as best it could to traditionally privileged positions in the "managing" and "writing" sectors of the administration of Egypt under the Ptolemies. Connections and indeed overlaps between this caste and the priestly establishment must have been a matter of course: Strabo's assertion that "the priests were conversant with the kings" (17, 1, 3; also 17, 1, 5) bolsters this statement.

Having lost the Chremonidean War, which lasted from the summer of 268 to 263/262, and (just before the war began) his loving *(Philadelphos)* sister and wife, Arsinoe, who had actively promoted it (Habicht 1997, 143–149), Ptolemy II set out to consolidate his Egyptian kingdom. Ptolemaic control over the southern Aegean was now at risk, and the Seleucid menace loomed large and near in Syria and Phoenicia (Bagnall 1976). The Second Syrian War, pitting Ptolemy II against Antiochus II, broke out around 260 and lasted until 253. Strict, clear-headed military and economic measures were needed; it is perhaps not a coincidence that a demotic ostracon from Karnak (dated between October 27 and November 25, 258), summing up instructions for a general survey of land (Bresciani 1978, 1983; Burstein 1985, 122–123n97), appeared only one year after the *Revenue Laws* papyrus. Even if these two documents were not an attempt at fiscal or economic codification (Bingen 1952, 3), they nevertheless presupposed or at least aimed at some kind of standard practice in the surveying of cultivable land and in the farming of taxes, which in turn assumed a well-defined geographical and administrative grid.

Different spheres of the Ptolemaic administration may be defined with reference to the following Greek verbal roots:

ag- (lengthened by vowel mutation: hence *ēg-*), for the "leading," in the first place, of army troops; hence the titles *strategos* and *hegemon* for the commanders of, respectively, larger and smaller units in the Ptolemaic army;

arch-, as found, for example, in the title *nomarches* ("nomarch" in its Anglicized form) for the management of all kinds of economic activities, foremost among them agricultural production and the collection of taxes;

graph-, as in *grammateus* ("scribe") and *antigrapheus* ("checking clerk") for the writing or recording of facts and figures, an essential operation in view of the correct assessment of exploitable resources;

oik- as in *oikos* ("house, household"), the whole of Egypt being conceived of as Ptolemy's household, to be governed by a *dioiketes* in Alexandria, whose functions were replicated by the *oikonomos* (one in each district).

In the demotic documents it was normal practice for the Egyptian officials who wrote them to employ the Egyptian equivalent for official titles (Clarysse 1987, 12): It thus seems possible to indicate the equivalents for the Greek *arch-* ("managing"; *sḥn*: "ordonner, équiper, protéger, confier": Héral 1990, 305; and see Sethe and Partsch 1920,

163) and the Greek *graph-* ("writing"; *shn*, as found in *sh n Pr-'3*, the "pharaoh's scribe," or *basilikos grammateus*; Kruse 2002, 11–22). On the other hand, the titles of *strategos* (demotic *s3trks*, in various spellings), *hegemon* (demotic *hgmn*), and *oikonomos* (demotic *3knwms*, in various spellings) are as a rule simply transliterated (Clarysse 1987, 21–32): This observation is consistent with the initial predominance of Graeco-Macedonian immigrants in the military and financial spheres.

At the central level, in Alexandria, the *dioiketes* acted as the king's chief finance and interior minister; the office of the *idios logos* ("special account") was in charge of the administration of nonrecurring income (Bagnall 1976, 5; Swarney 1970); a *hypomnematographos* and an *epistolographos* superintended the royal chancery (*P.Tebt.* III 703, introduction, 68–70): Various laws, regulations, orders, and instructions emanating from the king (*nomoi, diagrammata, prostagmata, programmata*: Lenger 1980, 1990) would originate from here, quite often as a reaction to petitions (*enteuxeis*) from his subjects.

The key figures in the Ptolemaic administration at the level of the nome are all listed in the address of an ordinance (*prostagma*) of November–December 263, introducing the edict (*programma*) by which the one-sixth tax (*apomoira*) on the produce from vineyards and orchards was directed to the cult of Arsinoe Philadelphos (traditionally, the native Egyptian temples were entitled to this share of the agricultural produce): "King Ptolemy to all *strategoi*, hipparchs, captains (*hegemones*), nomarchs, toparchs, *oikonomoi*, auditors (*antigrapheis*), royal scribes (*basilikoi grammateis*), libyarchs, and chiefs of police (*archiphylakitai*), greeting" (*P.Rev.* 37, 2–5). In this list, the first officials named are the army leaders (*strategoi*, hipparchs, *hegemones*), who oversaw the military control of the conquered territory, and last mentioned are the *archiphylakitai*, who were in charge of the day-to-day policing of all economic activities in the nome (Thompson 1997b). Between them are listed the civil officials (including those in charge of the oases of western Egypt: the libyarchs), who attended to routine administrative matters.

Table 22.1. The Basics of Ptolemaic Administration

	Branches of Administration			
Administrative units	οἶκος	ἄρχειν (*shn*)	γράφειν (*shn*)	ἄγειν
Alexandria/Rhakotis	dioiketes		hypomnematographos, epistolographos	
Nomos (*tš*), metropoleis	oikonomos	nomarches *p3 shn dnj.t*	basilikos grammateus, antigrapheus	strategos *s3trks*
Meris (*dnj.t*)		meridarches *p3 shn dnj.t*		
Topos/toparchy (*qh*)		toparches *p3 shn t3 qh*	topogrammateus	
Kôme		komarches	komogrammateus	

The basic structure of early Ptolemaic administration is summed up in table 22.1.

The *basilikos grammateus* ("royal scribe") was the pivotal figure in the administration of the nome (Kruse 2002); his immediate superior was the *strategos*. The task of a *basilikos grammateus* was to write down and keep written records of the facts and figures relating to all of the transactions in the nome; foremost among these were the census (by household, *oikia*, or fiscal category, *ethnos*: Clarysse and Thompson 2006) and the survey of cultivable and cultivated land. An accurate survey of the land (after the Nile flood) and of the produce (before the harvest) was an obvious prerequisite for the working out of the country's fiscal system (Verhoogt 1998, 2005). Important financial responsibilities therefore accrued to the "writing sector" of the early Ptolemaic administration, and this explains how the *basilikos grammateus* eventually came to replace the *oikonomos* (Kruse 2002, 890). No reference to an *oikonomos* is found in the late Ptolemaic and early Roman documents from the Herakleopolite published in the *BGU* series (*BGU* IV, VIII, XIV, XVI), with the exception of *BGU* XIV 2370, a somewhat earlier document (dated around 84/83 BCE) that provides an interesting *terminus post quem* for the disappearance of the *oikonomos*.

At the lower administrative levels of *meris, topos,* and *kômê* ("division, region," "place, area" and "village," respectively), *meridarchai* ("managers of a *meris*"), *topogrammateis* ("scribes of the *topos*"), and *toparchai* ("managers of the *topos*"), as well as *komogrammateis* (village scribes) and *komarchai* ("managers of the village") are found. A *topos* comprised a varying number of villages *(kômai)* and could be referred to by the name of its main center: "in the area of" (Greek *perì*) + village name; alternatively, its name might reflect geographical conditions: *Katô, Mesê, Anô,* with reference to the northern ("lower"), central or southern ("upper") location (e.g., in the Oxyrhynchite nome: Pruneti 1981) or even derive from historical circumstances: *Agêma,* for instance, was the name of a *topos* in the Herakleopolite nome that had been destined for occupation by soldiers of the homonymous special contingent of the Macedonian army (Falivene 1998, 37–39). In a third-century BCE demotic document from al-Hiba (CGC 50148, 6–7), the designation *p3 sḥn t3 qḥ* applies to the same official (Petosiris), who was referred to by the Greek title *toparches* in *P.Hib.* 75.2–3 (Müller-Wollermann 1992, 244); accordingly, *qḥ* should be taken as the Egyptian equivalent of *topos* (in this document, the *topos* Koites is meant), just as *sḥn* corresponds to *archein*. The term *toparchy (toparchia),* on the other hand, probably referred to a toparch's managing function *(toparches),* soon to be applied, as it were by metonymy, to the area in which he exercised this authority (one or more *topoi,* or parts thereof). In other words, one and the same official could be the *toparches* of more than one *topos;* consequently, a toparchy could be a larger entity than a *topos;* by the same token but on a smaller scale, a *komarches* could be in charge of more than one village *(kômê).*

As military conquest turned into military occupation of Egypt, a large part of the Graeco-Macedonian army was effectively demobilized. In lieu of their wages, army men were granted land: This was to all effects a payment in kind, one that turned them into landholders (or cleruchs: *klerouchoi*) and rentiers and made them "at home" *(katoikoi)*, finally settled in the Egyptian *chôra*. Significantly, the Egyptian language had no equivalent for this new institution; the word *katoikos*, therefore, was simply borrowed from Greek and transliterated in demotic characters (*gtwks*, and at least one more variant spelling: Clarysse 1987, 25). Cavalry settlers *(katoikoi hippeis)* received the largest land holdings—up to one hundred arouras for the "hundred-aroura men" *(hekatontarouroi)*. The names of these original settlers *(hoi prôtoi*: "the first" Graeco-Macedonian settlers in a nome: Uebel 1968, 167n3; Kramer 1991, 78) recur in land-survey documents long after they had left their landholdings (Falivene 2007), still grouped by their army unit, sometimes under the names of their respective commanders, the *hegemones* (Kramer 1991, 74–80; see also Boswinkel and Pestman 1982, 34–55). Crowning the same move from conquest to occupation of the land, a general *(strategos)* came to be at the head of the nome (Mooren 1984). Thus, the Ptolemaic army controlled and shaped the administrative system, which was in fact mapped onto the Egyptian land, resulting in a kind of cadastral reference system that lasted into the Roman period. This is what Strabo may have meant when he wrote that the smallest administrative divisions in the nome *(merides)* were the *arourai* (17.1.3); that is, rather than referring strictly to the Egyptian land measure, he was perhaps thinking of the names that remained attached to the original land holdings, or "fossil *klêroi*" (Zucker 1964; Falivene 1998, 273–288; 2007), long after they had been split into smaller units and variously reapportioned to new grantees.

The apportionment of land to new settlers and afterward the organization of land cultivation cannot have been immune to at least potential tensions with the preexisting organization of the Egyptian territory. The standard procedure for the granting of land to new settlers required that the land be apportioned in large tracts of ten thousand arouras either to a single grantee (in the mid-third century BCE, this was the rather exceptional case for the *dôrea* of the dioiketes Apollonios: see Clarysse and Vandorpe 1995) or for cleruchs: An agent known as a *muriarouros* (a "ten-thousand-aroura man") was in charge of preparing the land for distribution and cultivation (Clarysse 1997, 75). The superior of a *muriarouros* was in all likelihood the nomarch (*nomarches*, "manager of the nome"): Their special relation is shown in *P.Petr.* II 42, where they appear together, along with various other officials; it is further confirmed by the fact that the Ghoran cartonnage papyri concerning a *muriarouros* originate from the archives of *nomarchai* (Falivene 2000). Assuming that there was traditionally (and possibly still in the earliest stages of the Ptolemaic administration) just one *nomarches* in a nome, in time two changes apparently affected this official. On the one hand, a general of the invading army (a *strategos*) was put at the head of the nome; in addition, the nomarch's authority was reduced by dividing it among several nomarchs, each of whom was in charge of just a "portion" (Egyptian *dnj.t*, and in Greek, *moira, meris*; Héral 1990, 308–311; also Müller-Wollermann 1992, 245) of the nome; as many as seven nomarchs are attested for the Arsinoite nome in the third century BCE (*SB* XXIV 15937; Clarysse 1997, 70–72). The Egyptian title of these "plural" nomarchs was *p3 sḥn dnj.t*, and a more fitting Greek rendering would be *meridarches* (the Greek root *arch-* corresponds to the Egyptian root *sḥn*, just as *meris* is rendered as *dnj.t*). *Meridarchai* are in fact attested for the Herakleopolite nome by several documents dating from the first century BCE, including *BGU* XIV 2370; of the three *meridarchai* referred to in this document, at least one was responsible for more than one toparchy (Brashear 1980, 10). This shows that at the time the Herakleopolite was divided into *merides* (and these in turn into toparchies), just like the Arsinoites, where the three *merides* of Herakleides, Polemon, and Themistos are attested beginning in the third century BCE.

Some relatively late attestations for nomarchs in the Arsinoite district (dating from the 230s BCE; Clarysse 1997, 72–76) may be accounted for by supposing that the smaller, therefore more numerous, *merides* of the nomarchs were incorporated into three, gradually larger divisions not all at once but rather one nomarch at a time, insofar as each nomarch's task within the overall reclamation and resettlement plan of the Fayyum (see Thompson 1999a, b) was completed. This also is consistent with the fact that *muriarouroi* are not attested in documents after 247/246 (Clarysse 1992–1993, 216). Harimouthes, an Egyptian nomarch attested in the lower (i.e., northern) toparchy of the Oxyrhynchite nome at an early date (*P.Hib.* I 85, of 261 BCE) and reappearing in *P.Hib.* I 44 (of 253 BCE) in the position of toparch of the same toparchy, may be a case in point: While his job description remained apparently much the same, the shift in terminology may reflect a change in the administrative hierarchical structure; perhaps Harimouthes now had a superior, a *meridarches* at the head of a newly instituted *meris* that embraced more than one toparchy, and was thus made redundant as a nomarch. A process of this kind may explain the overlap (Clarysse 1997) between nomarchs and toparchs in the Fayyum in the 230s. The possibility for a nomarch *or* a toparch to function in each other's place is in fact explicitly stated in *P.Rev.* 41, 14–17, where *either* the nomarch *or* the toparch, in the capacity of "official in charge of the nome," is entitled to obtain a seed loan from the oikonomos "before the season comes for sowing the sesame and croton . . . if they so wish." Later on, "when the season comes for gathering the sesame, croton, and cnecus, the cultivators shall give notice to the nomarch and the toparch, or where there are no nomarchs or toparchs to the oikonomos" (*P.Rev.* 42, 3–7). Once more, nomarch and toparch (or just one of them) may be present—or indeed both may be absent, in which case their superior, the oikonomos, will act in their place; ideally (if theoretically), all three should preside on the assessment of the crops.

Even though there were Egyptians among the nomarchs (Pathembris and Horos are attested among the seven officials with this title in *SB* XXIV 15937), by the end of the process of reclamation and resettlement all three divisions of the

Arsinoite district were named after Greek officials: Once again, the apportioning of land to Greek settlers appears to have been coterminous with its renaming in Greek. According to much the same principle, the whole Fayyum came to be called "Arsinoe's district," although this had not yet occurred in the *Revenue Laws* papyrus (where it is still called *he Limne*, "the lake"), but all in all, the impression one gets from this document is that by the 250s the Graeco-Macedonian new-comers (first among them, their king) felt that they had gained command of the geographical and human landscape of Egypt and that, although they still needed (as they always would) cooperative Hellenizing Egyptians, they now knew how to adequately impose their requirements. If and when required, a Greek could now assume the position of "head manager" in the nome and perform this task effectively: At this stage, Egyptians may have been demoted from positions of authority they had previously (and traditionally) held as nomarchs. Indeed, the very title *nomarches* vanishes from our documents.

Again see table 22.1 for the basics of Ptolemaic administration.

ADMINISTRATION AND THE
PTOLEMAIC FISCAL SYSTEM

Adapting a practice that had been established in step with the development of a monetary economy within the Athenian empire (Préaux 1939, 450–459), the Ptolemies farmed out their taxes: During a yearly audit, tax farmers *(telonai)* would bid and pledge themselves for a given revenue, thereby acquiring the right to keep for themselves any surplus that might occur. They could also operate as a company, consisting of a chief farmer *(archones)* and his associates *(metochoi)*. It was possible to farm one or more taxes for one or more districts. A double surety was required in that somebody else must go bail *(enguetes,* "surety") for the tax farmer in case he became unable to compensate all or part of a deficit in the expected tax income.

Banks (*trapezai*) and granaries (*thesauroi:* basically, royal banks for the economy in kind), respectively under a *trapezites* ("banker") and a *sitologos* ("grain accountant"), were crucial in ensuring the deposit, exchange, and circulation of money and grain according to a complex agenda that we can reconstruct in detail on the basis of the *Revenue Laws* papyrus. *Trapezai* were farmed out (Bogaert 1994). The underlying principle (but not the scale and scope of activity, of course) was the same as that applied in the farming out of the exclusive trading license (i.e., a monopoly: *monopôlia*) for other, less ambitious commercial enterprises, such as the exclusive right to sell lentil soup in Choinotbis, a village in the Herakleopolite district (Uebel 1964). What a contractor of the trading license for oil (the *elaikê*) acquired, for instance, was an exclusive right to buy sesame, croton, and the produce of other oil plants at wholesale prices from the grower while these crops were still on the threshing floor; he would then sell the resulting oil at varying prices in Alexandria, the Libyan oases, and "all over the country in all the towns and villages" (*P.Rev.* 40, 14, 18).

With the right, however, came the obligation to buy and sell fixed quantities at fixed prices. The specification of prices is the focus of the *Revenue Laws* papyrus insofar as these texts represent an application of the law, not the laws themselves. As for expected quantities, these were established on the basis of a preliminary assessment of the produce. Before harvest time, the contractor and the cultivator appraised the crops in the presence of the oikonomos and his checking clerk, the *antigrapheus:* This was in fact the second inspection, following an earlier one to determine the number of arouras to be sown with oil plants under the responsibility of the nomarch and/or the toparch, the oikonomos, and the *antigrapheus,* all of whom were subject to a double fine (to both the royal treasury and the contractor) if, at the time of the second assessment, "they find that the right number of arouras has not been sown." The oikonomos and the *antigrapheus* might thus find themselves in the somewhat peculiar situation of fining themselves, hence the order that "the dioiketes shall exact the payment from them" (*P.Rev.* 41, 5–13).

The nomarch and the toparch, though liable for the fine for incorrect land assessment, are conspicuously absent during the second produce assessment, which tells us something about the limitations of their authority. They would apportion land to cultivators and designate it for the production of certain crops, and they were responsible for the results of these undertakings; in fact, they acted as the interface between the cultivators and the other parties, whether contractors or officials other than themselves, but they had no part in the evaluation of prospective produce, not to mention the fixing of prices for the various crops; in short, the nomarch and the toparch had no say in the financial decisions.

The same pattern applied at village level: Here only the komarch could allow the produce to leave the village, but only after the contractors had given him a sealed receipt that listed what they had bought from each cultivator (*P.Rev.* 40, 1–8) at the value decreed in the legal tariff (*P.Rev.* 39, 16–17). The komarch controlled the transactions between the cultivator and the contractor and ensured that the produce was sold by the cultivators to the contractors and to nobody else; he also made certain that the contractors paid the prescribed amount to the cultivators. But just how much produce was to be obtained and sold and at what prices was for others (the oikonomos and the *antigrapheus,* upon agreement with the contractor and the cultivator) to decide.

On the whole, the Ptolemies punctiliously pursued a "can't lose" fiscal and economic strategy aimed at ensuring that the Crown would in any case receive the expected revenue; any deficit had to be compensated by a class of middlemen. This class comprised not just the contractors but also the cultivators *(georgoi),* who were not actually workers of the land (the ancient counterpart of the *fellahin*) but rather their employers, who leased large tracts of land from absentee landholders (Bingen 1978, 1983).

Whether this sophisticated system was a viable one and how long it lasted are different issues: It could evidently work only as long as the middlemen found it advantageous. A well-known document (*P.Tebt.* III 703; transl. Austin 1981, 432, no. 256) from the end of the third century BCE, possibly a circular from the dioiketes to an oikonomos being "sent to the nome" (1.258), hints at problems arising at various stages in the very same procedure envisaged by the *Revenue Laws* papyrus and recommends (11.222–230) the following: "Take especial care that no act of extortion or any other misdeed is committed. For everyone who lives in the country must clearly know and believe that all such acts have come to an end and that they have been delivered from the previous bad state of affairs." The Ptolemies may have been unable to conceive of a different system for exploiting the land and the people of Egypt (Bingen 1978, 11), but they also probably had no choice because of the limited number of their own people in Egypt, as well as the resistance they encountered (or would have met) on the part of the local population and establishment (especially the priestly class), had part of the Egyptian elite not been involved in the complex and controlled "outsourcing" that I have outlined.

LATER DEVELOPMENTS:
THE ROMAN PERIOD

Nomes were sometimes split, leading to the creation or reestablishment of smaller districts: The Koite and Neilopolite, for instance, were at different times (late Ptolemaic and early Roman period, respectively) carved out of the southern and the northern Herakleopolite, respectively. The Antinoopolite was created by Hadrian. Between 137 and 254 CE the three divisions of the Arsinoite nome were reduced to two, those of Themistos and Polemon being under the same strategos and the *meris* of Herakleides under a different one (this arrangement lasted for about a century; thereafter, the whole Arsinoite was again under one strategos; Bastianini-Whitehorne 1987, 46–55). But despite these changes, the administrative map of Egypt—the articulation of the land into nomes, merides, toparchies, and villages, as well as the titles of the officials in charge of their administration—remained basically stable under Roman rule.

Beneath the appearance of continuity, however, important shifts in authority led to a redistribution of responsibility and power among old and new officials—first among these was the emperor's deputy, *praefectus Alexandreae et Aegypti* (Bowman 1986, 65–68)—and, at a more fundamental level, among the various components of the population of Egypt. The keyword here is *municipalization,* a "process...definitely and deliberately begun in the Augustan period with the creation of urban communities with 'Hellenic' landowning élites," leading to the formal constitution of town councils (*boulai*) in Egypt by Septimius Severus in 200/201 CE (Bowman and Rathbone 1992, 108). The *boulê* was to function as a compensation chamber between the central administration and the revenue-producing land: It did this by ensuring that the fundamental administrative operations of tax collecting and recordkeeping were adequately performed by local liturgical officials ("some from its own membership, some not, depending on the task": Bowman 1986, 71) under the supervision of the *strategos* and the *basilikos grammateus,* who for their part became career bureaucrats who were appointed by the government and served only outside their home district (Kruse 2002, 44).

In the reign of Philip the Arabian (244–249 CE), a reform of the taxation and administrative system took place that entrusted a commission of the "ten first men" *(dekaprotoi)* in the *boulê* with the administration of the nome. At the same time, the office of the *basilikos grammateus* was abolished (Kruse 2002, 940–952), and in fact, the whole bureaucratic line of "writing officials" appears to have been dismissed. As the *dekaprotoi* operated at the toparchy level, the *topogrammateis* must also have become redundant (latest dated attestation: *P.Laur.* I 4, 246 CE), while the *komarches* took over the functions of the *komogrammateus* (Thomas 1975, 115; Borkowski and Hagedorn 1978, 781–783). The limited number of *dekaprotoi,* combined with the heavy burden that went with their office, explains the rule of collegial responsibility for these officers, who were to operate by toparchy in boards of at least two (toparchies were paired off so that a team of at least four *dekaprotoi* was in charge at any one time; Bagnall 1978). The same principle of collegial responsibility apparently applied to toparchs and komarchs as well (Vitelli 1906 on *P.Flor.* I 2, 265 CE; see also Oertel 1917, 163). Some rearrangement of the toparchies (discussed later) must also have occurred in this reorganization.

"What the Romans had been trying to do for the past century, namely to make the local property-owning class responsible for the orderly and complete collection of the taxes owed to the central government" (Bagnall 1993, 55) was now accomplished. The *dekaprotoi,* however, soon found themselves caught in an "administrative web.... Responsible in every particular to their superiors, they were forced to make up losses by oppression" (Turner 1936, 11). In about sixty years, a new reform was carried out whose beginnings went back to Diocletian's reign (284–305); apart from the *dioiketes* himself (Hagedorn 1985), its "victims" included the *dekaprotoi,* the *strategos,* and indeed the nome itself as an administrative entity. The *dekaprotoi* were now to serve for a five-year term coincident with the five-year cycle of the newly instituted tax schedule *(epigraphê)* issued each year in the early summer (Bagnall and Thomas 1978, 186); in return, they were excused from renomination. Eventually, "at a date between 3 May and 2 July 302," the *dekaprotoi* ceased to function altogether (Thomas 1974, 68), and from 307/308 on, numbered toparchies were replaced by numbered *pagi,* each headed by a *praepositus pagi.*

LATER DEVELOPMENTS:
THE BYZANTINE PERIOD

The process that led to the creation of the new geographical and administrative grid by *pagi* may be summed up as follows. First, the number of toparchies was increased and their size reduced, with a view to making them more "manageable"; the resulting new toparchies were referred to by number, though naturally the traditional names persisted for a while: A few Fayyum documents from the third decade of the second century CE attest to this intermediate stage, when "toparchies are at the same time numbered and named after a village" (Derda 2003, 45). Second, the creation in the third century CE of the office of the *dekaprotoi* (whose area of responsibility was defined by toparchies) must have reinforced and stabilized the new grid of numbered toparchies. Third, at the beginning of the fourth century, as the *dekaprotoi* were being phased out, *pagi* became the new administrative unit, possibly overlapping the *numbered* toparchies, as distinguished from the older ones (those named after a village or with reference to either their location in the nome or some other special characteristic of their territory); this is suggested by the occasional interchangeability of the terms *pagus* and *toparchia* in certain fourth-century documents (Sijpesteijn and Worp 1978, 9–10); it also goes a long way toward explaining the often-observed discrepancies between the number of old toparchies and of *pagi* in the Oxyrhynchite (Pruneti 1989), Hermopolite (Sheridan 1998, 106–134), and Arsinoite nomes (Derda 2001).

The very existence of the nomes as administrative units was curtailed as a result of the introduction of the *pagi*. The cultural persistence of the nomes, however, is still apparent in the *Notitia Dignitatum,* a "register of civil and military offices of the Roman/Byzantine empire compiled in the 390s," in which "the towns of the delta are schematically represented and from them the traditional symbols of the various nomes emerge" (Bowman 1986, 81–82). In the capitals of the nomes (the *mêtropoleis* of old, now *civitates*) the *strategos,* now divested of many of his powers, acquired the new title of *exactor civitatis,* while his other responsibilities were diverted to the *logistes* (or *curator civitatis*) and later to the *defensor civitatis* (Thomas 2001, 1253; Kruse 2002, 952–953).

After 293/294, following the suppression by the junior emperor Galerius of a revolt in Coptos, the Thebaid became administratively separate from the rest of Egypt. This division was a lasting one and was carried over in the several successive attempts—throughout the fourth century and down to Justinian's *Edict* XIII (ca. 537/538)—at reorganizing the administrative structure of Egypt (Rouillard 1928; Lallemand 1964, 41–57; Bowman 1986, 78–79).

The inauguration of the new fifteen-year tax cycles (in which each year was called an indiction), which reckoned retrospectively from the year 312, tallied with the restoration of church property (313), which followed immediately upon the cessation of the official prosecution of Christians as soon as Constantine finally came to power. The church promptly affirmed itself as an alternative source of authority; it was within the (much-divided) Church of Egypt that the conflict between Alexandria and Constantinople acted itself out (Haas 1997; Heinen 1998). The foundation of Constantinople (formally celebrated on May 11, 330) at the same time undermined Alexandria's position as the principal city of the Greek-speaking east and reoriented Egypt eastward. The bishop, or patriarch of Alexandria, in fact became the most powerful figure in Egypt (Rouillard 1928, 229–239): Unlike officials who were but deputies of the distant emperor, he could claim and exercise direct authority in both Alexandria and the whole country by means of the bishops whom he appointed in the *mêtropoleis* and also through the village clergy (presbyters and deacons, the bishop's appointees). Inland, the country witnessed the "collapse of the institutional basis of separate Egyptian culture, the temples," and, running parallel to it, the dismantling of village institutions: "By the end of the fourth century it is normal to find presbyters and deacons as the representatives of the village population" (Bagnall 1993, 316). On the other hand, the existence of large landowners effectively favored "the integration of the villages into the city economy and society." Increasingly, these wealthy families were made responsible for village tax collection, thereby "leading to the privatization of public business and the bureaucratization of the private" (ibid., 318): in sixth-century Oxyrhynchus, the Apion family provides a well-known example of this double shift (Gascou 1985; Mazza 2001).

New ways of life and changed bureaucratic patterns are reflected in the administrative language, too: From the seventh century on, the term *kômê*, for "village," is replaced by *chôrion*, with an emphasis on a village as part of the countryside (the *chôra*), that is, the territory now integral to a *mêtropolis*. The pagarch (*pagarches* or *pagarchos*) first appears in our sources toward the end of the fifth century: He was responsible for collecting taxes from all subjects who were not exempted—on the strength of *autopragia*, or (fiscal) "self-determination"—from his authority (Liebeschuetz 1990). Since this function *(pagarchia)* was apparently attested before the officer who exercised it (Mazza 1995), one may suppose that the *praepositus pagi*, having lost control of too large a part of his *pagus*, was superseded by a new official, the *pagarch* (Rouillard 1928, 52–62), who also took on what had been a *komarch's* responsibilities.

Arab pagarchs are attested well into the eighth century CE, when they are found addressing, still in Greek, the local communities (Gonis 2004). The new conquerors—as Alexander and the early Ptolemies had been—were well aware of the importance of avoiding a breakdown of the administration (Rouillard 1928, 248; Grohmann 1959, 33–34; Christides 1993) if they were to consolidate their occupation of the Egyptian land.

BIBLIOGRAPHY

Austin, M. M. 1981. *The Hellenistic World from Alexander to the Roman Conquest: A Selection of Ancient Sources in Translation.* Cambridge: Cambridge University Press.

Bagnall, R. S. 1976. *The Administration of the Ptolemaic Possessions outside Egypt.* Leiden: Brill.

Bagnall, R. S. 1978. "The Number and Term of the Dekaprotoi." *Aegyptus* 58: 160–167.

——. 1993. *Egypt in Late Antiquity.* Princeton: Princeton University Press.

——, and D. W. Rathbone, eds. 2004. *Egypt from Alexander to the Copts: An Archaeological and Historical Guide.* London: British Museum Press.

Bagnall R. S., and J. D. Thomas. 1978. "Dekaprotoi and Epigraphai." *Bulletin of the American Society of Papyrologists* 15: 185–189.

Baines, J., and J. Málek. 2000. *Cultural Atlas of Ancient Egypt,* rev. ed. New York: Facts on File.

Bastianini, G., and J. E. G. Whitehorne. 1987. *Strategi and Royal Scribes of Roman Egypt: Chronological List and Index.* Papyrologica Florentina 15. Florence: Edizioni Gonnelli.

Bingen, J. 1952. *Papyrus Revenue Laws: Nouvelle édition du texte (Sammelbuch Griechischer Urkunden aus Ägypten,* Suppl. 1). Göttingen: Hubert & Co.

——. 1978. "The Third-century B.C. Land Leases from Tholthis." *Illinois Classical Studies* 3: 74–80.

——. 1983. "Les cavaliers catoeques de l'Héracleopolite au Ier siècle." In *Egypt and the Hellenistic World: Proceedings of the International Colloquium, Leuven, 24–26 May 1982,* ed. E. Van 't Dack, 1–11. Studia Hellenistica 27. Leuven: Studia Hellenistica.

Bogaert, R. 1968. *Banques et banquiers dans les cités grecques.* Leiden: A. W. Sijthoff.

——. 1994. *Trapezitica Aegyptiaca: Recueil de recherches sur la banque en Égypte gréco-romaine.* Papyrologica Florentina 25. Florence: Gonnelli.

Borkowski, Z., and D. Hagedorn. 1978. "Amphodokomogrammateus: Zur Verwaltung der Dörfer Ägyptens im 3. Jh. n.Chr." In *Le monde grec: Pensée, littérature, histoire, documents. Hommages à Claire Préaux,* ed. J. Bingen, G. Cambier, and G. Nachtergael, 775–783. Brussels: Éditions de l'Université de Bruxelles.

Boswinkel, E., and P. W. Pestman, eds. 1982. *Les archives privées de Dionysios, fils de Kephalas (P.Lugd.Bat. 22): Textes grecs et démotiques.* Leiden: Brill.

Bowman, A. K. 1986. *Egypt after the Pharaohs. 332 BC–AD 642: From Alexander to the Arab Conquest.* Berkeley: University of California Press.

——, and D. W. Rathbone. 1992. "Cities and Administration in Roman Egypt." *Journal of Roman Studies* 82: 107–127.

Boyaval, B. 1973. "Papyrus ptolémaïques inédits de Ghôran et Magdôla." *Cahiers des Recherches de l'Institut de Papyrologie et d'Égyptologie de Lille* 1: 215–216.

Brashear, W. M., ed. 1980. *Ägyptische Urkunden aus den Staatlichen Museen Berlin: Griechische Urkunden.* Vol. 14, *Ptolemäische Urkunden aus Mumienkartonage.* Berlin: Staatliche Museen Preussischer Kulturbesitz.

Bresciani, E. 1978. "La spedizione di Tolemeo II in Siria in un ostrakon demotico inedito da Karnak." In *Das ptolemäische Ägypten: Akten des internationalen Symposions 27–29 September 1976 in Berlin,* ed. H. Maehler and V. M. Strocka, 31–36. Mainz: Philipp von Zabern.

——. 1983. "Registrazione catastale e ideologia politica nell'Egitto tolemaico." *Egitto e Vicino Oriente* 6: 15–31.

Burstein, S. M. 1985. *Translated Documents of Greece and Rome. 3. The Hellenistic Age from the Battle of Ipsos to the Death of Kleopatra VII.* Cambridge: Cambridge University Press.

Calderini, A., and S. Daris. 1935–2007. *Dizionario dei nomi geografici e topografici dell'Egitto greco-romano.* 1.1. Cairo: Società Reale di Geografia d'Egitto-1.2. Madrid: Consejo Superior de Investigaciones Cientificas-2-5, Suppl. 1. Milan: Cisalpino-La Goliardica. Suppl. 2. Bonn: Habelt. Suppl. 3. Pisa: Giardini. Suppl. 4. Roma: Fabrizio Serra.

Christides, V. 1993. "Continuation and Change in Early Arab Egypt as Reflected in the Terms and Titles of the Greek Papyri." *Bulletin de la Société d'Archéologie d'Alexandrie* 45: 69–75.

Clarysse, W. 1987. "Greek Loan-Words in Demotic." In *Aspects of Demotic Lexicography: Acts of the Second International Conference for Demotic Studies, Leiden, 19–21 September 1984,* ed. S. P. Vleeming, 9–33. Leuven: Peeters.

——. 1992–1993. "A New Muriarouros in a Bilingual Text." *Enchoria* 19/20: 215–217.

——. 1997. "Nomarchs and Toparchs in the Third-century Fayyum." In *Archeologia e papiri nel Fayyum: Atti del Convegno Internazionale. Siracusa 24–25 maggio 1996,* 69–76. Syracuse, Italy: Istituto internazionale del papiro.

——, and D. J. Thompson. 2006. *Counting the People in Hellenistic Egypt.* Vol. 1, *Population Registers* (P.Count.). Vol. 2, *Historical Studies.* Cambridge: Cambridge University Press.

Clarysse, W., and K. Vandorpe. 1995. *Zenon, un homme d'affaires grec à l'ombre des Pyramides.* Leuven: Presses Universitaires.

Depauw, M. 2000. "Alexandria, the Building Yard." *Chronique d'Égypte* 75: 64–65.

Derda, T. 2001. "Pagi in the Arsinoite Nome: A Study in the Administration of the Fayum in the Early Byzantine Period. With an Appended Edition of *P.Aberd.* 164 descr. by Nikolaos Gonis." *Journal of Juristic Papyrology* 31: 17–31.

Derda, T. 2003. "Toparchies in the Arsinoite Nome: A Study in Administration of the Fayyum in the Roman Period," *Journal of Juristic Papyrology* 33: 27–54.

Drew-Bear, M. 1979. *Le nome Hermopolite: Toponymes et sites.* Missoula, Mont.: Scholars Press.

Falivene, M. R. 1991. "Government, Management, Literacy: Aspects of Ptolemaic Administration in the Early Hellenistic Period." *Ancient Society* 22: 203–227.

——. 1998. *The Herakleopolite Nome: A Catalogue of the Toponyms with Introduction and Commentary.* American Studies in Papyrology 37. Atlanta: Scholars Press.

——. 2000. "Sull'origine del *P.L.Bat.* XX Suppl. A (Progetto di dighe e canali per la doreà di Apollonios)." In S. Russo, ed. *Atti del V Convegno Nazionale di Egittologia e Papirologia, Firenze, 10–12 dicembre 1999,* 115–121. Florence: Istituto papirologico G. Vitelli.

——. 2007. "Patterns of the Greek Settlement in Egypt during the Ptolemaic Period: 'Old Settlers' in the Herakleopolite Nome." In B. Palme. ed., *Akten des 23. Internationalen Kongresses für Papyrologie, Wien, 22.–28. Juli 2004,* 207–214. Vienna: Verlag der Österreichischen Akademie der Wissenschaften.

Fraser, P. M. 1972. *Ptolemaic Alexandria.* Oxford: Clarendon Press.

Gardiner, A. H., ed. 1948. *The Wilbour Papyrus* I–III (IV, *Index,* by R. O. Faulkner, 1952). London: Oxford University Press.

Gascou, J. 1985. "Les grands domaines, la cité, et l'état en Égypte byzantine." *Travaux et Mémoires* 9: 1–90.

Gomaà, F., R. Hannig, and H. Pohlmann. 1991. *Tübinger Atlas des Vorderen Orient.* Vol. 3, 1, *Ägypten zur Zeit des neuen Reiches: Nordteil, Südteil.* Wiesbaden: Reichert.

Gonis, N. 2004. "Another Look at Some Officials in Early Abbasid Egypt." *ZPE* 149: 189–195.

Grenfell, B. P., ed. 1896. *Revenue Laws of Ptolemy Philadelphus. Edited from a Greek Papyrus in the Bodleian Library, with a Translation, Commentary, and Appendices.* Oxford: Clarendon Press.

——, A. S. Hunt, and J. G. Smyly. 1902. *The Tebtunis Papyri* I. London: Oxford University Press.

Grohmann, A. 1959. *Studien zur historischen Geographie und Verwaltung des frühmittelalterlichen Ägypten.* Wien: R. M. Rohrer.

Guéraud, O., and P. Jouguet. 1938. *Un livre d'écolier du IIIe siècle avant J.C.* Cairo: Imprimerie de l'Institut français d'archéologie orientale.

Haas, C. 1997. *Alexandria in Late Antiquity: Topography and Social Conflict.* Baltimore: Johns Hopkins University Press.

Habicht, C. 1997. *Athens from Alexander to Antony,* trans. D. L. Schneider. Cambridge, Mass.: Harvard University Press.

Hagedorn, D. 1985. "Zum Amt des *dioiketes* im römischen Aegypten." *Yale Classical Studies* 28: 167–210.

Heinen, H. 1998. "Das spätantike Ägypten (284–646 n.Chr.)." In *Ägypten in Spätantik-Christlicher Zeit: Einführung in die koptische Kultur,* ed. M. Krause, 35–56. Wiesbaden: Reichert.

——, W. Schlömer, and H. Pohlmann. 1989. *Tübinger Atlas des Vorderen Orient.* Vol. 5, 21. *Ägypten in hellenistisch-römischer Zeit.* Wiesbaden: Reichert.

Helck, W. 1974. *Die altägyptische Gaue (TAVO Beiheft B15).* Wiesbaden: Reichert.

Héral, S. 1990. "Deux équivalents démotiques du titre de *nomarches.*" *CdÉ* 65: 304–320.

Hombert, M. 1925. "Quelques papyrus des collections de Gand et de Paris." *Revue Belge de Philologie et d'Histoire* 4: 660–662.

Kees, H. 1961. *Ancient Egypt: A Cultural Topography,* ed. T. G. H. James; trans. I. F. D. Morrow. Chicago: University of Chicago Press.

Kramer, B., ed. 1991. *Corpus Papyrorum Raineri.* Vol. 18. Griechische Texte, 13, *Das Vertragsregister von Theogenis* (P.Vindob. G 40618). Vienna: Brüder Hollinek.

Kruse, Th. 2002. *Der königliche Schreiber und die Gauverwaltung: Untersuchungen zur Verwaltungsgeschichte Ägyptens in der Zeit von Augustus bis Philippus Arabs (30 v. Chr.—245 n. Chr.).* 2 vols. Munich: K. G. Saur.

Lallemand, J. 1964. *L'administration civile de l'Égypte de l'avènement de Dioclétien à la création du diocèse (284–382).* Brussels: Académie Royale de Belgique.

Lenger, M.-Th. 1980. *Corpus des Ordonnances des Ptolémées (C. Ord. Ptol.).* Brussels: Académie Royale de Belgique.

——. 1990. *Corpus des Ordonnances des Ptolémées: Bilan des additions et corrections (1964–1988). Compléments à la bibliographie.* Brussels: Fondation égyptologique Reine Elisabeth.

Liebeschuetz, J. H. W. G. 1990. *From Diocletian to the Arab Conquest: Change in the Late Roman Empire.* Aldershot: Ashgate.

Mahaffy, J. P. 1896. "Introduction to the Revenue Papyrus." In B. P. Grenfell, ed., *Revenue Laws of Ptolemy Philadelphus. Edited from a Greek Papyrus in the Bodleian Library, with a Translation, Commentary, and Appendices,* Oxford: Clarendon Press: xvii–lv.

Mazza, R. 1995. "Ricerche sul pagarca nell'Egitto tardoantico e bizantino." *Aegyptus* 75: 169–242.

——. 2001. *L'archivio degli Apioni. Terra, lavoro e proprietà senatoria nell'Egitto tardoantico.* Bari: Edipuglia.

Mooren, L. 1984. "On the Jurisdiction of the Nome Strategoi in Ptolemaic Egypt." In *Atti del XVII Congresso Internazionale di Papirologia*. Vol. 3, 1217–1225. Naples: Centro Internazionale per lo Studio dei Papiri Ercolanesi.

Mueller, K. 2003a. "Mastering Matrices and Clusters: Locating Graeco-Roman Settlements in the Meris of Herakleides (Fayyum/Egypt) by Monte-Carlo-Simulation." *APF* 49: 218–254.

———. 2003b. "Places and Spaces in the Themistou Meris (Fayyum/Graeco-Roman Egypt): Locating Settlements by Multidimensional Scaling of Papyri." *Ancient Society* 33: 103–125.

Müller-Wollermann, R. 1992. "Demotische Termini zur Landesgliederung Ägyptens." In *Life in a Multi-cultural Society: Egypt from Cambyses to Constantine and Beyond*, ed. J. H. Johnson, 243–247. Studies in Ancient Oriental Civilization 51. Chicago: Oriental Institute of the University of Chicago.

Oertel, F. 1917. *Die Liturgie: Studien zur Ptolemäischen und Kaiserlichen Verwaltung Aegyptens*. Leipzig: Teubner.

Palme, B. 1989. *Das Amt des ἀπαιτητής in Ägypten*. Vienna: Hollinek.

Parsons, P. J. 1967. "Philippus Arabs and Egypt." *Journal of Roman Studies* 57: 134–141.

Pestman, P. W. 1990. *The New Papyrological Primer*. Leiden: Brill.

Préaux, C. 1939. *L'économie royale des Lagides*. Brussels: Fondation égyptologique Reine Elisabeth.

Pruneti, P. 1981. *I centri abitati dell'Ossirinchite: Repertorio toponomastico*. Florence: Gonnelli.

———. 1989. "Toparchie e pagi: Precisazioni topografiche relative al nòmo Ossirinchite." *Aegyptus* 69: 113–118.

Rathbone, D. W. 1990. "Villages, Land, and Population in Graeco-Roman Egypt." In *Proceedings of the Cambridge Philological Society* 216, n.s., 36: 103–142.

Rouillard, G. 1928. *L'administration civile de l'Égypte Byzantine*, 2d ed. Paris: P. Geuthner.

Ruffini, G. R. 2007. "New Approaches to Oxyrhynchite Topography." In *Proceedings of the XXIV International Congress of Papyrology, Helsinki 1–7.8.2004*, ed. J. Frösén, T. Purola, and E. Salmenkivi, 965–978. Helsinki: Finnish Society of Sciences and Letters.

Samuel, A. E. 1966. "The Internal Organization of the Nomarch's Bureau in the Third Century B.C." In *Essays in Honor of C. Bradford Welles*. American Studies in Papyrology 1. New Haven, Conn.: American Society of Papyrologists: 213–229.

Sethe, K., and J. Partsch. 1920. *Demotische Urkunden zum Ägyptischen Bürgschaftsrechte vorzüglich der Ptolemäerzeit*. Leipzig: Teubner.

Sheridan, J. A., ed. 1998. *Columbia Papyri IX: The Vestis Militaris Codex*. American Studies in Papyrology 39. Atlanta: Scholars Press.

Sijpesteijn, P. J., and K. A. Worp. 1978. *Zwei Landlisten aus dem Hermupolites (P.Landlisten)*. Zutphen, the Netherlands: Terra.

Sottas, H. 1921. *Papyrus démotiques de Lille*. Paris: P. Geuthner.

Swarney, P. R. 1970. *The Ptolemaic and Roman Idios Logos*. American Studies in Papyrology 8. Toronto: Hakkert.

Talbert, R. J. A., ed. 2000. *Barrington Atlas of the Greek and Roman World*. Princeton: Princeton University Press.

Thomas, J. D. 1974. "The Disappearance of the Dekaprotoi in Egypt." *Bulletin of the American Society of Papyrologists* 11: 60–68.

——. 1975. "The Introduction of Dekaprotoi and Comarchs into Egypt in the Third Century A.D." *Zeitschrift für Papyrologie und Epigraphik* 19: 111–119.

——. 1982. *The Epistrategos in Ptolemaic and Roman Egypt*. Part 2, *The Roman Epistrategos*. Opladen: Westdeutscher Verlag.

——. 2001. "The Administration of Roman Egypt: A Survey of Recent Research and Some Outstanding Problems." In *Atti del XXII Congresso Internazionale di Papirologia*, ed. I. Andorlini, G. Bastianini, M. Manfredi, and G. Menci, 1245–1254. Florence: Istituto papirologico G. Vitelli.

Thompson, D. J. 1997a. "The Infrastructure of Splendour: Census and Taxes in Ptolemaic Egypt." In *Hellenistic Constructs: Essays in Culture, History, and Historiography*, ed. P. Cartledge, P. Garnsey, and E. Gruen, 242–257. Berkeley: University of California Press.

——. 1997b. "Policing the Ptolemaic Countryside." In *Akten des 21. Internationalen Papyrologenkongresses, Berlin 1995*, ed. B. Kramer, 961–966. Stuttgart: Teubner.

——. 1999a. "Irrigation and Drainage in the Early Ptolemaic Fayyum." In *Agriculture in Egypt: From Pharaonic to Modern Times*, ed. A. K. Bowman and E. Rogan, 107–122. Oxford: Published for the British Academy by Oxford University Press.

——. 1999b. "New and Old in the Ptolemaic Fayyum." In *Agriculture in Egypt: From Pharaonic to Modern Times*, ed. A. K. Bowman and E. Rogan, 123–138. Oxford: Published for the British Academy by Oxford University Press.

——. 2001. "*Ethne*, Taxes, and Administrative Geography in Early Ptolemaic Egypt." In *Atti del XXII Congresso Internazionale di Papirologia*, ed. I. Andorlini, G. Bastianini, M. Manfredi, G. Menci, 1255–1263. Florence: Istituto papirologico G. Vitelli.

Turner, E. G. 1936. "Egypt and the Roman Empire: The Dekaprotoi." *JEA* 22: 7–19.

Uebel, F. 1968. *Die Kleruchen Ägyptens unter den ersten sechs Ptolemäern*. Berlin: Akademie Verlag.

——. 1964. "*ΜΟΝΟΠΩΛΙΑ ΦΑΚΗΣ*: Ein bisher unbezeugtes Handelsmonopol frühptolemäischer Zeit in einem Jenaer Papyrus (*P.Ien.* inv. 900)." In J. Wolski, ed. *Actes du Xe Congrès International de Papyrologues*, 165–181. Warsaw: Comité des Sciences de la culture antique, Académie polonaise des Sciences.

Verhoogt, A. 1998. *Menches, Komogrammateus of Kerkeosiris: The Doings and Dealings of a Village Scribe in the Late Ptolemaic Period (120–110 B.C.)*. Leiden: Brill.

——. 2005. *Regaling Officials in Ptolemaic Egypt: A Dramatic Reading of Official Accounts from the Menches Papers* (P.L. Bat. 32). Leiden: Brill.

Vitelli, G., ed. 1906. *Papiri fiorentini: documenti pubblici e privati dell'età romana e bizantina. I (1–105)*. Milano: Hoepli.

Yoyotte, J., and P. Charvet. 1997. *Strabon: Le Voyage en Egypte. Un regard romain*. Paris: NiL Éditions.

Zucker, F. 1964. "Beobachtungen zu den permanenten Klerosnamen." In *Studien zur Papyrologie und antiken Wirtschaftsgeschichte Fr. Oertel zum achtzigsten Geburtstag gewidmet*, ed. H. Braunert, 101–106. Bonn: Rudolf Habelt Verlag.

CHAPTER 23

LAW IN GRAECO-ROMAN EGYPT: HELLENIZATION, FUSION, ROMANIZATION

URI YIFTACH-FIRANKO

INTRODUCTION

A wide variety of activity related to law, such as contracts, appeals, court proceedings, and legislative acts, were frequently documented on papyri. In Graeco-Roman Egypt these were recorded in a variety of languages over the millennium and a half from the Saite period to the early centuries of Arab rule. From the sixth century BCE to the first century CE demotic was used. With the Macedonian occupation of 332 BCE, Greek set in and was still in use long after the Arab occupation of 641. With the Roman occupation of 30 BCE Latin emerged for some purposes, and Coptic was used in legal documents from the sixth century on, becoming dominant after the Arab conquest.

In the period stretching from Alexander to the Arab conquest, then, a person who was documenting a legal activity could frequently choose from among more than one language. This choice of language was neither a mere technicality nor a matter of indifference, however. Very frequently, legal documents were authored by professional scribes, who in their writing adhered to long-standing traditions: Greek scribes used formulae imported from the Greek motherland by immigrants who had followed Alexander's conquest, while their Egyptian counterparts employed local formulas that predated the Greek occupation. The formulas used in either case were naturally different. Accordingly, the choice of language affected the nature of the institution.

The selection of a language also carried cultural implications. One would most naturally employ the legal institutions of one's ancestors and record them in the same language they had used. If one chose differently, there must have been important reasons to do so. In the early Roman period a will drawn up by a Roman citizen had to be written in Latin and follow strict formulaic rules to be valid. Accordingly, the acquisition of Roman citizenship entailed a change from Greek to Latin as the language of wills (Kaser 1971, 687n10; Wolff 2002, 157–159). A language might also be changed for reasons of expediency: In the Ptolemaic period a petition to a Greek official, such as the king, would be more effective if written in Greek than in Egyptian, so Greek petitions to the king are predominant from the start (Depauw 1997, 137).

Neither rule nor expediency necessarily governed other legal activities, however. In the Ptolemaic period the composition of legal documents in demotic was never banned. The contents of these documents were also, under certain conditions, enforceable in a court of law. Accordingly, in the Ptolemaic and much of the early Roman period, Greek and Egyptian scribal traditions coexisted and were eventually used by parties of Greek and Egyptian origin alike.

Still, in the course of the first century CE demotic disappeared from legal documents. This was a development of far-reaching consequence, for the demise of the demotic document went hand in hand with that of the formulaic tradition that found expression in its clauses. So far as the law of contract goes, in the following centuries Egypt became a Greek land, and those living there almost exclusively used Greek types of contracts authored by Greek scribes and following Greek formats. One of the objectives of this chapter is to discuss how and why this Hellenization took place. I maintain that it accompanied the rise of the office of the Greek public notaries—most conspicuously the *agoranomeion*—in the Egyptian *chôra* in the Ptolemaic and early Roman periods. Accordingly, I examine important landmarks in the evolution of the *agoranomeion* in that time frame.

The recognition that the contractual practices underwent their crucial phase of Hellenization in the first century CE highlights a striking paradox: With regard to the format of legal documents, never in the three centuries that Egypt was ruled by a Greek (i.e., Macedonian) dynasty was the country as Greek as it was when it became a Roman province. This recognition raises an important question: Did the Hellenization of Egypt advance at the same pace in other areas of life and society? This question will not, of course, be treated in this framework. Yet some positive results can be reached. Minutes of court proceedings from the second century CE sometimes refer to a certain manual called the "Law of the Egyptians," which served as a guideline in court proceedings that involved peregrines (i.e., those who did not hold Roman citizenship). The precepts contained in that guideline are of diverse origin—Greek and Egyptian alike—and were applied by and to the local subjects regardless of their ethnic origin. Thus, the contents of this manual at least do not evince the triumph of the Greek over the Egyptian element in the second century CE but instead reflect a fusion of the two into a new "code" of law that was applied by and to everyone in the province.

In 30 BCE Egypt became a Roman province and remained under Roman rule for almost seven hundred years. What effect did this Roman presence have on the legal landscape of Egypt? In 212 the Antonine Constitution turned the provincial population into Roman citizens. Formally, it subjected all its inhabitants to the precepts of Roman law. Yet did this change in status also mean a profound change in the legal practices in Egypt? To answer this I dedicate a short section to the question of Romanization. We now turn to the beginnings of the *agoranomeia*.

HELLENIZATION

Security and Sale

The *agoranomos* emerges in the Greek papyri for the first time in the mid-third century BCE. Some of the earliest attestations connect him with the foreclosure of securities for loans.[1] In loans, the creditor gives money and requires some security for its recovery, so the debtor grants him temporary title (though not necessarily ownership) to some of his assets until he repays the debt. What happens if the borrower does not return the money on time? The Ptolemaic lawgiver shows much interest in regulating this issue. According to a royal decree *(diagramma)*, presumably from around 275 BCE, the creditor cannot simply seize the asset (Wolff 2002, 51–52).

When the loan is granted, the debtor is expected to register the security with the *agoranomos*.[2] The entry is to report the nature of the object, its location, the identity of the creditor, the amount of money lent, and the date of expiry. If the debt is not settled on time or treated in a new contract, the *agoranomos* moves on to the *epikatabolê*, an official act that sets in motion the foreclosure procedure (Rupprecht 1995a, 426–428; 1997, 291–302). In addition, it is quite plausible that the decree that regulated foreclosures and defined the role of the *agoranomos* is also responsible for the very establishment of the *agoranomeia* in the *chôra* in the third century BCE. The *agoranomoi* were established in the *chôra*, then, in order to monitor foreclosures. Soon, however, they assumed new tasks.

When the Greeks first arrived in Egypt, there were no organized archives for Greek documents, so the settlers had to secure their transactions by other means. In the third century BCE, legal documents commonly assumed the form of a double document. Identical versions of the contract were recorded on the upper and lower halves of the same papyrus. The upper text was folded and then closed with the seals of the parties and the witnesses who were present at the act, while the lower half remained visible. Any change in the wording of the open part after the conclusion of the contract could be easily detected by breaking open the upper text and reading its contents. The instrument would then be deposited with the *syngraphophylax*, a private individual whose high social standing would ensure its safekeeping (Wolff 1978, 57).

By the late third century things began changing. Copies of privately composed legal documents were assembled in local (perhaps official) collections (Rupprecht 1995b, 37–49). Far more important for the present discussion is the aforementioned creation of the *agoranomeia*. According to my hypothesis, the *agoranomoi* were originally established in the *chôra* to monitor loans and securities. For that purpose they developed advanced bureaucratic skills. The general population was familiar with these skills and realized the potential advantages of registering contracts at this newly established public archive. Accordingly, once an *agoranomos* was present, other (especially valuable) transactions were recorded in his files as well. For the *agoranomos*, the registration meant a new source of income (*CPR* XVIII, pp. 30–31), so he likely welcomed the new practice.

This practice is attested in two spheres in particular: the law of marriage and the law of sale. A newly married bride frequently brought into her husband's house highly valuable assets—very frequently her only ones. The husband was to manage these assets with care in the course of the marriage and to return them to the wife or her family if the marriage ended. It was in the wife's best interest to ensure that he did so. Accordingly, when the *agoranomeia* emerge in the second half of the third century BCE, a new clause appears in marriage documents that obligates the husband to record the marital arrangements in the new archive within a specified period after his wife requested that he do so (Yiftach-Firanko 2003, 55–79).

An identical phenomenon is evident in the case of land sales. For the purchasers, a sale was a precarious matter. They paid good money for an object that could later prove defective in substance or title. In consequence, sale contracts from the late third century BCE contain an anticipatory clause similar to that found in contemporaneous marriage documents. The vendor is instructed to "give" *(dotô)* the purchaser a "deed of sale" *(ônê)* at an *agoranomeion* within ten days of the latter's request.[3] The purchaser's security needs would be satisfied by the registration of the act at any nearby *agoranomeion*. Accordingly, in *SB* XIV 11376 (239 BCE, Tholthis)—our earliest evidence of the practice from the Egyptian *chôra*[4]—the vendor is free to register the sale at any of the nearby *agoranomeia* of Oxyrhynchus and Herakleopolis.

At first, the registration was of no consequence for the legal position of the purchaser. All the buyer gained was probably yet another means of proving the conclusion of the contract and the act of payment, should his title later be challenged or prove defective. Still, the *agoranomoi* also issued a special certificate that reported the registration.[5] Since the same papyrus would frequently contain a confirmation of the payment of the conveyance tax *(enkyklion)*,[6] its issuance could well corroborate the assumption that the purchaser had procured title to the asset. Accordingly, when the state wished to secure the inalienability of an asset, one way was to prohibit the *agoranomoi* from performing the registration (*SB* XVI 12519.5, II BCE, Arsinoite).

In general, however, the state was interested in promoting the new practice. A complete and well-organized registry of sales would allow it to take cognizance of real rights and to increase its revenues from the conveyance tax. The registry would also enhance the legal certainty, for it would give potential buyers some indication of the legal position of the prospective object of sale. In order to achieve these goals, it was necessary first to standardize the registration. In *SB* XIV 11376 of 239 BCE, we recall, the vendor is at liberty to record the sale at any nearby *agoranomeion*. For the parties' security requirements this was quite sufficient. When necessary, they simply went back to the office where they had registered the sale and extracted proof of its registration. Yet this liberty prevented the state and members of the parties' community from keeping track of the act. For their needs, registering all of the acts performed in a given area in one registry seemed imperative. Accordingly, in *P.Köln* V 219—a memorandum issued by an unknown official in 209 or 192 BCE—the inhabitants of an unidentified village in the northeastern Arsinoite who wish to register sales are instructed to appear before a certain Herakleides in Philadelphia so that certificates *(chrêmatismoi)* may be issued "as customary."

The papyrus does not relate the position of Herakleides in Philadelphia or explain how he was supposed to treat the acts of sale. He may have been a collector of the conveyance tax, who was to take cognizance of sales before their registration by the *agoranomos* and to ensure thereby that the tax would be paid after the sale was registered.[7] Herakleides could also have been an *agoranomos* or an official with similar capacities who was posted in Philadelphia inter alia to make the registration procedure available to the inhabitants of its surroundings. On either hypothesis, *P.Köln* V 219 illustrates the great interest of the Ptolemaic state, in the late third or early second century BCE, in furthering and regulating the registration of sales in Egypt and in utilizing it as a means of taking cognizance of land conveyances in the *chôra*.

Most of our mid- and late Ptolemaic evidence on the registration of sales stems from the Pathyrite nome. The Pathyrite source material yields some sixty registration certificates issued between 134 and 88 BCE. The text of the certificates and their physical layout are exceedingly uniform. Just like *P.Köln* 219, this uniformity reveals a high degree of standardization, possibly by the state, of the registration of sales. The Pathyrite source material is important for yet another reason. Much of the source material relates to Egyptians. For these Egyptians, the composition by a Greek notary of a Greek instrument with its distinct Greek terminology meant a close, perhaps first encounter with Greek scribal traditions and through them also with Greek law. Accordingly, the creation of the *agoranomeia* played a key role in the dissemination of Greek law in the Ptolemaic *chôra*.[8] We now turn to the *anagraphê*.

The *Anagraphê:* Official List of Contracts

Written documentation of a contract played a key role in any legal dispute over its terms (Wolff 1978, 146–154). The record reported the legal act itself and also conveyed the terms on which it was made. For this purpose it usually applied routine clauses that went back to the Greek or Egyptian legal traditions in accordance with the language in which the document was issued. If the document was introduced in court, the judge had to be familiar with these clauses in order to consider and interpret them properly. Accordingly, one of the most important measures in the formation of the court system in early Ptolemaic Egypt was to direct disputes among Greeks, with their Greek documents, to the Greek court of the *dikastêrion* and those among Egyptians to the Egyptian board of the *laokritai* (Wolff 1970, 37–53).

The existence of an interpretative tradition in the courts also required the maintenance of some uniformity by the scribes; for the expedient administration of justice with regard to leases, for example, the judge had to find a similar scheme and content in every lease contract. Accordingly, *BGU* VI 1214 and *P.Ryl.* IV 572 exhibit a considerable effort by the state, in the early and mid-Ptolemaic period, to create a limited body of Egyptian scribes whose selection would be tightly controlled by the state. What is especially interesting for our purpose is that, at least according to a sound restoration in *P.Ryl.* IV 572.35, the *laokritai* were to be involved in the selection. In other words, the Egyptian judges were to exercise control over the nomination of the very scribes whose product would later guide them in their verdicts.

This system could be upheld only as long as the *laokritai* maintained their exclusivity in dealing with and interpreting Egyptian documents. If they had ever possessed such exclusivity, in the second century BCE it was largely lost.[9] Cases brought by Greeks and Egyptians alike were now freely judged by various state officials and judicial boards (i.e., the *chrêmatistai,* who gradually emerged as a regular court of law in the early second century BCE). In the new instances the judges were rarely Egyptians, and one wonders whether they could have dealt with a legal document in demotic without translation (Wolff 1970, 81–85). One solution was to have the Egyptian documents translated by the litigants themselves before submitting them to the court.[10] But a translation done privately could be prejudiced; thus, the state needed to take action.

By the mid-second century the *agoranomeia* had become established throughout Egypt; for roughly a century they had kept lists of documents, witnessed declarations by parties to transactions, and issued official papers recording these statements. They were now prepared for an additional task, perhaps the most important one. In the minutes of the legal hearing *P.Tor.Choiach.* 12.4.13–15 = *MChr* 31 = *UPZ* II 162 (117 BCE, Thebes), a *prostagma* is cited as having declared that Egyptian contracts that have not undergone *anagraphê* are "without authority" *(akyroi)*. *Akyros* implies not only invalidity but also—especially in the context of *P.Tor.Choach.* 12—inadmissibility as evidence in a court of law (Préaux 1965, 188–189). Accordingly, the *prostagma* states that an Egyptian document that was not subject to an *anagraphê* is not admissible in court.

The most direct Ptolemaic evidence of the *anagraphê* is provided by *UPZ* I p. 596 from 145 BCE. In this letter, Paniskos, a notary in the region of Peri Thêbas, reports to his superior the details of a procedure that was introduced in the preceding year: When Egyptian documents are introduced by an Egyptian temple scribe (*monographos*), a Greek extract is issued that summarizes the key elements of the transaction. Then follows the *anagraphê*—the registration of the transaction on a special list. Finally, a subscription is written on the Egyptian document that confirms the act of registration (Wolff 1978, 40–44; Pestman 1985a, 24–25; Rupprecht 1995b, 49–50).

Once the procedure was completed, the original document was returned to the parties, who then, and only then, could submit it as evidence before a court of law. From the perspective of the language barriers, the new measure did not remove the earlier difficulties entirely: All that a Greek-speaking judge now had was probably an Egyptian document with a short note in Greek that the document had undergone *anagraphê*, with few particulars of the transaction noted. More details, however, were potentially available to the judge from the Greek extract, whose creation is mentioned by *UPZ* I p. 596 as well. Perhaps this potential availability was enough for the litigants to give a reliable verbal account of the contents of the document they had submitted. Or were the litigants expected to submit the Greek extract as well? Either way, the *prostagma* placed any discussion of Egyptian legal transactions by a non-Egyptian court on much firmer ground than before.

For the *agoranomeia,* the *prostagma* had two major consequences. First, in *UPZ* I, p. 596 the Greek extract of the Egyptian document was issued by the notary and his assistants themselves. This necessitated, perhaps for the first time, the employment of a native speaker who also had some experience with Egyptian legal schemes and terminology. The same employee was also expected to be familiar with the Greek formulaic tradition and to be able to find the appropriate Greek rendering of the Egyptian terms. In the decades following the *prostagma* we find in Upper Egypt some "Egyptians" reaching the zenith of the scribal career, the office of the *agoranomos* itself (Wolff 2002, 71n1; 95; Pestman 1978, 310).[11] This was perhaps an outcome of the new requirement.

Second, in order to register demotic legal documents issued anywhere in Egypt, it was necessary to dispatch state scribes to the Egyptian hinterlands to carry out the task. The need became ever stronger when Greek double documents also became subject to the *anagraphê* around 120. Later on, around the beginning of the Roman period, the presence of the scribes in every corner of the *chôra* played a key role in the widespread dissemination of the Greek legal document and the consequent Hellenization of the law of contracts in Egypt (cf. below). In order to understand the change we need to return first to the second century BCE.

The "Agoranomic" Document

Through the *anagraphê* of Greek and Egyptian documents, the *agoranomoi* became exposed to a variety of documents and schemes that they now regularly read, excerpted, and registered. It was merely a matter of time until they started composing entire legal documents on their own. At first, the *agoranomoi* issued primarily those that related to their original scope of business (i.e., loans and securities).[12] By the late Ptolemaic period, however, they were in some areas composing every type of legal document, all of which they also stored in archives under their supervision. Earlier security measures were therefore considered redundant: Agoranomic documents do not report the presence of witnesses and only occasionally makes use of the double-document form (Wolff 1978, 83).[13]

Yet the appearance of the agoranomic document signifies more than just a shift from one form of document to another. In Pathyris, where most of the late Ptolemaic agoranomic documents stem from a milieu of Hellenized Egyptians, the change was probably not from one Greek form of documentation to another but from an Egyptian to a Greek documentation method. Accordingly, the availability of an *agoranomeion* played a key role in the gradual promotion of Greek law, perhaps at the expense of the Egyptian.[14]

Still, the immediate consequences of the change were rather modest. In the late Ptolemaic period the *agoranomeia* left their mark in limited areas. Best attested is the activity of the *agoranomeion* in Upper Egyptian Pathyris and Krokodilopolis, as well as in the city of Hermopolis, as the papyri of the archive of Dionysios, son of Kephalas *(P.Dion.)*, indicate: Legal documents from that archive stemming from the metropolis itself were composed in the *agoranomeion* (nos. 23–31). The archive of Dionysios also shows, however, the limits of the new position; once we leave the metropolis the old formats—Greek and demotic alike—resurface *(P.Dion.* 1–8, 9–22, 32–34).

It was the Romans who paved the way for the triumph of the Greek documentation methods. Demotic legal documents were still drawn up in the early Roman period; in some areas, such as family law, they were common enough to attract the attention of two governors in the late first and early second century CE.[15] In general, however, in the first days of their presence in Egypt, the Romans introduced new measures that in the long run brought about the demise of demotic as a language for legal documents (Depauw 2003, 89n157). If in the Ptolemaic period demotic documents were supposed to be registered in situ (cf. p. 547), the Roman documents authored by Egyptian *synallagmatographoi* were to be registered in the archive of the *Nanaion*, the temple of Isis in Alexandria (Wolff 1978, 51–52). Upon a plausible interpretation, the petition *SB* I 5232 (Soknopaiou Nesos, 15 CE)—the earliest account of the procedure—shows that a conveyance of real right was considered ineffective if it was documented by a demotic record that had not been registered (Rupprecht 2003, 484, 488; Jördens 2005, 45–46). The new complications generally made the composition of demotic documents unrewarding (Wolff 2002, 73).[16]

While demotic documentation methods became increasingly complex in the early Roman period, their Greek counterparts steadily became more accessible to the public. In the Ptolemaic era, the very few public notary offices that existed were perhaps located primarily in the metropoleis. Still, in the late Ptolemaic period some officials were registering privately composed documents in the villages (cf. p. 548). Their presence there prepared the ground for the establishment, at the beginning of the Roman period, of independent, permanent notary offices in villages throughout the Egyptian hinterlands. In the Arsinoite nome, village notaries *(grapheia)* became established in the more populated villages of Tebtynis, Theadelphia, and Karanis, but also in remote localities like Soknopaiou Nesos (Wolff 1978, 18–19; Jördens 2005, 46–48).

The case of Soknopaiou Nesos is particularly interesting, for the community remained an Egyptian priestly stronghold throughout the early Roman period (Hobson 1981, 402; Jördens 2005, 44–45, 50, 56). Here, the creation of the *grapheion* made Greek documentation methods more accessible to the public than they ever were in the Ptolemaic period. The *grapheion* scribes are known to have composed demotic documents as well. But in the case of the demotic document they also had to add a Greek subscription *(hypographê)* to the legal instrument in order to validate it. Consequently, by the end of the first century demotic was abandoned in legal documents (Depauw 2003, 104–105).

The foregoing does not mean that, in the centuries to come, the Greek public notaries remained the only places for the composition of legal documents. Quite the opposite is the case. Whenever the trouble and expenses arising from the involvement of the public notary were disproportionate to the importance of the transaction, this involvement was avoided. This was the case, for example, with leases through much of the Roman period (Yiftach-Firanko 2007). Yet even when the public notary was sidestepped, the old demotic forms were not reinstated. In those cases the authors of the document preferred Greek schemes that did not require the direct involvement of a public notary (Wolff 1978, 112–113, 117–119, 125). When in the late second century the *grapheia* were losing ground, it was these alternative Greek schemes, not the demotic ones, that were increasingly adopted for every type of transaction. As far as the law of contract goes, Egypt had now become a Greek land. Yet did Egyptian law disappear completely? By no means. As the next section explains, in some spheres of legal activity Egyptian practices were still followed in the second century CE.

FUSION OF LEGAL TRADITIONS: THE CASE OF "THE LAW OF THE EGYPTIANS"

The term "the law of the Egyptians" *(ho tôn Aigyptiôn nomos)* emerged in the Roman period. It is mentioned in no more than six papyri, most of them from the second century CE.[17] Still, as a survey of the most instructive of these sources shows, the importance of the term surpasses its modest attestation. In those sources, the law is reported to have allowed fathers to dissolve their daughter's marriage and take away her dowry against her will. The right, which is extensively discussed in the second-century CE petition *P.Oxy.* II 237, is recorded in literary sources from as early as fourth-century-BCE Athens (Harrison 1968, 30–32; Mélèze-Modrzejewski 1970, 332) and is generally assumed to be of Greek origin. As indicated by another papyrus, the court proceedings *SPP* XX 4 (124 CE, Ptolemais Euergetis?), the "law of the Egyptians" also allowed fathers to revoke wills made by their deceased sons and to inherit their property. The origin of this latter right is borne out by a third papyrus referring to the law—the collection of extracts of court proceedings from early second-century *P.Oxy.* XLII 3015 (after 117 CE, Oxyrhynchus).

Greek and demotic papyri amply record the Egyptian practice of parents "selling" their estate in advance to their children. After the sale the parents are allowed to use the assets but not to dispose of them without the children's consent. The unity of the family as an economic entity is thereby secured (Kreller 1919, 204–207; Pestman 1995, 80–81). The extent of this right is discussed in the extracts of *P.Oxy.* XLII 3015, in which the judges consider whether, after such a sale, the parents are still allowed to divide their property by will among their children and prospective intestate heirs. For this purpose they consult "the law of the Egyptians".

This is the background of the father's right to the estate of his predeceased son as discussed in *SPP* XX 4. In order to maintain the family unity as an economic entity it is necessary to limit not only the parents' right to dispose of their property but also that of their children: They, too, have to leave their assets within their family of origin. In order to meet this end, everything that predeceased children leave behind should devolve first upon their father and then, after his death, his closest next of kin. The family fortune will thus remain intact. Accordingly, while the rule regarding the daughter and her dowry (as discussed in *P.Oxy.* II 237) is of Greek origin, that relating to the estate of the deceased son reflects an Egyptian tradition. "The law of the Egyptians", then, is a collection of local practices of different ethnic backgrounds.

In fact, it is much more than this. *P.Oxy.* II 237 is one of the most important sources on "the law of the Egyptians". It is a petition submitted in 186 by Dionysia to the governor of Egypt against her father, Chairemon, who tried to dissolve her marriage and take away her dowry against her will. Dionysia claims that he did so unlawfully. To support her claim she adduces four precedents, three of which are minutes of court proceedings in which a Roman judge prevents a father from dissolving a marriage.

In these minutes the father's supposed authority is generally ignored: The wife alone should decide the course of her own marriage. This is the case in a sentence passed in 128 by the governor, T. Flavius Titianus, and in a ruling by the *epistrategos* Paconius Felix in 134. Yet, unlike Titianus, who simply ignores the law for its "inhumanity," Paconius Felix first allows its contents to be read in court. The fact that the "law of the Egyptians" could be *read* indicates that it was a written, tangible piece of evidence (Wolff 2002, 75n18). It was a collection of precepts of different origin—both Greek and Egyptian—that were adhered to in early Roman Egypt. In the aforementioned instance it is read in a court presided over by a Roman judge. This may well have been the reason for the creation of the law in the first place: to make provincial practices accessible to Roman judges whenever they heard cases involving non-Roman litigants.

Still, the law is more than just a written account of provincial practices. The fourth precedent in Dionysia's dossier is a response by a local legal expert, Ulpius Dionysodoros by name, to an official who was hearing a case in which a father was calling for the dissolution of his daughter's marriage. Dionysodoros, who is asked whether the father's action is lawful, recalls that fathers are allowed to dissolve their daughters' marriage only if they (i.e., the fathers) are united with their wives in an "unwritten marriage." Precisely the same restriction is made in *SPP* XX 4 regarding the father's right to his dead son's assets; the father acknowledges in this papyrus that he is entitled to the estate only because he (the father) was united with the son's mother in an "unwritten marriage." The same measure, then—the unwritten nature of the father's marriage—is used to curtail both the Greek authority over the daughter and the Egyptian authority over the son. This is hardly coincidental. Whoever curtailed the two capacities did so when they were joined in the same textual framework. This framework was, I suggest, "the law of the Egyptians". Accordingly, "the law of the Egyptians" was not just a list of rules. It was a legal treatise that was subject to adjustments that were made regardless of the different "national" roots of the provisions.

In fact, we may witness one such adjustment in the making in the aforementioned response of Ulpius Dionysodoros. A judge directs a question to the legal expert about a father's authority to dissolve his daughter's marriage. The legal expert, consulting the "law of the Egyptians", learns that this power has already been curtailed whenever the father is united with his wife in an unwritten marriage. Yet the expert goes further. He applies the curtailment to a circumstance not originally considered by the law—that of the father giving the daughter in marriage—and then issues his response according to his own new interpretation. It was perhaps through such responses that the law was developed and updated in the course of its existence. The response also indicates who was entrusted with that development—a close group of legal experts versed in local law, who acted as legal advisors in courts presided over by Roman officials. Their position was similar perhaps to that held, in the same period, by some Roman jurisprudents by virtue of the *ius respondendi*.[18]

"The law of the Egyptians" was created, then, in order to make provincial practices accessible to Roman judges. Yet once it was created, the public was not oblivious to its existence and did not hesitate to use its provisions regardless of the origin, as well as the ethnic, civic, and cultural affiliation, of the users. Accordingly, in the case of Dionysia, *P.Oxy.* II 237 reports the practice of Greek and Egyptian institutions alike. That of the latter is still more striking in view of her father's social standing: an ex-gymnasiarch of Oxyrhynchus and thus a representative of the Greek municipal elite (Mélèze-Modrzejewski 1970, 332). The precedents brought forward by Dionysia exhibit a mixture of Greek and Egyptian names. In the hearing before Titianus, the names are Greek and Roman, while in that before Paconius Felix they are markedly Egyptian. Finally, *SPP* XX 4 bears Greek or Hellenized names, although the institution itself seems Egyptian.

In conclusion, the source material dealing with "the law of the Egyptians" is indeed scarce. Yet what has come down to us reveals an institution of the highest importance for the legal history of Egypt as a Roman province. The law was a manual composed for the use of Roman judges. It was meant to give them some knowledge of non-Roman practices in the province. As such, it recorded practices of both Greek and Egyptian origin. The law was an object of ongoing study, interpretation, and development by a group of local legal experts who acted as consultants in provincial courts of law. The contents of the law were employed by all non-Romans. It was thus perhaps the first code of law that was applicable to all Egyptians regardless of their origin. Accordingly, just as the creation of a network of Greek notary offices brought about a formulaic unification of Egypt under Greek auspices, so did "the law of the Egyptians" bring about a unity of its own: a universal observance of precepts of various origin that were assembled in a manual prepared for use in the provincial courts of law.[19]

ROMANIZATION

In 30 BCE Egypt became a part of the Roman Empire and remained under Roman rule until the Arab occupation of 641. How did the Roman presence influence the legal landscape of Egypt in the course of these seven centuries? To what extent did it cause non-Romans to adopt the institutions of the *ius civile*?

In Rome, most enforceable claims had to be expressed in the language of the praetor's edict, which utilized highly professional terminology. To employ these terms themselves, litigants needed the help of Roman legal experts. They also had to cloak every suit in a distinctly Roman mantle. This need to Romanize suits was a major impulse for Romanization wherever actions were founded on an edict of a Roman magistrate, usually that of the *praetor urbanus* or on similar edicts of a provincial governor. This was not the case in Egypt, however. There, plaintiffs were at complete liberty to present their claims in court in any form they wished. The terms did not have to be particularly Roman, so legal language was not Romanized through the terminology of the suit. Nor was there room for special experts in Roman law who would explain how to use that language. Certainly, Roman officials could introduce Roman legal institutions and terms through their verdicts, and they occasionally did. In general, however, no predilection was shown towards the *ius civile* in comparison to other, non-Roman sources either with regard to peregrines or even in relation to the *cives Romani* (Wolff 1966, 38).

In theory, Roman law could have penetrated Egypt through the propagation of Roman schemes in legal documents. This is, we recall, the way Greek law came to the fore in the late Ptolemaic and early Roman periods. This, however, has never been the case with Latin. In most spheres of private law Latin documentation was at best marginal. Both Romans and non-Romans wrote their contracts in Greek and shaped them according to the same "schemes" that existed and were developed by scribes long before the Roman conquest (Wolff 2002, 163–165).

There was, however, one exception: the law of persons and family and the law of succession in particular. At least until 235 CE, wills of Roman citizens had to be written in Latin in order to be valid (ibid., 134). The rule was enforced in Egypt, and so, in first- and second-century Egypt, wills of Roman citizens are written in Latin. Romans put into use other elements of the law of succession as well (e.g., the acquisition of inheritances through the formal acts of the *cretio* and the *agnitio possessionis bonorum*), Roman legacy categories (*legatum* and *fideicommissum*), and the opening of wills before a public official. Roman citizens seem, then, to employ in Egypt, even if in an unrefined form, much of the hereditary system of the *ius civile* and the *ius honorarium*.

The law of succession is also a sphere in which we can establish a reception of Roman legal institutions by non-Romans in the early days of the empire. In 6 CE the *lex Julia vicesimaria* imposed a 5 percent tax on estates inherited by Roman citizens.

To enforce the collection of the new tax, all Roman wills were required to be opened at a special bureau set up at the emperor's shrine, the *Caesareum*, or at the *statio vicesimae hereditatium*. The opening of a will had to be attended by the witnesses who had been present at its composition. Non-Romans were not subject to this inheritance tax, but they deliberately adopted the new procedure for their own wills. In the second century CE Greek wills were subject to an official opening as frequently as Roman wills (Yiftach-Firanko 2002, 160–165). The case of the wills brings out, then, an important point. Roman legal institutions were rarely deployed by Romans in Egypt, but when they were, they influenced the practices of non-Romans as well.

In the third century, most inhabitants of the *imperium Romanum* became Roman citizens as an outcome of the Antonine Constitution of 212 CE. The constitution had one immediate effect. In Rome, one way of creating a contractual bond was through the act of *stipulatio*. The party who was to become the creditor asked the prospective debtor orally whether he were willing to undertake an obligation. The obligation itself was created by a positive answer and was enforceable in a Roman court through the *actio ex stipulatu* if the *stipulatio* was about a fixed sum of money and through a *condictio* if it was not (Kaser 1971, 542). Since the prospective creditor could incorporate in his question any lawful contents, the *stipulatio* was used for the creation of virtually any obligation. It could thus be used after 212 to make obligations of a non-Roman nature undertaken by the new Romans actionable in a Roman court; a clause recording the *stipulatio* was simply incorporated in the Greek legal documents. Greek contracts were thus adapted to the Roman contractual system.

Yet the insertion of the *stipulatio* clause into the Greek contracts did not really Romanize them. Many transactions recorded on Greek papyri from Egypt were enforceable in a Roman court even without the *stipulatio*. This was, for example, the case with sale and lease; these were consensual contracts, and the consensus could easily be extracted from the Greek contract as it stood. There were, however, some contracts for which the *nudus consensus* was not enough, nor could the Greek contract be reinterpreted in any other way that would make it enforceable according to Roman law (Pringsheim 1961, 251). The Greek scribes of the early third century may not have known the difference and probably did not care. They simply inserted the clause in every contract regardless of whether it was really necessary.[20] For them, if the insertion did not help, it certainly would not hurt. It certainly spared them the need of engaging the subtleties of the Roman contractual system. From this perspective, the appearance of the *stipulatio* clause may have checked, rather than promoted the Romanization of Greek contracts in Egypt.[21]

As in the earlier period, the law of family, status, and succession constitutes a different story. In the third and fourth centuries the *patria potestas,* the Roman dotal system, marriage, adoption, and manumission are mentioned directly or at least leave some traces in documents composed by the new Romans (Wolff 2002, 137–148; Arjava 1998, 155–159). In some cases, there is no real reception of Roman concepts. In 331 CE a constitution of Constantine the Great inflicted harsh punishments on spouses who divorced for any reason besides those listed in its text (*C.Th.* 3.16.1). The constitution was in all probability never enforced in Egypt, yet the news that the emperor in Constantinople did not approve of divorces did not escape its inhabitants. And so, in fourth-century petitions relating to domestic crises spouses accuse each other of an unlawful breakup. They never dispute their partners' right to end the marriage nor ask that the sanctions of *C.Th.* 3.16.1 be imposed on them. This is merely a rhetorical bid for the benevolence of the addressed official (Yiftach-Firanko 2001, 1338).

Other Roman regulations struck deeper roots in third-century Egypt. Greek and Roman adult women alike were required to have a formal guardian present for certain legal acts. Yet there was one difference: Unlike their Greek counterparts, Roman women were exempt from this tutelage as soon as they gave birth to three children (*ius trium liberorum*). Since this was the case with most women before the age of thirty, the tutelage became unnecessary for most. After 212 the Greek and Roman systems of guardianship fused. As a consequence, the *ius liberorum* affected all female inhabitants. The fact that it was enforced is clearly shown by a rapid decline of the tutelage in the third century CE (Arjava 1997, 29). In the case of tutelage and perhaps also in that of *patria potestas,* the Antonine Constitution meant an actual introduction of a Roman legal institution. Even in these cases, however, the introduced institution was adapted to the social mentality of the new Romans. Here, too, Romanization probably did not involve profound changes in Egypt's legal landscape.

CONCLUSION

The Ptolemaic kings of Egypt ruled a variety of ethnic groups that were diverse in language, culture, religion, and legal practices. In the Ptolemaic period no attempt was made to fuse these different elements into one "nation", nor was a single code of law ever created that was binding on the entire population of Egypt. The main themes, rather, were tolerance and even the protection of particular legal traditions. Among other things, both the Greek immigrants and the Egyptian population were allowed to maintain their own scribal traditions and to be judged in autonomous courts of law in accordance with their ancestral laws.

By the beginning of the Roman period, changes were under way. The autonomous courts of law had by then ceased to exist, and so had the earlier national codes on which they based their sentences. The second century CE witnessed the abandonment of demotic script in legal documents and the emergence of a new law, "the law of the Egyptians", which was applied by the entire population and consisted of Greek and Egyptian elements alike. The present chapter has sought to shed some light on that process by focusing first on the developments that brought about the triumph of Greek as the exclusive language of legal documents.

The Ptolemies never aimed at eliminating demotic as a language in legal documents, but a process set in motion in the third century BCE by a Ptolemaic king eventually led to that outcome. In the late third century BCE, *agoranomeia* were established in the capitals of the nomes throughout Egypt to allow the state to monitor foreclosure on assets placed as security for debts. Soon, however, the *agoranomoi* assumed new tasks.

In the third century BCE, most Greek documents were composed privately, that is, without the involvement of a public notary. The security provided by these documents was sometimes limited. Consequently, once the *agoranomeia* were established, they were also used for the registration of particularly valuable transactions: sale of real property and delivery of dowries at marriage. Because the record was written in Greek, whenever the parties were Egyptian, the act of registration was frequently an occasion on which they became exposed to Greek language and schemes. The state soon regulated the registration procedure and utilized it for its own purposes. An early piece of evidence of state intervention is provided by *P.Köln* V 219.

Soon the *agoranomoi* took on new tasks. In the second century, Egyptian documents were presented as evidence to Greek judges, who needed a reliable Greek account of their contents. The *agoranomoi* were charged with creating those accounts, as well as registering the contracts in their files. The new procedure further exposed Egyptians to Greek schemes used in the *agoranomeion* for the translation of their demotic acts. It also furthered the employment in the *agoranomeion* of Egyptian scribes who could perform those translations.

Around the same time, the *agoranomoi* also started recording legal documents of their own, and the fact that the document was composed by a public notary accorded it enhanced security. The agoranomic document was also drawn up in Greek, a fact that facilitated its use as evidence before Greek judges. In Pathyris in Upper Egypt, the outcome was a shift toward the agoranomic Greek instrument, especially in high-value transactions, particularly sales. This was yet another impulse for deploying Greek rather than Egyptian documentation methods.

A seemingly "anti-demotic" policy was manifested after the Roman conquest. The Romans imposed the deposition of demotic documents in Alexandria. They also created *grapheia* in the villages that made Greek instruments widely available in the nomes' hinterlands. The *grapheion* notary could also compose demotic documents, yet the imposition of the addition of a Greek *hypographê* to every demotic document made its composition unrewarding and brought about its demise in the following generations.

What gave raise to the new policy? Did it derive from a more general anti-Egyptian attitude on the part of the Romans? I think not. This is evident from the discussion of "the law of the Egyptians." This manual, the use of which in court is attested in the second century CE, consisted of Greek and Egyptian elements alike and related, as far as we know, to family law and the law of succession. There is no indication that regulations of Greek origin were treated more favorably by the law than Egyptian ones. In fact, even in the field of written contracts, Roman policy was neither nationally nor culturally motivated. For a Roman judge and administrator, having to deal with evidence in one foreign language, Greek, was challenging enough. An additional language would have been too much. Even so, demotic documents were never banned. Their composition was simply made unrewarding until it was abandoned altogether.

Finally, we come to Romanization. Egypt was under Roman rule for nearly seven centuries, but in the period discussed in this chapter the Roman presence did not influence people's legal practices as Greek presence had. In Egypt, the language of the courts was not particularly Roman, nor did Roman judges apply Roman legal concepts or institutions more than non-Roman ones in formulating their rulings. The Latin language and formulae were also not very common in legal documents. In general, Romans and non-Romans in Egypt issued the same Greek legal documents, applied local institutions and mechanisms, and usually administered justice according to the same non-Roman guidelines. Yet Roman law did leave its marks in certain areas: As elsewhere in the Roman empire, Roman citizens in Egypt followed major elements of the Roman law of succession, family, and personal status. In these areas, Roman concepts also influenced, probably as early as the first century CE, the practices of non-Romans.

The picture was not altered considerably even after 212, when the Antonine Constitution granted most inhabitants of Egypt the status of Roman citizen. Roman legal institutions continued to be more commonly applied in the law of succession, family, and status. In other areas such as contract law, the adjustment of local practices to Roman concepts was superficial and crude. The stream of Roman concepts into Egypt may have picked up the pace in the fifth century, a period that is beyond the scope of this discussion.

NOTES

1. *P.Enteux.* 61.11, *epilysis; P.Enteux.* 14.4 and *P.Tebt.* III.1 817 recto. 19–20, *epikatabolê.*

2. Cf., in particular, *P.Enteux.* 14, 15 (222 and 218 BCE, Magdôla), 61 (246–240 BCE, Ghoran), *P.Köln* V 219 (209/192 BCE, Arsinoites), *P.Tebt.* III.1 814 (227 BCE, Tebtynis) and 817 (182 BCE, Krokodilopolis), *MChr.* 233 recto (111 BCE, Pathyris).

3. Tholthis: *BGU* XIV 2398, 2399; *SB* XIV 11375 (all from 213–211 BCE); 11376 (239 BCE). Theogenis: *CPR* XVIII 25, 27 (both 232 BCE), and Wolff (1978, 195).

4. In the third century, Alexandrian landed property transactions were also registered in a special archive. Cf. *P.Hal.* 1.242–259, *BGU* VI 1213.9 (both III BCE), and Wolff (1978, 188–190).

5. See *P.Tebt.* III.1 814, col. I (239 BCE, Tebtynis).

6. For example, *BGU* III 999 (99 BCE, Pathyris).

7. In most late-Ptolemaic transactions in Upper Egypt the actual payment of the tax followed rather than preceded the registration. In *BGU* III 999, for example, the tax was paid seven months after the registration. The opposite case is reported in *P.Stras.* II 81 + 82 (115 BCE, Diospolis Magna). Cf. also Pestman (1985b, 56–57), who discusses diverging practices in the case of provisory sale.

8. In *P.Adler,* from the archive of Horos, son of Nechoutes, nearly all twenty-one Greek documents are *agoranomic*; fourteen are registration certificates.

9. This is shown in particular by the short-sighted and short-lived effort to reinstate the authority of the *laokritai: P.Tebt.* I 5.207–220 of 118 BCE (e.g., Wolff 1970, 87, 204; Mélèze-Modrzejewski 1975, 705–706).

10. Cf., for example, *P.Giss.* 37 (134 BCE, Pathyris).

11. Comp. Muhs (2005, 100–104), on first-century CE Tebtynis and Soknopaiou Nesos.

12. Cf., for example, *P.Mich.* II 182 (182 BCE, Krokodilopolis, Arsinoites).

13. Witnesses are still reported in agoranomic wills. Cf. Kreller (1919, 315).

14. Particularly in the case of sale documents. Loans and especially marriage documents and wills are still largely demotic in this period. Cf., for example, Pestman (1981, 299–304).

15. That is, M. Mettius Rufus (89–91 CE) and Ser. Sulpicius Similis (107–112 CE). Cf. *P.Mert.* III 101; *P.Oxy.* II 237.8.21–27 (109 CE).

16. In the second century, the edict *P.Oxy.* I 34 verso col. iii = *M.Chr* 188 (127 CE) imposed additional requirements. Cf. also *BGU* V 1210.221–228 (after 149, Theadelphia).

17. See *P.Oxy.* II 237.7.29 (186 CE); IV 706.7 = *M.Chr* 81 (73 CE?); XLII 3015.3 (after 117 CE, all from Oxyrhynchus); *P.Tebt.* II 488.21–27 (after 121/122 CE, Tebtynis); *SPP* XX 4.16 = *CPR* I 18 = *M.Chr* 84 (124 CE, Ptolemais Euergetis?).

18. Cf. *Digest* 1.2.2.49.

19. On the question of the fusion of the two legal traditions, cf. Mélèze-Modrzejewski (1964).

20. Cf., for example, the insertion in petitions or wills in which no obligation was created; in these, therefore, the clause was not required.

21. On the infiltration of Roman concepts into Greek contracts in the later Roman Empire, cf. Wolff (1956, 20–27).

BIBLIOGRAPHY

Arjava, A. 1997. "The Guardianship of Women in Roman Egypt." *Akten des 21. Internationalen Papyrologenkongresses, Berlin 1995. APF* (Beiheft 3): 25–30.

——. 1998. "Patria Potestas in Late Antiquity." *JRS* 88: 147–165.

Depauw, M. 1997. *A Companion to Demotic Studies.* Brussels: Fondation Égyptologique Reine Elisabeth.

——. 2003. "Autograph Confirmation in Demotic Private Contracts." *CdÉ* 78: 66–111.

Harrison, A. R. W. 1968. *The Law of Athens,* vol. 1. Oxford: Clarendon.

Hobson, D. 1981. "Greeks and Romans at Socnopaiou Nesos." In *Proceedings of the Sixteenth International Congress of Papyrology*, ed. R. S. Bagnall, G. M. Browne, A. E. Hanson, L. Koenen, 389–403. Chico, Calif.: Scholars Press.

Jördens, A. 2005. "Griechische Papyri in Soknopaiu Nesos." In *Tebtynis und Soknopaiu Nesos: Leben im römischen Fajum: Akten des Internationalen Symposions vom 11. bis 13. Dezember 2003 in Sommerhausen bei Würzburg*, ed. S. Lippert and M. Schentuleit, 41–56. Wiesbaden: Harrassowitz.

Kaser, M. 1971. *Das römische Privatrecht*, 2d ed., vol. 1. Munich: C. H. Beck.

Kreller, H. 1919. *Erbrechtliche Untersuchungen auf Grund der gräko-ägyptischen Papyrusurkunden*. Leipzig: Teubner.

Mélèze-Modrzejewski. J. 1964. "Réflexions sur 'le droit ptolémaïque.'" *Iura* 15: 32–56.

———. 1970. "La règle de droit dans l'Égypte romaine." In *Proceedings of the Twelfth International Congress of Papyrology*, ed. D. H. Samuel, 317–377. Toronto: Hakkert.

———. 1975. "Chrématistes et laocrites." In *Le monde grec: Pensée, littérature, histoire, documents: Hommages à Claire Préaux*, ed. J. Bingen, G. Cambier, and G. Nachtergael, 699–708. Brussels: Editions de l'Université de Bruxelles.

Muhs, B. 2005. "The *Grapheion* and the Disappearance of Demotic Contracts in Early Roman Tebtynis and Soknopaiou Nesos." In *Tebtynis und Soknopaiu Nesos: Leben im römischen Fajum: Akten des Internationalen Symposions vom 11. bis 13. Dezember 2003 in Sommerhausen bei Würzburg*, ed. S. Lippert and M. Schentuleit, 93–104. Wiesbaden: Harrassowitz.

Pestman, P. W. 1978. "L'agoranomie: Un avant-poste de l'administration grecque enlevé par les Égyptiens?" In *Das ptolemäische Ägypten: Akten d. internat. Symposions, 27.–29. September 1976 in Berlin*, ed. H. Maehler and V. M. Strocka, 203–210. Mainz am Rhein: von Zabern.

———. 1981. "Nahomsesis, una donna d'affari di Pathyris: L'archivio bilingue di Pelaias, figlio di Eunus." In *Scritti in onore di Orsolina Montevecchi*, ed. E. Bresciani, G. Geraci, S. Pernigotti, and G. Susini, 295–315. Bologna: CLUEB.

———. 1985a. "Registration of Demotic Contracts in Egypt: *P.Par.* 65; 2nd cent. B.C." In *Satura Roberto Feenstra: Sexagesimum quintum annum aetatis complenti ab alumnis collegis amicis oblata*, ed. J. A. Ankum, J. E. Spruit, and F. B. J. Wubbe, 17–25. Fribourg: University Press.

———. 1985b. "Ventes provisoires de biens pour sûreté de dettes: "Onai en pistei" à Pathyris et à Krokodilopolis." In *Textes et études de papyrologie grecque, démotique et copte*, ed. P. W. Pestman, 45–59. Leiden: Brill.

———. 1995. "Appearance and Reality in Written Contracts: Evidence from Bilingual Family Archives." In *Legal Documents of the Hellenistic World*, ed. M. J. Geller and H. Maehler, 79–87. London: Warburg Institute, University of London.

Préaux, Cl. 1965. "La preuve à l'époque hellénistique, principalement dans l'Égypte grecque." *La Preuve: Première Partie = Recueils de la Société Jean Bodin*, vol. 16, 161–222. Brussels: Editions de la Librairie encyclopédique.

Pringsheim, F. 1961. "Stipulationsklausel." In *Gesammelte Abhandlungen*, vol. 2, 194–256. Heidelberg: Universitätsverlag Winter.

Rupprecht, H.-A. 1995a. "Die dinglichen Sicherungsrechte nach der Praxis der Papyri: Eine Übersicht über den urkundlichen Befund." In *Collatio iuris romani: Études dediées á Hans Ankum à l'occasion de son 65e anniversaire*, ed. R. Feenstra, A. S. Hartkamp, J. E. Spruit, P. J. Sijpestein, and L. C. Winkel, vol. 2, 425–436. Amsterdam: J. C. Gieben.

———. 1995b. "Sechs-Zeugenurkunde und Registrierung." *Aegyptus* 75: 37–53.

——. 1997. "Zwangsvollstreckung und Dingliche Sicherheiten in den Papyri der ptolemäischen und römischen Zeit." In *Symposion 1995, Vorträge zur griechischen und hellenistischen Rechtsgeschichte (Korfu, 1.-5. September 1995)*, 291–302. Cologne: Böhlau Verlag.

——. 2003. "Die Streitigkeit zwischen Satabous und Nestnephis." In *Symposion 1999, Vorträge zur griechischen und hellenistischen Rechtsgeschichte (Pazo de Mariñán, La Coruña, 6.-9. September 1999)*, G, Thür, F. Javier (eds.), 481–492. Cologne: Böhlau Verlag.

Wolff, H. J. 1956. "Zur Romanisierung des Vertragsrechts der Papyri." *ZSav* 73: 1–28.

——. 1966. "Organization der Rechtspflege und Rechtskontrolle der Verwaltung im ptolemäisch-römischen Ägypten bis Diokletian." *TR* 34: 1–40.

——. 1970. *Das Justizwesen der Ptolemäer*, 2d ed. Munich: Beck.

——. 1978. *Das Recht der griechischen Papyri Ägyptens in der Zeit der Ptolemaeer und des Prinzipats*. Vol. 2, *Organisation und Kontrolle des privaten Rechtsverkehrs*. Munich: Beck.

——. 2002. *Das Recht der griechischen Papyri Ägyptens in der Zeit der Ptolemaeer und des Prinzipats*. Vol. 1:, *Bedingungen und Triebkräfte der Rechtsentwicklung*, ed. H.-A. Rupprecht. Munich: Beck.

Yiftach-Firanko, U. 2001. "Was There a 'Divorce Procedure' among Greeks in Early Roman Egypt?" In *Atti del XXII Congresso Internazionale di Papirologia, Firenze 1998*, ed. I. Andorlini, G. Bastianini, M. Manfredi, and G. Menci, 1331–1339. Florence: Istituto Papirologico G. Vitelli.

——. 2002. "Deeds of Last Will in Graeco-Roman Egypt: A Case Study in Regionalism." *BASP* 38: 149–164.

——. 2003. *Marriage and Marital Arrangements: A History of the Greek Marriage Document in Egypt, 4th Century BCE–4th Century CE*. Munich: Beck.

——. 2007. "The Rise of the Hypomnêma as a Lease Contract." In *Proceedings of the 24th International Congress of Papyrology, 1–7 August 2004 Helsinki*, ed. J. Frösén, T. Purola, and E. Salmenkivi, 1051–1062. Helsinki: Societas Scientiarum Fennica.

CHAPTER 24

EGYPTIAN RELIGION AND MAGIC IN THE PAPYRI

WILLY CLARYSSE

TRADITIONAL RELIGION: UNITY IN DIVERSITY

The Ancient Egyptian Worldview

Egyptian religion was based on a single worldview, which was realized in different ways in different localities. The ordered world was created by the gods out of the chaos at the beginning of time, but chaos remained present all around the world. It became visible in the ocean surrounding the inhabited lands, in the foreign countries ever ready to invade Egypt, in the desert on both sides of the fertile Nile valley, in death threatening all living things, and in social upheaval and revolt. The cosmic order ($M3^c.t$), reflected in the social order, was maintained by the gods who had created it, with the help of mankind. The gods had not completely withdrawn into the heavenly realm but remained available through their cult statues in the temples.

The temple was the house of the god (*ḥw.t-ntr*), where the god lived with his family (wife and child) and was served by the priests as representatives of the pharaoh. The often imposing building was a cosmos in miniature, with a star-studded roof supported by huge stone papyrus columns. The sanctuary with the divine statue was carefully protected from the forces of chaos all around: only pure priests (*wʿb*) were allowed to enter; on the entrance towers (pylons), the pharaoh is represented killing foreign enemies, symbolizing the forces of chaos (figure 24.1), and inside the entrance gates armed guards stand ready to destroy all demons who dare to enter the sacred realm. Just as Egypt is a cosmos—an ordered space—compared to the barbarian countries, so the temple is the center of order and cleanliness as opposed to the dirty streets of the surrounding town. In return for the daily offerings that the pharaoh presents on the walls and his representatives, the priests, lay before the shrine, the god keeps the whole world moving by making the sun come up and the Nile rise at the right moment.

The Egyptian temple has been compared, with some reason, to our nuclear power stations: Cosmic powers, both dangerous and life giving, are hidden inside

Figure 24.1. Pylon of the Edfu temple, showing King Ptolemy XII smiting the enemies. Photo by W. Clarysse.

and need to be kept under control. The statue is hidden in the temple's dark interior, and the common people are not allowed to pass beyond the sacred pylons. The statue of the god is washed, dressed, and offered food and drink by the higher priests, who have to be perfectly clean (circumcised, washed, and shaven). Only on festive occasions does the god, usually carried in a bark on a stretcher, make an appearance outside the temple. On such occasions he can be consulted by the believers, who lay down oracle questions along the processional street (figure 24.2a–b). Since the holy of holies is in fact close to the back side of the temple, the rear wall is sometimes decorated with a cult relief, and people come here to approach the god, whom they know to be present on the other side of the wall. Unlike churches or mosques, Egyptian temples are not places where people gather

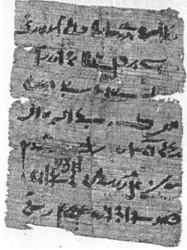

Figure 24.2a–b. Two oracle questions, one positive and one negative. Photo courtesy of the Ashmolean Museum, Oxford.

inside: Instead they watch at the front door and along the processional way (*dromos*); perhaps on special occasions some were allowed in the first court.

Side by side with the huge stone temples numerous mud-brick shrines were served by priests of lesser rank, often for lesser gods, saints, and sacred animals. They were less grand but more accessible than the major gods in their stone fortresses. In the Fayyum village of Kerkeosiris (ca. 1,500 inhabitants), for instance, no fewer than thirteen such shrines are attested, owning 6 percent of agricultural land (Crawford 1971, 86–90). Isis priests (*isionomoi*, demotic *in-wwy*) (Depauw 1998) and ibis raisers (*ibioboskoi*) were a typical feature of many villages. The two cults left an imprint on the landscape, as can be seen from the many toponyms including the words *isieion* and *ibion* (demotic *ʿḥy*) (Vandorpe 1991).

Figure 24.3. Bust of Sarapis. Graeco-Roman Museum, Alexandria (Bagnall and Rathbone, *Egypt: From Alexander to the Copts* [2004], 34). Reproduced by permission of the editors.

Local Variants

Against this broadly uniform background, each region has its own gods and adds its own accents. Thus, in Memphis the world is created by Ptah, in Elephantine by the ram-headed Chnum, and in Hermopolis by Thoth. In Edfu the sun god Horus, with the head of a falcon, fights the forces of chaos by killing a hippopotamus or a crocodile, whereas in the Fayyum the crocodile god Souchos is identified with the sun god and stands for the cosmic world order in the form of the yearly Nile flood. Whereas Amon in Thebes and Sarapis in Alexandria (figure 24.3) live with wife and child as a holy family (Amon, Mut, and Chonsou; Sarapis, Isis, and Harpochrates), Thoth is a bachelor, and Horus of Edfu lives in a long-distance relationship with Hathor, who once a year makes the trip of about fifty kilometers by boat from her own temple in Dendera to that of Horus.

Mummification and Afterlife

Mummification, burial, and mortuary cults are linked with the cult of Osiris, the god who was killed and resurrected (see Riggs 2005). The undertakers' business is the best-known branch of the temple activities, partly because mortuary priests often kept their papers in a tomb. Thus, several interesting family archives in both demotic and Greek have been found in tombs. In principle, the mummification priests, called *taricheutai* ("picklers" in Greek, *ḥry-ḥb* in demotic), who read from the sacred books during the funeral and those who looked after the tomb (*w3ḥ-mw*, translated as choachytes, "water pourers," in Greek)—are specialists each in their own field, but in practice the three tasks were usually in the hands of a single group of people. The funerary priests jealously guarded their territories, and in their title deeds tombs are treated as valuable assets on a par with houses and land. Mummification was not only for Egyptians, but, as was already the case with Joseph's father, Jacob, in Genesis, foreigners living in Egypt quickly adopted the custom. This is evident in the lists of the deceased kept by the choachytes and in the Greek-style mummy portraits of the Roman period.

Not only humans were mummified but also sacred animals, which were often ceremonially buried in huge subterranean catacombs. The *theagoi* (*ṯ3y-ntr*) had the honor of carrying the sacred animals to their tombs (Dils 1995) (figure 24.4), and the government contributed to the expenses with lavish gifts.

The Role of the Temples in Economy and Administration

The temples were also important landowners, sometimes in several nomes (Evans 1961). Grain, wine and oil were in theory produced for the cult of the gods, but the priests also profited. The temple factories also produced oil, fine linen (the

Figure 24.4. Theagoi carrying the mummified crocodile (Theadelpheia; now in the Alexandria Museum); plate from E. Breccia, *Monuments de l'Egypte gréco-romaine*, I.2, pl. 64 [1926]). Reproduced by permission of the Graeco-Roman Museum, Alexandria.

so-called byssus), and papyrus. Temple notaries, another source of income, painted their elegant cursive hieroglyphs (demotic) on large papyrus rolls with lots of blank space on all sides, whereas their Greek colleagues, who had to buy their papyrus from outside, filled their much smaller sheets with tiny, tightly packed letters. Native high culture was preserved in the temples, where the priests learned to read and write hieroglyphic, hieratic, and demotic scripts in the "house of life" and also practiced traditional sciences, such as mathematics, astronomy and astrology, medicine, dream interpretation, architecture, and so forth. In a recent survey (Ryholt 2005), it has been calculated that half of the Tebtynis temple library, with the remains of more than two hundred books, consisted of cultic texts, a quarter were narratives and a quarter scientific works.

In the pharaonic period the temples also functioned as wheels in the royal administration. They nominally owned large tracts of land, but in fact royal taxes on land were partly collected for the king through the temples. There was no opposition between temple and state: The temples were very much integrated into the royal administration. In the Graeco-Roman period this system was gradually replaced by a separate civil administration, and this contributed to the slow decline of the Egyptian temples.

At the pylon or temple gate (*rw.t-di-mȝꜥ.t*) justice was rendered both by native priests (*laokritai*) and by Greek officials. According to the hieroglyphic inscriptions, the god himself was available here for those who were seeking justice. This principle is illustrated by the numerous demotic temple oaths on ostraca: When the accusing party could not prove his case, the accused was allowed to deny the accusation by an oath (*ꜥnḫ*) invoking the local god. If the accused took the oath, the case was dismissed; otherwise he was considered guilty. In such cases there is no

Figure 24.5. Semtheus identified with Greek Herakles. Photo courtesy of the Ashmolean Museum, Oxford.

real distinction between priestly and divine justice: The priestly judges used the god to render justice. In Krokodilopolis, the capital of the Fayyum, this gate of justice is called "the northern gate" (*p3 r3 mḥty*), transliterated in Greek as (*P*)*remitieion*. Not only the Egyptian priests but even the Greek strategos rendered justice here, and the tribunal before the temple gate is even mentioned in some acts of Christian martyrs under Diocletian. Again temple and civil authorities work hand in hand (Quaegebeur 1993).

New Developments in Egyptian Religion

With the exception of the Theban temples in Karnak, Luxor, and the Theban west bank, tourists usually admire temples that were constructed in Graeco-Roman times. They were built according to the detailed guidelines provided by the "Book of the Temple" (Quack 2005), which is preserved in multiple copies, and at first sight it seems as if nothing has changed since time immemorial. But changes did take place, most of them so gradually that they escape attention, whereas some, like the growing state intervention and use of Greek, are easier to grasp. These developments become apparent when documents of different periods are compared.

Listening Gods

Whereas the traditional gods in their temple were out of reach for the ordinary people, popular forms of these very same gods were accessible at the back of the temple, at the entrance gate, or in small local shrines. People consulted them in case of illness (healing gods), when they had to make important decisions (oracle gods), or when a conflict had to be settled (divine justice). These gods turned their benevolent face to the visitor, and their ability to listen to the prayers was often expressed by multiple ears accompanying the divine picture. These same qualities are expressed by their typical names, such as *Nfr-ḥr* (Greek Nepheros), that is, Beautiful-of-face, or *Dhwty-sḏm* (Greek Thotsytmis), and even *Msḏr-sḏm* (Greek Mestasytmis), that is, Thoth-who-listens and The-ear-that-listens. The divine names return as personal names: Nepheros (fem. Tnepheros) is common in the Fayyum, and in the same region Mestasytmis is Hellenized as Mysthas and Akou-silaos (from Greek ἀκούω, "to listen") (see figure 24.7). Although this kind of personal piety goes back to the New Kingdom, it becomes widespread in the Graeco-Roman period, when the Egyptian listening gods (*theoi epêkooi*) become popular all over the Mediterranean world.

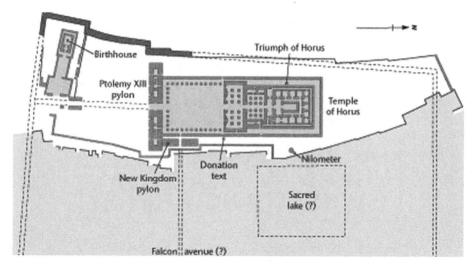

Figure 24.6. Ground plan of the Edfu temple (Bagnall and Rathbone, *Egypt: From Alexander to the Copts* [2004], 229). Reproduced by permission of the editors.

Animal Cults

A typical development of the later periods is the animal cult. Sacred animals had existed since at least the New Kingdom, but they rose in prominence in later times. They could be individual animals like the Apis, Mneuis, or Buchis bulls in Memphis, Heliopolis, and Hermonthis; the Hesis cow in Aphroditopolis (Atfih); or the twin crocodile gods in the Fayyum. Often, however, a whole species was considered sacred. Thus, ibises were raised on special farms (*ibiônes*), and it was forbidden to hunt the oxyrhynchus and lepidotus fishes not only in Oxyrhynchus but all over Egypt as well (Heinen 1991). Appian (*De animalibus* XII.7) describes the lion den in Leontopolis; the plural in the name of the city ("city of the lions") suggests that several sacred lions were kept in the local zoo.

Some sacred animals were living individuals in which the god manifested himself in this world. Bouchis is Montou, the sacred crocodile is Sobek (Souchos), and the Hesis cow is Isis (as is stated by the priests in *P.Zen. Pestman* 50.5). Moreover, the same god can be represented in a human form as Montou or Isis, or as a human with an animal head, in the case of Souchos. In the Fayyum the local crocodile gods in the villages (e.g., Sok-nopaios = Souchos, lord of the island; Sok-nebtynis = Souchos, lord of Tynis; Soknokonneus = Souchos, lord of Bakchias) were as many individualizations of the one god Souchos. But the sacred fishes of Neith in Esna are called *eidôla* or "images" of the goddess (Quaegebeur, Clarysse, and Van Maele 1985, 223), whereas Apis is the "herald" of Ptah, not Ptah himself. Similarly, the ibis birds and baboons were images of Thoth rather than Thoth himself. The relationship between sacred animal and god was therefore a complex one.

Figure 24.7. Votive inscription found in Pisa, Italy. Dedication by Flavius Pharnutianus Rufus about 100 CE. The name Pharnutianus shows his Egyptian background. Three pairs of ears are surmounted by crowns of Egyptian gods: the lotus of Harpochrates, the kalathos of Sarapis, and the cow horns, sun disc, and feathers of Isis (*SEG* XXVI 1143; there is also a plate in M. Guarducci, *Epigrafia greca*, vol. 3, Rome [1974], 69).

After death sacred animals, like humans, were mummified and buried and received a funerary cult. The burial was a great and costly occasion, with a mourning period of seventy days, as for humans. The expenses for myrrh and byssus needed for the burial of Apis were partly subsidized by the government and partly paid for by contributions from the temples all over the country (*P.Lund*. III 10 = *SB* 8750; 98 CE). The stone sarcophagus with the Apis bull was then hauled in procession from the city to the Serapeum, up the steep desert ridge, over a distance of three kilometers. Those who could attend the burial proudly left hundreds of commemorative small stelae in the tombs. In Ombos, the main local civil officials participated in the yearly burial of the ibises and hawks (*O.Joachim*), whereas, according to the inscriptions from Hermonthis, Queen Cleopatra herself attended the burial of Buchis (Goldbrunner 2004, 112–113, 152–155).

Egyptian "Saints"

Divinized individuals similarly functioned as intermediaries between the distant gods and the believers. They might be pharaohs of the past, like Amenemhat III of the Middle Kingdom (ca. 2000 BCE), who was worshipped in the Fayyum under the name Marres or Pra-marres ("pharaoh Marres") (Widmer 2002), or private individuals, such as Imouthes, the minister of King Djoser (ca. 2600 BCE) and architect of the step pyramid in Saqqara, and Amenothes, son of Hapu, the architect of King

Amenophis III (ca. 1375 BCE), both sages and healing gods. The cult of Amenothes in the famous temple of Deir el-Bahari in Thebes lasted until the mid-fourth century CE. Greek and demotic ostraca tell of us of his miraculous healings, and in the second century BCE the rules of his cult association were written down on a Greek papyrus (Quaegebeur 1977). Most local "saints," however, are far less conspicuous: In the list of the deceased buried in the necropolis and cared for by the choachytes, they are marked as "masters" (*p3 ḥry* in demotic; φρι in Greek) and "praised" (*ḥsy* in demotic; Ἁσιης, Ἑσιης in Greek) and no doubt received special treatment in death (ibid.).

Oracles

Oracles had also been known for many centuries in Egypt, but shortly before the Ptolemaic period a new type of oracle questions developed, by which the query was written down on two chits of papyrus, usually one positive and one negative. The structure of these questions remained unaltered for nearly a millennium, notwithstanding the changes in language (from demotic to Greek to Coptic) and religion (from Egyptian gods to Graeco-Egyptian gods to Christian saints and Christ himself). First comes an invocation of the deity, then the actual question in the form of a conditional sentence, positive or negative, then an imperative, asking for the decision of the divinity. A typical example is the demotic *P.Oxf.Griffith* 1 (Bresciani 1975; figure 24.2a–b): "(1) The servant Tesenouphis, son of Marres, says before his lord Soknopaios, the great god, and before Isis with the beautiful throne: (2) If it is good for me to plow the shore of the lake this year, year 33, (3) may this (piece of) writing be taken out for me."

The believer took the answer home with him, whereas the other chit remained in the temple and was eventually thrown away. Hundreds of these chits, often still sealed and unopened, were recently found in a rubbish dump near the temple of Tebtynis (*P.Zauzich dem.* 10, introduction). The popularity of this type of document is illustrated not only by the numerous papyri found all over Egypt but also by an edict in which the prefect forbade oracle consultation during the visit of the Emperor Septimius Severus: "Let no one pretend to know matters beyond human knowledge and profess (to know) the obscurity of future things either by means of oracular responses, i.e., written documents allegedly issued in the presence of the divinity, or by means of processions of statues or suchlike charlatanry" (*SB* XIV 12144).

Dreams

The gods could also give advice through dreams. Dream books are attested since the New Kingdom and occur also in demotic; they explain the meaning of dreams, taking account of the character or social position of the dreamer, as was to happen also in the later Greek dream book of Artemidoros. Often the believer spent the night in the temple expecting the god to send a dream that would provide a cure for illness or trouble (Malinine 1962). The most famous example of this phenomenon is the *katochos* Ptolemaios, who lived in the great temple of Sarapis in Saqqara for fifteen years. Ptolemaios and his younger brother Apollonios carefully listed their dreams day by day in Greek, in demotic, and even in Egyptian by means of Greek characters. But at a certain point Apollonios lost faith and wrote his brother a desperate letter that ended with this statement: "Never again can I hold up my head in Trikomia for shame that we have given ourselves away and been deluded, misled by the gods and trusting in dreams" (*Select Papyri* I 100). Others were more successful, and the Egyptian priest Hor from the Delta city of Sebennytos even managed to obtain a royal audience in Alexandria on August 29, 168, after he had predicted the retreat of the Syrian king Antiochos and the salvation of Egypt. Hor wrote his dreams in demotic on potsherds, which were found a few hundred metres from where his contemporaries Ptolemaios and Apollonios lived.

Katochê

Ptolemaios was a *katochos*, that is, he was possessed by the god and could not leave the temple precinct. He made a living by performing minor religious tasks, selling clothes and even soup, and perhaps even begging. The phenomenon of the *katochê* is still imperfectly understood, but it was certainly motivated by religion and not simply a form of temple asylum. Ptolemaios was in the power of the god, who communicated with him through his dreams. In these dreams he clearly longed to retrieve his liberty, but this apparently did not happen, as his archive was found in Saqqara, where he lived in or near the shrine of the Syrian goddess Astarte.

It cannot be proven that the *katochoi* were identical with those persons who dedicated themselves to a god, promising to pay a small monthly sum in exchange for protection against all kinds of demons and spirits (Clarysse 1988). Texts of this type have been found in Tebtynis and Philadelphia and may be linked to the temple's medicinal practices. Some Egyptian priests, especially those of Sachmet, were experts in traditional medicine, combining detailed knowledge (demotic and Greek manuals were found in the temples) with magic. Holy water was poured over statuettes of Horus, the master of the dangerous animals, and then drunk by the patients (figure 24.11); magical imprecations were sung in combination with effective drugs to drive away the malignant spirits. In order to have access to this alternative medicine, people had to pay a kind of insurance to the temple, making themselves "slaves" of the god for the rest of their lives.

GROWING STATE INTERVENTION

The Administration of the Temples

The internal organization of the temples was in the hands of the priests. They did not function throughout the year but were divided into at first four, then (from 237 BCE on) five groups (s3.w in Egyptian, φύλαι in Greek), who alternated in their duties to the gods. The leaders (sḥn.w, Greek ἡγούμενοι) of these groups were in charge of the temple and yearly choose a director (mr-šn, which in Greek could be transliterated as λεσώνης or translated as ἀρχιερεύς). In each temple the government installed a financial administrator, called an *epistates*. Originally he came from outside the temple, but quite soon the epistates also belonged to one of the priestly families. Priestly functions were usually passed down from father to son, but the newly installed priests had not only to conform to ritual prescriptions (they had, for instance, to be circumcised) but also to pay an entrance fee to the government.

Egyptians who entered the royal administration usually came from the native upper classes linked with the priests. The same families provided not only the prophets, *stolistai* and *hiereis*, who together constituted the higher clergy, but also the Egyptian notaries, scholars, doctors, and even civil servants. In many cases local grandees combined priestly and administrative titles and even military functions. It is often unclear whether these were priestly families entering the service of the Ptolemies or government officials gaining access to the temples. In the later period civil officials gradually took over some of the most important temple functions (Gorre 2009).

An interesting feature of the Roman period, when the temples became more self-centered, is the opposition between the higher and lower clergy, which resulted in several lawsuits in which *pastophoroi* (lower-rank priests) clashed with the *hiereis* (*SB* X 10564). The Gnomon of the Idios Logos also forbids priests to hold other positions (*BGU* V 1210), and government jobs were now clearly separated from temple functions.

The Temple in the Administration

As stated earlier, state and temple did not stand in opposition, but the temples were an integral part of the system. Since in pre-Ptolemaic times the reading and writing of the complicated hieroglyphic script were a near monopoly of the temples, the priests were at the same time the obvious organizers of the administration.

This ancient land-tenure regime under the administration of the local temple continued for some time in the Ptolemaic period, especially in Upper Egypt. According to the Edfu donation text, written in hieroglyphs on the outside wall of the temple, the temple owned no less than 3640 hectares, three quarters of which were in the nome of Edfu, the rest in other southern provinces. Within the Edfu nome about 20 percent of the land seems to have been owned by the god Horus (Manning 2003, 77). But in the demotic papyri of the Hauswaldt archive (third century BCE), temple land was sold by individuals and even auctioned off by the administration; thus, some temple land was in fact treated as private property and was only nominally owned by the temple. There were therefore two types of temple land, real temple land (sacred land), owned by the god and administered by his priests, and private land that belonged to the god's estate (*ḥtp-ntr*). The sacred land gradually came under state control and was confiscated in the Roman period. The private land (in fact, land passed down in hereditary lease) yielded no rent, but a small harvest tax had to be paid. Originally this tax was paid through the temple administration, but from 223 BCE on and especially after the great revolt (206–186 BCE) the tax went directly to the king. He partially compensated the temple for this loss of income by a subvention (*syntaxis*), from which the offerings to the gods could be paid. Since the tax was now levied by government officials and not by the temple administration, it was continually threatened with being used for other, more urgent secular purposes, notwithstanding promises in the royal decrees to keep "the revenues of the temples in place." Only for a tiny part of these lands did the temples continue to levy the harvest tax themselves, under strict government control, for specific purposes. This limited system of financial independence was finally abolished by the Emperor Hadrian in 123 CE (Vandorpe 2005).

In some places the temple continued to function as an intermediary between taxpayers and state far into the Roman period. Thus, in Soknopaiou Nesos taxes on oil production and weaving were first paid to the temple, which then passed them on to the fisc (Lippert and Schentuleit 2005b). Part of the produce was destined for internal use in the temple.

Priestly Privileges

In the Ptolemaic census lists, priests of all categories are listed separately. They make up between 5 and 10 percent of the village population in a strongly Hellenized area such as the Fayyum (Clarysse and Thompson 2006, 177–186). For most of these, the priesthood was an honorary status rather than a full-time profession, as appears from some bilingual surety contracts. Thus, a god bearer (*t3y ntr*, Greek *theagos*) of Souchos (figure 24.4) was a simple donkey driver (*P.Lille dem.* II 49) (Dils 1995, 155 n5), or an astronomer of Herishef becomes a cobbler in the Greek abstract (*P.Lille dem.* II 51). Nonetheless, being counted as a priest clearly involved fiscal privileges if only because this particular donkey driver or cobbler was not on the list when donkey drivers or cobblers were called upon for corvée works.

In the Roman period a limited number of priests were fully or partially exempted from works on the dikes and from the heavy Roman poll tax, the *laographia*, which normally amounted to at least 16 and even 32 drachmas a year, the equivalent of two to four weeks' wages. For each temple a quota was fixed. In

112 CE, for instance, Tebtynis was allowed 40 priests and 40 *pastophoroi*, Bakchias 64 priests (*BGU* XIII 2215, 113/4 CE), and Soknopaiou Nesos had more than 100 priests.

Priestly functions were clearly coveted. They were usually passed down from father to son but could also be sold off. When no heirs were available, the functions were sold by auction by the *idios logos* for thousands of drachmas (one drachma was equivalent to a worker's wage for one day) (*P.Lund.* III 10).

Temple Asylum

As sacred spaces, temples, like churches, might provide asylum for people who risked punishment by officialdom. No doubt this was the case for Egyptian temples in earlier periods also. Some even believe that the *katochoi* (or at least some of them) were in fact seeking asylum in the temple. In contracts of debt and surety, the debtor or person guaranteed often had to declare that he would not seek refuge in a temple.

The asylum inscriptions, in which the king guarantees the rights of the temple against encroachments by officials, are a typical phenomenon of the late Ptolemaic temples. Though they have been interpreted as signs of the increasing power of the temples, it is far more likely that they show that the temples needed royal help to guarantee their traditional rights against local grandees (Bingen 1989, 26–31).

Dynastic and Imperial Cults

When the Ptolemies organized the cult of the royal family around the tomb of Alexander the Great in Alexandria, the Egyptian temples took the hint and organized their own cults for the living royal couple, for some queens, and for the Ptolemaic ancestors (figure 24.8). This cult is a totally new feature in the temple decoration: Whereas the pharaoh normally confronts the gods as the representative of humanity, here his own ancestors stand on the side of the gods.

The cult is described in some detail in the priestly decrees, which were proclaimed during yearly gatherings of representatives of the whole Egyptian priesthood in Alexandria or Memphis. In the Canopus decree a fifth *phyle* is added to the traditional four, in honor of the reigning kings, and in the Rosetta Stone new divine honors are added to those that already exist. The elaborate crowns of the divinized queen Arsinoe or princess Philotera/Berenike, described in those texts, are also pictured on the temple walls and the statues. Here the priests as a group function more or less in the same way as the Greek poleis elsewhere in the Hellenistic world, voting divine honors for the king, a procedure that is definitely un-Egyptian. In pharaonic Egypt, the pharaoh did not pretend to be a god, and honors were not voted by his subjects (Clarysse 1999).

With Augustus, the queens disappear from the temple walls, but so also do the scenes of the royal cult. Though Augustus himself is called "son of the god," the Roman pharaoh is again a representative of humanity facing the gods and no more than that. The imperial cult took place in special temples *(Sebasteion, Hadrianeion)* in the metropoleis and was Greek in style. It was part of the daily routine of local officials (see, e.g., *BGU* II 362).

Collaboration

The privileged position of the priests in the tax system, their integration in the Ptolemaic administration, the royal subvention of the temples, and the elaboration of an Egyptian royal cult all led to a close cooperation of the Egyptian priesthood with the Ptolemaic regime. In their petitions the priests often insist on their task of bringing food and drink offerings to the divine royal family. The trilingual decrees stress again and again the legitimacy of the Macedonian dynasty, and insurgents are not only enemies of the gods, impious (*asebeis*) and ignorant, but are also accused of profaning and demolishing temples and divine statues. Probably these accusations were true, and many temples suffered during the revolts: Valuable assets were to be found there, and the priests had compromised themselves by collaborating with the foreign occupants (Véïsse 2004, 197–242).

On the other hand, part of the clergy may well have sympathized with the insurgents. The rebel kings Haronnophris and Chaonnophris were titled "loved by Amonrasonther, loved by Isis," and one can hardly doubt that they were proclaimed in the temple of Thebes. In 163, shortly after the revolt of Dionysios Petosorapis, the police searched for arms in the great Memphite Serapeum (*UPZ* I 5.10). And the prophetic literature, such as the potter's oracle and the oracle of the lamb, apparently anticipated a savior and a new golden age, which would bring an end to the "city on the sea" (Blasius 2002). Whereas the priestly princes of Memphis fraternized with the Ptolemies and officially crowned them in Memphis (Thompson 1988, 138–54), the lower clergy may have been more ambivalent in their loyalty.

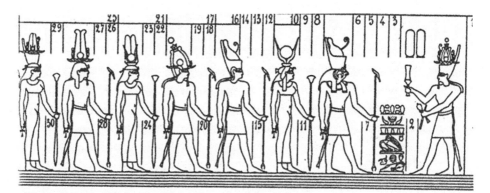

Figure 24.8.   Ptolemy IV making an offering to the gods of Edfu, followed by Ptolemy III, II, and I with their queens, as *synnaoi theoi.* Drawing from E. Chassinat, *Le temple d'Edfou,* vol. 1, 527, pl. XXXVIa, Paris (1897).

THE IMPACT OF GREEK

Interpretatio Graeca

When Herodotus gave Greek names to the Egyptian gods, calling Amon Zeus, Osiris Dionysos, and Neith Athena, this *interpretatio graeca* was just a way to explain to his readers the nature of these gods by an often superficial equivalence. Neith, for instance, was identified with Athena because of the martial characteristics of the two goddesses and the close link between the cities of Athens and Sais. In the Roman period, however, Neith is really represented as a Greek Athena, the red crown becomes a Greek helmet, and the shield with two crossed arrows develops into a wheel of fortune (figure 24.9). When Athena is represented on terracotta lanterns, the Greek goddess apparently inherits the celebrated lamp festival of Neith in Sais (Quaegebeur 1983, 318–321; Quaegebeur, Clarysse, and Van Maele, 1985, 218–220). In a wonder story about Imhotep, the son of Hephaistos (Ptah) (*P.Oxy.* XI 1381), the cult of the saint is rightly given a long Egyptian history, one that reaches back to the Old Kingdom and the reign of Mycerinos. But at the same time Imhotep is Asklepios, and the author of the story is miraculously healed through a dream, as in the temples of the Greek god of medicine. The author wants "every Greek tongue to tell the story of the god and every Greek man to honor Imouthes the son of Ptah." Greek and Egyptian god have become inextricably intertwined.

The *interpretatio graeca* of Egyptian deities often becomes apparent in personal names. Many people in antiquity had double names, which they could use alternately, depending on the circumstances. The most famous of these is perhaps Simon-Petros; Simon is his Jewish name, while Petros ("the rock") promotes him to the leading figure among the apostles, the first pope. When the two names of a person belong to different languages, one can be simply the translation of the other, as in Didymos (Thomas, "the twin"), or, much later, Schwartzert (Melanchton, "black earth"). In Graeco-Roman Egypt, this kind of double name often yields information about the Greek interpretation of Egyptian religion. In their simplest form, double names can be simple translations, such as Hatres/Phatres and Didymos "(the) twin"; Pbekis and Hierax, "the falcon"; Mersis and Pyrrhos, "the red one"; Mysthes and Akousilaos, "(the god) who listens"; or Thaesis and Isidora, "the one who belongs to Isis/the one given by Isis." They can also convey the equivalence of Greek and Egyptian gods, as in Dionysios and Petosorapis (Dionysos = Osorapis); Apollonia and Senmonthis (Apollo = Montou); Paniskos and Psemminis (Pan = Min); or Imouthes and Asklepiades (Imhotep = Asklepios). Sometimes theological speculation is involved, as in Semtheus alias Herakleodoros (in terracottas the Egyptian child-god *Sm3-t3wy* or Semtheus, a form of Harpochrates, is often depicted with a club, like Greek Herakles, fig. 24.5), or Herais alias Tiesris

Figure 24.9. Egyptian Neith as Greek Athena, with her son, the sphinx god Tutu. Vienna 5077; drawing from J. Quaegebeur, *Studia Hellenistica* 27 (1983): 309. Reproduced by permission of *Studia Hellenistica*.

(Hera corresponds to Egyptian Mout, whose temple has a characteristic moon-shaped sacred lake called *išrw* = *esris* in Egyptian).

Hellenization of the Gods

The Hellenization of the gods is evident not only in their names but can also be seen in their dress and their mythology. Whereas on the temple walls the gods and the king are represented in the traditional fashion with kilts, staffs, wigs, and crowns, they can also take on a Greek face. The Sarapis cult may have functioned as a model here: Sarapis is shown as a Greek Zeus or Hades (with the three-headed Kerberos at his feet), with a classical hairstyle and beard, a Greek coat, and Greek sandals. The only Egyptian element is the kalathos on his head, a vase-shaped container with vegetable motifs, showing his fertility function (see figure 24.3). A wooden board found at Tebtynis shows us a divine triad that includes Soknebtynis and Min (figure 24.10). Soknebtynis is an enthroned Zeus-like figure, while Min is a standing young man (with no beard). Soknebtynis can be identified as the crocodile god because he holds a little crocodile in his lap; Min is recognizable because he holds his penis in his hand. They look like Greek gods, except for some Egyptian attributes (crowns, scepters, crocodile). In the thousands of terra cotta statues found in houses and tombs, Sarapis, Isis, and Harpochrates are usually shown in Greek form. The child Harpochrates, nude or with a Greek cloak, often wears an Egyptian crown or the lock of youth. When he wears a club he is identified with Greek Herakles, who, like Horos, demonstrated his power as a baby by killing or chasing the snakes sent by hostile gods (Seth and Hera, respectively). Here Greek and Egyptian myths are becoming intertwined. Harpochrates holds his finger to his mouth, the traditional Egyptian way of representing a child (figure 24.5). But this attitude was reinterpreted by later writers as a symbol of silence and wisdom.

The Greek Dioskouroi, Kastor and Polydeukes, are well attested through personal names, and their cult has often been considered a rare example of a purely Greek cult in Egypt. An oracle question to the Dioskouroi, however, found in the Egyptian temple of the crocodile god Souchos in Bakchias, and the double name Dioskourides alias Psansnos, "the one of the Dioskouroi, alias the two brothers" show that here, too, Greek and Egyptian cannot be separated. The twin crocodiles, which are represented suckling the goddess Neith in the traditional imagery, have become grecized as Kastor and Polydeukes, or the sons of Zeus have been Egyptianized as crocodile gods (Quaegebeur 1983, 312–316).

The Oracles

The Hellenization of the gods can be seen quite clearly in the oracle questions mentioned earlier (Valbelle and Husson 1998). The earliest demotic oracle questions are all addressed to Egyptian gods. The oldest example known to us comes from Memphis and probably even precedes the arrival of Alexander. Most Ptolemaic chits come from the Fayyum and are addressed to Sobek (Souchos). In Soknopaiou Nesos, Souchos is closely linked (married) to the goddess Isis Nepherses, "Isis with the beautiful throne." In other parts of Egypt other gods come to the fore, e.g., the hippopotamus goddess Thoeris in Oxyrhynchus or the ibis of Thoth in Hermopolis. The earliest of these papyri are written in demotic, but already in the third century BCE many questions in Tebtynis are written in Greek. Often the Greek text is written with a brush, not with a reed pen, which shows that the writers, no doubt local priests, were Egyptians. They wrote in Greek because this was the language of the better-educated classes, and the god was of course part of this upper-class world.

In the Roman period demotic disappears, and the Egyptian gods are now always addressed in Greek. Moreover, Soknopaios is now identified with Ammon, an oracle god who enjoyed wide fame with the Greeks for many centuries (Alexander even went to visit him in Siwa). In Oxyrhynchus, Sarapis reigns supreme, a Greek Dionysos-Hades grafted upon the cult of Osiris-Apis. Sarapis is now

Figure 24.10. Soknebtynis-Kronos (with a small crocodile on his lap) and ithyphallic Min in Tebtynis. From *Egyptian Religion, the Last Thousand Years: Studies Dedicated to the Memory of Jan Quaegebeur* (OLA 84, Leuven, 1998), 244. Reproduced by permission of the editor.

identified with Zeus and Helios, the Greek chief god, and the Greek sun god (and oracle god) Apollo. The syncretistic view allows gods from different backgrounds to merge their functions and to become each others' equivalents. Egyptian gods receive a Greek name and a Greek iconography and even take over bits and pieces of Greek mythology, all the while retaining their Egyptian essence.

Astrology in the Greek Fashion

The ceiling of one room in the temples of Esna (200 BCE), Dendera (60 BCE), and Shenhur (Roman period) is decorated with a representation of the sky, depicting the constellations of the Greek zodiac, the planets, and the zodiacal signs (fishes, twins, lion, scales, etc.). Images in traditional Egyptian style render a Greek astronomical view of the cosmos based on Babylonian astronomy, to which are added the thirty-six decans of Egyptian origin. In the Roman period the zodiac sometimes replaced the sky goddess Nut on the inner side of the lid of sarcophagi. Astronomy and astrology were widely practiced by the learned Egyptian scribes, but it is only in the Ptolemaic period that the first astronomical papyri are found in temple surroundings. Horoscopes in Demotic (38 BCE–171 CE) and in Greek (10 BCE–508 CE) register the positions of heavenly bodies in the zodiac for the birthdate of individuals. Only exceptionally is this followed by a prediction, as in *P.Oxy.* IV 804: "It contains dangers. Be careful for 40 days because of Ares." The horoscopes found in the temple of Medinet Madi (Narmouthis) show that the priests were involved in this enterprise (Jones 1999).

Greek Texts in and around Egyptian Temples

The walls of the Egyptian temples are covered with sacred hieroglyphs, but Greek texts gradually appear at the gates and even inside the sacred enclosure of the temples. Thus, the great trilingual decrees were, as they say, set up by the priests "in the most conspicuous place in the temples of first, second, and third rank." As early as the late Ptolemaic period Greek stelae in front of the gates or around the temple indicated the area of asylum.

In the late Ptolemaic and early Roman period, private individuals who contributed to the building of gates, walls, and chapels inside the temple often advertised their benefactions by way of Greek inscriptions. The most conspicuous example is perhaps Parthenios of Coptos, of whom no fewer than twenty-five stelae have been found—in hieroglyphs, demotic, Greek, and a mixture of these (Farid 1988). Greek building inscriptions were even engraved on the architectural elements of the temple, for example, over the doorway (*I.Fay.* II 105, 107; second century BCE). In the late Ptolemaic period the hymns to Isis-Thermouthis by Isidoros were inscribed on the vestibule pillars in the forecourt of the Narmouthis temple (Davoli 1998, pl. 109; *I.Métriques* 175). The Greek verses in hexameters and elegiac distychs celebrate Isis as a goddess for the entire world, but they also remind the reader of the Middle Kingdom origin of the temple and identify Pharaoh Sesoosis (Sesostris) with the divinized Poremanres (Amenemhat III). In 96 BCE Herakleodoros, son of Sostratos, and his family dedicate the vestibule and the sphinxes in front of it with two other Greek inscriptions on the same pillar, right above the hymns (*I.Fay.* III 158–159). In Narmouthis as elsewhere, temple constructions are no longer namelessly attributed to the reigning pharaoh; rather, sponsors want to see their names advertised. This is a Greek way of self-promotion, and most of the inscriptions are also in Greek.

In the Ptolemaic temple of Philae in the deep south, Greek dedicatory inscriptions by officials (especially the local garrison commander), dating mostly from the second century BCE, decorated the wall leading from the quay to the temple, but the priests themselves also publicized the privileges they received from the kings in Greek form. In the first century BCE and in the Roman period, most of the inscriptions are private *proskynemata* to Isis on the great pylon left by pilgrims, both in Greek and demotic (Dietze 1994). Greek "acts of worship" are common in all temples; even Stotoetis, a cutter of hieroglyphs, scratched his name in Greek (*I.Fay.* III 168).

Pilgrims approaching the great Serapeum of Memphis and walking along the alley of sphinxes would perhaps not notice the hundreds of Greek inscriptions scribbled on the back of the sphinxes (Rogge-Harrauer 1999), but they could not miss the Greek chapel with Corinthian capitals (the *lychnaption*) at the end of the dromos and two groups of Greek statues, one including Dionysos, the other representing Greek poets and philosophers, of whom Pindar, Protagoras, and Plato can be identified thanks to inscriptions on their bases (Lauer and Picard 1955). Inside the temple wall the visitors would pass the shrine of Astarte, in which the Greek *katochos* Ptolemaios kept his little archive, including several works of Greek literature. Near the entrance of the temple they could also see the colorful advertisement of a Cretan dream interpreter, written in Greek iambics under an Apis bull. The nameless Cretan was accredited "by an order of the god" (Cairo stela 27567; Thompson 1988, pl. VII).

Papyri found inside the temple similarly show the increasing presence of Greek. The priests of Tebtynis copied their literary works in demotic on the back of Greek administrative documents. In their houses were found Greek documents, as well as fragments of Homer and Euripides, medical and astro-nomical texts, and even philosophical works (van Minnen 1998; Ryholt 2002). Two jars full of ostraca, found in a room inside the temple wall of Narmouthis, are quite puzzling. Some are Greek, others demotic, but demotic signs are found in the Greek texts and vice versa, which is odd because the two scripts go in different directions. The texts were probably written in a school context; in this temple school of the second century CE the two languages were inextri-cably intermixed (*O. Narm.* I and II).

The End of Egyptian Religion

The One God and the Many

In traditional polytheism the major gods had clearly defined fields of activity, both geographical (Souchos was, for instance, worshipped in the Fayyum and in Kom Ombo, Ptah in Memphis, Khnum in Elephantine and Esna, Amon in Thebes) and functional (Isis is the mother goddess, Hathor specializes in sex, Sakhmet sends and cures illnesses; Thoth, the scribe of the gods, is also the god of wisdom; Osiris takes care of the afterworld; Horos is both the sun and the young king, etc.). But many gods functioned as creator gods, many could merge with the sun-god Re, most goddesses were spouses and mothers, and so on. In the Late Period, moreover, visiting gods could share a temple, as *synnaoi theoi,* with the main deity and then assume some of his characteristics. In wisdom literature the abstract idea of "the gods" or even "God" coexisted with individual gods. Major gods could take over the names and roles of minor gods, as Osiris did with Sokar in Memphis or with Chenti-Amenti in Abydos.

This phenomenon became ever more prominent. Thus, in the litanies in honor of Isis, nearly all female goddesses, Egyptian as well as Greek, become manifestations of a universal goddess, "Isis with the ten thousand names" *(myrionymos)*. Similarly, Sarapis takes over the roles of Osiris, Hades, Dionysos, Zeus-Ammon, and Apollo, and he is addressed in the oracle questions as "Zeus Helios Sarapis." In the terracottas the child-god Harpochrates not only wears the royal double crown but also bears the solar nimbus or the club of Herakles (figure 24.5). All Egyptian gods are great, twice great, three times great *(trismegistos),* and their universal power is expressed by all kinds of symbols: animal heads, knives, staves, crowns, wings, snakes, and uraei.

Thus, new gods who had not played any important role in the traditional temple cult could come to the fore. Harpochrates, who functions as a child of the major gods in the temples, now becomes a "great god" in his own right, as is clear from the hundreds of magical stone stelae in which he is portrayed trampling crocodiles and holding snakes and scorpions in his hand. Water poured over the stela and collected in a small basin had a healing power (figure 24.11) (Sternberg-El Hotabi 1999). Bes, who kept the evil powers away from the mammisi, the god-king's birth chamber in the temple, now receives a cult of his own. A typical example of such a new god, who gained access to a temple cult only in the Roman period, is Tutu (figure 24.9): He is represented as a striding sphinx with a serpent tail, turning his head to the viewer; animal heads in his neck and on his chest (crocodile, ram, lion) show the god's demonic powers. Sometimes he is coupled with his mother, Neith (Athena), and the wheel of fortune; he also controls fate. However, he is also linked to Amon-Re and the solar cult. His popularity is attested by numerous votive stelae that were set up in the temples and by the frequent personal names Totoes and Tithoes, but only one temple dedicated to him is known, that at Kellis in the Dakhleh Oasis (Kaper 2003).

Religion without Temples

The near absence of temples and cult personnel equates Tutu with the demons of whom he is the master. Demons were widely feared and propitiated in Greco-Roman times. We meet them in the demotic self-dedications, in magical papyri, and especially in onomastics. This is illustrated by personal names such as Herieus,

Hry.w, "the benevolent (ones)," which can be translated in Greek as Euphron (Clarysse 1991); Panetbeus, *Pa-n3-ḏb3.w,* "the one of the avenging gods," or Panechates, *Pa-n3-ḥty.w,* "the one of the *ḥty* demons." When named after these dangerous demons, a child was placed under their protection. Because of the high infant mortality rate, children were considered to be under constant threat of the "evil eye." On mummy portraits they sometimes wear a collar with an amulet in a small container, and in private letters their names are often preceded by the word *abaskantos,* "may jealousy, i.e., the evil eye, not touch them" (Bonneau 1982).

Oracles, dreams, and astrology were originally linked to the temple (or rather to the forecourt of the temple, the only place accessible to the general public). But in some instances the link with the temple may have weakened: Thus, the Cretan dream interpreter was not a priest of Sarapis, and the *katochos* Ptolemaios also seems to have functioned as a private interpreter of his own dreams and those of his friends. Oracle questions could be written by priestly scribes, but the believers themselves could also interpret the movements of the sacred bark in the procession or of the holy Apis bull in his court. Thus, the so-called oracle of Astrampsychus, which first appeared in the third century CE, was a do-it-yourself oracle, containing a list of ninety-one questions and 910 answers. Originally written in Greek, it was very popular through translations (and Christianization) in Latin and most European languages (Stewart 2001).

The most prominent aspect of religion outside the temples is no doubt found in magical papyri. Although magic (i.e., the scientific exploitation of the divine powers) existed for centuries both in Egypt and in Greece, magical papyri are a typical feature of the late Roman and Byzantine periods. On the one hand, there are magical handbooks, such as the magician's library found at Thebes, which comprises both Greek and demotic papyri (Tait 1995); on the other hand, hundreds of texts on papyri, ostraca, and lead tablets contain practical applications of the handbooks to individual situations: amulets against illnesses and the evil eye, as well as love charms and spells to make a horse lose a race. In some cases the written charm is coupled with a doll on which the magical rites had been performed (du Bourguet 1980).

Egyptian Religion within Christianity

Christianity is distinguished from pagan religion by its ideology of aggressive monotheism, its abolition of sacrifices, and its scientific approach based on a sacred book. As we have seen, the strict polytheism of traditional Egyptian religion had already given way to different forms of henotheism, by which different gods took over each other's roles to such an extent that they tended to merge. Instead of absorbing the traditional gods, Christianity demonized them. It did not actually deny their existence but turned them into malicious demons. In addition, Decius

Figure 24.11. Horos cippus,
Brussels, Musées Royaux
d'Art et d'Histoire, E. 4995.
Photo copyrighted by the
IRPA-KIK, Brussels.

(250 CE), who ordered every citizen of the empire to sacrifice food and drink offerings (θύειν καὶ σπένδειν), had already perceived that sacrifices made a real difference: Whereas ancient religious festivals implied an abundant meal for the whole community, Christians offered the body and blood of Christ only in a symbolic way. The poor were cared for in a different manner—Christian charity. Egyptian religion did use written texts (e.g., the Book of the Dead, the Book of Breathing, and the Book of the Temple), but there was not one fundamental charter of belief like the Bible or the Qur'ān.

Not everything in the new religion, however, was new to the Egyptians: Pharaoh was the son of god and of his earthly father, like Jesus; the creation of the world by the divine logos is also found in the theology of Ptah; the resurrection of the dead was foreshadowed by the cult of Osiris; the Eucharistic meal was similar to the sacred meals in the temples of Sarapis and Thoeris (Youtie 1948); the Holy Trinity could be compared with the divine families in the temple; even the expectation of a messianic king was not unknown, as appears from the names of the rebel pharaohs Haronnophris and Chaonnophris (Véïsse 2004, 99, 247).

In one or two generations' time, between 300 and 360, Egypt shed its traditional religions and went over massively to Christianity. In the first half of the fourth century the old and the new religions coexisted for a while, as can be seen in Panopolis, in Philae, or in the Khargeh Oasis. But the drastic change in onomastics from pagan names based on the Egyptian gods to Christian names, mentioning "god" (Theo- and -noute names), abstract virtues (e.g., Eusebios, Eulogios), biblical persons (e.g., Elizabeth, Johannes), and saints (e.g., Petros and Paulos, Kosmas and Damianos) illustrates the pervasiveness of the transformation (Bagnall 1993, 280–281). The last inscriptions recording the rise of the Nile in a traditional religious context date from 295 CE, in 320 CE the son of a priest is still circumcised, the last Buchis bull is buried in the reign of Constantius (340 CE), the last bloody sacrifice is attested in Deir el-Bahari in the second quarter of the fourth century, and in 336 CE a priest of Zeus and Hera is still appointed in Oxyrynchus (ibid., 261–273). According to Ammianus Marcellinus, the Emperor Julian was present at the enthronement of an Apis bull in 362 CE. In any case, by the end of the fourth century pagan religion had disappeared from public view, and Egypt had become a Christian country famous for its hermits and monasteries.

The old religion lived on in the new to a limited extent. Thus, the cult of the Virgin Mary with the little child, Jesus, took over the iconography from the earlier Isis cult. Mary became the new *theotokos*, "mother of the god." Of course, she has her hair decently covered, in opposition to the sexy hairstyle of Isis. Christian knights like Georgios, Victor, or Apa Claudius, sitting on horseback and piercing a demonic figure with their lance, take over the role of Horos and Heron. Mummification continues for a while against the opposition of the ecclesiastical authorities. The rising of the Nile is now celebrated in the church, which also takes over the age-old custom of delivering oracles. Magic and astrology still flourish, and here the gods live on as demons that have to be manipulated or overpowered. But these, like the survival of the old Egyptian ankh symbol for the life-giving cross (Cramer 1955) are poor remnants of the old religion in a new world (Frankfurter 1998).

BIBLIOGRAPHY

Bagnall, R. S. 1993. *Egypt in Late Antiquity*. Princeton: Princeton University Press.

Bingen, J. 1989. "Normalité et spécificité de l'épigraphie grecque et romaine de l'Egypte." In *Egitto e storia antica dall'ellenismo all'età araba: Bilancio di un confronto*, ed. L. Criscuolo and G. Geraci, 15–35. Bologna: CLUEB.

Blasius, A., ed. 2002. *Apokalyptik und Ägypten: Eine kritische Analyse der relevanten Texte aus dem griechisch-römischen Ägypten*. Leuven: Peeters.

Bonneau, D. 1982. "L'apotropaïque 'Abaskantos' en Égypte." *RHR* 199: 23–36.

Brashear, W. M. 1995. "The Greek Magical Papyri: An Introduction and Survey. Annotated Bibliography 1928–1994." In *Aufstieg und Niedergang der Römischen Welt: Geschichte und Kultur Roms im Spiegel der neueren Forschung*, vol. 2, 18.5, 3380–3684. Berlin: de Gruyter.

Bresciani, E. 1975. *L'archivio demotico del tempio di Soknopaiu Nesos nel Griffith Institute di Oxford*, I. Testi e documenti per lo studio dell'Antichità. Milan: Istituto editoriale Cisalpino.

Clarysse, W. 1988. "A Demotic Self-dedication to Anubis." *Enchoria* 16: 7–10.

———. 1991. "Hakoris, an Egyptian Nobleman and His Family." *Ancient Society* 22: 235–243.

———. 1999. "Ptolémées et temples." In *Le décret de Memphis*, ed. D. Valbelle and J. Leclant, 41–62. Paris: Fondation Singer-Polignac.

Clarysse, W., and D. J. Thompson. 2006. *Counting the People in Ptolemaic Egypt*. Cambridge: Cambridge University Press.

Clarysse, W., and H. Willems, eds. 1998. *Egyptian Religion: The Last Thousand Years*, OLA 84–85. Leuven: Peeters.

Cramer, M. 1955. *Das altägyptische Lebenszeichen im christlichen (koptischen) Aegypten*. Wiesbaden: Harrassowitz.

Crawford, D. J. 1971. *Kerkeosiris: An Egyptian Village in the Ptolemaic Period*. Cambridge: Cambridge University Press.

Davoli, P. 1998. *L'archeologia urbana nel Fayyum di età ellenistica e romana*. Naples: Procaccini.

Depauw, M. 1998. "The isionomos or *in-wwy*." In *Egyptian Religion: The Last Thousand Years*, ed. W. Clarysse and H. Willems, 1131–1153. Leuven: Peeters.

Dietze, G. 1994. "Philae und die Dodekaschoinos in ptolemäischer Zeit." *Ancient Society* 25: 63–110.

Dils, P. 1995. "Les *ṯȝj* (*n3*) *ntr.w* ou θεαγοί. Fonction religieuse et place dans la vie civile." *BIFAO* 95: 153–171.

Du Bourguet, P. 1980. "Une ancêtre des figurines d'envoûtement percées d'aiguilles, avec ses compléments magiques, au Musée du Louvre." *Livre du Centenaire de l'I.F.A.O. 1880–1980*, 225–238. Cairo: Institut Français d'Archéologie Orientale.

Dunand, F., and F. Zivie-Coche. 1991. *Dieux et hommes en Egypte, 3000 av. J.-C.–395 apr. J.-C.: Anthropologie religieuse*. Paris: Armand Colin.

Evans, J. A. S. 1961. "A Social and Economic History of an Egyptian Temple in the Greco-Roman Period." *Yale Classical Studies* 17: 143–283.

Farid, A. 1988. "Die Denkmäler des Parthenios, des Verwalters der Isis von Koptos." *MDAIK* 44: 13–65.

Frankfurter, D. 1998. *Religion in Roman Egypt: Assimilation and Resistance.* Princeton: Princeton University Press.

Goldbrunner, L. 2004. *Buchis: Untersuchung zur Theologie des heiligen Stieres in Theben zur griechisch-römischer Zeit.* Monographies Reine Elisabeth 11. Brussels: Fondation Egyptologique Reine Elisabeth.

Gorre, G. 2009. *Les relations du clergé égyptien et des Lagides d'après la documentation privée.* Stud. Hell. 45. Leuven: Peeters.

Heinen, H. 1991. "Thoeris und heilige Fische: Eine neue griechische Inschrift für Ptolemaios X. Alexander I." In *Hellenistische Studien: Gedenkschrift für Hermann Bengtson,* ed. J. Seibert, 41–53. Münchener Arbeiten zur Alten Geschichte 5. Munich: Editio Maris.

Jones, A., ed. 1999. *Astronomical Papyri from Oxyrhynchus (P.Oxy. 4133–4300a).* Memoirs of the American Philosophical Society 233. Philadelphia: American Philosophical Society.

Kaper, O. E. 2003. *The Egyptian God Tutu: A Study of the Sphinx-god and Master of Demons with a Corpus of Monuments.* Orientalia Lovaniensia Analecta 119. Leuven: Peeters.

Lauer, J.-Ph., and C. Picard. 1955. *Les statues ptolémaïques du Sarapeion de Memphis.* Publications de l'Institut d'Art et d'Archéologie de l'Université de Paris 3. Paris: Presses universitaires de France.

Lippert, S., and M. Schentuleit, eds. 2005a. *Tebtynis und Soknopaiu Nesos: Leben im römerzeitlichen Fajum.* Wiesbaden: Harrassowitz.

——. 2005b. "Die Tempelökonomie nach den demotischen Texten aus Soknopaiu Nesos." In *Tebtynis und Soknopaiu Nesos: Leben im römerzeitlichen Fajum,* ed. S. Lippert and M. Schentuleit, 71–78. Wiesbaden: Harrassowitz.

Malinine, M. 1962. "Une lettre démotique à Aménothes fils de Hapou." *Revue d'Egyptologie* 40: 37–42.

Manning, J. G. 2003. *Land and Power in Ptolemaic Egypt: The Structure of Land Tenure.* Cambridge: Cambridge University Press.

Quack, J. 2005. "Die Ueberlieferungsstruktur des Buches vom Tempel." In *Tebtynis und Soknopaiu Nesos: Leben im römerzeitlichen Fajum,* ed. S. Lippert and M. Schentuleit, 105–115. Wiesbaden: Harrassowitz.

Quaegebeur, J. 1977. "Les saints égyptiens préchrétiens." *OLA* 8: 129–143.

——. 1983. "Cultes égyptiens et grecs en Egypte hellénistique: L'exploitation des sources." In *Egypt and the Hellenistic World: Proceedings of the International Colloquium Leuven 24–26 May 1982,* ed. E. Van 't Dack, P. Van Dessel, and W. Van Gucht, 303–324. Studia Hellenistica 27. Leuven: Peeters.

——. 1993. "La justice à la porte des temples et le toponyme Premit." In *Individu, société et spiritualité dans l'Egypte pharaonique et copte: Mélanges offertes au Professeur Aristide Théodoridès,* ed. C. Cannuyer and J.-M. Kruchten, 201–220. Ath–Brussels–Mons: Association montoise d'Egyptologie.

Quaegebeur, J., W. Clarysse, and B. Van Maele. 1985. "Athêna, Nêith and Thoêris in Greek Documents." *ZPE* 60: 217–223.

Riggs, C. 2005. *The Beautiful Burial in Roman Egypt: Art, Identity, and Funerary Religion.* Oxford: Oxford University Press.

Rogge, E., and H. Harrauer. 1999. *Kunsthistorisches Museum Wien. Aegyptische-Orientalische Sammlung. 11 Statuen der 30. Dynastie und der ptolemäisches-römischen Epoche.* Mainz am Rhein: von Zabern.

Ryholt, K. 2005. "On the Contents and Nature of the Tebtynis Temple Library." In *Tebtynis und Soknopaiu Nesos: Leben im römerzeitlichen Fajum,* ed. S. Lippert and M. Schentuleit, 141–170. Wiesbaden: Harrassowitz.

Sauneron, S. 1988. *Les prêtres de l'ancienne Egypte.* Paris: Édition Perséa.

Sternberg-El Hotabi, H. 1999. *Untersuchungen zur Ueberlieferungsgeschichte der Horusstelen: Ein Beitrag zur Religionsgeschichte Aegyptens im 1. Jahrtausend v.Chr.* Aegyptologische Abhandlungen 62. Wiesbaden: Harrassowitz.

Stewart, R. 2001. *Sortes Astrampsychi.* Vol. 2, *Ecdosis altera.* Munich: Saur.

Tait, W. J. 1995. "Theban Magic." *Papyrologica Lugduno-Batava* 27: 169–182. Leiden: Brill.

Thompson, D. J. 1988. *Memphis under the Ptolemies.* Princeton: Princeton University Press.

Valbelle, D., and G. Husson. 1998. "Les questions oraculaires d'Egypte: Histoire de la recherche, nouveautés, et perspectives." In *Egyptian Religion: The Last Thousand Years,* ed. W. Clarysse and H. Willems, 1055–1071. Leuven: Peeters.

Van Minnen, P. 1998. "Boorish or Bookish? Literature in Egyptian Villages in the Fayum in the Graeco-Roman Period." *Journal of Juristic Papyrology* 28: 99–184.

Vandorpe, K. 1991. "Les villages des ibis dans la toponymie tardive." *Enchoria* 18: 115–122.

——. 2005. "Agriculture, Temples, and Tax Law in Ptolemaic Egypt." *CRIPEL* 25: 165–171.

Veïsse, A.-E. 2004. *Les "révoltes égyptiennes": Recherches sur les troubles intérieurs en Egypte du règne de Ptolémée III à la conquête romaine.* Studia Hellenistica 41. Leuven: Peeters.

Widmer, G. 2002. "Pharaoh Maâ-Rê, Pharaoh Amenemhat, and Sesostris: Three Figures from Egypt's Past as Seen in Sources of the Graeco-Roman Period." In *Acts of the Seventh International Conference of Demotic Studies, Copenhagen, 23–27 August 1999,* ed. K. Ryholt, 377–393. Copenhagen: Carsten Niebuhr Institute of Near Eastern Studies.

Youtie, H. C. 1948. "The Kline of Sarapis." *Harvard Theological Review* 41: 9–29 = *Scriptiunculae,* vol. 1, 487–509. Amsterdam: Hakkert, 1973.

CHAPTER 25

THE PAPYRI
AND EARLY
CHRISTIANITY

DAVID G. MARTINEZ

AFTER Alexander the Great brought Egypt into the fold of the Macedonian empire in 332 BCE, Greek began to take root in that country as the language of business, commerce, and government as it did in other parts of his realm. This situation did not change when Egypt came under Roman control after 30 BCE. Two events, one occurring during Greek rule in Egypt and the other during Roman rule, brought about a new status for the great world language. The first was the translation of the Septuagint, the Greek version of the Hebrew Bible, produced in Egypt, starting early in the Ptolemaic dynasty (Jellicoe 1968, 29–73). The second was the advent of Christianity and the vigorous production and dissemination of Greek Christian scriptures and other sacred material in Egypt and throughout the Mediterranean world.

For Diaspora Jewish communities and Christians in Egypt and elsewhere, the Septuagint became far more than a Greek rendition of a sacred Hebrew text. It assumed a life and momentum of its own as an inspired document, and Philo characterized the legendary seventy-two Jewish scholars who produced it "not as translators, but as prophets and hierophants" (*de vita Mosis* II 40). Moreover, Augustine demanded that Jerome base his Latin version of the Old Testament on the holy translation rather than the original Hebrew.[1] Early Christian texts completed what the Septuagint had started. The world language thus became the language of sacred scripture,[2] and by and large, the same koinê Greek idiom (tempered at times by bilingual influence) in which the earliest Christians of Egypt filed their petitions with the government, jotted down their receipts of sale, and composed their private letters was the language in which they read their Bible.[3] The two parts of this chapter reflect Greek in its capacity as the language of the sacred, as well as of daily life in early Christianity.

CHRISTIAN LITERARY PAPYRI

The earliest Christian documents on papyrus are biblical and literary. In examining this material, let us first consider the most frequently read texts of this sort in Egypt, ranked here by the number of separate copies.[4]

Psalms:	209
Matthew:	50
John:	45
Genesis:	36
Exodus:	29
Acts:	25
Shepherd of Hermas:	23
Daniel:	22
Romans:	20
Luke:	19
Isaiah:	18
Hebrews:	15
I Corinthians:	14
Origen:	14
Ecclesiasticus:	13
Revelation:	13
Jeremiah:	12
Mark:	12

A list such as this has limited and largely symbolic value.[5] We of course do not know how many copies of such works remain unidentified and unpublished. In addition, it may seem strange that an elegant codex that contains almost all of Matthew's gospel and a scrap of papyrus used as an amulet with fragmentary remains of Matthew's paternoster each counts as one copy. The latter state of affairs is legitimate, however, since two such documents provide distinctive and different kinds of evidence for the use of that biblical book. With regard to the former problem, comparison of this list with a similar one using van Haelst's 1976 catalogue shows that, although the number of copies of individual works has fluctuated over thirty years, the general distribution of what were the most popular biblical and Christian documents in Egypt has not changed very much.

Criteria for Determining Christian Ascription

By a vast margin the Psalter emerges as the most frequently read text from the Greek Bible in Egypt. This and other Old Testament books were of course read by Hellenized Jews living in Egypt as well as Christians. Sometimes it is impossible to ascribe with any certainty a papyrus to one tradition or the other. Various factors, however, such as the presence of contracted sacred names (*nomina sacra*), codex format, types of script, and various conventions of writing numbers, make it likely to a greater or lesser degree that most of the copies of works from the Greek Old Testament from Egypt come from Christians rather than Jews.[6] The first two of these criteria merit more than brief mention.

The codex,[7] made of either papyrus or parchment, is the form of presentation that resembles the modern book in contrast to the older format of the roll (chapter 11), the latter consisting of sheets glued together side by side and wound around a dowel of wood, bone, or metal,[8] with the writing only on the internal side or "recto" (the side with the fibers running horizontally). The codex was produced by stacking pages on top of each other and folding them down the middle, with writing continuing from front to back. Many earlier codices are of the "single quire" type, that is, one stack of folded sheets. As the format grew more sophisticated, the refiners of this style assembled a number of smaller folded stacks, or quires, and sewed them together at the back. Whereas Christians greatly preferred the codex format to the roll, at least for the scriptures, from the earliest times their literature appears in Egypt (i.e., the second century CE), we know of very few fragments of codices datable before the fourth century whose Jewish ascription is verifiable or at least made likely on other grounds.[9] Until more evidence on early Jewish codex copies emerges, these observations allow us to affirm that, for the second and third centuries, a Greek copy of the Old Testament in codex format, absent other indicators for or against, is *likely* to be of Christian origin.

The presence of *nomina sacra* in papyrus documents affords surer evidence of Christian authorship.[10] In the early centuries CE Christian scribes began writing certain sacred words (or words to which sacred meaning was extended) in abbreviated form with an overstrike. They practiced this most frequently on about fifteen words, of which the following four were the most frequently and consistently abbreviated from early times: θεός ($\overline{\theta c}, \overline{\theta v}$), κύριος ($\overline{\kappa c}, \overline{\kappa v}$), Ἰησοῦς ($\overline{\iota c}, \overline{\iota v}$), Χριστός ($\overline{\chi c}, \overline{\chi v}$).[11]

The most vexing issues connected with this convention continue to be its ultimate origins and the related problem of why words that belong to a fairly set corpus are abbreviated and others just as theologically "charged" (such as *logos*) are not. The early investigator L. Traube (1907) sought to explain the practice as a

Hellenistic Jewish corollary to the abbreviated writing of the Tetragrammaton. Scholars of documentary Greek texts have understood it in terms of conventions of abbreviation in inscriptions and nonliterary papyri. Others have traced it to Christian scribes who began with either κύριος or θεός as a surrogate for the Tetragrammaton, extending the technique from those to other words.[12] Contesting Traube's thesis of Jewish origins, C. H. Roberts notes that among Greek papyrus and parchment copies of the scriptures, which are demonstrably Jewish, the presence of these abbreviations is negligible.[13] He describes the roster of abbreviated words, particularly with regard to the four primary terms , as embodying an "embryonic creed of the first church" (1979, 46), originating from the Christian community in Jerusalem and representing a common stock of Christian beliefs. This formulation suggests the possibility that one or more authoritative texts, which had a creedal flavor, set (or at least helped to set) the roster.[14]

Septuagint/Old Testament

Psalms is striking not only for number of copies but also for the antiquity of many of them. It is widely held that the earliest Christian biblical papyrus is the Rylands Gospel of John fragment, P52 (discussed later). One of our earliest papyri of Psalms, however, certainly rivals and possibly usurps that title: Bodl. MS. Gr. bibl. g. 5 (P),[15] a codex fragment that preserves parts of Ps. 48.20–49.3; 49.17–21 (figure 25.1a–b). The editors, Barns and Kilpatrick (1957), date the script from the end of the first century to the end of the second. The codex format at this early date makes Christian ascription likely.[16]

Various factors drive the overwhelming popularity of this book among Christian readers in Egypt. Liturgical papyri and other materials reveal the abundant use of the Psalms in corporate worship and private devotion, as well as their impact on liturgical language (Schermann 1912, 196–201). Monks in the Pachomian community were expected to learn the Psalms;[17] recitation and/or reading of them formed a vital part of the daily office of monastic groups.[18] On a theological level, the authors of the New Testament (Hurtado 2006, 28), as well as the early fathers, including those from Egypt, found in the Psalms a treasure trove of Christological prophecy, typology, and allegory.[19] Origen authored a number of exegetical works on the book, including probably his earliest commentary (about 222 CE), which reached Psalm 15 (16).[20] Didymus produced an exhaustive exposition, some of which survives in the Tura papyri (discussed later). Under Athanasius's name we have fragments of scholia to the Psalter.[21]

In addition, as Christians sought a voice for their own literature alongside (but by no means replacing) the classical standards for schools,[22] the Greek Psalter served as a worthy parallel to Homer in its antiquity, poetic power, and didactic value.[23] Of the approximately thirteen documents that use biblical material for instruction, collected by Cribiore (1996) in her catalogue of school exercises, eight come from the Psalms. For example, P.Lond.Lit. 207 preserves on its recto side

Figure 25.1a–b. Bodl. MS. Gr. bibl. g. 5 (P), recto and verso: fragment of
a codex that presents parts of Ps. 48.20–49.3; 49.17–21. Photo courtesy of
the Bodleian Library, University of Oxford.

Psalms 11.7–14.4, written in a large and elaborate capital script, which the editors date to the third/fourth century, with dots added by another hand above the letters for syllable division to the end of Ps. 13.[24] On the verso is written Isocrates' *ad Demonicum* 26–28, in a different hand of the same general date, described by Cribiore as that of a teacher, also with dots but between the letters and probably added by the same hand that wrote it.[25] The syllabic dots in both passages point to an educational context, and the fact that the Psalms text contracts κύριος, θεός, and ἄνθρωπος as *nomina sacra* strongly argues for Christian provenance. Texts such as this lend a measure of documentary confirmation to the views of the earlier Greek fathers, particularly Origen and the fourth-century Cappadocians, who encouraged Christian students to study Greek literature alongside biblical texts.[26]

In yet another respect, for Christians the Psalter held a position similar to that of Homer, that is, as an ancient poetic text of magical power. This to some extent applies to the book as a whole; however, certain Psalms, especially LXX 90 (91), had particular prestige. There are now at least twenty-five texts from Egypt that preserve all or parts of 90 (91) and have been identified either certainly or possibly as magical amulets dating from the fourth to the tenth century.[27]

Of the Greek Old Testament after Psalms, Genesis and Exodus claim the greatest number of separate copies. For example, *P. Yale* I 1 (van Haelst 1976, 12) preserves Gen. 14.5–8 on the recto and 12–15 on the verso. Its codex format and convention of writing numerals as symbols, which differs from the normal Jewish practice, makes it likely that it is from Christian rather than Jewish hands (Roberts 1979, 78). The original editor, C. Bradford Welles, dated the script to the last quarter of the first century CE and regarded it as the oldest evidence for the codex and the earliest Christian document. Most palaeographers, however, have assigned the text to the late second or early third century.[28] *P.Amh.* I 3, in addition to preserving on the recto side one of the earliest Christian private letters (discussed later), on the verso gives us possibly the oldest Greek text of Genesis 1.1–5 (Grenfell and Hunt assign the script to the late third/ early fourth century), copied in both the LXX and in the version of Aquila (van Haelst 1976, #3). Musurillo (1956, 126) identifies this text as an amulet, but reusing a letter for two different versions of exactly the same passage rather suggests an educational function (Aland 1976, #Var 35 p. 360; see figure 25.3 below).[29]

New Testament

We are immediately struck by the extent to which the survival rate of separate copies of Matthew, John, and Acts exceeds that of Pauline and other epistolary literature. The gospels, with and without Acts, were sometimes grouped in a single codex separate from the epistolary section of the NT, which was also, as we shall see, at times so grouped. The facility of the format for clustering related genres of literature surely fostered its rise to popularity.[30] One of the earliest such gospel/Acts codices, *P. Chester Beatty* I or P45 (incorporating a separately published fragment, *P.Vindob.* inv. G. 31974), comprises fragments of thirty leaves of a codex that originally contained around fifty-five leaves, dating to the third century (van Haelst 1976, #371). This manuscript probably, as another Egyptian gospel codex, Codex Washingtonianus (ibid., #331), definitely did, placed the gospels in the so-called Western order: Matthew, John, Luke, and Mark.[31] The evidence of magic further reinforces the conception of the four gospels as an authoritative and powerful textual unit. Their opening verses were considered particularly potent formulae and were employed as amulets, interlaced with Ps. 90 (discussed earlier) and other texts of power.[32]

Papyrological evidence has favored the gospel of John with early survivals, the most famous of which is P52 (Jn. 18.31–33, 37–38).[33] It was C. H. Roberts (1935) who first dated this fragment to the early part of the second century, judging it the oldest copy of any part of the NT and the earliest Christian papyrus. Although the roster of papyrologists and other scholars who agree or mostly agree with Roberts's assessment is impressive,[34] it is not unanimous. Notably E. G. Turner (1977, 100) cautioned that the late second century also presents viable palaeographic parallels, and more recently B. Nongbri (2005), in an exhaustive examination of previously offered, as well as newly adduced evidence, has made the same argument, extending the possibilities into the early third century. Indeed, early dating for P52 and implications drawn from it have sometimes proven overzealous.[35] Small and fragmentary documents make it difficult for us to form a palaeographic "big picture," always more important for dating than individual letter shapes. For texts such as this it is safer to posit a broader spread, such as "early second to early third century."[36]

Although the Pauline epistles lag behind the two best-attested gospels and Acts and even the three best-represented OT books in number of copies, they boast one of the earliest and fullest papyrus codices, *P. Chester Beatty* II, supplement (P46; van Haelst 1976, #497) (figure 25.2). The surviving eighty-six leaves, which are divided between the University of Michigan and the Chester Beatty Library (Dublin),[37] comprise nine epistles ascribed to Paul in order by size: Romans (beginning at 5.17), Hebrews,[38] 1 and 2 Corinthians, Ephesians, Galatians, Philippians, Colossians, and 1 Thessalonians. The codex is a single-quire[39] type, and judging from what we know of that format, we may determine that the original (probably of about 104 leaves) lacked all or part of 1 and 2 Timothy and Titus since the missing leaves at the end could have accommodated 2 Thessalonians but not the pastorals (Epp 2002, 495–502). Majority scholarly opinion favors an early third-century date of the script.[40] This splendid document may not, however, be the earliest papyrological evidence for literature under Paul's name. That distinction should likely go to a small fragment of a codex, *P.Ryl.* I 5 (van Haelst 1976, #534), which preserves a few verses of a book that P46 likely omits, Titus 1.11–15, 2.3–8, which some scholars date to the second century.[41] P46's incorporation of Hebrews

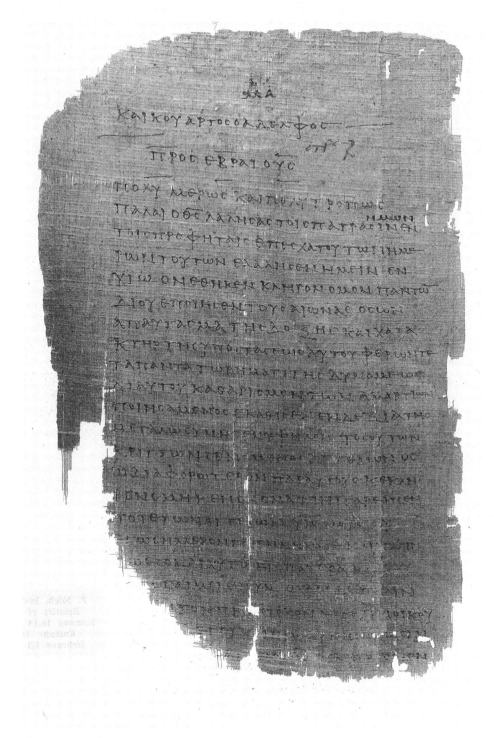

Figure 25.2. Chester Beatty Biblical Papyrus II (P46; third century); leaf 41, which comprises the last words of the epistle to the Romans (from 16.23; this manuscript transposes the doxology of 16.25–27 to the end of chapter 15) and the opening of the epistle to the Hebrews. After the end of Romans, the notation roughly calculates the length of the book as "1,000 lines" for the purpose of paying the scribe. Image reproduced by permission of the Papyrology Collection, Graduate Library, University of Michigan.

as Pauline, as well as its likely omission of the pastoral books, and this early fragment of one of those books, which may have been part of a larger collection, provide evidence for emergent attitudes toward canonicity and authorship.[42]

Biblical Papyri: Some Observations

In the two previous sections we have observed that the best-attested books of the Greek Bible among Egyptian Christians are Psalms, Matthew, John, Genesis, and Exodus. The penchant for the Fourth Gospel has generated considerable discussion on a number of fronts, especially with regard to the alleged "Gnostic" coloring of the early Egyptian church. For example, K. Aland (1967, 99–103) has argued that the popularity of John in Egypt evinces a dominant strain of Gnosis since John was the preferred gospel of Gnostics. However we may assess the influence of Gnosticism in Egypt on other grounds, the papyrological data on the gospels do not support it.[43] Even if we limit our survey to the earliest papyrus copies (between approximately the second to early fourth centuries), the difference between the number of copies of John (seventeen) and Matthew (fourteen) is not great. When our investigation extends into later antiquity and other media besides papyrus, reflected in the list that introduced this section, Matthew slightly trumps John. Thus, we cannot in any real sense speak of a favoritism toward John either in number or antiquity of copies, regardless of whether this gospel was any more popular among Gnostics than in catholic/orthodox communities.[44]

What is more striking is the preponderance of Matthew and John over Luke and Mark.[45] The perception may have been that the content of the other Synoptics was already accommodated in Matthew, and that Matthew and John, the two eyewitnesses, fully articulated the polarity of "somatic" and "spiritual" respectively, in their portrait of Jesus, to use the terms of Clement of Alexandria.[46] We may reasonably see the somatic/spiritual pattern emerging in the three dominating Old Testament books as well, with Genesis and Exodus revealing the great narratives of creation, the patriarchs, and Moses and with the Psalms providing spiritualizing and doxological reflection on these events as *Heilsgeschichte*.

Apocryphal Literature

Of the substantive remains of Apocryphal materials on papyrus (van Haelst 1976, #568–620), the following documents are among the earliest and most significant. The first published Oxyrhynchus papyrus (van Haelst 1976, #594), which preserves several logia of Jesus and dates palaeographically to the early third century, was later identified as a Greek fragment of the Gospel of Thomas, based on the 1945 discovery of a full Coptic translation among the Nag Hammadi finds. A few years later, two other third-century papyri from Oxyrhynchus were published and subsequently identified as belonging to the same work.[47] That the text of these fragments differs at points from that of the Coptic probably indicates that more than one Greek edition of the Gospel of Thomas circulated in antiquity (Cameron 1992, 535).

Of a similar date as *P.Oxy.* I 1 are the Jesus logia of *P.Lond.Christ.* 1 (*P.Egerton* 2),[48] which consist of two codex leaves and fragmentary remains of a third, preserving about ninety lines of text with an additional fragment of one of the leaves published by M. Gronewald (*P.Köln* VI 255), adding four new lines of text, and supplementing six others. Bell and Skeat, the original editors of *P.Lond.Christ.* 1, dated the hand to the mid-second century. Gronewald notes that the new Cologne fragment exhibits apostrophe between consonants, a palaeographic trait not common until the third century.[49] In content, the papyrus, in its versions of Jesus' "Search the scriptures" dialogue with the Pharisees, the cleansing of the leper, and the answer to the question about paying taxes, displays an interweaving of Johannine and synoptic accounts (Jn. 5.39, 45; Jn. 9.29 et al.; Mk. 1.40 ff and parallels; Mk. 12.13 ff and parallels; see Porter 2006, 326 f). In addition, in a lamentably fragmentary section, it preserves a miracle story "on the bank of the Jordan" involving sowing and reaping, found in none of the canonical gospels. If, as seems likely, the author knew the New Testament gospels, he probably had none before him as a written text but reproduced tracts of them from memory (Jeremias 1963).

Patristic Literature

Of the rich patristic literature that flourished from the second to the eighth century, the papyri present us with wealth in some cases and bewildering dearth in others.[50] The polarities are well illustrated by the prominent and prolific early authors who lived in Egypt. Of the five great Alexandrian fathers of the first five centuries, Clement (ca. 150–ca. 215), Origen (ca. 185–ca. 254), Athanasius (ca. 296–373), Didymus (ca. 313–398), and Cyril (d. 444), Origen and Didymus survive in appreciable quantities, mainly due to one spectacular find in 1941. A huge cache of papyri in a cave in Tura, about twelve kilometers south of Cairo, yielded more than two thousand papyrus pages, including eight codices, palaeographically dated to the sixth or seventh century and probably belonging to the nearby monastery of Saint Arsenios.[51] The Origen material preserved among the Tura codices (182 pages) includes large sections of the theological treatises *Contra Celsum, de Pascha,* and *Dialogus cum Heraclide,* as well as his homily on the "witch of Endor" episode in I Sam. (LXX I Reg.) and his commentary on Romans.[52]

The majority of the Tura papyri, however (1,118 pages), preserve works of Didymus the Blind, namely extensive portions of his exegetical treatises on Genesis, Job, Psalms, Ecclesiastes, and Zacharias, as well as smaller fragments, including a *dialogos* with a heretic, the only example of nonexegetical writing we have in this group, and a small section of his commentary on John (covering 6.3–6.33), the only piece of New Testament exegesis we have from Didymus anywhere.[53] The Psalms and Ecclesiastes commentaries are actual lectures to advanced students and thus offer us an invaluable glimpse into what might be called a university classroom of fourth-century Alexandria.[54] These commentaries richly illustrate what some Christian school texts considered earlier suggest: the integration of biblical and classical texts in the Christian school curriculum in Egypt.[55]

Aside from the Tura finds, the most notable survival of the Alexandrian theologians is fifty-two well-preserved pages of a codex from the sixth–seventh century found in El Deir (north of Hawara in the Fayyum), containing a large section (books 6–9) of Cyril's treatise *de adoratione et cultu in spiritu et veritate*, which is now spread among collections in Dublin, London, Paris, and Vienna (van Haelst 1976, #638). No papyri have yet surfaced of the works of the great Athanasius, a formidable presence in some documentary texts.[56] A few lines from Clement's *Stromata* VI 8 survive on a fragmentary papyrus in Cologne.[57]

Some of the earliest Christian authors, including those known as the Apostolic Fathers, are the most poorly represented. The papyri give us not a single fragment of Clement of Rome, Polycarp, or Papias; moreover, no copies of the two early examples of apologetic literature, the works of Justin Martyr and the Epistle to Diognetus, survive. The *Didache*, Ignatius, and Barnabas each rate a single Greek papyrus.

Conversely, one of the documents among the "Apostolic Fathers" canon boasts more copies than any other non-biblical text and more than many biblical ones: *The Shepherd of Hermas*. With the recently published Oxyrhynchus fragments (*P.Oxy.* LXIX 4705–4707) we now have twenty-three different papyrus copies of this enigmatic author from a fairly wide geographic distribution.[58] As C. H. Roberts (1979, 22) remarks, "[*The Shepherd of Hermas*] popularity in provincial Egypt may give us a better insight into the character of the churches than anything else." He says this with regard to the intense Jewish coloring of the work, which, according to him, looms large also in early Egyptian Christianity (in contrast with the Gnostic strain that some have seen as predominant). More specifically, the treatise, with its emphasis on purity of heart, which induces purity of action, and its correlating of goodness and evil with angelic and demonic beings, is reminiscent of the thought of the monastic leader Pachomius. *The Shepherd* may have furnished, if not a textbook, at least inspiration for monastic ideals (Rousseau 1985, 136–38).

The practical focus of *The Shepherd* also lends itself to an educational context; both Eusebius (*hist. eccl.* III 3.6) and Athanasius (*ep. fest.* 39) attest that *The Shepherd* was used for the instruction of catechumens (Staats 1986, 107). It would not be difficult to view the work as a kind of Christian corollary of Isocrates' *ad Demonicum*.[59] Also, whether or not one judges the work as an apocalypse, *The Shepherd* breathes the spirit of the apocalyptic throughout (Osiek 1999, 10–12). We see the affinity of Egyptian Christians for apocalyptic literature from the stature of the books of Daniel and Revelation in the papyri.[60] In addition, the first literary evidence of Christianity in the Arsinoite nome is Eusebius's account (*hist. eccles.*

VII 24) of Dionysius, bishop of Alexandria (elected 248), paying a pastoral visit to the Christians in the region in order to teach them the true meaning of Revelation and refute the false interpretation of a local bishop, that the book promised an earthly millennium of carnal pleasure.[61]

CHRISTIAN DOCUMENTARY PAPYRI

When we come to documentary evidence, a disappointment immediately confronts us: Whereas on the literary side we have several papyri whose scripts editors and other scholars have dated with a degree of confidence to the second century, there are no documentary Christian texts indisputably assignable to that early period. In fact, even for the first part of the third century, the volume of identifiably Christian nonliterary papyri is meager and at times controversial. The fact that certain "monotheistic" expressions and other types of religious language appear in both Christian and non-Christian private letters and other documents complicates the task of identification considerably.[62]

This difficulty finds ample illustration in the case of *P. Harris* 107. The editor (with reservation) and other scholars have dated the hand to the early third century, and some have judged it one of the earliest, if not the earliest, Christian private letters.[63] In it a certain Besas addresses his mother, "Heartiest greetings in God. Above all I pray to God the Father of the truth and to the Comforter, the Spirit, that they protect (διαφυλάξωσιν) you in soul, body, and spirit; for your body, health (ὑγείαν); for your spirit, happiness (εὐθυμίαν); and for your soul, eternal life (ζωὴν αἰώνιον)." Besas then instructs that his garment be sent "for the Pascha festival" (εἰ<ς> τὴν ἑορτὴν τοῦ Πάσχα). In addition to other aspects of the letter, the fact that the prayer apparently invokes the dyad of Father and Spirit (but omits any reference to the Son) has raised the possibility of Gnostic or Manichaean identity.[64] Earlier defenders of a Christian provenance, however, have argued for τῆς ἀληθείας as a Christological title based on John 14.6 ("I am the way, *the truth*, and the life").[65] The entire invocation could thus amount to a Trinitarian formula that corresponds to the human psychological triad of "soul, body, and spirit," which itself, despite the different order of the terms, recalls the Pauline blessing of I Thes. 5.23 ("May your spirit, soul, and body be kept sound and blameless"), as in other Christian papyri.[66]

More recently, Gardner, Nobbs, and Choat (2000) have reasserted the Manichaean identification of the letter, dating it late third or early fourth century and arguing from cogent parallels to its phraseology found in the recently published Manichaean Greek and Coptic papyri of the Kellis collection and in other Manichaean literature. The authors mount a strong (but to my mind not decisive) case that the letter is Manichaean rather than Christian. The date is crucial, since Manichaean provenance requires that it be late third century at the earliest. Although, as I have already mentioned, palaeographic dating must be allowed a generous spread, the most convincing parallels to the papyrus' script are documentary hands of the earlier third century rather than the third/fourth-century school hands adduced by Gardner, Nobbs, and Choat (2000).[67]

Manichaeans at Kellis and elsewhere indeed seem to have adopted "God of truth" as a kind of watchword. The phrase, however, also occurs in a well-known Psalm (LXX 30(31).6), frequently commented on and alluded to by Alexandrian exegetes and other church fathers, sometimes with specific reference via John's gospel to "Truth" as a Christological title.[68] The fact that it occurs ten times in the fourth-century liturgical compilation known as the "Prayers of Serapion" suggests that it could have had currency in other Egyptian liturgical traditions both then and earlier.[69] With regard to the letter's elaboration of the Pauline trichotomy ("body, soul, spirit," here in the order common in Egyptian Christian liturgies: "soul, body, spirit"), for which Gardner, Nobbs, and Choat (ibid.) adduce parallels from the Coptic Kellis Manichaean texts, it is also the case that similar language appears in the Serapion compilation (1 Johnson [p. 50]; 13.19 Funk). In addition, collocations such as "body, soul, and spirit," as well as $(\delta\iota\alpha)\phi\upsilon\lambda\acute{\alpha}\sigma\sigma\epsilon\iota\nu$ ("protect"), also occur in magical texts (the latter especially in the imperative as a common amuletic formula).[70]

This modest rebuttal to the evidence of Gardner, Nobbs, and Choat (ibid.) does not refute their claim, but it does at least suggest for *P. Harris* 107 and the Kellis Manichean texts that the phrases common to both could have their ultimate source in the language of liturgy and protective magic. The reference to Easter in this letter could accommodate either Christian or Manichaean provenance.[71]

Another letter, *P.Amh.* I 3 (264/282 CE; Naldini 1998, #6; figure 25.3a–b), portrays a series of complicated commercial maneuvers in which church officials, at the highest and lowest levels, play a role. The fragmentary nature, however, of the papyrus, due in part to its being trimmed down when reused for biblical passages (discussed earlier), frustrates our best attempts to discern the exact nature of their participation. The lacunae deprive us of the names of the sender or recipient. The writer (now in Rome) addresses certain parties who work with (or for) him in the Arsinoite nome and advises them on business matters that involve, among other things, buying dry goods in the Arsinoite and selling them in the capital. The moneys from these transactions are to be paid to church officials. The papyrus specifically mentions Maximus, the current bishop of Alexandria, and a lector whose name is lost. The two may constitute an ecclesiastical polarity: the bishop as the highest church official and the lector the lowest, the first stage of the clerical *cursus honorum*.[72] Involved in the transactions are also Theonas, probably Maximus's successor, and Preimeiteinos, an associate of the bishop whose clerical status (or lack thereof) is not as certain.

Figure 25.3a. *P.Amh.* I 3 (Pierpont Morgan Library Pap. G. 3) recto. A private letter dated to 264/265–282/283 CE, describing business transactions involving clergy. Above the second column of the letter in the margin is written in a late third/early fourth-century hand Hebrews 1:1. Photo courtesy of the Pierpont Morgan Library, New York.

To my knowledge, this papyrus provides our earliest attestation of Christian clergy in a dated Christian text. In its mutilated state it does not reveal whether the bishop and his associates function as mere depositories for the funds or play a more active and engaged role in the business at hand. The latter scenario, if true, should cause no surprise. We know from later papyri that bishops frequently had their roots in and moved among the affluent classes. According to land registers from the Hermopolite nome (dated to 350–375 CE), some of them owned considerable tracts of property.[73]

Moving from the realm of private to public documents, we come to two of the earliest nonliterary papyri that mention the word "Christian." *P.Oxy.* XLII 3035, an "order to arrest" (or summons; see Gagos and Sijpesteijn 1996), dated to February 28, 256, from the president of the city council, describes the wanted man as

Figure 25.3b. *P.Amh.* I 3 (Pierpont Morgan Library Pap. G. 3) verso. Genesis 1:1–5 in the versions of the Septuagint (lines 1–9) and Aquila (lines 10–16), early fourth century. The scribe who produced this passage may be the same one who produced the Hebrews passage on the recto. Photo courtesy of the Pierpont Morgan Library, New York.

"Petosorapis, son of Horos, a Christian" ($X\rho\eta\sigma\iota\alpha\nu\acute{o}\nu$, that is, $X\rho\eta\sigma<\tau>\iota\alpha\nu\acute{o}\nu$; the editor, P. Parsons, notes another example of this spelling[74]). It is not certain whether his faith is the reason for the summons or merely incidental. If the former, the papyrus could pertain to the persecution under Valerian;[75] this text, however, dates a year before that emperor's actions against believers. This is not to say there may not have been smaller persecutions by individual authorities or that Petosorapis's faith was not somehow involved. The designation, however, may be no more than an individualizing description, such as those that specify profession, which occur in directives such as these.[76] The papyrus shows incidentally that some Egyptian Christians had no problems with traditional theophoric names (Petosorapis means "given by Sarapis"; Pestman 1994, 32, 46).

Probably the earliest public document that mentions a Christian in Egypt, *P.Vindob.* inv. G 32016,[77] which dates to the early third century CE, comprises a list of nominees for liturgical office in Arsinoe, the capital of the Arsinoite nome in Middle Egypt. Each entry typically provides the name of the nominee, a second name by which he is known, his father's and grandfather's names, the district of the metropolis where he lives, and the net worth of his property (one had to own a certain amount of land to be considered for this office). Following these standard items, a different clerk adds a further descriptive phrase that one could call "other" or "miscellaneous," to give the superior officer in charge of ranking the nominees further information on which to base his decisions. About one of them, a certain Antonius Dioscorus, the first clerk records, "Antonius Dioscorus, son of Origen, Alexandrian" (the district and property designations are lost); then the second clerk adds, ἔστ(ι) Διόσκορος Χρηστιανός, "Dioscorus is a Christian." It is likely that the clerk intends this characterization as a liability rather than an advantage (van Minnen 1994, 76). Nevertheless, the evaluator of the nominees ranks Dioscorus second in qualifications for the office.[78]

At a minimum this text tells us that Christians, although periodically suffering persecution under the Roman authorities, participated in public life and local government in Egypt from an early date. Through their economic means and social position, they were competitive for public office despite a skeptical and at times hostile political atmosphere. With regard to social status, Dioscorus possesses distinct advantages. He has a Roman-style double name, with a Roman gentilicium and a Greek cognomen (a distinction possessed by no other nominee for this particular liturgy), as well as Alexandrian citizenship. These factors may have merited him (or perhaps imposed upon him, since many wished to avoid such public service) a high place in the ranking, despite a likely attempt by one of the clerks to scuttle his candidacy by marking him as a Christian (ibid.).

The four pieces here considered, some of our earliest documentary papyrological evidence for Christianity in Egypt, present a microcosm of the issues that such texts raise: the relationship of the church with the world (especially with the civil establishment), the emerging Christian clergy and spiritual elites, the increasing influence of Christian writings on daily life, and the obscure shadings between orthodoxy and heresy. The following topics explore these issues further.

Persecutions of Christians

Although earlier regimes conducted localized cases of persecution (Frend 1965, 389–398), no general edict against the faith emerged until the reign of Decius in 249.[79] In that year the emperor ordered all subjects to sacrifice to the gods and document their act with petitions or requests for state certification. Refusal could bring death, as the first attested martyrdom from the edict, that of Pope Fabian

(January 250), shows.[80] Forty-five applications for such certificates, called *libelli*, have survived on papyrus, of which thirty-four are from the town of Theadelphia. A very typical example is *P.Mich.* III 157, dated to June 17, 250 CE:[81]

> [first hand] To the officials in charge of the sacrifices, from Aurelius Sakis of the village Theoxenis, with his children Aion and Heras, temporarily residents in the village Theadelphia. We have always been constant in sacrificing to the gods, and now too, in your presence, in accordance with the regulations, we have sacrificed and poured libations and tasted the offerings, and we ask you to certify this for us below. May you continue to prosper.
>
> [second hand] We, Aurelius Serenus and Aurelius Hermas, saw you sacrificing.
>
> [first hand] The first year of the Emperor Caesar Gaius Messius Quintus Traianus Decius Pius Felix Augustus, Pauni 23.

The fact that we do not have Decius's actual edict and cannot be sure of its precise wording has led some historians to question whether it was actually a directive against Christians or a traditionalist emperor's attempt to shore up the piety of a beleaguered state (Rives 1999). Christian authors certainly believed the former,[82] and the structure of the *libelli* lends some support to that view. The formulaic phrase in these documents, "we have always been constant in sacrificing to the gods" (vel sim.), seeks to avoid any suspicion of the forbidden faith. Also, the declarations are quite meticulous in affirming that the participant performed the slaughter, libations, and sacrificial meal, the three-tiered ritual of ancient pagan sacrifice, which one may observe as early as the *Iliad* and *Odyssey*. It is also likely that similar mandates by later emperors were directed against Christians, as we are about to see.

The "order to arrest" (discussed earlier) does not provide conclusive information about hostilities against Christians under Valerian (253–260), and the same can be said for other papyri from that period (for a possible exception see Whitehorne 1977). We are on firmer footing with regard to the persecutions advanced by Diocletian and his fellow tetrarchs, sometimes called the "Great Persecution" (303–305 in the western part of the Roman Empire; 303–312 in the eastern part; Frend 1992, 673). Diocletian conducted these actions by a series of edicts,[83] the first of which apparently provided for the destruction of Christian churches and scriptures.[84] On a more social level, the first edict ordered that Christians of the upper classes lose their station, and those holding civil jobs be reduced to slavery. The "infrastructure" part of that edict finds ready illustration in *P.Oxy.* XXXIII 2673, dated to February 5, 304. In this document a lector affirms on oath to the president of the town council and his associates that the church possesses no goods whatsoever, "neither gold nor silver nor money nor clothes [vestments?] nor beasts nor slaves nor lands nor property either from grants or bequests." Thus, not only was the church itself demolished and disbanded (he calls it ἥ ποτε ἐκκλησία, "the former church"), but it had also been forced to yield all of its possessions, of which the lector claims the church has none, "excepting the bronze implements,[85] which were found and delivered to the *logistes* to be carried down to the most glorious Alexandria in accordance with what was written by our most illustrious prefect Clodius Culcianus."

We learn from the third/fourth-century Christian apologist Lactantius (*de mortibus persecutorum* 15.5[86]) that Diocletian's first edict also involved a command to sacrifice. In this case one had to sacrifice to the gods in order to gain access to the courts, a measure designed to bar Christians from the legal establishment. An early fourth-century private letter, *P.Oxy.* XXXI 2601,[87] demonstrates how an enterprising believer might evade this requirement: "Kopres to his sister Sarapias, very many greetings. Before all else, I pray for the good health of you all before the Lord God. I want you to know that we arrived on the 11th. It became known to us that those who present themselves in court are being made to sacrifice. I made power of attorney in favor of my brother." After several other lines he concludes on the verso side: "Deliver to my sister from Kopres. Amen." The word "amen" is written in cryptogram form, ϙθ, that is, the numeral 99, the numerical value of the letters of the word spelled in full ($a=1+\mu=40+\eta=8+\nu=50$). This isosephism, like the obscure χμγ, becomes part of a stock of cryptograms and symbols that increasingly appear in fourth-century or later Christian documents, frequently at the beginning and end.[88] Kopres also shows his faith by casting the words "Lord God" in abbreviated form with the overstrike, κυρί(ῳ) θ[(ε)ῷ, but he does so in a way that reveals either carelessness or ignorance of the accepted standards in literary texts.[89]

Kopres evades the sacrificial test imposed by Diocletian by composing a "deed of representation" or "power of attorney" for one he calls "my brother" (ἀποσυστατικὸν ἐποίησα τῷ ἀδελφῷ μου), that is, he authorizes him to appear in court in his place.[90] Is this "brother" a pagan friend, as the editor P. Parsons suggests, and, if so, why the designation "brother"? We must bear in mind that "brother" had a broad currency of usage, and it may have been possible to apply it to a pagan associate without being misunderstood.[91] It is also possible that "brother" could be taken literally, a real blood relative who was not a Christian and would not have had difficulty performing the ritual on Kopres's behalf. Regardless of his identity, it is clear that Kopres suffers no crisis of conscience in employing him in this manner (Judge and Pickering 1977, 53). He also seems to portray the whole affair as an annoyance rather than a major obstacle, and the fact that later in the letter he sends for his family indicates that he does not consider this present manifestation of Diocletian's hostilities as having reached the deadly proportions that came later (Parsons ad loc.).

Monasticism

Monasticism originated in Egypt.[92] Early Egyptian monastic life reveals both the ferment of prayerful contemplation and the turmoil of controversy. This polarity finds full expression in three dossiers of letters from the mid-fourth century addressed to influential monks: the archives of Paieous (330s), Papnouthios (probably early 340s), and Nepheros (mainly 350s),[93] all likely associated with the same monastic community, which had emerged from the Melitian Schism.

Melitios, bishop of Lykopolis, took issue with Peter, bishop of Alexandria, for adopting what he considered overly lenient measures for the return of those who had lapsed from the faith during a lull in the Diocletianic persecution (around 306). Mounting acrimony led to Peter's excommunicating Melitios. The official persecution increased momentum, issuing in Peter's martyrdom and Melitios's exile. When the latter eventually returned to Egypt, he founded a schismatic church and ordained clergy. Eventually the Melitian bishops could compete with their Catholic counterparts in numbers and influence, and monasteries arose that were connected with the Melitian separatists. The council of Nicaea (325) saw a reconciliation brokered between the schismatics and Peter's successor, Alexander, which recognized the legitimacy of the former's clergy; but hostilities erupted again when the more stringent Athanasius assumed the see (328). In time, because of opposition to Athanasius, the Melitians allied themselves politically with an Arian party, thereby enabling him and their other enemies to brand them, for the most part unfairly, as Arians themselves.[94]

The first of these dossiers mostly originates from or is addressed to Apa Paieous (Apa, "father"), the head (or one of the heads) of a large Melitian community, the monastery of Hathor in the Upper Cynopolite nome. In one of the letters, *P.Lond.* VI 1914, dated to 335 CE, we meet the formidable figure of Saint Athanasius and, as we would suspect, in no positive light. The writer, Kallistos, a Melitian monk or cleric, recounts his and his colleagues' sufferings at the hands of Athanasius and his circle. He begins his narrative with Isaac, the bishop of Letous, an opponent of Athanasius and apparently a Melitian himself or at least a sympathizer, who was dining at an army camp in Alexandria with Heraiscus, who was likely the Melitian bishop of Herakleopolis Magna.[95] When drunken partisans of Athanasius try to seize Isaac, he escapes with the help of sympathetic soldiers, but Athanasius's hit squad manages to assault and beat to the point of death four other "brothers" who were coming into the camp. They continue their reign of terror by intimidating and roughing up any in the area who were offering housing and refuge to the Melitian monks, including Heracleides, manager of a local "lodge" (μονή).

The harassment of the Melitian brothers was getting on successfully, but, as Kallistos continues to report, things start to unravel. First comes the heartfelt repentance of the officer in charge, the *praepositus castri*, who aided Athanasius's gang, expressed in "a report to the bishop: 'I sinned and was drunken in the night, in that I maltreated the brethren.' And he also on that day put on a love feast [ἀγάπην],[96] although he was a pagan ['Ελλην], because of the sin that he committed." In addition, Athanasius receives word that a plot to rescue one of his well-known supporters, a monk named Makarios, whom the emperor himself had arrested, has failed, resulting in the further arrest of another ally, Archelaos. One is tempted to hear a note of relish, as Kallistos remarks twice during his description, "Athanasius is getting very downhearted."[97] Any elation which he and other Melitians may feel over Athanasius' hard times is tempered by persisting difficulties of their own. Despite the *praepositus*' repentance, the brothers continue to be denied access to Heraiscus (Hauben 1981, 453).

Other letters reveal the monks and monasteries in the more characteristic light as agents and centers of intercession and healing. In *P.Lond.* VI 1926 (= Horsley 1987, 245–250), from the second of the three archives, a woman, "Valeria in Christ," addresses the monk Papnouthios: "I beg and entreat you, most valued father, to ask for me [help?] from Christ and that I may obtain healing; for by ascetics and the devout revelations are shown. For I am beset with a great disease consisting of terrible shortness of breath. For so I have believed and do believe, that if you pray for me, I will receive healing. I beseech God, I beseech also you, remember me in your holy prayer. Granted that I have not come before your feet in body, I have come to your feet in spirit."

The need for healing from spiritual ills also finds its locus in petitionary letters to monks. In *P.Lond.* VI 1917 a repentant sinner writes in Greek so fractured as to be almost incomprehensible: "To you then I write—Apa Paieou, that you may lift up your hands to our Master God in the semblance of a cross . . . that God may [erase] the bond of my sins by your most secure, most holy prayers." He continues, "A transgression from the devil has come upon me," apparently in the form of violating a covenant made between him and several monks. The writer seems further to describe his lapse as follows: "I abode, being tempted, in the vegetable garden."

Just what the sin, the covenant, and the garden were, the lacunae of the papyrus at this point and the obscurity of the language do not reveal. We may think of the writer as making a commitment (the διαθήκη?) to enter monastic life but being detained by the enticements of the world (the garden?); this, however, is only a guess. At any rate he addresses the great leader of the monastery:

> By all means therefore beloved . . . night and day entreat the Lord of all—all those who are in the Son, being in the Father, and he that is in the Father is in the Son—that he may restore me into your hands . . . And not only did I write this, but I wrote also . . . [he mentions other monks, including those with whom he had made the covenant], that they may lift up most holy hands to God with all their hearts, in the semblance of a cross, and may not cut me off . . . but . . . be compassionate and merciful, being zealous on my behalf to God. By all means then beloved, write from cell to cell [κατὰ μονήν] and to Apa Sourous and to Apa Pebe, that they also may be merciful for me and may call upon God with zeal.

Despite his poor command of Greek, he reveals some knowledge of the scriptures and sensitivity to "insider" buzz phrases and practices of the monks. In his penitent prayer, "that God may [erase] the bond of my sins," he invokes the dramatic Pauline metaphor of the *cheirographon*, totally erased (not just crossed out) by divine mercy (Col. 2.14) and monastic intercession. His ungrammatical description of the people of the Lord as "those who being in the Son are in the Father, and the one who is in the Father is in the Son" recalls Johannine passages (e.g., Jesus' description of his relationship with the Father in John 10.38 and 17.21) and may reflect the manner in which the community spoke of itself. Similarly, the convention of praying with lifted hands "in the semblance of a cross" may reveal insider knowledge of devotional practice.[98] At any rate, he feels that he has offended the entire community, and so his petition is community wide. He asks Paieou not only for his prayers, but also to circulate his petition for forgiveness and prayer "from cell to cell," invoking the combined and concentrated intercession of the entire monastic guild not only in Paieou's monastery but also in Melitian groups beyond it.[99]

The writers of these letters view the monks as the religious corollaries of the officials with whom they were accustomed to file their petitions in epistolary form, imploring them to redress their grievances. The phrase so familiar from those documents, "If you do this, I will have received justice," finds striking parallel in the words quoted earlier by the asthmatic Valeria: "If you pray for me, I will receive healing."

And so, as I hope the two parts of this chapter have demonstrated, the written word on papyrus provided many early Christians of Egypt a vital conduit for both sides of the divine-human dialogue. It bore the oracles of God in the form of the New Testament and the inspired Septuagint; it also conveyed the far more fragile human word to God, as believers addressed their petitions to the monks as the nome- and village-level brokers of divine mercy and spiritual power.

ACKNOWLEDGMENTS

I am grateful to Peter van Minnen for reading an earlier draft of this article and offering many helpful suggestions. I also thank J. Chapa and S. Charlesworth for allowing me access to their unpublished articles.

NOTES

1. *Ep.* 28.2; Kelly (1975, 217 f). As Christians increasingly claimed the LXX as their sacred text, Jews began to turn from it in favor of the Hebrew or other Greek versions (Jellicoe 1968, 74–99, esp. 74–76).

2. Homer, although a sacred text, never quite reached the level of "scripture"; the *Orphica* may have come closest (Burkert 1985, 297).

3. For Aramaic, Hebrew, and Septuagintal influence in NT Greek, see Black (1967); Moulton and Howard (1929, 413–485); for Coptic influence on Roman and Byzantine documentary papyri see Gignac (1976, 46–48). Both non-literary papyrus documents and the different books of the NT display a broad range of linguistic competence and stylistic sophistication. We should avoid two often-made but misleading generalizations: first, that the language of the NT is predominately "popular" or "vulgar" (see Wifstrand 2005, 71–77), and second, that it evinces a distinctive dialect, sometimes called "Jewish Greek" (see Horsley 1989, 5–40; 2003, 1–78).

4. The following list was compiled from the Leuven Database of Ancient Books. Included are all copies from Egypt on papyri and other media (parchment, wood tablets, ostraca, etc.). The list excludes material later than the ninth century.

5. See also the lists just for papyrus texts by Hurtado (2006, 19–24) (limited to the second and third centuries) and Llewelyn (1994, 257–259).

6. Roberts (1979, 74–78), responding to Treu (1973, 138–144). Treu called these criteria into question, as have others, notably R. Kraft; see his extensive online discussions and material at http://ccat.sas.upenn.edu/rs/rak/earlylxx/jewishpap.html.

7. Turner (1977); Roberts and Skeat (1983); Blanchard (1989); Gamble (1995, 49–66); Hurtado (2006, 43–93). Shorter treatments in Gamble (1992); Llewelyn (1994, 249–256); Metzger and Ehrman (2005, 12–14).

8. Separate sheets of papyrus which were not part of rolls, or sheets of various animal skins were also used for shorter texts, especially for Christian (and non-Christian) documents of the more "subliterary" type, such as amulets (for example, Daniel and Maltomini 1990, 53–112) and liturgical material (such as Martinez 1999) and for bits of literature for educational purposes (see Cribiore 1996). Sometimes such sheets were reused, such as the late third-century hymn to the Trinity P.Oxy. XV 1786 (van Haelst 1976, #962; Pöhlmann and West 2001, 190–194), the earliest Christian hymn with musical annotation, written on the verso of a list of grain deliveries. For a concise overview of the distinction between the formats (codex, roll, and sheet) see W. Clarysse, Leuven Database of Ancient Books, Help page, http://www.trismegistos.org/ldab/help.php, s.v. bookform.

9. P.Oxy. IV 656 (van Haelst 1976, #13) seems indisputable; more controversial are P.Oxy. VII 1007 (van Haelst 1976, #5) and P.Berol. 17213 (van Haelst 1976, #15). See Roberts 33 f., 76–78.

10. Traube (1907); Paap (1959); Roberts (1979, 26–48); Hurtado (2006, 95–134); S. Charlesworth (2006). Shorter treatments in Metzger (1981, 36 f.); Metzger and Ehrman (2005, 23 f).

11. Roberts's first group (1979, 27), with their nominative and genitive forms are given here (abbreviating was done in all grammatical cases). Roberts has placed the remaining eleven into two other groups as to the frequency and consistency of their abbreviation, and it should also be said that in the earliest period both the words abbreviated and the style of abbreviating were in flux (Bell and Skeat, 1935, 2–4; Roberts 1979, 27–28, 36–37).

12. On these views and in general, see Metzger (1981, 36–37).

13. Roberts (1979, 28–34). But see also Horsley (1983, 96; 1987, 189); R. Kraft provides discussion and images at http://ccat.sas.upenn.edu/rs/rak/lxxjewpap/kyrios.jpg.

14. For example, consider the last sentence of Peter's famous Pentecost speech, delivered in Jerusalem, in Acts 2.14–36: "Let all the house of Israel know with certainty that God has made Lord and Christ this Jesus whom you crucified." The sentence embodies in a kind

of creedal form (Bruce 1990, ad loc.) the four most frequently abbreviated words and includes two others often abbreviated ('Ἰσραήλ and σταυρός in the verb ἐσταυρώσατε). The entire Pentecost speech comprises most of the fifteen significant words.

15. See van Haelst (1976, #151); Aland (1976, #AT68).

16. Other Psalm papyri that have been dated to the second century or early third, with their van Haelst (1976) numbers, are as follows: *P.Ant.* I 7 (#179), *P.Bodm.* XXIV (#118), *P.Leipz.* inv. 170 (#224), *PSI* VIII 121 (#174). Not in van Haelst: *PSICongr.XX* 1; *P.Barc.* inv. 2 (Roca-Puig 1985, 7–16).

17. *Praecepta,* 139–140 (Boon 1932, 49 f.; cf. Veilleux 1981, vol. 2, 166); Rousseau 1985, 81n20.

18. In Pachomian literature see *Praecepta* 8, 15, 142 (Boon 1932, 15 f., 50 f.; Veilleux 1981, vol. 2, 146 f., 166). For John Cassian's description (*Inst.* II 4) of the Egyptian monastic practice of twelve psalms at vespers and twelve at nocturns, see Chadwick (1968, 58). For the office of the ψάλτης see Wipszycka (1996, 248–251).

19. See in general Devreesse (1970) and Martinez (1999, 6n14).

20. On the fragments of this work see Nautin (1977, 262–275). For Origen's later exegetical work on Psalms, see Gribomont (1992, vol. 2, 722).

21. For these and the controversy as to their authorship see ibid.

22. For Greek education in Egypt in the Hellenistic, Roman, and later periods see Cribiore (1996, 2001).

23. For Homer see Cribiore (1996, 49; 2001, 194–197, 204–205). Neither Homer in particular nor classical literature in general were ever supplanted, even as Christians began to introduce biblical material in the curriculum (Reynolds and Wilson 1991, 48–51; Henner, Förster, and Horak 1999, 51n31).

24. Van Haelst (1976, #109); Cribiore (1996, #297).

25. *P.Lond.Lit.* 255 = Cribiore (1996, #298).

26. Reynolds and Wilson (1991, 49–50). The Bodmer and Chester Beatty papyri may have come from a single library at Panopolis, possibly the property of a school where classical and Christian authors were read (Bagnall 1993, 103–104, and cited lit., esp. in n382). For similar combinations of the Psalms and classical literature, see the school notebooks published by Boyaval (1975 = Cribiore 1996, #396; IV CE) and Parsons (1970 = Cribiore 1996, #388; late III CE). The last-mentioned text also illustrates a culture of bilingualism (Greek and Coptic) in Christian education in late-antique Egypt (Cribiore 1999, 281–282; Bagnall 1993). Also in this regard see the notebook *MPER NS* IV 24 (= Cribiore 1996 #403; Henner, Förster, and Horak 1999 #42; IV/V CE).

27. La'da and Papathomas (2004, esp. 107–110); Wasserman (2006, 149 n. 41); Daniel and Maltomini (1990, 73).

28. For the controversy see Emmel (1996, 290). Conversely, Pestman (1994, 31–32) approves of Welles's dating.

29. In the upper margin of the recto, above the second column of the letter, is Hebrews 1.1 (van Haelst 1976, #536). On the reuse of papyri for school texts and the complicated issue involving the "front" and "back" of these documents, see Cribiore (1996, 60–62).

30. Gamble (1992, 1068; 1995, 63); Skeat (1997, 31).

31. If Skeat (1997) is correct that the late second-century fragments P4, P64, and P67 constitute our earliest gospel codex, it may also have displayed the Western order (p. 19; Metzger and Ehrman 2005, 53). Peter Head (2005), however, has called into question Skeat's understanding of these fragments.

32. For example, *PGMP* 19 and *BKT* 6.7.1 (= van Haelst 1976, 731; La'da and Papathomas 2004, #10).

33. *P.Ryl.* III 457 = van Haelst (1976, #462).

34. Namely F. G. Kenyon, W. Schubart, H. I. Bell, A. Deissmann, U. Wilcken, and
W. H. P. Hatch (see intro. to *P.Ryl.* III 457; Metzger and Ehrman 2005, 56).

35. Nongbri (2005, passim, esp. 30n22), and cf. Turner (1977, 3 f).

36. Other very early papyrus copies of John include *P.Oxy.* L 3523 (P90), late second
century (Llewelyn 1994, 242–248), and *Papyrus Bodmer* II (P66) (= van Haelst 1976, #426;
Metzger and Ehrman 2005, 56–57; Comfort and Barrett 2001, 376–468). For the latter, the
early third-century date assigned by the original editors is confirmed by Turner (1987, 108,
#63). Earlier dates in the second century have been argued by Hunger (1960, 12–33); Cavallo
(1967, 23); and Seider (1970, 121).

37. The Michigan leaves were published by Sanders (1935); the entire manuscript, both
Michigan and Dublin leaves, was published with an edition of plates by Kenyon (1934, 1936, 1937).

38. For the Pauline character of Hebrews and this position in the order of the epistles,
see Metzger and Ehrman (2005, 55); Hatch (1936).

39. Bonner (1934, 7–12); Metzger and Ehrman (2005, 54–55).

40. For instance, Wilcken (around 200) and Kenyon. Others date it earlier or later
(Comfort and Barrett 2001, 204–206).

41. For instance, Roberts, Bell, and Skeat (Roberts 1979, 13; Roberts and Skeat 1983,
40 f.; cf. Comfort and Barrett, 2001, 135). Others, however, prefer a date in the third century
(see van Haelst 1976; Aland 1976, #NT 32).

42. On the general point see Hurtado (2006, 35–40).

43. This point was argued by Prof. Juan Chapa in a paper he presented at the 25th
International Congress of Papyrology in Ann Arbor, Michigan, in the summer of 2007.
I have depended on Chapa's work for much of the material in this paragraph. See also his
preface to the just published John fragments, *P.Oxy.* LXXI 4803–4806.

44. This was likely not the case either in Egypt or elsewhere; see Hill (2004, esp. 148–
166, 289–293). Earlier C. H. Roberts questioned the extent of Gnostic influence in early
Egypt on a number of grounds, including that pre-fourth-century papyrus texts yield scant
evidence for the movement (1979, esp. 52, 72–73).

45. Llewelyn (1994, 260–262) also tabulates evidence that shows that these books were
the two most frequently quoted in patristic writings.

46. *Apud* Eusebius *hist. eccles.* VI 14.7. I thank Juan Chapa for this reference (see note
43 above).

47. See *P.Oxy.* IV 654, 655 = van Haelst (1976, #593, 595). For the three *P.Oxy.* Gospel
of Thomas fragments, see Lührmann (2000, 106–129). For their physical properties see
Hurtado (2006, 81–83). For other *P. Oxy.* Apocryphal fragments, see Epp 2005, 511 f.

48. Van Haelst (1976, #586); Llewelyn (2002, 99–101); Lührmann (2000, 142–153).

49. Turner (1987, 11n50, 108). There are, however, a few earlier examples, and Turner
himself has not called the second-century date of this papyrus into question (1977, 3 and
tables on 144).

50. In general see Aland and Rosenbaum (1995); Rosenbaum (1981); Treu (1974).

51. In general see Horsley (1987, 196–198); van Haelst (1976, 229 f. on #643).

52. Aland and Rosenbaum (1995, 408–413, 452–460, 467–516); van Haelst (1976,
#683—687); Horsley (1987, 196).

53. Aland and Rosenbaum (1995, 57–162); Nelson (1995, vi–vii, 203–204); cf. Horsley (1987, 196–197); van Haelst (1976, #643–647).

54. For Didymus's pedagogy and the educational context in which he worked, cf. Nelson (1995, esp. ch. 1); Horsley (1987, 197); Layton (2004, 13–35).

55. Among the Greek authors cited in these two commentaries are Aristotle, Democritus, Homer, Isocrates, Plato, Pythagoras, Solon, and Zeno. See Nelson (1995, 86–119, 187–188); Horsley (1987, 197).

56. There is, however, a graffito from the sixth–seventh century that preserves forty-one fragmentary lines of his *Epistula ad monachos* (van Haelst 1976, #625).

57. *P.Köln* VII 297 to be used with Aland and Rosenbaum (1995, 40–46, KV 9a). For another papyrus doubtfully attributed to him, see Aland and Rosenbaum (1995, 39, KV 9); van Haelst (1976, #636).

58. See Gonis's introduction to these texts; Aland and Rosenbaum (1995, 232–310, KV 29–42); van Haelst (1976, ## 655–668). The rich papyrological evidence meshes with the inclusion of *The Shepherd* in the Codex Sinaiticus and its esteem by Clement and Origen in showing how important this book was in Egypt (Staats 1986, 107).

59. One of the earliest of the Hermas papyri, *P.Mich.* II 130 = van Haelst 1976, # 657 (ed. late II, approved by Roberts 1979, 14, questioned by Aland and Rosenbaum 1995, 278n3), has features such as the use of lectional signs and the reuse of a documentary text, which may point to school use (Aland and Rosenbaum 1995, 276, 279n7).

60. As to Revelation, among the oldest are *P.IFAO* II 31 (Hagedorn 1992), late II, early III; *P. Chester Beatty* III (van Haelst 1976, #495), early III; *P.Oxy.* LXVI 4499, late III, early IV (see Parker 2000).

61. Lane Fox (1986, 265–268); Kyrtatas (1987, 175–178); van Minnen (1994, 77).

62. On this point see Epp (2005, 761–763). The earliest Christian letters are from the third and fourth centuries. Attempts to identify various second-century or second/third-century letters as Christian (Naldini 1998, #1–4) have run afoul of inconclusive evidence. On this point and for the difficulties in determining criteria for designating letters as Christian see Wipszycka (1974); Llewelyn (1992, 169–177, on *P.Oxy.* XLII 3057).

63. See van Haelst (1976, #1194); Naldini (1998, # 5).

64. For a good survey of scholarly views on the text see Winter (2000, 48–54).

65. Crouzel (1969, 138–140), who also connects the idea with Origen, but see Naldini (1998, 427).

66. Namely, another Christian letter, *P.Oxy.* VIII 1161 (IV) = Naldini (1998, #60), and a Christian amulet (Daniel and Maltomini 1990–1992, #30). On these (and the document under discussion) see Horsley (1981, 102 f).

67. For example, Seider (1967 #41, Tafel 25).

68. Didymus frag. in Pss. (Ps. 30.6) 270, 22. Also LXX Esdra 4.40; cf. Basil *adv. Eunomium* V (PG 29, 757B): "Blessed be the God of truth, who is the Father of the Truth, Christ."

69. That is, Serapion of Thmuis, a fierce opponent of the Manichaeans. The prayers, however, likely had multiple authors. For this controversial document see Johnson (1995, esp. 154 f, 159 f for "God of truth"). Johnson suggests that the phrase "may serve as a characteristic expression of an editor of the text" (155). For other liturgical and hymnic examples, see *P. Dêr Balizeh*, fol. 1, verso 14 (van Haelst 1976, #737); Romanos *cant.* 25 κβ´ 1; Ghedini (1940, 210).

70. On "soul, body, and spirit" see Naldini (1998, 427); Horsley (1981, 102 f; 1987, 38 f). For magical texts see Martinez (1991, 90 on line 36 f). On (δια)φυλάσσειν see Delatte and Derchain (1964, index s.vv.); Delgado (2001, s.vv.).

71. For Πάσχα as "Easter," cf. Lampe s.v. For the Manichaean practice of the festival, cf. Gardiner, Nobbs, and Choat (2000, 123 f). The request for the garment may be routine; it could be connected with baptismal ritual, which was practiced on Easter in the early church (see the description of the baptized as "clothed in the garment of salvation, Jesus Christ," Cyr. H. *catech.* 19.10; Lampe 1961 s.v. ἱμάτιον).

72. That is, if what we know about lectors elsewhere may be applied to Egypt; see Lampe (1961, s.v. ἀναγνώστης 2); Wipszycka (1996, 238–248); Naldini (1998, 428 f).

73. *P.Herm.Landl.*; see Horsley (1983, 156 f); Bagnall (1993, 292).

74. For a full discussion see Luijendijk (2005, 173 f.; also forthcoming 2009).

75. Healy (1905). For shorter accounts see Parsons (ad loc.); Navarra (1992).

76. Such a description, the editor, Parsons, notes, could indicate that Petosorapis "did not conceal his religion and indeed could be identified by it" by the inhabitants of his village. Luijendijk (2005, 225–227; 2009 forthcoming), however, suggests that, since the word "Christian" occupies the position we would normally expect the name of an occupation to hold in a list of this kind, it may be that the word is a type of professional designation, i.e., "Christian clergyman" (see also her discussion of Sotas the Christian [2005, 172–174]).

77. This text was published by P. J. Sijpesteijn (1980), as was an additional part of it by the same editor in 1990. For an important discussion see van Minnen (1994, 73–77).

78. In the left margin of the papyrus by each entry a different writer has written a number by each name.

79. Rives (1999); Pohlsander (1986); Frend (1965, ch. 13); more briefly, Horsley (1982, 180–185).

80. Horsley (1982, 183); Di Berardino (1992); Cross and Livingstone (1997, 594).

81. The translation is that of the editors, A. E. R. Boak and J. G. Winter. Most of the *libelli* have been collected by Knipfing (1923); of these, the present text (with, however, misreadings) is no. 35 (p. 385 f). It has also been published with a brief introduction and commentary by Pestman (1994, 236 f, no. 62).

82. For example, Cyprian of Carthage in the *Epistulae* and *de lapsis*, and the fragments of Dionysius, bishop of Alexandria; for specific references and discussion see Horsley (1982, 183–185).

83. For the scheme of the edicts, our sources for them, and further bibliography see Cross and Livingstone (1997, 483, s.v. Diocletian, and 1258, s.v. persecutions); Frend (1992, 673).

84. The text of this edict has not survived and must be reconstructed from various sources (Frend 1965, 495 f; 1992, 673; Creed 1984, xxii–xxiii, with comments on Lactant. *de mort. pers.* 13, 94).

85. Reading at line 22 ὕλην instead of πύλην, which is printed in the original edition; see Rea (1979).

86. On this text see Pestman (1994, 254).

87. Ibid., #69; Naldini (1998, #35).

88. Neither occurs in papyri before the fourth century. However, °θ has literary attestation that dates it as early as the late second century (see the editor on this text, line 34), but it is unusual in Christian letters. For χμγ, which has frustrated attempts at explanation, see especially Tjäder (1970); Horsley (1982, 177–180); and Llewelyn (1997, 156–168). Other

Christian symbols in papyrus documents include the labarum ☧; staurogram (⳨ see Llewelyn 1997, 166*n*39; Hurtado 2006, 135–154), and various forms of the Christian cross.

89. See the editor on line 5 and Turner's comment, which he cites here: "One must bear in mind that in private letters the use of a *nomen sacrum* is surely always imitative, and the reason for writing it very likely unknown to the writer—unless he is himself a reader of good written texts (NT, etc.) or a professional scribe of such." See also Roberts (1979, 27 f); Pestman (1994, 32).

90. In general, see P. Parson's introduction to this text, Taubenschlag (1955, 505–508), and the introduction to *P.Oxy.* XIV 1642, where the one given power of attorney is also called "brother."

91. The word can be a near equivalent to "colleague"; Arzt-Grabner (2002, 187).

92. See the general treatments and bibliography in Bagnall (1993, 293–303); van Minnen (1994, 78–85). See also the essays collected in part III of Wipszycka (1996, 279–403). The first papyrus to mention a monk is *P.Coll. Youtie* II 77, republished as *P.Col.* VII 171 (324 CE), in which the monk Isaac, along with a deacon Antoninos, helps a certain Aurelius Isidoros survive an assault; on this papyrus see Judge (1977; idem in Horsley 1981, 124–126, #81); Wipszycka (2001).

93. Most of the texts in the first two archives are edited in *P.Lond.* VI; the third in *P.Neph.* For details see Bagnall (1993, 308); van Minnen (1994, 79 f).

94. For a fuller account of the Melitian schism and church, see Bell in *P.Lond.* VI 38–45; more recent discussion and bibliography in Bagnall (1993, 306–309); Hauben (1998), and on doctrine and orthodoxy especially 334–346; Harmless (2004, 35, 94–95).

95. Van Minnen (2001) made this identification, on which see Hauben (2004).

96. For the love feast as possibly distinctively Melitian, see Hauben (1998, 342 f).

97. Indeed, his troubles multiplied. The same year Athanasius was summoned to Tyre to answer for his ruthless conduct against the Melitians and his insubordination, most likely in part based on his and his followers' activities described in this letter. He was stripped of his ecclesiastical position and, after an unsuccessful appeal to Constantine, exiled to Trier (Simonetti 1992, vol. 2, 855).

98. The Pachomian community also assumed this stance while reciting the paternoster (Harmless 2004, 128; I thank Nick Marinides for this reference).

99. Some of the monks he asks to pray for him are in the "Upper Country," possibly the Thebaid, the editor, Bell, conjectures (81).

BIBLIOGRAPHY

Aland, K. 1967. *Studien zur Überlieferung des Neuen Testaments und seines Textes.* Arbeiten zur neutestamentlichen Textforschung. Vol. 2. Berlin: de Gruyter.

——. 1976. *Repertorium der griechischen christlichen Papyri.* Vol. 1, *Biblische Papyri.* Berlin: de Gruyter.

——, and H.-U. Rosenbaum. 1995. *Repertorium der griechischen christlichen Papyri.* Vol. 2, *Kirchenväter-Papyri (Teil 1: Beschreibungen).* Berlin: de Gruyter.

Artz-Grabner, P. 2002. "'Brothers' and 'Sisters' in Documentary Papyri and in Early Christianity." *Rivista Biblica* 50: 185–204.

Bagnall, R. S. 1993. *Egypt in Late Antiquity.* Princeton: Princeton University Press.

Barns, J. W. B., and G. D. Kilpatrick, eds. 1957. "A New Psalms Fragment." *Proceedings of the British Academy* 43: 230–232.

Bell, H. I., and T. C. Skeat, eds. 1935. *Fragments of an Unknown Gospel and Other Early Papyri.* London: Trustees of the British Museum.

Black, M. 1967. *An Aramaic Approach to the Gospels and Acts,* 3d ed. Oxford: Clarendon Press.

Blanchard, A., ed. 1989. *Les débuts du codex: Actes de la journée d'étude.* Turnhout: Brepols.

Bonner, C. 1934. *A Papyrus Codex of the Shepherd of Hermas.* Ann Arbor: University of Michigan Press.

Boon, D. A. 1932. *Pacomiana Latina.* Louvain: Bibliothèque de la Revue d'Histoire.

Boyaval, B. 1975. "Le cahier scolaire d'Aurelios Papnouthion." *ZPE* 17: 225–235.

Bruce, F. F. 1990. *The Acts of the Apostles: The Greek Text with Introduction and Commentary,* 3d ed. Grand Rapids, Mich.: Eerdmans.

Burkert, W. 1985. *Greek Religion.* Cambridge, Mass.: Harvard University Press.

Cameron, R. 1992. "Thomas, Gospel of." In *Anchor Bible Dictionary,* ed. D. N. Freedman, vol. 6, 535–540. New York: Doubleday.

Capasso, M., R. Savorelli, R. Pintaudi, and M. Gigante. 1990. *Miscellanea Papyrologica in occasione del bicentenario dell'edizione della Charta Borgiana.* Papyrologica Florentina 19. Florence: Gonnelli.

Cavallo, G. 1967. *Richerche sulla Maiuscola Biblica.* Florence: Edizioni Gonnelli.

Chadwick, O. 1968. *John Cassian,* 2d ed. London: Cambridge University Press.

Charlesworth, S. 2006. "Consensus Standardization in the Systematic Approach to Nomina Sacra in Second- and Third-century Gospel Manuscripts." *Aegyptus* 86: 37–68.

Comfort, P. W., and D. P. Barrett, eds. 2001. *The Text of the Earliest New Testament Greek Manuscripts,* 2d ed. Wheaton, Ill.: Tyndale House.

Creed, J. L. (ed.). 1984. *Lactantius: De mortibus persecutorum.* Oxford: Clarendon Press.

Cribiore, R. 1996. *Writing, Students, and Teachers in Graeco-Roman Egypt.* American Studies in Papyrology 36. Atlanta: Scholars Press.

———. 1999. "Greek and Coptic Education in Late Antique Egypt." In *Ägypten und Nubien in Spätantiker und Christlicher Zeit,* vol. 2, 279–286. Wiesbaden: Reichert.

———. 2001. *Gymnastics of the Mind.* Princeton: Princeton University Press.

Cross, F. L., and E. A. Livingstone. 1997. *The Oxford Dictionary of the Christian Church,* 3d ed. Oxford: Oxford University Press.

Crouzel, H. 1969. "La lettre du *P.Harr.* 107 et la théologie d'Origène." *Aegyptus* 49: 138–143.

Daniel, R. W., and F. Maltomini. 1990–1992. *Supplementum Magicum,* 2 vols. Papyrologica Coloniensia XVI.1–2. Opladen: Westdeutscher Verlag.

Delatte, A., and P. Derchain. 1964. *Les intailles magiques Gréco-Égyptiennes.* Paris: Bibliothèque nationale.

Delgado, L. M. 2001. *Léxico de magia y religión en los papiros mágicos griegos.* Diccionario Griego Español, Anejo 5. Madrid: Consejo Superior de Investigaciones Cientificas.

Devresse, R. 1970. *Les anciens commentateurs grecs des Psaumes.* Vatican City: Biblioteca apostolica vaticana.

Di Berardino, A. 1992. "Fabian." In *Encyclopedia of the Early Church*, ed. A. Di Berardino and A. Walford, vol. 1, 315. New York: Oxford University Press.

———, ed., and A. Walford, trans. 1992. *Encyclopedia of the Early Church.* 2 vols. New York: Oxford University Press.

Emmel, S. 1996. "Greek Papyri in the Beinecke Library." *ZPE* 112: 289–291.

Epp, E. 2002. "Issues in the Interrelation of New Testament Textual Criticism and Canon." In *The Canon Debate*, ed. L. M. McDonald and J. A. Sanders. Peabody, Mass. Hendrickson.

———. 2005. *Perspectives on New Testament Textual Criticism.* Leiden: Brill.

Freedman, D. N., ed. 1992. *The Anchor Bible Dictionary.* New York: Doubleday.

Frend, W. H. C. 1965. *Martyrdom and Persecution in the Early Church: A Study of a Conflict from the Maccabees to Donatus.* Oxford: Blackwell.

———. 1992. "Persecutions." In *Encyclopedia of the Early Church*, ed. A. Di Berardino and A. Walford, vol. 2, 671–674. New York: Oxford University Press.

Gagos, T., and R. Bagnall, eds. 2001. *Essays and Texts in Honor of J. David Thomas.* American Studies in Papyrology 42. n.p.: American Society of Papyrologists.

Gagos, T., and P. J. Sijpesteijn. 1996. "So-called 'Orders to Arrest.'" *BASP* 33: 77–97.

Gamble, H. Y. 1992. "Codex." In *The Anchor Bible Dictionary*, ed. D. N. Freedman. Vol. 1, 1067–1068. New York: Doubleday.

———. 1995. *Books and Readers in the Early Church: A History of Early Christian Texts.* New Haven, Conn.: Yale University Press.

Gardner, I., A. Nobbs, and M. Choat. 2000. "*P. Harr.* 107: Is This Another Greek Manichaean Letter?" *ZPE* 131: 118–124.

Ghedini, G. 1940. "La lettera *PHar.* 107." *Aegyptus* 20: 209–211.

Gignac F. 1976, 1981. *A Grammar of the Greek Papyri of the Roman and Byzantine Periods.* Vols. 1 and 2. Testi e documenti per lo studio dell'antichità 55.1 and 55.2. Milan: Istituto editoriale Cisalpino–La Goliardica.

Gribomont, J. 1992. "Psalms, Book of." In *Encyclopedia of the Early Church*, ed. A. Di Berardino and A. Walford, vol. 2, 722–723. New York: Oxford University Press.

Hagedorn, D. 1992. "*P. IFAO* 31: Johannesapokalypse 1.13–20." *ZPE* 92: 243–247.

Harmless, W. 2004. *Desert Christians: An Introduction to the Literature of Early Monasticism.* Oxford: Oxford University Press.

Hatch, W. H. P. 1936. "The Position of Hebrews in the Canon of the New Testament." *Harvard Theological Review* 29: 133–151.

Hauben, H. 1981. "On the Melitians of *P. London* VI (*P.Jews*) 1914: The Problem of Papas Heraiscus." *Proceedings of the XVI International Congress of Papyrology*, ed. R. S. Bagnall, G. M. Browne, A. E. Hanson, and L. Koenen, 447–456. Chico, Calif.: Scholars Press.

———. 1998. "The Melitian Church of the Martyrs." In *Ancient History in a Modern University*, ed. T. W. Hillard, R. A. Kearsley, C. E. V. Nixon, and A. M. Nobbs. Vol. 2, 329–349. Grand Rapids, Mich.: Eerdmans.

———. 2004. "Heraiscus as Melitian Bishop of Heracleopolis Magna and the Alexandrian See." *JJP* 34: 51–70.

Head, P. 2005. "Is P4, P64 and P67 the Oldest Manuscript of the Four Gospels? A Response to T. C. Skeat." *New Testament Studies* 51: 450–457.

Healy, J. 1905. *The Valerian Persecution: A Study of the Relations between Church and State in the Third Century A.D.* Boston: Houghton, Mifflin and Company.

Henner, J., H. Förster, and U. Horak. 1999. *Christliches mit Feder und Faden: Christliches in Texten, Textilien, und Alltagsgegenständen aus Ägypten.* Nilus Bd. 3. Vienna: Österreichische V.-G.

Hill, C. E. 2004. *The Johannine Corpus in the Early Church.* Oxford: Oxford University Press.

Horsley, G. H. R., ed. 1981, 1982, 1983, 1987, 1989. *New Documents Illustrating Early Christianity,* vols. 1–4. North Ryde, NSW: Ancient History Documentary Research Centre, Macquarie University.

——. 2003. *Η ΕΛΛΗΝΙΚΗ ΤΗΣ ΚΑΙΝΗΣ ΔΙΑΘΗΚΗΣ.* Thessaloniki: Publication Department of Aristotelian University of Thessaloniki.

Hunger, H. 1960. "Zur Datierung des *Papyrus Bodmer* II (P66)." *Anzeiger der österreichischen Akademie der Wissenschaften, phil.-hist. Kl.* 4: 12–33.

Hurtado, L. 2006. *The Earliest Christian Artifacts: Manuscripts and Christian Origins.* Grand Rapids, Mich.: Eerdmans.

Jellicoe, S. 1968. *The Septuagint in Modern Study.* Oxford: Clarendon.

Jeremias, J. 1963. "An Unknown Gospel with Johannine Elements." In *New Testament Apocrypha,* ed. E. Hennecke and W. Schneemelcher and trans. R. Mcl. Wilson, 94–97. Philadelphia: Westminster.

Johnson, M. E. 1995. *The Prayers of Serapion of Thumis.* Orientalia Christiana Analecta 249. Rome: Pontificio Istituto Orientale.

Judge, E. A. 1977. "The Earliest Use of Monachos for 'Monk' (*P. Coll. Youtie 77*) and the Origins of Monasticism." *Jahrbuch für Antike und Christentum* 20: 72–89.

Judge, E. A. and S. R. Pickering. 1977. "Papyrus Documentation of Church and Community in Egypt." *Jahrbuch für Antike und Christentum* 20: 47–71.

Kelly, J. N. D. 1975. *Jerome: His Life, Writings, and Controversies.* New York: Harper & Row.

Kenyon, F. C. 1934, 1936, 1937. *The Chester Beatty Biblical Papyri,* fasc. 3.1, *Pauline Epistles and Revelation, Text;* fasc. 3, supp. 3.1, *Pauline Epistles, Text;* fasc. 3, supp. 3.2, *Pauline Epistles, Plates.* London: E. Walker.

Knipfing, J. R. 1923. "The Libelli of the Decian Persecution." *Harvard Theological Review* 16: 345–390.

Kyrtatas, D. J. 1987. *The Social Structure of Early Christian Communities.* New York: Verso.

La'da, C. A., and A. Papathomas. 2004. "A Greek Papyrus Amulet from the Duke Collection with Biblical Excerpts." *BASP* 41: 93–113.

Lampe, G. W. H. 1961. *A Patristic Greek Lexicon.* Oxford: Clarendon.

Lane Fox, R. 1986. *Pagans and Christians.* London: Penguin.

Layton, R. A. 2004. *Didymus the Blind and His Circle in Late-antique Alexandria: Virtue and Narrative in Biblical Scholarship.* Urbana: University of Illinois Press.

Llewelyn, S. R. 1992, 1994, 1997, 2002. *New Documents Illustrating Early Christianity,* vols. 6–7, North Ryde, NSW: Ancient History Documentary Research Centre, Macquarie University; vols. 8–9, Grand Rapids, Mich: Eerdmans.

Lührmann, D. 2000. *Fragmente apokryph gewordener Evangelien in griechischer und lateinischer Sprache.* Marburger Theologische Studien 59. Marburg: N. G. Elwert.

Luijendijk, A. 2005. "Fragments from Oxyrhynchus: A Case Study in Early Christian Identity." Th.D. diss., Harvard University, Cambridge, Mass.

——. 2009. *Greetings from the Lord: Early Christians in the Oxyrhynchus Papyri.* Cambridge, Mass.: Harvard University Press (forthcoming).

Martinez, D. G. 1991. *P. Michigan XVI: A Greek Love Charm from Egypt.* Atlanta: Scholars Press.

Martinez, D. G. 1999. *P. Michigan XIX: Baptized for Our Sakes: A Leather Trisagion from Egypt (P. Mich. 799)*. Stuttgart: Teubner.

Metzger, B. M. 1981. *Manuscripts of the Greek Bible: An Introduction to Greek Palaeography*. New York: Oxford University Press.

——, and B. D. Ehrman. 2005. *The Text of the New Testament: Its Transmission, Corruption, and Restoration*, 4th ed. New York: Oxford University Press.

Moulton, J. H., and W. S. Howard. 1929. *Grammar of New Testament Greek*, vol. 2. Edinburgh: T. & T. Clark.

Musurillo, H. 1956. "Early Christian Economy: A Reconsideration of P. Amherst 3 (a)." *CdÉ* 31: 124–134.

Naldini, M. 1998. *Il Cristianesimo in Egitto: Lettere private nei papiri dei secoli II–IV*, 2d ed. Fiesole, Italy: Nardini.

Nautin, P. 1977. *Origène: Sa vie et son œuvre*. Paris: Beauchesne.

Navarra, L. 1992. "Valerian." In *Encyclopedia of the Early Church*, ed. A. Di Berardino and A. Walford, vol. 2, 860. New York: Oxford University Press.

Nelson, A. B. 1995. "The Classroom of Didymus the Blind." Ph.D. diss., University of Michigan, Ann Arbor.

Nongbri, B. 2005. "The Use and Abuse of P52: Papyrological Pitfalls in the Dating of the Fourth Gospel." *Harvard Theological Review* 98: 23–48.

Osiek, C. 1999. *The Shepherd of Hermas*. Hermeneia. Minneapolis: Fortress Press.

Paap, A. H. R. E. 1959. *Nomina Sacra in the Greek Papyri of the First Five Centuries* AD. Papyrologica Lugduno-Batava VIII. Leiden: Brill.

Parker, D. C. 2000. "A New Oxyrhynchus Papyrus of Revelation: P115 (*P. Oxy.* 4499)." *New Testament Studies* 46: 159–174.

Parsons, P. J. 1970. "A School-Book from the Sayce Collection." *ZPE* 6: 133–149.

Pestman, P. W. 1994. *The New Papyrological Primer*, 2d rev. ed. Leiden: Brill.

Pintaudi, R., ed. 1980. *Miscellanea Papyrologica*. Papyrologica Florentina 7. Florence: Gonnelli.

Pöhlmann, E., and M. West. 2001. *Documents of Ancient Greek Music: The Extant Melodies and Fragments Edited and Transcribed with Commentary*. Oxford: Clarendon.

Pohlsander, H. A. 1986. "The Religious Policy of Decius." *Aufstieg und Niedergang der römischen Welt: Geschichte und Kultur Roms im Spiegel der neueren Forschung*, vol. 2, 16.3: 1826–1842. Berlin: de Gruyter.

Porter, S. E. 2006. "Textual Criticism in the Light of Diverse Textual Evidence for the Greek New Testament: An Expanded Proposal." In *New Testament Manuscripts*, ed. T. J. Kraus and T. Nicklas, 305–337. Leiden: Brill.

Rea, J. 1979. "*P. Oxy.* XXXIII 2673.22: ΠΥΛΗΝ to 'ΥΛΗΝ!" *ZPE* 35: 128.

Reynolds, L. D., and N. G. Wilson. 1991. *Scribes and Scholars: A Guide to the Transmission of Greek and Latin Literature*, 3rd ed. Oxford: Clarendon Press.

Rives, J. B. 1999. "The Decree of Decius and the Religion of Empire." *JRS* 89: 135–154.

Roberts, C. H., ed. 1935. *An Unpublished Fragment of the Fourth Gospel in the John Rylands Library*. Manchester: Manchester University Press.

——. 1979. *Manuscript, Society, and Belief in Early Christian Egypt*. Schweich Lectures of the British Academy, 1977. London.

——, and T. C. Skeat. 1983. *The Birth of the Codex*. London: Published for the British Academy by the Oxford University Press.

Roca-Puig, R. 1985. *Dos Pergamins Bíblics*. Barcelona: Graphos.

Rosenbaum, H.-U. 1981. "Patristik und Papyrologie." In *Proceedings of the XVI International Congress of Papyrology*, ed. R. S. Bagnall, G. M. Browne, A. E. Hanson, and L. Koenen, 633–642. Chico, Calif.: Scholars Press.

Rousseau, P. 1985. *Pachomius: The Making of a Community in Fourth-century Egypt*. Berkeley: University of California Press.

Sanders, H. A. 1935. *A Third-century Papyrus Codex of the Epistles of St. Paul*. Ann Arbor: University of Michigan Press.

Schermann, T. 1912. *Ägyptische Abendmahlsliturgien des erstens Jahrtausends*. Studien zur Geschichte und Kultur des Altertums 6. Paderborn.

Seider, R. 1967–1990. *Paläographie der griechischen Papyri*, vols. 1–3. Stuttgart: Hiersemann.

Sijpesteijn, P. J. 1980. "List of Nominations to Liturgies." In *Miscellanea Papyrologica*, ed. R. Pintaudi, 341–347. Papyrologica Florentina 7. Florence: Gonnelli.

———. 1990. "A New Part of *P. Vindob*. G 32016: List of Nominations to Liturgies." In *Miscellanea Papyrologica in occasione del bicentenario dell'edizione della Charta Borgiana*, ed. M. Capasso et al., 503–506. Papyrologica Florentina 19. Florence: Gonnelli.

Simonetti, M. 1992. "Tyre: Councils." In *Encyclopedia of the Early Church*, ed. A. Di Berardino and trans. A. Walford, vol. 2, 855. New York: Oxford University Press.

Skeat, T. C. 1997. "The Oldest Manuscript of the Four Gospels?" *New Testament Studies* 43: 1–34.

Staats, R. 1986. "Hermas." *Theologische Realenzyklopädie* 15: 100–108.

Taubenschlag, R. 1955. *The Law of Greco-Roman Egypt in the Light of the Papyri, 332* B.C.–*640* A.D., 2d ed. Warsaw: Pañstwowe Wydawnictwo Naukowe.

Tjäder, J.-O. 1970. "Christ, Our Lord, Born of the Virgin Mary." *Eranos* 68: 148–190.

Traube, L. 1907. *Nomina Sacra*. Munich.

Treu, K. 1973. "Die Bedeutung des Griechischen für die Juden im römischen Reich." *Kairos* 15: 123–144.

———. 1974. "Papyri und Patristik." *Kairos* 16: 97–114.

Turner, E. G. 1977. *The Typology of the Early Codex*. Philadelphia: University of Pennsylvania Press.

———. 1987. *Greek Manuscripts of the Ancient World*, 2d ed., ed. P. J. Parsons. London: University of London, Institute of Classical Studies, Bulletin Supplement 46.

Van Haelst, J. 1976. *Catalogue des papyrus littéraires juifs et chrétiens*. Paris: Publications de la Sorbonne.

Van Minnen, P. 1994. "The Roots of Egyptian Christianity." *APF* 40: 71–85.

———. 2001. "*P. Harrauer* 48 and the Problem of Papas Heraiscus in *P. Lond* VI 1914." *Tyche* 16: 103–105.

Veilleux, A., trans. 1980–1982. *Pachomian Koinonia*. 3 vols. Kalamazoo, Mich.: Cistercian Publications.

Wasserman, T. 2006. "P78 (P. Oxy. XXXIV 2684): The Epistle of Jude on an Amulet?" In *New Testament Manuscripts*, ed. T. J. Kraus and Tobias Nicklas. Leiden: Brill.

Whitehorne, J. E. G. 1977. "*P. Oxy*. XLIII 3119: A Document of Valerian's Persecution?" *ZPE* 24: 187–196.

Wifstrand, A. 2005. *Epochs and Styles: Selected Writings on the New Testament, Greek Language, and Greek Culture in the Post-classical Era*. Wissenschaftliche Untersuchungen zum Neuen Testament 179. Tübingen: Mohr Siebeck.

Winter, F. 2000. "Frühes Christentum und Gnosis in Ägypten." *Protokolle zur Bibel* 9: 47–70.

Wipszycka, E. 1974. "Remarques sur les lettres priveés chrétiennes des iie–ive siècles (à propos d'un livre de M. Naldini)." *JJP* 18: 203–221.

——. 1996. *Études sur le christianisme dans l'Égypte de l'antiquité tardive*. Studia Ephemeridis Augustinianum 52. Rome: Institutum Patristicum Augustinianum.

——. 2001. "*P.Coll.Youtie 77* = *P.Col.* VII 171 Revisited." In *Essays and Texts in Honor of J. David Thomas*, ed. T. Gagos and R. S. Bagnall, 45–50. American Studies in Papyrology 42. n.p: American Society of Papyrologists.

CHAPTER 26

MANICHAEISM AND GNOSTICISM IN THE PAPYRI

CORNELIA RÖMER

PAPYROLOGICAL finds have enriched our knowledge not only of early Christianity (chapter 25) but also of some religions outside the Christian church. The rediscovery, editing, and translation of the holy books of these religions fifteen hundred years or so after they had to be hidden from the eyes of government and church officials have aroused wide scholarly interest and even encouraged or generated contemporary religious movements or currents, both inside and outside Christianity.

With Constantine's adoption of Christianity in 312 CE and its acquisition of official status after he completed his domination of the Roman Empire in 324, the church began a long process through which imperially sanctioned councils not only determined what constituted Christian orthodoxy and what was heretical but could use state power against those deemed heretics. A variety of other religious movements that had flourished in Egypt and elsewhere around the Mediterranean Sea in the first three centuries CE, many still or newly popular in the fourth century, came to be considered heretical. Their adherents were persecuted, their books were sometimes burned, and it is only by chance that we have any texts or artifacts remaining from those groups, whose members would in many cases have called themselves Christians. For a long time, our knowledge of other nonpolytheistic religions and religious groups besides Christianity and Judaism derived from the writings of the church fathers, whose views were naturally partisan. Epiphanius, who was bishop of Salamis on Cyprus in the fourth century, wrote three books titled *Panarion*—which means "medicine chest"—in which he lists about eighty heretical groups from Adam down to his own time and warns right-thinking Christians about the immoral practices and aberrant beliefs of Valentinians, Bardesanians, and Manichaeans, to name just a few. His "medicine chest" was supposed to contain effective remedies against the dangers of those heretical beliefs. Some names of the leaders of these groups are still on the index of the Vatican today even though their beliefs have been consigned to history.

What made these beliefs different from the Christian creed was more than the different way in which they understood the relationship of humankind to the one God or how the three parts of the Holy Trinity can be understood in a monotheistic system as a single God. Questions like these had troubled the early Christian church for quite some time; the church fathers' answers attempted to explain the secrets of the Holy Trinity by using the means and thought patterns of Greek philosophy. Fights over the relationship of Father and Son culminated in the struggle over the teachings of Arius, who was deacon in Alexandria in the early fourth century CE. He preached that Christ could not be equal to God but had to be a creation; otherwise, the One God would have suffered because he created his son from himself.

The Gnostics and other "heretical" groups whom Epiphanius and other church fathers talk about are different. Their concepts of God and salvation were less a result of sophisticated philosophical strategies for explaining the world and God than a mixture of various traditions, including Jewish, Egyptian, and Persian ones, which were believed to make salvation possible. These "heretics" may have believed in Christ as the savior of all humanity, but they could not believe in the uniqueness of Christ. Even though many of them claimed Christ as their savior, they still had a different understanding of what led to salvation. The apostle Paul had stressed in his letter to the Romans (10, 9–13) that it was faith that allowed people to receive the blessing of salvation. Gnostics believed that it was gnosis, or recognition of our situation in the world. In their view, the human condition was not embedded in the wonderful creation of the One God, which is what "real" Christians believed. For them, creation was both alien and hostile to the human race. They rejected the Old Testament and its God. Gnostics saw themselves and the entire world as an entity of two parts, of which one, the body, was dark and mortal, and the other, which contained the light, consisted of sparks from the realm of light from which people and all organic material come and must finally return. Every human being was thus involved in the final task of the huge machinery to recreate a status in which the dark parts on the one side and the light parts on the other would one day exist in two completely different entities and thus recreate the beginning of the world before the deadly mixture came to be in people and all organic beings. In this scenario, Christ was only one of the messengers sent from the realm of light to save humanity (but not creation) and to teach it about the final aim of the separation of light and darkness, not only the salvation of each individual.

Figure 26.1. Mani, drawing by F. C. Burkitt based on a
wall fresco found at Khotscho near Turfan, from F. C.
Burkitt, *The Religion of the Manichees (1925)*.

The basic structure of these beliefs, which united the different gnostic groups,
led to a wide variety of practical approaches on how to achieve the final aim. The
church fathers, such as Epiphanius in his *Panarion* and others, were appalled in
particular by the Gnostics' condemnation of creation. But the fact that much of
their teaching was in many respects not so far from Christian dogma as the church
fathers wanted their followers to believe must also have disturbed the advocates of
the "real" Christian church. In some of these Gnostic systems, Christ was the main
savior figure; in others it was the forefathers of the Old Testament who guaranteed
salvation; in Manichaeism it was the new Messenger of Light, the apostle Mani,
who, coming after Christ, would finally give the right revelation to the people and
excel Christ in doing so (figure 26.1).

As in Christianity, the ideas of these religious groups, too, show the deep
uncertainty about the human situation in the world, which was characteristic
around the turn of the millennium, and reflect attempts to give the world a new

structure so as to envisage new strategies for salvation. It seems that the whole Mediterranean basin was at that time convinced that this world was not the best but that a new, different, and better world would come, whether on the Last Day, as the Christians believed, or at the end of this world, when light and darkness would be separated forever. The role of creation as such was important to both views of the world; for Christians, creation was God's gift to human beings to use for their benefit during their mortal lives; for the Gnostics, creation was the machinery that enabled people to overcome the world in its present state because only through the mixture of light and darkness in the world and in themselves would they be able to separate the two by making the mind triumph over the body.

This chapter deals with religious groups such as these as they existed in Egypt in the Roman and late antique periods. (Traditional Egyptian religion, still vital in the early centuries of the Christian era, is discussed in chapter 24.)

Papyrology has played a decisive role in our understanding of the religious movements of the first centuries CE in Egypt and elsewhere in the Mediterranean. Because of the discoveries of papyri, we have had a chance not only to look into the original writings of some of these "heretical" groups and see them functioning in their social contexts but also to learn from private letters how their followers behaved in their proper religious and social environment. Papyri and parchments that contain both the literary texts in which these groups believed and a variety of documents allow us to create a new picture of the "heretics" and their beliefs beyond that offered by Epiphanius and his *Panarion*.

The Gnostic Writings from Nag Hammadi, Oxyrhynchus, and the Area of Panopolis

In late 1945 an Egyptian farmer found a large jar that had been abandoned near a cliff close to his village. The name of the village was Nag Hammadi, situated on the left bank of the river Nile, somewhat south of Abydos, at the point where the river bends toward the east at an angle of 90 degrees. The jar contained thirteen ancient books, manufactured from papyrus and covered by leather bindings that were still intact (figure 26.2). The veracity of this account of the discovery of the Nag Hammadi Codices depends entirely on what the finder of the jar told the police and scholars; it is up to us to decide how much of it we want to believe.

The thirteen codices arrived on the Cairo antiquities market, and all but one, the Codex Jung, which was first purchased by the Zurich-based foundation of the

Figure 26.2. The Nag Hammadi Codices in their original covers.

famous psychoanalyst, were incorporated into the holdings of the Coptic Museum in Cairo. The Codex Jung has in the meantime returned to Cairo as well.

The codices of this find are all written in the Coptic language. Dated documents that were torn and recycled to strengthen the leather bindings of the books show that the codices were bound and most likely copied some time after the middle of the fourth century CE. The texts themselves are older, although how much older is difficult to ascertain; there is, however, no doubt that they were originally written in Greek and were translated into Coptic at some point in the later third or early fourth century CE. Even more difficult to establish is when they were first created in Greek, but it is unlikely that any of them (apart from a fragment of Plato's *Republic*) goes back beyond the first century CE.

Why did these books end up in a jar near a cliff? The explanation of this riddle might, it seems, be connected to their content. Most of the writings, fifty-one treatises altogether, some of which are in several different versions, are Gnostic in the sense described earlier. The assumption is that these books were once part of a library for which orthodox Christians were searching and that they were therefore hidden from the searchers. This is especially likely because some of the papyrus pieces that reinforce the bindings clearly come from a monastery. The fact that the famous monastery of Pachomius was situated in the village of Chenoboskion, not far from Nag Hammadi, has made this idea even more enticing to many scholars. Were these books once owned by the monks of the earliest monastery in Egypt, founded by Pachomius in 325? This idea, which has attracted both positive and negative reactions from scholars, can neither be proved nor refuted. Pachomius (and probably most of his followers) spoke Coptic, but we know from his biography that Greek-speaking men from Alexandria joined the community in Upper

Egypt. Pachomius is said to have learned Greek himself but expected the new-comers to learn Coptic (*Vita* in Greek, 361). The Greek texts may have been brought upriver by those who wanted to join and been translated for use in the monastery. Against this assumption is the fact that the Sahidic dialect in which these texts are written is not uniform, which seems to indicate that the translation was done in different places. The question remains whether the monks of a monastery would have been open minded enough to keep these texts in their library—or, rather, sophisticated enough to appreciate the codices' contents. When we look at catalogues of monastic libraries as they are preserved in papyri from late antiquity (Otranto 2000), we find that these lists contain only volumes of the Old and New Testaments, legends of saints, and writings of the church fathers but no works whose titles might reveal heretical content. But those lists all come from the fifth or sixth centuries, when the uniformity of the Christian creed had been ordained and sealed, and were compiled for official use; they may have omitted titles not considered appropriate for reading by adherents of the orthodox beliefs of the official Christian church. It is more likely, however, that those later libraries had been cleansed of everything not orthodox (the "heretical" volumes having been removed to caches outside the monasteries, as may have happened in the case of the Nag Hammadi Codices). The question of the ownership of the Nag Hammadi Codices thus remains open.

Whoever collected these books must have had an interest in the explanation of the world as the Gnostics saw it. He must also have been interested in secret writings, like those so-called Hermetic texts in which the god Hermes Trismegistus explains the world (Codex VI 6, 7). The fact that a (bad) Coptic translation of a small part of Plato's *Republic* (588b–589b) also fills several pages of one of the codices makes their owner still more interesting to us (Codex VI 5).

The *Apocryphon of John* occupies a prominent place among the other treatises. It appears in three different versions in the codices of Nag Hammadi (Codex II, 1; III, 1; IV, 1; figure 26.3). A fifth-century Coptic codex housed in the papyrus collection in Berlin, which was known long before the Nag Hammadi library was found (Codex 8205), also contains a version of this treatise. It must have been very popular in Gnostic circles; Irenaeus, the bishop of Lyon, probably knew of this text when he composed his antiheretical book, *Contra Haereses*, in 185 CE.

According to its title, the *Apocryphon of John* presents itself as a secret revela-tion of John, the son of Zebedee, who meets the resurrected Christ far away from all human dwellings in the desert. This setting for a secret encounter has numerous precedents in Jewish revelation literature. What Christ tells John is a mythological narrative about the creation, the Fall, and the salvation of humankind. He explains the existence of evil in the world and reveals a way in which people can escape this unworthy condition, which came about through the mixture of light and darkness. Much of the content is phrased in the vocabulary of Greek philosophy. God is perfect and has no connection to the evil world. "He is the invisible Spirit; it is not

Figure 26.3. Nag Hammadi Codex II, 28–29, *Apocryphon of John*.

right to think about him as a god or something similar. For he is more than a god, since there is no one above him, nor does anyone lord it over him. He exists in nothing inferior, for everything exists in him" (Codex II, 1–3; *NHLE* 100). From this perfect entity emanate Christ and Sophia, who encourage humans to return to the original condition, which existed before light and darkness were mixed. The female entity, Sophia, plays an important role, as do female entities in general in Gnostic systems. Evil comes into the world when Sophia disobeys God and brings forth the monster Yaldabaoth, who—as himself a mixture of the light particles inherited from his mother and earthly parts of darkness—creates the world. From here, the struggle between light and darkness begins, which is the condition of humankind, according to all Gnostic systems. Finally, Christ is sent to save humanity by reminding people of their heavenly origin. Christ speaks: "Arise and remember that it is you who hearkened and follow your root, which is I, the merciful one, and guard yourself against the angels of poverty and the demons of chaos and all those who ensnare you, and beware of the deep sleep and the enclosure of the inside of Hades" (Codex II 1, 31; *NHLE* 116). He then gives orders to John to write down everything he has just said and to give these words to his (John's) companions.

Of a different flavor is the Gospel of Thomas, presented only once in the codices from Nag Hammadi (Codex II, 2). This gospel is a collection of 114 sayings of Jesus, of which many find more elaborate parallels in the Gospels of Matthew, Mark, and Luke. The discussion of the origins of the New Testament gospels and a possible source, "Q," which may have contained a more primitive and no longer extant version of them was enormously stimulated by this new text. Some of those sayings that do not parallel those in the New Testament have a Gnostic character. Saying 83 runs as follows: "The images are manifest to man, but the light in them remains concealed in the image of the light of the Father. He will become manifest, but his image will remain concealed by his light" (Codex II, 2, 47; *NHLE* 127).

The sayings are introduced as "the secret sayings which the living Jesus spoke and which Didymus Judas Thomas wrote down" (*NHLE* 118). They are thus presented as belonging to an esoteric circle. But no particular Gnostic group can be identified in which these sayings might have been compiled. The Manichaeans' interest in this gospel must have been considerable, since one of their first missionaries was called Thomas, and the concept of a heavenly "twin" (*didymos* is the Greek word for "twin") was popular with the Manichaeans as well (mentioned later).

The Gospel of Thomas—like the other texts in the Nag Hammadi Codices— was clearly translated from the original Greek into Coptic. In this case, we also have parts of the Greek sayings preserved in papyri that do not belong to the Nag Hammadi find. Three papyri found at Oxyrhynchus contain twenty-one of Jesus's sayings, which are the same as those from Nag Hammadi. These papyri date to the beginning or the middle of the third century CE and are thus about one century older than the Nag Hammadi manuscripts. When British papyrologists B. P. Grenfell and A. S. Hunt first published *P.Oxy.* 1 with eight *logia Iesu* (sayings of Jesus) in 1897, they did not have the complete Coptic text with its title from Nag Hammadi. Grenfell and Hunt's publication sparked a vivid discussion, for they claimed that these sayings are extracts from a collection of Christ's sayings, not passages from a narrative gospel (which the Nag Hammadi Codex confirms); that the sayings are not heretical (which is a matter of the reader's viewpoint); that they are independent of the four Gospels in their present shape (which the codex confirms); and that they may go back to the first century CE (which may be correct, but the Nag Hammadi codices give no further help in answering this question).

For papyrology, the discovery of the *logia Iesu* at Oxyrhynchus and their publication in 1897 is a decisive historical date. This sensational find made papyrology and its heroes, Grenfell and Hunt, popular not only in Britain but also worldwide and enabled them to continue their work in Oxyrhynchus in the hope of finding more material that would bring people closer to the secrets of the New Testament texts. This hope was fulfilled some years later, when two further fragments with *logia* were found and published in 1904 in volume four of *The Oxyrhynchus Papyri*. That these texts were indeed "heretical" in the eyes of the Christian church from the fourth century on became manifest only when the complete Coptic version was found at Nag Hammadi.

While the background of the Nag Hammadi find is still obscure, the findspot of the *logia,* the town of Oxyrhynchus in Middle Egypt, is one of the best-known towns of Roman Egypt (see chapter 2). Not surprisingly, in this lively environment all manner of different Christian groups would develop. As early as the end of the third century, Oxyrhynchus had at least two churches (*P.Oxy.* I 43v). Besides the *logia Iesu* from the Gospel of Thomas, some additional theological fragments were excavated here by Grenfell and Hunt, which surely once belonged to a member of a Christian community in which gnosis, not faith, was believed to lead to salvation. Interestingly, *P.Oxy.* I 4, which has only twenty-nine lines, some of which are very fragmentary, contains a theological treatise in Greek about the "upper and the lower soul" and mentions the "prison of the body," thus revealing its Gnostic background. *P.Oxy.* I 4 is dated to the late third or early fourth century.

Of the same date is *P.Oxy.* VIII 1081, which—like the *logia Iesu*—turned out to be a Greek version of a complete Coptic Gnostic text called the *Sophia Jesu Christi,* preserved in Nag Hammadi Codex III and in the great Berlin Codex 8502 (mentioned earlier). The main topic of the *Sophia Jesu Christi* is the existence of an invisible, supercelestial region inhabited by the Father and to which those will return who know the Father in pure knowledge.

The Berlin Codex, which dates to the fifth century CE, was most likely found somewhere around Panopolis in Upper Egypt. Thus, we have for the *Sophia Jesu Christi* the same situation as for the *logia Jesu:* one textual witness in Greek, dating to about the third century or earlier and coming from the highly Hellenized city of Oxyrhynchus, with its close connections to Alexandria, and two later Coptic versions from the fourth and fifth centuries that come from Upper Egypt. Taking into consideration the ambiguity of archaeological finds, which depend on a number of factors, a pattern seems to repeat itself here in showing how the shift from Greek to Coptic developed first in the Hellenized centers of the north and spread to the more rural Egyptian regions farther south. The same situation exists with regard to the *Gospel according to Mary,* first discovered in a small Greek fragment of the early third century excavated at Oxyrhynchus (*P.Ryl.* III 463) and found in its Coptic translation in Berlin Codex 8502.

The Greek versions, which undoubtedly were the original ones, circulated in places like Oxyrhynchus (and certainly Alexandria) as late as the third century; afterward, the Coptic versions spread and prevailed. Both the Codex Askevianus (of the late fourth century), which contains the difficult text of the *Pistis Sophia,* and the Codex Brucianus (of the same date), with the *Books of Jeû,* two great Gnostic Coptic codices now in the British Library and the Bodleian Library, fit the same pattern.

The transition from Greek to Coptic in the Gnostic writings is paralleled by a change in the relative importance of the two languages in Christian literature. There is no apparent difference in this development between the Christian and the "heretical" writings. The earliest Coptic manuscripts of the New Testament date to the late third or early fourth centuries CE, the period when the Gnostic writings, too, were translated into the indigenous tongue.

The close parallels between the holy texts of these competing and conflicting groups are also apparent in the way their books were made. Christians and Gnostics copied their books into codices, not onto rolls. As a book form, the roll was gradually abandoned after the second century CE; there is not a single New Testament or Gnostic text written on a new roll. Hand in hand with the preference for this recently introduced book format goes the custom of abbreviating the so-called *nomina sacra* in certain ways, such as taking the first and last letters of the names of Jesus or God or the word for "spirit" or "master" and indicating the abbreviation by putting a line over the remaining letters. No difference in the copyists' style of writing can be detected. The scribes were most likely not trained for only one community but worked for whoever employed them. Pagan texts of the time also do not show different styles of writing. At that time, scribes of pagan texts did not use the abbreviated *nomina sacra*. Only Christians and heretics shared common features in their holy books.

MANICHAEISM IN EGYPT

From the fourth century on, the most successful religion apart from Christianity was Manichaeism, and it remained so for several centuries. Fortunately, we are better informed about the religion of Mani than about any other Gnostic system. Our knowledge is based to a large extent on papyrological material that was excavated in Egypt. Yet, in this case, the finds from Egypt are rivaled by those made in the oasis of Turfan in northern China, where climatic conditions have preserved Manichaean texts and wall paintings that complete the picture of what was once a world religion in the true sense. Languages in which Manichaean writings are found range from Greek, Latin, and Coptic to Chinese, Middle Persian, and Uigur, a Turkic language spoken in the region of the Northern Silk Road. When Christianity became the official religion around the Mediterranean, Mani's followers were persecuted. His religion traveled with the merchants along the Silk Road, and it eventually became the state religion in the Uigur Empire, where it flourished until the mid-ninth century. But Mani also had numerous followers in Italy and North Africa, the most prominent of whom was Augustine, who for eight years found in this Gnostic system the answer to the question of how evil comes into the world.

The singularly wide diffusion of this religious system meant that Manichaeans encountered the myths and beliefs of many contemporary cultures, which had an impact on the character of Manichaeism in different places: In Europe its followers gave their creed a consciously Christian flavor, and in the East it had certain Buddhist characteristics. The very versatility of Mani's religion added to its success. The Manichaean writings found in Egypt, written on papyrus or parchment, all have very close affinities to Christianity.

From its beginning, Manichaeism played an important role in the study of the history of religions. Augustine wrote fervent invectives against his former coreligionists. In his *Panarion,* Epiphanius dedicated an extensive essay to this dangerous enemy of Christianity. The finds at Turfan, where at the beginning of the twentieth century German, British, and French archaeologists excavated Manichaean monasteries, stimulated new interest. But it was the discoveries in Egypt that made the study of Manichaeism a lively field of scholarly research during the second half of the twentieth century and beyond. New finds continue to come to light in the oases of the western desert and elsewhere.

The Cologne Mani Codex

Scholars had long seen Manichaeism as a religion dependent mostly on Zoroastrian traditions, but the discovery of a small parchment book that now belongs to the papyrus collection of Cologne University in Germany provided a new basis for the understanding of Mani's cultural and religious background. The Cologne Mani Codex (figure 26.4) is unique in not only its content but also its extraordinary size. It measures only 3.8 × 4.5 centimeters, and each page contains twenty-three lines written in a careful bookhand in which the letters do not exceed a height of more than one millimeter. Even though the codex may have shrunk from its original size (the difference in size cannot be very great), it is still remarkable that scribes were able to put such tiny, neat letters onto the parchment. They were probably well trained for small writing, as were the cutters of gems in antiquity, who had to produce miniature figures on very small surfaces. They may also have used small bottles filled with water, which served as magnifying glasses. The date of this miniature book is still debated, but on palaeographical and historical grounds, the fifth century CE seems more likely than the eighth or even ninth century. The place where the codex was found in Egypt is not certain either, but Upper Egypt and the region around Lykopolis seem most likely.

The 192 pages of the codex, some of which are very fragmentary, contain the biography of the founder of Manichaeism. The text is written in Greek, a translation apparently made in Egypt from the original Aramaic. The style of composition adds to the uniqueness of this example of a biography from late antiquity. Through excerpts from writings by his first disciples, we follow Mani's life. Each citation is headed by the name of the disciple—some of them known also from other

Figure 26.4. The Cologne Mani Codex, pp. 58 and 63 (enlarged).

Manichaean sources. As eyewitnesses (or at least claiming to be), the disciples report both the events that involve their master and his very words. The authenticity that this procedure asserts corresponds to Mani's claim of the superiority of his religion, which was based on the importance he gave to the recording of everything he said and did. For instance, Mani said, "Indeed, all the (apostles), my brethren who came prior to me: (they did not write) their wisdom in books the way that I, I have written it. (Nor) did they depict their wisdom in the Picture (-Book) the way (that I, I have) depicted it. My church surpasses (in this other matter also), for its primacy to the first churches" (*Keph.* 370, 16–375, 15; Gardner and Lieu 2004, 265–268). Mani's religion was as much a religion of the book as Christianity. The holiness of books in Manichaeism may help us to understand the singularly small size of the Cologne Mani Codex. As the product of an extremely difficult scribal process, the book itself would have counted as proof of the holiness of its content and of the followers' dedication to the religion's founder, whose life was told in its pages.

The Cologne Mani Codex is far from complete. When we first meet Mani, he is already four years old, and we lose sight of him on the last extremely fragmentary pages, when he is twenty-six. The remaining years of his life must be reconstructed from other sources. Mani was born in 216 in the city of Seleucia-Ctesiphon in Mesopotamia; when he was four years old, his father took him away from his mother to live with him in a community of baptists on the lower Euphrates. Here Mani experiences his first revelations, which are brought to him by a heavenly twin. The twin is the key to Mani's religious system. He describes him in these words (Cologne Mani Codex 24; Gardner and Lieu 2004, 51): "*I received him* (my twin) piously, and I obtained him as my own property. *I believed him* that he belongs to me and that he is a good and useful counselor. *I recognized him,* and understood that I am he from whom I was separated. I have borne witness that I myself am he and am completely the same." As in every Gnostic system, human beings come from the realm of light, to which they must return. Mani's belief was that, at death, he would be reunited with his heavenly twin and that not only he himself but all human beings as well have a twin with whom they will be one again after death (with some restrictions, as we will see later). Also of interest in Mani's song about the twin is the sequence of *receiving, believing,* and *recognizing,* which in the climax describes the steps that lead to full gnosis.

Even as a child, Mani has also learned that all plants contain particles of light that human beings are not allowed to harm if they want to become perfect Manichaeans. Plants weep when they are harvested, and trees talk in anger when they are cut, making their sufferings clear. For Mani's followers, his biography must have been an entertaining yet still serious book to read or listen to. His biography is a pious narrative with a folkloristic tone.

The baptists with whom Mani and his father lived are described as members of a Jewish-Christian community on the Shat el-Arab River. The Cologne Mani Codex thus demonstrates for the first time that, besides the Persian religion of

Zoroaster (and maybe more important than it), Christianity and Judaism were the most powerful roots of Manichaeism.

At the age of twenty-four, Mani received a second great revelation from his twin, and after a dramatic discussion with the baptists, he left them and embarked on his missionary travels, which took him from Mesopotamia, through Persia, and ultimately as far as India. In this passage again, the codex reflects a number of folkloristic elements, such as when Mani meets a hoary hermit whom he converts or when he appears before a king and his attendants and convinces them all of the truth of his teachings.

Upon returning to Mesopotamia, Mani is welcomed by the Sassanid king, Shapur I, who supported his religion. Here the Mani Codex breaks off. We know the rest in much less detail from some sources in Middle Persian. Shapur's successors were less favorably disposed, and in 276 Mani died in a prison in Seleucia-Ctesiphon after the priests of the Zoroastrian cult, who recognized him and his religion as a serious rival, had denounced him at court.

What made Mani's religion so successful? Certainly the charisma of its founder played a role, as did his determination to promote his religion more vigorously than all others before him, claiming that he was the real Apostle of Light after Zoroaster, Jesus, and the apostle Paul. He believed that the time of the oral transmission of teachings was over (which had led to terrible controversies in Christianity) and that everything he had said and done should be written down. This was a new and decisive shift away from the spoken word to words that existed in writing and were therefore eternal. The folkloristic flavor of his biography, as we see it in the Cologne Mani Codex, may have added to the popularity of his teaching, as his painted book, which showed the creation of the world and the fight between light and darkness, also certainly did. In the Persian tradition, Mani is still called the "Painter." Another advantage of Mani's church was its strict hierarchic structure, with one supreme leader, twelve teachers, seventy-two bishops, and so on, who were sent out wherever a Manichaean church was founded. In the fourth century, a Manichaean teacher was established in Egypt (mentioned later).

On the other hand, the difficulty of his system was the strict asceticism that it expected of those who wanted to become *electi*, the chosen ones, who would advance the task of the separation of light and darkness. To collect as many light particles in themselves as possible, the *elects* had to avoid harming light particles in any living entity. Thus, they were not allowed to harvest plants, cut trees, bake bread, or even touch (they would have said "to beat") water. Naturally, they were not allowed to marry or have sex. Their food was preferably organic material that contained a high percentage of light particles. Melons were considered a particularly powerful source. As elects they wandered around, begging for their daily food, and were allowed only to pray and sing or to copy the holy books. This upper class of Manichaeans was supported by the *catechumens*, who fed and housed them.

Catechumens could not expect to play a decisive role in the separation of light and darkness but could hope to be reborn as elects in future lives (Mani had taken the belief in the transmigration of souls from his Buddhist experience in India). The lifestyle dictated to the elects probably stimulated a system of housing to which these wandering ascetics could turn. It has been argued that the earliest monasteries (the oldest one that is clearly dated is that founded in Egypt by Pachomius in 325) had their roots in Manichaean guesthouses for their elects.[1] But the Christians made of these guesthouses something completely different. On the one side we find the lonely elects, unable to support themselves and expecting only to be fed and clothed, and on the other side were the monks, who were dedicated to a communal life of work and prayer in which everything was to be shared.

Mani's religion was likely introduced in Egypt during his lifetime. Some texts in Middle Persian (Gardner and Lieu 2004, 111) tell of the first missionary, Addaius, who "came as far as Alexandria." He and other missionaries may have reached Egypt by ship across the Red Sea from the Shat el-Arab River rather than overland through the desert to Alexandria. Traveling by ship, they would have first reached the regions of Upper Egypt before going downstream to Alexandria, and indeed it seems that the strongholds of Manichaeism were in Upper Egypt in the area around Lykopolis (today Assiut), from where Manichaeism reached the oases in the western desert. Most of the papyrological finds concerning Mani's religion in Egypt originate from the region around Lykopolis or most likely came from there.

Between 277 and 297 the neo-Platonist Alexander of Lykopolis wrote a well-informed treatise against the Manichaeans. He may have had personal encounters with Manichaean missionaries. A letter written on papyrus, most likely by the bishop of Alexandria, also dates to the end of the third century. In it he warns Christians not to trust the Manichaeans and stresses the absurdity of their teachings (*P.Ryl.* 469; Gardner and Lieu 2004, 114–115); he condemns the "stupidity" of the ascetic practices of the elects and quotes the prayer they repeat before eating: "Neither have I cast the bread into the oven. Another has brought me this and I have eaten it without guilt." He continues: "Whence we can easily conclude that the Manichaeans are filled with much madness."

Better than the literary antiheretical works, this letter shows the Christians' genuine concerns about the then new religion originating in Mesopotamia. It attacks the Manichaeans for practices that were fundamental to their concept of salvation. This behavior was openly displayed by the elects when they wandered from place to place to ask for alms. Where Manichaeans were at home, the figure of the uncombed and smelly elect became a common feature in everyday life and provoked feelings of dismay and much mockery. It is surprising that we hear rather little of attacks or difficulties in the private letters of Mani's followers.

The Manichaean Codices from Medinet Madi (Fayyum) and the Private Documents from Upper Egypt and the Oases

Even though the first large find of Manichaean texts was made in the Fayyum, the Coptic dialect in which these texts are written reveals that these books originated in the Lykopolis area. In 1929, farmers in the southwestern Fayyum were plundering mud-brick houses of the Roman period on the ancient site of Narmouthis (today Medinet Madi) in hopes of finding fertilizer for their fields. They discovered a box filled with seven codices still bound in their wooden covers. From the antiquities market in Cairo, four volumes were brought to Berlin, while the other three became part of the Chester Beatty collection in Dublin. This find, made forty years before the Cologne Mani Codex became known, provided new insight into what Manichaeism was and how "Christian" it could be. The codices contained two of the canonical works of Mani's religion: the *Kephalaia of the Teacher* (the main teachings of Mani, which once consisted of 520 pages with at least 172 chapters, now in Berlin; some very small fragments in Vienna) and the *Epistles* of Mani (Berlin). From his pupils there were the *Synaxeis of the Living Gospel* (Berlin). The find also included a *Psalm Book* (once containing more than 600 pages; Dublin), *Homilies* (Dublin), and a *Church History* of at least 250 pages (formerly in Berlin, now lost). Coptologists recognized that these texts had been translated from a Syriac original and had been copied into the codices around 400 CE. Besides the fact that many of the pages of these Manichaean books are horribly worn or quite fragmentary, the entire codex of the *Church History* disappeared from Berlin at the end of the Second World War. In a preliminary report Carl Schmidt and Hans Jakob Polotsky had said enough about the content of this codex to make apparent its affinity in style and content to what we have now in the Greek Mani Codex in Cologne (Schmidt and Polotsky 1933).

Jesus plays an important role in the *Kephalaia of the Teacher*, Mani. In chapter 8, Mani talks about the path that Jesus took in his descent to earth, incorporating the Christian concept of salvation into the Manichaean cosmos and bringing together Christ and the Manichaean entities from the realm of light (8, 36, 27–37, 27; Gardner and Lieu 2004, 218–219): "Once again, the Light-Man speaks to the congregation that is sitting in front of him: When Jesus the son of Greatness came to this world, at the time that he unveiled the greatness, he boarded ten vehicles! He journeyed in the universe by them. The first vehicle is the light ship, since he received instructions from the Ambassador there. The second carriage is the ship of the First Man, since his dwelling is established there. The third is the Pillar of Glory, the Perfect Man, since he shone forth there. . . . After he had assumed these ten, he came and manifested himself in the flesh. He chose the holy church in four vehicles. One is all the holy brothers. The second is the pure sisters. The third is all the catechumens, the sons of the faith. The fourth is the catechumens, the daughters of the light and truth." A large portion of the codices from Medinet Madi is now available in new editions and translations.

Until fairly recently, papyrological finds that illustrated Manichaean life in Egypt beyond the scriptures of its church were rare. Only two letters are recognized (not without dispute: see chapter 25) as having been written by followers of Mani. The first, *P.Harr.* I 107, is a late third or early fourth-century letter of unknown provenance written by a certain Besas to his mother. In it the son sends greetings to his mother and refers to the "Father, God of Truth" and the "Paraclete Spirit."[2] The other letter comes from fourth-century Oxyrhynchus (*P.Oxy.* XXXI 2603) and awaits republication.[3] A Manichaean background has been proposed. On a high intellectual level, the writer of this letter recommends his brethren to be received by the addressees, using the image of a mirror as an argument for mutual trust. At the end he sends greetings to the "brethren with you, both *elect* and *catechumens.*" A third Manichaean letter is currently being prepared for edition. It comes from Oxyrhynchus and also contains greetings to elects and catechumens. A Manichaean community is thus attested in Oxyrhynchus at least for the fourth century. Some small Syriac fragments written in a specifically Manichaean script add to this picture (Burkitt 1925, 111–119).

A more detailed idea of how Manichaeans lived in their religious communities and also participated in the daily life of their (most likely predominantly) Christian environment has been provided by the excavations in the Dakhleh Oasis, about 180 kilometers southwest of Assiut. Since the early 1990s, Australian scholars have uncovered the remains of the ancient village of Kellis (figure 26.5). Manichaeism is attested there until the late fourth century, when the village was abandoned. In addition to letters, literary texts written on papyrus or wooden boards have also been found. Both kinds of texts are presented in either Greek or Coptic; of special interest is a word list that gives Manichaean technical terms in both Syriac and Coptic. This word list has again stimulated debate about whether indeed all Manichaean texts went through two stages of translation, first from Syriac into Greek and then into Coptic, or whether they were directly translated from Syriac into Coptic.

Literary texts from Kellis include a Greek version of a psalm already known from the Coptic psalm book from Medinet Madi, some of Mani's epistles in Coptic, which were lost in the Medinet Madi codices, and a very interesting prayer in Greek, titled "Prayer of the Emanations." It lists all of the divine entities that play a role in the separation of light and darkness and are sent down by the Father of Light to rescue the first man and mankind. Whether these Greek texts are versions that were used at an earlier stage and then abandoned, or whether both languages were used side by side remains undetermined.

The Manichaeans of Kellis also wrote in Greek or Coptic in their private lives (figure 26.6). We have more than thirty private letters written in Coptic by followers of Mani (more may yet be published) and one in Greek that is undoubtedly of Manichaean background. It is a striking feature of the Coptic letters from Kellis that many of them have the addressee's name written in Greek (as if the "letter carrier" would understand that language better) and that the salutations are also phrased in Greek, while the main corpus of the letter follows in Coptic. Most

Figure 26.5. House 3, Room 6, at Kellis with ancient material scattered on the floor.

of the Coptic letters were found in "House 3," thus acquainting us with one Manichaean household in the middle of the village. No elect is named as such: The people in House 3, both men and women, all seem to have been catechumens. That the senders (and recipients) of these letters were followers of Mani is clear from the references to the elect, the catechumens, and the Paraclete. It seems that the theological idea of Mani or his twin (ultimately the same person) as the Paraclete whom Jesus had announced (John 14:26) was common knowledge in the Manichaean communities. The private letters from Oxyrhynchus also refer to the founder of the religion as the Paraclete.

   The tone of the letters is solemn, with people often talking piously with one another. The letters from the family archive of Makarios, which date to between 350 and 370, are characteristic. When Makarios receives letters from his sons, who were dwelling at the time in the Nile valley, we even get a glimpse of the highest Manichaean official in Egypt. "I will go with the Teacher to Alexandria" (*P.Kell Copt.* 29.13–15), we read there, or "my brother Piene is learning Latin with the Teacher" (*P.Kell.Copt.* 20.24–26). Is it possible that Piene was preparing to become a Manichaean missionary in the west? Books and their production play an important role in the lives of these people. Books (unfortunately without any titles) are exchanged (*P.Kell Copt.* 20, 36; 26, 28 ff) and copied (*P.Kell.Copt.* 22, 66; 24, 36; and 34, 23). Despite this interest in the Holy Scriptures, however, the letters say nothing about the realm of light and its

Figure 26.6. *P.Kell.Copt.* 25, letter by Matthaios to his mother, Maria (from House 3, Room 6, at Kellis).

messengers, in contrast to the "Prayer to the Emanations" (mentioned earlier), which shows the importance of the myth in the Manichaean church, as does the psalm book from Medinet Madi. Being a Manichaean was serious business; the act of providing alms to the elect is referred to in two letters: *P.Kell.Copt.* 15 and *P.Kell.Gr.* 63. For these people, their church is the "Holy Church," and some of them may have had to suffer for their beliefs. The warnings not to let a letter fall into the hands of "someone," as well as the need for secrecy, do not necessarily refer to the difficult circumstances of the person as a Manichaean but rather to the position of a Manichaean believer in a difficult family situation. The appearance of a magical spell that accompanies one letter is astonishing because magic in all forms was prohibited to the Manichaeans; this particular spell is a curse to be used to separate a loving couple.

Further finds may even better illustrate the coexistence of Christians and Manichaeans in this environment. The excavation of the Manichaean monastery that is mentioned in an account book of rents found at Kellis but has not yet been located could also give us new insight into the relationship between elects and catechumens in their daily lives. The twenty-first century might bring the lives of these persecuted people even more into focus through the books and private letters that still await excavation.

NOTES

1. Koenen (1983) has strongly argued for this connection between Manichaean houses and the early monasteries.
2. The main arguments for a Manichaean background of this letter are found in Gardner, Nobbs, and Choat (2000, 118–124, and plate III).
3. Lieu (1994, 98n316).

BIBLIOGRAPHY

Nag Hammadi

Otranto, R. 2000. *Antiche liste di libri su papiro.* Rome: Edizioni di storia e letteratura.
Robinson, J. M., ed. 1990, rev. ed. *The Nag Hammadi Library in English, Translated by Members of the Coptic Gnostic Library Project of the Institute for Antiquity and Christianity.* Leiden: Brill. Cited in the text as *NHLE.*
Till, W. C., ed. 1972. *Die gnostischen Schriften des Koptischen Papyrus Berolinensis 8502,* 2nd ed. Berlin: Akademie Verlag.
Turner, J. D., and A. McGuire, eds. 1997. *The Nag Hammadi Library after Fifty Years: Proceedings of the 1995 Society of Biblical Literature Commemoration.* Leiden: Brill.

Veilleux, A. 1980. *Pachomian Koinonia*. Vol. 1, *The Life of Saint Pachomius and His Disciples*. Kalamazoo, Mich.: Cistercian Publications.

Manichaeism

Burkitt, F. C. 1925. *The Religion of the Manichees*. Cambridge: Cambridge University Press.

Gardner, I., A. Alcock, and W.-P. Funk, eds. 1999. *Coptic Documentary Texts from Kellis*, vol. 1 (=*P.Kell. V*). Dakhleh Oasis Project Monograph 9. Oakville, Conn.: Oxbow.

Gardner, I., and S. N. C. Lieu, eds. 2004. *Manichaean Texts from the Roman Empire*. Cambridge: Cambridge University Press.

Gardner, I., A. Nobbs, and M. Choat. 2000. "*P. Harr.* 107: Is This Another Greek Manichaean Letter?" *ZPE* 131: 118–124.

Koenen, L. 1983. *Manichäische Mission und Klöster in Ägypten*. In *Das Römisch-byzantinische Ägypten*, 93–108. Aegyptiaca Treverensia 2. Mainz am Rhein: P. von Zabern.

———, and C. Römer, eds. 1988. *Der Kölner Mani-Kodex: Über das Werden seines Leibes*. Opladen: Westdeutscher Verlag.

Lieu, S. N. C. 1994. *Manichaeism in Mesopotamia and the Roman East*. Leiden: Brill.

Schmidt, C., and H. J. Polotsky. 1933. *Ein Mani-Fund in Ägypten*. Berlin: Akademie der Wissenschaften.

CHAPTER 27

THE FUTURE OF PAPYROLOGY

PETER VAN MINNEN

In this final chapter I take a look ahead. In doing so I draw heavily on two position papers I have given at international papyrological congresses: in Copenhagen in 1992 (Van Minnen 1993) and in Vienna in 2001 (van Minnen 2007; such congresses are held under the auspices of the Association Internationale de Papyrologues every three years). In the first presentation, which dealt with the history of papyrology, I made the past normative; in the second ("The Millennium of Papyrology (2001–)?"), I made the future normative. In this chapter I again do the latter because readers are more indulgent when it comes to the future; the past has to be manipulated too much to be acceptable as normative.

Papyrologists have made predictions or projections about their future before, but they have usually been reluctant to commit themselves too far (see McGing 2006, 246–248). The title of my first paper ("The Century of Papyrology [1892–1992]") actually derives from one of the earliest predictions about papyrology ever made: By 1900, Ludwig Mitteis and Theodor Mommsen (see Martin 2000; Gonis 2006) had both claimed that the twentieth century would be the "century of papyrology," just as the nineteenth century had been the "century of epigraphy." In my first paper I discussed how accurate this prediction had been and suggested ways in which papyrologists could improve their communication with other disciplines. The present handbook goes a long way toward doing just that.

In the second paper, I calculated how much work remains to be done. I concentrated on the editing of unpublished texts, what I called the "core business" of papyrologists. Even if only half of all unpublished texts in the more than 1,400 known collections worldwide from "Aachen to Zutphen" (an estimated 1,000,000–1,500,000, of which almost half are held by the Egypt Exploration Society) are publishable, it would still take papyrologists ten times as long as it took them to publish the estimated 72,500 published texts in the hundred years since about 1895 (broken down into 50,000 Greek and Latin documents; 7,500 Greek and Latin literary texts; as well as 7,500 Coptic; 3,500 demotic and abnormal hieratic; 3,000 Arabic; and 1,000 Aramaic and Pehlevi texts). Hence, the "millennium of papyrology."

My statistics on literary and documentary texts from papyri and ostraca published or republished in five-year periods from 1890 to 1999 (van Minnen 2007, 714) can be updated as follows. In the period 2000–2004, about 4,500 texts were published or republished, and 2005 and 2006 were exceptionally good years, with about 1,500 and 2,500 texts published or republished. The total of published texts now stands at about 80,000.

On average, 12 volumes (monographs) with papyrus texts come out every year, and this has been the case since about the mid-1970s. There is every reason to believe that this publication rate, with an average of about seven hundred Greek and Latin texts published each year, as well as texts in other languages at irregular intervals, is going to continue in the foreseeable future. At least the five-year period since 2000 has confirmed the prediction I made in 2001.

In these statistics I ignored "normal" hieratic papyri because they date from before the papyrological "millennium and a half" (from the earliest abnormal hieratic and demotic papyri in the early seventh century BCE to the latest Greek papyri in the late eighth century CE). I also ignored papyri with texts in yet other languages such as Syriac, Armenian, and Gothic because there are only a handful of such texts to begin with. A Punic papyrus of the sixth century BCE can be added to the list of oddities: an amulet found inside a bronze case with the head of a falcon at Tal-Virtù, near Malta (on this "Maltese falcon," see Rocco 1975).

Editing the unpublished texts in collections worldwide and republishing texts in need of revision will keep papyrologists busy for centuries at least. That much is clear. Given the tendency, more marked in the past than at present, to publish relatively more Greek literary papyri than other papyri and relatively more Greek and Latin documentary papyri than papyri in other languages, as well as relatively more Ptolemaic and early Roman documentary papyri than documentary papyri from late antiquity, the current backlog in the publication of documentary papyri, especially those from late antiquity and/or in other languages, is even bigger than that for the kinds of papyri that have traditionally received more attention from papyrologists. But none of this changes the bottom line: There are enough papyri of every kind, from any period and in any language, to keep papyrologists busy for quite some time.

The only problem I see is not that there are not enough texts but that there are not enough papyrologists. By increasing their number, one could reduce the amount of time it will take to publish the remaining texts, but that will not be easy. Papyrologists who edit texts use a number of specialized skills they have acquired in the course of a decade or more. Ideally, the acquisition of the philological skills (knowledge of Greek and/or other ancient languages) should take place before the acquisition of the specialized skills (palaeographical, editorial, and historical) needed to read, edit, and use papyrus texts, but this is not always possible. It is also not easy to speed up the process, and increasing the numbers of trainees at the limited number of institutions that actually offer courses and other forms of training in papyrology is a financial and logistical problem.

In recent years, a consortium of ten institutions in North America has started a series of papyrological summer institutes of the kind that was very successful in the 1960s. The expectation is that this will continue after the current round (2003–2012; for announcements see http://www.papyrology.org/). Shorter summer programs are occasionally organized at a variety of European institutions. All of this is aimed at making a generation of younger students of the ancient world at least aware of papyri and in some cases to "convert" them to papyrology (for a case of "enforced apostasy" from papyrology, see *P.Merton* II, p. vii). The pool of potential "converts" may decline or expand, depending on the general level of enrollment in subjects such as the classics, ancient history (with Greek and Latin), Egyptology, and classical Arabic. If, say, enrollments in the classics go down, papyrologists will have to make a greater effort to reach students before they settle for "Homer and Vergil" (and not much else). It seems likely that Egyptology and classical Arabic will attract increasing numbers of students in the foreseeable future. Papyrologists will need to make sure that their material can be used responsibly by ancient history students who have little or no knowledge of ancient languages (they are appearing in increasing numbers) by streamlining the way they present papyrus texts and making translations widely available.

Papyrologists do or could do many other things besides editing and "disseminating" texts. In fact, I earlier calculated the number of editors of papyrus texts in the last decades of the twentieth century at only sixty-five (van Minnen 2007, 707), whereas a couple of hundred papyrologists usually show up at international congresses. Clearly, papyrology cannot be so narrowly defined as to exclude most of its practitioners.

There are very few full-time papyrologists, scholars who do nothing else: Most teach ancient Greek or ancient history besides. What do all of these papyrologists do? They edit and reedit texts from papyri and/or with their help study some aspect of the ancient world (e.g., its literature or the social history of Egypt in the Graeco-Roman period). Sometimes they even go to Egypt to dig up more papyri and to find out more about the context from which they derive. There have always been such papyrologists, but early on, they did a lot of harm while doing a lot of good: They dug up hundreds of thousands of papyri, which will keep papyrologists busy for another millennium, but they also destroyed the original context from which these papyri derived without recording it properly. Since the 1930s, better recordkeeping at excavations in Egypt has generated a huge quantity of additional data to match what one reads in the texts. A lot of this still needs to be explored, adding enormously to the task at hand, but the most recent excavations will no doubt result in models for using data from older excavations, which are often incomplete in any case.

In the section that follows, I start with the immediate context from which the papyri derive as physical objects. In the section after that, I concentrate on the texts written on them, and in the final section I focus on the wider context that produced the texts.

PAPYRI AS ANCIENT ARTIFACTS

Papyri and ostraca have been found mainly in Egypt and less so in other parts of the ancient world. Early on, papyri were dug up by the local population and by papyrologists in search of papyri (and little else). Early archaeologists followed their trail, but it was not until the 1930s that serious excavations (not just to find more papyri but also to record the finds in context) were undertaken. World War II disrupted this promising development for decades. In the last couple of decades, however, new excavations have been undertaken with remarkable success (for a survey see Bagnall 2001).

The first serious excavations concentrated on sites on the outskirts of the Arsinoite nome, such as Karanis and Tebtynis, which had yielded many papyri before. Special circumstances there have preserved much organic material. In the course of the Roman period, the gains on the desert made in the early Ptolemaic period were lost, and many sites on the outskirts were returned to the desert for a millennium and a half. In recent years, the expansion of agriculture in Egypt has regained some of these losses, but there are still sites left to search for papyri and other materials (see the urgent call for "rescue" excavations in Gallazzi 1994), which will allow a detailed reconstruction of many aspects of life in these towns based not just on texts but also on the whole range of materials found. This has always been the goal of serious excavations in the Arsinoite nome, but so far none has delivered on its promise (I outlined a strategy to come to grips with the early excavations at Karanis in van Minnen 1994). In the future, however, one may expect to be able to put the various kinds of materials so far studied in isolation from one another back together once the excavators sit down to make sense of the whole.

In recent decades, the focus has shifted somewhat to sites in the Eastern Desert and in the oases in the Western Desert. The former are mainly, but not exclusively, Roman army camps and the like, which have so far yielded large quantities of ostraca and a wealth of other materials (on the exemplary work at Mons Claudianus see, e.g., *O.Claud.* III). Excavations on the Red Sea coast have revealed, for example, Berenice, a town of major importance to the trade with East Africa and India from the early Ptolemaic period to late antiquity (see Wendrich et al. 2003). Sites in the oases of the Western Desert are even more promising because they tend to be more "normal" towns, such as one finds in the Nile valley, except for the oases' special hydrological circumstances (on Kellis, the best-published site so far, see the *Dakhleh Oasis Project: Monograph* series).

We have already begun to understand quite a bit more about the Roman army system in the Eastern Desert, mainly through the work of Cuvigny (see also chapter 2). In the near future one can also expect to learn quite a bit more about sites in the Western Desert (e.g., Mothis), which have so far not been foremost in the study of Graeco-Roman Egypt. For the delta, however, one will probably never know much about the kinds of things taken for granted in the Nile valley and the Arsinoite nome and presumably soon in the oases of the Western Desert because the water table there was raised as early as the nineteenth century—before papyrological excavations had started—and this development has continued apace ever since. The archaeology of nonorganic materials there will make some progress, but that is not papyrology.

What the expansion into the desert areas and the exploration of new sites in the Arsinoite nome and even the Nile valley will do to papyrology is mainly twofold. In the first place, it will redress an annoying imbalance. Ever since the end of the nineteenth century, papyrologists have drawn mainly on the same finds from a limited number of sites. All of the statistics so far produced (see Rémondon 1966 through Habermann 1998) therefore show the same kinds of bias. Expanding into new territories will generate at least new biases to match the old ones.

Second, the exploration of new sites will continue to add to the stock of unpublished material. As a matter of fact, more papyri and ostraca are currently found each year than are published by papyrologists. For as long as more are found in Egypt, the daunting backlog of 1,000,000–1,500,000 unpublished items will therefore not diminish, no matter what papyrologists do.

An added effect of the expansion into new territories is a more traditional one: Artifacts, including papyri, will disappear from excavations and reappear on the market (cf. chapter 21). Nowadays, responsible institutions no longer invest in "hot" papyri, but there is too much money in irresponsible hands. "Hot" papyri often lack a provenance, and the context in which they were found is deliberately effaced.

Once papyri are retrieved, they need to be conserved on site and in the museum where they will be kept. Conservation of papyri has taken a turn for the better since the mid-1970s, and this will no doubt continue in the foreseeable future. Another phenomenon that is also likely to go on indefinitely is the increased access to information about and images of papyri. First Yale University, then the University of Michigan, pioneered the electronic cataloguing of papyri in their collections. Then a more ambitious project was pioneered at Duke University, where the largely unexplored collection was conserved, catalogued and digitized. By the end of 1995, Duke was the first collection to go online as a whole—to go "public." At that point, a collaborative effort linking the most important collections in the United States got under way, the Advanced Papyrological Information System (APIS). The much larger collections at Yale, Michigan, the University of California–Berkeley, Columbia University, and Princeton University, later joined by others around the globe, have made many more images of and much more information about papyri in their collections available. My guess is that currently about 10 percent of all published texts are now accounted for in APIS-type projects, the bulk of these in APIS itself. I use the term "accounted for" advisedly as not all projects provide the same level of detail or coverage for published texts. Coverage of unpublished material in APIS-type projects is much spottier.

All of this material is accessible through the Web sites of the individual collections, but most of it is also available as a whole at the Web site at Columbia University (http://www.columbia.edu/cu/lweb/projects/digital/apis/; now also at http://www.papyri.info). As time progresses, ever more papyri in collections worldwide will become accessible in some form through digitized images, and incomplete records will be added to over time. The quality of papyrological work that deals with published texts will improve because it will be possible to base it not just on the information in the printed edition but increasingly also on high-quality images. This has already revolutionized the work with texts from certain collections, and the same will happen with all of them.

Making images of unpublished papyri available will definitely make it possible for outsiders without access to the originals to work on a "virtual collection." This has already led to the publication by papyrologists from all over the world of dozens of papyri at Duke University.

One possible effect of APIS-type efforts to make images of papyri available in bulk is to give the renewed interest in palaeography a boost (see chapter 5). Palaeography is more than a dating tool, but even as a dating tool it is badly in need of revision. For some "papyrologies" (e.g., Coptic papyrology), a careful study of dated texts could generate the chronological backbone.

PAPYRI AS TEXTS

Most papyrologists are mainly interested in the texts written on papyri. True, they sometimes interact with originals, but the texts are the main thing papyrologists worry about. There is nothing wrong with that. Texts are the papyrologist's facts (cf. Youtie 1963). Most of them study papyri because they have a passionate interest in the past and because they are trained to construe that past from texts. Texts indeed provide a meaningful link with the past because they are bits of communication. When reading, one listens in on a conversation of long ago, as it were. I do not deny that one can also "read" other artifacts and that in a postprocessual world pots do have a soul (contrast Wilamowitz-Moellendorff's *obiter dictum* that "Töpfe haben keine Seele": Wilamowitz-Moellendorff 1913, 5). But most papyrologists are not archaeologists but philologists by training, and therefore this section on texts is twice as long as the one on papyri as artifacts.

Texts are also accessible to anyone who knows the ancient language they are in or can use translations responsibly. This means that potentially all students of the ancient world can, if only occasionally, become papyrologists. The problem with this has always been mainly twofold. In the first place, most papyrological publications are obscure, certainly in comparison with epigraphical publications, where the great series (*IG, CIL*) at least provide a home for the bulk of the texts. Only *The Oxyrhynchus Papyri* can claim a somewhat similar status, mainly because of the way this series has been marketed since the end of the nineteenth century. Many libraries otherwise devoid of papyrological publications have a set of *P.Oxy.* The recent development of electronic tools has brought most published papyrus documents in Greek and Latin and some in Arabic within the reach of all. In some cases, translations are available as well, either through APIS-type projects (which deal with the material collection by collection) or through a comprehensive database (as for Arabic documentary papyri). Eventually all documentary papyrus texts will become available with translations linked to them in some form. If making the papyrus texts more "user-friendly" (through descriptions that retrace the flow of the text and especially annotated translations) is done responsibly, chances are that papyrus texts will be used responsibly by future generations of scholars, even those who do not have the specialized skills to deal with the material directly in the original languages.

In the second place, papyrus texts are difficult for outsiders to access because of the special formatting imposed on the representation of texts in printed form. These are purely conventional (the so-called Leiden system) and limited in number but evidently a major obstacle for many. Things here have been further complicated since the 1980s. In putting the printed texts of Greek and Latin documents on papyri and ostraca into electronic form in the Duke Data Bank of Documentary Papyri (DDBDP), additional interventions in their representation were rendered necessary. The orthography of many words had to be corrected—a "smart" searching program that would recognize aberrant forms did not yet exist. All kinds of other information (e.g., on scribal corrections or corrections of readings in the various *addenda et corrigenda* to the printed editions) were inserted with the help of other kinds of formatting.

Originally, the DDBDP was meant as a huge index to the printed volumes, but when it was completed (for the time being) in June 1996, its original purpose had long been superseded. It had turned out to be not just a huge index but also the premier tool for editors of Greek and Latin documentary papyri. Increasingly, papyrus collections had been exhausted as far as complete and legible documents were concerned. Around the time this was happening, the DDBDP made it possible to identify and publish even fragmentary texts with confidence. The relatively simple searching program allowed one to recognize a few words or even a string of letters as deriving from a particular type of document, for which one then found more complete parallels in the DDBDP. This is the most important function of the most important tool papyrologists currently use, and it will remain that indefinitely. I think the exceptionally prominent status of this electronic tool warrants a few additional comments.

When the DDBDP first went online (now at http://www.papyri.info), a user-friendly interface changed the way the texts are represented in significant ways. Even papyrologists now think that what the interface shows on the screen is the text they can quote. It is nothing of the sort, however, because the DDBDP was never meant to give the text but merely to provide an index to the printed texts. The formatting is so different from the one found in most printed editions that only those with a trained eye can "read" the heavily doctored DDBDP "texts" as such by "retranslating" what they see on the screen (a little bit like "reading" *PSI* volumes and "translating" the symbols { } and < > used there to their exact opposite to match the way they are used elsewhere). It will take the concerted effort of generations of papyrologists to rectify this in the DDBDP itself, and they would still need a smart indexing program to navigate the results.

Ideally, the texts in the DDBDP should also reflect current critical understanding of the texts by incorporating corrections to the printed texts made after the *editio princeps*. This has already happened to some extent. In the mid-1990s, corrections to older text editions published up to 1920 were in fact incorporated from the *Berichtigungsliste der griechischen Papyrusurkunden* I–IX and other sources (e.g., *Chrest.Mitt.* and *Chrest.Wilck.*) in an effort to correct the critical imbalance in the corpus of published texts. Older text editions contain relatively many misreadings, and it would have been misleading to include their texts as they were originally printed without taking the many, often substantial published corrections into account. The revision of older editions included in the DDBDP will have to continue as more volumes of the *Berichtigungsliste* come out (so far, X and XI). Essential help can also come from APIS-type projects, which should review texts published from papyri in their collection also with an eye to their electronic representation and the incorporation of corrections from the *Berichtigungsliste* and other sources. Where they have not yet done so, they would have to go over the substantial body of material already covered a second time.

A reality check might be helpful at this point: It takes several papyrologists currently five years to reedit 500 Greek documents critically and responsibly. To do this for all 55,000 published Greek and Latin documents would take them half a millennium. Not all texts are in need of reedition right away, but all of them *will* be within the next half millennium. Part of the effort that is going into APIS-type projects is aimed at supplying help that is lacking in some editions. Ideally, future (re-)editions should provide from the start all the kinds of help one might possibly need. To this end, in the appendix to my paper for the papyrological congress in Vienna (van Minnen 2007, 712–714),[1] I have presented several sets of "ten commandments" for preparing, publishing, and using papyrus editions that should go a long way toward standardizing and improving current editions.

To educate users (papyrologists, as well as outsiders) about what currently constitutes a text in papyrology, there is a desperate need for a "diplomatic" handbook for the various "papyrologies" in existence. Such handbooks exist for medieval documents (e.g., Guyotjeannin, Pycke, and Tock 1993 for Latin documents) but not for ancient texts. Handbooks for Greek and Latin, demotic and abnormal hieratic, Coptic, and Arabic documentary papyri are an urgent desideratum, perhaps less so for Aramaic and Pehlevi. Handbooks for the literary papyri (with known or new texts) in the main languages are also needed. The older handbooks take too much for granted, and the newer ones often provide more bibliographical coverage than information that one cannot find elsewhere.

There is nothing wrong with having different sets of common practices for documents (as opposed to literary texts) or even for new literary texts (as opposed to known ones), but users have never been told this (e.g., the "Note on the Method of Publication and Abbreviations" printed in every volume of *P.Oxy.* lists practices used for the documents but not for the literary texts that immediately follow).

The DDBDP currently does not include all Greek and Latin documentary texts that fall within its definition. Some documentary texts were omitted because they were mistaken for literature (e.g., dream reports); others were excluded because they were mistaken for inscriptions (e.g., the texts on larger sherds in *O.Douch*). Moreover, a whole category of texts, often called "subliterary" (e.g., magical texts), has been omitted even when they contain documentary material as well (unlike magical handbooks, individual spells refer to actual people, who may also occur in "regular" documentary texts). It would be better if this material were also available in database form, either in the DDBDP or in a separate database (or both). Some of the Greek magical texts on papyrus have now made it to the Thesaurus Linguae Graecae, where they can be searched; the more "literary" subliterary texts can be searched at http://cpp.arts.kuleuven.be/. For the entire corpus of magical texts on papyrus there is now a printed dictionary (Muñoz Delgado 2001), but this is not as useful as a fully searchable database. For the time being, "regular" literary papyri (Homer, etc.) do not have to be included in a separate database. Standardized texts

1. The stray quotation at the top of p. 714 ("inconsistency is too common to be criminal") goes with the four sets of "ten commandments" on pp. 712–713.

of these are already searchable in the TLG. But within the context of APIS-type projects, literary texts need to be included as full texts, thereby making it possible for textual critics to manipulate the texts of each witness.

The many APIS-type projects pose problems of their own, not least in that they contain unique scholarly content not found elsewhere. They are extremely labor intensive and not easy to keep up. That is one of the structural differences with the databases construed from published texts such as the DDBDP. APIS-type projects and the publication-based projects will therefore develop side by side for the foreseeable future rather than in tandem. The former will, however, provide a critical check on the latter, and the latter will be a useful repository of all kinds of useful information for the former. Fairly simple links between the two kinds of projects will not absolve users from doing most of the work of piecing the information together themselves.

The "great leap forward" in the use of papyrus texts happened in the mid-1990s, when the DDBDP replaced the awkward dictionaries and indices used until then, and images of the published papyri in at least some collections (University of Michigan, etc.), as well as other kinds of help, started to become available for instant use by scholars working away from the collections. Increasingly, APIS-type projects will add more images and other information for each item included in their collections. In addition to images of at least the published texts, they will also provide translations, copied or updated from the publications or newly made, introductions that retrace the flow of the texts, and copious annotations, all of which may be lacking in the printed editions. The images are primarily aimed at specialists, but the translations and other aids can be used by a far greater number of scholars. Even those not ordinarily engaged in papyrological research can start using papyri responsibly (for an example, see Dijkman 2003, a study of the village scribe in Roman Egypt based on the limited number of translated documents available in APIS). Eventually all of the collections will thus be covered. The moment when images and translations of all published papyri will be available electronically to the entire scholarly community is not too far off. That would complete the "great leap forward" made possible by the digital revolution of the mid-1990s.

PAPYRI AS FACTS

Papyrus texts exist in many forms, as is clear by now, but whichever kind is used, papyrologists still need to integrate the data and turn the texts into usable facts. In my paper at the international congress of papyrologists at Copenhagen in 1992 (van Minnen 1993), I sketched the various ways in which this is or could be done. Here I can highlight only a few of these (see now also Bagnall 1995). Even so, this section is again almost twice as long as the one on papyri as artifacts, and this should come as no surprise coming from the pen of a papyrologist with historical inclinations.

Sometimes papyrologists literally have to put the pieces back together. If fragments of one papyrus have been dispersed over several collections, a composite text has to be devised or even published before one can use it well for some other purpose. This alone takes as much time as editing an unpublished text. More commonly, single items from a larger cache of documents have been dispersed over several collections, and these have to be put back together. Papyrologists have increasingly focused on these so-called archives, caches of papyri deliberately put together in antiquity (see Martin 1994). It is best not to be too strict in the application of the term *archive* as texts may have been found together not because they originally formed part of the same "archive" (or library) but because they were deliberately discarded together, as in *genizas*, or more accidentally, as in dumps. Even such seemingly hodgepodge caches can be interesting if studied as a whole, as I showed in the case of a traditional Egyptian *geniza:* the so-called temple library from Tebtynis that contained hieratic and demotic literature (in actuality discarded books from a variety of mostly private libraries) (see van Minnen 1998, 168; disputed by Ryholt 2005). The composition of a dump can also be interesting. The more recent excavations carefully record the stratigraphy of dumps, and even for the older excavations (e.g., Karanis) data exist to reconstruct (somewhat more imaginatively, to be sure) how the dumps there came about.

As a by-product of APIS-type projects, more data will become available about the acquisition of papyri in various collections. This will provide ever more scope for "museum archaeology" (see chapter 10), which indicates the possible links between texts by tracing them back to the same dealer or even purchase (e.g., as part of the German *Kartell,* which bought papyri for several collections in Germany in the early twentieth century; cf. chapter 3).

For the time being, putting texts from a single archive together will remain the painstaking work it has always been. Archives can reveal a lot more about ancient society than a single text. A family archive allows one to reconstruct the life of a family over several generations (e.g., *P.Fam.Tebt.,* to cite an early example of this kind of thing) and often gives one a better idea of the family's social position. Likewise, individual items from an official archive are often baffling, but once they are reassembled, they become meaningful or at least understandable. The publication of *P.Polit.Iud.* has finally cleared up the role of the Jewish *politeumata* in Ptolemaic Egypt.

Apart from texts that were deliberately put together in antiquity, there are others one can assemble oneself. Putting similar texts (or those that relate to a particular social institution) together in a series often allows a more convincing picture to emerge. The prime example is the corpus of wet-nursing contracts in *C.Pap.Gr.* I. Much more can be done with this material now but only because of the work that went into assembling the texts from a wide variety of sources.

Larger archives or types of texts for which too many examples exist will be more difficult to assemble, but the potential of the electronic medium will allow more progress in this area. The very large Zenon archive from the third century BCE was captured before the development of electronic tools in the so-called *Guide to the Zenon Archive* of 1981. Similar projects have been contemplated for other large archives. The Dioscoros archive of the sixth century CE is on the verge of being captured electronically. Fournet has gathered images and other data on all of the published and most of the unpublished texts. Once this detailed and painstaking work is available to other scholars, they will be able to produce much better work, whether they are researching some aspect of late Roman society based on texts in the archive or reediting a particular type of text. Fournet himself has done the latter for the poems of Dioscoros (*P.Aphrod.Lit.*, section IV) and is about to publish a reedition of the petitions from the archive. It will not be possible to reedit all of the texts belonging to the Dioscoros archive in one go, but they deserve to be reedited according to modern standards, and the scholarly world will gradually come around to do just that.

A papyrological conference held in December 2005 in Strasbourg focused on the Dioscoros archive, and there it was clear how much is unknown, how much papyrologists think they know but do not really, and how much they do know but have so far failed to put together. Connecting the dots the way it was done at this conference is bound to change our understanding of late antiquity in many ways. The concerted approach of the Dioscoros archive by papyrologists of different persuasions has already been helped by the electronic tools in existence, especially the DDBDP, but the electronic tool devised by Fournet will be of even greater assistance. The Dioscoros archive is dispersed over many collections, most of which are not currently contemplating APIS-type projects. Fournet's database is a kind of virtual APIS-type project, a database that captures an ideal "collection": the archive as it was originally discovered.

I have used the Dioscoros archive merely as an example. All archives (currently over 400) are in the process of being captured in the Leuven Homepage of Papyrus Archives (http://www.trismegistos.org/arch/index.php). This is less detailed than Fournet's database for the Dioscoros archive, but all the kinds of things that database contains could potentially also be made available for the other archives.

Papyrologists collect texts from printed or electronic sources to write synthetic accounts of various aspects of the ancient world (see chapter 21). I would like to stress two points: the importance of expanding the database for any of these aspects and the focus on Egypt.

In the first place, for any aspect of the ancient world, the number of available papyrus texts is not yet closed by any means. So far only a small portion of all papyri have been made accessible to scholars, as I explained earlier. For any topic the available database can and will be expanded by a factor of five or (sometimes much) more. This is more important than one thinks. Adding yet another tax receipt is by itself not going to change our knowledge of the ancient world substantially, and even if minor improvements are made to our knowledge by the continued editing of similar papyrus texts, at some point the law of diminishing returns (cf. McGing 2006, 248) kicks in.

But all of this depends on the kind of returns one expects. Even simply increasing the quantity of the available evidence for any aspect of the ancient world is going to improve the quality of what one knows about it. Numbers provide a greater statistical reliability for the conclusions one draws from the evidence. Traditionally students of the ancient world have had to be satisfied with a limited data set for almost everything they were interested in and with an ever-increasing level of sophistication in the interpretation of the same evidence. What papyrus texts offer papyrologists is a much better deal. Not only will there be an ever-increasing scope for sophistication in the interpretation of papyrus texts, as with any other type of evidence, but papyrologists will also be able to put more and more data in series and derive statistically better conclusions from them. Numbers do count. An example of a consensus papyrologists seem to have reached not as to the overall interpretation of the findings but as to the quality of the interpretation is the statistical use of the data included in the census documents from Roman Egypt (Bagnall and Frier 1994). With nearly 300 census documents and more than 1,000 individuals, the conclusions are far more interesting than with, say, 30 documents and 100 individuals. Just imagine how much more secure the conclusions will be when there are 3,000 census documents listing 10,000 individuals. That day will come, and future papyrologists will be able to apply much more sophisticated statistical procedures and see whether a chronological division of the material provides insights into the demographic development over time (at present, a chronological division of the data would undercut their statistical usefulness because there is no critical mass for each of the shorter periods one can distinguish within the first three centuries of Roman rule).

In the second place, one should not forget that the majority of papyrus texts come from Egypt and illustrate its history—social, cultural, or otherwise. It is true that papyrus texts have come to light in places outside Egypt as well. Nonetheless, we should not lose sight of the difference of scale. For Egypt, the number of available texts on any topic is just about overwhelming. Elsewhere one is at best dealing with useful snapshots. The Latin ostraca from Bu Njem (*O.Bu Njem*) reveal a great deal about a Roman army unit, about the literacy of its peculiar brand of society, and so on. But in Egypt there are multiple "Bu Njems," and in Libya itself the major source of information even on the Roman army is not the ostraca but inscriptions, and it is the same for many aspects of ancient life outside Egypt. In other parts of the ancient world, inscriptions will always be a more important (or at least more numerous or diverse) source of information than papyri or ostraca.

For many papyrologists, "Egypt" used to mean "Greek-speaking" Egypt. Texts in some form of Egyptian, abnormal hieratic, demotic, and Coptic were the domain of Egyptologists and Coptologists. Likewise, the abundant parallel documentation in Arabic for early Arabic Egypt was the domain of Arabists. In practice, few Egyptologists, Coptologists, and Arabists cared about papyri. Since the 1960s, however, things have changed quite a bit. Not that there are now large numbers of Egyptologists, Coptologists, and Arabists editing unpublished texts from papyri (the demotists are the largest group, and they are up against the smallest number of unpublished texts), but most papyrologists, classicists by training, have become aware of the fact that they can ignore the parallel documentation in languages other than Greek and Latin only at their peril. The demotists have led the way. In more recent years, very promising developments have taken place in Coptic and Arabic papyrology. Efforts to collect Coptic documents not published in monographs have resulted in three sturdy volumes on the model of the Greek *Sammelbuch,* and Arabic papyrology now has its own series of international congresses and a database (http://orientw.unizh.ch/apd/project.jsp).

Substantial descriptive databases are available for published Greek and Latin documents (the Heidelberger Gesamtverzeichnis, or HGV, http://aquila.papy.uni-heidelberg.de/gvzFM.html); for published demotic and abnormal hieratic documents (http://www.trismegistos.org/daht/index.php); and for published Coptic documents (http://dev.ulb.ac.be/philo/bad/copte/base.php?page=accueil.php). More important, papyrologists need DDBDP-type databases for languages other than Greek and Latin because they must be able to search the published texts in the original language. So far only Arabic has tried to follow in the Greek and Latin footsteps of the DDBDP. The much smaller corpus of published documents in Arabic makes it likely that one will see the completion of this database very soon. It will provide an enormous stimulus to the publication of more Arabic documents, of which there are relatively many in existing collections worldwide. I realize that there are difficult problems for demotic and Coptic (just think of the various Coptic dialects or the competing ways of transliterating demotic), but none of this is insurmountable (a smart indexing program could solve these problems). It will never take more than a fraction of the time it took to compile the original DDBDP with its 50,000 published Greek and Latin documents to capture the 17,000 published documents in other languages or the 8,000 literary texts or the 5,000 recently published Greek and Latin documents.

The focus on Egypt brings me back to the first section of this chapter—on papyri as artifacts. A greater awareness of the fact that the papyri come from somewhere in Egypt and that it makes a difference whether one can identify that place either from the text or from its archaeological provenance will improve the quality of papyrological scholarship. Even if the general provenance of the majority of texts is known (mainly thanks to the old excavations at Oxyrhynchus and in the

Arsinoite nome), increasingly more papyri will have a more precise provenance as archaeological information becomes available for newly found texts.

If I may draw one conclusion from the foregoing, it is that there is now more to do than anyone imagined in the 1970s. Papyrologists have come to realize that the number of unpublished texts far outstrips that of published texts and that the number of publishable texts is now far larger than ever before, mainly because the DDBDP for Greek and Latin documents (and eventually similar databases for documents in other languages) allows papyrologists to make sense of fragmentary texts. Papyrologists have also come to realize that it is useful to provide at least limited access to unpublished material in collections and even more access, especially in the form of images, to published materials; they also now recognize that it is often easy enough to collect the dispersed information on published texts in electronic form, which is especially useful as it can quickly make information about the bulk of the published material available. Papyrologists have also learned that it pays to reassemble texts from excavations or archives and to redo older text editions with the help of the tools now available.

For each of these realizations, there is a matching prediction. In the foreseeable future, the number of unpublished texts in collections around the globe will be reduced by 4,500 in each five-year period (except that more texts will continue to be found in Egypt). The total number of published texts will pass the 100,000 mark by about 2030, if one does not count unpublished texts accessible in some form through APIS-type projects. The total number of publishable texts is currently about ten times as many as have been published, and this material will keep papyrologists busy for at least a millennium. An updated version of the DDBDP, a version that includes the older material inadvertently excluded in the current version, as well as parallel databases for documents in other languages and for other types of texts, will make the work of papyrologists easier, better, and more comprehensive. Increased access to images of published and unpublished papyri will make all kinds of papyrological work better and more reliable and will also allow papyrologists to do more work away from physical papyrus collections. Electronic access to unpublished texts will also allow the discovery of more links between them or with published material than hitherto, when the discovery of such links was mainly serendipitous. Virtual guides to archives or dossiers will soon provide the same kind of services as the *Guide to the Zenon Archive,* as well as even better services: Texts and images, not just data about the texts, will also be provided. Better data from excavation and a renewed attempt to come to terms with older excavations will enable a clearer grasp of the context from which papyri derive. Virtual collaboration between papyrologists at different institutions will result in better work because many archives and dossiers and certainly many types of texts add up to too many items for one papyrologist to handle alone.

Still, the most important conclusion from all of this is the need for better communication. Papyrologists use different sets of common practices to represent texts in print. These "tricks" have never been fully explained and have often scared potential users away. In the digital era the problem has been compounded because the digital medium has increased the confusion. The development of electronic tools has added enormously to the number of such practices. A "text" in the DDBDP is not the same thing as a text in printed form, and one text can appear as multiple discrete "dates." It is electronically possible to smooth out all of the mismatches, but my prediction (that it will take half a millennium to do so) is surely more realistic than the expectation that technology will somehow fix our problems for us or that the input of "volunteers" will revise texts efficiently and promptly. What we need in the short run is a "diplomatic" handbook for each kind of text (literary, documentary, etc.) and for each language that explains the mismatch between texts and "texts" and all the other things papyrologists either take for granted or, in too many cases, are not even aware of themselves.

The future is indeed normative and delightfully so. If papyrologists do even half of the things I have listed in the previous paragraphs (preferably in less than half a millennium), one will be rewarded with an ever better knowledge of all kinds of aspects of life in the ancient world and especially with the unexpected: The history of papyrology is not (only) unremitting drudgery (and ever more of it is on its way, for at least a millennium) but (as Keenan shows in chapter 3) also an unbroken string of exciting discoveries that usually take one completely by surprise (as did the text I reedited in van Minnen 2000). The past will continue to surprise into the distant future as far as the eye can see.

BIBLIOGRAPHY

Bagnall, R. S. 1995. *Reading Papyri, Writing Ancient History.* London: Routledge.

———. 2001. "Archaeological Work on Hellenistic and Roman Egypt, 1995–2000." *American Journal of Archaeology* 105: 227–243.

———, and B. W. Frier. 1994. *The Demography of Roman Egypt.* Cambridge: Cambridge University Press.

Dijkman, J. 2003. "De dorpsschrijver in Romeins Egypte." *Tijdschrift voor Geschiedenis* 116: 5–30.

Gallazzi, C. 1994. "Trouvera-t-on encore des papyrus en 2042?" *Proceedings of the 20th International Congress of Papyrologists,* ed. A. Bülow-Jacobsen, 131–135. Copenhagen: Museum Tusculanum Press.

Gonis, N. 2006. "Mommsen, Grenfell, and the 'Century of Papyrology.'" *ZPE* 156: 195–196.

Guyotjeannin, O., J. Pycke, and B.-M. Tock. 1993. *Diplomatique médiévale.* Turnhout: Brepols.

Habermann, W. 1998. "Zur chronologischen Verteilung der papyrologischen Zeugnisse." *ZPE* 122: 144–160.

Martin, A. 1994. "Archives privées et cachettes documentaires." *Proceedings of the 20th International Congress of Papyrologists*, ed. A. Bülow-Jacobsen, 569–577. Copenhagen: Museum Tusculanum Press.

———. 2000. "Das Jahrhundert der Papyrologie?" *APF* 46: 1–2.

McGing, B. 2006. "Papyri." In *The Edinburgh Companion to Ancient Greece and Rome*, ed. E. Bispham, T. Harrison, and B. A. Sparkes, 238–250. Edinburgh: Edinburgh University Press.

Muñoz Delgado, L. 2001. *Léxico de magia y religión en los papiros mágicos griegos*. Madrid: Consejo Superior de Investigaciones Científicas, Instituto de Filología.

Rémondon, R. 1966. "L'Égypte au 5ᵉ siècle de notre ère: Les sources papyrologiques et leurs problèmes." *Atti dell'XI Congresso Internazionale di Papirologia*, 135–148. Milano: Istituto Lombardo di Scienze e Lettere.

Rocco, B. 1975. "Un talismano bronzeo da Malta contenente un nastro di papiro con iscrizione fenicia," *Studi Magrebini* 7: 1–18.

Ryholt, K. 2005. "On the Contents and Nature of the Tebtunis Temple Library: A Status Report." *Tebtynis und Soknopaiu Nesos: Leben im römerzeitlichen Fajum*, ed. S. Lippert und M. Schentuleit, 141–170. Wiesbaden: Harrassowitz.

van Minnen, P. 1993. "The Century of Papyrology (1892–1992)." *BASP* 30: 5–18.

———. 1994. "House-to-house Enquiries: An Interdisciplinary Approach to Roman Karanis." *ZPE* 100: 227–251.

———. 1998. "Boorish or Bookish? Literature in Egyptian Villages in the Fayum in the Graeco-Roman Period." *JJP* 28: 99–184.

———. 2000. "An Official Act of Cleopatra (with a Subscription in Her Own Hand)." *Ancient Society* 30: 29–34.

———. 2007. "The Millennium of Papyrology (2001–)?" *Akten des 23. internationalen Papyrologenkongresses*, ed. B. Palme, 703–714. Vienna: Verlag der Österreichischen Akademie der Wissenschaften.

Wendrich, W. Z., R. S. Tomber, S. E. Sidebotham, J. A. Harrell, R. T. J. Cappers, and R. S. Bagnall. 2003. "Berenike Crossroads: The Integration of Information." *Journal of the Social and Economic History of the Orient* 46: 46–87.

Wilamowitz-Moellendorff, U. von. 1913. *Sappho und Simonides: Untersuchungen über griechische Lyriker*. Berlin: Weidmann.

Youtie, H. C. 1963. "The Papyrologist: Artificer of Fact." *Greek, Roman, and Byzantine Studies* 4: 19–32.

Index

Page numbers in bold indicate figures.